EASTERN EUROPE!

TOMEK JANKOWSKI

EASTERN EUROPE!

Everything You Need to Know About
the History (and More!) of a Region
that Shaped Our World and Still Does

TOMEK JANKOWSKI

New Europe Books

Published by New Europe Books, 2013
Williamstown, Massachusetts
www.NewEuropeBooks.com

Copyright © Tomek Jankowski, 2013
Cover design © Oscar Boskovitz, 2013
Interior design by Justin Marciano

ISBN: 978-0-9850623-2-3

Cataloging-in-Publication Data is available from the Library of Congress.

Printed in the United States of America on acid-free paper.

Dedicated to my wife, Magda,
for putting up with me and all the books

TABLE O' CONTENTS

	page
Foreword	XIII
Introductory FAQ	XV
Acknowlegments	XX
Table o' Figures	XXII
SECTION I	1
A Few Words About a Word	2
A Note on Pronunciation	5
A Word (or Two) about Time	5
Languages	9
Geography	24
Religion	32
SECTION II	45
Introduction: A Prehistory	46
Introduction: History	51
Introduction: Classical Eastern Europe	57
Chapter 1: Setting the Stage, 500–800 CE	68
A. Western Rome	68
B. The Avars	73
C. The Slavs	74
D. The First Slavic States	75
E. The Bulgars	77
F. The Dacians and Vlachs	78
G. The Khazars	80
H. (A Bunch of) Finns and Balts	82
Special Insert: The Steppe	85

Chapter 2: The Origins of States, 800–1242 CE 88

A. The Franks. 88

B. Moravia Magna and Bohemia 94

C. The Bulgarians 96

D. The Rus 97

E. The Magyars/Hungarians 100

F. The Slovenes and Croatians 103

G. Duklja, Raška, and the Serbs. 104

H. The Poles 105

I. The Pechenegs 110

J. The Cumanians. 110

K. The Lithuanians 111

L. The Finale: 1239–42 111

Special Insert: Peoples of Eastern Europe—The Jews 117

Chapter 3: The Medieval Years, 1242–1600 CE 120

A. The Mongol Empire, the Golden Horde, and Tartars 123

B. Bulgaria 126

C. Serbia 126

D. Montenegro 128

E. Bosnia & Herzegovina 129

F. Croatia. 130

G. The Republic of Ragusa/Dubrovnik 130

H. Albania 131

I. The Byzantine Empire 133

J. The Ottoman (Turkish) Empire 135

K. Wallachia, Moldavia, and Transylvania 137

L. Hungary. 140

M. Bohemia. 143

N. The Teutonic Knights and Schizoid Prussia 145

O. Lithuania and the Eastern Slavs. 148

P. Livonia and the Balts. 149

Q. Poland as Catalyst. 151

R. Novgorod, Muscovy, and the Russians. 154

S. Halych-Volhynia: A Kingdom in Galicia 157

Special Insert: Peoples of Eastern Europe—The Germans . . 159–161

Chapter 4: The Dawn of a New Age, 1600–1800 162
A. Bohemia 162
B. The Principality of Transylvania 166
C. Wallachia and Moldavia 168
D. Montenegro 169
E. The Swedish Empire 170
F. The Polish-Lithuanian Commonwealth 173
G. The Ukrainians and Belarussians 179
H. Ottoman Empire 183
I. Russia 186
J. Of Austrians and Habsburgs 192
K. Prussia 195

Special Insert: Peoples of Eastern Europe—The Gypsies . . 199–201

Chapter 5: The Very, Very Long 19th Century,1800–1914 . . 202
A. Introduction 203
B. The Ottoman Empire as Doorstop 208
C. Serbia's Front Row Seat 213
D. Montenegro Hits the 19th Century 218
E. Romania is Born 218
F. Bulgaria's Raw Deal 222
G. Albania as Accident 225
H. The Italian Risorgimento and Irridentism 227
I. Pan-Germanism and How Fritz (and Helga) Got their Mojo . . . 228
J. Pan-Slavism and Pie in the Sky 231
K. The Austrian Dilemma and Hungary 233
L. Russia, the Hope and Prison of Nations 240
M. Dawn of the Dead: The Poland That Just Won't Go Away . . . 247

Special Insert: Peoples of Eastern Europe—The Muslims . . 253–255

Chapter 6: The Great War, and a Magic Year, 1914–1939 . . . 257
A. The War 258
B. Paris, 1919 263
C. The Ottoman Empire Goes Out in Style 265
D. Austria-Hungary as a Bug on the Windshield 268
E. Serbia and History 272

F. Montenegro is Pushed Off the Cliff 274

G. The Failed Superstates I: Yugoslavia 274

H. Bulgaria Tries 1913 Over Again 277

I. The Failed Superstates II: Romania 280

J. Albania: Let's Try That Again 283

K. Hungary Loses the War . . . Again 285

L. The Failed Superstates III: Czechoslovakia 289

M. Ukraine: With Friends Like These 294

N. Belarus Gets Its 15 Minutes . . . Literally 298

O. Libre Baltica: Lithuania, Latvia, and Estonia 299

P. Russia and How Russians Do Change 303

Q. The Failed Superstates IV: Poland 310

Chapter 7: War! 1939–45 317

A. The War as You Probably Don't Know It 321

B. About the Numbers Used in this Chapter 326

C. An Overview of the War 328

D. Poland and The Art of Not Being 331

E. The Baltics and a Bad Neighborhood 336

F. The Czech Lands Revert to the 17th Century 339

G. Slovakia Is Born, Sort of 342

H. Hungary Embraces Its Inner Tar Baby 343

I. Romania Guesses Wrong 346

J. Yugoslavia, Serbia, and 1914 All Over Again 349

K. Croatia's Dark Side 351

L. Albania Tries to Keep Its Head Above Water 353

M. Bulgaria: Third Time a Charm? 355

N. The Soviet Union Wins by Knockout in the 9th Round 357

O. The Holocaust 362

Special Insert: Home is Where the Border is! 368–371

Chapter 8: The Frying Pan, the Fire, etc., 1945–92 374

A. Introduction: The Cold War, or This Town Isn't Big Enough . . . 379

B. The Warsaw Pact: The Farm Animals Unite 388

C. Yugoslavia: Exit, Stage Left 392

D. Albania as an Island 395

E. Bulgaria Finally Gets Something in Return 398

F. Romania Goes Off the Deep End 401

G. Hungary and Its Food-Based Ideologies 404

H. Czechoslovakia, Just East of Eden 409

I. East Germany as the Runt of the Litter 413

J. Poland, the Perennial Pain in the Butt 417

K. The Soviet Union, Keeping Up with the Joneses 425

Chapter 9: Easy Come, Easy Go: 1989–92 433

A. Introduction: Ashes to Ashes, We All Fall Down 436

B. Poland and the Ghosts of 1980: The First Steps 438

C. The Hungarian "Refolution" 440

D. East Germany Goosesteps into Oblivion 441

E. Elvis is Dead, but Czechoslovakia Goes Velvet Anyway 443

F. Bulgaria Knows Peer Pressure When It Sees It 445

G. Asking for a Light in the Romanian Powderkeg 446

H. Albania and Frost in Hell 447

I. Playing Fiddle on the Deck of the Titanic: the Soviet Union 450

J. Libre Baltica, Part II 452

K. Agonia: The Many Deaths of Yugoslavia 452

Epilogue 461

Reference 469

    Musical Chairs, or Place Names in Eastern Europe 469

    Eastern Europe in Numbers 472

    Mrs. Jankowska's Homemade Pierogis 498

Notes 501

Bibliography 545

Index 565

About the Author 598

FOREWORD

In 1989, as a young scholar from Hungary, I was one of the fortunate few among my compatriots who had the opportunity to study in the United States. The rapid changes that were occurring in Eastern Europe captured the imagination of many fellow students. I remember a German student suggesting that the students of Indiana University form a European Club. "Good idea," I thought, "Perhaps we are on the map of Europe, after all." That student then designed an emblem we could use on T-shirts. It turned out to be an outline of the European continent, but at one glance, it became apparent that Eastern Europe was missing.

We now know that the Western world was highly apprehensive about the fall of Soviet power in Eastern Europe and continental reunification was not envisioned at all. We were not part of the Western mental map of Europe. Perhaps the situation has improved somewhat today, but "Europe" for many Americans (and Germans, Frenchmen, British, and Italians) still means *the West*. Eastern European contributions to world civilization can't be told in just a few lines: the list includes artists, writers, musicians, scientists, scholars, film makers and more. To mention a couple: did you know that Andy Warhol's parents and brothers were born in Slovakia, or that Rubik's Cube comes from Hungary?

The author of this book used to be a student of mine at Janus Pannonius University in Pécs, Hungary, where he lived and taught for years. Led at first by his Polish ancestry, he immersed himself in history and along the way developed a devotion to the study of Eastern Europe. As we used to talk over many a *korsó* of beer (need I explain?), careful not to clink our glasses lest we violate a national taboo stemming from the 19th century, young Tomek and I would mull the region's almost complete absence from the West's consciousness. Now he has produced a unique portrait of Eastern Europe, from Szczecin all the way down to Trieste and beyond, one that would give a professional historian pause. This book is a veritable intellectual feat, not only because the author seems to be at home in languages, history, and literature as diverse as, say, Bulgarian and Hungarian, but mainly because his book conveys what it means to be European and Eastern European at the same time. *Eastern Europe!* is a guide through the millennium-long maze of wars, strange customs and habits, and seemingly impenetrable languages of a region that has been largely shaped by external powers but has also left its imprint on the world.

This is a must-read for all who want to learn about and understand this forgotten part of Europe.

László Borhi

—Senior Researcher, Institute of History of the Hungarian Academy of Sciences; Visiting Professor, Central Eurasian Studies, and Chair Professor, Hungarian Studies, at Indiana University, Bloomington; author of *Hungary in the Cold War, 1945–1956*[1]

iNTRODUCTORY FAQ

Q: Why am I reading this?

A: I have a few assumptions about why you're reading this. They fall into the following categories:

- You're in the dentist's office and it's either this book or the June 1995 copy of *Cosmopolitan* you've already read over the last nineteen appointments.

- You've inherited a surname with lots of extra letters you're sure you're mispronouncing.

- You're dating someone who has inherited a surname you're sure you're mispronouncing, and it's really starting to irritate his/her parents.

- Someone close to you is in the military and is currently stationed in one of those countries with a severe vowel drought.

- You accidentally moved pictures of your boss you'd "tweaked" in Photoshop™ onto the company intranet, and now you're the office manager for your company's Albania branch.

- There's a Ukrainian church near your home that sells the most amazing pierogis on Saturdays, and you're trying to pry the recipe out of those little old ladies with the babushkas.

- You're a government employee who was just tasked with researching some detail about Trghksbjndkltsylvania or Phgdvnmtrzcdograd.

- Junior just called from his/her exchange program in Prague, and you couldn't tell from his/her slurred speech whether the country was famous for its beers or bears, so you figure you'd better pay him/her a visit.

- You have a crucial exam tomorrow morning for a 400-level class and you're hoping to God this book explains who Tycho Brahe was, what he did, and when and where he did it.

- Well, whatever your reasons for reading this book, we're here to help.

Q: What is Eastern Europe?

A: You would think the answer would be easy; just grab a map of Europe and look at the eastern half—but it's not quite that simple. Defining Eastern Europe throughout history is sort of like playing the proverbial wack-a-mole game. The Romans thought of Eastern Europe as everything east of what they controlled—which meant the Balkans were a core and integral part of Roman civilization, while Britain was an outlying barbarian border territory. The breaking of the Roman Empire into eastern and western halves muddled the East-West border somewhat, but Charlemagne's empire put a stake on the Elbe and Danube rivers as the West's outer eastern boundaries. (This meant that Vienna was a border town, while modern cities like Berlin and Copenhagen were in the barbarian East.) The Great Schism in Christianity, the Steppe invasions, the Ottoman Empire, the rise of the German empires, the rise of Russia—and its *doppelgänger*, the Soviet Union—all kept reshaping and redefining Eastern Europe for each new generation.

The term "Eastern Europe" only came into use in the late-18th century as an increasingly prosperous and powerful (and self-aware) Western Europe wanted to distinguish itself from the backwards, decaying medieval relics in the east. In the late-17th century, Pope Innocent XI proclaimed Poland *antemurale christianitatis* (Rampart of Christendom) but in the early-19th century the great Austrian statesman Prince Metternich famously declared "*Asien beginnt an der Landstraße*" (Asia begins at Province Street)—referring to the road beginning at Vienna's eastern gate leading eastward into Hungary.

A common thread throughout all these changes has been that Eastern Europe—and *who* is Eastern European—has always been defined by others. Today's Eastern Europe, for example, derives from the Cold War of 1945–89 and Stalin's Iron Curtain. This is a book about peoples who only fairly recently came to think of themselves as "Eastern Europeans," but who nonetheless have always been fully engaged in European history and have even, on occasion, played important roles.

For the purposes of this book I have defined "Eastern Europe" as that region of Europe that has spent its entire history surrounded by competing civilizations, between Western Europe, Central Asia, the Middle East, and North Africa, sometimes benefiting immensely through social, economic, or technological gains—but with the trade-off of occasionally serving as somebody else's battlefield. While some states in Eastern Europe managed to become strong enough to challenge outside powers on occasion, none were ever completely able to overcome the region's role as a crossroads, and Eastern Europeans have always had to balance as best as possible—whether between Byzantines and Franks, Habsburgs and Turks, or Soviets and the West.

So, to sum things up in answer to the question of "What is Eastern Europe," the answer is: it depends.

Q: Why haven't I seen much about Eastern European history in books with titles like, A History of Europe? Eastern or otherwise, it's still Europe, isn't it?

A: Good question. Western libraries are filled with books claiming to tell the history of "Europe," but by "Europe" they really mean *Western* Europe. British historian Norman Davies puts it this way:

> The title of "Europe," like the earlier label of "Christendom," therefore, can hardly be arrogated by one of its several regions. Eastern Europe is no less European for

being poor, or underdeveloped, or ruled by tyrants. In many ways, thanks to its deprivations, it has become more European, more attached to the values which affluent Westerners can take for granted. Nor can Eastern Europe be rejected because it is "different." All European countries are different. All West European countries are different. And there are important similarities which span the divide. A country like Poland might be very different from Germany or from Britain; but the Polish experience is much closer to that of Ireland or of Spain than many West European countries are to each other. A country like Greece, which some people have thought to be Western by virtue of Homer and Aristotle, was admitted to the European Community; but its formative experiences in modern times were in the Orthodox world under Ottoman rule. They were considerably more distant from those of Western Europe than several countries who found themselves on the wrong side of the Iron Curtain.[1]

Q: OK, so my company has posted me to Eastern Europe. Why should I waste time reading about Eastern European history? Why not just get one of those little phrase books?

A: Well, if you want to be successful dealing with Eastern Europeans, you will need to speak their language—and I don't mean Bulgarian. Actually, learning at least some Bulgarian might be helpful, but the point is that Eastern Europeans have a different relationship with their past than Westerners do, particularly Americans. The past for Eastern Europeans is not restricted to dry, dusty books on shelves that only a few socially maladjusted nerds read; the past is a living part of life for Eastern Europeans, and their discussions about the present are often clothed in the language of the past. For the average American, the American Revolution of 1775–83 was thousands of years ago, but for the average Eastern European, the 1389 battle of Kosovo Polje or the 1410 battle of Grunwald haven't quite ended yet. True, the historical *accuracy* of their memories may be suspect, but it is important for you to know and understand the references they use. To quote historian Lonnie R. Johnson:

> Developing a sense for what could be called the subjective dimensions of Central Europe—the (usually pretty good) stories that Central Europeans tell about themselves and the (usually pretty bad) ones they tell about their neighbors—is important to understanding the region. Some of the problems Central Europeans have with themselves and with one another are related to the fact their history haunts them.[2]

Q: Good God—does this mean I'm going to have to inject some reference to medieval battles into all my conversations with Eastern Europeans? I'm in business, for Pete's sake!

A: No, relax. It is just important to understand that history permeates everyday life and thinking for Eastern Europeans, and not having at least a basic understanding can lead to missed references or a social faux pas like clinking beer glasses in a Hungarian pub. Bad move.

Q: Does this mean I'm going to be reading about . . . Slavs?

A: Well, yes, we will be exploring some Slavic peoples and their histories but many, *many* other peoples as well. Eastern Europe and its heritage is not just about Slavs, but also includes Hungarians, Germans, Romanies (Gypsies), Cumanians, Arabs, Romans, Jews, and so many others.

It was common in the West at the turn of the 20th century to say that Western Europe was primarily a Germanic and Latin realm, while Eastern Europe was Slavic. The real difference between Western and Eastern Europe (as far as ethnic groups are concerned) is that Eastern Europe has far greater ethnic diversity than Western Europe. And, even worse, weaker state and institutional development in Eastern Europe—a product of historic political instability in the region—blurred the lines between some ethnic groups. For instance, nobody doubts the differences between French, Dutch, and Germans (though in truth all three derive from pretty much the same groups of peoples) but Eastern Europeans still argue whether Lemkos are Ukrainians or if Macedonians or Bosnjaks[3] really exist or not.

Through its relative political stability, Western Europe has achieved sharper (if ultimately superficial) distinctions between its various ethnic cultures than Eastern Europe. The West learned this lesson painfully in 1919 when it tried to reorganize Eastern Europe for its own purposes. It was kind of like herding cats.

Q: Will there be any sex or violence in this book?

A: Admittedly, it will be a little weak in the sex department, but we do promise lots of senseless, gratuitous violence. As a Hungarian professor once told me, "Those Eastern Europeans who wanted boring, calm, predictable lives emigrated, but those of us who wanted exciting and interesting lives, we stayed!"

Q: OK, so I'm going to read your history. Exactly how much history will this book cover? After all, Eastern Europe's history pretty much begins in 1918, right?

A: Nope. The early Bulgarian, Czech, and the parent civilization to the Russian, Ukrainian, and Belarussian states all existed by the time Alfred the Great first united Anglo-Saxon England in 890 CE. The Hungarian, Croatian, and Polish states followed shortly after. This book covers some 1,516 years—beginning with the death of the Greco-Roman "Classical" world—and blathers on until about the beginning of the 21st century.

Q: Will there be many names or terms in funny, unpronounceable languages? I can't even say "Schenectady."

A: Well, yes, there are going to be a lot of new names and terms, most in languages you're not familiar with. But don't panic. This book contains pronunciation guides right in the text.

USELESS TRIVIA: USELESS TRIVIA!

If you've ever worried that you hadn't destroyed enough of your brain cells through alcohol abuse in college and that you might have lots of pointless extra storage capacity under your skull, we're here to help! Throughout this book are little boxed-off sections like this one called "Useless Trivia" inserts that are filled with interesting but utterly useless historical, cultural, or other completely senseless facts about Eastern Europe that you can use to amaze your friends. I doubt these will even show up in any popular game shows. Still, these little factoids can be fun and, if nothing else, they can serve as placeholders in your memory until something more important comes along, like remembering *Gilligan's Island* episodes. Here's an example, below.

USELESS TRIVIA: I'M PRETTY SURE THAT THING IS COPYRIGHTED . . .

In August 1947 Western diplomats (and let's face it, some spies) were intently watching a Soviet Tupelev-4 long-range bomber make its world debut at an airshow just outside Moscow. Normally these Western observers would be focusing on the aircraft's capabilities but on this day they were actually just trying to see if it was really a Soviet plane. When they watched multiple versions of the Tu-4 fly by, however, their worst fears were confirmed: it really *was* a Soviet plane.

In the summer of 1944, three American B-29 "Superfortresses" were damaged while bombing Japanese industrial targets and were forced to land in the Soviet Union. These American long-range bombers were the most advanced technology of the day, far beyond Soviet capabilities. The American crews were released but Stalin kept the planes and ordered his engineers to take the planes apart, study them, and build an exact Soviet replica model. Both Washington and London believed that Soviet science was too primitive for this feat and suspected in 1947 at the airshow that the Tu-4s flying before them were actually those three damaged American B-29s—but modifications proved that the Soviets had succeeded and the Tu-4 was real. This meant that the Soviet air force could now reach such American targets as Chicago. The Soviets built some 800 Tu-4s before upgrading to more advanced models.[4]

ACKNOWLEGMENTS

Who knew it would be so much work writing a book? When I started this project, I had a full head of thick, luxurious hair, and now people in the oncoming lane get sun glare from my scalp. OK, maybe I'm exaggerating but just a bit.

In any event, because misery really does love company, I spread the pain as I got in well over my head and handed copies of my manuscript to any victim—I mean friend—who came within thirty feet of me. Actually, some lived in other states or even countries but were foolish enough to open my e-mails. Anyway, this means I am highly indebted to a lot of folks who slogged through my numerous typos, tortured grammar, endless run-on sentences, constant irrelevant tangents, and legions of mistakes. Each time I got a manuscript back drenched with red ink like a bloody murder victim, I twitched and writhed in agony from these thousand stab wounds—my baby!—but this book is far better for their efforts, and I am truly grateful to those of you who did so. Professor László Borhi has been a longtime inspiration and source of encouragement. I would also like to thank Dr. John Ashbrook, Assistant Professor of History at Sweet Briar College, and Dr. Nate Weston, Professor of History at Seattle Central Community College, for reviewing my manuscript and providing helpful feedback. Gratitude also goes to Tricia and Anne Marie Saenger, Dennis Pack, Anastasia and Will Colby, Allison Barrows and Romas Brandt, and László & Ildikó Olchváry, as well as longtime friend Paul Olchváry for his faith and patience. I am also indebted to Sharon Price for her technical aid in creating a far more professional-looking Independence Chart, as well as Derek Smith for helping out with some technical issues. Putting the bibliography together was a mind-numbing exercise, but my darling sister-in-law Joanna Dybciak-Langworthy volunteered, along with my wife, Magda, and together the deed was finished.

If there are any remaining mistakes, omissions, or boring tangents, I can assure you that these folks are not to blame. The fault lies with me and my fat typing fingers alone.

Tomek E. Jankowski
Londonderry, New Hampshire, 2013

The passenger terminal and the lighthouse, Varna, Bulgaria (Image © Angelina Dimitrova / Shutterstock)

TABLE O' FIGURES

page

Figure 1. Eastern Europe in 2013 8

Figure 2. The Indo-European Language Family Tree 9

Figure 3. The Indo-European Language Family 10

Figure 4. A Basic Breakdown of the Indo-European Language
Groups in Modern Europe 11

Figure 5. A Breakdown of the Slavic Language Group 14

Figure 6. Breakdown of the Finno-Ugric Language Family in
Eastern Europe 18

Figure 7. A Modern-day Language Map of Eastern Europe
with 2009 State Borders 20

Figure 8. Eastern Europe's Language Map in 1922 with
Contemporary State Borders 21

Figure 9. Eastern Europe and its geography 24

Figure 10. The General Cultural Regions of Eastern Europe . . 28

Figure 11. Central Europe vs. East Central Europe in 2010 . . . 29

Figure 12. The Major River Systems and Regions of Eastern
Europe. 30–31

Figure 13. The General Religious Borders of Eastern Europe . . 33

Figure 14. The Spread of Agriculture in Late Stone Age Europe . . 46

Figure 15. The Celtic Settled Regions of Europe, c. 800 BCE
with Modern-day Country Names. 50

Figure 16. The Independence Chart 52

Figure 17. An Independence Chart for Select Western
European Countries 53

Figure 18. The Persian Empire, c. 500 BCE 60

Figure 19. The Roman Empire Under Emperor Trajan,
117 CE 63

Figure 20. The Farthest Extent of the Umayyad Arab Empire,
c. 750 CE 66

Figure 21. Eastern Europe Timeline, 500–800 CE 69

Figure 22. Comparative Western Europe Timeline, 500–800 CE. . 70

Figure 23. Eastern and Central Europe in the mid-7th
Century CE 71

Figure 24. The Farthest Extent of Slavic Settlement in the
Late-7th Century 75

Figure 25. The Khazar Khaganate/Empire in c. 814 CE 81

Figure 26. The Steppe in Eastern Europe and Asia. 85

Figure 27. Eastern Europe Timeline, 800–1242 CE 89

Figure 28. Comparative Western Europe Timeline,
800–1242 CE 90

Figure 29. Eastern Europe in 814 CE 91

Figure 30. The Farthest Penetration of the Vikings,
800–1100 CE 98

Figure 31. Eastern Europe in 1000 CE 109

Figure 32. Western and Eastern Pomerania in 2012 113

Figure 33. Eastern Europe Timeline, 1242–1600. 121

Figure 34. Comparative Western Europe Timeline,
1242–1600 122

Figure 35. The furthest extent of the Mongolian Empire,
c. 1250 (including the Golden Horde): 123

Figure 36. Eastern Europe in c. 1242 125

Figure 37. Eastern Europe in 1350 132

Figure 38. Eastern Europe in 1500 138

Figure 39. Eastern Europe Timeline, 1600–1800. 163

Figure 40. Comparative Western Europe Timeline,
1600–1800 164

Figure 41. Eastern Europe in 1625 166

Figure 42. The Swedish Empire in 1650 172

Figure 43. The Ottoman Empire in 1600, with Modern
Borders 184

Figure 44. Eastern Europe in 1750 193

Figure 45. Charles V's Habsburg Empire, c. 1550. 194

Figure 46. Prussia and Brandenburg in 1750 197

Figure 47. Eastern Europe in 1800 203

Figure 48. Eastern Europe Timeline, 1800–1914. 204

Figure 49. Comparative Western Europe Timeline,
1800–1914 205

Figure 50. Eastern Europe in 1900 217
Figure 51. Eastern Europe Timeline, 1914–39 256
Figure 52. Eastern Europe in May, 1914 261
Figure 53. Eastern Europe in 1924 269
Figure 54. Eastern Europe Timeline, 1939–1945. 319
Figure 55. Allied and Axis Deaths in World War II. 321
Figure 56. World War II Fatalities by Global Region 322
Figure 57. Total World War II Fatalities in Europe 323
Figure 58. Total Civilian World War II Fatalities in Europe . . 324
Figure 59. Top 10 Countries in the World in Terms of % of
Population Killed in World War II 325
Figure 60. Where the Axe Fell in the Holocaust 363
Figure 61. Eastern Europe Timeline, 1944–1991. 377
Figure 62. Eastern Europe in 1960 383
Figure 63. A Divided Europe: NATO vs. the Warsaw Pact
in 1980. 391
Figure 64. Eastern Europe Timeline, 1988–92 434
Figure 65. Comparative Global Changes Timeline,
1970–2000 435
Figure 66. The Populations of Eastern Europe in 2012. 472
Figure 67. Comparing Populations: Western vs.
Eastern Europe (2012) 473
Figure 68. Eastern Europe's Population by Region (2012) . . 473
Figure 69. Europe's Top 30 Countries by Population (2012). . 474
Figure 70. 35 Largest European Cities by Population
(c. 2010) 475–476
Figure 71. Minorities as a % of Population Across
Eastern Europe (2010) 477
Figure 72. The Ethnic Breakdowns of Bosnia-Herzegovina
and Montenegro, 2010. 478
Figure 73. Languages in Eastern Europe at Home and
Abroad (2009) 480
Figure 74. Literacy Levels Across Europe in 2011 481
Figure 75. The European Union in Eastern Europe in 2012 . . 483
Figure 76. NATO in Eastern Europe in 2012 485
Figure 77. CIA World Factbook Ranking of

Eastern European Economies by GDP-PPP in 2011 487

Figure 78. GDP-PPP in Eastern Europe by Region (2011) . . . 488

Figure 79. GDP-PPP Growth in Eastern Europe
(2011, estimated) 488

Figure 80. Eastern Europe Across Various Economic
Indices, 2010 490–91

Figure 81. Broadband Internet Penetration of European
Countries, 2011 492

Figure 82. Traditional Alcohol Consumption in
Eastern Europe 494

Figure 83. The Consumption of Pork vs. Beef for Select
Countries 497

"Faced with the question 'What are Hungarians like?,' the respondents [to an essay contest held for non-Hungarians] observed, among other things: Hungarians devote a staggering amount of attention to the past; indeed they pour out into the streets, flagrantly and loudly, several times a year in an effort to conjure up notable historical events."
  —from the foreword to *The Essential Guide to Being Hungarian*[1]

Section I

Wherein we take a look at some of Eastern Europe's key attributes today, and get a sense for the lay of the land, as it were. So put on your rubber gloves and snap 'em tight; we're going in.

The first concerns central and eastern Europe. If you came from there, and I assume that almost all of you do, you are citizens of countries whose status is doubly uncertain. I am not claiming that uncertainty is a monopoly of central and eastern Europeans. It is probably more universal today than ever. Nevertheless, your horizon is particularly cloudy. In my own lifetime every country in your part of Europe has been overrun by war, conquered, occupied, liberated, and reoccupied. Every state in it has a different shape from the one it had when I was born. Only six of the twenty-three states which now fill the map between Trieste and the Urals were in existence at the time of my birth. [...]

It is perfectly common for the elderly inhabitant of some central European city to have had, successively, the identity documents of three states. A person of my age from Lemberg[1] or Czernowitz[2] has lived under four states, not counting wartime occupations; a man from Munkács[3] may well have lived under five. [...] In more civilized times, as in 1919, he or she might have been given the option which new citizenship to choose, but since the Second World War he or she has been more likely to be either forcibly expelled or forcibly integrated into the new state. Where does a central or eastern European belong? Who is he or she? The question has been a real one for great numbers of them, and it still is. In some countries it is a question of life and death, in almost all it affects and sometimes determines their legal status and life chances.

—British historian Eric Hobsbawm (1917–2012), himself raised in 1920s Vienna and Berlin, in a lecture given to students at the Central European University, in Budapest, in 1993[4]

A FEW WORDS ABOUT A WORD

And that word is . . . "state." What is a state? For Americans, it's one of the fifty things below the national (federal) government that they have to pay lots of taxes to—but that's because the original American states actually thought of themselves as thirteen separate countries joining together. I have to use that term a bit differently in this book, though.

A state is simply a political structure with a definite leader who controls a specific territory. The problem is that we're about to cover *fifteen hundred years* of history—which is sixty generations, if we assume one generation is twenty-five years—and states changed a lot over that time. Take for instance a state on the early steppe, when a tribe or clan, using marriage, alliance, and war, managed to convince other nearby tribes to join together and recognize the first tribe's leader as their ruler. That's a state; it has one boss, it controls a certain territory (which usually means it can tax or collect tribute in that territory, and others can't), and the ruler is responsible for all decisions regarding relations with outside tribes, trade, and war.

States like that tended not to last long, but over time as they grew larger and more sophisticated, their rulers usually found that instead of relying on their family and close friends to deal with crime, foreign relations, and other issues, they needed specialists to deal with the hard stuff; and so you had the first government and ministers—the minister of finance, the foreign minister, etc. And, of course, these specialists soon needed help keeping track of everything they were doing, and so you had the first bureaucrat. This happened all over the world, not just Europe. In fact, until the 18th century, the country with the most evolved and elaborate government bureaucracy was China. That's an important point to remember: European state development historically lagged behind many other civilizations, like those of the early Islamic Arab empire(s).

The great moment for European statehood came with the two truces signed during the horrific Catholic–Protestant wars sparked by the Protestant Reformation, in 1555 at Augsburg and in 1648 at Westphalia. These two peace agreements established the idea of *state sovereignty*, which meant that states were no longer just playthings belonging to aristocrats. States had their own legal, independent rights. Naturally, the question then arose across Europe of what exactly a state was for if it didn't just belong to aristocrats: this discussion among Europe's intellectuals is called the *Enlightenment*, and it lasted for about 150 years. The founding documents of the United States of America, the Declaration of Independence and the Constitution, are products of the Age of Enlightenment.

The thing about Europe is that it is a small nubby isolated peninsula sticking off the western end of the Eurasian landmass, and worse, this little peninsula is jam-packed with peoples and countries. A major theme in European state history from the days of Charlemagne to the European

Union is the constant and intense competition among all these relatively equal little states, as David C. Kang describes:

> States engaged in the "great game" of the balance of power, alliances, and conquest whenever possible. The slightest advantage was to be seized; the slightest weakness was exploited. States constantly jockeyed with one another to survive, and survival meant conquest.
>
> [. . .] Because European states were constantly under threat of attack, being bigger and more powerful enhanced a state's chances of surviving. Thus states strove and competed to become as powerful as possible. Yet, if one state became too big, it would threaten to take over the entire system and conquer all the other states. In response, other states tended to join together against the stronger power, flocking to the side of the weak, in order to keep any one state from dominating the system and conquering everyone else. This European pattern gave rise to one of the most enduring concepts in international relations: balance of power.[1]

But this intense competition also led to the strengthening of the state, which in turn led to an increasing centralization of authority and power in states in the 17th, 18th, and 19th centuries. By today, we live in a (political) world almost entirely organized around nation states. In the 14th century, trading cities from all across northern Europe fed up with pirates and high taxes banded together to form the Hanseatic League, which had its own navy and armies, and occasionally even fought against its own countries. A few centuries later, however, the idea of cities in different countries banding together was impossible because national governments—countries—had become stronger. Likewise, in the 13th century whole regions of France—like Burgundy, Aquitaine, and Anjou—were effectively independent, although they were technically recognized as parts of France; each had their own armies and often ignored or defied Paris. Just a few centuries later, however, in the late 17th century King Louis XIV commanded every square inch of French soil. The difference between these two time periods is that of medieval versus early modern Europe. Medieval kings spent a lot of time just keeping their kingdoms together. We take strong central governments, national laws, national armies, flags, currencies, national post offices, and so on for granted nowadays, but in medieval Europe, wealthier aristocrats had their own armies—sometimes larger than the king's—and printed their own currencies (minted in precious metals). Mail was sent through merchants and travelers who happened to be going that way, and you had to hope it got there. The rise of strong central governments with *gendarmes* (police), bureaucrats, public services, and year-round armies changed everything.

So you see the problem: comparing 19th century Britain to 12th century Poland or the 16th century Ottoman Empire is very difficult because they were based on very different ideas, and organized very differently. This is why I will use this simple, generic term "state" to refer to any political structure that controlled a definite territory in Eastern European history, from the Cumanian khanate to Frederick the Great's Prussia to Gottwald's communist Czechoslovakia.

Castle Square in the Stare miasto (Old Town), Warsaw, on April 13, 2013. Though the city dates to the 10th century, none of the buildings in this picture are older than the 1950s, courtesy of German efforts to destroy the city entirely in World War II.

(Image © marekusz / Shutterstock.com)

A NOTE ON PRONUNCIATION

"Boy, those French, they have a different word for *everything*!"
—comedian Steve Martin

Let's face it, you're about to wade into an ocean of foreign names, all written in weird and unfamiliar languages—some in different alphabets. I've thought long and hard about how best to give you an idea of how to pronounce them, and I think it would be easiest to simply follow each new term with an approximate pronunciation, using American English phonetic (sound) pronunciation. For instance, after the Romanian city of Targovişte, you would see "*(tar-go-VEESH-teh)*," or the Polish-Lithuanian dynasty name *Jagiełło*, you would see "*(yah-GYEH-wo)*". The emphasized syllable will be in capital letters. There are some sounds in Eastern European languages that do not exist in English—like the Hungarian "gy" or the German "ö"—but we'll do our best to get around those. For instance, in reverse, modern-day Greeks call the United States' capital Βάσινγκτον (vass-EENG-tohn) because they don't have the "w" or the "sh" sounds. Close enough.

I think this is the easiest approach, and while not quite exact, at least an Eastern European will know what you mean. Think about this in reverse; when I was a student in Hungary many years ago, a businesswoman once began talking to me about something called "kunuff-huff." I had no idea what "kunuff-huff" was, and she was quite surprised that I didn't know—until she wrote it down, and I realized that she was pronouncing the popular business term "know-how" in a Hungarian way. If someone had just told her to pronounce it like "(nó-háú)," I would have understood her right away—and even been somewhat impressed, since she did not speak English.

There are some cases where a common English name or equivalent exists for an Eastern European name, and in those cases I will either use the Eastern European name but will put somewhere in parentheses the English equivalent, like "*Kraków* (Cracow)," or just go with the common English term, like Moscow—which in Russian is actually Москва (MOSK-vah)—or Warsaw, (*Warszawa*; var-SHAH-vah in Polish), or Bucharest (*Bucureşti*; boo-koor-ESHT-tee in Romanian). In most cases, though, we'll try to stick with the Eastern European original.

A WORD (OR TWO) ABOUT TIME

A funny thing happened while I was away as a student. I was living in a country where the communists were still in power but clearly on the way out. One of the early things to go was a writing convention in history: the communists, who were very practiced atheists—at least in the daylight—forced people to stop using the age-old expressions "B.C." (Before Christ) and "A.D." (*Anno Domini*, Latin for "In the Year of Our Lord), referring to the Western convention of using Jesus' life as a milestone in our measurement of time. Instead, the communists forced people to use the more bland (but functional, I suppose) terms *i.e.* (*időszámításunk előtt*, "Before Our Era") and *i.sz.* (*időszámításunk szerint*, "In our Current Era"). It was in the end a fairly harmless change, but nonetheless, before the door could slap the posterior of the last comrade on his way out, many people insisted on switching back to the pre-1945 *Kr.e.* (*Krisztus előtt*, "Before Christ") and *Kr.u.* (*Krisztus után*, "After Christ"). Fair enough, though it was really a package deal: as the communist regimes crumbled, many things were being changed. Street and even some city names reverted back to their precommunist names from the 1940s. Imagine 60% of the street names in your home city suddenly changing overnight to something they were called forty years ago. Overnight, maps became useless.

If that wasn't confusing enough, imagine my surprise upon returning to the U.S. in the mid-1990s, when I learned that in my absence, the more familiar "B.C." and "A.D." had been replaced by "BCE" (Before the Common Era) and "CE" (Common Era). My first reaction was that all these changes were getting just a little too creepy, but with some reflection I grudgingly came to understand and accept the point. And so, throughout this book I will be using the new convention, which I hope you, my gentle readers, will understand. If it's any consolation, consider that the Western year 2012 is year 1433 AH for Muslims—in other words, 1,433 years after the Hijra, or the year the Prophet Mohammed moved from Mecca to Medina, which would be 622 CE (or A.D. 622 for us old-timers) in the Western calendar.[1] Meanwhile, the Western Gregorian year 2012 is the year 5772 AM for observant Jews, who measure time from when they believe the world was created. It's all relative.

Speaking of the Gregorian calendar, I use it, well, religiously throughout this book for apples-to-apples comparisons of dates. The first Western calendar was created in Roman times and named after Julius Caesar some 2,050 years ago. Pope Gregory XIII updated it in the late 16th century to more accurately measure time and keep the calendar in sync with the seasons—hence the Gregorian calendar. Catholic countries adopted it immediately but Protestant countries, suspicious that this new calendar was some Papal trick, stalled for a while. They eventually did recognize that it was indeed more accurate, however, and adopted it. The British Empire (including its American colonies), for instance, adopted the Gregorian calendar only in the mid-18th century. This difference between the two calendars today is not great—thirteen days—and only becomes dramatic for our purposes here during the early 20th century when Tsarist Russia (which still stuck to the old Julian calendar at that point) slid into revolution, and the Bolsheviks later adopted the Gregorian calendar—well, eventually. This is why we talk about the Russian "February Revolution" of 1917, which actually took place in early March of 1917 (by the Gregorian calendar), and the military parades celebrating the so-called "Great October Revolution" in the Soviet Union were held each year on November 7. This is just to remind you that while I am using a single calendar throughout the text to give you a timeline, many of the peoples I'm describing often organized and measured time very differently than we do now.

The Prague astronomical clock (Pražský orloj) in Prague, the Czech Republic

(Image © vicspacewalker/Shutterstock)

Figure 1. Eastern Europe in 2013

LANGUAGES

There's no way around it. Eastern Europe is chock-full of languages, and they will seem, for the most part, strange and completely foreign to people whose experience with foreign languages tends to be with Spanish or French. But there is hope! Most languages in Eastern Europe are related to one another, meaning they developed from a common source. In fact, most languages spoken in Europe today—Eastern *and* Western—are related. They belong to the Indo-European language family, whose speakers cover almost all of Europe and a large chunk of Asia (as well as the Americas and beyond).

Figure 2. The Indo-European Language Family Tree[1]

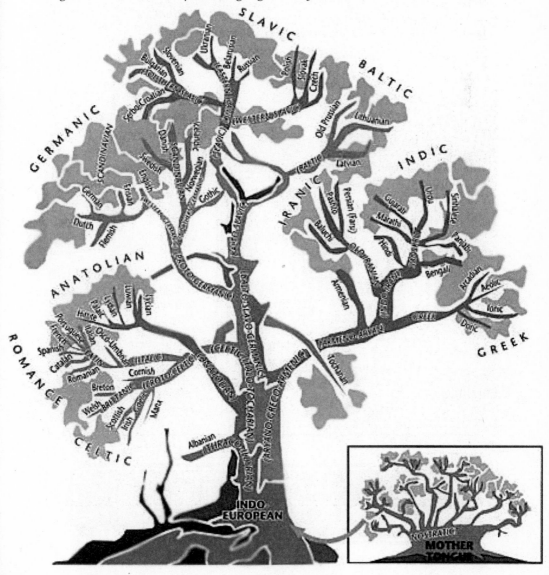

The Indo-European language family is the largest language family in the world, with just a little less than half of the planet's population speaking an Indo-European-derived language as their native tongue. It is believed this language family originated in Anatolia (modern-day central Turkey) around 7,000 BCE, with its speakers eventually spreading to Iran, India, and the Russian Steppe, and westward throughout Europe and beyond. Modern-day linguists began to uncover this huge language family at the end of the 18th century when they realized the similarities between Greek, Latin, and Sanskrit (the ritual language of the ancient Aryans in northern India). Here is a basic breakdown of the modern-day Indo-European languages, portrayed as a family tree:

Figure 3. The Indo-European Language Family

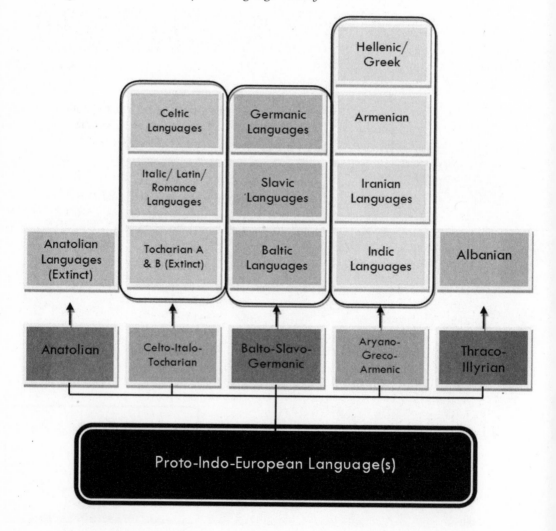

Figure 2 (page 9) looks complicated but it basically shows, like a genealogical family tree, how the various subgroups (or branches) of languages evolved from an Indo-European parent language (or group of parent languages). If you start from the base and work your way up, there are essentially four major branches that grow out of the main trunk—the Anatolian, the Celto-Italo-Tocharian, the Balto-Slavo-Germanic, and the Aryano-Greco-Armenic "branches." There's actually one more, a small, stubby one off to the side called the Thraco-Illyrian branch as well, but more on that one later. It might be a little easier to think about it this way:

Figure 4. A Basic Breakdown of the Indo-European Language Groups in Modern-day Europe

Super-Groups	Groups	Modern Surviving Examples in Europe
Celto-Italo-Tocharian	Celtic	Breton, Cornish, Irish Gaelic, Manx, Scottish Gaelic, Welsh
	Italic/ Latin/ Romance	Catalonian, French, Friulian, Italian, Portuguese, Romanian, Spanish (Castillian), Vlach/ Aroman
Balto-Slavo-Germanic	Baltic	Latvian, Lithuanian
	Slavic	Belarussian, Bosnian, Bulgarian, Croatian, Czech, Kaszub, Macedonian, Polish, (Great) Russian, Serbian, Slovak, Slovenian, Sorbian/ Wendic, Ukrainian
	Germanic	Danish, Dutch, English, Faroese, Frisian, German, Icelandic, Norwegian, Swedish
Aryano-Greco-Armenic	Hellenic/ Greco	Greek
	Armenic	Armenian
	Indic	Romany/ Roma (Gypsy)
Thraco-Illyrian	Albanian	Albanian

The Anatolian languages are now all extinct, and include some of the earliest Indo-European languages we know about, like ancient Hittite. The Celto-Italo-Tocharian languages broke into two, and possibly three groups of languages: the Celtic languages, the Italic (sometimes called "Latin" or "Romance") languages, and possibly Tocharian, an ancient language (or group of languages) spoken in what is today western China but which is now extinct. The Balto-Slavo-Germanic languages gave birth to, as you've probably already guessed, the modern-day Baltic, Slavic, and Germanic languages. The Aryano-Greco-Armenic languages gave birth to several language groups: the Indic languages (which as the name implies includes several languages of the northern Indian subcontinent, such as Hindi, Urdu, Punjabi, Kashmiri, and Nepali), the Iranian languages (of which modern-day Farsi or Persian is only one example, with many now extinct including ancient Scythian, Sarmatian, and Alani), the Armenic languages of which only modern-day Armenian now remains; and likewise, the Hellenic or Greek languages of which only modern-day Greek exists, although once many Hellenic languages existed (e.g., Ionian, Doric, and Mycenaean). Modern-day Romany, the Gypsy language, is considered an Indic language. Thraco-Illyrian is a theoretical language group whose sole surviving member is modern-day Albanian.

What does all this mean for us? For our purposes, it tells us that the languages you see above are all sibling languages that developed from a common ancestral language and are related to one another. The Indo-European language family spans Europe, so that in fact only a handful of languages in modern-day Europe—e.g., Basque, Estonian, Finnish, Hungarian, and Turkish—are *not* from the Indo-European language family. There are a few important things to remember about this language family:

- The Indo-European language family has its roots in the Middle East and Asia, where its languages today span modern-day India, Pakistan, Iran, and parts of Afghanistan. The ancient Aryans were very different from how the Nazis pictured them.

- It is also important to remember that no matter which category a language is classified in, all languages are significantly influenced by other languages and other language families. For instance, English is a Germanic language, but its vocabulary borrowed a lot of vocabulary from medieval French and Latin, as well as Danish and the Celtic languages. Indeed, by now English has borrowed from just about every language on the planet, thanks in large part to commercialism and colonialism.

Languages are always changing and evolving, and there is no such thing as a "pure" language.

- Finally, language does not equal (≠) ethnicity. A good example would be modern-day Canadians and Americans, the majority of whom speak English as their native language—though many Canadians and Americans do not have any English ancestry. It is easy to imagine ancient romantic Germanic or Slavic warrior ancestors, but in reality premodern Europeans (and others) mixed and mingled a lot. Just because grandpa grew up speaking Italian doesn't mean you should automatically expect to be able to trace his ancestry back to ancient Rome; DNA tests could surprise you with a patchwork of Latin, Celtic, Germanic, Slavic, Balkan, African, Middle Eastern, or other lineages.

USELESS TRIVIA: OUR GIFT TO ETYMOLOGY!

The number of words in English originating from Eastern European languages are few and deal mostly with some form of food, like "paprika," "pierogi," and "borsht." English has managed to borrow *some* terms, however: *coach*, for instance, comes from the Hungarian town Kócs (pronounced like "coach"), where the wheel-spring suspension was invented in the 15th century to be used by almost all horse-drawn vehicles—like stage*coaches*, later train *coaches*, and so on. Another Eastern European–derived word came into English when a 1930s Czech science-fiction writer, Karel Čapek, coined a term to refer to dronelike slaves living under a dictator. He used the Czech term for work, *robota*, which became "robot" in English—a machine that does menial labor.

The Slavic languages

When two Greek brothers, Constantine and Methodius, traveled 770 miles (1,240 km) to the Czech lands in the 9th century CE from their hometown on the Aegean Sea, they spoke a local Slavic dialect fairly close to modern-day Bulgarian and Macedonian, and yet they were able to communicate with the Slavs (i.e., early Czechs) 770 miles away in Prague. The Slavic languages are the closest of all the Indo-European languages, maintaining still today a surprising level of mutual comprehensibility despite spanning half a continent and a host of different historical foreign influences.

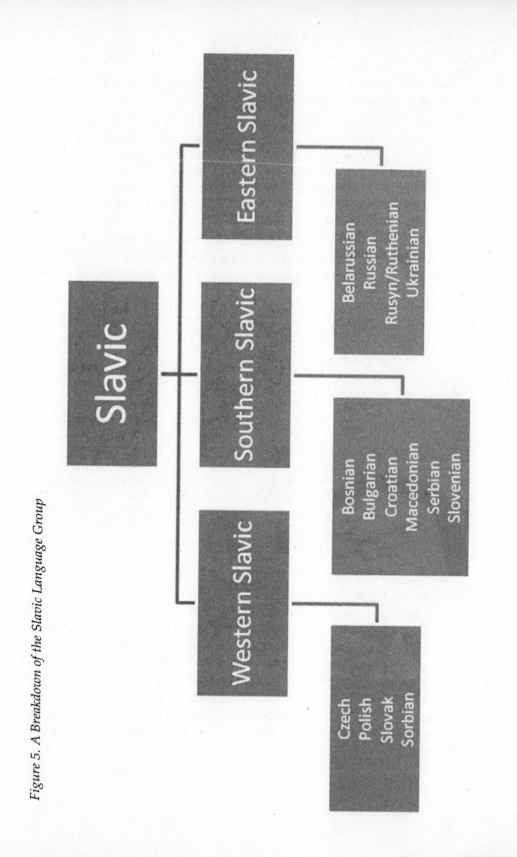

Figure 5. A Breakdown of the Slavic Language Group

The Slavic languages are broken into three different groups, and these language groups are seen as representing three very different cultural realms as well. (See Figure 5.) The first group is the Western Slavic languages, which today include Polish, Czech, and Slovak. They are geographically the most western (located largely in Central Europe) but culturally and historically their speakers have also been the most closely tied to the West. The Western Slavic languages typically have had strong influences primarily from German, Latin, French, and Italian. All of the Western Slavic languages are written in the Western "Latin" or "Roman" alphabet, just like English.

The next group is the Southern Slavic languages, which today are Bosnian, Bulgarian, Croatian, Macedonian, Serbian, and Slovenian. While this Balkan-centered cultural realm has had some influences from the West (e.g., Rome, Venice, France, Germany), its primary cultural origins lay with the East (Byzantium, the Ottoman Empire). As we'll see later, for several centuries in the Dark Ages there was little difference between the Western and Southern Slavic languages, but in the late-9th century the Magyars (whose non-Slavic language we'll examine later) invaded Europe and cut the Slavic world in two, separating the Western and Southern branches. Modern-day Czech, for instance, a Western Slavic language, still shares some grammatical features with the Southern Slavic languages. Half of the Southern Slavic languages are written in the Western "Latin" alphabet (Slovenian, Croatian, Bosnian) and half are written in the Cyrillic alphabet (Bulgarian, Macedonian, Serbian).

USELESS TRIVIA: CAN YOU SPELL "EFFICIENT"?

The Cyrillic alphabet (Аа, Бб, Вв, Гг, etc.) may look strange to Westerners who are used to the Roman Latin alphabet (Aa, Bb, Cc, Dd, etc.), but the Cyrillic alphabet was carefully adopted (largely from the Greek alphabet) specifically for the Slavic languages. This means that there are far fewer spelling variations than languages like English or French typically have, in part because their use of the Latin alphabet developed "organically"—meaning gradually, over time and with little interference from authorities. For example, in English, the "f" sound can be written *f* ("fun"), *ph* ("phone"), or *gh* ("rough"), while in Serbian, it can only be written with one letter: ф (*Филаделфија*, "Philadelphia"; *Француска*, "France"). This means that Russian or Bulgarian school children have far fewer spelling issues, simply because there are often fewer spelling options. English, with its legacy archaic Germanic spellings ("night" and "two") and the influence of medieval (Norman) French, is more challenging in this respect.

The third and last branch comprises the Eastern Slavic languages, which today include Belarussian, Russian, and Ukrainian. These languages all derive from a civilization that flourished in what is today Ukraine, Belarus, and western Russia 800+ years ago called (*Kieven*) *Rus*, and the language spoken by that civilization: Rusyn. Through Rus, all three languages have inherited strong influences from the Byzantines: Greek Orthodox Christianity, the Cyrillic alphabet, and much Greek vocabulary. Because of the Byzantine use of Bulgarian priests to help Christianize Rus in the 11th and 12th centuries, there were early on some strong Southern Slavic influences as well on the Eastern Slavic languages. Conversely, though originally born from medieval Bulgarian and Macedonian, Old Church Slavonic is often associated with the Eastern Slavic languages because of its long use by the Russian Orthodox Church, during which time it had absorbed many traits and influences from medieval Russian.

A note about languages of the former Yugoslavia: linguists still debate exactly what languages exist in this region. For decades under the Yugoslav state, a single, unified "Serbo-Croat" language was taught in Yugoslav schools (written in Serbia in the Cyrillic alphabet, and in Croatia in the Latin alphabet), but since the breakup of Yugoslavia local nationalists have denied the existence of a single, unified Serbo-Croat language, instead claiming that Serbs, Croats, and Bosnians all speak different languages. Still, when Serbia, Croatia, and Bosnia negotiated the Dayton Peace Accords in 1995, no interpretors were needed between their representatives. This goes to show that politics often plays a role in determining what is recognized as a language. Western Europe is not exempt from this phenomenon; the real differences between modern-day Dutch, Flemish, and the German dialect *Plattdeutsch* (*Plattdüütsch*, also known as Lower Saxon) have more to do with political borders than linguistics. The emergence of Catalonian as distinct from Spanish is a similar issue. As the linguist Max Weinreich once put it, "A language is a dialect with an army and a navy."

USELESS TRIVIA: BUT WHAT *DIDN'T* THEY CHANGE!

In 1917, immediately after seizing power, the Bolsheviks turned to reforming the Russian language so illiterate Russian peasants could learn to read and write more quickly, dropping five letters from the Russian Cyrillic alphabet in the process. Lenin also favored replacing the traditional Russian Orthodox Julian calendar with the more modern Gregorian calendar, but after Lenin's death Stalin instead created a strange five day week, then later a six day week calendar. Only in 1940 did Stalin relent and adopt the Gregorian calendar, but it's odd that the militantly atheistic Stalin, who was not shy about shooting priests or burning down churches, reverted to the traditional Russian name for Sunday: Воскресенье (Voss-kreh-SSEH-nyeh), "Resurrection Day."

The Baltic Languages

Once represented by dozens of languages stretching on a modern-day map from Moscow to Berlin, the Baltic language family has been reduced in recent centuries to just two representatives, Latvian and Lithuanian. It was once believed by linguists that the Baltic languages were somehow directly linked to the ancient proto-Indo-European language, but both this idea and even the notion of a proto-Indo-European mother language have since been rejected as simplistic. Nonetheless, the Baltic languages have retained numerous archaisms lost by many of their sibling Indo-European languages and are therefore much-studied by linguists. Interestingly, despite the nonsense propagated by Nazi ideology in the 20th century, the Baltic languages' closest relations within the Indo-European language group are the Slavic and Germanic languages. These three families are intimately related and share a common linguistic ancestor (or group of language ancestors). Both Lithuanian and Latvian are written today in the Western "Latin" alphabet (like English) and have particularly rich literary traditions.

Romanian

Many are surprised to learn that Romanian is an Italic or "Romance" language derived from Latin. A Romance language in Eastern Europe? *Ce n'est pas possible!* But it is true. Now, like all of the other Italic languages, Romanian also has a substantial non-Latin heritage—believed in Romanian's case to be primarily from the *Dacians*, a people thought to be related to the ancient Thracians and Illyrians of the pre-Roman Balkans. There are also influences from other language groups (e.g., Greek, Bulgarian, Turkish, and French) but it is nonetheless a dyed-in-the-wool Romance language, every bit as much as Italian or French. In fact, knowing some Italian or French would be extremely helpful if you visit Romania. Romanian is the product of the ancient Roman Balkans, or better put, the collapse of the ancient Roman Balkans. (This is all explained in more detail in Chapter One.) Modern-day Romanian contains a fairly hefty borrowed Slavic vocabulary—"Yes" and "No" in Romanian are *Da* and *Nu*, respectively—but don't let that fool you; a phrase the Romanians like to use to refer to themselves says it all: *O insulă a latinităţi intr-o mare de slavi*—A Latin island in a sea of Slavs.

Other Language Families and Groups?

While most European languages today belong to the Indo-European language family, not all do. In Eastern Europe there is another large language family—the Finno-Ugric language family, which is represented by several modern-day languages in the region. (See Figure 6.) This language family is said to have originated in the Ural Mountains (in modern-day Russia) about 5,000 years ago, with the Ugric branch gradually spreading southward along the Urals toward the Black Sea, while the Finno-Permic branch moved toward the Baltic Sea and eastern Scandinavia. Some Finno-Ugric speakers, like the Hungarians, migrated into Europe fairly recently in historic times. Livonian (spoken in northern Latvia) is considered a dying language, with only a few hundred native speakers today. "Ostyak" and "Vogul" may sound like Star Trek galactic races, but they are actually small tribes in the eastern Urals. Modern-day Hungarians and Finns make much of the fact they are (very distant) linguistic cousins.

Figure 6. Breakdown of the Finno-Ugric Language Family in Eastern Europe

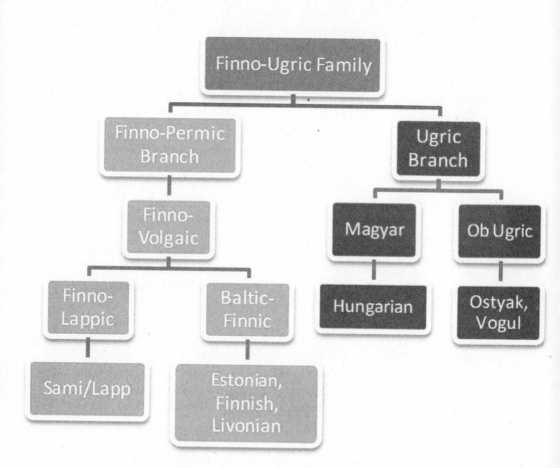

USELESS TRIVIA: ENGENDERING LANGUAGE!

Most Indo-European languages use genderized nouns, meaning that every noun is assigned a gender (masculine, feminine, or neuter). If you've ever studied German, for instance, you've had to memorize which nouns had "Der" (masculine form), "Die" (feminine or plural form) or "Das" (neuter form) definite articles. Hungarian, which as you know by now is *not* an Indo-European language, goes in the opposite extreme. Not only does it not have genderized nouns, but it only has a single personal pronoun. In simple English, this means that Hungarian only has one word—*ő*—to cover *he and she*. The sentence *Ő ment haza* can mean both "He went home" or "She went home."

The Turkic languages are definitely derived from some larger Uralic (i.e., Ural Mountain-born) language family, although the relationship of the Turkic languages to language families such as the Finno-Ugric family has not been fully sorted out yet. The modern Turkic languages span from the Balkans to Central Asia to northern China and everywhere in between. Turkish is only one of the Turkic languages, with Azeri (of Azerbaijan), Kyrgyz, Uighur, Uzbek, Kazakh, Tartar and many others thrown in the mix as well. In the 20th and 21st centuries Turkey has supported a sort of "Pan-Turkism" among the Turkic peoples living across Europe and Asia in support of their cultural and political rights.

Another important group is the Semitic languages, which are represented in Eastern Europe through Hebrew, Yiddish, and even Aramaic. Hebrew was used by European Jews primarily as a ceremonial language, but Yiddish—a hybrid of medieval Hebrew, German, and Slavic—was a living language throughout the region for a thousand years until its near destruction in the Holocaust. Aramaic, a sister language to Hebrew (and probably Jesus' native tongue), still has some tiny legacy pockets of speakers located in Russia and Ukraine. Ladino, the Spanish-Arabic-Hebrew hybrid language of Sephardic Jews, is also represented in Eastern Europe primarily in Bulgaria, Macedonia, Turkey, and Greece as a legacy of the Ottoman years in which many Sephardim fled the Spanish *Reconquista* to the relative safety of the Ottoman Empire and its bustling southern Balkan commercial centers.

Language Maps

The language map of Eastern Europe has always been messy, never matching political borders. But while the map in Figure 7 may seem chaotic, it is in fact the "cleanest" language map ever for the region. The reason is primarily World War II, and the postwar large-scale ethnic cleansing that took place all across the region as governments forced ethnic boundaries to match new political ones. During the 20th century, *tens of millions* of Eastern

Europeans were ethnically cleansed at some point. Still, we can see leftover pockets of Polish speakers in Lithuania, Belarus, and Ukraine, while a few million Hungarian speakers live outside of Hungary. With the collapse of the Soviet Union in 1991–92, some 15-20 million Russians suddenly found themselves living outside of Russia in Ukraine, Belarus, Moldova, the Baltic states, the Caucasus, and Central Asia. If anything, Figure 7 is vastly *simplified*. Still, at least the conflicts in the former Yugoslav regions become clearer. And as the region continues to attract immigrants, one commonly encounters Arabic, Chinese, Armenian, Swahili, or Laotian speakers as one walks a typical Eastern European street as well.

Figure 7. A Modern-day Language Map of Eastern Europe with 2009 State Borders

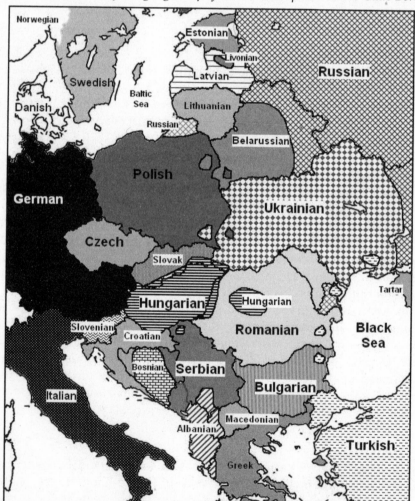

In Figure 8 we have the language borders of 1922 (with contemporary state borders), and we can see a lot more diversity—though even this is simplified.

Still, we can see a whole century's worth of ethnic conflict in the making. In the new age of nation states, multiethnic states like Poland, Czechoslovakia, Yugoslavia, and Romania were under siege from within. Also, along the Turkish coastline you can see that Greek was spoken—until the devastating events of 1922. Islands of German and Yiddish-speakers still dot Eastern Europe, while the center of gravity for the Polish-speaking world was decidedly more eastward. Italian was still heard along the Dalmatian coastline, and the Baltic languages competed with German and Russian. Wilno (Vilnius) was primarily a Polish-speaking city, Breslau (Wrocław) was German, Fiume (Rijeka) was Italian, and Lwów (Lviv) was mixed Polish, Ukrainian, and Yiddish—though just four years earlier it was known as Austrian Lemberg.

Figure 8. Eastern Europe's Language Map in 1922 with Contemporary State Borders

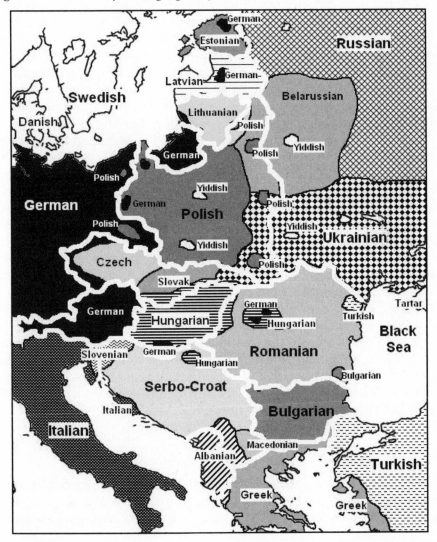

Alphabets

Writing things down is an important part of a culture's development, allowing folks to get a receipt from a purchase, sign contracts, or read sacred religious texts. Alphabets pretty much have developed in lock step with civilization, and go back to the oldest urban centers around the world. Most cultures didn't so much develop their own native alphabets as borrow one from neighboring influential cultures, and so Eastern Europe's history includes the use of the Roman Latin alphabet, the Hebrew alphabet, the Greek alphabet, the Arabic alphabet, the Cyrillic alphabet—perhaps the only one native to Eastern Europe—and more. The region's history is also replete with ancient sacred runic alphabets and scripts from pagan times such as the various Germanic runic *Futharks* that are still found in stone, wood, and bone carvings from England to Poland, and there's the old Turkic Steppe runic *Rovás* (RO-vosh) script brought by the early pagan Magyars into the Carpathian Basin. Runic scripts tended to be seen as magical and were usually only used for certain occasions, but hey, writing is writing.

In the 19th century, as medieval utility gave way to modern-day nationalism, alphabets were formalized and often made to fit new conceptions of national identity. Many languages in Eastern Europe outright switched alphabets. For instance, Turkish was written in the Arabic script until the Turkish republican authorities—who wanted to break from the country's Muslim Ottoman legacy—switched to the Latin alphabet in the early 1920s. The Glagolatic[2] and Cyrillic alphabets saw some use in the early Czech and Croat kingdoms, particularly among Christians. Romanian was originally written in the Bulgarian Cyrillic alphabet until modern-day Romanian patriots switched to the Latin alphabet. Moscow had forced Romanians in Soviet Moldavia to write their language in the Cyrillic alphabet. In the 19th century Lithuanian was written with the Polish Latin alphabet but Russian authorities tried to impose the Russian Cyrillic alphabet, inspiring a native underground adaptation of the Latin alphabet that modern-day Lithuanian still uses. Speaking of Polish, in 1945 some enthusiastic Polish communists wanted to switch Polish to the Cyrillic alphabet, to the horror of most Poles. In the early 20th century, Albanian was written in four alphabets: the Arabic, Cyrillic, Latin, and Greek alphabets. In the early 1920s, Lenin forced several Soviet Central Asian and Caucasus languages to switch to the Latin alphabet only to have Stalin force them in the 1930s to switch to the Cyrillic alphabet. Historically, Serbs and Croats have used the both Latin and Cyrillic alphabets at different times, or in different regions.

Language and Culture

Finally, an interesting phenomenon impacting nearly all languages across the region is its (recent) totalitarian past. By the time of World War II, all of the cultures of the region had developed rich literary traditions, but hardly had a few more years passed than Soviet-imposed communism permeated all aspects of life, including the languages. Orwellian fiction became a daily reality for Eastern Europeans as Stalinist regimes across the region distorted the meanings of words, creating legions of powerful-sounding but ultimately empty phrases. Learning to use the regimes' doublespeak in public, and incorporating its upside-down world of twisted meanings became a crucial survival technique every Eastern European had to master. The regimes fell in 1989–92, but their impact on how Eastern Europeans speak and communicate, and ultimately think, is still being felt decades afterward, as many prominent writers across the region have lamented:

> Writers and philosophers have long recognized that totalitarianism contains within itself an important language element. And the communist regimes of Central Europe were no exception. The native languages of the region—including Czech—experienced a violent upheaval in the meanings of old words, a torrent of newly created words, and the widespread introduction of what can only be called "empty phrases." The result of this was not limited to the post-1948 coup period or the post-1968 "normalization" period. If language forms our thoughts (and vice versa), then totalitarianism has marked us in a fundamental way, has marked our imaginations, our associations, and our unconscious thought patterns.[3]

14th-century fortress of King Charles I Robert (of Anjou)—on the Danube River bend, near the modern-day border with Slovakia. (Image © oldm/Shutterstock)

2. GEOGRAPHY

Figure 9. Eastern Europe and its geography[1]

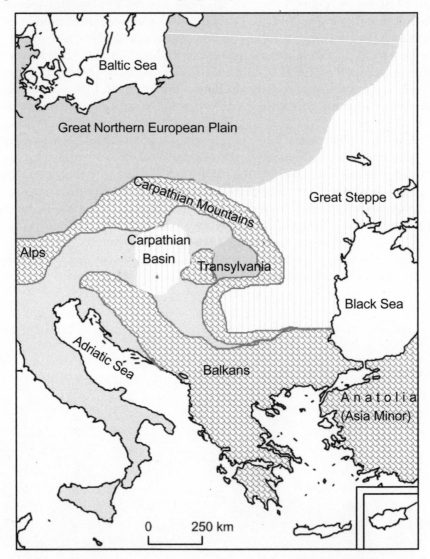

"Anyone born in a luckier place and time must say: there, but for the grace of geography, go I."

—Timothy Garton Ash[2]

Eastern Europe is a big place and there are shelves full of books describing in minute detail the various combinations of dirt, rock, and water that Eastern Europeans have to stand on, climb over, or wade through. For our purposes though I'll just point out a few of the more significant features that have had an impact on local history. For starters, though this may seem obvious, Europe is a big peninsula, with Western Europe at the tip of it. In order for the ancestors of most of those people currently living in Western Europe to get there, they had to pass through *Eastern Europe* first. In particular, there were four routes that most invaders/immigrants passed through:

- **Northern European Plain:** If you put your finger on the northern Ural mountains in Russia and move it westward across northern Russia, Belarus, then Poland, continuing westward through northern Germany, Belgium, and France until you finally hit the Bay of Biscay—in effect, the Atlantic Ocean—your finger has just traced what is called the Great Northern European Plain. This is a very long plain that is mostly flat, or with a few small gentle rolling hills, and which has only a few river systems interrupting it. If you're an eastern army looking to enter Europe, this plain is a Route 66 right into the heart of Europe with few physical obstacles. This plain has played a HUGE role in Polish and German history. During the Cold War, the United States feared this plain because the USSR had such a large advantage in tanks and this plain was perfect for an armored attack.

  To get a sense of the role this plain has played in the region's history, here is a snippet on its effects in Polish affairs:

  Legend has it that one fine spring morning, in the Dark Ages, three Slavonic brothers, Czech, Lech[3], and Rus, set out to find new homes. Czech founded the Czech nation in the first good clearing they came to. The other two carried on until Lech saw an eagle building its nest, took it as a sign from the gods, and founded Gniezno,[4] the first capital of Poland. Rus traveled on.

  Lech's choice must rank with the ten worst decisions in history. Most of Poland is a flat open plain described by military experts as an "ideal spot for a battlefield" (a feature exploited today by rental rather than invasion, for NATO maneuvers, among others).[5]

- **The Carpathian Basin:** As the Alps peter out just west of Vienna, another mountain range picks up a few miles away just east of nearby Bratislava: the Carpathian Mountains. Smack in the middle of Eastern Europe they form a large ovular shape like a huge stone cradle, wrapping around a vast, flat grassland called the Carpathian Basin. The Carpathians begin in western Slovakia and flow eastward along the northern border with Poland into Ukraine, where they gently slope southward into Romania. Suddenly, in central Romania, they jut westward toward Serbia, though they fall off before reaching the border. The protective "walls" of the Carpathians—with easily-defended mountain passes surrounding a wide grassland ideal for horses—made this basin a no-brainer first stop for many Steppe tribes invading Europe, like the Huns or Goths. The little triangular region formed at the southeastern end of the "hook" in modern-day Romania is a microcosm of the larger basin, and has therefore had an even more interesting history; it is known as the "forest-bordering land," or, in Latin, Transylvania.

- **The Balkans:** The Balkans comprise a peninsular land bridge between Europe and Anatolia, and, in effect, between Europe and the Middle East and Asia. The Balkans have therefore hosted countless merchant caravans and armies for thousands of years moving between Europe and Asia. In fact, early hominids (human ancestors) may have first entered Europe through the Balkans, as well as many critical prehistoric populations and technologies. The crucial defining geographical feature of the Balkans is its mountains ranges and indeed, the Balkans takes its name from the Balkan Mountains. The breaks and passes through the mountain ranges have served as highways for traders and warriors, and have hosted the feet of ancient Thracians, Celts, Goths, Persians, Greeks, Romans, Turks, and Italians, among so many others for millennia. The Balkans are often characterized as violence-prone and wartorn, but in truth, despite the occasional headline-grabbing foreign invasion or nationalist unrest, much of Balkan history is really about a broad mosaic of peoples living side by side peacefully, comingling and just getting on with life.

USELESS TRIVIA: BREAKING UP IS HARD TO DO!

What exactly is "Balkanization"? "Balkanization" was first used by Western Europeans in the 19th and early 20th centuries to describe the collapse of the old empires in the Balkans and the rise of nation states. In 1800, four empires covered almost the entire map of Eastern Europe. However, within just a few years the Ottoman empire (which ruled most of the Balkans) began to crumble, and annoyed Western Europeans had to start learning the names of "new" countries like Romania, Serbia, and Greece that were seemingly popping up like popcorn. To 19th century Westerners, it seemed irrational that Balkan peoples would want their own independent nation states—Does Europe really need a Bulgaria?—but as the Ottoman Empire slowly gave way, the West was forced to accommodate the new states. In fact, a large part of the West's policies toward Eastern Europe in the 19th and 20th centuries have been defined by the West being forced to grapple with the breakdown of empires in the region (and the resulting messiness and disorder), to the West's strategic chagrin.

- **The Steppe:** The Steppe—sometimes called the Great Steppe, the Russian Steppe, the Central Asian Steppe, or the Pontic Steppe—is a huge geographical feature stretching across Central Asia and spilling into Europe. We deal with the Steppe in much more detail later in a special insert after Chapter 1, but for now this description should suffice:

North of the Caucasus the situation was rather different. Here a vast expanse of steppe, extending from China to Europe, provided a corridor for constant movement and migration throughout time. This zone of open steppe with forest steppe to the north was dissected by the great rivers, the Volga, Don, Dnepr, Bug, Dnestr, and the lower reaches of the Danube. Through this zone moved bands of horsemen-pastoralists, unnamed in deep prehistory but later appearing in a variety of historical texts as Cimmerians, Scythians, Sarmatians, Alans, Huns, Magyars, Bulgars, and Mongols. All made some cultural impact on Europe, threading their way along the Danube corridor or being deflected northward around the Carpathian mountains to the plains of northern Europe. The intensity and nature of that impact, especially in the prehistoric period, provides an opportunity for lively debate! None, however, will deny the significance of the steppe communities on developing European culture.[6]

Within Eastern Europe are a few cultural regions, shown in Figure 10. These regions are not absolute and there is much arguing over them, but they are commonly referred to nonetheless. The first is Central Europe (shown in black), which is the region with the longest cultural exposure to the West. Some refer to this region as "German Europe" because of the old German/ Prussian and Austrian imperial realms, but this is misleading; French, Italian, Flemish, and other (Western) cultural influences have also played an important formative role in this region. Second is the Balkans (in dark gray). This region has the most eclectic history of all Europe, and its defining influences come from the Byzantine and subsequent Ottoman Turkish civilizations. Then comes the Baltics (in white), who've spent centuries mired in German, Danish, Polish, Swedish and Russian history. Finally, we have what I call the "Eastern Slavic- or Russian-focused" region (in light gray). This is a peripheral region of Eastern Europe whose origins lay in the Kieven Rus civilization, and the subsequent Muscovite Russian imperial civilization.

Again, these regions are general and many countries span more than one. Croatia, Slovenia, and sometimes even Hungary[7] straddle the Balkans and Central Europe, while Greeks prefer to think of themselves as being part of "Southern Europe," which includes Portugal, Spain, Italy, and Malta—ignoring the centuries-old common Balkan historical and cultural traditions Greeks share with neighbors Bulgaria, Serbia, and Albania. While Poles prefer to think of themselves as Central Europeans, some regions of Poland today are culturally closer to the Baltics, while others teeter on the Eastern Slavic world. Ukraine, Moldova, and Romania each sit astride multiple regional zones—Central Europe, the Balkans, and the Eastern Slavic realm—though they are often only identified with one. Again, this is just a general guide for you to understand the common cultural markers Eastern Europeans use.

> Central Europe therefore cannot be defined and determined by political frontiers (which are inauthentic, always imposed by invasions, conquests, and occupations), but by the great common situations that reassemble peoples, regroup them in ever new ways along the imaginary and ever-changing boundaries that mark a realm inhabited by the same memories, the same problems and conflicts, the same common tradition.
>
> —Czech writer Milan Kundera, "The Tragedy of Central Europe"[8]

Figure 10. The General Cultural Regions of Eastern Europe

What exactly do you mean, "Central Europe"?

Figure 11 examines the concept of Central Europe. Developed originally by Pan-Germanists in the late-19th century to distinguish then–German-dominated Europe from what they saw as the Anglo-French West, "Latin" Southern Europe (Spain, Portugal, Italy), and "Slavic" Eastern Europe, the concept of *Mitteleuropa* (Meet-TEL OY-rope-ah; "Central Europe") has changed much since. During the Cold War, (West) Germany and Austria became "Western," and to most Western Europeans "Central Europe" came to mean Alpine Western Europe—eastern France, Switzerland, (West) Germany, Austria, and northern Italy. However, in the 1970s and 80s anticommunist dissidents in Poland, Czechoslovakia, Hungary, and the Slovenian and Croatian republics of Yugoslavia revived the notion of themselves being *Central Europeans* (rejecting "Eastern Europe"), resurrecting the pre–World War I usage that included all of the German and Austro-Hungarian imperial domains as "Central Europe." (See figures 44 and 45.) Some began to use the term *East Central Europe*, which meant those parts of Central Europe caught on the wrong side of the Iron Curtain. Again, these definitions should never be taken too seriously, but this just goes to show that throughout the 20th century, someone mentioning "Central Europe" in 1900, 1940, 1960, or 1999 may be referring to very different groups of countries.

Figure 11. Central Europe vs. East Central Europe in 2010

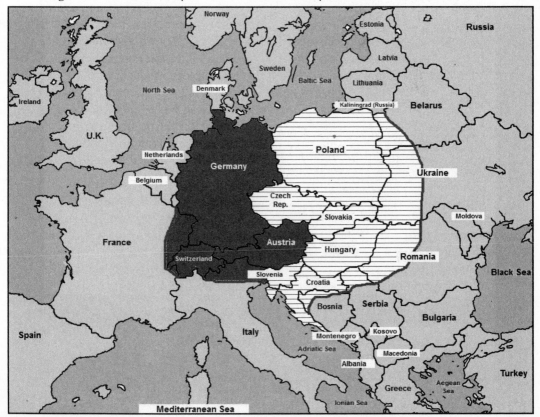

Figure 12 (i.e., 12a & 12b) portrays some of the most important rivers in Eastern Europe as well as some important and often-referenced historic sub-regions. These historic subregions more often than not cross modern-day national boundaries, and have played a role in more than one people's history.

Figure 12a. The Major River Systems of Eastern Europe

Figure 12b. The Major Regions of Eastern Europe

USELESS TRIVIA: THE SILVER STANDARD!

15th-century Europe suffered from a silver shortage caused by a trade imbalance with Asia: Europeans had (re-)discovered the Orient and were importing spices, textiles, and porcelains as fast as their ships could carry them, but Europe produced nothing that Asians wanted, and therefore had to pay hard cash (i.e., silver) for everything they bought in Asia. To the rescue in the late 15th century came a very rich silver mine discovered near the present Czech town of Jáchymov (Yah-KHIM-off), known in the West by its German name, Joachimsthal (Yo-AH-kheemz-tahl). The ending "-thal" (rhyming with "doll" and with the "h" silent) in old German meant "valley," like for instance in "Neanderthal," so Joachimsthal meant "Joachim's Valley." Anyway, so successful were these *Thalers* (as they became known) that when silver began to flood into Europe decades later from Spanish silver mines in Peru, the South American silver coins were also called *Thalers*. The "Thalers" name became attached to many silver-based currencies across Europe for centuries. Well, in 1785, the newly-born United States also chose the Thaler as the name of its own new currency, tweaking the spelling to reflect local pronunciation: the U.S. dollar.

3. RELIGION

Religion, like languages, adds yet another dimension of dizzying diversity to Eastern Europe, and just as any language maps—no matter how detailed they may seem—are necessarily simplified compared to the real situation on the ground, so too is any attempt to portray religion in the region, ultimately glazing over lots of complexity. Religion has played a crucial role in shaping Eastern Europe. Unfortunately, Eastern Europe has a reputation for religious fanaticism, but this is because the region—true to its crossroads heritage—has served as the front lines for the clashes of Popes, Patriarchs, and Sultans.

Three major religious worlds meet in Eastern Europe: Western "Roman" Christianity, Eastern Orthodox Christianity, and Islam. The chasm in mainstream Christianity between Roman and Byzantine Christianity slashes through Eastern Europe like a festering wound, forming a purple Velvet ecumenical curtain that stretches from the Adriatic to the Baltic. Both sides, Catholic and Orthodox Christianity, have long since shattered into many smaller Christianities, the Catholic world because of theological revolt and the Orthodox as each new country demanded its own national church free from the Greeks—but still today, both sides eye the other suspiciously across this "Velvet Curtain" (shown as a black and white stripe in Figure 13).

Figure 13. The General Religious Borders of Eastern Europe

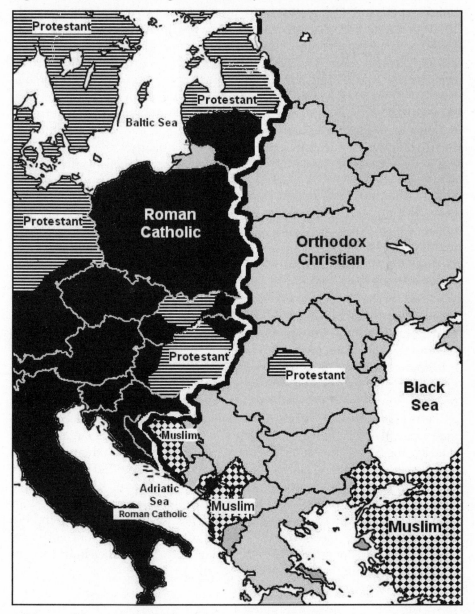

Pre-Christian Eastern Europe and Paganism

The three "Abrahamic" religions—Judaism, Christianity, and Islam—have been fundamental in shaping Eastern Europe for the past three thousand years, if we take the Jewish communities nestled in the northern Greek Black Sea trading towns into consideration. People have been living in Eastern

Europe for *tens* of thousands of years, however; what kind of spiritual or religious beliefs did they hold before the Torah, cross, or crescent? The problem is that we know very little about those pre-Christian beliefs, other than a few surviving snippets from a handful of chronicle entries or archaeology. In the 19th century, all across Europe Romanticists sought out and unearthed pre-Christian beliefs and artifacts in an attempt to reconnect to some imaginary pure, primordial ethnic past, but they all too often tried to force what they found into a preconceived religious (and ethnic) mold. Modern-day religions are highly structured and hierarchical, and more importantly, very clearly defined, their rituals and practices being nearly universal to believers. In the pre-Christian era, however, gods, myths, beliefs, rituals, and practices varied greatly not just from ethnic group to ethnic group but often region to region, from clan to clan, settlement to settlement. All too often the term "pagan" implies a uniform group of people with defined beliefs, when in reality it describes anyone with pre-Christian or pre-Islamic spiritual beliefs. "Pagan" (*paganus*) originally meant something like "hick" or "redneck" to Romans, and urbane Roman Christians readily applied it to those who stuck with the old Roman polytheistic state religion.

From a strictly historical perspective, we actually know very little about the spiritual beliefs of pre-Christian (and pre-Islamic) Eastern Europeans outside of the Romans and Greeks, and how these beliefs played out in the daily lives of those who held them. We have a smattering of information like for instance about the ancient Magyar *Turul*, a mythical falcon (common in the myths of the Steppe peoples) that delivers messages between people and the gods. We know the name of some Slavic gods such as Perun, Triglav, and Svarog. However, though they are indeed associated with the early Slavs, we're not sure how "Slavic" they really were. (During the Slavic invasions of Dark Ages Europe, in the 6th and 7th centuries, many non-Slavic peoples accompanied Slavs into Europe and were later assimilated. What spiritual practices did they have? What happened to them when they assimilated? Some of the Slavic gods can seemingly be traced back to ancient Iranian gods. How and when did the Slavs inherit these gods?) Some have worked hard to reconstruct these ancient belief systems but those attempts are at best conjecture. Sometimes in history we are forced to admit that we just don't know.

Christianity

The spread of Christianity in Eastern Europe pretty much marched along in lock-step with the foundation of the first states. Even in some cases where states existed prior to Christianization, modern-day countries still often trace their origins to the date of their Christianization, as in the case of Poland where schoolchildren today learn the date 966 CE as the beginning of Poland—though we know Poland existed at least a few years prior. This odd phenomenon is due to the fact that "Christianization" did not only refer to what people did on Sunday mornings; it also meant being politically, economically, and socially integrated into the system of Christian states in Europe. The longest holdouts were the Baltic and Finnic peoples, who managed to maintain their pagan practices well into the 15th century despite years of active "persuasion" by German, Polish, Danish, Swedish, and Russian swords.

A crucial way in which Christianity influenced the region (and its early history) was through the very active rivalry between the Western and Eastern Christian churches in the first several centuries of Eastern European history. At the time, Eastern Europe was crawling with Western- and Eastern-affiliated agents trying to spread their own brand of Christianity and convince local rulers to sign up with their side. An important tool of persuasion was the army; both sides had their patron empires—Western Christianity the Frankish Empire, and Eastern Christianity the Byzantine Empire—that weren't shy about occasionally calling in the heavy artillery—literally—to make a theological point. Many Eastern European states at one time or another "switched sides"; Czechs and Hungarians at one point reached for Orthodox Christianity while the Serbs and Bulgarians also flirted with Roman Catholicism. There certainly was a destructive side to this rivalry but a competent and adept ruler in Eastern Europe was often able to exploit it, playing one side against the other to local advantage.

USELESS TRIVIA: MEDIEVAL TANKS!

The Hussite Wars in Bohemia brought an amazing person onto the European stage, Jan Žižka (YON ZHEESH-kah), who by all accounts was a military genius centuries before his time. Fighting on the side of the Hussites, Žižka used unorthodox tactics to repeatedly defeat much larger Catholic German, Czech, and Hungarian armies throughout his extraordinary five-year (1419–24) military career, before dying of the plague. Žižka is most famous for inventing "battle wagons," horse-drawn wagons covered with thick wood "armor" and latched windows (for rapid opening and closing) containing small cannons and expert archers that were whipped around battlefields like modern-day tanks as mobile heavy firepower support. Indeed, the Hussite Wars gave birth to an arms industry, and Bohemia became famous for innovative, quality firearms and armor. The words "pistol" and "howitzer" in English, for instance, likely derive from medieval Czech: *pis'tala* ("little tube") and *houfnice* ("catapult"). The modern-day Czech Republic continues the tradition and military historians still today study Žižka and his military feats.

How did we end up with Western and Eastern Christian churches? Both agree on all the theological essentials; it was over questions of primacy and power that things went sour, as we shall see.

Western Christianity

Christianity had spread to the Roman Empire shortly after Jesus' life, thanks to saints Peter and Paul, but for the first few centuries Christians spent most of their time dodging Roman persecution. The church was finally legalized in the early-4th century, but at a time when the Empire was coming apart at the seams (giving rise to a lot of apocalyptic literature). When the Western half of the Roman Empire collapsed in the late-5th century, Christianity in Western and Central Europe almost disappeared though important centers of Christian worship and scholarship remained scattered here and there. By the 8th century under Frankish protection, the Rome-based church was able to spread and re-assert itself throughout Europe, playing a crucial role in the Frankish Empire and, later, its successors (e.g., France and Germany). It is difficult to overestimate the extent to which the church helped shape Western and Eastern Europe in its first millennium, not only through religious instruction but through the spread of literacy, education, scholarship, spreading basic hygienic practices, and serving as a conduit for diplomacy for medieval Europe's many feuding princes and petty warlords. In fact, the church's success became a problem as the church grew more prosperous and powerful, creating formal hierarchies and imposing standardized beliefs and practices—generating dissidents like St. Francis, and eventually leading to the Protestant Reformation.

Roman Catholicism's long history in Eastern Europe should be a surprise to no one, but few Westerners know that religious dissent has a long history in the region as well: the Protestant Reformation raged in the East as well as the West. In fact, a century before Martin Luther nailed his famous 95 theses on his church door in Germany, a Czech cleric named Jan Hus (YON HOOSS; "Jan" = John) was preaching the reform ideals of heretical English dissident John Wycliffe in Bohemia (present-day western Czech Republic). Hus and was tricked into appearing before a church council but was arrested and ultimately burned at the stake in 1415. His followers, the "Hussites,"[1] rose in rebellion and were eventually able to establish Europe's first recognized (proto-)Protestant denomination, Hussitism, which coexisted with Roman Catholicism in Bohemia for two centuries until Catholic forces destroyed it in 1620.

> ## USELESS TRIVIA: OLD SCHOOL!
>
> Medieval Bosnia was a Christian state, but one that adhered to a heretical form of Christianity. For centuries Popes struggled to suppress the Bosnian heresy, though they also struggled with their rivals, the Byzantine/Orthodox camp, for Bosnia's soul. In the 15th century, using nearby Hungary as leverage, the Popes in Rome finally managed to break the Bosnian church and impose standard Catholic rites, but just in time for the Ottoman invasion, which would lead to five hundred years of Muslim rule. Some historians have speculated that resentment against Rome's destruction of the native Bosnian church may have led to the surprisingly large-scale conversion of Bosnians to Islam.

Protestantism made strong inroads into Eastern Europe. Lutheranism spread among Germans settling in Eastern European cities, while Calvinism spread rapidly in the 16th and 17th centuries among literate aristocrats, craftsmen, and merchants in the region. Still today, about a fifth of Hungarians belong to a Calvinist denomination called *Református* (REH-fourmaht-oosh; "Reformism") that once swept the country. In fact, 17th century Transylvania, then a semi-independent country led by its Reformist Hungarian aristocracy, fought on the Protestant side in the Thirty Years' War (1618–1648). Germans, Danes, and Swedes injected Lutheranism into Estonia and Latvia. Lutheranism also played an important role in Slovak history. And despite the modern-day association of Poles with Roman Catholicism, 16th-century Poland had such a large mixture of Roman Catholics, Protestants, Christian Orthodox, Jews, and Muslims that it was forced, simply for the sake of public order, to enact religious toleration laws.

Eastern Orthodox Christianity and the Second Rome

The Eastern Orthodox Christian church has played an equally crucial role in the early history of Eastern Europe. The great break in European Christianity that created the two competing faiths, Western ("Catholic") and Eastern ("Orthodox") Christianity, began with a 3rd-century CE decision to split the Roman Empire into two parts, an eastern half and a western half, each with its own emperor and capital. This was the result of civil wars in the empire, the barbarian invasions that had overwhelmed the borderlands, and rampant corruption in the empire's old (western) power centers. One man in the early-4th century was able to overcome great odds and civil war to have himself declared sole Emperor of the (reunited) Roman Empire: Constantinus I (Constantine)—but he promptly moved his capital to the *eastern* half of the empire, to the city later named after him, Constantinople.

This Constantinus was the same emperor who legalized Christianity in the Roman Empire, who organized the Council of Nicaea in 325 CE (from which the modern-day Nicaean or "Nicene" Creed derived) to lay the modern theological foundations for Christianity, and who himself converted to Christianity on his deathbed in 337 CE. He created a basic problem for later Christians, however: was the old Roman imperial capital, the city of Rome (and its bishop), the real head of the Christian church? Or was the new Roman capital at Constantinople, with *its* bishop—where the church was legalized and eventually made the official Roman state religion—the head? Throughout the 4th and 5th centuries after the split, the Western half declined rapidly until it finally ceased to exist in 476. The city of Rome had deteriorated so much that even the last few Western Roman emperors abandoned it and ruled from Milan or Ravenna in northern Italy. The Eastern Roman Empire continued to thrive, however. For a while the Christian bishop of Rome (i.e., the Pope) recognized the authority of the bishop in Constantinople (i.e., the Patriarch) but in the 8th century a rupture took place that eventually led to the Great Schism of 1054, breaking Christianity into two competing churches. To this day, both churches insist that they are the *real* Christian authority, the one true church.

USELESS TRIVIA: YOU SAY TOMATO . . .

Who were the Byzantines? Historians today often still disagree. The problem isn't really who they were, but who they *weren't*. It all began when the Roman Empire split in two and, briefly reunited in the 4th century under Constantine, and the imperial capital moved to the eastern half in 330 CE. The problem is that Westerners never quite accepted this move of the imperial capital to the East, the abandonment of Rome for Constantinople. When Westerners talk about the collapse of the Roman Empire, they really mean the *western half* of the Roman Empire, which officially died in 476 CE. The eastern half of the empire lived on for some time longer—a thousand years longer, in fact, until 1453. Many Westerners refuse to accept this eastern half of the empire as truly "Roman," though in its early years it continued to use Latin as its official language, as well as Roman laws, institutions and customs, calling itself the *Imperium Romanorum*, the Roman Empire. In the decades after the collapse of the western half of the empire, however, the eastern half instituted legal reforms and over time, as the empire's core Balkan urban centers contained many Greeks, the official state language became Greek. Over the centuries, as it evolved the eastern empire became less and less recognizably "Roman" though it still continued, until the end of its days, to refer to itself (in Greek) as the Βασιλεία Ρωμαίων; the Roman Empire. Because its capital city, Constantinople, was founded on the site of an ancient Greek province called Βύζανς (Byzans), Westerners derisively called this eastern empire the

Byzantine Empire. Generally speaking, modern historians see the distinction between "Eastern Rome" and "Byzantium" as being between the Classical ("Roman") period (c. 300–600 CE) and the medieval ("Greek") period (600–1453), although the Byzantines themselves never recognized that distinction.

For Orthodox Christians, Constantinople became a "Second Rome" that sheltered the church and its teachings through very dark times, when Roman civilization collapsed in the West and Christianity was almost wiped out there (6th–8th centuries). The city of Rome itself was sacked and destroyed repeatedly in these times by scores of invaders, despite a 7th-century attempt by the Eastern Romans to re-establish Roman rule in Italy. The empire remained powerful in the East, though, centered in the Balkans and its ancient East-West trade routes for centuries more, and holding back even worse invaders originating in the Middle East or Central Asia, allowing Western Europe to slowly rebuild itself. This "Second Rome" (Constantinople) sent out scores of missionaries among the pagan peoples who settled Eastern Europe and the old Roman borderlands, Christianizing them and slowly incorporating them into a distinctly Christian and European family of countries.

Incidentally, both the Catholic Poles and the powerful medieval dynastic family the Habsburgs[2] in the 16th and 17th centuries, each ruling over large numbers of Orthodox Christians, managed to convince at least some of their Orthodox subjects to "switch sides." The Poles convinced some Ukrainian Orthodox, the Habsburgs some Romanian Orthodox, to recognize the Pope in Rome as the ultimate head of their churches, in exchange for being allowed to keep most of their own Orthodox rituals. These groups became known as "Uniates" or "Greek Catholics," and still survive today although in the 20th century the communist regimes tried ruthlessly to stamp out the Uniates in their respective realms in very bloody fashion. Both churches owe their survival in those grim times to members who emigrated to North America, where they could keep traditions (and clergy) alive.

The Third Rome(s)

In 1453, the Ottoman Turkish Sultan Mehmed II overcame the once impenetrable walls of Constantinople, destroying the Byzantine Empire. The young (Russian) Muscovite state came to see itself as the third heir to Rome, after Rome (the city) and Constantinople. The Muscovites declared that now Moscow was the seat of Christianity, and Moscow's rulers henceforth took to calling themselves "Caesar"—in Russian, *Tsar*. They weren't alone; the medieval German empire that arose in the 10th century also saw itself as the reincarnation of the (Christian) Roman Empire—hence, its name, the "Holy Roman Empire"—and its rulers also called themselves "Caesar"—in German, *Kaiser*.

USELESS TRIVIA: BUT DID HE EVER WEAR A RED SUIT?

Nicholas of Myra was born along the Anatolian coast of what today is western Turkey in the late-3rd century CE, in what was then the Eastern Roman Empire. Nicholas was a tireless proponent of Christianity, a real fire-and-brimstone kind of guy, eventually becoming the Bishop of Myra. He is still today the subject of many Orthodox Christian icons in Russia, Bulgaria, Macedonia, Greece, and Turkey, and among Christian Arabs of the Levant (e.g., Syria, Lebanon, Israel). Western Christians were impressed by Nicholas as well; in 1087 Italian mercenaries broke into his tomb in a Byzantine chapel in Myra and stole his bones, bringing them back to Bari, in Italy, where they are still enshrined today.

Many years later, the Germanic peoples of northern Europe somehow came to transfer some of their pre-Christian legends of a kindly hermit who gave gifts to children to Nicholas—and thus was born the legend of Saint Nicholas, who through mispronunciations of the German *Sankt Nikolaus* (St. Nicholas) or the Dutch *Sinterklaas*, became the English *Santa Claus*. The real St. Nicholas attacked and destroyed pagan shrines, famously destroying in particular a temple dedicated to the Roman goddess Diana at Artemis (in modern-day Turkey), whose sacred day was December 6—which the Christian church then later made, in his honor, St. Nicholas's feast day. Across Europe today on December 6, St. Nick visits in the wee hours while the day is still dark and leaves small chocolates or other treats for children to delight in on waking up in the morning. It was only in the early 19th century that the legend of St. Nicholas (and Santa Claus) became associated with Christmas.

Orthodox Christian Heresy: Bogomils

In the early 10th century, a priest or scholar showed up in Bulgaria professing a new twist on Christianity, which he called Bogomilism. There is debate as to what exactly Bogomil meant ("Bog" = "God" in Slavic languages) and what its beliefs actually were, but it is generally accepted that its founder (name unknown) was influenced by the Persian religion Manichaeism, and possibly Zoarastrianism as well. Despite attempts by both the local Bulgarian church and the authorities in Constantinople and Rome to quash Bogomilism, it survived in Bulgaria until the Ottoman conquest of the late-14th century, and even spread to neighboring Serbia and Bosnia. In fact, though there is little evidence, some historians have wondered whether the Bogomils somehow may have influenced the heretical Cathars of 13th-century western France. The Cathars were destroyed by the Albigensian Crusade of 1243–44, in which their headquarters, the castle of Montsegur along the Spanish frontier, was besieged by the French king and the Cathars massacred shortly thereafter at Montsegur, their mountainous stronghold on the Spanish frontier.

USELESS TRIVIA: JEWISH HERESIES

Eastern Europe wasn't just a hotbed of Christian heresy, it bred Jewish dissident movements and sects as well. Out of Poland came the Jewish sexual apostates the Frankists, while Lithuania's *Litvaks* became major supporters of the *Haskalah*—a sort of Jewish "Enlightenment" that espoused secular study and assimilation into larger European society. Lithuania also hosted the anti-Hasidic *Misnagdim*. The Hasidic movement itself began in Polish Ukraine, including the *Breslovers*. Russia's Jews gave us the proselytizing Hasidic Lubavitchers. In the 17th century an Ottoman-born Rabbi, Sabbatai Zevi, led a brief but surprisingly strong Jewish messianic movement that swept Jewish communities in the Ottoman Balkans as well as the Polish-Lithuanian Commonwealth and Ukraine. Jewish theological scholarship continued unabated long after the mass of European Jewry moved eastward, and Eastern Europe has played a large role in the evolution of modern-day Judaism and Jewish identity.

Art

From our modern-day perspective one of the benefits of overlapping civilizations and their competing religions has been a region-wide heap of beautiful art and architecture, the result of a very intense propaganda war waged by all religions for centuries. Simply put, Eastern Europe is littered with stunning paintings, sculptures, décor, architecture, castles, palaces, temples, fortresses, gardens and so much more, all relics of a millennium's worth of religious rivalries. Modern-day Eastern Europe is of course cashing in on these relics in the form of a bustling tourist industry. From the great cities and commercial centers to the smallest villages, priests, reverends, rabbis, and imams all waged holy crusades and jihads against one another (and their own respective heresies) from which the region has inherited a huge cache of devotional art and architecture which in many ways still stylistically defines the region's cities. Despite their struggles for theological exclusivity, modern-day Eastern Europe is a dynamic amalgamation of these styles and influences, with the region's architecture, foods, music, and customs today bearing the echoes of Rome and Persia, Paris and Constantinople, Baghdad and Bremen.

USELESS TRIVIA: THE BIBLICAL BALKANS . . . ?

In the summer of 2010, Bulgarian archaeologists excavating the 5th-century CE church ruins on a small island off the southern Bulgarian Black Sea coast called *Sveti Ivan* (*Свети Иван*)—"St. John"—found two small boxes buried beneath the altar. One had an inscription in Greek dedicated to St. John and with his birthday (June 24) inscribed on it, while the second contained animal and human bones. Were the human bones the remains of St. John the Baptist? To everyone's astonishment, DNA and radiocarbon tests confirmed the bones as belonging to a Middle Eastern man who lived in the 1st century CE.

Now, there were a lot of men in the Middle East in the 1st century CE, and churches and museums all over the world claim to have relics of John the Baptist. Still, it's an interesting thought. How did they get to a small church off the Bulgarian coast? Archaeologists believe they were brought to the church—then not far from the capital of the Eastern Roman Empire—from the Roman Middle East in the 4th or 5th century.

Judaism and Islam

Judaism and Islam have also played important roles in Eastern Europe, and to a degree far greater than in Western Europe, but these two groups are dealt with in special sections in between chapters. It should not be forgotten that Eastern Europe has plenty of Jewish synagogues and Muslim mosques, some merely remnants of what once was but some still functioning. The *Staronova synagoga* (Old-New Synagogue) is a hauntingly simple but beautiful synagogue still in use today in Prague some eight centuries after it was built. Since the fall of communism throughout Eastern Europe, Jewish temples closed since 1945 have been opening again, restoring 19th-century (or older) artwork and architecture and reviving congregations long thought lost. And even outside of those areas more traditionally Muslim in modern-day Eastern Europe (Bosnia, Turkey, Albania), there have been new signs of Muslim life, such as the restoration and refurbishing of the 16th-century Yakovali Hassan Pasha mosque in Pécs, Hungary. Its restoration was partially financed by the Turkish government as a museum and functioning mosque (complete with a minaret). There are also active mosques today in Belarus, left over from the days of Polish rule when Muslim Tartars were resettled.

USELESS TRIVIA: WHIRLING AND TWIRLING!

Sufism is a mystical branch within Islam that emphasizes the individual path to union with Allah (over the community-driven path, via *Shari'a* or holy law), sort of like an Islamic form of Jewish Qabbalah. Sufism gave birth to the mystical dervishes, whose famous whirling dances sought mystical and divine inspiration through physical disorientation, a common religious practice. Many famous Muslim soldiers from the Ottoman empire were Dervishes including the dreaded Ottoman slave-soldiers, the Janissaries. Sufists of the 20th century fell out of grace with Turkish republican authorities, however, and in 1925 the Bektashi Dervish Sufists had to move their headquarters from Istanbul to Tiranë (Tee-RAH-nuh), the capital of the new Albanian kingdom.

Ultimately, there is also the reality that Eastern Europe has not been immune to the modern trends in religion that have swept Western Europe in the 20th century, namely, that for whatever broad brush we may paint the peoples of the region—Poles as Roman Catholics, Bosniaks as Muslims—the truth is that church and mosque attendance has been falling dramatically ever since World War II. Though still often invoked on ceremonial occasions and holidays like Christmas, religion is playing less and less of a role in the every day lives of Eastern Europeans, even in those areas where religion is seen as crucial to ethnic identity. As elsewhere in the modern world, buildings of worship each week in Eastern Europe typically host shrinking crowds of elderly people. Some in (and outside) the region attribute this rising tide of secularism to the communist years, but if anything, the communist attempt to suppress religion may have actually delayed the spread of secularism in Eastern Europe, as religious communities and clergy often played a role in resistance to state tyranny. Anthropologists, sociologists, and historians (and others) all offer different explanations for the spread of modern secularism, but however one explains it, religion has played a crucial role in the formation of Eastern Europe and the societies that live there today, but it would be a mistake to see those formational forces of the past as still the defining components of modern-day Eastern Europe, as influential as they once were.

USELESS TRIVIA: I SEE DEAD PEOPLE!

The Christian tradition of All Soul's Day likely dates back to pagan times, but Christians attribute the holiday itself to the monks of Cluny in eastern France, who in the 10th or 11th centuries made it a day of solemn commemoration for the dead. Its modern-day American off-shoot is, of course, Halloween. But in Central Europe, it still persists as a solemn holiday. At dusk on All Saints Day (November 1), Central Europeans head to their local cemeteries with small candles and place the candles on the graves of departed friends and relatives, so that by nightfall the cemeteries are a sea of little dancing lights.

Széchenyi square in Pecs, Hungary—home to a Roman Catholic church that was formerly the Gazi Kasim Mosque, one of the northernmost onetime mosques in Europe. (Image © Northfoto/Shutterstock)

SECTION II

Wherein we take a look at Eastern Europe's history, where its peoples (past and present) came from, and what forces shaped the region to be what it is today. This is also the part that tells you where all those street and beer names came from.

> *Kas var dziesmas izdziedāt,*
> *Kas valodas izrunāt?*
> *Kas var zvaigznes izskaitīt,*
> *Jūras zvirgzdus izlasīt?*
> *(Who can sing all the songs,*
> *Who can utter all the languages?*
> *Who can count all the stars,*
> *Or collect the grains of sand on the shore?)*
> —Latvian folk song[1]

Riga, Latvia (Image © Aleksey Stemmer / Shutterstock)

A. INTRODUCTION: PREHISTORY

In the Beginning: Beginning with the beginning in history is always a problem, because you have to decide exactly when the beginning was. Humans and their ancestors have been in Eastern Europe for tens of thousands of years, but at which point did they become "Eastern Europeans"? Calling a Neolithic person an Eastern European is like calling someone from the Lenape/Delaware Indian tribe in the 16th century a New Yorker. Was there an *Eastern* in prehistoric Europe?

Figure 14. The Spread of Agriculture in Late Stone Age Europe[1]

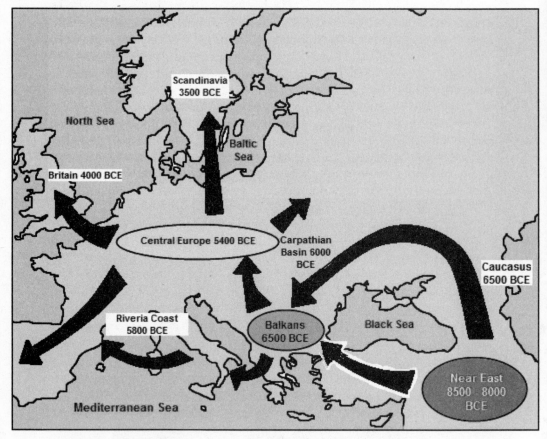

In Figure 14 we see how agriculture is believed to have spread into Europe during the Neolithic, or Late Stone Age. This map is a generalization that simplifies what was likely a complicated process even within specific regions, but nonetheless, the basic flow from the western Middle East (i.e., Near East) to the Balkans through either Anatolia (modern-day Turkey) or the Caucasus and the Steppe are well established. The dates signify the approximate earliest local beginnings of agriculture. There were two basic outflows from the Balkans, northward into the Carpathian Basin and from there to Central Europe (and beyond), and another by sea to the coastal regions of the northern Mediterranean in what is today coastal Italy, France, and Iberia.

An important clue comes from the fairly new field of genetics, which tells us that modern-day Europe's population is surprisingly (genetically) homogeneous, moreso than that of any other continent. Despite all the ethnic groups and countries, most present-day Europeans derive from just a handful of ancestral groups. And geneticists also confirm what the linguists have already told us—namely, that these groups span the "East-West" divide; prehistoric Europeans didn't recognize an Eastern or Western Europe. Now, the further eastward in Europe one goes, the greater level diversity in DNA haplotypes (i.e., DNA gene groupings) one finds, but that just reflects a point I made earlier which is that Europe as a whole is a peninsula with Western Europe at its tip.

Put another way, Western Europe is connected to the Middle East, North Africa, and Asia by . . . Eastern Europe. An important implication of this fact is that for the first several thousand years of European history, an awful lot of the peoples, technologies, trade goods, and languages that eventually came to make up modern-day Western Europe *probably flowed through Eastern Europe first*. This may go all the way back to the very dawn of *homo sapiens*—modern-day humans—as many theories claim that modern humans (or our immediate predecessors, *homo erectus*) first entered Europe via either the Russian Steppe from Asia or the Balkans from the Middle East.

Figure 14 is an example of how Eastern Europe has served as the conduit through which people and their ideas have flowed into Europe for thousands of years. Most know that the Late Stone Age, the Neolithic, gave way to the Bronze Age around 3000 BCE, giving rise to the Aegean Sea–focused Minoan and ancient Greek civilizations that kicked off the Classical Age. However, the Bronze Age was preceded by the *Chalcolithic* or Copper Age, and its origins (in Europe) lay in modern Bulgaria around 3500 BCE, spreading like the agricultural societies northward to Central Europe and beyond. (Some archaeologists believe the Danube to have been a critical corridor for the flow of goods, technologies, and languages into prehistoric Central Europe from the Balkans.) This was the first metallurgical revolution for Europe, and its origins are in the Balkans. Indeed, in the summer of 2012, archaeologists discovered the ruins of what is to date the oldest prehistoric town in Europe, in Provadia, Bulgaria, about 21 miles (35 km) west of Varna. This settlement of 350 people is believed to date to between 4700 and 4200 BCE, or about 1,500 years *before* the start of the ancient Greek civilizations.[2] This just highlights the crucial role Eastern Europe has played in Europe's historical development before the formation of stable states in the medieval era. For millennia ancient trade routes criss-crossed Eastern Europe, while the Indo-European languages—whether they came originally by fierce Iranian Steppe warriors or docile Balkan farmers—also most likely entered Europe first through Eastern Europe. Eastern Europe is a *sine qua non* for European civilization.

USELESS TRIVIA: KEEPING UP WITH THE SKIS!

What's with the "-ski" last name endings? Do all Eastern European family names end that way? Or even all Slavic names? Well, in short, no. Slavic names that end in "-ski" are actually *adjectives*, or more specifically adjectives made from nouns. "Jankowski" (Yahn-KAWF-skee), for instance, is simply an adjective based on the name "Jan" (John). And as adjectives in the Slavic languages, surnames reflect the gender of their owner: a female member of the Jankowski family has the last name "Jankow*ska*." (The "-ski" ending is a masculine adjective ending form.) For instance, in Russian Lenin's wife was named Nadyezhda *Krupskaya*, but her father was Konstantin *Krupsky*.

But just how *Slavic* is that *-ski* ending, really? This is actually an old Indo-European family relic, and still survives in other Indo-European languages like the Germanic languages, for instance: *Danske* is Danish for "Danish," while "Swedish" in Swedish is *Svenska* and *Íslenska* is "Icelandic" in Icelandic. It even survives in modern English (a Germanic language) as *-ish*—as in *English, reddish, noon-ish,* etc.—deriving from the Old English *-isc* and the Gothic *–isks*.[3] But it entered modern English in another way as well, imported from medieval French: Bureaucracy run amok is called "Kaf*kesque*" (re: Franz Kafka), while something badly distorted from its intended or original form is called "grot*esque*." Think about that the next time you crack a brew*ski*.

Of course, nobody knew they were in Eastern Europe back then, because Eastern Europe wasn't Eastern Europe yet—in the same way New York wasn't New York yet—but sheer geography dictated that most of the basic elements that went into making European civilization had to flow first through Eastern Europe. This also means that Eastern Europe, from its earliest days, has an extremely complex, eclectic, and diverse history. Archaeologists and linguists in Eastern Europe today spend a lot of time sorting out the physical and cultural debris from thousands of years of constant flows of humanity through the region, attempting to sort out who was who and what belonged to whom (and when).

USELESS TRIVIA: THAT FRANK SINATRA LOOK

A Danish team of geneticists led by Dr Hans Eiberg at the University of Copenhagen discovered in 2008 that a single mutation in a gene called OCA2 arose sometime 6,000-10,000 years ago in humans living along the northwestern coast of the Black Sea (modern-day coastal Romania, Ukraine) giving them, for the first time in human history, blue eyes. Before this mutation, all humans had brown eyes, which most still do today. However, migrations from the Black Sea area spread this mutation across Europe, so that today about 40% of Europeans have blue eyes.

To give you an example of some of that diversity, let's take a look at a people many are surprised to learn lived at one point in Eastern Europe: the Celts. That's right—cue the Clannad music. Around 800 BCE the Celts began spreading into Western Europe from either Central Europe or possibly even the Steppe, eventually settling as far westward as Portugal and Spain, but remaining as far eastward as modern-day southern Poland, Ukraine, Slovakia, Czech Republic, Hungary, Croatia, Romania, and Bulgaria. Bagpipes are a common instrument throughout these areas.

The Celts at this time were divided into many tribes and spoke many languages, and had no common state or organization other than occasional loose alliances. The Celtic peoples are associated with the spread of Iron Age technology, and they've left their place names all across the region. For instance, the name for the historic western Czech province, "Bohemia," derives from the Celtic *Boii* tribe that once inhabited the same real estate. The Danube River is believed to have gotten its name from the ancient Celts, as did the River Rába that flows from Austria to Hungary. Cities like Vienna, Bled (Slovenia), Legnica (Poland), Roman-era Pécs (Hungary), and the Galatia region of central Turkey are also believed to have derived their names from the ancient Celts. In 2009, Polish archaeologists discovered the remains of an ancient 3rd-century BCE Celtic village near Kraków (KRAH-koof; Cracow). There are even historical indications that the Celtic Lugian tribe in what is today southern Poland requested and received Roman military aid in their struggles against the encroaching Germanic peoples in the late-1st century CE. Indeed, the continued migration of peoples from the east—especially the Germanic peoples—and the growth of the Roman empire pushed the Celts westward and northward out of Eastern Europe, until they were confined largely to Spain, France, and the British isles, where their descendents still live today. In recent years, particularly in the Czech Republic, Celtic festivals have sprung up, some as nothing more than Irish or Scottish friendship festivals (and an excuse to guzzle beer), but some as forlorn efforts to try to "reclaim" a "lost" Celtic heritage.[4] Just keep in mind that you have to say *pivo* to order beer in Prague nowadays, not the Irish Gaelic *beoir* or the Welsh *cwrw*.

Figure 15. The Celtic Settled Regions of Europe, c. 800 BCE with Modern-day Country Names

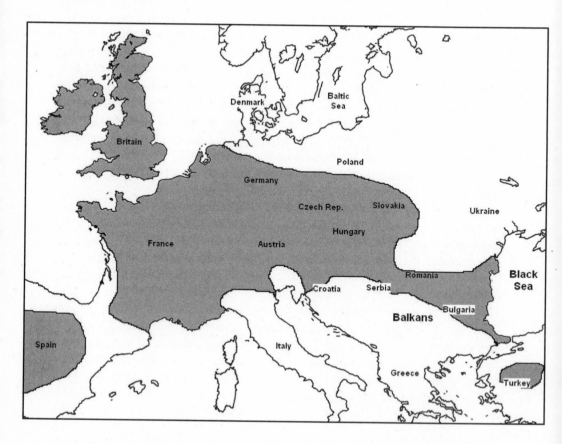

USELESS TRIVIA: FUN SCIENCE PROJECTS AT HOME!

In 1933, a local schoolteacher, Walenty Szwajcer (Vah-LEN-tih SHVY-tser), was taking his students on a country excursion to nearby Lake Biskupin (Bee-SKOO-peen) in central Poland when he noticed something sticking out of the water. Szwajcer contacted noted archaeologist Józef Kostrzewski (YOO-zef Cost-ZHEF-skee), who examined the site and immediately organized an excavation. What Kostrzewski found was the stunningly well-preserved remains of an 8th century BCE wooden fortified settlement from the late Bronze Age and early Iron Age. The site was named after the lake, and so today Polish schoolchildren learn about ancient "Biskupin" and take field trips there. Archaeologists link the site with the prehistoric Lusatian culture people of the late Bronze Age and early Iron Age, who lived from about 1300 to 500 BCE in what are today Poland, Slovakia, the Czech Republic, Austria, and Germany. Although 20th-century nationalists from all these countries have tried to claim the Lusatians as their own ancestors—during World War II, Nazi archaeologists from the *SS Ahnenerbe* tried to claim Biskupin as an "ancient Germanic" site—the truth is known today to be much more complex and nuanced. Today the site has been reconstructed and is open to the public as a museum, with young archaeologists-in-training spending summers in residence learning Bronze Age technologies and living practices while sharing their knowledge with schoolchildren and tourists.[5]

The point of this section has been to show that any attempt to understand Europe's prehistory requires some in-depth understanding of Eastern Europe's geography and prehistory, such was the contribution made by the region to the continent's development. It is no exaggeration to say that Britain or France would not be what they are today were it not for the peoples, ideas, and goods that once flowed through ancient Bulgaria and Ukraine. In the late-20th century, it became common in the West to refer to the countries of Eastern Europe as "New Europe." However, while there is some validity to this label in the sense of the belated establishment of sovereign nation-states in the region in modern times, in at least one respect Eastern Europe is really the Old Europe, through which wafted the very earliest seeds of civilization to the rest of Europe.

B. INTRODUCTION: HISTORY

Before we get to the history, let's talk a little about, well, history, at least in Eastern Europe. Every people, every region in Eastern Europe has a very unique history all their own but there is a general flow to history in the region. It is this flow which we're going to examine in Figure 16, the Independence Chart, which shows relative periods of independence and dependence for a select group of Eastern European countries.

Figure 16. The Independence Chart

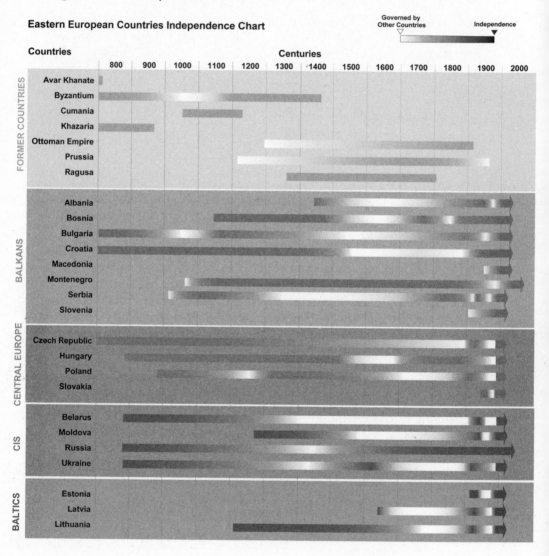

First, let's talk about how to read the Independence Chart1. This is an attempt to show the length of time over the past 1,200 years or so that each country (or people) in the region has been in control of its (their) own destiny.

Simply, the darker the bar, the more independent the country at that time. Conversely, the lighter the bar, the more dependent (meaning a foreign power has some level of influence or control in the country) the country is. A completely white bar or space means the country either doesn't exist or is completely controlled by foreign elements. The countries profiled are grouped on the left by region. CIS refers to the Commonwealth of Independent States.

Now, this chart is of course heavily based on interpretation—my interpretation, specifically—but it will give you the general gist nonetheless. For instance, if you look at Russia, Belarus, and Ukraine, you'll notice each has a dark strip stretching from the late-9th century to the early-13th century; these all represent ancient Rus, out of which all three of these modern-day countries evolved. Another example would be Romania, whose darkened bar from the early-14th to the early-16th centuries represents old Wallachia (Val-LAKH-ee-yuh), whose territory forms the core of modern-day (southern) Romania. Let's compare this to a similar chart done for a few Western European countries, past and present.

Figure 17. An Independence Chart for Select Western European Countries

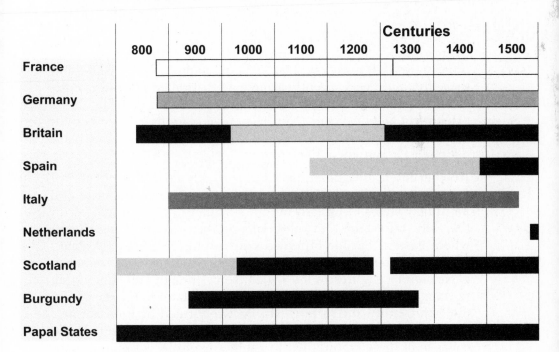

So what do these Independence charts tell us? Well, a few important things:

- When comparing Eastern Europe and Western Europe, it becomes clear that while many countries in both regions were created in about the same time period, those in Western Europe have enjoyed a much more stable and far less broken history of statehood. Statehood and self-government in Eastern Europe, even for the more successful countries, has been historically erratic, with consequences for the development of state institutions.

The history of the Poles, the Czechs, the Slovaks, the Hungarians has been turbulent and fragmented. Their traditions of statehood have been weaker and less continuous than those of the larger European nations. Boxed in by the Germans on one side and the Russians on the other, the nations of Central Europe have used up their strength in the struggle to survive and to preserve their languages. Since they have never been entirely integrated into the consciousness of Europe, they have remained the least known and the most fragile part of the West—hidden, even further, by the curtain of their strange and scarcely accessible languages.
—Czech writer Milan Kundera, "The Tragedy of Central Europe"[2]

- Even within Eastern Europe, there is a chasm of difference between those states that have long histories—no matter how broken—and those that only very recently achieved self-rule. Modern-day Eastern Europeans distinguish the two categories through the terms "Historical Nations" and "Non-Historical Nations." As you might suspect, these terms have engendered no small amount of petty nationalist acrimony in the region.

- Another interesting point this chart shows is the general historical flow in the region. The 9th to the 11th centuries saw the birth of a lot of new states in Eastern Europe—actually, all of Europe—with the 13th, 14th, and 15th centuries seemingly being a high point where Eastern Europe brimmed with strong, locally ruled states. Then came the 16th and 17th centuries, which saw the dramatic expansion of empires in the region, some foreign and some local, putting a dramatic damper on independent states in the region. By the 19th century, the region was effectively ruled by four empires, but further into the 19th century and in the early-20th century, the collapse of these empires led to another explosion of independent states. The interwar years proved challenging, however, and after the very unpleasant years of 1939–45 and the almost-as-unpleasant Cold War, we had 1918 redux in 1989–92 as another empire collapsed in the region. The little arrows pointing boldly into the 21st century are an optimistic hope for stability and prosperity in the region. Western Europeans today tend to glorify the 17th, 18th, 19th, and early 20th centuries of their histories but you can see on this chart why Eastern Europeans tend to reach further back to medieval times for their lost mythical "golden ages."

USELESS TRIVIA: YOUR HERO OR MINE?

"One day Nasreddin Hodja was riding his donkey backwards, facing towards the back. 'Hodja,' the people said, 'you are sitting on your donkey backwards!' 'No,' he replied. 'It's not that I am sitting on the donkey backwards, I'm just interested in where I have been coming from more than where I am going, my friends."[3]

Nasreddin Hodja was a *mullah*[4] who lived in the 13th century Seljuq Sultanate of Rum (modern-day central Turkey). Little is known about the historical Nasreddin, but stories about both his great wisdom and occasional foolishness have spread far over the centuries. Today stories about Nasreddin are known in the Arab world, Iran, Central Asia, Armenia, India, and China as well as of course his native Turkey. Through the Ottoman Empire, his stories also spread in the Balkans so that today Romanians and Bulgarians embrace Nasreddin as their own. His stories have spread as far as Russia and even, through the Adriatic trade, to Italy. Compendiums of his fables and wit have been published throughout the Middle East, the Balkans, and Russia. The American writer Mark Twain even included a story about Nasreddin in his 1880 anthology *Library of Humor*. Meanwhile, the city of Bukhara in Uzbekistan has a statue of Nasreddin riding his donkey backward.

- Nonetheless, as Norman Davies pointed out in the Introductory FAQ, there are some historical commonalities that span the East-West divide in Europe: Spain, Italy, and Scotland (among others) also have erratic state histories and each mythologizes as their respective "golden ages" periods much further back in history, much like many of their Eastern European peers.

USELESS TRIVIA: WHO IS "US" ANYWAY?

According to the 2009 Belarussian state census, Belarus's overall population shrank from a little over 10 million ten years ago to about 9.5 million in 2009. Now, populations all across Europe are dropping, but a decline of 5% should make you nervous. Still, the census also showed that Belarussians, as a portion of their country's population, actually increased from 81% in 1999 to 84% in 2009. (Russians as a minority declined from 11% to 8%.)[5] Belarus for the Belarussians, right?

Well, it depends what you mean by "Belarussian." In the 2009 census *barely half*—53%—of Belarussian citizens claimed *to speak* Belarussian (as opposed to 74% in 1999), and even worse, only 23% use it regularly at home. Belarussian is a dying language in its own country. How is it possible that the number of Belarussians is growing in the country, but their language is dying? Again, it depends what you mean by "Belarussian." First, the Soviet-nostalgic dictatorship of Alexander Lukashenko promotes Russification in Belarus. But as well, many who identified themselves as ethnic Russians in 1999—some of whose families have lived in Belarus since the 19th century—have since started calling themselves Belarussians, though they still speak Russian. This all adds up to a changing sense of what it means to be "Belarussian," and that like Irish Gaelic to the Irish, the Belarussian language is becoming less and less a component of that identity.

This historical lack of stability or consistency with both governments and states in Eastern Europe has created a slight and subtle terminology difference in the region. Americans in particular use the words "country" and "nation" interchangeably, as if they mean the same thing. Well, for Americans, who've only known one country and one government for most of their history, they *are* the same thing. To begin with, Europeans in general separate state from government, which explains why they have both presidents (or, in constitutional monarchies like Britain, the Queen) *and* a prime minister; the president or monarch is the head of *state*, while the prime minister is the head of the *government*. But Eastern Europeans take this concept even further. A country is an organized political entity, with its own borders, government, and so on. The United States, South Africa, Peru, etc.—these are countries. A *nation*, though, is different. The two can coincide, but not necessarily. A *nation* (to Eastern Europeans) is a group of people who belong to the same ethnic group, speak the same language, and have a shared history together, whether they live in the same country or not. Now, as any cultural anthropologist will tell you, ethnicity is a very slippery thing to define, but it is nonetheless a core base identity unit in modern-day Eastern Europe. For instance, modern-day Hungary (i.e., the country) has about ten million citizens, but the Hungarian *nation* consists of about *thirteen million* people, three million of whom live *outside* of Hungary's borders. The subtle difference between these terms still manages to generate lots of political ulcers in Eastern Europe, and confusion for those outside the region.

Street scene in Cluj Napoca, Romania (photo by the author)

C. INTRODUCTION: THE CLASSICAL AGE IN THE EAST, OR "EASTERN EUROPE – THE PREQUAL"

When someone mentions the Classical Age, you probably picture a guy in a toga lounging next to a Doric (or maybe Ionian) column eating grapes. More importantly, you probably think of the Classical civilizations—Greece, Rome, maybe Egypt—as being the parent civilizations for the West. That is true in some respects, but the Classical Empires did not recognize a Western or Eastern Europe, and sent their soldiers, diplomats, scholars, merchants, engineers, and colonists stomping through both. As we've already seen, prehistoric Eastern Europe was crisscrossed by ancient trading routes and the Classical empires often followed these same routes into Eastern Europe in a bid to dominate them, or they sometimes stormed into Eastern Europe in pursuit of some annoying barbarians. As always, Eastern Europe was then, as now, a meeting place where clashing empires, civilizations, and peoples met, fought, and occasionally traded. In particular we're going to examine four ancient Classical civilizations that left their mark on Eastern Europe: the Greeks, Persians, Romans, and Arabs.

The Greeks, and a Lot of People Named "Helen"

Somewhere between the 3rd and 2nd millennia BCE, an Indo European–speaking people began to filter southward into the Balkans from the northern Black Sea region. By about 1600 BCE, these peoples had coalesced to form the Mycenaean civilization in what is today central and northern Greece, and they—the first Greeks—overran the nearby Minoan civilization in Crete, quickly spreading throughout southern Greece and western Anatolia. Mycenaean Greek civilization flourished until about 1200 BCE, when new waves of Greek invaders from the north—the Dorians—laid waste to Mycenaean cities, leading to a general civilization collapse in the Greek world. After a few centuries known as the Greek Dark Ages, some important Greek city states began to arise such as Athens and Sparta, and by about 600 BCE, what we call today Classical Greece was in full swing with the likes of Plato, Aristotle, and Socrates wandering about spouting stuff we still read today. Greeks ventured throughout the Mediterranean and settled the shorelines of what are today southern Italy and Sicily, France, Spain, Turkey, Libya, and Egypt. As the Persian Empire began to push into Greece proper in the 6th and 5th centuries BCE the Greek city states, led by Athens and Sparta, united to drive the foreigners out but when the Persian threat receded, the allies turned on one another in the infamous Peloponnesian War (431–401 BCE). The result was Greek civilization laid low, and by the mid-4th century BCE a northern semibarbaric Greek kingdom called Macedon was able to overrun most of Greece.

The Macedonian king who conquered Greece was named Philip, but his son, Alexander (allegedly) had his dad murdered in 336 BCE, and immediately went out and conquered himself a massive empire—an empire that, when he died in 323 BCE, included what are today Greece, Macedonia, Bulgaria, Turkey, Syria, Lebanon, Israel, Jordan, Egypt, Iraq, Kuwait, Iran, Afghanistan, and chunks of Pakistan and India. His vast empire quickly fell apart but his generals and administrators were often able to maintain control in the smaller successor states that emerged, leading to what is called the Hellenistic Age. In the Hellenistic Age, Greece itself reverted to city states and small, local kingdoms but Greek dynasties ruled states across what are today Turkey, Syria, Lebanon, Jordan, Israel, and Egypt. (Egypt was ruled by the descendants of one of Alexander's bodyguards, Ptolomy, from about 300 BCE to 31 BCE; Cleopatra was the last "Ptolomaic" ruler of Egypt.) During the Hellenistic Age, Greek culture spread throughout the eastern Mediterranean and Middle East, and the Greek language was used like English today, as the language of diplomacy, business, and trade. This is why, for instance, the books of the New Testament of the Bible were written in Greek. In any event, the Hellenistic Age came to end when a new power arose out of the west. By about the time of Jesus, Greece and the eastern Mediterranean region were firmly ruled by the Roman Empire though in many ways Greek culture heavily influenced Roman civilization and the eastern Mediterranean for centuries to come.

The Persians

In the West the Persians are often portrayed as villains, as the evil Orientals who tried to conquer the "Western" Greeks. In reality, the Persian Empire ruled parts of the Balkans (including some Greek lands) for centuries, and Greeks at times often allied with the Persians against other Greeks. The famous Greek resistance to Persia began when the Persians began to encroach on turf controlled by the growing Athenian and Spartan empires. The Persian Empire also served as an important source and conduit for trade, ideas and technologies that helped shape the Greek, and later Roman and post-Roman worlds. In any event, at about the same time as the Mycenaean collapse in 1200 BCE, another Indo-European people were filtering into what is today Iran, the ancient Iranians. For several centuries they were ruled by foreign empires such as the Assyrians, but in the early-7th century they created the first of several Iranian empires. This first phase was called the Medean Empire (after the Iranian Mede tribes who ruled it), which ruled much of modern-day Iran and would stretch westward into modern-day Turkey. It lasted for a century until the ruler of a regional kingdom in the Medean Empire called *Parsa* (hence *Persian*) rebelled and overthrew the Medes. Cyrus the Great (as he was known) founded the Persian Empire, though his empire is also called the *Achaemenid* Empire, after Cyrus's family dynasty. In any event, Cyrus's empire soon stretched eastward into India and encompassing all of Iran, and westward into Mesopotamia

(Iraq), the Levant (Syria, Jordan, Lebanon, Israel), Egypt, Turkey, and even into the Balkans, to the Danube Delta on the Black Sea in what are today eastern Greece, Macedonia, Bulgaria, Romania, and Ukraine. That's a point worth repeating, that Persian soldiers were once stationed on the Danube River.

Figure 18. The Persian Empire, c. 500 BCE

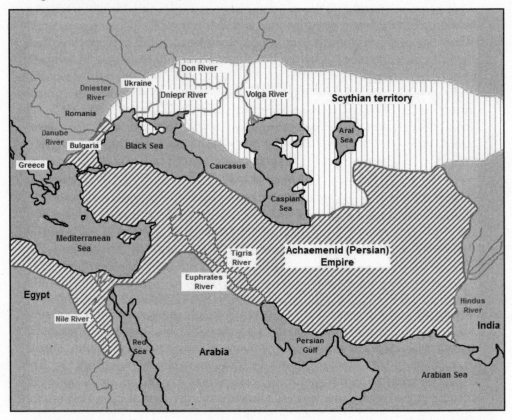

Cyrus's empire was destroyed by Alexander the Great in 330 BCE, but was succeeded by the Parthian Empire in about 250 BCE, which lasted almost 500 years, until 224 CE. The Parthians caused the Roman Empire a lot of grief as the two competed for what are today eastern Turkey, Armenia, and Iraq. The Parthian Empire became the Sassanid Empire in 224 CE, the last of the pre-Islamic Persian Empires.

USELESS TRIVIA: BEFORE THE 300 THERE WERE 700,000! SORT OF.

The heroic Spartan-led Greek resistance to a massive Persian invasion at Thermopylae in 480 BCE has inspired many modern-day writers and film-makers, but few know that the story behind those legendary events that took place on that narrow Greek mountain pass began in Eastern Europe.

Rewinding back thirty-four years, we find that the Persian "king of kings," Darius I, had a problem with raids from Scythian warriors along his northern frontier, which bordered the Steppe. He had tried to confront the Scythians head-on but to no avail, so in 514 BCE Darius tried another tactic: he decided to surprise them from behind. He assembled a massive army—700,000, according to the Greek historian Herodotus, though most historians think this number too big—and marched west through Anatolia (modern-day Turkey) into Europe, crossing the Danube River in what is today Bulgaria, then northward through modern-day Romania and Moldova into Ukraine. The Scythians simply melted into the vast expanse of the Steppe, with Darius following precariously behind. Herodotus claims Darius made it as far as the Volga River in modern-day Russia before giving up and turning back, though again, some doubt he got that far. As he retreated through Ukraine—faulty maps left Darius unaware of shorter routes home through the Caucasus—the Scythians continuously raided and harassed his dispirited army. Apparently neither Napoleon nor Hitler had ever bothered reading Herodotus.

After Darius's broken army retreated back to Persia, the Athenians began to stir up trouble among the Greeks ruled by the Persians along the Anatolian coast, leading to an Ionian Greek Revolt in 499 BCE, which Darius tried unsuccessfully to suppress. He died in 486 BCE, leaving the mess to his son, Xerxes. It was Xerxes I who invaded Greece in 480 BCE, leading to that fateful battle at Thermopylae.

Just as the Parthians jousted with the Romans, the Sassanids fought several wars with the Byzantines as the two empires struggled for what are today Turkey and the Levant. The Sassanid Empire was overrun and destroyed by the Muslim Arab armies that exploded out of Arabia in the mid-7th century CE. Though not considered a Persian empire per se, in the 10th century the descendants of a Turkic Khazar general named *Seljuq* (SELL-jook) settled in what was then a Persian kingdom ruled by Turkic slave-soldiers called *Mamluks* (Mam-luke), and shortly seized power to create the Seljuq Empire.

The Seljuq dynasty was Turkic in origin and indeed imported Turks from the Steppe into what is today Turkey to fight the Byzantines, but it ruled its vast (Muslim) empire from what is today Iran and "went native" after some time, becoming Persianized. None of the Persian empires ruled as much territory as Cyrus's original Achaemenid Empire, but all kept steady pressure on the civilizations of Anatolia, the Levant, the Caucasus, and the Black Sea, fighting and trading with Greeks, Romans, and Byzantines.

The Roman Empire

The city of Rome, by legend, was founded in 753 BCE and was ruled for a couple of centuries by an Etruscan dynasty as a monarchy until these kings were overthrown in 509 BCE and a republic created. The Roman Republic went through a period over the next three centuries of rapid expansion, and indeed most of the territories associated today with what would become the Roman Empire were really conquered during the republic period. In any event, the Republic faced and survived many crises but a series of civil wars and the ambitions of a ruthless and power-hungry general named Julius Caesar in the last decades of the 1st century BCE doomed the republic. Its institutions weakened or destroyed, the republic gave way in 27 BCE when Caesar's nephew, Octavian, was able to seize complete power as *Imperator* (Emperor) *Caesar Augustus*; the Roman Republic became the Roman Empire.

The Empire reached its greatest territorial extent under Emperor *Traianus* (Trajan) in the early-2nd-century CE, ruling over most of what is today Western Europe (excluding Germany, eastern Austria, Scotland, and Ireland), in Eastern Europe the Balkans, then Turkey, the Caucasus, southern Crimea, the land around the Tigris and Euphrates rivers in Mesopotamia (modern-day Iraq) as far as the Persian Gulf, the Levant (modern-day Syria, Lebanon, Jordan, Israel), Egypt, and what are today northern Libya, Tunisia, Algeria, and Morocco.

With constant waves of invaders from the Steppe and growing corruption at home, the Roman Empire began a slide into decline in the 3rd century CE, finally being broken in two—Western and Eastern empires—in 285 CE. Two emperors in the 4th century, Constantine and Theodosius, each managed to unite the Empire but both ruled it from the *eastern* half, in the Balkans. After Theodosius the Empire split again, never to reunite. The Western Roman Empire slid swiftly into oblivion, finally succumbing to barbarian rule in 476 CE. This is the event most in the West associate with the "fall of the Roman Empire." However, as discussed in the Religion section, the Eastern Roman Empire (referred to in the West as the *Byzantine Empire*) prospered and continued on for another 977 years, until it was destroyed by the Ottoman Turks in 1453.

Nevertheless, the collapse of Roman civilization in Western and Central Europe was cataclysmic and led to a centuries-long collapse in food production, trade, literacy, and technical skills. Europeans would not be

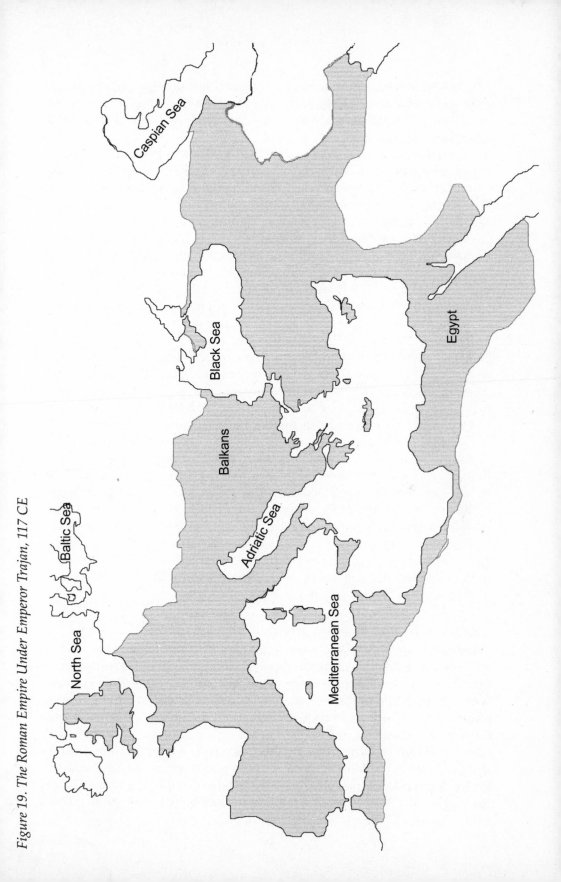

Figure 19. The Roman Empire Under Emperor Trajan, 117 CE

Caspian Sea

Black Sea

Egypt

Balkans

Baltic Sea

Adriatic Sea

North Sea

Mediterranean Sea

able to recreate some Roman engineering and technological feats until the 18th or 19th centuries—1,400 years after the Western Roman collapse—and the desire to emulate Rome was a powerful driving force behind medieval European politics.

After declaring the Republic in 509 BCE, the Romans focused on expanding in Italy and subjugating their neighbors—Latium in central Italy, the Greeks in southern Italy, and the Celts in northern Italy. In the 3rd century BCE, Rome became involved in a major slugfest called the Punic War (264–241 BCE) with the ancient Phoenician civilization (and its largest outpost, Carthage) in the western Mediterranean, and when it was over the victorious Romans turned their attention to the eastern Mediterranean, to the Greek lands. To support those efforts but also to secure the wealthy trade routes that stretched into Asia, Roman armies spent the 2nd and 1st centuries BCE conquering the Balkans and incorporating them into the Roman world.

Over time Romans came to see the Balkans not as alien conquered territory but as "home turf." Twenty-two Roman emperors were born in the Balkans,1 and its trade routes became vital for the Empire. Several provinces were carved out of the Balkans: Noricum (modern-day Slovenia, southern Austria), Illyricum (which was later broken up into Dalmatia and Pannonia), Dalmatia (modern-day Bosnia and Croatia), Pannonia (modern-day western Hungary), Macedonia (modern-day Albania, Macedonia, northern Greece), Moesia (modern-day Serbia and northern Bulgaria), Dacia (modern-day Romania), Thrakia (modern-day European Turkey, southern Bulgaria and eastern Greece), Epirus (modern-day northern Greece) and Achaia (modern-day central and southern Greece). Roman power began to fade in the Balkans in the early 4th century CE as Rome was forced to abandon territories to invading barbarians[2] from the Steppe. The Byzantines tried to restore Roman rule in the region after the 5th century but were never fully successful, though they played a critical role in stabilizing the post-Roman Balkans and helping the region recover from the chaos and tumult of the (Western) Roman collapse.

Classical Arabia and the Islamic Empire

In the early-7th century CE, a new religion exploded out of Mecca and Medina in the Arabian desert. Led by the Prophet Muhammed, Arab Muslim forces initially subdued all of the Arabian Peninsula by the 630s CE, then, under what are described as the four successor Caliphs (after Muhammed), Arab armies surged forth and conquered what are today Iran, Iraq, the southern Caucasus, eastern Turkey, the Levant (Syria, Lebanon, Jordan, Israel), Egypt, and eastern Libya. It was at this juncture that Islam fell into disunity and civil war in the 650s, splitting into the Sunni and Shiite sects that still persist today. Still, a powerful new dynasty arose in 661, and by 750 CE the Umayyad (OO-my-yahd) Arab Empire had added all of North Africa

(*Maghreb*: "the western lands"), Spain (*Al Andalus*), and in the east what are today Afghanistan, Pakistan, Turkmenistan, Uzbekistan, and Tajikistan to the Islamic Empire. Umayyad Arab armies repeatedly invaded the Byzantine Balkans and the Caucasus, as well as the Frankish lands in Western Europe, occupying Nimes, Narbonne, and Avignon in the 720s before being driven back after the famous Battle of Poitiers in 732 CE by the Franks. For centuries Arab raiders attacked towns along the northern Mediterranean shore and in the Adriatic, taking loot and slaves. An Arab force destroyed the city of Rome's harbor area in 846, and looted the Vatican.

The Umayyad dynasty gave way to the Abbasid (AHB-bah-sid) dynasty in 750—although a branch of the Umayyads survived in Arab and Berber Spain, creating the independent *Qurtuba* (Cordoba) Caliphate. The Abbasid dynasty ruled their vast empire from Baghdad, transforming that city into a major center for scholarship, science, and trade. Indeed, early Islam encouraged scholarship, and Muslim cities like Cordoba, Timbuktu, and Baghdad became leading science and scholastic centers. Muslim scholars preserved, translated, and further developed ancient Greco-Roman and other Classical texts that were lost to the Christian European world after the Western Roman collapse.

Christian Europeans rediscovered these texts during the Crusades in the east and Spanish *Reconquista* in the west, igniting the European Renaissance. But those European Crusaders and Conquistadors also discovered a superior material culture in the Muslim lands, igniting a hunger in Christian Europe for exotic foods, spices, and goods only available through trade with the east. The Abbasids in particular were consummate merchants, and Arab traders sailed the Mediterranean and even traversed the Volga and Dnieper, playing a vital role in Christian Europe's rediscovery of the ancient Asian trade routes.

In the 10th century a new dynasty arose out of North Africa to challenge the Abbasids, the Fatimids (FAH-tih-mids). The Fatimids initially managed to overrun most of North Africa (including Egypt), but were defeated by the Abbasids by the late-12th century. A more serious challenge came out of the east in the 13th century, however, as the Mongol Empire invaded the Middle East. In 1258 the Mongols destroyed Baghdad and, in the process, the Abbasid dynasty.

The rise of the Mongol threat posed another problem for the Islamic Empire, however. Both the Abbasids and a brief Egyptian dynasty in the 12th-13th centuries called the Ayyubids had taken to capturing Turks and forcing them to fight as slave-soldiers. These slave-soldiers, or *Mamluks*, became increasingly important in Arab society and played a crucial role in repulsing a major Mongol invasion at Ain Jalut (modern northern Israel) in 1260. The Mamluks then drove out the remaining Christian Crusader states in the Levant, succeeding by 1302. They used their prestige from these victories to seize power across the Arab world, and soon Egypt, Syria, and other Arab lands were ruled by their former Turkish Mamluk slaves. The Mamluk era ended the Classical era of the Arab Islamic Empire, though the Mamluks themselves were soon overcome and conquered by the rising Turkish Ottoman Empire in the 14th century.

Figure 20. The Farthest Extent of the Umayyad Arab Empire, c. 750 CE

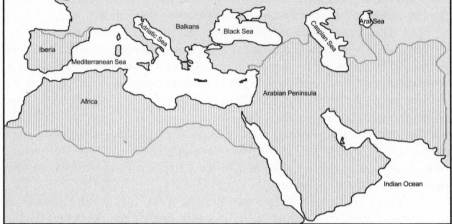

The Indian Ocean Basin Trade

Trade is a critical ingredient to the Eurasian story. Ever since prehistoric times, the various peoples of Eurasia managed to move goods across amazing distances. Large caches of Roman coins have been found in China, for instance. At times when armies marched or civilizations collapsed, trade would ebb or dry up altogether, sometimes for centuries, only to revive later. One of the most famous examples was the Silk Road which stretched from China to Europe through Central Asia, Persia, and the Middle East. Another dramatic example is the Indian Ocean trade network that revived after the horrific Mongol conquests of the 13th century.

The Mongols inadvertently relinked regions not connected since Roman times, and ancient trade routes quickly sprang back to life. The unification of India under Moghul Muslim rule in the 15th and 16th centuries in particular led to an explosion in seaborn trade, with Muslim merchants traveling to East African ports like Kilwa, Sofara, and Raphta as well as to the many Red Sea and Persian Gulf ports of the Middle East, and eastward to Southeast Asia, Indonesia, Malaysia, the Philippines, and Japan.

In the early 15th century, Ming China constructed a legendary fleet of massive ships (whose size Europeans would not be able to replicate until the 19th century) led by Admiral Zheng He that traveled to India, the Middle East, and East Africa in seven epic voyages (1403–33), trading exotic goods and establishing diplomatic relations. Since the Crusades (11th-14th centuries),

Europeans had become aware of these eastern trade routes, and European merchants such as Marco Polo (mid-13th century) risked life and limb traversing land routes to India and China, but these were dangerous and unreliable.

In Eastern Europe, the Slavs living along the Dnieper and Volga Rivers and others such as the Volga Bulgars traded with the Arab world. Soon Vikings discovered these trade routes and took them over, giving birth to the first large-scale medieval European trade network with access to the East, via the Baltic Sea. Baltic trade flourished until Italian merchants carved more direct routes through the Mediterranean and Black Seas in the 13th century. These Mediterranean routes were strangled by the rise of the Ottoman Empire in the 15th century, however, forcing Europeans to take some fairly radical steps to reopen them and regain access to the Indian Ocean and, by extension, the Far Eastern trade networks.

The Gateway of India in Mumbai (formerly Bombay), India. It was built by the British Raj in 1911 to commemorate King George V's visit to India. (Image © Sam DCruz / Shutterstock)

Professor: "This is America, the famous USA. Nothing but lunatics! And every one of them pretending to be happy."
Serfer: "You're wrong. They're not pretending, they *are* happy, they are. And the greatest joy for Americans is that they believe in their happiness and want nothing else—while you (Poles), you only pray, whine, and scare the world with those sad faces of yours. All the concentration camps, all the cemeteries, all the monuments; maybe we should tear them all down and build parking lots! Maybe that would help!"
Potejto: "But we've had too many wars, too much poverty. . . ."
—scene from the 1997 Polish film *Szczęśliwego Nowego Jorku (Happy New York),* directed by Janusz Zaorski, about Polish immigrants struggling to adapt to life in the U.S. in the 1990s

1. SETTING THE STAGE 500–800 CE

CHAPTER SUMMARY

With the final collapse of the western half of the Roman Empire at the end of the 5th century, chaos reigns throughout much of Europe. Small islands of civilization survive here and there in the West, but for the most part Western and Central Europe are reduced to a cultural desert where Christianity, literacy, and security have all but disappeared. The eastern half of the Roman Empire survives, however (as the Byzantine Empire), and over the next several centuries it plays a crucial role in rebuilding civilization in Europe. Meanwhile, barbarians continue to flow into the ruins of Roman Europe, and amid all the violence and chaos a few groups manage to establish states that bring some sorely needed stability: the Franks in Western Europe, and the Avars, Bulgars, and Khazars in Eastern Europe. The papacy in Rome, threatened by Germanic Lombard barbarians and Arabs, cuts a deal with the Franks for protection in exchange for political legitimacy (with the church recognizing Frankish rulers as heirs to the old Roman Empire): this is the seed from which the modern West is born. The Avars, in turn, bring with them into the very heart of Europe a people from the northeastern forests, the Slavs.

Soon, amid the rubble, we begin to see the inkling of the first states in Eastern Europe.

CHAPTER GUIDE
A. Western Rome 68
B. The Avars 73
C. The Slavs 74
D. The First Slavic States .75
E. The Bulgars 77
F. The Dacians and Vlachs .78
G. The Khazars 80
H. (A Bunch of) Finns and Balts 82

A. Western Rome

Imagine waking up one day and finding all the police gone. All of them. You might at first rejoice because now you have no fear of a speeding ticket, until you remember that now there's nobody to protect you or your family. Now imagine the post office empty and closed. No more mail. Then you discover there's no more fire department. Electricity, water, and gas; all utilities just stop. No more phones, land line or cell. The satellites orbiting above simply go dark. With no police or army, chaos breaks out, and local

Figure 21. Eastern Europe Timeline, 500–800 CE

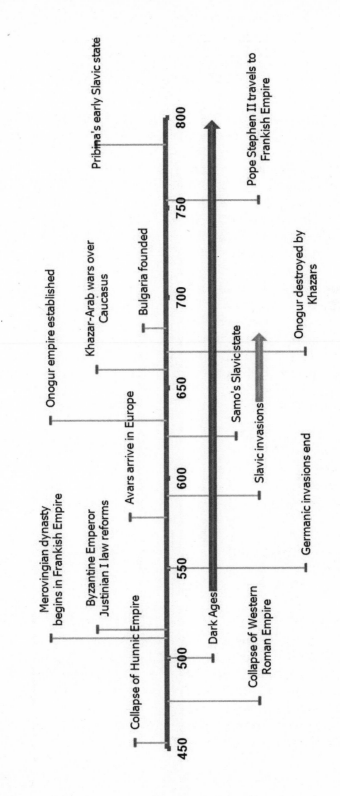

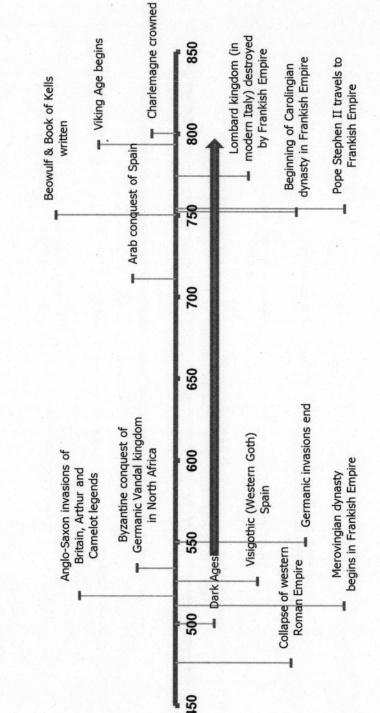

Figure 22. Comparative Western Europe Timeline, 500–800 CE

stores are looted by frenzied mobs. Traffic between towns grinds to a halt as gas runs out—which means no more food or supplies are being brought in to your town. You notice that there are no more planes flying above. The local hospital is abandoned (and looted). There are no more authorities or governments, no more clean drinking water or functioning sewers. You are now isolated from the rest of the world, and you had better start scrounging for tonight's dinner. The money in your pocket is now worthless too. Internet? E-mail? All gone. The planet over, centuries' worth of accumulated advanced communications technology all fall silent.

We are so dependent on civilization that we take much for granted. It never occurs to most of us to worry about where next week's breakfast will come from, or whether our neighbor will murder us. We flick a switch and the electricity comes on, as we expect it to. Winter, once deadly to our ancestors, is for us just an inconvenience, and we expect to come home each day (in our well-heated cars) to a comfortable house. Our food and most of the things we use in our daily lives come to us from far away, sometimes even from other continents. Imagine them all suddenly gone.

Figure 23. Eastern and Central Europe in the mid-7th Century CE

1,500 years ago, when our story begins, Roman citizens living west of the Danube River woke up to the world I just described. They of course didn't have cars, cell phones, or planes, but their civilization collapsed all the same and it was as traumatic for them as it would be for you. It didn't happen overnight—indeed, it took decades, even centuries—but Roman society broke down, security disappeared (meaning robbers and gangs preyed on the weak), trade routes collapsed (so much for the food and other goods such as textiles and medicines they had carried), starving mobs reduced cities to war zones, and communication between different parts of the old empire collapsed as well. A few of the larger aristocratic estates or towns created their own security forces, and people flocked to these small islands of civilization, but chaos reigned. Within just a couple generations of the western Roman collapse, writing and Christianity almost disappeared. Roads, bridges, dams, canals, public buildings, forts, and walls fell into disrepair and crumbled; farms were abandoned. Starvation, disease, and violence all became widespread.

USELESS TRIVIA: TREE SAP, DEAD FLIES, AND JEWELRY!

In his book *Geographia*, written sometime between 148 and 170 CE, the Greek geographer and astronomer Ptolemy, living in Roman Egypt, wrote about an ancient trade network stretching at least back to Neolithic (i.e., late Stone Age) times that spanned most of northern and Central Europe to the Mediterranean, and beyond: the Amber Road. Amber had no practical use, but its decorative beauty and, for some, spiritual power was enrapturing, compelling merchants to risk their lives traversing the deep, dark northeastern forests where amber was found: the coastline of the eastern Baltic Sea, what are today Poland, Kaliningrad (Russia), Lithuania, Latvia, and Estonia. Baltic amber has been found in the tombs of Egyptian Pharoahs as well as the graves of ancient prominent Britons of the Stonehenge-builders era, and made it as far east as ancient Assyria (modern-day Iraq and Syria). Roman artifacts regularly turn up along the ancient amber trade routes in Poland, far from Roman borders, as a testament both to eager Roman merchants who plied these trails and the trade in Roman goods conducted by the ancient amber collectors of the Baltic coast. In 2010 a poignant indicator of the extent of the Baltic trade routes popped up when German archaeologists found a large cache of silver coins, jewelry, and bars from the Arab lands (with Arabic inscriptions) buried in German Pomerania on the site of an early-7th-century Slavic village.[1] Amber still washes up on Baltic beaches today.

This is the beginning of what Westerners call the Dark Ages, the period between the collapse of the Western Roman Empire and the re-establishment of civilization in Western Europe three hundred years later. In Western Europe, there were no countries (yet); only Celtic or Germanic tribes living in the countryside (outside central and parts of southern Italy), or very frightened Romans (e.g., Latin speakers) cowering in the cities, and along the southern shorelines were some Greek and other communities. The Germanic *Völkerwanderung* (Great Migration of the Peoples) had begun already in the time of Julius Caesar (mid-1st century BCE) but the real show got underway as the Roman Empire began to weaken in the early 3rd century CE. Germanic peoples streamed into Europe from the Steppe in waves, landing in the Balkans and the Carpathian Basin, and shuffling across the Northern European Plain through modern-day Germany, France, Spain, and even on into North Africa (modern-day Morocco, Tunisia). By the time of the western Roman collapse in 476 CE, much of northern Europe, from Scandinavia to Britain to Iberia, was chock full of Germanic peoples or at least ruled by them.

B. The Avars

The eastern Roman, or *Byzantine* Empire was able to hold on to the Balkans south of the Danube River in the decades before the western Roman collapse, but the Carpathian Basin was quickly lost to waves of invaders from the Great Steppe: the Huns, then, after Attila's death in 453, waves of Germanic peoples. The Ostrogoths (Eastern Goths) stuck around the longest, building an empire stretching from modern-day southern Italy (including Sicily), the northern Balkans, and the Carpathian Basin—including modern-day Hungary, Slovakia, and Romania—but the Byzantines managed to drive them out in 562. Just when peace seemed at hand, a Turkic tribal confederation called the Avars showed up on Byzantium's doorstep from the Great Steppe.

The Avars quickly took over the Carpathian Basin, which with its wide, flat grasslands was perfect for their horses, and they booted out the (Germanic) Lombards who had since moved in. (We'll be meeting the Lombards again later.) By 578 CE, the Avars—led by their most famous *khagan*, or emperor, Bayan (BAH-yahn)—had themselves an empire that stretched from modern-day Austria,[2] Hungary, and Slovakia to Bulgaria in the south and the Prut River (dividing modern-day Romania and Moldova) in the east. The Avar *khaganate*—or Steppe empire—lasted another two centuries until 810 when two of its enemies, the Franks in the west and the Bulgars to the south, both fed up with Avar raids, ganged up and destroyed the Avar state.

The Avars are important because during their two centuries of rule in the Basin they helped to stabilize Eastern Europe politically and economically after the calamity of western Rome's collapse, slowing down the flow of peoples and armies from the Steppe into Europe. But they are remembered in history for something else. Successful Steppe empires were like rock stars, attracting large numbers of groupies who followed them for security and economic opportunities. The Avars were accompanied into Europe by a number of different peoples, one of which would completely change the face of Eastern Europe, especially since the Avars had just pushed many Germanic peoples westward.

C. The Slavs

In the sixth century, the Slavs took possession of the arterial route from Aquileia on the Adriatic to Constantinople, a road that had kept this part of the empire, alone in the east, strongly linked to Latin-speaking Italy. In this way they finally moved into the Balkan territories of the Roman empire, including [. . .] Greece itself. In that traditional center of the civilised world they were to be diffused and assimilated by the residents; but farther north, their relative numbers were far more overwhelming. By the seventh century the Slavs had been left in linguistic possession of most of eastern Europe, where they are to this day.[3]

The actual origins of the Slavs is in debate, with different theories claiming they originated in the modern-day Czech Republic, central Poland, western Belarus, Ukraine, northern Russia, southern Russia, the Carpathian Basin, or Serbia. What is known is that by the late 6th century, Slavs had already started seeping into the Balkans from the east when the Avars showed up, and the Byzantines took the opportunity of the Avars' arrival to hire them to boot the Slavs out of Byzantine territory. The Byzantines at the time had just gotten caught up in a nasty war with the Sassanid Persian Empire in the east—even back then the Middle East was a major headache for world leaders—and it seemed natural for Byzantium to reach for an outsourcing solution by hiring the Avars to do some barbarian pest control.

Unfortunately for Byzantium, after some initial battles the Avars and Slavs realized they had more in common than not, so they joined forces instead and began raiding and pillaging the "target-rich" Byzantine Balkans. Over the next century until about the 670s, waves of Slavic speakers—without any central organization—poured into Eastern Europe, first into the Balkans with the aid of the Avars, as far southward as Athens itself with many Greek cities like Thessaloniki[4] being besieged or laid waste by Slav-Avar assaults. Then they continued westward to the Adriatic, and finally northward to the Baltic

Sea, reaching as far west as the modern-day Danish border and the modern-day German cities of Hamburg and Bremen. One theory, for instance, about the origins of Berlin, Germany's capital city, is that it was originally a Slavic settlement, its name deriving from *br'lo*, Slavic for "swamp" or "bog."

In Figure 24 we see the farthest extent of Slavic settlement by the end of the Slavic invasions of the 6th and 7th centuries, facilitated by the Avar partnership. As was usually the case in this era, the "Slavs" who invaded and settled Eastern Europe likely included many other peoples who just "joined the fun" and later were eventually absorbed into the larger Slavic language and culture(s).

Figure 24. The Farthest Extent of Slavic Settlement in the Late-7th Century

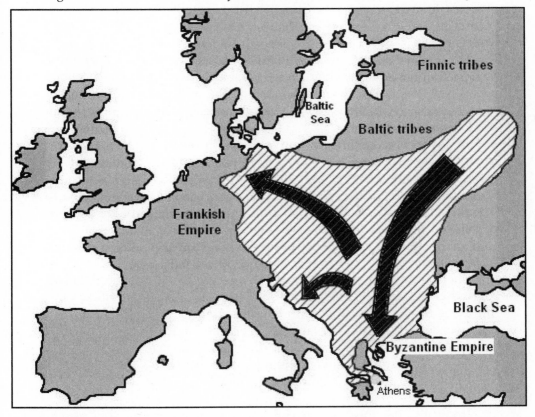

D. The First Slavic States

Where was the first Slavic state founded, and by whom? Truth is, we don't know. History and archaeology are a bit vague on this point—they don't call it the Dark Ages for nothing—but here are a few examples of some of the earliest Slavic states we *do* know something about. Up until now, the Slavs we've been talking about have been strongly linked historically to the Avars, but there is another shadowy group of Slavs called the *Antes* or *Antis* (pronounced like your *auntie* Edna). They show up in a few records in the 6th century, and the Eastern Roman bureaucrat Jordanes describes them as living north of the Black Sea between the Dniester and Dnieper rivers—although some experts dispute this—and he describes them as being well organized and having towns.

After an Avar attack in 602 the Antes disappear from the records—perhaps the attack was fatal?—so we really don't know much about them, but it may be they who deserve the credit for creating the first Slavic state(s) in the form of a tribal confederation. In any event, Jordanes referred to another group of Slavs, the ones in cahoots with the Avars, which he called the *Sclaveni*, and it is with them that we will be mostly concerned.

In 623, some of the Carpathian Basin Slavs had had enough of Avar rule and revolted, choosing as their leader a Frankish merchant named "Samo" (SAH-mo). The Franks were a Germanic tribe who had set up house in old Roman Gaul (modern-day France and western Germany) about whom we'll learn more later.

In any event, Samo went native, learning the Slavic language and customs (including taking on a dozen wives) and founded a state in what is today the eastern Czech Republic and Slovakia—although some place his state more in eastern Austria. Samo's Slavs even managed to repulse an invasion by a Frankish army in 631, only to implode and collapse after he died in the 660s. We know little else of Samo's state, and can only point to it as evidence that at least some Slavs were beginning to learn statecraft.

There is another possible early Slavic state we know about, called Carinthia or *Karantanija* (Car-on-TAHN-ee-yah), founded by Slavs living in the eastern Alps shortly after Samo's state in the late-7th century—some believe the Karantanians were actually refugees from Samo's collapsed state—in modern-day northern Italy, southern Austria, and Slovenia. Modern-day Slovenians regard the ancient Karantanians as their ancestors. Karantanija did not last long before it too succumbed to the Franks.

Ironically, the most successful Slavic state by far in this period wasn't started by Slavs, though they eventually became its masters. It was started by an outside invader who conquered the eastern Balkans, ruling over a sea of Slavs—only to embrace and merge with them to such an extent that today we consider their descendants—modern-day Bulgarians—a Slavic people.

USELESS TRIVIA:
WHEN MYTHOLOGY HITS THE OPEN ROAD!

In the 13th century, between 1282 and 1285, a chronicler to the Hungarian court of King László IV named Simon Kézai (SHEE-mon KAY-zye) included in his book *Gesta Hungarorum* ("Deeds of the Hungarians," in Latin) a story of the *Csodaszarvas*, the Mythical Stag. This legend told of two brothers, Hunor and Magor, who ended up chasing a mythical white stag, and while they never quite caught the stag—apparently they were poor hunters—through a series of adventures they did manage to grab some real estate and wives, in the process founding two nations: the Huns (Hunor), and the Hungarians (Magyars = "Magor"). Describing this legend, Simon went on to link the Hungarians and the Huns, claiming that the Hungarian occupation of the Carpathian Basin in 895 CE was in reality a *re-occupation*, since the Hungarians' brothers, the Huns, had occupied that same turf 400 years before. This myth of the Hun-Magyar link has lived among some Hungarians, but unfortunately, it's all a load of huey. Modern-day linguists, archaeologists, and historians have decisively debunked Kézai's Magyar-Hun link.

Chroniclers were literate men who recorded the events of their times, making a living from the fact they could read and write, a rare skill in medieval Europe. Some were monks, laboring away in isolated monasteries. Others, like Simon Kézai, were court chroniclers, essentially PR people or *propagandists* who ran medieval spin machines for princes or kings, often referencing fanciful myths or legends to buff up the boss's street creds to help legitimize his policies. The critical difference between chroniclers and modern-day historians is *train*ing. The job requirement for a chronicler was simply literacy, but modern-day historians are taught to critically analyze evidence. A historian is sort of like a traffic cop carefully investigating an accident decades or centuries after it happened, but a chronicler was more like a witness to the accident whose king or bishop (i.e., "the boss") happened to be driving one of the cars. This means that while medieval chronicles can still often be helpful, they need to be taken with a grain of salt.

E. The Bulgars

The ancient Bulgars were a Turkic-speaking people who descended from the Ural Mountains in the 2nd century CE, first into the lands north of the Caspian and Black seas before breaking up into several groups. In the early 7th century (632), the great Bulgar *khan* (a Steppe king or leader) Kubrat (or Kuvrat; KOO-braht - or - KOO-vraht) established *Onogur* (OWN-o-goor; "Land of Ten Arrows / Tribes") or what is also called Great Bulgaria, a Steppe empire that stretched from his capital on the Sea of Azov to possibly as far west as the Danube River. This powerful, though fleeting empire, was destroyed in 670 by the nearby Khazar empire and once again Bulgars were scattered to the winds. Two of these scattered Bulgar groups in particular are of interest to us; one group migrated to the confluence of the (southern) Volga and Kama rivers and ruled there an independent state for six centuries until 1241 when they were destroyed by the Mongols. They became known as the Volga Bulgars, and with extensive trade links to Baghdad and the Arab world, they adopted Islam. It is believed the modern-day Chuvash people are descendants of the ancient Volga Bulgars.

The second group, led by a khan named Asparukh (or Isparikh, depending on who you ask; Ah-SPA-rookh, Ee-SPA-reekh), migrated westward into modern-day Moldova where they first came into contact with Byzantium and after a short (but sharp) two year war, in 681 the Byzantines allowed the creation of a Bulgar state in what is today southern Romania and northern Bulgaria. These Bulgars did not find this land empty, as we've already seen. It was wall-to-wall with Slavs. Little is known about how the process of merging took place, but it seems from Byzantine sources and the archaeological record that very quickly the Turkic Bulgars allowed Slavs to attain high offices in the new state, and within a century or so, there were no more differences between Bulgars and Slavs; the two had become one people.

To this day, Bulgarian is one of the most unique of the Slavic languages because of its early non-Slavic pedigree. For instance, in all of the Slavic languages except Bulgarian, the main personal pronouns are the same: *On* (He) and *Ona* (She). (In Cyrillic, "он," "она"). But in Bulgarian, they are: той (tuh-y; "he") and тя (tyah, "she"). Byzantine emperor Leo III came to appreciate his Bulgarian neighbors when Bulgarian Khan Tervel helped save Constantinople from a massive Arab invasion in 718, attacking and mauling Arab forces from behind.

Some more exciting things happen with the Bulgar state in the 800s, but that's the next chapter.

F. The Dacians and Vlachs

The Dacians (DAH-chans) are a people whose origins are obscured by history, so that we just don't know much about them. There is almost no evidence of their language left, just a few place names we think they left behind. Modern-day Romanians claim descent from the Dacians, and have even named their nationally manufactured car the "Dacia".[5]

We do know *some* things about the Dacians, though, which are widely accepted by scholars. The Dacians were an ancient people living in the southeastern Balkans who *may* be—we're not really sure—derived from or related to the ancient Thracians and their cousins the Illyrians, whose western Balkan empire the Romans destroyed and conquered in 168 BCE. The relationship between these three ancient peoples—the Dacians, Illyrians, and Thracians—is controversial because so little evidence survives, but the argument is not purely academic: modern-day Romanian (the language) seems to have a(n ancient, pre-Roman) historical relationship with Albanian, leading some to theorize that both languages may possibly derive from ancient Dacian.

Anyway, the Dacians established a kingdom in the decades immediately preceding the collapse of the Roman Republic in the 1st century BCE in what is today Romania, eastern Hungary, Moldova, and northern Bulgaria, and their most powerful king was Burebişta (Boo-reh-BEE-shtah), who reigned at about the same time as Julius Caesar. In 101–106 CE, the Romans invaded and conquered Dacia, creating the Roman province of *Dacia*. (The Romans were very imaginative with their province names.)

The collapse of Roman power in the Balkans in the 3rd and 4th centuries was just as calamitous as elsewhere in the empire, as civilization crumbled and barbarian armies overran once prosperous cities. The Dacians disappear from history at this point, although maybe "disappear" isn't quite the right word:

> What was the fate of the indigenous population? Many were killed, while others were carried off beyond the Danube as captives (some of whom were ransomed and returned), or fled to walled cities or to the islands. Still others withdrew to the mountains or remote regions, and their descendants reappeared later as Vlachs or Albanians who begin to turn up in written sources in the eleventh and twelfth centuries.[6]

The Roman Balkans was filled with many different peoples, Dacians among them, and it seems that when Roman control over the region gave way, many of these peoples fled into the mountains of the southern Balkans for safety from the horse-riding invaders of the Steppe. There, over centuries, these peoples melded together to form, in the western Balkans, modern-day Albanians, and in the eastern Balkans—where Latin was used among the different peoples as a *lingua franca* (common language): Vlachs.

The term *Vlach* seems to have been a common term in the post-Roman Balkans for shepherds, and indeed the Vlachs became pastoralists during their long centuries in the mountains, tending to sheep and goats. Vlachs lived throughout the southern Balkan mountain ranges, eventually emerging into Greece, Albania, Serbia, and Bulgaria—all these countries still today have Vlach minorities—but the majority of them lived in Bulgaria and would carry the imprint of Bulgarian culture for centuries to come. Indeed, Romanian was written in the Bulgarian Cyrillic alphabet until the early-19th century.

A final point worth making is that few Vlachs ever called themselves "Vlachs"; most Vlachs referred to themselves as "Romans," or a variation like the *Aromans* of Epirus in modern-day northwestern Greece. This is how medieval Wallachia (Vlachia) eventually became modern-day "Romania."

G. *The Khazars*

The Khazars started their career as a Turkic people caught up in a gigantic early Turkic empire called the *Tujue* (Too-JOO-weh) or *Göktürk* (Gook [like "book"]-tewrk) empire. This early eastern Turkic empire was centered north of China in the early 6th century CE but may have extended as far west as the Black Sea. When this empire imploded in the mid-7th century, its western half was divvied up between Kubrat's Bulgar ("Great Bulgaria") and the Khazar empires. Within just a couple decades, though, the Khazars were able to crush *Onogur* (as we saw in the Bulgar section) and impose their rule from the Aral Sea in the east to modern-day Moldova in the west, though their capital and cultural center was always in the northern Caucasus.

Though few know their name today, the Khazars played an extraordinarily important role in early European history simply by defending their borders; the Khazars held back the extremely aggressive and expansionist Arab empire(s), repeatedly halting Arab invasions into the Caucasus and Central Asia throughout almost all of the 8th century. This was the period when the Arab Umayyad armies were overrunning the Middle East and North Africa, even crossing in 711 CE the Straits of Gibraltar into Spain.

A successful Arab invasion of what is today southern Russia, and perhaps far beyond, would most certainly have had a severe impact on Eastern European, and European, history. The dual role, in fact, that Khazaria and Byzantium played in turning back the constant Arab invasions of Eastern Europe (through Russia and the Balkans) is indeed often forgotten by Westerners.

Figure 25. The Khazar Khaganate/Empire in c. 814 CE

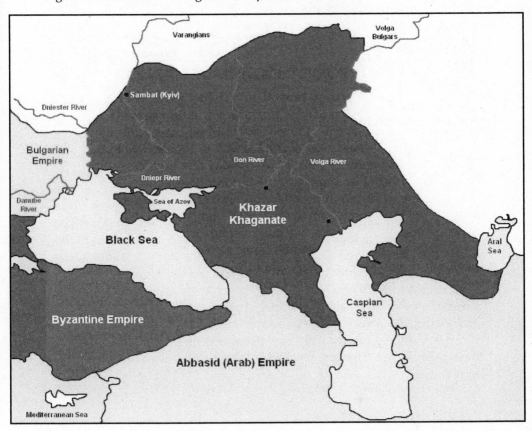

But the Khazars also provided some other benefits to Eastern Europe, such as serving as sort of an incubator for other peoples caught up in their empire, teaching them all the arts of running a state; e.g., government, diplomacy, war, and finance. In this way, future Eastern European groups like the Bulgars, Hungarians, and Cumanians learned much from their years of captivity in the Khazar empire. As well, when the Umayyad caliphate gave way in the Arab world to the Abbasid dynasty, relations between the Arabs and Khazars over time improved, and the Khazars became an important prism for trade between Eastern Europe (reaching as far afield as Scandinavia) and both Byzantium and the Arab world. This had a very direct impact developmentally on Eastern Europe.

USELESS TRIVIA: MAZEL TOV!

The Khazars have an odd distinction in world history; they are the only known country, outside of ancient Israel and Judea themselves, to voluntarily adopt *Judaism* as their state religion. At some point in the early 9th century, the Turkic Khazar elite converted to Judaism—many sources from all over Europe and the Middle East confirm this—and invited rabbis from the Jewish communities embedded in the Greek Black Sea towns to come and proselytize in the Khazar lands and build synagogues. It is not certain how many Khazars converted. Some sources claim all of them did, but other evidence, including some archaeological evidence, suggests that at least in some parts of the Khazar empire only the elites converted, but nonetheless Jewish ritual objects are frequently found in the graves of important Khazars. The early graves of ancient pre-Christian Bulgars and Hungarians, who were once ruled by the Khazars, also sometimes contain Jewish ritual objects. It is believed that the reason behind the decision to convert to Judaism may have been linked not so much to divine inspiration as to a certain geopolitical reality—namely, the Khazar lands were bordered on the south by a very aggressive Arab Islamic empire, and in the west by an equally aggressive Christian Byzantine empire; surely, it would have been in the Khazars' interest to choose a neutral religion? Shalom, indeed!

H. (A Bunch of) Finns and Balts

Somewhere in the dark, thick forests, somewhere among the many lakes and rivers, somehow in the often frozen land of the midnight sun on the eastern Baltic shores lurked two groups of peoples who would both have an important impact on Eastern European history. The Finnic peoples, half of the Finno-Ugric language family who are believed to have originated in the northern Ural Mountains some 5,000 years ago, spread over 3,000 years not only into what is today northern Russia, Finland, and Estonia but also eastward into northern Siberia. By Roman times these Finnic tribes—Vepsians, Mordvinians, Sami (i.e., Lapplanders), and Karelians—occupied not only the northern lands associated with modern-day Finns but much of what is central European Russia today, carefully keeping to the safety of the forested lands north of the Steppe.

By the period at the end of this chapter, c. 800 CE, Finnic tribes were feeling the pressures of expanding Slavic settlements and were being pushed northward deeper into the Baltic forests—but, as some studies are suggesting, not without first imparting some important civilizational knowledge to their Slavic neighbors. Indeed, as we'll see in Chapter 2, the Finnic ancestors of the modern-day Estonians and Livonians are mentioned in chronicles as having played a decisive (and often overlooked) role in the establishment of Kieven Rus.

Meanwhile, Indo-European-speaking peoples had flooded the southern Baltic Sea shoreline roughly from modern-day Courland in Latvia to Pomerania along the modern-day Polish-German border, clinging especially to the Vistula, Narew, Niemen, and Daugava rivers.[7] The Baltic peoples lived fairly quietly for centuries in the sheltering isolated forests along the eastern Baltic shoreline but the neighborhood went decidedly bad when in the late Roman era Germanic peoples began to move in from the east, and on their heels Slavic peoples.

The Balts were consummate traders and had developed a fairly extensive and sophisticated commercial network in the eastern Baltic region complete with bustling port cities like *Truso* (modern-day Elbląg; ELB-long) in Poland, or *Kaup* (Cowp; modern-day *Моховое*/ Mokhovoyeh in Russian Kaliningrad). These Baltic commercial centers attracted, among others, Roman merchants who sought that golden-brown jewel of the Baltic Sea: amber. The Balts also had to contend with Scandinavian raids as well as commercial competition from Vikings, who established competing trade centers on the Estonian and Latvian coasts such as Grobin (modern-day Grobiṇa, Latvia).

The real troubles for the Baltic and Finnic peoples, however, began as the Crusades in the Holy Land went sour. Since the 12th century Saxons, Slavs, and Danes had been raiding the Baltic and Finnic lands, joined occasionally by the Holy Roman Empire, Sweden, or Poland. However, when some Crusader armies were kicked out of the Middle East by Muslim victories in the late 12th and early 13th centuries, (recently unemployed) Crusaders were attracted to the pagan eastern Baltic region. Pope Celestine III declared a formal crusade against Baltic and Finnic pagans in 1193, kicking off the Northern or Baltic Crusades.

Fanatic Crusaders flooded the pagan eastern Baltic lands, destroying their towns, laying waste to their trade networks, and ultimately reducing the Balts and Finnic peoples from dozens of tribes down to just a handful. One of these, the Lithuanians, was born of a coalition of Baltic tribes who united to confront the Crusaders in the early-13th century, but that story is for future chapters. For the next several centuries, the Baltic and Finnic peoples were forced to grapple with a series of Danish and German Crusader states, as well as with the occasional Polish, Russian, or Swedish incursion.

USELESS TRIVIA: BUNCH OF PHILISTINES

The Baltic peoples clung to their native pre-Christian pagan beliefs and practices longer than most others, in the face of medieval German Crusader, Danish, Polish, Swedish, and Russian pressure to Christianize. Eventually, of course, the Christians won out and today most Balts are either Lutherans (Estonians, Latvians) or Catholics (Lithuanians). However, they didn't go without a fight, and Christian monks, missionaries, and soldiers plied their faith in the eastern Baltic lands at great personal peril.

The memory of those struggles has not completely faded, however, and many modern-day Balts, while firmly practicing Christians, regard the struggle for the old gods as an important part of Baltic identity. In this vein, in 1979 (i.e., in the Soviet era) a group of Lithuanian artists led by Jonas Stanius (YO-nass STAH-nyoos) began carving elaborate wooden sculptures of old Baltic pagan gods, spirits, demons, and legends on a hill outside the Lithuanian town of *Juodkrantė* (Yoo-awd-KRANT-ay)[8] on the Baltic Sea. With some hundred figures and more being added each year since, Raganų Kalnas (Witches Hill) has become a major attraction in the region and has even inspired a revival of some pre-Christian festivals.

So far, we've mentioned all these *Steppe* peoples (e.g., Huns, Goths, Avars, Bulgars, Magyars/Hungarians, and Khazars) with their seminomadic societies and very horse-centered armies, but we haven't really talked about *what* or *where* the Steppe was, and why it was so important to European and Asian history.

THE STEPPE

So, what is a steppe? As you may—or may not—recall from your high school geography lessons, it's a long, flat expanse with tall grass and very few trees. If you were standing in a steppe region, you'd be able to see very far in all directions. It's kind of like a desert and it is quite dry, though with slightly more rain than a desert—a mere technical detail, but it's the difference between lots of grass and sand dunes. Geography aside, steppes tend to encourage certain kinds of human lifestyles because, let's face it, there's only so much you can do with grass. Peoples living in steppe regions tended to be semi- or fully nomadic, meaning they roamed a lot and live in temporary, collapsible structures (i.e., tents) made from animal skins. They usually survived by herding animals, and had strong tribal or clan structures.

Figure 26. The Steppe in Eastern Europe and Asia

Now, on the particular steppe we're talking about—and it's a BIG one—the peoples living there quickly made the horse the center of their lives, relying on horses for shepherding, for traveling the Steppe's vast distances, and for war. The importance of the horse in the culture of the Steppe peoples during the Steppe culture's golden age of c. 1000 BCE to 1300 CE is illustrated by European chronicles which describe amazing Steppe warriors who could twist around backwards in their saddles—while their horses were *running at full gallup*—and shoot an arrow at fantastic distances with deadly accuracy. It is no mistake that Europeans eagerly adopted the stirrup from the Steppe peoples. Indeed, the Steppe peoples may have been the first humans to domesticate the horse.

USELESS TRIVIA: WAS THERE ANYTHING STRANGE ABOUT THOSE PILLAGERS?

In the late-19th century, Russian archaeologists began excavating the graves of ancient Scythian warriors across the southern Steppe in what are today Russia, Ukraine, and Moldova dating to the 6th and 5th centuries BCE. Many of these graves had escaped the notice of robbers, so they still contained rich treasures. The curious thing about some of these ancient warriors was *that they were women*. Some archaeologists thought the warrior dress and weaponry were perhaps a suitable burial for the *wife* of a warrior, but a detailed survey of the graves by German archaeologist Renate Rolle in the 1980s showed that the weapons were all sized and shaped specifically for women and studies of the bodies and weapons by international archaeologists Jeannine Davis-Kimball and Elena Fialko proved fairly conclusively that these women fought for a living. Were Scythian women the mythical Amazons?

The Amazons were mentioned by the 5th-century BCE Greek historian Herodotus when he described a tribe of wild Sarmatian (related to the Scythians) warrior women who rode horses into battle. However, none of these graves contained horses, and their weapons were more suitable to fighting on foot rather than on horseback. It may be that these women were trained soldiers who defended the homestead while the armies (i.e., men) were off fighting elsewhere. This still doesn't discount the potential Amazon link, however, because some of these warrior women were buried with the relics of children; Herodotus mentions that the Amazons gave up *horse-mounted combat* when they married, but not necessarily all forms of combat. The idea of women leading mounted charges in vicious Steppe combat startled the ancient Greeks as it still startles us today, but history suggests that it shouldn't.

Strict Steppe clan hierarchies gave Steppe generals better control of their armies, allowing them often to use far more sophisticated strategies and tactics than their urban (i.e., European) enemies whose armies were typically motley collections of armored knights, mercenaries and peasant conscripts. This expertise with horses and command structures explains why for generations Steppe peoples like the Huns were able to devastate Europe with such ease, despite the fact Europe also had horsemen. It was comparing weekend warriors to the professionals.

So, where exactly is this steppe? As I mentioned, it's a big one. It begins in modern-day Manchuria, in northeastern China, and stretches westward across northern China and Mongolia, through northern Central Asia (mostly modern-day Kazakhstan) and southern Russia, past the Aral Sea, still westward past the northern Caspian Sea, continuing westward still past the northern Black Sea shore through southern Ukraine, finally ending at the Danube Delta on the western Black Sea where modern-day Ukraine, Romania, and Bulgaria meet. (See Figure 26.) This is one HUGE expanse of mostly flat, rolling grasslands.

When you think of a German, you may think of a plump blonde-haired guy wearing Lederhosen drinking from a stein, but in the 5th century you would have had a hard time telling the difference between a Goth and a Hun. The extreme Steppe environment shaped cultures in similar ways, which when coupled with the large amount of intermingling and cultural mixing that occurred on the Steppe, well, means that modern-day archaeologists, linguists, and historians still spend lots of time trying to tell them all apart. Byzantine bureaucrats and medieval European diplomats and generals had the same problem.

The Steppe is important in European (especially Eastern European) history because for some 2,300 years, from about 1000 BCE to the early 13th century CE, there was a massive and almost constant westward flow of humanity across Eurasia, scraping and grinding like a vast human glacier past all the great civilizations—China, Central Asia, India, Persia, the Middle East, Byzantium—before finally depositing them abruptly (and violently) at the end of the Steppe in Europe, in the Carpathian Basin, the Great Northern European Plain, or the Balkans. Constant waves of nomadic tribes—whether Iranian (e.g., Cimmerians, Scythians, Sarmatians, Alans, Iazians), Turkic (e.g., Huns, Avars, Bulgars, Pechenegs, Cumanians) Germanic (e.g., Goths, Gitae, Vandals, Franks), or Finno-Ugric (e.g., Magyars)—fought their way or were pushed westward by this massive conveyer belt stretching from China to Europe whose momentum was maintained by constant military pressure from the civilizations along the way.

Indeed, it wasn't until the early 20th-century that explorers realized how big the Great Steppe was, and connected historical events in northern China with events later in Europe.

2. THE ORIGINS OF STATES 800-1242 CE
THE SNOWBALL STARTS DOWNHILL

CHAPTER SUMMARY

The Frankish, Byzantine, Bulgarian, and Khazar empires emerge as the largest (and most important) states in Europe during this era, with the Franks and Byzantines feverishly competing throughout Eastern Europe for souls to save. It was not long before the region's tribes begin to emulate their imperial neighbors, and within a few decades of the beginning of this period some of the first Eastern European states appear. Eventually, two loosely connected systems, a Frankish system of Western Christian states and a Byzantine system of Orthodox Christian states arises, and the new states gradually come to mirror the social, economic, and political structures of their respective imperial sponsors (i.e., the Franks or Byzantines). This leads to a period of relative prosperity throughout the region, but this is short-lived as a catastrophic event in 1239–42 devastates Eastern Europe to a degree not to be seen again until the twentieth century.

CHAPTER GUIDE
A. *The Franks* 88
B. *Moravia Magna and Bohemia* 94
C. *The Bulgarians* 96
D. *The Rus* 97
E. *The Magyars/Hungarians* 100
F. *The Slovenes and Croatians* 103
G. *Duklja, Raška, and the Serbs* 104
H. *The Poles* 105
I. *The Pechenegs* 110
J. *The Cumanians* 110
K. *The Lithuanians* 111
L. *The Finale: 1239–42* 111

When last we left our heroes, things were a mess. However, out of the Dark Ages' primordial soup was emerging a new world, one that would be far more recognizable to you today than the one just a century before it.

A. The Franks

When did the West begin? It all depends on how you define "the West." Many think of the ancient Greeks and Romans as "Westerners" because they laid the philosophical foundations for the modern West, but they did not think of themselves as Westerners any more than Christopher Columbus considered himself a citizen of the European Union. When the ancient

Figure 27. Eastern Europe Timeline, 800–1242 CE

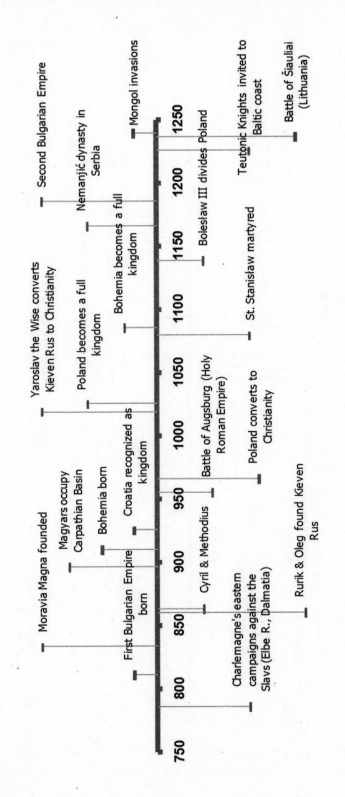

Figure 28. Comparative Western Europe Timeline, 800–1242 CE

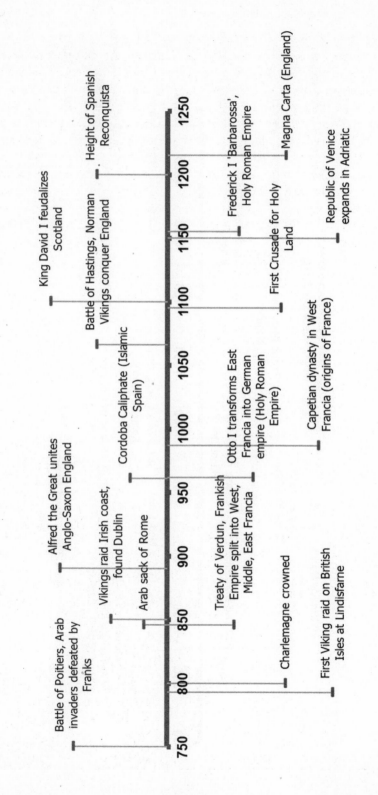

Greeks or Romans looked for their equals, they looked to the Mediterranean world of such peoples as the Persians, Egyptians, and Carthaginians. Greeks and Romans saw the parts of Western, Central, and Northern Europe beyond their political boundaries (and control) as a dark wilderness of uncivilized barbarians, not as lands inhabited by fellow "Europeans." The mere coincidence of living on the same landmass did not impress the ancient Greeks and Romans enough to make them feel some affinity for those barbarians. For our purposes, we'll pin the West's origins to a priest's long walk in the thick mists of post-Roman Dark Ages Europe, which ended with a wedding of sorts between two worlds that needed each other badly. It was a marriage of convenience, to be sure, but as shotgun weddings go, this one turned out to be quite successful for all parties concerned.

Figure 29. Eastern Europe in 814 CE

The story begins with our old friends the Lombards, the Germanic people who had been pushed out of the Carpathian Basin by the Avars in Chapter 1. They had moved westward and settled in northern Italy (yes, *Lombardy*, named after them), and by the mid-8th century had expanded throughout much of Italy and had taken to picking on the Christian bishop of Rome (who only later would become called "Pope"), Stephen II. To boot, Umayyad Arabs, fresh from their conquest of the *Maghreb* (North Africa), were raiding Sicily, Sardinia, and the Italian coast, even occupying Syracuse temporarily in 740. The city of Rome was in danger and Stephen needed help, but the Byzantines and the Patriarch in Constantinople—technically Stephen's boss—had their own hands full with the Arabs and other threats. Desperate for aid, he put on his galoshes, packed a lunch, and started trudging northward.

The Franks were a federation of Germanic tribes that had migrated to Roman Gaul in 11 BCE and were recognized as official allies (*foederati*) by the Romans in the 4th century CE, by which time they controlled most of what is today France and western Germany. The Franks helped the Romans defeat Attila and his Huns at the Battle of Chalons/Catalun in 453 CE. A powerful dynasty known as the Merovingians took over the Frankish federation in the 5th century—it was a Merovingian Frankish army that attacked Samo's Slavic state in 631 CE in Chapter 1—and they ruled the growing Frankish empire until being overthrown in 751 by one of their own bureaucrats, Pepin the Short, who made himself king.

Pepin did two important things. First, three years later, in 754, he received a curious visitor from Rome—the bishop of Rome, in fact, our Stephen II. Stephen told Pepin of the troubles with the Lombards and the Arabs, and the two cut a deal: Stephen would recognize Pepin as legitimate ruler of the Franks in return for Frankish "muscle power" to be used against Stephen's (i.e., the Church's) enemies. This brought the shattered remnants of the old Greco-Roman Mediterranean Classical world into union with the powerful, new northern European barbarian world of the Germanic tribes. It was a marriage made in heaven, and the resulting security allowed the Christian Church to spread in the West while also giving the Papal seal of approval to Frankish expansion. The Franks trounced the Lombards, and even helped the Papacy in Rome break free from Byzantine control. The West was born.

The second important thing Pepin did was have a son, Charles. Charles took the agreement with the Popes seriously. He expanded Frankish borders eastward and undertook a major series of campaigns in the years 785–804 to push the Slavs—who raided Frankish towns—back across the Elbe River. (But he also sometimes allied with Slavs against enemies, like Widukind's troublesome Saxons.)

Still today some Western Europeans regard Charles's eastern border, the Elbe River, as the cultural border between Western and Eastern Europe. Charles was rewarded for all this on Christmas Day in the year 800 by being crowned emperor by Pope Leo III, as if Charles were the emperor of a revived western Roman Empire. We know him through history as "Charles the Great," or, in French, *Charlemagne*. The Byzantine emperor was forced to recognize Charlemagne and his Frankish Empire as an equal, and the modern-day European Union venerates him as one of the first true Europeans.

USELESS TRIVIA: WHAT DO YOU MEAN, WE'RE EXTINCT?

Charlemagne's battles to push the Slavs back eastward across the Elbe River in the late 8th century were only the first shots in a very long struggle which is often portrayed in modern-day histories as "German vs. Slav," but in reality it was states vs. tribes. The settled states, the Frankish and later German empires, joined by Bohemia and Poland, more often than not cooperated with one another to conquer and Christianize the pagan Slavic and Baltic tribes living between them. These efforts took centuries.

So what happened to all these Slavic groups? Most were indeed conquered and disappeared from history, either being "Germanized," "Polonized," or "Czechified." Some still survive, today, however, like the Sorbs. The Sorbs—also called "Wends" or Lusatians—are a Western Slavic people living in modern-day southeastern Germany near the Polish and Czech borders, the remnants of the Frankish-era "Polabian Slavs." By 1900 there were still about 150,000 Sorbs, but 20th century German nationalists put a severe dent in their numbers, though still some 60,000 survive today. Increasingly only older Sorbs still speak Sorbian, as younger Sorbs tend to blend into mainstream German culture.[1]

Another group of Western Slavs who survived the early medieval Polish-German pressure to assimilate are the Kaszubs (KAH-shoob; or "Kashubs," or even "Cassubians" in English), several hundred thousand of whom still live in the Pomerania region of northwestern Poland, and still speak Kaszub (or *Kaszëbë*). Economic pressures and Prussian *Germanization* campaigns compelled many Kaszubs to emigrate abroad in the early 20th century, mostly to the Americas.[2]

Charlemagne's eastern policy was ambitious. He subdued the remaining Germanic tribes and, using the Elbe River as his holding line, established his "Eastern March" military defensive district at the southern end of the Elbe ("Eastern March" = *Östermark* = *Österreich* = Austria). When these borders were set, he extended Frankish rule further eastward by subjugating the Slavs living in what is today Slovenia and Croatia. In 810 he worked with the Bulgarians to destroy the Avar khanate. Charlemagne's policies did not stop where his armies did, however; he sent forth missionaries and agents to spread both Roman Christianity and Frankish interests throughout Eastern Europe, in heated competition with Byzantine missionaries and agents.

When Charlemagne died in 814, his massive empire was divided into three parts among his three grandsons. In short, the westernmost part, which was principally filled with Celts and Latin-speaking peoples (as well as obviously the Germanic Franks) eventually became France. (The modern-day German name for France is still *Frankreich*, which translates literally as "Kingdom of the Franks," and for centuries after the Crusades medieval Arabs referred to all Christian Europeans as *Faranji* – Franks.) The easternmost portion of Charlemagne's empire, populated mostly by Germanic peoples, eventually became Germany.

B. Moravia Magna and Bohemia

In the late-8th century, a small nascent Slavic state arose around the modern-day western Slovak town of Nitra, ruled by a warlord named Pribina (Pree-BEE-nah). In 833 a Moravian (eastern Czech) Slavic warlord named Mojmir (MOY-meer) overran Nitra and established his own empire, called Greater Moravia or *Moravia Magna* (in Latin), centered in today's eastern Czech Republic.

Mojmir was succeeded in the 840s by Rastislav, who continued to expand the state's boundaries but more importantly began to develop his state's relations with the Franks. Rastislav understood that Moravia's survival required its conversion to Christianity, but feared Moravia would just be absorbed into the Frankish empire if he wasn't careful, so he purposely reached for the Christianity that was farther rather than nearer—that of Byzantium. Rastislav invited the Byzantines in 862 to send missionaries to Moravia, and two brother-missionaries from Thessaloniki (in modern-day Greece) were sent.

In 870, however, Rastislav was deposed by the Franks who shut down the Byzantine-rite church in Moravia. Sviatopluk (Svyaht-O-plook), Rastislav's nephew, took over and managed to maintain Moravian independence from the Franks while extending Moravian borders in all directions, ultimately controlling what is today the southern regions of Poland (including Vratislav [modern-day Wrocław, Poland] and Kraków), what are today the Czech Republic and Slovakia, as well as western Hungary and parts of Austria and Slovenia. The archaeological record shows a dramatic jump in the material well-being of Moravia's cities under Sviatopluk, with foreign trade flourishing.

USELESS TRIVIA: THE GRASS IS ALWAYS GREENER . . .

In 862, feeling that Frankish priests were getting a little too cozy in his empire, the Moravian ruler Rastislav asked Byzantium for Christian missionaries. The Byzantines sent two Greek brothers, Constantine and Methodius, both of whom were raised in Thessaloniki (which back then had a mixed Greek and Slavic population), and both of whom could speak Slavic. They arrived in 863, and began translating the Bible into the Slavic language. The brothers used the Glagolitic alphabet, which their disciples in Bulgaria later simplified to create the Cyrillic alphabet used by modern-day Russians, Bulgarians, Serbs, and so on. (Constantine changed his name to "Cyril" shortly before his death, so the Cyrillic alphabet is named after him.) The brothers' successful work among the Moravians managed to irritate local Frankish missionaries, however, and the two were summoned to Rome in 867 to explain themselves. They actually managed to convince the Pope of the value of their work, though Cyril fell ill and died before leaving Rome. Methodius returned to Moravia and continued his missionizing, but he was finally expelled from Moravia in 885 by the Frankish faction. His disciples, expelled from Moravia, founded seminaries in Bulgaria that later played a crucial role in the spread of Christianity to Kieven Rus. Though Moravia and even Croatia remained in the Western Christian "camp," both Cyril and Methodius are still remembered and honored today in both lands by many plaques and monuments, and in 1979 Pope John Paul II—a Pole—made the brothers patron saints of Europe.

Sviatopluk's undoing was his choice of allies against the Franks, but more on that later. Moravia established institutions and traditions of government, church and diplomacy—and resistance to German control—that served as a model for successive Eastern European states over the next two centuries. (Indeed, as we'll see later, the Czechs would play a role in establishing both the Polish and Hungarian states.) In the 880s, Sviatopluk expanded Moravian control into Bohemia (modern-day western Czech Republic), but after his death the Slavic warlords of Bohemia rose up and organized their own state under the leadership of the Přemysl (Psheh-MIH-sel) family.

Thus was Bohemia born. The first true (Christian) Bohemian prince, Václav I (VAH-tslav; on whom the English Christmas carol "Good King Wenceslas" is based)—established the Bohemian capital at Prague (925–932) and while not quite completely free of German control, Václav still managed to maintain Bohemian autonomy. Bohemia soon joined the

German "Ottonian" Empire in the mid-10th century as a duchy, but in 1085 Bohemia was recognized as a full kingdom. Přemyslid rule in Bohemia lasted until 1306.

USELESS TRIVIA: THAT OL' TIME RELIGION

When Constantine (later Cyril) and Methodius began their Christian mission among the Slavs, they needed somehow to communicate the texts of the Christian Bible and rituals to the largely illiterate Slavs of the 9th century. The two Greek brothers set out translating everything. Their translations of both the Christian mass and Bible were eventually used all across the Slavic world, although the Pope and the Franks would later expunge the brothers' Slavic liturgy from Bohemia and Croatia, replacing it with Latin. Still, it played a vital role in the Christianization of the Slavic world.

In fact, Constantine and Methodius's Slavic liturgy is still in use (in modified form), some 1,100 years later. Now known as *Old Church Slavonic*, the brothers' translations are a regular part of mass and liturgy in the modern-day Bulgarian, Macedonian, Serbian, and Russian Orthodox churches, much as Latin survived in use in Roman Catholic churches. For instance, Russian Orthodox liturgical chants are often sung in Old Church Slavonic, not Russian. You can even see Old Church Slavonic inscriptions on the walls of the Roman Catholic cathedral in Zagreb, a legacy of Constantine and Methodius's mission in medieval Croatia. Old Church Slavonic was originally based on old Bulgarian, though it has since absorbed other influences as well, particularly medieval Russian.

C. The Bulgarians

In the early-9th century, Bulgaria was ruled by a khan (king) named Krum (KROOM). In 810 Krum collaborated with the Franks to destroy the Avar empire and rewarded himself by seizing the southern half of the Carpathian Basin (much of modern-day Romania, eastern Hungary and eastern Serbia). Shortly afterward he boldly provoked a major war with Byzantium by seizing the Byzantine city of Serdica (modern Sofia, Bulgaria), and his victories in that war over the next few years transformed Bulgaria from a local Byzantine satellite state into a major regional power. The First Bulgarian Empire was born. One of Krum's successors in the early-10th century, Simeon I, was strong enough to march into Constantinople itself and have himself crowned "Caesar (Tsar) of all Bulgarians and Romans"—making Bulgaria equal to Byzantium.

This was the pinnacle of Bulgarian power. It was in this period that Bulgaria accepted Christianity, and though it wavered for some years between Western and Eastern rite Christianity, the founding of an independent Bulgarian Orthodox Church in the late-9th century sealed the deal. In the early-10th century, Bulgaria ruled much of the Balkans and was, along with the Byzantine and Frankish empires, one of the most powerful states in Europe.

However, Bulgaria experienced a serious decline in the late-10th century (at a time when Byzantine fortunes were reviving), particularly after an attack from Kieven Rus in 969. Disaster came when the Byzantine emperor Basil II surprised and destroyed a Bulgarian army at Balasita in 1018, and had the eyes gouged out of most of the surviving 15,000 Bulgarian prisoners, granting himself the title Βουλγάροκθονοσ (Bulgar-oak-THONE-oss), "Slayer of the Bulgarians."

This debacle spelled the end of the First Bulgarian Empire, and the country entered a long period of Byzantine rule lasting for almost two centuries. Independence was recovered in 1185 when two Vlach brothers, Asen and Peter, led a successful anti-Byzantine revolt, leading to the establishment of the Second Bulgarian Empire. Though not as strong or influential as its predecessor, the Second Bulgarian Empire nonetheless led to a Bulgarian cultural renaissance of sorts, relatively free of Byzantine interference as Byzantium had troubles of its own—the fated Fourth Crusade and the founding of the Latin Empire. Bulgaria's borders once again stretched from the Black Sea to the modern-day Albanian coast, and at one point reached as far north as modern-day Belgrade (Serbia). This Bulgarian empire would survive for many centuries, though its first century saw its strongest growth and stability.

D. The Rus

When you think of Vikings, the image that usually comes to mind is of a blonde-haired, stocky, shirtless guy wearing a horned helmet and wielding a battle axe, or rowing one of those famous Viking long ships with a dragon head prow. Scary stuff. But the Vikings, while very capable of the kind of violence they are famous for, could also be surprisingly sophisticated in their economic pursuits. The Vikings made fierce merchants and accountants as well as raiders and warriors.

The exploits of Norwegian and Danish Vikings are well known in the West. During the Age of Vikings (c. 750–1100 CE), ragged hordes of these fierce Nordic warriors set out from Scandinavia and terrorized much of coastal Europe, invading the British Isles, France, the Iberian Peninsula, and sailing far to the west, discovering Iceland, Greenland, and even Vinland (modern-day Newfoundland and Labrador in Canada). Their plundering

Figure 30. The Farthest Penetration of the Vikings, 800–1100 CE

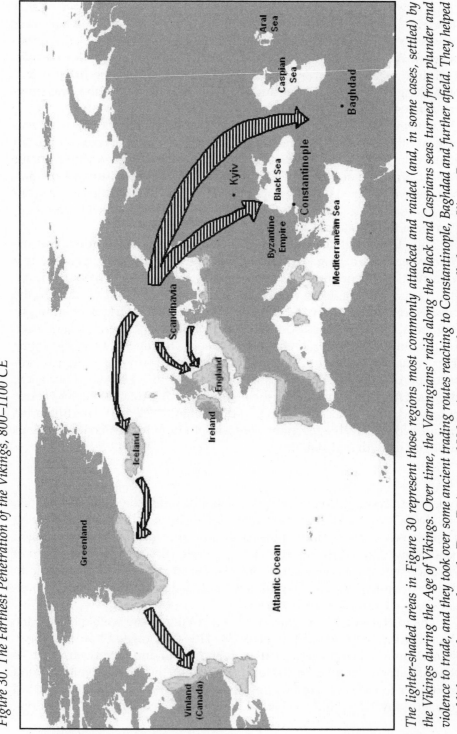

The lighter-shaded areas in Figure 30 represent those regions most commonly attacked and raided (and, in some cases, settled) by the Vikings during the Age of Vikings. Over time, the Varangians' raids along the Black and Caspians seas turned from plunder and violence to trade, and they took over some ancient trading routes reaching to Constantinople, Baghdad and further afield. They helped establish several states along the Don, Dniepe,r and Volga river routes that eventually became Kieven Rus.

ships even penetrated the Mediterranean. Fewer Westerners, however, know of the Vikings' *eastern* exploits.

In the mid-7th century Swedish Vikings began exploring the waterways southward beyond Finland, especially the major rivers: the Don, Dnieper, and Volga. These Vikings called themselves *Væringjar* (Vayr-EENG-yahr), which in English is usually "Varangians," but the Finnic peoples who lived throughout modern-day northwestern Russia called them *Ruotsi* (Roo-OTT-see), "the rowers," from which our name for them probably derives: the *Rus*. The Varangians, over time, took over major trading networks stretching from Scandinavia to Byzantium, Persia, and the Arab lands beyond the Caspian and Black seas. The Byzantines even hired some of them as mercenaries, as the Byzantine emperor's *Varangian Guard*.

USELESS TRIVIA: NOT EXACTLY *ROOTS* . . .

The whole point of the Varangians' traversing the incredible lengths of the Don, Dnieper, and Volga rivers from Scandinavia to Central Asia and the Middle East was trade, but trading what? Well, initially they traded Arctic fur pelts for Arab silver, but over time they expanded their catalog to include slaves. Before the Atlantic slave trade that plundered Africa in the 15th–19th centuries, by far the largest slave network in the world centered on the trade of Slavic peoples as slaves.

The word 'slave' (*sclavus, esclave*) derives from the name of peoples beyond the eastern frontier—Slavs. Lines of manacled war prisoners from the eastern campaigns were a frequent sight on the roads of Francia. They were en route to Mediterranean ports and the Islamic lands beyond.[3]

In the 8th–12th centuries Varangians, Franks, Byzantines, Italians, and (later) Germans sold captured Slavs in Mediterranean ports or Baghdad to the Muslim world, where they were sent to North Africa, the Middle East, or to Indian Ocean traders. Arab corsairs also raided the Adriatic coast for Slavic and Greek slaves until the 11th century. The spread of Christianity among Slavs, the rise of Kieven Rus, and the Crusades largely put an end to this trade. Still, the name "Slavs" came to mean *slaves* in many modern languages—e.g., English, French (*esclave*), German (*Der Sklave*), Dutch (*slaaf*), Swedish (*slav*), Danish (*slave*), Italian (*schiavo*), and Spanish (*esclavo*). The Mongols, Tartars, and Ottoman Turks continued the tradition (on a much smaller scale) for centuries more until the 18th and 19th centuries.

According to legend, in the mid-9th century local Slavic and Finnic tribes asked a Varangian known as *Rørik* (or Rurik; ROOR-ik) to end local strife and establish a confederation of Varangians, Slavs, and Finnic peoples based around Lake Ladoga and Novgorod (New City). After his death, his kinsman Oleg vastly expanded the state's borders, including conquering the city of Kyiv (in Russian: Kiev) in the 880s. Thus was born Kieven Rus. By the mid-10th century the Varangians had "gone native" and under Grand Prince Svyatoslav I, Kieven Rus had become a vast (Eastern Slavic) empire. Svyatoslav destroyed the Khazar empire in 968. The subsequent princes Vladimir (980–1015) and Yaroslav the Wise (1019–1054) brought Byzantine Orthodox Christianity to Kieven Rus, adopted the Cyrillic alphabet for the Eastern Slavic Rus language, imported artisans and missionaries from Byzantium and its allies (remember Methodius's seminaries in Bulgaria?), developed a written legal code (*Русска Правда*; ROO-Skah PRAHV-dah, "The Justice of Rus"), and built schools and monasteries across Rus. These years, 950–1100, are considered the golden age of Kieven Rus. Despite these successes, however, Kieven Rus's vast territory and dependence on trade with the declining Abbasid Arab and Byzantine empires took their toll, and over the next couple of centuries the rulers of Kieven Rus faced political fragmentation. By 1224, the authority of the rulers in Kyiv was weak and quickly fading to nil.

There is a common habit of referring to Kieven Rus as "early Russia" or "medieval Russia," but this is inaccurate. This is kind of like calling the Roman Empire "early Italy." This is important, because Kieven Rus was an Eastern Slavic civilization that—just as Roman civilization gave birth to the Italian, French, Spanish, and other peoples—fathered the modern Ukrainian, Belarussian, *and* Russian peoples. A bit later we'll get into how the three Eastern Slavic sibling peoples were eventually to separate.

E. The Magyars/Hungarians

Originating in the Ural Mountains in what is today Russia about 6,000 years ago and migrating slowly southward until landing on the southern Volga on the Great Steppe near the Caucasus, the ancient Magyars found themselves ruled by the Khazar empire in the 8th century CE. The many Turkic loan words in modern Hungarian about politics, agriculture, and animal husbandry attest to this Khazar period being an intensive learning experience for the Magyars. In 830 CE, a revolt broke out in the Khazar empire and the Magyars fled westward to the land between the Dnieper and Dniester rivers (modern-day Ukraine), and this land they called *Etelköz* (Land Between the Rivers"; EH-tell-kooz).

After settling in Etelköz in the early-9th century, the Magyars began receiving offers from the Moravians (remember *Moravia Magna*?), who ruled the nearby Carpathian Basin at that time, for mercenary services.

The Moravian ruler Sviatopluk used Magyar mercenaries—whose devastating Steppe cavalry no European army could stop—in his wars against the Franks, the Bulgars, the Byzantines, and others. Unfortunately for Sviatopluk, the Magyars he hired took note of the wide Carpathian Basin grasslands they passed through on each mission, and they became familiar with most of Central and Eastern Europe's main travel routes during their Moravian campaigns. This became a problem for Sviatopluk in 895–896 when the Magyars' enemies, the Bulgarians and Pechenegs, ganged up and invaded Etelköz, driving the Magyars out. Thanks to their intimate familiarity with the region, the Magyars—led by Árpád (AHR-pod), whose dynasty would rule Hungary until 1300—quickly occupied much of the Carpathian Basin, easily overwhelming Moravian defenses.[4] Thus was Hungary founded and Moravia Magna destroyed, allowing Bohemia to rise from its ashes. A thousand years later in 1896, Habsburg Hungary celebrated a millennium of Hungarian statehood with great pomp and ceremony, building many of the monuments and attractions tourists flock to see in modern-day Budapest.

Initially, around 896, the Magyars behaved like the Steppe people they were, like the Huns, Goths, and Avars before them: they raided and pillaged surrounding lands. Thanks to Sviatopluk's campaigns the Magyars were familiar with Europe's geography, and they plundered as far as Paris and even Iberia. From the perspective of many people in Europe this behavior got old very quickly, and it fell to the Eastern Frankish king—by now we can call him "German"—Otto I, to do something about it. In August 955, in a fierce battle near the River Lech (like "Blech!"), at Augsburg in southern Germany, he managed to shatter weary Magyar forces returning from a campaign, and even captured two of their most senior commanders.

A couple of things came out of this battle. The first was that the Germans were so stunned by this victory that Otto was declared emperor of Germany on the spot by his victorious army. Otto's battlefield elevation to emperor status was officialized a few years later, in 962, and his empire eventually became known (in Latin, the official language of medieval Western Europe) as *Sacrum Romanum Imperium*, "the Holy Roman Empire," in 1024. The second important thing to come out of the defeat at Augsburg/Lechfeld was a Magyar identity crisis. Magyar armies had known setbacks before, but not this bad. Luckily, a father and son team, Crown Prince Géza (GAY-zuh) and his son Vajk (Vike)—who, after converting to Christianity, became *István* (EESHT-vahn; "Stephen")—understood that Magyar survival meant conversion to Christianity and integration into the Christian European state system.

USELESS TRIVIA: MEDIEVAL EASTERN EUROPE IN KENTUCKY!

The Hungarian royal crown has a strange history, as crowns go. The one St. István (Stephen) received in 1000 CE has been lost to history. The current one is believed to be two different crowns fused together, the lower part a Byzantine crown from c. 1070 and the upper part probably from the Pope (since its inscriptions are in Latin). It was carried to safety in 1241 with king Béla IV (BAY-luh) when he fled the Mongol invasion, and was buried on the field at Mohács (MOW-hotch) in 1526 so it wouldn't fall into victorious Turkish hands, it was buried again at the village of Orsova (OAR-show-vuh) in 1849 to hide it from the advancing Russians who were crushing the 1848–49 Hungarian Revolution, and on a cold September night in 1944 during World War II, when Russians were again invading Hungary, the crown was once more being scurried away by its official guardians to protect it.

Its guardians escaped Budapest with the crown and made their way to Mattsee (Mott-ZAY), a small Austrian village near Salzburg, where they waited. In early May 1945, the American 7th Army took Mattsee, and some very surprised G.I.s found themselves being given a thousand year old royal crown by a small group of dignitaries who spoke a strange language. The Hungarian royal crown was shipped to the United States, where, with the onset of the Cold War, it was held secretly in a secure vault at Fort Knox in Kentucky. In 1978, as a conciliatory gesture in the détente era of the Cold War, U.S. President Jimmy Carter ordered the crown given back to (then-communist) Hungary, along with studies the U.S. had performed authenticating its history. Today it is on display in the Hungarian Parliament building.

The Magyars invited German priests into the country and made the northern city of Esztergom (EH-stair-gum) a center for missionizing. Géza himself likely died a pagan in 997 but he started the ball of Christian conversion rolling, and his son finished the job by getting Hungary upgraded on Christmas day in 1000 CE to full Christian kingdom status. To celebrate this, Hungarians made István a saint after he died and hacked off his right arm as a sacred relic, which is displayed today in a cathedral named after him (*Szent István Bazilika*; St. Stephen's Basilica) in Budapest.

By now you may be wondering why the Hungarians are sometimes called "Magyars" and sometimes "Hungarians." Well, it's like this: First of all, Hungarians call themselves *Magyars* (MUH-djyuhr), possibly derived from the Hungarian word *mondani*, "to speak"—as in, "those who can talk." (This was a common way for peoples to name themselves; the Slavs' name may derive from the Slavic term *slovo* (word) or *slava* (honor, glory), and their name for Germans—*Niemiec*—means "those who *can't* speak.")

It's less clear where "Hungarian" comes from. It may stem from 9th- and 10th-century Europe's confusion of the Magyars with the 5th century Huns (because from Europe's perspective, they both looked and acted alike). Or it may stem from Kubrat's 7th century Great Bulgaria empire, which was also known by a Turkic name, *Onogur* (OWN-oh-goor; "Land of the Ten Arrows," i.e., tribes). As the Steppe Magyars moved westward slowly, peoples they passed (like the Slavs) may have associated them with the defunct Onogur empire. The modern Slavic name(s) for Hungarians (e.g., in modern Polish – *Węgier* ["Ven-gyair"], Russian – *Венгер* ["vyengyer"]) *may* derive from Onogur, and the Slavs may have brought it westward to the Germans (*Ungarisch*), then the French (*Hongrois*), and so on. Maybe.

F. The Slovenes and Croatians

As we've seen, the Franks in the early-9th century had established control over most of the northern Dalmatian coastline on the Adriatic Sea. In 818, a Slavic duke, Ljudovit (LYOO-do-veet), led a revolt among the coastal Slavs against the Franks but was defeated. He fled, and his defeat sealed the fate of the Slavs on the northernmost shores of the Adriatic, the ancestors of the modern-day Slovenes, who were doomed to 1,100 years of being ruled by Germans; that is, by the Eastern Franks, the Holy Roman Empire, then the Habsburgs. Slovenia emerged only in 1918, to help create Yugoslavia. Despite Ljudovit's defeat, however, the Franks' hold on the coast further down in Dalmatia began to slip and a number of small Slavic coastal states formed. Several of these states, which had inherited Christianity from the Franks, united in 845 under Trpimir (Terp-EE-meer) to form the first Croatian state, which was recognized by the Franks as a duchy. Under Tomislav I (who was from the Trpimir family line), Croatia became a full kingdom in Christian Europe in 925 and expanded its borders to include the modern-day Istrian Peninsula in the north, the Drava river in the east (Slavonia), and the coastal city of Dubrovnik in the south.

USELESS TRIVIA: CAN A GUY GET AN *OŽUJSKO* HERE?

In the mid-10th century CE, Egypt was ruled by the great Abbasid dynasty, which ruled the Arab lands from Baghdad. However, a new power had arisen in the *Maghreb* (western) deserts of North Africa, a new Berber dynasty called the Fatimids, and they were on the march. In July 969 they sent forth a huge army led by their greatest general (and former slave), *Jawhar as-Siqilli*—"Jawhar the Sicilian," or as he was also known, Jawhar *al Rumi,* "Jawhar the Roman"—who defeated the Abbasid forces and occupied their Egyptian capital, Fostat. In preparation for the arrival of his boss, the Fatimid ruler Caliph El-Moez Li-Dinallah from what is today Tunisia, General Jawhar founded a new city to serve as the new Fatimid capital and he named it *al-Qahira*—Cairo—meaning "The Victorious."

   Not much is known about this legendary Fatimid general, Jawhar as-Siqilli. However, he was known by many names, among them *al-Saqlabi,* "the Slav," as well as *ibn Anton,* "Son of Anton"—a common Slavic name. Croatian legends claim Jawhar was born in Cavtat (TSAV-tot), a small Croatian village on the southern Dalmatian coast, and was captured by Arab raiders and taken to Arab-ruled Sicily as a slave. (In the 8th–11th centuries, Arab pirates and slave traders commonly raided the northern Mediterranean coastline, including the Adriatic Sea, taking loot and Christian captives to Arab-ruled Sicily, the Middle East, or North Africa.) Some sources claim Jawhar was Greek, others an Italian native of Sicily ("Roman"), but is it possible that Cairo was founded by a Croat?

After Tomislav's death in 928, however, the Croatian kingdom began to split apart and its neighbors began grabbing real estate. It staggered on until the death of King Zvonimir (ZVOH-nyee-meer) in 1089, after which civil war broke out over the succession. Hungary annexed what was left of Croatia in 1102, and for the next several centuries Croatia's fate was tied to Hungary. It retained many of its own institutions, including its parliament (the *Sabor;* SAH-boar) and its ruler, the *Ban* (BON)[5], and had wide autonomy, but for all intensive purposes Croatia shared the fate of the Hungarian kingdom.

G. Duklja, Raška, and the Serbs

Serbia's early medieval history, like the Germans', is a whole jumble of little states. The early Serbian tribes migrated into the Balkans in the mid-7th century and modern-day Serbs have legends of statehood dating from that time, but in reality the earliest Serbian state probably dates from the 9th century. The Byzantines encouraged Prince Vlastimir to create a Serbian state based in Trebinje (Tre-BEEN-yeh; in modern-day southern

Herzegovina) to counter growing Bulgarian power in the Balkans. Vlastimir's state didn't last long, but one of his relatives, Časlav (CHAH-slav), reasserted Serbian independence from Bulgaria briefly in the 10th century.

During Časlav's reign, Serbia was imbued with heavy Byzantine cultural influences, including Orthodox Christianity. After Časlav's state splintered apart, three principal Serbian states emerged: Duklja (DOOK-lee-yah), Zahumlje (Za-HOOM-lyeh), and Raška (RAHSH-kah). Initially Duklja was dominant, with its ruling dynasty often controlling the other two, but by the late-11th and early-12th centuries, Byzantine interference and civil wars had broken Duklja's power, allowing Raška to emerge as the primary Serbian state. Raška began to collect all the smaller Serbian states under one roof, especially after the Nemanja (written: Немања, Neh-MAN-yah) dynasty, led by Stefan Nemanja, came to power in 1166. Serbia was born. The Nemanja dynasty would later shepherd Serbia through its golden age in the late-14th century.

When the Byzantine emperor Manuel Comnenus died in 1180, the Serbian *Grand Župan* (*Велики Жупан*; Vel-EE-kee ZHOO-pahn, "Grand Duke") Stefan Nemanja chucked all caution aside and began expanding Serbia's borders to roughly the modern-day Macedonian-Serbian border in the south, and the Serbian-Bosnian border in the north, to the city of Niš (NYEESH) in the east. This is important to remember because *modern-day* Serbia's core political and cultural center is in its north, around the city of Belgrade.

In this period, however, Belgrade belonged to Hungary, and Serbia's political and cultural center was in what is now southern Serbia. In any event, one of Stefan Nemanja's sons, Sava (later St. Sava), managed to secure his father's preference for the Orthodox Church in Serbia (over Roman Catholicism), and the Nemanjić dynasty went on to rule Serbia in increasing greatness throughout the 13th century. Serbia flourished in this era and indeed, its greatest years were still ahead, as we'll see in the next chapter. In 1217, Serbia was recognized as a full kingdom.

H. The Poles

Like the Serbs, modern-day Poles have legends of a Poland much older than it really is, including the myths of princes Ziemowit (ZHEM-o-veet) and Ziemomysł (ZHEM-o-Mihsh-el; *ziemia* in Polish means "territory") ruling a mythical Poland in the 9th century. However, modern-day archaeology suggests no organized state existed until at the earliest the 940s. What is today southern Poland, from about Kraków westward, was ruled in the 10th century by Bohemia. North of this area, however, sandwiched between the Bohemians in the south and the Baltic tribes on the seacoast, were a collection of restless Slavic Lechitic[6] tribes known as the *Polanie*[7] (po-LAHN-yeh) who would build the first Polish state on the broad, flat central Polish plains in the early or mid-10th century.

In this period, it was common for Arab diplomats and merchants to publish stories of their travels abroad, and one such diplomat, *Ibrahim ibn Iaqub* (Ee-brah-heem Ee-ben YAH-koob), from Islamic Spain, traveled throughout Central Europe in the mid-10th century. It is not clear if he actually visited Poland or just wrote down tales he heard in neighboring Bohemia, but ibn Iaqub in 963 CE mentioned Poland and its ruler, a "Mesko" (actually, *Mieszko* in Polish; MYESH-ko).

Some historians believe either Mieszko himself or his father or grandfather created the first Polish state shortly before ibn Iaqub wrote about Poland. Regardless, in 966 Mieszko quickly sized up Poland's neighborhood and did two crucial things: He married the daughter of the (far more powerful, and Christian) Bohemian king, and applied directly to the Pope in Rome for conversion to Christianity, thereby making sure he gave his neighbor, Otto I (Remember him? The German Holy Roman Emperor who defeated the Magyars at Lechfeld in 955?), no excuse to interfere in Poland.

Mieszko was recognized as a Duke (meaning Poland was now a Duchy in Christian Europe) in 966, and his family dynasty, the Piasts (PEE-yahst), would continue to rule Poland until 1370. Well, sort of. You'll see. Anyway, Mieszko's son, Bolesław (BOW-leh-swahff), succeeded him and dramatically expanded Poland's borders to include modern-day Lusatia (Germany), Silesia, and Pomerania. His crowning achievement—pun intended—was being crowned king of Poland in 1025, getting Poland upgraded to full kingdom status in Christian Europe.

USELESS TRIVIA: MAYBE YOU SHOULD CONSIDER A DIFFERENT VOCATION.

Legend has it that King Henry II of England bellowed out one day while sitting in his court in 1170, "Will no one rid me of this turbulent priest?" He was referring to the Archbishop of Canterbury, who had incessantly argued with the king over lands and privileges. Four English knights overheard their king and took this outburst as an order, promptly marching over to Canterbury Cathedral and hacking the archbishop—Thomas Becket, or *Thomas à Becket*—to little ecumenical pieces. The martyred Thomas was soon made a saint, and Henry—who actually hadn't wanted the archbishop murdered—spent the rest of his life in St. Thomas's shadow.

Well, Poland has its own Thomas Becket—indeed, the patron saint of Poland, St. Stanisław (Stah-NYEE-swaff) of Szczepanów (Shcheh-PAN-oof). About nine decades before Thomas Becket, Stanisław was bishop of Kraków and also constantly quarreling with *his* king, Bolesław II (BO-leh-swaff). According to legend, at one point Stanisław even resurrected a deceased landowner to testify in front of the king about a land dispute.

Well, by 1079 Bolesław had had enough and he (unlike Henry II) actually *did* order his knights to murder the bishop, but they refused—you don't want to mess with a guy who can raise the dead. So, Bolesław himself murdered Stanisław as he was celebrating mass, cutting him to pieces. Horrified barons deposed Bolesław and he had to flee the country.

Bohemia also had its Christian martyrs, like Vojtěch (VOY-tyekh) of Prague, who chose the name "Adalbert" after being ordained a priest. It was Adalbert, as the bishop of Prague, whom Pope John XV sent to pagan Hungary in 977 to baptize Prince Géza and his son Vajk—later King *István* (Stephen). Afterwards, Adalbert went on a mission to the pagan Baltic peoples living along what is today Poland's Baltic shore. When he arrived, he decided to demonstrate Christian power by chopping down trees in one of the pagan Brusi's sacred groves, which so impressed the Baltic peoples that they took an axe to Adalbert. The Polish king ransomed his body back, though decades later some of his bones were taken back to Prague. St. Adalbert was revered in Poland, the Czech lands, and Prussia for centuries.

One of Hungary's first saints, St. Gellért (GHEL-ayrt), achieved his sainthood in an even more gruesome manner. Born in Italy but made a bishop in Hungary by King István (EESHT-von) in the early 11th century, what is known is that Gellért was caught by a rampaging mob in the midst of a pagan uprising in 1046. Details are sketchy, but some sources claim the pagans stoned him to death; others say they stuffed him into a barrel filled with spikes and threw him over a cliff; while still other accounts say they simply speared him. However he died, Saint Gellért has the hill he was martyred on in modern-day Budapest (with a nice statue) and even a hotel with a spa named after him for all his troubles.

This first Polish kingdom grew rapidly over the 11th century, conquering the cities of Wrocław (German: Breslau) and Kraków (Cracow) from the Bohemians, making the latter the Polish royal capital, and even trashing Kyiv. Indeed, early Piast Poland's last king, Bolesław III (Krzywousty), whose ruled spanned the years 1107–1138, was ironically one of its most powerful. Poor Bolesław just made a bad choice, but it was, unfortunately, an *important* one. Laying on his deathbed in 1138, he "pulled a Charlemagne" and divided his kingdom among his five sons, who then fought over the grand prize.

Thus was Poland ripped apart in 1138, not to be reconstituted again until 1300. For the next 160+ years, there was no king or central authority in Poland, and after a while the local Piast nobles all got used to not having anyone in Kraków give them orders or collect taxes from them. Several Piasts tried over the next 160 years to re-establish the kingship, but the regional nobility always thwarted them. Even without any national government, a couple of important groups entered Poland and Polish history in this time of political fragmentation:

- **Jews:** Many Roman Jews had found haven in Western Europe as the Franks established a stable state, but with a spreading and increasingly institutionalized church came the spread of anti-Semitism, forcing many Jews to flee eastward into the German lands and beyond. There they found opportunities (and protection) in the newly established states of Eastern Europe, especially Poland. See the special section on Jews after this chapter for more detail.

- **Crusader Germans:** The Baltic lands—filled with, well, Baltic-speaking peoples (who, more importantly, were not Christians)—became at the beginning of the 13th century the subject of intense interest for several German crusader armies, many of which by coincidence had just gotten booted out of Jerusalem and needed gainful employment. Two main groups stand out:

USELESS TRIVIA: HAMLETSKI!

In 1015, a young prince named Knut (sometimes written "Cnut" or "Canute" in English), brother to Harold, king of Denmark, sailed from his native land with a large army of both Danish and Norwegian Vikings (and others) to seek his fortune. With an estimated 10,000 men at his command—a large force by Viking standards—he landed in northern Anglo-Saxon England and proceeded over the next two years to conquer the whole country. By 1017, Knut was undisputed king of England. Two years later Knut's brother died and so he inherited the throne of Denmark as well, and later he sent forth yet another army to conquer Norway, so that by 1028 all three countries—Denmark, England, and Norway—were ruled together by King Knut.

Why are we talking about this in a book on Eastern Europe? Because Knut's father, Svend *Tveskæg* (Sven the Two-bearded), who had been king of Denmark from 986 to 1014, was married to Gunhilda, Knut's mother. "Gunhilda" was actually the Danish name she adopted after marrying Sven; her birth name was allegedly *Świętosława* (SHVYENT-o-swah-vah); she is identified in several chronicles as a "Slavic princess" from Pomerania, and in one as the daughter of Duke Mieszko I of Poland. This means that from 1017 to 1037, England's king was half Slavic, possibly a Pole, and possibly even the nephew of Poland's first king, Bolesław (Bo-LEH-swaff) I (996–1025). There are even hints that Knut had Polish soldiers with him during his invasion of England in 1015, a gift from his alleged uncle.

- **The Livonian Brotherhood:** Known in German as Schwertbrüderorden (Brothers of the Sword), this was founded in 1202 by German priests attemping to convert the Finnic tribes in modern-day Estonia and Baltic tribes further south in modern-day Latvia such as the ancient Curonians, Semigales, and Latgales.[8] These German missionaries came under increasing attack from obstinate and ornery local pagans so, working closely with the king of Denmark (who swiped northern Estonia as his compensation), the Livonian Brotherhood in turn imposed its rule over the Baltic lands with an iron fist. This, at least, was the plan until they were defeated in 1236 by a coalition of fed-up Baltic peoples at the Battle of Saule (SOW-leh),[9] in either modern-day Lithuania or Latvia. The remnants of the Livonian Brotherhood were then absorbed into the next group.

Figure 31. Eastern Europe in 1000 CE

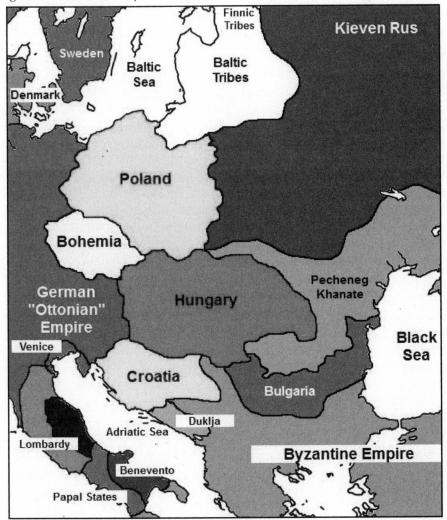

- **The Teutonic Knights:** After being ejected from Jerusalem in 1211, the Ordo domus Sanctæ Mariæ Theutonicorum Ierosolimitanorum, (Order of the Teutonic House of Mary in Jerusalem)—or, for short, the Deutscher Orden ("German" or "Teutonic Order")— sauntered back into Europe and got itself a job from the Hungarian king protecting Transylvania from Cumanian raids, only to get ejected by the Hungarians when the Knights tried to steal Transylvania for themselves in 1225. By sheer luck, another ruler had a pesky neighboring pagan raiding problem, too, one Duke Konrad who ruled the northern Polish region of Mazowsze (Mah-ZOFF-sheh; Mazovia). He hired the Teutonic Knights in 1225 to help deal with a neighboring Baltic tribe, the Brusi, and the Order quickly moved into the southern Baltic coastal region and set up shop. We'll be seeing much more of these guys in the next chapter.

I. The Pechenegs

The Pechenegs were a Turkic Steppe people who established in the late-9th century a short-lived but powerful empire on the Steppe. Their foremost enemies were Rus, Khazaria, Bulgaria, and the Byzantine Empire, though they are most famous for their wars against Rus. The Pecheneg khan Kurya's (COOR-yah) most famous exploit was the ambush of the Rus prince Svyatoslav I in 972 and making a drinking cup from Svyatoslav's skull, but the Pechenegs would pay dearly for that extravagance. Rus's power was growing, and over the first several decades of the 11th century Rus armies inflicted great defeats on the Pechenegs. In the late-11th century, the weakened Pechenegs were ejected from their lands by newcomers from the east, the Cumanians, and scattered to the four winds. Some Pechenegs were resettled in Hungary and Bulgaria as auxiliary military forces, and eventually assimilated.

J. The Cumanians

The Cumanians (also known as the *Polovtsy*, from Russian), were a Turkic tribe that established a large empire on the Steppe stretching from modern-day Kazakhstan to the Romanian-Bulgarian border in the 11th century. They made a living by raiding Kieven Rus, Hungary, Bulgaria, and the Byzantine Empire. As was usual for Steppe empires, theirs was less an ethnic group than a confederation of different Steppe peoples that had found it profitable to work together raiding and plundering others. In fact they had absorbed many Pechenegs when they conquered the Pecheneg lands.

The Cumanians (like the Magyars before them) also leased themselves out as mercenaries for the various European states, for instance taking part decisively in the 1185 Bulgarian uprising that established the independent Second Bulgarian Empire. At the height of Cumanian power, the royal dynasties of Kieven Rus, Hungary, and Bulgaria all mixed and intermarried with the Cumanian ruling elite. Although their empire lasted nearly two centuries, the Cumanians were sort of "shooting stars" in Eastern Europe, suddenly appearing and, after shining brightly for a while, disappearing. Before disappearing, though, they did do some things that would have an impact on the region, strangely enough all of it while their empire was in the midst of its own demise. Many Cumanian refugees eventually settled in Bulgaria and Hungary, where they served for centuries as light cavalry before eventually assimilating. Modern-day Hungary still has two counties and several towns named after the Cumanians, and the name "Cumanian"—*Kun* in Hungarian—is still a common family surname.

K. The Lithuanians

The Lithuanians are a Baltic people, and in the 12th century they found themselves wedged between increasingly aggressive neighbors: Crusader Germans and Danes to the north and west, Poles to the west, and Kieven Rus to the south and east. Though chronicles as early as 1009 mention the Lithuanians, the earliest origins of the Lithuanian state is the end of the 12th century, as Lithuanian tribes began to organize to defend themselves against incursions from German Crusaders and Kieven Rus. These tribal confederations cemented into a Lithuanian state in the 1230s under its exceptional leader, Mindaugas (MEEN-dow-gahss). He fended off a Crusader German invasion in 1236 at the Battle of Saule (SOW-leh), shattering the German Livonian Brotherhood in the process. Mindaugas began building a Lithuanian empire by taking territory from the Kieven Rus successor states, and in 1253 he was crowned King of Lithuania, and recognized by the Pope. Mindaugas had nominally converted to Christianity but the country later lapsed back into Lithuanian paganism, though some of his family, ruling over Eastern Slavs, converted to Orthodox Christianity. By the time of his death, in 1261, Mindaugas had transformed a backward Baltic tribal state into a major regional power.

L. The Finale: 1239–1242

In the early-9th century the Magyars had lived near the Volga under the Khazars, before fleeing westward into Europe. For centuries afterward rumors persisted that some Magyars had remained behind in the Volga region. These rumors prompted Hungary's King Béla (BAY-luh) IV to dispatch Julián (YOO-lee-ahn), a Dominican friar, to explore the eastern lands and seek out these survivors. In 1236, after a long journey through Cumania and the southern Rus lands, Julián found himself standing in the Volga Bulgar khanate among a Magyar-speaking people. Elated, Julián made his way back to his king in Hungary and reported his find. Equally elated, Béla dispatched Julián once more to persuade the surviving Magyars to move to the Kingdom of Hungary, to finally unite the whole Magyar nation in its new Carpathian home. Julián immediately left but when he reached the Rus city of Suzdal in 1237 he met a few straggling members of the lost Magyar tribes, and they implored Julián to turn back and flee for his life. In the intervening time since his last visit, a great power had arisen out of the east and invaded the Volga Bulgar lands, slaughtering and scattering nations. The Volga Magyars were no more, Julián was told, and he had best return and warn his sovereign of the coming storm. Julián had just seen a preview of what was about to befall Eastern Europe, its worst single military disaster until the 20th century. Julián did as advised, and reported back to his king that the Mongols were coming.

In 1219 Genghis Kha'an10, who had united several disparate Steppe tribes in Mongolia to create a powerful nomadic empire, turned his attention away from northern China, which he had just conquered, and sent a force to invade the Islamic Khwarizmian empire in Central Asia.[11] Soon the Mongols were on the Black Sea, and Genghis sent two trusted generals, Jebe (JEH-beh) and Subedei (SOO-beh-day), with a powerful army northward into the Caucasus, where they easily crushed several ancient kingdoms. On June 16, 1223, the Mongols defeated a combined Cumanian-Kieven Rus force at the River Kalka, but despite this stunning victory the Mongols withdrew. They came back a few years later, however, dispatched by Genghis Kha'an's successor Ögedei (OO-geh-dye), determined to spread the Mongol domains westward. In 1229 this army defeated the Cumanians again at the River Yaik, though the Cumanian Khan Köten (KOO-ten) was later able to fend off the Mongols near the Black Sea, temporarily halting their advance. Ögedei, however, sent one of Genghis Kha'an's grandsons, Batu (BAH-too), with a massive army to claim the western lands, and it was this army in 1237 that laid waste to the Volga Bulgar lands and scattered the "lost" Volga Magyars, among many other peoples. In 1238 the Cumanians were forced westward by the Mongols, and they cut a deal with the Hungarian king that allowed them to settle within his kingdom (1239). Béla hoped to use the famous Cumanian light cavalry in his defenses but events would conspire against this. Soon the Kieven Rus cities of Ryazan, Vladimir, Suzdal, and Yaroslavl were burning as the Mongols laid waste to Kieven Rus.

USELESS TRIVIA: MONGOL TERROR AS TOURISM!

The Easter week holiday in Poland is a very solemn time, but the first Thursday after the Roman Catholic Feast of *Corpus Christi* in Kraków brings back the Mongols. Sort of. During the *Festiwal Lajkonika* (Lajkonik Festival), a *Lajkonik* (ligh-KO-nyeek), an actor dressed satirically as a mounted Mongol (or Tartar) warrior parades through the streets of Kraków humorously prancing and jousting with gathered crowds. To be "attacked" (bonked on the head by his lance) by the Lajkonik is seen as good luck. The spectacle ends with the Lajkonik collecting faux ransom money from the mayor, and some speeches and poetry about Kraków's continued prosperity over the next year— and then lots of eating and drinking. As well, everyday in the *Rynek Główny* (the main square of Kraków) one can hear the famed bugler atop *Kościół Mariacki* (St. Mary's Church), who plays a sorrowful medieval *hejnał* song on his bugle, stopping dramatically in mid-note at one point in deference to a legend of a bugler who was cut down by a Mongol arrow to the throat as he tried to warn the city's population of the coming sack of the city in 1241. Local city firefighters provide the buglers for this tourist attraction on a rotating basis nowadays, and it is broadcast live on national radio each day.

In December, 1240, as the Mongol forces were reducing the Rus capital Kyiv to ashes, King Béla refused a Mongol demand that Hungary submit. Months later, in early February 1241, the Mongols launched a two-pronged invasion of Eastern Europe, with a northern force aimed at Poland and a southern force invading Hungary. In Poland, with no central authority to coordinate the country's defense, city after city fell: Lublin (LOO-bleen), Sandomierz (Sahn-DO-myesh), and by early March, Kraków itself. By the end of March the Mongols were besieging Wrocław, only to abandon it when they learned a Bohemian army was on its way to help the Bohemian king's brother-in-law, Prince Henryk (HINE-rick) II *Pobożny* (The Pious), of Silesia, who was holed up nearby at Legnica (Leg-NYEE-tsah; in German: "Liegnitz"—LEEG-nits). Henryk had collected an impressive array of allies to help defend Legnica: Teutonic Knights, French Knights Templar, and other European mercenaries.

The Mongols moved swiftly to confront Henryk before aid arrived and, through a common Steppe ruse of feigned retreat, managed to draw out and destroy Henryk's forces at Legnica in April 1241. The last major bastion of resistance in Poland had fallen. After their victory at Legnica—which ended with Henryk's severed head being paraded around on a pike—the Mongols turned southward into Bohemia where, after halfheartedly besieging Bohemian King Václav I at Olomouc (Ol-OH-mo-oots; German = *Olmütz*) fortress, they continued southward to rejoin the main Mongol forces in Hungary.

At about the same time that Mongol forces were crushing the European force at Legnica in Polish Silesia, another Mongol army was busily destroying a Hungarian army at Mohi (MO-hee) on the Sajó (SHUH-yo) River in modern-day northeastern Hungary. The Hungarian king, Béla IV, had tried to muster enough forces to confront the Mongols but internal strife and the murder of the Cumanian Khan, Köten, by suspicious Hungarian nobles—which prompted Béla's Cumanian allies to abandon Hungary to its fate—led to disaster at Mohi. Béla himself managed to escape, fleeing westward across Hungary with the Mongols in hot pursuit. The Mongols then launched smaller invasions of the Balkans, devastating the Bulgarian and Serbian lands and ravaging the Adriatic Dalmatian coast. One Mongol army even turned toward Austria, halting for unknown reasons at Wiener Neustadt, just east of Vienna. About half of Hungary's population was killed during the invasion, including an estimated 80% of the peasants living on the Great Plain.

Then, out of the blue, they simply left, in March 1242. A messenger had arrived from Mongolia in December 1241, informing Batu that the great Kha'an Ögedei had died, and that Batu should report immediately back to Karakorum (the Mongol capital) for the traditional *quriltai* (Mongol leadership council) to choose the next Mongol Kha'an. Europe did not know this and was stunned as Mongol forces withdrew. After the tragic Battle of Legnica, the Grand Master of the Teutonic Order wrote a letter to King Louis IX of France telling him that Legnica was lost, and that nothing stood in the way of the Mongols and Paris. Historians today argue whether this was true or not, but some insist that the Polish-German army that faced the Mongols in Silesia that day in April 1241 was as formidable as any in Europe at the time. We'll never know if the Mongols could have successfully continued westward into Western Europe, or if they intended to. Was the invasion simply a test of Europe's defenses, a practice run for a future full-scale event that was never to take place? Were the Polish and Hungarian campaigns a Mongol probe of the Carpathian Basin and Northern European Plain as invasion routes? Or was it simply revenge against Hungary for harboring the Cumanians, who had humiliated the Mongols? Did the Mongol discovery of the Carpathian, Alpine, and Balkan mountains discourage further advances, given their need for wide grasslands for their horses? We'll never know.

USELESS TRIVIA: MEDIEVAL MULTICULTURALISM!

Pomerania—which in old Slavic means "land by the sea"—resides on the southern Baltic seashore and is in many ways a typical Eastern European region with roots in the histories of many peoples and nations. By Roman times Pomerania was filled with Baltic peoples, but soon came the Germanic peoples, and on their heels the early Slavic peoples. By the year 1000 CE, Pomerania was wall-to-wall with Slavs. For a couple of centuries, a pseudo-independent Slavic duchy existed in Pomerania that clung stubbornly to paganism despite raids by Vikings and attempts by the neighboring Polish kingdom and the Holy Roman Empire to impose Christianity. By the mid-11th century the Poles did conquer much of Pomerania, but Poland imploded in 1138. Decades later western Pomerania succumbed to Danish conquest. (The *Gesta Danorum* chronicle of 1201 describes in detail the Slavic pagan temples ordered destroyed by Danish King Valdemar I in 1168.[12]) Denmark took over all of Pomerania, but by the late 13th century it lost the eastern half to the rising German (Holy Roman imperial) land of Brandenburg. Both Brandenburg and the Danes brought German immigrants into Pomerania.

When the Thirty Years War ended in 1648, Sweden gained western Pomerania from Denmark. The future Russian Tsarina Catherine the Great was born a German princess in 1729 in the Pomeranian city of Stettin,[13] then part of Brandenburg-Prussia. During the Napoleonic Wars, Prussia managed to grab western Pomerania from Sweden, completing the German takeover of all of Pomerania. In the late 19th century, Otto von Bismark's Prussia (and later Germany) tried to purge Pomerania of its multiethnic past by attempting to forcibly "Germanize" Pomerania's Poles, Slavs, Swedes, Danes, and others.

At the end of World War I, in 1918, Pomerania remained in Germany but, now bordering a reborn Poland, was a major source of tensions for the two countries. After World War II, with German defeat, came the horrific expulsion of all Germans from eastern Pomerania so that today Pomerania is again (artificially) divided, between German western *Pommern* (Pomerania) and Polish eastern *Pomorze*. However, peoples such as the Kaszubs serve to remind us of Pomerania's eclectic heritage. And yes, if you're wondering, those little beige, foofy dogs with the same name—Pomeranians—originated in Pomerania as well.

Figure 32. Western and Eastern Pomerania in 2012

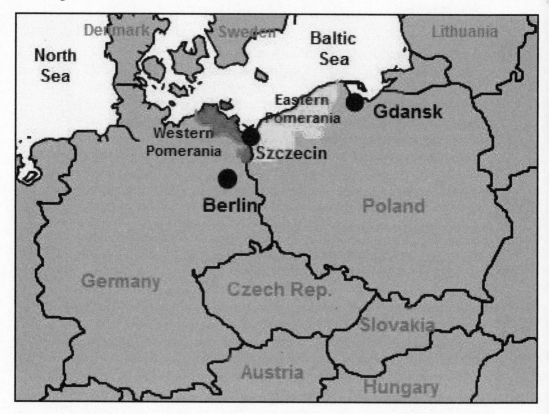

Priest: It follows God created the universe, therefore He exists.
Boy: And yet Spinoza didn't believe in the Holy Trinity.
Priest: Spinoza was a Jew.
Boy: What's a Jew?
Priest: You never saw a Jew? Here. I have some sketches. These are Jews.
Boy: No kidding. They all have these horns?
Priest: No, this is the Russian Jew. The German Jew has these stripes.

—scene from Woody Allen's film *Love and Death*, 1975, set in 1812 Russia

Any attempt to understand European history, much less Eastern European history, requires delving into Jewish culture and history. Conversely, so too does any attempt to understand Jewish or even Israeli history require some background in Eastern Europe. Here is a brief introduction to what I call "Jewish Eastern Europe."

After a series of (unsuccessful) rebellions against Roman rule in the late-1st and early-2nd century CE, Jews were largely ejected from their homelands in Judea and Israel, in what is called the *Diaspora*. Jews quickly filled the Roman Empire's cities, but when it fell into ruin and collapse, they flocked (like everyone else) to the remaining civilizational bastions. Those Jews who made their way to Umayyad Arab Spain, which in the 8th–11th centuries was a prosperous and powerful Arab state known as the Cordoba Caliphate, became known as *Sephardim* (*Sepharad* = "Spain" in Hebrew). They eventually came to speak a Hebrew-Latin-Arab hybrid language known as *Ladino*. Those Jews who opted for the Frankish or German states became known as *Ashkenazim* (Hebrew for "German"), and over time they developed a language that was a hybrid of Hebrew, medieval German, and Slavic called *Yiddish*. The growth of Western (Frankish) institutions meant the spread of the Christian church in Western Europe, and as it became more institutionalized it took to demonizing and demonstrating against Jewish communities; anti-Semitism marched hand-in-hand with the growth of Western society. Soon, by the 12th and 13th centuries, Jewish communities were being attacked and expelled from Western Europe in droves. Most fled eastward in the 13th and 14th centuries, until, to quote historian Max I. Dimont, "By 1500, the Jewish center of gravity [in Europe] had completely shifted to Eastern Europe."[1]

Within Eastern Europe, medieval Poland became the star attraction for Jews, and in 1335 the Polish king Kazimierz III *Wielki* (the Great) granted Jews specific legal rights. (A town named after the king became the center for Jewish life in Poland, and today as the Kazimierz district of Kraków, it is still a cultural center for Polish Jews.) Jews prospered in Poland but as Poland entered a period of decline in the 18th century, Jewish communities found themselves increasingly exposed to violent historical forces. In 1795, when the Polish-Lithuanian Commonwealth was destroyed, Russia inherited Poland's Jews, and Catherine II "the Great" immediately set up a restrictive zone in the former eastern Polish lands called the Pale of Settlement (*Черта оседлости*; CHAIR-tah o-SYED-lost-tyee), for Jews. Jews in Russia saw their poverty and political marginalization reach new lows.

In the mid-19th century, Russia introduced a new word to the Jewish vocabulary, погром (pogrom), an orchestrated but very violent riot led by local authorities terrorizing and murdering Jews, while seizing or destroying their property. It is not clear when pogroms began, but after the assassination of Tsar Alexander II in 1881 by anarchists, waves of pogroms swept across Russia, victimizing many thousands of Jews.

As medieval Christian fanaticism gave way to modern nationalism, Jewish communities across industrializing Europe found themselves under attack as never before, but nowhere more so than Russia, from which a mass Jewish exodus began in the 1880s. The Americas were a favored destination, but they were far away and very expensive to get to. Russian Jews flocked to the much less dangerous Habsburg empire and beyond, and large Yiddish-speaking colonies suddenly sprang up in many 19th-century Central and Western European cities. Many Jews tried assimilating into their host societies, but nationalists from Paris to St. Petersburg reacted with political parties espousing blatantly anti-Semitic platforms. World War I and the postwar economic woes and political disappointments only made matters worse. Per historian Tony Judt, himself a descendant of just such Jewish refugees:

> Since Ukrainians, Slovaks, Belarussians and others faced their own challenges in defining and securing a national space distinct from that of their neighbors, the presence of Jews could only complicate and antagonize, offering a target for expressions of national insecurity. Even in the Habsburg monarchy, what Jews had really been part of was an urban civilization contained within a rural empire; once the latter was broken up after World War I and redefined by national spaces in which towns and cities were isolated islands in a sea of agrarian life, Jews lost their place.[2]

The Cold War froze most historical discussion on the Holocaust in Eastern Europe, so that today many countries in the region are grappling with the Holocaust and their role in it. While the vast majority of Eastern Europe's Jews died in the Nazi death camps, some *did* survive. During the Stalinist years (1944–53) in Eastern Europe, as elsewhere, some Jews found hostility when they returned to their homes, so most either emigrated (to the Americas or British Palestine/Israel), or assimilated into their adopted homelands even further, abandoning their Jewish identities altogether. In postcommunist Eastern Europe, some Eastern Europeans, particularly in Poland, have been startled to learn through uncovered documents, modern-day DNA tests, or frank disclosures from relatives that their parents or grandparents had once been practicing Jews.[3] This has led to a resurgence in interest in

Jewish culture in parts of Eastern Europe, particularly former large centers of Jewish populations such as Kraków or Budapest. Ironically, given communist ideology, Soviet rule in Eastern Europe had included a form of anti-Semitism masked under the euphemisms "anti-Zionism" and "anticosmopolitanism."

Israel and Eastern Europe—Long-Lost Siblings?

It should, then, not be surprising that Israel and Eastern Europe have much in common, indeed to the extent that Israel can in many ways be considered an honorary Eastern European country. During the Israeli War for Independence in 1948, there were so many Polish Jews in the *Haganah* (הגנה), the early Israeli army, that army orders had to be issued in both Polish and Hebrew; many assimilated Polish Jews couldn't understand Hebrew. Of all the Israeli prime ministers, Yitzhak Rabin (1974–77) was the first *not* born in either Poland or Ukraine, and the three prime ministers who followed Rabin—Menachem Begin, Yitzhak Shamir, and Shimon Peres—all had Polish childhoods. Some, like Begin and Shamir, applied skills they had learned in the early 1940s Jewish anti-Nazi underground resistance in occupied Poland to the Israeli War for Independence. Just as the influence of Polish Jews in Israel began to wane in the 1980s, the Soviet Union allowed a million Soviet Jews to emigrate to Israel—guaranteeing an Eastern European influence with the likes of Natan Sharansky in Israel for decades more to come.

The Boskovice (bos-KO-veets-eh) Synagogue, built in 1698 and recently restored, located in Moravia (eastern Czech Republic). The town of Boskovice once contained Moravia's largest Jewish community. (Image © SeanPavonePhoto / Shutterstock)

3. THE MEDIEVAL YEARS
1242-1600 CE
THINGS GET INTERESTING

CHAPTER SUMMARY

This period sees the rise of Central Europe from the ashes of the Mongol invasion, with strong state development and growing economic and political integration with Western Europe, all the while shielded from the worst effects of the Golden Horde's Tartar raids by the growth of a massive Lithuanian empire. In this era some of the Central European states will become for a time significant players on the European stage, and will rise in some respects, if only fleetingly or superficially, to levels of development on a par with their Western counterparts. Meanwhile, the Balkans will head in the opposite direction, gradually succumbing to the expanding Turkish Ottoman Empire and in the process, decoupling from the rest of Europe and Christendom to be politically and economically integrated into the Islamic world. The front line between the Christian and Muslim worlds jutted into the heart of Europe, and Eastern Europe once again found itself an unwilling battlefield.

CHAPTER GUIDE

A. The Mongol Empire, the Golden Horde, and Tartars 123
B. Bulgaria 126
C. Serbia 126
D. Montenegro 128
E. Bosnia & Herzegovina 129
F. Croatia 130
G. The Republic of Ragusa/Dubrovnik 130
H. Albania 131
I. The Byzantine Empire 133
J. The Ottoman (Turkish) Empire 135
K. Wallachia, Moldavia, and Transylvania 137
L. Hungary 140
M. Bohemia 143
N. The Teutonic Knights and Schizoid Prussia 145
O. Lithuania and the Eastern Slavs 148
P. Livonia and the Balts 149
Q. Poland as Catlyst 151
R. Novgorod, Muscovy, and the Russians 154
S. Halych-Volhynia: A Kingdom in Galicia 157

Figure 33. Eastern Europe Timeline, 1242–1600

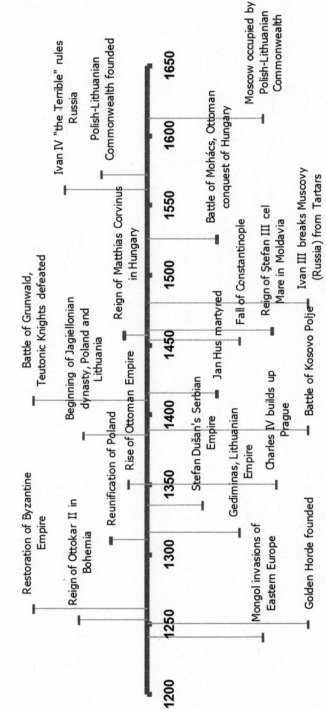

Figure 34. Comparative Western Europe Timeline, 1242–1600

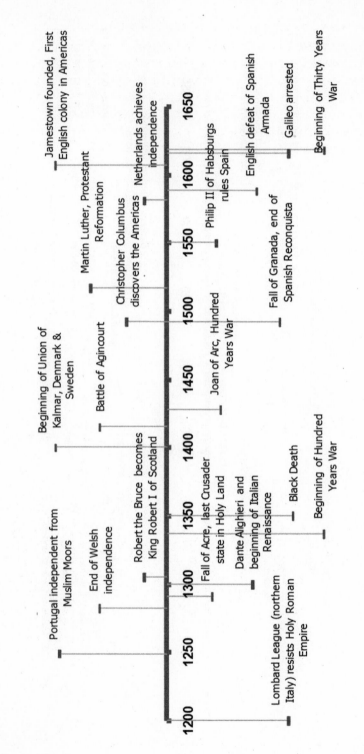

A. *The Mongol Empire, the Golden Horde, and the Tartars*

From the moment Genghis Kha'an realized he wasn't feeling well in 1227, his empire began to show some cracks, but it managed to survive Genghis by almost seven decades. And even then, some of its parts managed to survive into the 18th century. For some decades after Genghis it still continued to grow, forming the world's largest land empire ever, and—until the British surpassed it in the 19th century—the largest empire the world had ever seen. (See Figure 35 for a dramatic illustration.)

After withdrawing from Eastern Europe in 1242, Batu learned on his way back to Karakorum that his cousin and rival Güyük (GOO-yook) had already been made Great Kha'an, so Batu decided it would be better for his health *not* to return home. He established a new Mongol state—still answering to Karakorum—on the lower Volga River in lands inhabited then by a Turkic people, the Kipchaks. Batu's state was therefore named the Kipchak Khanate, though it is better known to history as the *Golden Horde*.[1] At first, the Horde closely controlled the affairs of the former Kieven Rus lands, and Rus princes were forced to travel to Batu's capital at Sarai on a regular basis to pay tribute and have their policies approved. Though never again on a scale akin to 1239–42, the Horde's armies continued to strike terror throughout Eastern Europe, launching devastating raids in the 13th and 14th centuries.

Figure 35. The furthest extent of the Mongolian Empire, c. 1250 (including the Golden Horde):

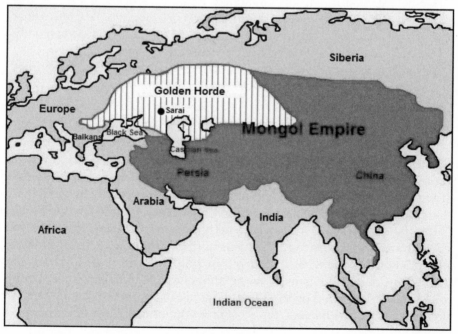

In 1294, the last great kha'an, Kublai Kha'an (whom Marco Polo had most likely visited in his travels), died and the Mongol Empire finally came apart, giving way to many smaller successor states. The Golden Horde continued to prosper, however, living on tribute collected from its Kieven Rus vassals and plunder taken from neighboring states. It reached its period of greatest power in the first half of the 14th century under Uzbeg (or Uzbek) Khan, who converted the Horde to Islam. Most of the Horde's leaders were descendants of Batu, a Mongol, but the Golden Horde ruled over a sea of Turkic peoples. The Chinese referred to the Turkic peoples west of China as "nomads"—*ta-ta* in Chinese—so over time this name stuck to the Turkic peoples of the Horde: *Tartars*.

USELESS TRIVIA: A PROBLEM WITH FREE MARKETS . . .

The town of Theodosius (modern-day Feodosiya/*Феодосія*, Ukraine) rose in ancient times as an important Greek trading center on the Black Sea, on the eastern shores of Crimea, but it was conquered by the Mongols in the 13th century. The emerging Italian city-state of Genoa bought it from the Golden Horde in 1266, and soon Theodosius—renamed Caffa by its new Genovese owners—was again a major trading port on the Black Sea. However, times change and in 1343 the Golden Horde was besieging the city, unsuccessfully. The Horde's army had fallen victim to the Bubonic Plague and was disintegrating, but the Horde's leader, Janibeg, turned this to his advantage when he had the corpses of his plague-ridden soldiers flung over the walls of Caffa into the city, in what is recorded as one of the first acts of biological warfare. Genoa eventually sent a force that saved Caffa and the war with the Horde ended in 1347, but in the meantime ships carrying goods and people (and rats) from Caffa had traveled to Adriatic ports and Italy itself, introducing the Black Plague to Europe. For four years the plague spread across Europe, killing an estimated 45-50% of Europe's population before subsiding in 1351.

The Golden Horde fell into civil war and disarray in the late-14th century, from which it never quite recovered. It enjoyed a brief revival under Khan Toqtamish (TAWKH-tom-eesh), but his efforts were undone by another Turkic empire from the east (modern-day Uzbekistan), founded by the brilliant strategist Timur (Tamerlane), who was trying to recreate the Mongol Empire. (Timur's empire lasted from the 1360s until his death in 1405, and stretched from Central Asia to what are today Iran, Iraq, Syria, eastern Turkey, and the southern Caucasus. His reign was extremely violent, killing millions.) The Golden Horde limped on for a few more decades before dissolving in 1438 into a few smaller khanates, the most powerful of which was the Khanate of

Crimea. The Crimean Khanate continued the tradition of Tartar raids into Eastern Europe for centuries more—fighting as allies or mercenaries for/against Poland-Lithuania, Muscovy/Russia, or the Ottoman Empire—until Russian armies penetrated to the Black Sea in the late-18th century, finally conquering and destroying the Khanate of Crimea in 1783.

Figure 36. Eastern Europe c. 1242

B. Bulgaria

The Mongol invasion had not left Bulgaria unscathed, and despite the weakness of its traditional enemy, the Byzantine Empire, in the 13th century Bulgaria continued to suffer from raids across its long border with the Mongol lands. About the time relief finally arrived in the mid-14th century in the form of a Polish-Hungarian offensive that pushed the Tartars away from Bulgaria's borders, Bulgaria developed another geopolitical headache in the form of a newly rising Serbia.

Stefan Dušan's growing Serbian empire initially began grabbing Bulgarian territory, but soon found common cause with the Bulgarians as anti-Byzantine allies. This wasn't quite the boon for Bulgaria that it might seem, however, as Dušan's growing power provoked the Byzantines into doing something so many weakened rulers across the Middle East had also done in recent decades: they hired the Turks.

In 1354, the first Ottoman mercenary troops entered the Balkans in Byzantine service, and they never quite left. They shoved the Byzantines aside and overran Bulgaria (conquering Plovdiv in 1362 and Sofia in 1382), before dealing the Serbian empire a fatal blow in 1389 at Kosovo Polje. In 1396, the last Bulgarian holdout, Vidin, fell, and Bulgaria began five long centuries of Ottoman Turkish rule.

C. Serbia

After centuries of living in the shadow of either Bulgaria or the Byzantine Empire, Serbia began its ascent as a major force in the Balkans under kings Stefan Dragutin and his son, Milutin, in the late-13th and early-14th centuries. In 1331, Prince Stefan Dušan (Душан; DOO-shahn) rebelled against his father, king Stefan III Uroš (OO-roesh), and his subsequent reign is seen today as medieval Serbia's golden age. Dušan wanted to revive the Byzantine Empire under Serbian leadership, and to that end he conquered what is today Albania, most of Greece, and the southern Dalmatian coast. He also raised the Serbian Orthodox Church to a status equal to the (Greek) Church in Constantinople, established a new legal code, and built schools, churches, and monasteries all over his realm, including the castle complex on Gornje (Mount) Nerodimlje (GORN-yeh NAY-ro-deem-lyeh) in Kosovo from where Stefan Dušan and, later, his son Stefan V Uroš, ruled Serbia in the summertime. Serbia's capital had been Skopje (SKO-pyeh; Macedonia's capital today), but under Dušan, Kosovo became the empire's political and cultural center.

In 1345 Dušan was able to declare himself "Tsar of the Serbs and the Greeks." He died in 1355 as he was preparing to conquer Constantinople. He was buried in southern Kosovo near modern-day Prizren, though his remains now lay in Belgrade's St. Mark's Church (Црква Светог Марка).

The year before Dušan's death, the Byzantines brought Ottoman troops into the Balkans as mercenaries to counter the Serbs and Bulgarians, but the Turks instead turned to conquest. Dušan's successors, beginning with his son, were weak and the kingdom began to disintegrate. Ottoman forces invaded Serbia, leading to the Battle of Kosovo Polje (Kosovo Field) on June 28, 1389 in Kosovo.

While Serbian forces succeeded in mauling the Ottoman army, the Serbs themselves suffered disastrous losses—including the country's ruler, Prince Lazar. (A Serbian nobleman did manage to assassinate Ottoman Sultan Murad I after the battle in revenge.)

Nevertheless, the Ottoman Turks simply brought up reinforcements and in short order southern Serbia (the core of Stefan Dušan's empire) was under direct Ottoman rule, though a rump Serbian state survived for a while in the north, paying an annual tribute to the Turks. After suffering defeat at Belgrade in 1456 by the Hungarians, the Ottoman Turks occupied the rest of Serbia in 1459. From then until the 19th century, Serbia reluctantly served as a battleground for Bosnian, Venetian, Hungarian, Habsburg, and Turkish armies.

USELESS TRIVIA: A ROSE BY ANY OTHER NAME . . .

Like the past of many Eastern European cities, Belgrade's reaches deep into the mists of the Bronze Age, and the feet of many peoples and nations have walked its streets. It all began some 7,000 years ago in modern-day Belgrade's northern suburb, *Vinča*, (VEEN-cha) where an advanced Bronze Age civilization laid the city's initial foundations. After periods of Greek and Illyrian occupation, the Celts built a city on the site they called *Singidūn* in the 3rd century BCE, only to have the Romans conquer it three centuries later, calling it *Singidunum*. As Roman rule collapsed in the Balkans in the late-5th century CE, the Byzantines and invading Steppe peoples competed for control over the city, eventually ceding it in the late-6th century CE to the Avars and Slavs, who called it *Belgrad*. In the 13th century Hungary took it over (calling it *Nándor-fehérvár*), dramatically fending off an Ottoman Turkish invasion at the city's walls in 1456. The Turks did finally overcome the city's defenses in 1521, however, and the Ottoman Empire ruled Belgrade until the 19th century. Though medieval Serbia had looked southward to Skopje or Kosovo for its capital, throughout the Ottoman centuries Belgrade became a quintessentially Serbian city and, after 1804, it became the nucleus for a reviving Serbian nation—as it still is today.

D. Montenegro

With the weakening of Serbia after Stefan Dušan's death in 1355, the old Serbian coastal state of Duklja—which by the 12th century had become known by the name of one of its regions, *Zeta* (ZEH-tah)—broke away in 1360. Initially Zeta grew to rule northern Albania and parts of Kosovo, but the Zetans were constantly under threat from the Ottoman Turks, Venetians, and Hungarians. In 1421, the Crnojević dynasty (Tser-no-YEH-veetch; *Crna* = "black") came to power, and allied Zeta with Venice against the Turks. That alliance came to a disastrous end with the Ottoman conquest of Zeta in the late-15th century. It was during that war that the Zetan capital was moved up into the less-accessible mountains, to its present-day capital of Cetinje (Tseh-TEEN-yeh). It was also during the Crnojević period that Zeta became known as *Crna Gora* (TSER-nah GOR-ah; "Black Mountain"), which the Venetians translated into Italian as *Montenegro*.

Initially the Turks ruled the country directly but its mountainous topography and rebellious Slavic inhabitants soon convinced the Turks to instead just collect tribute from them. When the Crnojević dynasty fled the Turks into Venetian exile, they left the Montenegrin Orthodox Archbishop, Vavil (VAH-veel), in power and he transformed Montenegro into a strange theocratic state ruled by the vladika (*владика*; VLAH-dee-kah), the archbishop-ruler. For the next three centuries, Montenegro continued to be ruled by its vladika, never completely able to escape Turkish rule—Cetinje suffered brutal Ottoman occupations in 1623, 1687, and 1712—but also rarely subjected to direct Ottoman rule like many of its Balkan neighbors.

USELESS TRIVIA: WHO ARE THOSE PEOPLE WITH THE NICE RUGS?

Westerners are often surprised to learn that before the 20th century, many Eastern European cities had large Armenian quarters. How did this happen, when Armenia is on the other side of the Black Sea, buried deep in the southern Caucasus Mountains? Armenia has a longer history than most of its European and Asian neighbors, adopting Christianity in 301 CE. However, the last Armenian kingdom, the Cilician Kingdom, was conquered by the Ottoman Turks in 1524, provoking an exodus of Armenians into Eastern Europe and the Ottoman cities of the Balkans. In this way Central Europe and the Balkans quickly acquired large Armenian communities, and Armenian merchants joined Jewish and Greek colleagues in commercial activities spanning Ottoman and Christian Eastern Europe. Most Armenians eventually assimilated, melting into the majority populations and leaving behind a cultural legacy such as surnames that end in "-ian" (e.g., Katchaturian, Sarkissian, and Egoyan).

E. Bosnia & Herzegovina

The Yugoslav implosion wars of the 1990s convinced many that Bosnia & Herzegovina were just extensions of Croatian or Serbian history, but they should be seen like Austria, which has its own history and traditions despite its cultural links with Germany. Bosnia & Herzegovina indeed has much to do with the early origins of both Serbia and Croatia, but to quote historian Noel Malcolm:

> All that one can sensibly say about the ethnic identity of the [medieval] Bosnians is this: they were the Slavs who lived in Bosnia."[2]

USELESS TRIVIA: NOT A BASIS FOR ETHNIC PURITY!

It is important to remember that in the medieval era, Europeans looked at ethnicity very differently from how we do today. As the historian Charles King describes it (in reference to the Caucasus):

> Categories such as 'Georgian' and 'Armenian', among others, have existed for centuries and perhaps even for millennia. However, that is not the same as claiming that these categories have always meant identical things to the people who used them, nor is it to say that the social groups to whom these labels applied have existed in an unbroken line from the foggy past into the present. In the days before border guards, passports, and censuses, the boundaries between states and the bonds among the people who inhabit them were far more fluid than they are today.[3]

Medieval European states were like corporations, owned and operated for the benefit of their aristocrats. When wars, famines, or plagues killed off their peasants or townspeople—in other words, their workforce and tax base—they often just imported replacements from somewhere else. Medieval Eastern European history is filled with countless examples of rulers importing farmers, merchants, craftsmen, or soldiers from elsewhere in Europe to resettle depopulated regions. Many of these immigrants brought new industries, skills, or crops to Eastern Europe. Germans, Frenchmen, Italians, Flemish, Scots, and others flocked to medieval Eastern Europe for centuries as immigrants seeking tax breaks or land grants, eventually melting into the larger population while leaving behind some odd customs and surnames.

Bosnia emerged as a Banate[4] in 1180 when Ban Kulin (KOO-leen) created an independent state, but almost immediately Bosnia came under great pressure from neighboring Hungary. The Mongol invasion of 1241–42 spared Bosnia a complete takeover by Hungary, but the country was effectively partitioned for the next century by Hungary, Serbia, and the Byzantine Empire.

In the early-14th century, however, Bosnia re-emerged under the control of the Roman Catholic Kotromanić (Ko-tro-MAH-neetch) family, and very quickly managed to expand to most of the Dalmatian coastline, including neighboring Orthodox Christian *Hum* (Herzegovina).[5] The Kotromanić dynasty ushered in independent Bosnia's "golden age" under Stjepan II and Tvrtko (TVURT-ko) Kotromanić, during which Bosnia's silver, copper, and gold mines turned Bosnia's cities into important trade centers.

By the early-15th century, Bosnian and Serbian mines produced one-fifth of Europe's silver. Bosnia became a full kingdom in 1377, but its fortunes began to wane after Tvrtko's death in 1391. The Ottomans invaded in 1463, finally conquering the entire country by 1482.

F. Croatia

Croatia's fortunes in the 14th, 15th, and early 16th centuries were firmly tied to Hungary. Although with a considerable amount of autonomy and self-government, the Croatian *Bán* (BON) was appointed (or confirmed) by the Hungarian king, as were many policies of the Croatian state. After the Battle of Mohács (MO-hotch) in 1526,[6] Croatia was decoupled from Hungary by its new Habsburg rulers and ruled directly from Vienna. The Habsburgs would control Croatian affairs until 1918.

G. The Republic of Ragusa/Dubrovnik

It is difficult in our modern age of strong nation states to imagine an era when countries were weak, and regions or even cities could be strong enough to rival countries. One such case was the Croatian city of Dubrovnik. As the Croatian kingdom began to splinter apart in the 11th century, Dubrovnik was broken off and absorbed into the Byzantine Empire. At this time, though its Slavic population called it *Dubrovnik*, it was known in the West by its Latin name *Ragusium*, or Ragusa.[7] In 1205 the rising naval power Venice seized Dubrovnik, and it served as an important Venetian naval base and port for a century and a half. During this time—in which Dubrovnik became a major port of entry for the 1348 Black Death into Europe—Dubrovnik's sailors learned the Venetian trade networks and ports of call.

This became a problem for Venice when Hungary took over Dubrovnik in 1358, and Dubrovnik suddenly became a threat to Venice's domination of the very profitable trade in the Adriatic and eastern Mediterranean. Dubrovnik's ships plied the seas under Hungarian protection in the 14th and early-15th centuries, making serious inroads into Venetian business. Dubrovnik's submission to Ottoman rule in 1458 only multiplied the city's fortunes, moreover, as the Turks also left the city relatively alone. The Turks not only afforded Dubrovnik's ships protection from the vengeful Venetian navy but also granted Dubrovnik's merchants exclusive access to exotic Ottoman ports (with trade networks stretching to India and beyond) closed to Venice. 15th-century Dubrovnik blossomed into a very wealthy city.

But it got even *better*. Dubrovnik's seafaring prowess became legendary, and Dubrovnik's sailors were sought all across Europe for their expertise. Their knowledge attracted the attention of one rising power in the early-16th century in particular, Spain, as the Spanish struggled to overcome Portugal's head-start in the New World and the vital trade routes to the Far East. Throughout the 16th century, Dubrovnik ship builders helped Spain perfect ocean-going vessals, and Dubrovnik sailors frequently accompanied Spanish voyages to the New World. It is even likely that there were Dubrovnik sailors on some of the ships of the 1588 Spanish Armada, which tried to subjugate Elisabeth I's England.

Unfortunately, the development of Atlantic trade with the New World and alternate routes to the Far East undermined the Adriatic trade networks Dubrovnik depended on, and both Dubrovnik and Venice declined rapidly in the 17th century. Both struggled through the 18th century before succumbing to Napoleon's ambitions, Venice in 1797 and Dubrovnik in 1808. At the Congress of Vienna in 1815, both were annexed by Austria, although in 1866 Venice joined the newly unified Italy. Dubrovnik rejoined Croatia after World War I, and has shared Croatia's fortunes ever since.

H. Albania

Secluded, mountainous Albania is seemingly about as isolated as the Balkans gets, and yet throughout its history it has often somehow managed to be in everyone's way. Illyrians, Greeks, Romans, Byzantines, Bulgarians, Serbs, Normans, Venetians, Croats, Spaniards, Turks, Italians, Germans, and so many others have at some time or other discovered that their goals required controlling Albania. The name "Albania" isn't even Albanian; it's assumed to derive from the Illyrian *Albanoi* tribe. Albanians call their country *Shqipëria* (Shkip-UR-ree-ah)—"Land of the Eagles," referring to its mountainous origins. Albania's major coastal cities—e.g., Berat (BAYR-ott), Durrës (DEWR-us), Vlorë (VLOR-uh), and Sarandë (SAR-an-duh)—were founded by the great Adriatic maritime empires, and these coastal cities did not become ethnically Albanian until the collapse of the Adriatic trade networks in the 17th century, as most Albanians kept to the mountains.

Figure 37. Eastern Europe in 1350

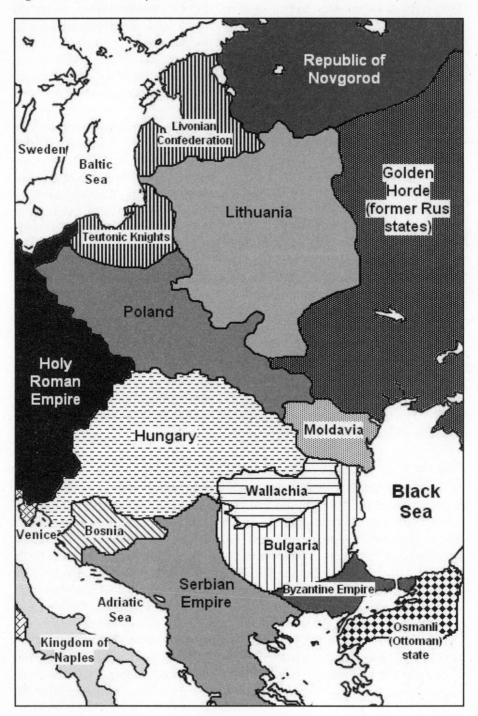

Albania began its history under Byzantine rule, which lasted until the late 11th century when the Serbian states began to encroach. Throughout the 11th century, the Byzantines and Serbs had to fend off repeated attempts by the French Normans—who ruled nearby southern Italy and Sicily—to seize the Albanian coastal cities.

When the Latin Empire was proclaimed in 1204, a Byzantine prince, Michael Comnenus, allied with Albanian tribal leaders and drove the Latins out of Albania and northwestern Greece, where Michael founded the Despotate of Epirus. The Albanian tribes lived fairly unmolested for the next several decades, even after the Byzantine restoration in 1261, but in 1272 the French Anjou dynasty—which had since inherited southern Italy—invaded and managed to seize the Albanian coastal cities, establishing the Kingdom of Albania under Charles I (of Anjou).

It was not Byzantine armies but Serbian, those of Stefan Dušan, who eventually drove the Anjous out, and Albania was annexed to the Serbian Empire in 1336. As Dušan's empire disintegrated after his death in 1355, however, local tribal leaders and noblemen—both Serbian and Albanian—began to feud, and endemic warfare forced many Albanians to flee southward into the flatlands of Greek Epirus and Kosovo, until the Ottoman Turks overran Albania in 1385.

Albania remained a part of the Ottoman Empire until 1443, when the Janissary son of an Albanian tribal leader, Gjergj Kastrioti (Gyerg Kahstree-OH-tee), led a revolt that drove the Ottomans out. He is better known by his Turkish name, *Skander-beg* (*Skander* = "Alexander," *beg / bey* = a Turkish landed bureaucratic title, like "earl"). Skanderbeg's independent Albania lasted barely beyond his death (1468), until 1478, when the Ottomans reoccupied the country.

I. The Byzantine Empire

In 1204 the Byzantine Empire and its capital, Constantinople, were duplicitously taken over by Franco-Venetian crusader armies on their way to the Holy Land, who founded the "Latin Empire." The Byzantine Empire survived through three successor states, two in Anatolia (modern-day western Turkey; the empires of Nicaea and Trebizond) and one in western Greece (Despotate of Epirus). The Latin Empire ruled Thrace. The Latin Empire was never very cohesive, however, and it was with surprising ease that a small reconnaissance force of Byzantine infantry recaptured Constantinople in 1261.

The Byzantine Empire was even blessed with a particularly competent postrestoration emperor, Emperor Michael VIII Palaeologus, who moved to rebuild the empire's economy and army—but it was too little too late, and upon his death in 1282 civil wars broke out. These wars gutted what little was left of the Byzantine Empire, and it entered the 14th century on the verge of collapse. Stefan Dušan, with his Serbian Empire, tried to take over the ailing Byzantine Empire as much to save it as to conquer it, but his efforts fell short and in the process he provoked the Byzantines into hiring the Ottoman Turks as mercenaries.

USELESS TRIVIA: GO EAST . . . NO, I MEAN WEST, YOUNG MAN!

Constantinople's mighty walls in 1453 stretched around the city for twelve miles and had withstood countless invaders for more than a thousand years. However, the Ottoman army that besieged the city in April and May 1453 was different. Some 80,000 strong (against the Byzantines' force of 7,000), Sultan Mehmed II's army boasted some of the best military and engineering minds of Eurasia, whose methods would be copied across Europe. Moreover, Mehmed's army brought a new technology, massive siege artillery.[8] The city's ancient walls cracked and crumbled under the strain of the bombardment, opening breaches through which Ottoman forces surged despite the valiant efforts of the Byzantine defenders. Emperor Constantine XI was killed in the fighting, and his city, Constantinople, was overwhelmed by Mehmed's forces.

News of Constantinople's fall to the Ottoman Turks took weeks to spread across Europe, and it prompted a small country on the Atlantic seaboard, Portugal, to redouble its efforts to find a sea route to the Far East around Africa. Since the late-14th century, Ottoman conquests in the Middle East and Balkans had restricted or shut down ancient land trade routes between Europe and India and the Far East, making the supply of Eastern wares unreliable and very expensive for Europeans. Portugal sent explorers to scout the African coast and see if they could get around it to India, finally succeeding in the 1480s. This success, in turn, prompted Portugal's rival, the newly united kingdom of Castille-Aragon (Spain), to finally accept the offer of an Italian explorer from Genoa to instead sail *west*ward around the world to the East and its riches. Christopher Columbus set sail in 1492, changing world history.

In 1354, Ottoman Turkish forces entered Europe to defend the Empire from Serbia, but instead the Turks soon overran much of the Balkans before being halted by the Hungarians. In 1396, a collection of Hungarian, French, and German knights—led by the Hungarian king, a future Holy Roman Emperor—attempted to relieve the Byzantine Empire by invading the Ottoman Balkans but were disastrously defeated at Nicopolis (southern Greece). By the mid-15th century the "Empire" had shrunk to little more than the city of Constantinople, which Ottoman Sultan Mehmed II besieged and conquered in May 1453. With it died the last remnants of Byzantine (and Roman) civilization.

J. The Ottoman (Turkish) Empire

In the 10th century a massive Turkic-Persian empire founded by a former Khazar general named Seljuq (SELL-jook) stretched from what is today Iran to China. A century later, the Seljuq Empire invaded the Byzantine lands, defeating a Byzantine army at Manzikert (modern-day Malazgirt, Turkey) in 1071. Now ruling much of Anatolia, the Seljuqs set up a province called the *Sultanate of Rum* (pronounced like "room"; Turkish for "Rome"). They also settled large numbers of Turks from the Steppe in Rum (Anatolia) to guard the Byzantine frontier. By the late-13th century, the Seljuq Empire was crumbling and the settler Turks began taking over the Sultanate of Rum. From among them arose a talented leader named Osman (OESS-man), who began conquering Byzantine lands and founded the *Osmanli* (or *Ottoman*) Empire.

In 1324 the Ottomans seized the Byzantine city of Bursa (modern-day northwestern Turkey) and made it their capital, while expanding their borders to the Aegean Sea. In 1354 the Ottoman army was hired as a mercenary force by desperate Byzantine authorities to fend off the threat of Serbian conquest, but the Turks took this opportunity to conquer much of the Balkans for themselves.

This turned out to be a very good move, because the armies of Timur (also known as "Tamerlane") arose from what is today Uzbekistan and invaded the Levant[9] and destroyed Ottoman forces at the Battle of Ankara in 1402. The Ottoman Sultan's sons were able to take refuge in the Ottoman Balkans until Timur died a short time later, and his empire fell apart. After restoring their empire, the Ottomans continued their march into the Balkans, taking Constantinople in 1453. But they were halted at Nándorfehérvár (Belgrade) three years later by the Hungarians. Throughout the 15th century Hungary proved a formidable enemy, repeatedly thwarting Ottoman plans for expansion in Europe.

USELESS TRIVIA: TRAVEL THE WORLD!
SEE EXOTIC PEOPLES! AND KILL THEM.

There was a long tradition among Turks of using captured enemy soldiers as mercenaries. In the 14th century the Ottoman Turks took this concept to a new level when they began demanding as tribute from their Christian Balkan subjects a percentage of their male children to be enslaved for either administrative or military duty. Now, while it's never fun being a slave, not all slaves are created equal, and these Christian children, though forced to convert to Islam, were an elevated form of slave and actually often held positions of great power. Some Christian Balkan families even welcomed the *devşirme* (DEV-sheer-meh; the system of selecting Christian boys) as a career opportunity for junior.

Those boys slated for military service received standardized training that was revolutionary for its time, and indeed, they were among the earliest military forces in medieval Europe to wear state-mandated uniforms. They were called *yeniçeri* (YEN-ee-jerr-y; "new soldiers"), or in English, *Janissaries*, and their iron discipline and fanaticism made them a feared military force across Europe and the Middle East for centuries. However, with the erosion of the Sultan's authority in the 18th century the Janissaries became increasingly corrupt, leading to their violent dissolution in 1826.

In 1526, however, Ottoman forces caught Hungary in a period of internal division and easily defeated an impromptu Hungarian army at Mohács (MOE-hotch; modern-day southern Hungary), removing a final obstacle to Ottoman expansion in Europe. Ottoman forces surged up the Danube River into Central Europe and laid siege to Vienna in 1529, though they had to abandon it after an outbreak of the plague in their camp. Most of Hungary was now an Ottoman province, while the Turks also jousted regularly with the Venetians for control of the Adriatic and Aegean seas. By the mid-16th century, the Ottoman Empire stretched from Persia in the east to the Arabian lands and Egypt in the south, the Balkans, the Caucasus, and what is today southern Ukraine and southwestern Russia. Ottoman armies were feared across Europe, and Ottoman Sultans expected that soon all Christendom would fall to them.

K. Wallachia, Moldavia, and Transylvania

Although the Ottoman invasion spelled disaster for most Balkan states, the early Romanian states ironically were born in this period and managed to carve out a fairly successful existence despite being surrounded by hungry and meddlesome neighbors. Alarmed by constant Tartar raids, Poland and Hungary teamed up in the early-14th century to drive the Golden Horde back across the Dniester River. Hungary then worked with local Vlach (Romanian) nobles to create Wallachia and Moldavia as buffer states, but both—Wallachia in 1330 under Basarab I (Bah-sah-ROB) *cel Mare* (the Great) and Moldavia in 1359 under Bogdan I—soon rebelled and broke away from Hungarian control.

The two Romanian states still had a bad neighborhood to contend with, however, and Wallachian ruler Mircea *cel Bătrân* (Meer-CHAY-ah chel BAH-tron; "the Elder"), who ruled from 1386 to 1418, had to fight off several Ottoman invasions, working with both Hungary and Poland and even taking part in the doomed 1396 Battle of Nicopolis.

USELESS TRIVIA: DOES THIS MEAN WE CAN MARRY OUR COUSINS?

Basarab is a legendary figure in early Romanian history, which is why a 2012 DNA study by the Genographic Project caused so much outrage and disappointment in Romaniap; for it concluded that modern-day Romanians with the "Basarab" surname are not necessarily related to one another or, worse, to the legendary historical Basarab (or his reported descendants, such as Vlad III "Dracula"). European medieval dynasties, in the name of political necessity, often took "shortcuts" to keep the throne in the family. In other words, a successful dynasty like the Basarab dynasty sometimes spread its name farther than its genes.[10]

Venetian and Genovese ships frequented Wallachia's Black Sea ports, though the Ottoman pressures took their toll and Wallachia started to decline after Mircea's death in 1418, especially after the Ottoman Turks closed the Black Sea to Western ships in 1453. The mid-15th century did manage to produce Wallachia's most famous ruler, however, Vlad III *Țepeș* (TSEH-pesh, "the Impaler") Dracula, but despite Vlad III's infamous resistance to the Turks, Wallachian rulers since Mircea's final years paid tribute to the Ottomans while struggling to maintain at least some autonomy.

Figure 38. Eastern Europe in 1500

Moldavia was initially shielded from direct Ottoman intervention by Wallachia, but as the Turks crept up the Black Sea coast Moldavia allied with the Poles in 1394, beginning a long tradition of Polish influence (and interference) in Moldavian affairs. The most famous Moldavian ruler is Ștefan III *cel Mare* (SHTEH-fon chel MAH-ray; "Stephen the Great"), who began his rule at a time when Ottoman power was on the rise throughout the Balkans, in 1457. He managed to repulse invasions from Hungary (by King Mátyás I, or "Matthias Corvinus") in 1467 and several by the Ottomans over the next decade. In 1471, seeing Wallachia weakening, Ștefan installed a close ally on its throne. He tried to maintain Moldavian-Wallachian independence, but in 1484–86 the Turks invaded again, seizing the Moldavian Black Sea coast and burning down his capital, Suceava (Soo-CHAY-ah-vah). With no help from Christian Europe, Ştefan threw in the towel and offered tribute to the Ottomans. After the Battle of Mohács in 1526, the Turks permanently stationed troops in Moldavia and Wallachia, severely limiting their sovereignty.

In 1599, the Turks supported the rise of Mihai *Viteazul* (MEE-high Vee-tay-AH-zool; "Michael the Brave") in Wallachia, but he went rogue on the Turks by occupying formerly Hungarian Transylvania, and the following year he seized Moldavia. Viteazul was murdered in 1601 (ending the almost 300-year reign of the Basarab dynasty in Wallachia), and the Turks quickly reasserted their authority in Wallachia and Moldavia, while Transylvania became a semi-independent tributary state. Still, Viteazul is remembered today by modern-day Romanians as the first ruler who united the three basic regional components of modern-day Romania: Wallachia, Moldavia, and Transylvania.

USELESS TRIVIA: VAMPIRES!

When the Romanian communist regime of Nicolae Ceauşescu was overthrown in 1989, eager Transylvanians welcomed the first Western tourists into what must be one of Europe's most naturally beautiful regions, only to be confronted with baffling requests to see the vampire's castle and crypt. Some of those at the receiving end of such requests being entrepreneurial and quick to adapt, almost overnight the Transylvanian equivalent of "Washington slept here" signs sprang up everywhere. Vampire mythology, of course, is as old as human civilization, stretching back to ancient Sumeria, India, and China.

Bram Stoker's 1897 novel *Dracula* was based on the 15th-century Vlach (Romanian) prince Vlad III Ţepeş (TSEH-pesh; "the Impaler") Dracula, a particularly nasty ruler famous for shishkebabing his enemies while valiantly resisting the Turks. Vlad III actually ruled Wallachia, not Transylvania (though he was born there), and was a fairly weak ruler dependent on the fickle sponsorship of his much stronger neighbor, Hungary. And while famous for fighting the Turks, he did so less to save Wallachia from Turkish rule than to keep his own butt sitting on the Wallachian throne. In 1462, the Turks overcame Wallachia's defenses, but they just installed Vlad's brother, Radu, on the throne and left.

To Stoker, Transylvania seemed far away and exotic, a perfect setting for his vampire, but the region's past is much more complex than vampire myths. Transylvania is where the Balkans and Central Europe meet, where the Roman Christian, Orthodox Christian, and for a long time, the Muslim quarters of Europe met, mingled, and occasionally fought. No wonder Stoker's Dracula wanted to move to London!

L. Hungary

When the Mongols withdrew in 1242, they left behind a country in ruins and severely depopulated. Reconstruction was hindered by internal strife, however, which hampered the Árpád dynasty for its final decades until it went extinct in 1301. Hungarian aristocrats, hoping to end the strife, reached for an impartial foreign dynasty to rule the country: the French Anjous (AHN-zhoh). The first Anjou ruler of Hungary was Charles I Robert, known in Hungarian as *Károly I Róbert* (CAR-oy ROW-bayrt). Károly Róbert had a major impact on Hungary, solidifying the state structure and laying the institutional foundations for Hungary becoming a major regional power. Among his many achievements, Károly Róbert convened meetings in 1335 and 1339 at one of his fortresses on the Danube River bend (in modern-day northern Hungary, close to the Slovak border) called Visegrád (VEESH-eh-grahd) with the kings of Bohemia and Poland to coordinate foreign and economic policy between the three kingdoms.[11] When the last Hungarian Anjou king died in 1382, he left his successor a powerful country well prepared to meet the growing Ottoman challenge in the Balkans.

The Anjous were succeeded by a member of the powerful Luxembourg dynasty named Sigismund (Zsigmond [ZHEEG-mond] in Hungarian) who also became Holy Roman Emperor in 1433, as well as king of Bohemia and four other countries. Though successful in many regards, he is best remembered for the failed joint Hungarian-French crusade in 1396 that ended in disaster at Nicopolis. Upon his death in 1437, Hungary accepted a king from the Polish Jagiellonian (Yah-gyeh-LONE-ee-an) dynasty, Władysław (Vwah-DIH-swahff), who had also been king of Poland since 1434. Known to Hungarians as *Úlászló I* [OO-lahs-low], he is also most famous for his greatest failure, a grand crusade to liberate the Balkans of the Turks, led by the very able Hungarian general and voivode of Transylvania, János (YAH-noesh; "John") Hunyadi (HOON-yuh-dee), in 1444.[12]

This crusade, though initially successful, met decisive defeat at Varna on the Black Sea (modern-day Bulgaria), with the young twenty-year-old Jagiellonian king cut down in the battle. Today in the city of Varna there is a memorial on the hill where *Władysław Warneńczyk* (Polish for "Władysław of Varna") was slain.

USELESS TRIVIA: WHERE BAD REPUTATIONS GET THEIR START

People like to feel special, and nothing makes them feel special like belonging to an exclusive club. That's why throughout human history there've always been elitist clubs and secret societies with complex handshakes and nifty decoder rings. Sigismund I, king of Hungary and future Holy Roman Emperor, started just such an exclusive club. To become Holy Roman Emperor he needed to hobknob with other movers and shakers across Europe, and so his club was founded in 1408 as a knighthood to defend the Cross and was based around the motif of St. George slaying the mythical dragon. Its name was, in Latin, *Societatis draconistrarum*, Order of the Dragon. Sigismund's club did the trick because he became Holy Roman Emperor in 1433. After he died in 1437, it just kind of fizzled out.

It did manage to leave its mark on history, however. In 1431, Sigismund decided to induct the prince of Wallachia, Vlad II—a valuable ally against the Turks—into the club. As a public mark of being in this exclusive club, Vlad was allowed to use the personal title "the Dragon," which in Romanian is *Dracul*. His son, who was also inducted into the group, used the title "Son of the Dragon": Vlad III Dracula. Thus are legends born, just waiting for an eager Irish fiction writer.

János Hunyadi survived the battle and returned to Hungary, where he was made regent (meaning, the ruler in place of a king). When he died of the plague just months after halting a Turkish invasion at Belgrade in 1456, his son, Mátyás (MAH-tyash; "Matthew"), was elected King of Hungary, riding his father's famous coattails. Mátyás became the most powerful and famous of Hungary's kings, and his long reign—1457–90—is fondly remembered today.

Better known by his Latin name, *Matthias Corvinus* ("Corvinus" = "the Raven" in Latin, from the family's coat of arms that featured a raven), Matthias patronized the Renaissance arts and sciences (building the largest library in Renaissance Europe, which is why so many publishers and bookstores in Hungary today are called "Corvina" or have a raven somewhere in their logo), leading a major architectural revolution and building campaign across the country. Some ascribe his enormous interest in artistic extravagance to an attempt to cover up with pomp and distracting beauty the fact that Mátyás was not of royal lineage, and had a dubious claim to the throne. His military exploits could not be doubted, however, as he expanded Hungary's borders to their greatest extent, seizing western Austria and large chunks of both Bavaria and Lusatia from the Holy Roman Empire, and successfully thwarting Ottoman schemes in the Balkans. From 1485, Mátyás ruled his Hungarian empire from Vienna, which he had captured from the Habsburgs.

USELESS TRIVIA: RINGING BELLS!

In Europe today, you know it's noon when church bells ring; or, in many towns across North America, firehouse sirens blare. You have a 15th-century Hungarian general to thank for this. In 1456, fresh from their conquest of Constantinople three years earlier, Ottoman Turkish armies surged northward up the Danube River into Central Europe. Christian Europe shook as the Turks seemed unstoppable, threatening the Holy Roman Empire and possibly even Papal Italy. However, General János Hunyadi saved the day when he organized the defenses on Hungary's southern border and repulsed a massive Ottoman land assault against Nándorfehérvár (modern-day Belgrade), saving the city and Europe. It would be seventy years before the Turks would attempt another invasion of Central Europe. To celebrate this great victory, Pope Calixtus III ordered church bells across Christendom to toll every day at noon, as they do still today.

The problem with strong leaders like Mátyás is that eventually they die, and the empire they built withers. After Mátyás's death in 1490, his territorial gains were lost one by one, and Hungary's influence waned rapidly. In 1526 the country's king—Lajos (LUH-yoesh; "Louis") II, another Jagiellonian—died fleeing the battlefield at Mohács (MOE-hotch) as Ottoman forces finally broke Hungarian power. Lajos had been king of Bohemia as well as Hungary, so his death created a power vacuum across East Central Europe that the Habsburgs capitalized on by seizing both the empty Bohemian and Hungarian thrones, retaining a thin slice of northern Hungary (calling it "Royal Hungary") with its capital at Pozsony (PO-zhone; modern-day Bratislava, the capital of Slovakia).

To counter external influence from Catholic Rome and the Habsburgs, the Turks encouraged the spread of a smaller, decentralized Protestant Christian denomination in occupied Hungary, the neo-Calvinist *Református* (Reformist) faith, to which about one-fifth of modern-day Hungarians still belong. As Hungary was absorbed into the Ottoman Empire and minarets and Turkish baths sprang up in the country's changing urban centers, Hungary became like Serbia an unwilling host to the front line battles between Christian and Muslim Europe, though Hungarian aristocrats often vacillated between both sides.

USELESS TRIVIA: CONQUEST AND SLAUGHTER AS CHILDREN'S RHYMES!

Children's nursery rhymes the world over often have a nasty political or historical background hidden in their innocent-sounding stanzas, but here's an old one from Hungary, echoing from a brutal past:

Katalinka, szállj el	**Little Katy, Flee Away**
Katalinka, szállj el,	Little Katy, flee away,
jönnek a törökök.	The Turks are coming.
Sós kútba tesznek,	They'll throw you in a salted well,
onnan is kivesznek,	Then they'll take you out,
kerék alá tesznek,	They'll put you under a wheel,
onnan is kivesznek.	Then they'll take you from under it.
Ihol jönnek a törökök,	The Turks are coming here now,
mindjárt agyonlőnek.	And soon they'll shoot you dead.[13]

M. Bohemia

Bohemia emerged from the Mongol invasion with little damage (compared to its neighbors). Since the 10th century Bohemia had become increasingly closely drawn into the Holy Roman Empire but not as a conquered land, rather as a full voting member and, since Bohemia was already a kingdom, a high-ranking one. In 1253, Ottokar II—still of the Přemyslid (Psheh-MIH-sleed) dynasty—became King of Bohemia, and one of its most celebrated kings. Among his first achievements was to participate in the 1255 Northern Crusade with the Teutonic Order against the Baltic tribes, during which he ruthlessly laid waste to the Baltic port city of *Tvangste*. The Teutonic Knights later rebuilt and named it "The King's Mountain" (*Königsberg* in German) in Ottokar's honor.

Ottokar expanded Bohemia's borders to include Silesia and much of eastern Austria, whose native Babenberg dynasty had recently died out. He also had ambitions to become Holy Roman Emperor, and he almost succeeded in a vote in 1273 but lost to Rudolf of Habsburg. Nonplussed, Ottokar raised a large army and attempted to dethrone Rudolf I by force, but it all came crashing down at the Battle of Marchfeld (in modern-day Moravia, eastern Czech Republic) in August 1278, when Rudolf's forces (with Hungarian aid) crushed the Bohemian army. Ottokar was found slain on the battlefield. The Habsburgs seized control of Austria from Bohemia, and kept it (for the most part) until 1918.

USELESS TRIVIA: MEDIEVAL LAWS THAT STILL MATTER!

Sometimes medieval history can seem quaint, though hardly relevant. It was a long time ago, after all. Well, an American company found out just how real medieval history can still be. It all started with a Czech brewery founded in 1895 called Budějovický Budvar, based in the western Bohemian city of České Budějovice (CHES-kay Boo-DYAY-o-veets-eh). The trouble began a century later, in the 1990s, when the company began exporting its beers and ales to the U.S. market. Founded in Habsburg times, its beers in the 1990s still used their German name: České Budějovice is *Budweis* (BOOD-vice) in German, and a beer from Budweis is called a *Budweiser*. You see the problem. German immigrants Eberhard Anheuser and Adolphus Busch had founded a brewery in St. Louis in 1876 and sold a beer with that same name. Faster than you can say "copyright infringement," Anheuser-Busch lawyers sued Budějovický Budvar in the 1990s. Unfortunately, Anheuser-Busch came up against a 13th-century edict by Bohemian King Ottokar II granting *any* brewery in České Budějovice the right to use the "Budweiser" name—a law modern-day courts upheld. Hit with the double-whammy of the EU's Protected Geographical Indication laws (which protect products named after locations), Anheuser-Busch eventually worked out a global distribution compromise with Budějovický Budvar.

The Přemyslids continued their rule of Bohemia until 1310, when the last Přemyslid died and someone from the Luxembourg family dynasty was chosen, John I, as king. There isn't much about John to report other than he had a son, Charles (*Karel* in Czech), who is revered by modern-day Czechs. Charles I became king of Bohemia in 1346 after his father, John, was killed and Charles himself wounded on the battlefield at Crécy in France in the Hundred Years' War. He loved his home city, Prague, and invested it with great art and architecture; many of the beautiful buildings and monuments tourists flock to see in modern-day Prague were built in Charles's day. He also founded Charles University, one of the earliest universities in Central Europe.

But Charles went on to bigger and better things, as he was elected Holy Roman Emperor (as Charles IV) in 1355. He was urged as Holy Roman Emperor to move his imperial capital to Rome but he refused, and so for a few decades until his death in 1378, Prague effectively became the political capital of Western Christian Europe and a major scientific and cultural center as well. You can visit his crypt in Prague's *Katedrála sv. Víta* (St. Vitus Cathedral).

USELESS TRIVIA: ASTRONOMY DOMINE!

In late August 2006, the International Astronomers' Union (IAU) met in Prague, the capital of the Czech Republic, to make a fateful decision about the status of Pluto as a planet. Unfortunately, Pluto got the thumbs-down, but for all the controversy, some were wondering why exactly the IAU would be meeting in Prague in the first place. Is it because astronomers are a notoriously cheap bunch?

Well, there may be *other* reasons too. Two of Europe's most famous early astronomers, Tycho Brahe and Johannes Kepler, both lived and worked in Prague in the late-16th and early-17th centuries, though neither was a native; Brahe was a Dane and Kepler was Austrian. Prague was at the time still in the top circuit of Holy Roman imperial cities, and a major cultural—and scientific—center of Europe. While in Prague, Brahe and Kepler rubbed elbows with many notable scholars and scientists of their day. Both dedicated themselves to improving the work of another revolutionary Eastern European astronomer, Nicholas Copernicus, who had lived and worked a full century earlier in Poland.

In the early-15th century a rebellious priest, Jan Hus (Yon Hooss; *Jan* = "John"), preached in Bohemia the radical ideas of the English theologian John Wycliffe about church reform, which made Hus very unpopular in some circles. He was invited by the Church to defend his views at the Council of Constance in Italy, but despite being granted official protection by the Holy Roman Emperor, Hus was arrested, tried, and executed in 1415. His followers rose up in revolt but were defeated at the monumental Battle of Lipany (Lee-PON-ih) in 1434. However, so numerous were his followers—called *Hussites*—that an accommodation was reached that legalized Hussitism, making Bohemia the first de facto Protestant country in Europe, eighty years *before* Martin Luther in Germany.

Trouble for the Hussites came in the form of the Ottoman conquest of Hungary in 1526, which ended with the death of Ludvik (Louis) II, who had been king of both Bohemia and Hungary. This meant that the exceedingly pro-Catholic Habsburgs gained control of the Bohemian throne. The Hussites—who began to fracture into increasingly radical splinter groups—lasted another century before the inevitable confrontation took place, sparking the Thirty Years' War, but that's for the next chapter.

N. The Teutonic Knights and Schizoid Prussia

Prussia is greatly misunderstood today, mostly because of Nazi mythology (and Allied propaganda) from the 20th century about Prussian militarism. However, the same Prussia that produced *Friedrich die Große* (Frederick the Great) also produced the great humanist philosopher Immanuel Kant.

So, to the beginning: The Teutonic Knights, as noted in Chapter 2, had been hired by the Polish ruler of Mazovia (modern-day northeastern Poland), Konrad, in 1225 to help tame the neighboring pagan Balts. These people called themselves *Brusi* and they spoke a language akin to modern-day Latvian and Lithuanian, a Baltic family language. The Brusi resisted the Order fiercely, but superior organization and equipment won the day and in fairly short order the Brusi's lands in what is today northern Poland and Russia's Kaliningrad province were conquered by the German crusaders.

The Teutonic Order—led by its visionary leader, *Hochmeister* (Grand Master) Hermann von Salza—established the *Ordensstaat* state (The Order's State) and began importing immigrants from the German lands. Over time, the new German settlers took on the Brusi name, at least as the Germans pronounced it—*Prußen* (PROO-ssen), later *Preußen* (PROY-ssen)—which is where the name *Prussia* comes from.[14] In no time the Order's famous red-brick cities began springing up along the southern Baltic—Marienburg (modern-day Malbork, Poland), Allenstein (modern-day Olsztyn, Poland), Memel (modern-day Klaipėda, Lithuania), Königsberg (modern-day Kaliningrad, Russia)—while some Polish cities like Gdańsk (German: Danzig) and Bydgoszcz (German: Bromberg) were also seized.

The *Ordensstaat* grew rapidly in the 13th century into a major regional power, and its knights' white tunics and shields with large black crosses emblazoned on the front became an infamous symbol of (German) crusader power in Eastern Europe. Indeed, the Order seemed to quickly forsake its calling as a Christianizing crusader army, and appeared to become more interested in grabbing real estate, as William Urban notes:

> The crusade had once been a matter separate from the state, so that they [the Teutonic Knights] could discuss the conversion of Mindaugas's Lithuanians without first conquering his lands; it was sufficient to be present at his coronation. Unfortunately, the acquisition of West Prussia and Danzig had changed the Poles from traditional allies to mortal enemies, so that the Teutonic Knights came to see further territorial conquests as the best means of protecting themselves. Once they had convinced themselves that they would be safe only if they held onto all of Prussia—and Samogitia as well, to secure the land route to Livonia—they were doomed. Changing times found them petrified in old ideas."[15]

USELESS TRIVIA: WHOSE HISTORY, AGAIN . . . ?

Red-brick Marienburg castle was built on the Nogath (NO-got) River[16] by the Teutonic Knights and became their capital in 1309. Despite the disastrous defeat at Grunwald in 1410, its mighty walls withstood a Polish siege, but after the Teutonic Knights' era had passed Marienburg lost its luster and by the 18th century, it was a decaying Prussian army barracks. The Napoleonic Wars left the castle in ruins, so Prussian antiquarians in the 19th century rebuilt the fortress as a museum, and the Nazis enshrined it as a virtual holy site of German history in the 1930s, but Nazi defeat in 1945 left the old medieval castle in ruins again—more so as the Soviet army used it for artillery practice. In the 1960s the Polish communist government began rebuilding the fortress, and today the *Muzeum Zamkowe w Malborku* (Castle Museum in Marienburg)[17] hosts extensive collections not only related to the Teutonic Knights and medieval warfare, but to the castle and its role in Crusader, Polish, Prussian, and German history.

By conquering their neighbors' territory, the Order made many new enemies, compelling the peoples of the Baltic region to organize against them: Lithuania, Poland, and Novgorod. But the Order's wars of expansion created another problem as well, one often overlooked in histories: its own immigrants. The problem was that what's often good for war is not necessarily good for the economy, and soon Prussia's German peasant and merchant settlers began to complain loudly about the huge tax levies the Order imposed to finance its military campaigns.

As we'll see, the Order's refusal to address this basic conflict of interests in its realm would eventually lead to its downfall, but from the beginning two parallel Prussias developed: one an aggressively expansionistic and militarized state led by soldier-monks bent on territorial conquest, the other a collection of more commercially-minded peasants, craftsmen, and merchants who preferred financial pursuits. The former had ambassadors at all the courts of Europe and leveraged them for support for its constant land claims, while the latter joined the Hanseatic League and developed commercial ties stretching from Novgorod to Spain.

O. Lithuania and the Eastern Slavs

As we last left Lithuania in Chapter 2, Mindaugas (Meen-DOW-gass) had managed to organize Baltic tribal resistance to the Livonian Brotherhood, most famously crushing them at the Battle of Saule (SOW-leh; *Schaulen* to Germans) in 1236. Mindaugas went on to organize a Lithuanian state through careful tribal alliances and good old-fashioned conquest, halfheartedly adopting Christianity, though shortly after his death the country reverted to traditional Lithuanian paganism. (This meant that the Papacy in Rome rescinded its earlier recognition of Lithuania as a Christian kingdom.) In 1316 the greatest of Lithuania's early rulers, Gediminas (Geh-dee-MEE-nahss), came to power, and Lithuania's borders expanded rapidly southward to the shores of the Black Sea, swallowing up many of the western Rus lands. By the 1330s, the Lithuanian Empire was Europe's largest country (by territory).

As Gediminas quickly found himself the ruler of a vast empire, he did something remarkable. The empire he'd just conquered was mostly inhabited by Eastern Slavs, who easily outnumbered Lithuanians. Gediminas pragmatically decided *not* to impose the Lithuanian language on his new subject peoples, instead adopting *their* language, Ruthenian,[18] as the official state language of the Lithuanian empire and granting these Eastern Slavic peoples cultural autonomy.

By allowing the former Rus peoples to maintain their own language(s) and culture, Gediminas inadvertently laid the foundations for two new nations. Those eastern Rus peoples who still lived under Mongol/Tartar rule eventually were drawn into the orbit of Muscovy (Moscow), which became the nucleus of a new post-Kieven Rus civilization, Russia; but the western Rus peoples who were cut off from their eastern brethren for centuries by Lithuanian conquest (and later Polish, Hungarian, and Habsburg rule) came over time to form the modern Belarussian and Ukrainian peoples.

Upon Gediminas's death in 1341, his son Algirdas (all-GEER-dahss) took over, and Lithuania expanded as far eastward as the city of Smolensk. However, for all Lithuania's successes under Algirdas, it faced growing threats with the rise of the Teutonic Order, Poland, and Muscovy. When Algirdas died in 1377, he was succeeded by his son, Jogaila (Yo-GUY-lah), who had to first murder his uncle Kestutis

(Kes-TOO-teess) and exile his cousin Vytautas (Vih-TOW-tahss) before he had complete power. Jogaila is a legendary figure in the region. By the 1380s, he realized that he ruled a creaky empire surrounded by powerful enemies and, amazingly, Jogaila turned to one of those enemies for help.

P. Livonia, Crusaders, and the Balts

After the defeat of the Livonian Brothers of the Sword at the Battle of Saule in 1236, the remnants of this shattered German crusading organization were absorbed by the Teutonic Knights in Prussia to the south and reorganized as the *Livonian Order*. The new Order then established the Confederation of Livonia, whose territory covered most of modern-day Latvia and Estonia. (Denmark sold northern Estonia to the Order in 1346. The modern-day Estonian capital "Tallinn" takes its name from *Tanni linn*, old Estonian for "Danish city.") Ruled from its capital at Üxküll (OOKS-kool; modern-day Ikšķile in central Latvia), the Livonian Confederation—often in cooperation with Denmark or Sweden—waged holy war against Baltic, Finnic, and Slavic pagans, as well as Russian "schismatics" on occasion.

The Livonian Confederation soon ran up against the same problems as the Teutonic Knights in Prussia, however, in that its imported German colonists had commercial interests in mind that often conflicted with the crusading focus of the Order. Indeed, many cities of the Livonian Confederation, including Riga (modern-day Latvia's capital), Dorpat (modern-day Tartu), Windau (modern-day Ventspils), and Reval (modern-day Tallinn) joined the Hanseatic League and used the League's power against the Order.

Unlike their peers to the south in Prussia, however, the Order in Livonia got smart and organized a diet (small parliament) at Walk (Valk) in 1419 to head off internal conflicts between the Order, the Church, and the urban commercial centers. This sane move helped keep the Livonian Confederation together for another century and a half, long outlasting their peers in Prussia. This last German crusader state was destroyed by Muscovy's Ivan IV ("the Terrible") in the 1558–83 Livonian War, and its lands were partitioned between the war's victors, the Polish-Lithuanian Commonwealth and Sweden.

USELESS TRIVIA: HANSE AND GRETEL

In the high Middle Ages (c. 800–1300), the Baltic Sea was one of Europe's economic hot spots, with merchant ships from all over northern Europe crowding the Baltic's ports in search of exotic goods from as far away as Central Asia and India. The abundant merchants were actually a problem; besides competition, port cities also set arbitrary taxes and fees, and it also encouraged pirates who made a fat living by preying on the heavily laden merchant ships. Somebody had to do something.

Well, in 1267, somebody did. Based on earlier precedents between German cities, the city of Lübeck formed the *Hanse* (HAHN-zeh; "guild," like a trade union) which eventually expanded to include commercial cities like Stettin, Danzig, Kiel, Antwerp, Edinburgh, Riga, Tallin, Novgorod, Brugge, London, York, Stockholm, and even inland cities on major river routes such as Kraków and Köln (Cologne). The Hanse, or *Hanseatic League*, as it is known in English, grew to some 170 member cities around the Baltic and North seas at its height in the 14th century.

The Hanseatic League wasn't just a group of accountants who argued taxes or fees with trading ports, moreover; it was a potent military power with its own armed forces, backing up its negotiations with large navies. It also vigorously hunted pirates and even waged wars against countries, forcing King Valdemar IV of Denmark at sword point, for instance, to share his kingdom's trade profits with the League in 1370.

The Hanseatic League played a major role in the development of Baltic trade, but it was born in an age when states were weak and cities or organizations like the League could throw some weight around. By the 16th century, however, states were growing stronger in Europe and some were fed up with the League's mafialike tactics. That, coupled with the rise of Muscovy (eclipsing Novgorod, the League's very wealthy eastern linchpin), and the shift of trade from the Baltic to the Adriatic and Mediterranean seas all combined to weaken the League, though it managed to limp on until 1669.

Q. Poland as Catalyst

As we saw in Chapter 2, Poland arose and converted to Christianity in the mid-10th century, building a modestly successful state until one of its most powerful kings, Bolesław (Bo-LEH-swaff) III, divided it among his sons in 1138, fracturing the country for a century and a half. The Mongol invasion of 1241 very thoroughly devastated Poland, leaving most of its cities in ruins. Reunification came only in 1304 when Władysław (Vwah-DIH-swaff) I *Łokietek* (Wo-KYEH-tek; "the Short") of the Piast dynasty managed to drive several foreign armies from core Polish territories—losing Silesia to Bohemia, Pomerania to Brandenburg, and the entire Baltic coastline to the Teutonic Knights in the process—but uniting Poland again. Only in 1320 did he finally get papal recognition as king of a reunited and restored Poland. When he died in 1333, his son Kazimierz (Kah-ZHEE-myesh; "Casimir") III became king. Kazimierz III *Wielki* (VYEL-kee; "the Great") instituted critical legal and military reforms, earning the nickname the "Polish Justinian."[19] He led a major rebuilding program of Polish cities, infrastructure (e.g., roads, bridges), and fortifications. It was Kazimierz who attended King Charles Robert's conferences at Visegrád (VEESH-eh-grod) in Hungary, and, as noted in the Jewish Eastern Europe insert, Kazimierz also granted immigrant Jews in Poland critical feudal legal rights.

Kazimierz died childless in 1370, leaving the Polish throne—by agreement—to the Hungarian Anjous, who ruled the country until 1382, at which point the youngest daughter of the late Anjou king became ruler of Poland. A twelve-year-old Anjou princess at the time, then named Hedwig (HED-veeg), she is still venerated today by Poles for her piety; Polish girls are commonly named in her honor—as *Jadwiga* (Yahd-VEE-gah), her name in Polish.[20]

As Jadwiga ascended the throne, Poland received an unusual offer from an unusual source. Lithuania's (twenty-six year-old) ruler, Jogaila, offered to marry Jadwiga and convert himself and his country to Western Christianity in exchange for being made (co-)ruler of both countries. Poland's nobility, wary of the growing threat of the Teutonic Knights, accepted Jogaila's offer and so in 1385 the Union of Krewo (KREH-vo) was signed, uniting Poland and Lithuania under a single ruler. Both countries kept their own administrations, laws, and armies, but were ruled by the same person, Jogaila, who adopted a Polish "Christian" name, *Władysław* (Vwah-DIH-swaff), thereby becoming King Władysław II Jagiełło (Yah-GYEH-wo; "Jogaila" in Polish) as well as Grand Duke of Lithuania. His dynasty—the Jagiellonian (Ya-Gyel-LONE-ee-an)—ruled both countries until it went extinct in 1572, ushering in an era of strength and prosperity for both.

USELESS TRIVIA: KING KAZIMIERZ III THE GREAT IN POPULAR CULTURE!

"Today is history. The young will ask with wonder about this day. Today is history and you are a part of it. When, elsewhere, they were footing the blame for the Black Death, Kazimierz the Great, so called, told the Jews they could come to Cracow. They came. They trundled their belongings into this city, they settled, they took hold, they prospered. For six centuries, there has been a Jewish Cracow. By this weekend, those six centuries, they're a rumor. They never happened. Today is history."

—speech by the character Amon Goeth (played by Ralph Fiennes), commandant of the Nazi concentration camp at Płaszów in Nazi-occupied Poland, to his SS guards on the camp's opening day; from Steven Spielberg's 1993 film *Schindler's List*

It should be clear by now that an OK Corral–style showdown was brewing between Poland and Lithuania on the one hand, and the Teutonic Knights on the other. It finally erupted in 1410, when the Teutonic Order provoked a war to disrupt the Polish-Lithuanian alliance. Jagiełło (Jogaila) was forced in 1401 to recognize his exiled cousin, Vytautas (Vih-TOW-tass), as Grand Duke of Lithuania, and the Order assumed these cousins with a bitter past would never reconcile. But both understood the threat posed by the Order and cooperated closely.

The result was the Battle of Grunwald (GROON-valt),[21] which took place in July 1410 in what is today northern Poland with an estimated 50,000 combatants (compared to some 40,000 soldiers in the Battle of Agincourt in France five years later in 1415). It ended in a disastrous defeat for the Teutonic Order, with 80% of its leadership (including Grand Master Ulrich von Jungingen) killed in the fighting.

The Order's power in Eastern Europe was broken but not completely extinguished, and its deluded leadership tried to restore its lost power through futile wars over the next several decades against the allies. The Order paid for these wars through oppressive taxation, which drove Prussian merchants in 1440 to form the *Preußischer Bund* (Prussian Union). The *Bund* revolted in 1454 against the Order and requested that Poland (with its much lower taxes and less invasive administration) take over Prussia, and so began the Thirteen Years' War, which ended in 1466 with Prussia being divided in two: western "Royal" Prussia being ruled directly by Poland, and eastern "Ducal" Prussia left to the Order but with feudal obligations to Poland.

The weakened Teutonic Order provoked another war in 1520–21 that it lost, ending with Ducal Prussia also being absorbed into Poland. The Order dissolved, faced with not only Polish rule but the spread of Lutheranism as well, though later religious orders would revive its name. Prussia emerged from Polish rule in 1657.

USELESS TRIVIA: MEMORIES OF GRUNWALD

In late August and early September 1914, in one of the first battles of World War I, the German *Reichswehr* (imperial army) successfully repulsed two much larger Russian armies invading East Prussia (modern-day northeastern Poland). The German victory was an example of brains over brawn. Gen. Paul von Hindenburg, one of the three German commanders behind the great victory, insisted in his cable to Berlin with news of the victory that the battle be named "The Battle of Tannenberg." Why?

In a strange reading of history, von Hindenburg declared that his victory had wiped away the 504-year-old "stain of defeat" inflicted on Germans by the "Slavs,"[22] referring to the medieval battle fought between Poland, Lithuania, and the Teutonic Order. Early-20th century German nationalists saw an epic struggle between German and Slav for control of Central and Eastern Europe, and they viewed that defeat of 1410 as a Wagnerian blow by "slavdom" in a German national *Götterdamerung*,[23] for which von Hindenburg busily created the mythology of revenge in 1914.

Weimar Germany erected a monument on the (1914) battlefield in 1927 and Hindenburg himself was buried there in 1934—although in the waning days of World War II, in 1944, as Soviet troops advanced westward across Poland, the monument was dynamited by retreating Nazi forces and his body brought back to the Reich, where it was found by U.S. forces in an abandoned salt min*e in 1945.*

Lithuania, though benefiting immensely from the union with Poland, was also very keen to maintain its political and cultural independence in the same way early Poland had feared being absorbed by the Holy Roman Empire. Vytautas, Jagiełło's cousin, is one of modern-day Lithuania's great medieval heroes. He forced Jagiełło to renegotiate the union in 1413 (Union of Horodło; Hor-O-dwaw), giving Lithuania greater rights. Still, over time

Lithuania's institutions came to mirror Poland's. The Jagiellonian dynasty ruled Poland and Lithuania until its last king, Zygmunt (ZIG-moont, "Sigmund") II, died in 1572. This union had proven a great success. The Polish-Lithuanian economies began to grow as ships from all over Europe filled their ports to buy timber and grain. When Zygmunt II saw the end coming for the dynasty with no heir, he negotiated the Union of Lublin in 1569. Before, Poland and Lithuania were two countries united by a common dynasty, but in 1569 they became one country, though Lithuania staunchly defended its own rights. Known as the *Commonwealth*, (*Rzeczpospolita* to Poles, *Žečpospolita* to Lithuanians), it dominated Eastern Europe for the next century.

R. Novgorod, Muscovy, and the Russians

The Rus lands were severely devastated by the Mongol invasion, and continued to suffer under the rule of the Golden Horde. The city-state of Novgorod, however, deflected a direct Mongol invasion in 1239 by offering submission and tribute as the Mongol armies approached. Novgorod became in the 1240s a wealthy city, well connected to the rest of Europe by trade, and it would serve over the next two centuries as a beacon of light for the Eastern Slavic peoples living under the Horde.

A republic, Novgorod expanded its borders in all directions and proved its military prowess to fellow Rus princes by repulsing in 1240 a Swedish invasion at the River Neva, and spectacularly defeating two years later the Teutonic Knights on the weak spring ice of Lake Peipus—both victories attributed to Novgorod's Alexander Nevsky. As one of 13th-century Europe's largest cities, Novgorod hosted a large number of resident European and Central Asian merchants and was a leading member of the Hanseatic League.

In its early years, the Golden Horde controlled its Kieven Rus territories closely, with Rus princes forced to travel to Sarai annually to pay tribute, reaffirm their allegiance, and seek approval for their policies. However, by the mid-14th century, as the Horde began to weaken and as Lithuania overran the western Rus lands, the Horde reorganized its Rus subjects around a growing city on a northern tributary river of the Volga called Moscow, even tasking Moscow after a while with collecting tribute in the Horde's name from Moscow's fellow Rus lands.

Moscow was a fairly new city, founded in the 12th century and growing wealthy quickly on the Volga River trade, dominating the Vladimir region by the early-14th century. By the late-15th century Moscow, or *Muscovy* as the state that formed around Moscow became known, was a formidable power and managed to defeat rival Novgorod in the contest for domination of the Rus lands. Moscow also overthrew Tartar rule when Grand Duke Ivan (EE-vahn; "John") III faced down a large Tartar army on the banks of the Ugra River in November 1480. Declaring the "Gathering of the Russias" policy—a drive for Muscovy/Russia to rule all the former Kieven Rus lands, generating conflicts with neighboring states and peoples well into our own times—Ivan III transformed Muscovy into Russia, and is seen as the "Father of Russia."

Russia closed the 16th century with its last ruler of the Rurik dynasty, and easily the worst: Ivan IV. Remembered as Ivan "the Terrible" (*Иван Грозный*; EE-vahn Groz-nee), he managed some successes, such as his conquest of the Kazan Khanate, one of the Golden Horde successor states that often raided Russia. He is better remembered for his failures, however, like for instance the ill-advised Livonian War that Ivan launched in 1558 to seize some warm water ports on the Baltic. It started wellm with Ivan shattering the Livonian Confederation, but ended more than twenty years later in 1583 in defeat after Poland-Lithuania and Sweden drove Russian armies from the Baltic.

Ivan the Terrible is most remembered for the *Oprichnina*, however. After being terrorized through his long regency by corrupt boyars[24] happy to be rid of Ivan's powerful predecessor Vassily III, he struck back later in his adulthood by dividing the country in two—his part, called the *Oprichnina*, and the rest, called the *Zemshchina*. He flooded the Oprichnina with his agents who terrorized and mass-murdered boyars, priests, and peasants indiscriminately.

By the time Ivan dismantled the Oprichnina in 1572, Russia lay in ruins and depopulated—and utterly subordinate to Ivan's will. Ivan discarded his predecessors' title "Grand Prince of Moscow" in favor of the bold "Tsar of all the Russias," but the accumulated effect for Russia of Ivan's reign was a ruinous ruler who squandered Moscow's great wealth and probably delayed Russia's active entry onto the European political stage a full century. Ivan died in 1584 but was forced to appoint a regent, Boris Godunov, for his sons. Boris eventually had himself declared Tsar in 1598, provoking civil wars that would last for almost a generation, known to Russians as the "Time of Troubles" (*Смутное время*; SMOOT-no-yeh Vrem-yah).

USELESS TRIVIA: ОПРИЧНИНА

In late 1564, the Grand Prince of Muscovy, Ivan IV, was in a bad mood. Emerging from a chaotic period of boyar (aristocratic land-owner) rule during Ivan's regency, the boyars only accepted Ivan's full ascension to the throne with restrictions. Ivan was not happy about this, and had decided essentially to pick his marbles up and go home; he announced his resignation and headed off to his private estate for an early retirement. Mindful of the chaos that had nearly torn Muscovy apart during Ivan's regency, the boyars begged him to change his mind. Ivan responded that he would return, but only on condition.

The result: Oprichnina (*Опричнина*; Oh-preech-NYEE-nah). The Russian state's lands were divided into two: one half Oprichnina, the rest Zemshchina (*Земщина*; zyemsh-CHEE-nah). In the Oprichnina, Ivan IV ruled with absolutely no restrictions at all—no legal restrictions, no church restrictions, and no interference from the boyars. The Oprichnina rapidly turned into a mass blood-soaked prison, where Ivan's agents terrorized, tortured, and murdered the inhabitants, including boyars and priests. Ivan had been careful to choose Russia's most productive and wealthiest lands for his Oprichnina. The population in the Oprichnina fell dramatically as peasants and boyars alike either fled or were murdered by the *Oprichniki*, Ivan's all-powerful agents. In 1572 a Tartar force invaded Muscovy but the Russian army had been too weakened by Ivan's reign of terror to defend the land; Moscow was burned to the ground. In the wake of this defeat the Oprichnina was disbanded, though with Ivan's opposition obliterated, the Oprichnina had already fulfilled its purpose anyway.[25]

Russian rulers since Ivan IV have used his example to develop their own secret organizations—the Tsarist *Ok*hrana (Tsarist secret police), the KGB, the modern-day FSB—to undermine anyone who could limit the ruler's authority, allowing Russian rulers to be despotically powerful still today. This has severely stunted Russian state institutional development, with obvious social and economic consequences. There have been Russian patriots and democrats who have tried to restrain state power through legal reforms, but they have all had to struggle against the legacy of the Oprichnina.

S. Halych-Volhynia: A Kingdom in Galicia

The break-up of Kieven Rus, which began in the 12th century but which was clinched by the Mongol invasions of the 1230s, resulted in a whole gaggle of successor states. Histories today often portray Russia as the sole inevitable outcome of that process, but in reality, many successor states arose from the rubble of Kieven Rus and it is only a matter of luck that Muscovy came to be the one that dominated the rest. As an example, here is the story of Halych-Volhynia (HOLL-eetch Vol-HIN-yah), an Eastern Slavic post-Rus state that arose in what is today western Ukraine and that briefly became an important regional power.

In 1199, a Kieven prince named Roman the Great (*Роман*) hobbled together some Rus territories based around an old western Rus commercial center, Halych (HAHL-eetch; or in Ukrainian *Галич*, "KHAL-eetch"[26]), forming the principality *Halych-Volhynia* (HAHL-eetch Voll-HIN-yah). Roman quickly conquered Kyiv and most of what is today western Ukraine and southeastern Poland. In modern-day histories this state is sometimes called "Halych," "Galicia," or even "Ruthenia." Roman's son Danylo (Dah-NIH-lo), with the aid of the legendary Rus figure Mstislav (Mist-EE-slav) the Bold, drove Hungarian invaders out in 1221 and re-established Halych-Volhynia.

Halych was devastated by the Mongol invasion in 1239–42, but it was far enough from Batu's capital at Sarai to be relatively independent. In 1253, Danylo (or *Данило Галицький*, "Danylo of Halych") was crowned King of Halych-Volhynia by an archbishop sent from Rome, which meant that Halych-Volhynia was a full kingdom in the eyes of (Western) Christian Europe.

Danylo died in 1264, and was succeeded by his son Lev I, who moved the capital to Lviv and extended Halych's borders as far as the Black Sea. Under Danylo and Lev, Halych's trade spanned Europe. Despite papal recognition, Halych remained Orthodox Christian with deep ties to Byzantium and its fellow former Rus lands to the east ruled by the Golden Horde. Lev's grandsons, Andrei and Lev II, joint kings of Halych-Volhynia, were both killed fighting the Tartars in 1323, and Halych's ruling Rurikid line died out in 1349. Poland, Lithuania, and Hungary then partitioned Halych-Volhynia, forever erasing it from Europe's map.

USELESS TRIVIA: EASTERN EUROPEANS IN TIGHTS!

The Carpathian Mountains form a sort of stone cradle smack in the middle of Eastern Europe, and while history has tended to pay attention to the many peoples who formed states on the open plains of the Carpathian Basin, less attention has been paid to those who stayed in the higher elevations. The Carpathians, like so many other mountains, served as a place of refuge and as such gave birth to a long line of outlaws, some acting like Robin Hood while others more resembled Che Guevara.

Juraj Jánošík (YOO-rye Yah-NO-sheek), a Slovak peasant, led a band of outlaws in the Tatry Mountains along the modern-day Polish-Slovak frontier (northern Carpathian Mountains), robbing both Habsburg and Hungarian magnates in Royal Hungary and Polish aristocrats across the border in Poland in the later 17th century. Jánošík was captured and met a gruesome end, but still today Czech, Slovak, Polish, and Hungarian children all read tales of brave Jánošík, many of which have been made into films. Similarly, the Transylvanian György Dózsa (Jyerdj DO-zhah; *Gheorghe Doja* to Romanians) led an unsuccessful peasant revolt in 1514, though his *kuruc* (KOO-roots) soldiers took to the hills and raised his banner in resistance long after his capture and execution. Meanwhile, Ukrainians have their Oleksa Dovbush (*Олекса Довбуш*) from the late-18th century and Usteem Karmalyuk (*Устим Кармалюк*) of the early-19th century. In the southern Carpathians, Iancu Jianu (YAN-coo ZHYAH-noo) led a band of *hajduks* (HIGH-dukes)[27] in resistance to Phanariot rule in early-19th century Ottoman Wallachia. The hills weren't alive with just the sound of music. . . .

PEOPLES OF EASTERN EUROPE: THE GERMANS

Q: Why do Eastern European cities have so many trees?
A: Because German soldiers like to march in the shade.

The 20th century was a pretty exciting century as centuries go—and not in a good way—and so not surprisingly it colors much of how we see earlier centuries. In particular, the behavior of Germany in the years 1914–45 have obscured the German role in Eastern Europe. Any objective review of Eastern European history, however, must count Germans among the peoples who have had an important impact in all respects on life in the region—and not only as foes, conquerors, or invaders, but also often as farmers, miners, craftsmen, priests, missionaries, lawyers, merchants, bankers, academics, and more. There is no doubt that Germans have often competed with other Eastern Europeans for real estate, but the often-quoted historical concept of *Drang nach Osten* ("Push to the East") is overstated. The vast majority of Germans living in Eastern Europe in the 20th century were the descendants of settlers who were willingly recruited by Eastern European rulers to live there. This is not to say that 19th and 20th century German history hasn't had a *Lebensraum* theme, or that Hitler didn't see Eastern Europe primarily as colony-fodder, but only to point out that Hitler, Bismark, Frederick the Great, and Hermann von Salza notwithstanding, there is also a long record of cooperation between Germans and Eastern Europeans. Indeed, today Germany is considered a "Western" country, but before mass expulsions after World War II destroyed this element, a large component of the German nation was *native* to Eastern Europe:

> In 1945 one of the largest forced removals of human beings in world history brought centuries of German settlement in the former Prussian provinces east of the Oder-Neisse and in the Sudetenland to an end. As a result of the devastation in eastern Germany during the last months of the war, mass flight and expulsion, and the redrawing of her eastern borders, Germany became a much more western country.[1]

Through the Frankish Empire, the Holy Roman Empire, the crusading states, the Hanseatic League, Prussia, Austria, and modern-day Germany, Germans have had an immense impact in shaping the state institutions and economies of Eastern Europe. The first legal codes in many Eastern European states were adopted from German cities, particularly Magdeburg. Many of the first churches throughout the region were also linked initially to German diocese or bishoprics. German merchants often plied Eastern European ports. In modern-day Czech, Polish, and Hungarian, some of the vocabulary for government, politics, and religion is derived from Medieval German. Of course, this all begs the question of just how much Eastern Europe has in return helped shape present-day Germany (and Austria), but that's for another book. Let's take a look at where Germans in the region have primarily lived:

- The cities of medieval Poland, Bohemia, and Hungary: Artisans, craftsmen, clergy, merchants, and adventurers flocked to the growing cities of medieval Eastern Europe, bringing with them skills, money, network connections, and German styles and culture.

- Western Bohemia, Poland: In the first centuries after the formation of Bohemia, Poland, and the German states, settlers from all three cultures penetrated into the lands then existing between them: the Sudeten Mountains, Silesia, and Pomerania. For many centuries, German, Czech, and Pole lived, farmed, and mined for the most part peacefully alongside one another.

- Hungary and Romania: At crucial junctures in Hungarian history, German immigrants formed two large communities, one in southwestern Hungary (Schwabs; in today's Baranya County, and its capital Pécs) and the other in urban Transylvania (Saxons). When the Romanian communists were overthrown in 1989, many Transylvanian Germans fled to West Germany.

- The eastern Baltic lands: Medieval German crusaders conquered what was seen as Christian Europe's last frontier, leaving behind a German rural baronial class that ruled the Latvian and Estonian lands well into the 20th century, though often serving different masters.[2]

- 17th century Russia: Peter I the Great invited many Westerners to move to Moscow and St. Petersburg during his reign, forming the *Немецкая слобода* (Nyeh-MYETS-kee slo-BO-dah; "the German Quarter") in Moscow, comprising merchants and craftsmen in the Tsar's service.

A 19th-century collection of statues in the main courtyard of Marienburg Castle (modern-day Malbork, Poland) of four great Grand Masters of the Teutonic Knights. From left to right: Hermann von Salza, Siegfriend von Feuchtwangen, Winrich von Kniprode, and Albrecht von Hohenzollern (Brandenburg)–Ansbach. (Photo by the author)

USELESS TRIVIA: WHERE DOES THE
EAST BEGIN AGAIN . . . ?

Slavs settled the region now known as Schleswig-Holstein in the 7th century and founded in the 9th century a town called Ljubice (LYOO-bee-tseh; "Lovely City") on the Baltic but in some tussles with local Slavic tribes, Saxons, and Danes, Ljubice was ravaged by war. In the mid-12th century the Saxon Count Adolf II of Holstein founded the city of Lübeck nearby, and over time its German population absorbed Ljubice—though Lübeck also adopted many Slavic laws and customs. Lübeck was for some time the only free Holy Roman imperial city east of the Elbe, and the largest German port on the Baltic. Lübeck also played a prominent role in the founding of Riga in Crusader Livonia. Fundamentally a merchant city, Lübeck had frequent disputes with neighboring states over trade issues, and in 1267 founded the Hanseatic League, a band of trading cities that challenged the power of kingdoms and pirates for several centuries in the Baltic. Medieval Lübeck's wealth and importance waned as trade moved from the Baltic to the Adriatic, but Lübeck's history is another important link between Germany and Eastern Europe.

- 18th-century Russia: Catherine II the Great (herself a German native of the Brandenburg coastal city Stettin) invited German farmers to settle deep in southern Russia along the Volga. Stalin deported these "Volga Germans" to Kazakhstan during World War II, and after the collapse of the Soviet Union in 1991 many of these Volga Germans fled "back" to Germany.[3]

The West has traditionally learned about Eastern Europe through German eyes—which means of course that the West has traditionally had a German bias in its view of Eastern Europe. This shows strongly for instance in how often the West has adopted German names for Eastern European cities. Warsaw derives from the German *Warschau* (VAR-show), while Cracow comes from the German *Krakau* (KRAHK-ow). Moscow (*Москва*; MOSK-vah in Russian) is *Moskau* (MOS-cow) in German. Prague in Czech is *Praha*, but in German *Prag*. Romania's capital is *Bucureşti* (Boo-coor-ESH-tee), but in German is *Bukarest*. The German imprint on Eastern Europe is apparent in modern-day English.

4. THE DAWN OF A NEW AGE 1600-1800
MOSTLY, A PRETTY BAD ONE, AT LEAST FOR EASTERN EUROPE

SUMMARY

This chapter opens with Eastern Europe being dominated by a few powers, the Polish-Lithuanian Commonwealth, the Ottoman Empire, Sweden, and the Habsburgs. The first two have increasingly powerful enemies, however, as well as some lingering internal political issues. By the end of this chapter, both will have been eclipsed by Russia, a new power in the region whose rise from obscurity is both an amazing and ominous tale. Europe in this period undergoes a huge transformation, beginning this chapter as feudal Christendom and ending as early modern Europe. But, alas, Eastern Europe will largely be excluded from these changes, remaining hopelessly mired in feudal social and economic conditions, in some cases well into the 20th century. The Ottoman Empire will take another stab at the conquest of Central Europe, laying the groundwork for the Islamic-Western confrontation that plays out still in our own times. Almost none of the Eastern European states we've examined so far will survive to see the next chapter.

CHAPTER GUIDE
A. Bohemia 162
B. Transylvania 166
C. Wallachia and Moldavia 168
D. Montenegro 169
E. The Swedish Empire 170
F. The Polish-Lithuanian Commonwealth 173
G. The Ukrainians and Belarussians 179
H. Ottoman Empire 183
I. Russia 186
J. Of Austrians and Habsburgs 192
K. Prussia 195

A. Bohemia

In the previous chapter we saw that Bohemia had effectively become Europe's first Protestant state with the legalization of Hussitism in 1437, and that the Habsburgs had inherited the Bohemian throne in 1526 when Ludvik II (Louis II, a Jagiellonian) perished at the Battle of Mohács against the Turks. These two events put Bohemia on a collision course with the most powerful dynasty in 16th and 17th century Europe. Things came to a head in 1618 when Bohemian aristocrats rejected the (newly elected) Habsburg Holy Roman Emperor,

Figure 39. Eastern Europe Timeline, 1600–1800

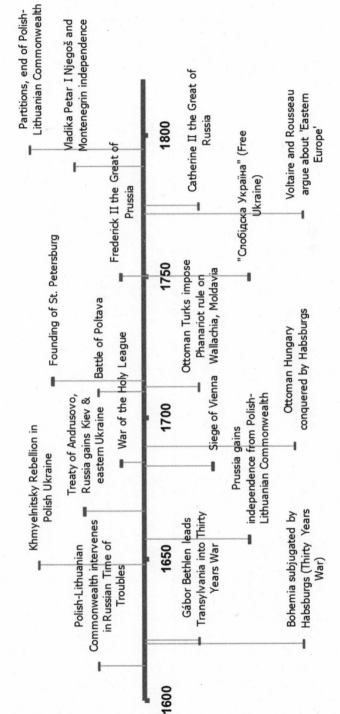

Figure 40. Comparative Western Europe Timeline, 1600–1800

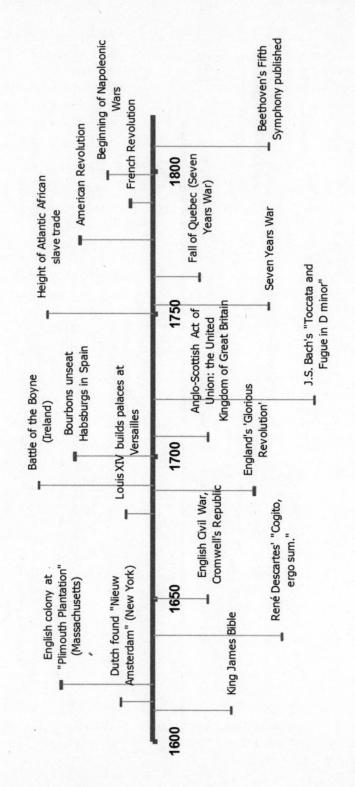

Ferdinand, as their king, and chose instead a Protestant prince, the German Elector Friedrich V of the Palatinate,1 in his place. Unimpressed, Ferdinand (now Holy Roman Emperor Ferdinand II) sent two envoys to Prague to straighten the Bohemians out, but when they arrived they were promptly tossed out the third storey windows of Prague Castle—though luckily both landed in a pile of horse "stuff" on the street and survived.[2]

USELESS TRIVIA: BEADS OF SWEAT!

If you've seen Native American folk art, you know that glass beads play a huge role. Sewn onto fabrics, clothes, and ceremonial items, beads are used by nearly all the Native peoples of North America, though the Plains Indians' art is most famous. Originally, Native artists used shells, coral, stones, metals, wood, or animal bones and quills for décor but when Europeans showed up with glass beads, Native Americans were mesmerized and they became a major trade staple for centuries.

The Dutch offered the Delaware Indians glass beads (among other offerings) to "purchase" Manhattan in 1626—but where did they get them from? In medieval Europe, glass beads were first made in Venice, but by the 15th century the Venetians began employing cheaper Bohemian laborers, many of whom brought Venetian methods back to Bohemia. Over time, Bohemian glassmakers arose as rivals to Venice and developed their own methods and styles. A majority of the glass beads Europeans brought to the New World in the 17th–19th centuries were from Bohemia, the most popular being *Sprengperlen* (German for "broken beads," or *Korálky* in Czech) and what were erroneously called "Russian beads." They were used by both Natives and American settlers as an inexpensive colorful décor for their clothes and homes. Bohemian glass is still made today in the Czech Republic.

The result was something we call the Thirty Years' War, in which Catholic and Protestant Europe fought each other viciously for several decades until both sides were exhausted and much of Central Europe lay in ruins. The first phase of the war began with Ferdinand II's invasion of Bohemia in 1618, culminating in defeat for the Protestant Bohemians at the Battle of Bilá hora (Bee-lah Hore-ah; "White Mountain") in November 1620. The Thirty Years' War continued on with Danish, Swedish, then French phases until 1648, but after 1620 Bohemia lay prostrate before Ferdinand's wrath. Most infamously he executed twenty-seven Bohemian Protestant noblemen in Prague's main square in 1621, but the Habsburgs' brutal revenge reached into every corner of the country. Bohemia, once a leading voice in the Holy Roman Empire, was reduced to the status of a Habsburg puppet kingdom until 1918.

Figure 41. Eastern Europe in 1625

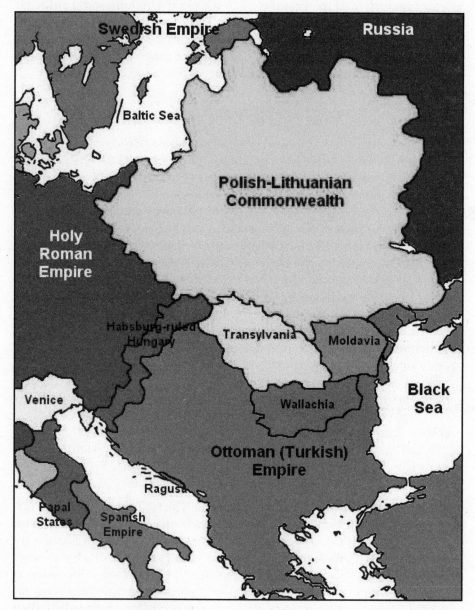

B. The Principality of Transylvania

After Hungary's defeat at Mohács in 1526, Transylvania was detached from defeated Hungary and ruled by the Turks, though often with Habsburg, Polish, and Wallachian meddling. The country was still led by its Hungarian aristocracy, with its cities dominated by "saxon" Germans and the countryside filled with Hungarian, Romanian, and other peasants. Under the rule of the Hungarian Báthory (BAH-tor-ee) family in the late-16th century, the Principality of Transylvania expanded northward to control about one-third of eastern Hungary, including what are today eastern Slovakia and western Ukraine.

In 1599, Transylvania was briefly conquered by the Wallachian ruler Mihai Viteazul, but after having him murdered in 1601, the Habsburgs took over and launched bloody anti-Protestant and anti-Orthodox pogroms across the land. In 1604, however, Hungarian nobleman István Bocskay (BOACH-keye) managed to eject the Habsburgs from Transylvania (which reverted to Ottoman vassal status), securing (relative) independence for Transylvania and sparing the land further religious strife.

USELESS TRIVIA: YOU CAN CHOOSE YOUR FRIENDS, BUT . . .

By all accounts, István Báthory (EESHT-von BAH-tor-ee; or *Stefan Batory* to Poles) (1533–1586), the Hungarian ruler of Transylvania and eventually the first king of the Polish-Lithuanian Commonwealth, was a genuinely nice guy who had it all together. He was intelligent, quite social, politically and militarily gifted, and a fair and moral man driven by strong Christian values. That's why it's so unfair he had Erzsébet (AIR-zhay-bet) Báthory as his niece, forever staining the Báthory name in history.

Erzsébet (Elizabeth) was Stefan's sister's daughter, and she was renowned for two things: first, her beauty, and secondly, the fact that she was a nutcase. She married a commander in the Habsburg army who set her up in a castle in Csejte (CHAY-teh), in Habsburg-ruled Royal Hungary (modern-day Čachtice [Chakh-TEE-tseh], Slovakia) while he left to battle Turks. Unfortunately, her husband died in 1604 while away at war, leaving Erzsébet alone in the castle. Well, for whatever reason, she snapped and began torturing and murdering dozens—possibly *hu*ndreds—of young Slovak peasant girls, and most gruesomely, draining their bodies to bathe in their blood. She was caught by Habsburg authorities in 1610, and bricked up alone in her bedroom as punishment. She was found dead in 1614. Despite this monster, the Báthory dynasty is remembered fondly in the region and Stefan Batory's tomb in Poland receives many admiring visitors and memorial flowers still today.

In 1613 Gábor Bethlen (GAH-bore BET-len) became Prince and ruler of Transylvania (with help from the Ottomans). When the Thirty Years' War began in 1618, Bethlen allied with the Protestants, and his armies fought in several campaigns in Habsburg Hungary, Bohemia, and Austria over the next few years. Some aristocrats saw Bethlen as the guy who could rejoin Habsburg Hungary, Ottoman Hungary, and Transylvania, effectively reuniting the old kingdom of Hungary and restoring its independence, but few would openly support Bethlen until he decisively defeated the Habsburgs. Unfortunately, poor coordination among the Protestant allies prevented exactly that, convincing Bethlen to make peace with the Habsburgs in 1626.

The Protestants enticed Bethlen to rejoin the war in 1629 but he died of natural causes before his armies could march. His successors in Transylvania, the Rákóczy (RAH-ko-tsee) family, for the most part stayed out of the rest of the war though Transylvania was a Protestant signatory at the Peace Treaty of Westphalia, ending the war in 1648. After György (JYOORJ; "George") II Rákóczy allied with Sweden and invaded the Polish-Lithuanian Commonwealth in 1657—which ended in disaster—the Turks reasserted their authority in Transylvania and put the Rákóczys on a short leash.

The sun really set on Transylvania's independence, however, with the War of the Holy League (1683–1699), during which Habsburg armies overran Ottoman Transylvania and Hungary, annexing both with the Treaty of Karlowitz in 1699. Ferenc II (FEH-rents; "Francis") Rákóczy led an anti-Habsburg uprising in 1703 in both Transylvania and Hungary that at first went well but was suppressed by 1711. The nonplussed Habsburgs expelled the Rákóczys, detached Transylvania from Hungary, and ruled it directly from Vienna.

C. Wallachia and Moldavia

The Ottoman Turks kept an eye on both Moldavia and Wallachia after the challenge from Mihai Viteazul in 1601, but they were both still ruled by native princes and had *some* control over their own affairs. That changed, however after an unsuccessful Russian invasion led by Tsar Peter I "the Great," which met defeat by Ottoman forces at the Battle of Stanileşti (Stan-EEL-esh-tee) in July 1711. The Turks reacted decisively: the complicit Moldavian prince, Cantemir (Kahn-TEH-meer), very wisely fled to Russia, but the Turks caught and executed the Wallachian prince, Brîncoveanu (Breen-ko-vay-AH-noo).

Both were quickly replaced by *Phanariot* rulers. The Phanariots were a class of wealthy Greek merchant families in the late 17th and 18th centuries who took their name from a district of Ottoman-ruled Constantinople called *Phanar*, a section of the city then still populated mostly by Greeks. Phanariots had made their wealth by cooperating with the Ottoman authorities and facilitating trade and banking throughout the Ottoman realm.

After the Russian invasion, the Turks banished native Romanian princes from positions of power in Wallachia and Moldavia, relying instead on the Greek Phanariot rulers who answered directly to Constantinople and had no local loyalties. It would ironically be a different group of Greeks working secretly with Romanian nationalists a century later who would help Romanians overthrow Phanariot power—but that's for the next chapter.

USELESS TRIVIA: EASTERN EUROPE MEETS THE CHESAPEAKE

Most Americans know the basic story of Captain John Smith, who helped establish and lead the first successful English colony in North America at Jamestown, Virginia in 1607. What few Americans know about Smith, however, is how he got the "Captain" bit. In the late-16th century, a young John Smith fled a dull craftsman's life in England for adventure, finding it in the form of a mercenary's life in Eastern Europe. Smith fought against the Ottoman Turks, first for the Habsburgs in Royal Hungary, then the Báthorys in Transylvania, and finally for Wallachia. It was the Habsburgs who bestowed the rank of captain on Smith for his valor. While in Wallachia, he beheaded three Turkish officers in a duel, and later had their severed heads depicted on his family coat of arms (which he carried later in Virginia). At one point he was captured by the Turks and sold off to Tartars as a slave, but he managed to escape Crimea back to England. Incidentally, a surviving inventory from the *Mary and Margaret,* a supply ship that arrived in Jamestown in October 1608, lists among its passengers "eight Dutch-men [i.e., Germans] and Poles," who were craftsmen hired to set up local industries. Indeed, records indicate that many Poles, Czechs, and other Eastern Europeans were brought to Virginia over the first few decades.

D. Montenegro

Ruled since the early-16th century by the *vladika*, the archbishop-prince, Montenegro continued as a pseudo-Ottoman vassal state into the 18th century, enduring both several Ottoman invasions as well as spasms of anti-Muslim hysteria, such as the great massacre of Slavic converts to Islam on Christmas Eve, 1709. The 18th century brought two important changes for Montenegro, however. The first was the discovery of an important ally against the Turks—namely, Russia, whose forces would help Montenegro achieve complete independence from the Ottoman Empire finally in 1789 under the legendary Vladika Petar I Njegoš (PAY-tar NYEH-goesh) of the Petrović (Peh-TRO-veetch) dynasty. The second was a gradual breakdown in the vladika's authority, as tribal blood feuds began to consume the country.

It would be left to Petar I's successors to finally create a modern-day state in Montenegro, though the Napoleonic Wars brought great suffering to the country and led to endemic internecine tribal warfare.

E. The Swedish Empire

In 1600, Sweden was a sparsely populated backwater, a quaint Scandinavian kingdom overshadowed by powerful neighbor Denmark. In 1523, led by Gustav Vasa, Sweden had won its independence from the Danish-dominated Union of Kalmar, a personal union (through the Danish royal family) between Denmark, Norway, and Sweden created in 1397. In revenge Denmark hobbled Swedish trade by limiting Swedish shipping in the western Baltic—and access to the wealthy ports beyond in Western Europe. In 1587 Swede Sigismund III Vasa was elected king of the Polish-Lithuanian Commonwealth, and when his father, King Johan (YO-hahn; "John") III Vasa died in 1592, Sigismund became king of Sweden, too.

The problem was that Sigismund was a Roman Catholic, and his ancestor Gustav Vasa had made Lutheranism the state religion in Sweden decades earlier. Sigismund promised to uphold Lutheranism in Sweden, but the Swedish aristocracy didn't buy it, and in 1599 his uncle, Karl (Charles), overthrew Sigismund as King of Sweden and eventually took the throne himself as Karl IX. This split in the House of Vasa led to decades of pointless wars between the Commonwealth and Sweden.

Karl IX began to modernize the feudal Swedish army, leaving his son with a powerful (though small) military force. His son became one of Sweden's greatest kings, Gustav II Adolf Vasa, known to Europe by the Latin version of his name—*Gustavus Adolphus*. He inherited the throne in 1611 when his father died, and his dad's army came in handy because while Denmark had effectively closed the western Baltic to Sweden, the eastern Baltic was wide open for exploitation and conquest.

Sweden, which already ruled Finland, launched a series of wars that resulted in the seizure of Estonia and Livonia (including Riga) from the Commonwealth and the Ingria region3 from Russia by the 1620s. After Danish defeat at Wolgast in 1629, Gustavus Adolphus entered the Thirty Years' War on the Protestant side, winning a series battles against Habsburg imperial forces until the King himself was killed in the Battle of Lützen in 1632.

Leaderless, the Swedish army was driven out of southern Germany by imperial forces until France entered the war in 1635 on the Protestant side. Swedish forces became infamous for laying waste to Catholic German areas, leaving a wide swath of destruction. When the war ended in 1648, Sweden gained western Pomerania from Denmark, and several German territories.

Though at the height of its power, the Swedish Empire in 1648 had been weakened by almost nonstop wars of conquest since the beginning of the century, thinning Sweden's already sparse population and taxing its economy, despite steady economic growth since the 1590s. Unfortunately, Sweden's first non-Vasa king, Karl X Gustav, continued the tradition of overseas wars by intervening in 1655 in the Polish-Lithuanian Commonwealth's Cossack rebellion that had broken out in 1648.

At first, Swedish armies achieved stunning successes and overran much of Poland4 and Lithuania—some Protestant Lithuanian aristocrats even tried to break Lithuania from the Commonwealth and join Sweden—but by the end of 1655 Commonwealth forces rallied and the fortunes of war turned. After a series of battlefield reversals, by 1659 the Swedes were completely driven from Commonwealth territory and the Commonwealth even sent forces to help Brandenburg and Denmark recover some territories from the Swedes. The Treaty of Oliva (*Oliwa* in Polish) in May 1660 ended the war with no border changes. Sweden's prestige and its finances were a shambles from the war.

Karl Gustav's son, King Karl X, fought brief wars in the Holy Roman Empire and against Denmark but largely focused on rebuilding his empire's economy, giving Sweden a needed respite. His son, however—Karl XII—used Sweden's resulting growing prosperity to build up the Swedish army and navy. This provoked Sweden's enemies to gang up in 1700, so that in the Great Northern War Sweden faced Russia, the Polish-Lithuanian Commonwealth, and its partner Saxony, and Denmark.

The allies did not coordinate their efforts, however, so that Karl was able to easily defeat a Russian invasion of Ingria at Narva in November 1700 before turning against first Denmark, then Saxony. Each was crushed, and when Karl turned against the Commonwealth, its aristocrats refused to support their Saxon king Augustus II (through personal union) and he had to flee for his life as Swedish forces chased him across Poland to Saxony in 1702. However, these victories had allowed Karl's remaining enemy, Peter I "the Great," and Russia to recover and reorganize Russian forces after the defeat at Narva.

Enlisting some cossacks led by Ivan Mazepa, Karl invaded Russia in 1707. But he suffered a series of defeats until meeting disaster at the Battle of Poltava in 1709. Karl fled the battlefield to the Ottoman Empire. The war dragged on in the form of naval battles until 1721—Karl died trying to invade Norway in 1718—but the Great Northern War broke the Swedish Empire. Sweden lost Ingria, Livonia, and Estonia to Russia, western Pomerania to Brandenburg-Prussia, and its remaining German territories to other German states. No longer a power in the Baltic region, a weakened Sweden fought a couple of wars with Russia later in the 18th century, losing territory each war, until finally losing Finland to Russia in 1809.

Figure 42. The Swedish Empire in 1650

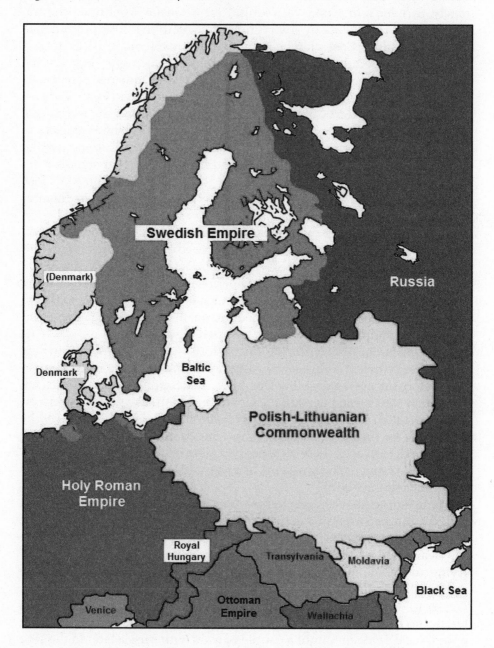

F. The Polish-Lithuanian Commonwealth

"You love liberty; you are worthy of it; you have defended it against a powerful and crafty aggressor who, under the pretence of offering you the bonds of friendship, was loading you down with the chains of servitude. Now, wearied by the troubles of your fatherland, you are sighing for tranquillity. That can, I think, be very easily won; but to preserve it along with liberty, that is what I find difficult It is in the bosom of the very anarchy you hate that were formed those patriotic souls who have saved you from the yoke of slavery."

—Jean-Jacques Rousseau, *Considerations on the Government of Poland and on its Proposed Reformation*; April, 1772[5]

"It is supposed that it was you, sire, who imagined the partition of Poland, and I believe it, because there is some genius in that."

—Voltaire, in a letter to Frederick II, king of Prussia; 1772[6]

If you're in reach of your stereo or computer at this point, I might suggest some good background music to this next section, which was actually composed for this period: Henryk Górecki's *Muzyka staropolska* ("Music of Old Poland," which is sometimes translated erroneously as "Old Polish Music"). It is very discordant and even a bit grating, but it does convey the power, pomposity, and yet structural chaos and frailty of the old Polish-Lithuanian Commonwealth. In any event, the Polish-Lithuanian Commonwealth's history can generally be divided into three periods: 1572–1648, when it was a leading power in Eastern Europe, politically, economically, and militarily; then 1648–1700, when it nosedived into a rapid decline and suffered multiple calamities—some external, others self-inflicted; and finally 1700–1795, when the Commonwealth existed as a mere shell of its former self, with widespread corruption, collapsing institutions, and frequent interference from foreign powers.

When Zygmunt II, the last Jagiellonian, died in 1572, the Commonwealth's nobility decided to elect a foreign king who had no local base of support. One of the first was the (Hungarian) Prince of Transylvania: István Báthory (or *Stefan Batory*, Bah-TOR-ee; as he's known to Poles), who proved a good steward of the Commonwealth and also was very adept at foreign policy as he worked closely with Sweden to defeat Ivan IV's Russia in the Livonian War. When Batory died in 1586, the Commonwealth's nobility chose a Catholic member of the otherwise Protestant Swedish royal family, the *Vasas* (VAH-zah; written in Polish *Waza*), whose dynasty would rule the Polish-Lithuanian Commonwealth for the next century, until 1672.

USELESS TRIVIA: THE RENAISSANCE IN EASTERN EUROPE?

Eastern Europe has a reputation for being backward and shrouded in a permanent cultural darkness, but did the European Renaissance somehow penetrate that darkness? In a word: Yup. The Renaissance (meaning, in French, "the Rebirth") was a rediscovery by Europeans of their Classical heritage, compelling them to study and emulate the ancient Roman and Greek arts (which focused on the human form and natural subjects, instead of the religious subjects favored by medieval Europe). Modern science and philosophy were born, as well as an interest in all things human. The Renaissance began slowly in northern Italy in the late-12th century, then spread over the next several centuries into northern Europe (France, Germany, the Low Countries, and Britain) and beyond. By 1400, nearly all of Christian Europe blazed with a new light of discovery, and our modern world grew out of that light.

The Renaissance did not skip Eastern Europe. It arrived both by foreigners—Italian, French, German, Flemish, Spanish, and other artists, architects, doctors, professors, poets, scientists, and others flooded Eastern Europe as wealthy Eastern European kings, aristocrats, churches, universities, and cities all paid for their services—and via Eastern Europeans who flooded the great universities of northern Italy, Germany, France, and Spain and brought their learned arts back to their home countries. Poland, Bohemia, and Hungary boast some of Central Europe's earliest universities, and most towns outside of the Balkans still bear some artistic imprint of the Renaissance, while schoolchildren today also learn about the likes of Renaissance men such as Jan Kochanowski, Weit Stoss, and Janus Pannonius.

One consequence of this choice was that it set the Commonwealth on a collision course with fellow (Protestant) Vasa-ruled Sweden, leading to a series of wars throughout the 17th century. In 1596, the Vasas moved the Polish capital from old, stuffy Kraków to prosperous and growing Warsaw. The first Vasa ruler, Zygmunt (TSIG-moont; "Sigismund") III, is most remembered for his meddling in the Russian "Time of Troubles" (see the Muscovy/Russian section of Chapter 3), invading Russia in 1609 and defeating the Russian army at Klushino in July 1610, then occupying Moscow for two years until Russian boyars organized a new army in November 1612 and drove Commonwealth forces out of Moscow. Polish-Lithuanian forces still held on to Smolensk, however, and fended off a Russian attempt to retrieve it in 1632–34.

USELESS TRIVIA: SPREADING OUT!

No Eastern European state ever took part directly in the European Age of Discovery or the Atlantic trade that exploded in the 16th and 17th centuries. Well, no Eastern European state, that is, *except one*.

After the Livonian War (1558–82), what is today modern-day western Latvia was ceded to Poland-Lithuania. The Commonwealth created the Duchy of *Kurzeme*, or Courland, and granted it wide autonomy. In 1641, Courland's most famous ruler, Jacob Kettler, became duke. Jacob was ambitious, and he established ship-building yards and local industries, along with mid-17th century Europe's largest merchant fleet. His ships sailed all over Europe, and under his reign, Courland's two major ports, Windau (VEEN-dow; modern-day Latvia's Ventspils) and Libau (LEE-bow; modern-day Latvia's Liepaja), became the busiest ports in 1650s Europe. But Jacob didn't stop there. He founded a Courland colony on the Caribbean island of Tobago, using this settlement as a trading port for ivory, gold, furs, and spices. In 1651, he also founded Fort Jacob on St. Andrews Island in the Gambia River in western Africa (modern-day Gambia), trafficking in a whole host of exotic African items (though not slaves). True to his Baltic German crusading heritage, Jacob also dispatched Lutheran missionaries to the Caribbean and Africa.

Courland had some tough neighbors, however, and in the midst of the war between Poland-Lithuania and Sweden in 1655–60, Jacob was imprisoned by the Swedes, while the English and Dutch seized his colonies in Africa and the Caribbean. The fort on Andrews Island—renamed James Island by the English—was transformed into a prolific slave-trading center. Courland was later absorbed by Russia.

The next Vasa, Władysław (Vwah-DIH-swahff) IV, took over the throne upon his father's death in 1632 and presided over both the Commonwealth's golden age and the beginning of its decline. Most of his reign was quite peaceful, but toward the end of his life, in 1648, Polish-ruled Ukraine exploded after decades of attempts by the Polish *szlachta*[7] and Catholic Jesuits to feudalize and Catholicize Ukraine's Cossack population. The Cossack rebels were led by the very competent commander *Bohdan Khmyelnitsky* (BOKH-dan Hmyel-NYEETS-kee; in Ukrainian *Богдан Хмельницький*).

The war went through several phases: the Cossack phase (1648–51), which ended at the Battle of Beresteczko (Bare-eh-STECH-ko) with Cossack defeat—but which provoked Russian and Swedish invasions. After near-collapse, the Commonwealth rallied and drove the Swedes out by 1660 (the Treaty of Oliwa), and the Russians by 1667 (Treaty of Andruszów [an-DROO-shoof] or *Andrusovo* in Russian). Prussia negotiated its independence from the Commonwealth in 1657 (Treaty of Wehlau; VAY-low) in exchange for its loyalty in the war against Sweden. In desperation, in 1672 the Cossacks negotiated an Ottoman intervention that the Commonwealth managed to fend off by 1676.

Although the Polish-Lithuanian Commonwealth emerged victorious and had driven all foreign armies from most of its soil—Russia grabbed eastern Ukraine, and the Turks held a fortress in southern Ukraine—its cities lay in ruins, the treasury was empty, its economy shattered, and a generation of the Commonwealth's best young men lay buried in graves across the country. The Commonwealth was a broken power.

After the abdication of the last Vasa, Jan II Kazimierz (John II Casimir), in 1672 the Commonwealth chose a hero from the war against the Turks, Jan (John) Sobieski (So-BYEH-skee), as King Jan III Sobieski. Sobieski was one of the last truly independent kings of the Commonwealth and one of its most famous—streets all across the Western world are named after him. His most famous exploit was to personally lead the Polish forces that came to the aid of the Habsburgs in September 1683, when the Ottoman Turks again invaded Central Europe and laid siege to Vienna.

After days of brutal infantry combat between the Turks and the Habsburg's allies, Sobieski himself led the cavalry charge that broke the Turkish lines and sent Ottoman forces in panicked retreat back into Ottoman Hungary. The Ottoman Grand Vizier's tent, complete with his wealth and titles of office, were abandoned in the chaos and can still be seen today on exhibit in Kraków, Poland.

But Sobieski then signed the exhausted Commonwealth up for the Habsburg-led project to liberate the whole Balkans of the Turks, and so in 1684 Poland-Lithuania joined the Habsburgs and Venice in the War of the Holy League (1684–99), though it could ill afford to, and the country gained nothing for its efforts.

USELESS TRIVIA: THE CONSEQUENCES HIDING
IN THOSE DUSTY HISTORY BOOKS!

So, the War of the Holy League (1684–99) is just another war in Eastern Europe's history, right? No shortage of those. Well, yes, but it did have some important consequences, even for us today.

On the lower end of the scale, there are legends claiming that coffee was introduced to Europe when the Allied armies surged into the abandoned Ottoman camp outside Vienna and discovered this Middle Eastern delight among the Ottoman supplies. This is unlikely, given that the Venetians and others had been trading with the Turks for centuries by 1683. One casualty of the war was the ancient Parthenon atop the Acropolis in Athens, which the Turks used for gunpowder storage; a stray Venetian cannonball hit it, there was a tremendous explosion, and the rest is history. Oops. But there were more important consequences. For instance, beginning with the War of the Holy League in 1684 the Serbian lands changed hands repeatedly in a series of Habsburg-Ottoman wars lasting until 1739 which led to a massive flight of Serbian refugees northward into the Habsburg domains. The Habsburgs resettled these Serbs along the border in Croatia, granting the refugees land in exchange for military service against the Turks. Called the *Militärgrenze* (Military Border), it was these Serbian enclaves deep in Croatian territory that revolted some three centuries later in the 1990s to "rejoin" Serbia.

A final impact of the war was on the Ottoman Empire itself. The Treaty of Karlowitz is a watershed in Ottoman history as the end of the period of Ottoman expansion (1350–1699) and the beginning of a long, painful period of Ottoman imperial contraction. In 1450, Ottoman armies were dreaded throughout Europe, but in 1683 they were facing very different European foes whose equipment, organization, and training far outstripped the Ottoman Empire's feudal military machine. The Muslim world reacted with dismay and fury at these humiliations, giving birth to two basic responses: those who sought to modernize, and those—like Muhammad ibn Abd-al-Wahhab (the 18th-century founder of the Wahhabist Muslim movement) who rejected modernization as de facto Westernization, instead seeking a return to a mythical ideal past of the early Arab empires. This debate still rages today in the Muslim world.

Sobieski[8] died in 1697, and from there on out, it was all downhill. The Commonwealth's nobility next chose a personal union with neighboring Saxony in the form of King Augustus II. He managed to get the Commonwealth involved in the Great Northern War of 1700–21, which essentially achieved its goal of destroying the rival Swedish Empire but also ended with Russian armies occupying Poland-Lithuania.

The Commonwealth was now a Russian puppet. The 18th century was a long period of sharp decline for the Commonwealth, not only of its former influence and power but in real economic and social terms as well. Its cities, once flourishing with trade from all over northern Europe, decreased in population and fell into decay.

The Russians did not always have to resort to the threat of arms to control the Commonwealth; many of the Commonwealth's nobility were happy to accept bribes from St. Petersburg for their votes in the *Sejm*[9] to produce laws absurdly advantageous to Russian interests. The Commonwealth's social institutions unraveled and disintegrated and the country slid into anarchy. 18th-century Europe came to see the Commonwealth as what we would call today a "failed state."

The inevitable happened in 1772 when Catherine II "the Great," Russian Tsarina, decided to drop the façade and just grab some of the Commonwealth's territory outright (with Prussia and Austria), in what became known as the First Partition. In 1791, under the leadership of Tadeusz Kościuszko (Tah-DAY-oosh Kosh-CHOOSH-ko), veteran of the American Revolution, the Commonwealth tried to reform itself into a constitutional monarchy, relying heavily on the model of the recently adopted U.S. Constitution (1787). The new constitution was passed on May 3, 1791, thereby giving modern-day Poland its national day.

The Russians, whose influence in the Commonwealth depended on the old, corrupt system, invaded in 1792, crushing Kościuszko's government and leading to the Second Partition in 1793 with Prussia. In 1794 Kościuszko led a mass uprising that initially achieved some impressive victories (such as at Racławice [Rah-tswah-VEE-tseh] in April, 1794), but the famous Russian General Viktor Suvorov (of later Napoleonic War fame) crushed the insurrection. In 1795, 226 years after its creation (and 409 years after the first Polish-Lithuanian union), the Polish-Lithuanian Commonwealth was destroyed by the Third Partition, which saw Lithuania, Belarus, and Polish Ukraine annexed by Russia, and Poland itself being divided between Russia, Prussia, and the Habsburgs.

USELESS TRIVIA: THE BENEFITS OF (SOMEBODY ELSE'S) BRAIN DRAIN!

As many Polish-Lithuanian nobles fled the First Partition in 1772, some found their way a few years later to the British colonies of North America, then in revolt against their mother country. One of the most famous was Kazimierz (Casimir) Pułaski (Poo-WAH-skee), who helped create the first American cavalry corps, and also helped standardize disciplined training of the new Continental Army. He fought in several battles of the American Revolution, including the battles of Brandywine and Charleston, and was wounded leading a cavalry charge in the Battle of Savannah in October, 1779, dying a couple of days later aboard an American schooner, *The Wasp*, in Savannah harbor.

Another famous refugee from the Commonwealth was Tadeusz (Thaddeus) Kościuszko (Tah-DAY-oosh Kosh-CHOOSH-ko), who upon arrival was appointed head engineer of Washington's army and became close friends with Thomas Jefferson. His military expertise contributed to the victory at Saratoga in 1777, and he helped design the fortifications for West Point. He left the American army in 1783 as a Brigadier General to return to Poland, where he became a national hero. He is buried today in Wawel Castle in Kraków, Poland, with full Polish—and American—military honors.

G. The Ukrainians

The term "Ukraine" was originally just a regional name, like Central America or Siberia, used at first to describe only the Dnieper River area, and it came from the Slavic word *kraj* (pronounced like "cry"), which means "region" or "country." "U-kraj-na" (Oo-CRY-nah; in Polish = *Ukraina*, in Russian = *Украйна*; in modern-day Ukrainian = *Україна*) meant something like "in the frontier lands" or "in the wild country." Although many Kieven Rus-successor states like Halych-Volhynia are often called "early Ukraine," Ukrainian history really begins with the Treaty of Lublin of 1569 between Poland and Lithuania, which created the Commonwealth. Prior to 1569, the Lithuanians had ruled Ukraine since the early-14th century, but Lithuanian rule was benevolent, allowing its Eastern Slav subjects wide autonomy.

A weakening Lithuania gave Ukraine to Poland in 1569, however, and the Poles—with their more developed feudal system—set out attempting to feudalize and Catholicize Ukraine. The Ruthenian (Eastern Slav) reaction to those efforts laid the foundations for a modern-day Ukrainian identity.

The land Poles were trying to feudalize—meaning great landowners created large estates and tried to force Cossacks and other free farmers to become peasants to farm them—was something like the American Wild West with outlaws, bandits, Ruthenian peasants, Tartars, Turks, Polish settlers, adventurers, and, ultimately, the Cossacks. Southern Ukraine, the Steppe region, was only tenuously controlled by the Poles, so convicts, slaves, rebellious impoverished peasants, and adventurers from all the surrounding territories in Europe and Central Asia as early as the 14th century made their way there to escape justice, poverty, or persecution.

They eventually established their own freestyle communities, called a *sech* (setch) (or, in Ukrainian, *sich*), which were like the Gold Rush towns of 1850s California: beyond the reach of any law, overflowing with vice, and extremely well armed. The larger seches banded together and formed disciplined military forces to raid neighboring Polish, Turkish, or Russian territory. The Turks called these raiders *qazaq* (guerillas), which became in Russian *kazaki* (*казаки*), which became in English, "Cossacks." The Cossacks became famous and fearsome horse-riding mercenaries (in the Steppe tradition) who were loyal to themselves alone, often allying with or against the Turks, Poles, Tartars, and Russians at different times.

The breaking point came in 1648, when the Cossack *Hetman* (leader[10]), Bohdan Khmyelnitsky, led his rebellion against the Commonwealth. Initially, Khmyelnitsky managed to drive Polish forces out of Ukraine, and in 1649, he returned triumphantly to Kyiv to a rapturous welcome by its Orthodox Ruthenian population. However, by 1651 Commonwealth armies returned and crushed the Cossack forces at Beresteczko (Bare-eh-STECH-ko). Refusing to accept defeat, Khmyelnitsky turned to Russia, signing in 1654 the Treaty of Pereyaslav, which effectively transferred rulership of Ukraine to Russia.

The Russian intervention initially brought relief to Ukraine, but the Commonwealth rallied and reversed the Russian military gains in the 1660s, leading to the 1667 Treaty of Andrusovo, which divided Ukraine between Russia and the Commonwealth. This infuriated the Cossacks, and their new leader Petro Doroshenko then negotiated an alliance with the Ottoman Empire in a bid to gain control of all of Ukraine. But the Commonwealth repulsed repeated Ottoman invasions.

When peace came in 1681, Ukraine was in ruins and still divided. The autocratic and absolutist rule of the Russian tsar also came as an unpleasant surprise for many Cossacks, and tensions grew in eastern Ukraine as Russian agents, bureaucrats, and soldiers flooded the land. Historian Timothy Snyder notes:

> The Cossack rising was grounded in the realities of the Commonwealth: while rejecting the inequality Polish institutions had created in Ukraine, it presumed the existence of rights that the Commonwealth protected.[11]

But if the Cossacks provided the underpinnings of Ukrainian political identity, another key player provided the cultural: the Ukrainian Orthodox Church, led in particular by Petro Mohyla (1632–47) and Sylvestr Kosiv (1647–57). In the late-16th century, there was an ill-fated effort on the part of the Commonwealth and some Ruthenian Orthodox clergy to counter the growing influence of the Russian Orthodox Church in Ukraine. Warsaw hoped to (re)connect Ukrainians to the Roman Catholic Church by letting them keep their unique rites and rituals in exchange for recognizing the Pope in Rome.

Known as the Union of Brest of 1596, these "Greek Catholics" or "Uniates" sparked a backlash as some Ruthenian clergy refused to break with the Orthodox Church and its head in Constantinople. This in turn inspired a major cultural revival among the Orthodox of Polish Ukraine throughout the 17th century, led primarily by Metropolitan Mohyla, followed later by Kosiv. When Khmyelnitsky marched triumphantly into Kijów (Kyiv) in 1649, Metropolitan Kosiv greeted him as a savior of Orthodoxy in Ukraine and in turn declared an independent Ukrainian Orthodox Church.

After the 1654 Treaty of Perejaslav, the Ukrainian Orthodox clergy surprised their Russian counterparts with the high level of education of their priests, who had sharpened their rhetorical skills through years of theological jousting with Polish Catholic Jesuits. This was not enough to save the church, however; very shortly after the 1667 Treaty of Andrusovo, the Tsar moved quickly to suppress the Ukrainian Orthodox Church and absorb it into the Russian Orthodox Church.

USELESS TRIVIA: YOUR PASSPORT, PLEASE!

Litwo! Ojczyzno moja! ty jesteś jak zdrowie.
Ile cię trzeba cenić, ten tylko się dowie,
Kto cię stracił. Dziś piękność twą w całej ozdobie
Widzę i opisuję, bo tęsknię po tobie.

(Lithuania! My Homeland! You are like my own health to me.
Your value as a treasure can only be appreciated
By those who have lost you. Today I am contemplating your great beauty
And singing your praises because I long for you.)

These are the opening words of Adam Mickiewicz's (Meets-KYEH-veech) epic 1834 poem *Pan Tadeusz* (Pahn Tah-DAY-oosh; "Sir Thaddeus"), which established Mickiewicz as one of the great classical Eastern European poets of the 19th century. Born in what is today Belarus, Mickiewicz was accepted by St. Petersburg literary circles but his politics got him in trouble with the Russian authorities and he fled abroad. He traveled Europe, befriending the great German writer Johann Goethe, and eventually settled in Paris where he taught university courses on Slavic literature. Always very conscious of Russian rule of his homeland, at the outbreak of the Crimean War in 1853 he tried to organize a brigade to liberate his homeland, but he died of cholera in 1855 in an Ottoman army camp. He was buried in Paris, though his body was moved to Kraków in 1900.

The question about Mickiewicz is *his identity*. Mickiewicz spoke and wrote in Polish as his native language, but many modern-day Lithuanians regard Mickiewicz—his name written as *Adomas Mickevičius* (Meets-keh-VEETCH-ee-ooss)—as a Polonized Lithuanian, who, after all, wrote about his *Lithuanian* homeland. Many modern-day Belarussians, however, refer to him as *Адам Міцкевіч* (Ah-dom Meets-KEH-veetch), and note that by "Lithuania," he meant the Grand Duchy of Lithuania, the Lithuanian half of the Polish-Lithuanian Commonwealth—which included Belarus, Mickiewicz's real homeland (according to Belarussians). So, was Mickiewicz Polish, Lithuanian, or Belarussian? The answer is that we can't really say, because Mickiewicz relied on an older form of identity that preceded our modern notions of ethnicity. There are many famous Eastern Europeans—Copernicus, Hunyadi, Stoss, Petőfi, Skanderbeg—who defy our modern notions of ethnic identity, though nationalists try to make them fit into modern identity molds like the proverbial square pegs in a round hole.

After the 1654 Treaty of Perejaslav, the Ukrainian Orthodox clergy surprised their Russian counterparts with the high level of education of their priests, who had sharpened their rhetorical skills through years of theological jousting with Polish Catholic Jesuits. This was not enough to save the church, however; very shortly after the 1667 Treaty of Andrusovo, the Tsar moved quickly to suppress the Ukrainian Orthodox Church and absorb it into the Russian Orthodox Church.

During the Great Northern War (1700–21), the leader of the Cossacks, Ivan Mazepa (Mah-ZEH-pah), rebelled against Russia when he felt St. Petersburg was disregarding Ukrainian interests, only to suffer defeat (along with his new Swedish allies) at the Battle of Poltava in 1709. Modern-day Ukraine honors him on its currency, but Mazepa's adventure convinced the Russians that even those seches who had remained loyal could not be trusted.

Distracted by events elsewhere, the Russians allowed Ukraine to develop fairly freely for the first few decades of the 18th century, a period remembered fondly by Ukrainians as "Free Ukraine" (Слобідска Україна; Slo-BEED-skah Oo-CRY-nah). But inevitably Tsarina Catherine II the Great abolished Free Ukraine in 1765 and its autonomous rights, making it a Russian province. Cossack leaders were opted into the lower ranks of the Russian nobility, while obstinate Cossacks who refused to give up their lifestyle were resettled in newly acquired Kuban region by the Sea of Azov. The remaining seches were forcibly dissolved, and all Cossack privileges were abolished. The resettled Cossacks along the Ottoman border became something more akin to the French Foreign Legion, a military organization tightly controlled by Russia and used in its wars throughout the 19th and 20th centuries. These latter Cossacks, however, while rugged and brave, had nothing of the freedom nor mobility of their ancestors, and they served only one master: the Tsar.

H. The Ottoman Empire

In Figure 43, you can see that the Ottoman Empire (the lands in vertical black stripes) in 1600 encompassed much of the Balkans, the Middle East, the lands around the Black Sea, and North Africa. In the 14th century, the Ottoman Turks had created one of the world's great military machines, which included the *Janissary* slave-soldiers whose strict regimented training and use of firearms was revolutionary. European medieval armies tended to be seasonal motley feudal collections of knights or aristocrats, mercenaries, and peasant conscripts who only stuck around as long as annual taxes could sustain them, after which they melted away. In the Janissaries, the Ottomans had created one of the world's first truly professional (and year-round) military forces, and they were devastating in battle. By the 17th century, however, Christian Europe was undergoing a big transformation, and its armies were becoming increasingly deadly foes for the bewildered Turks. As the Europeans struggled to manage their new vast and far-flung overseas colonial empires, they were forced to develop crucial improvements not only in military training and technology, but also in finance, logistics, and administration, in the process transforming medieval feudal states into modern-day countries. Despite its earlier ingenuity, the Ottoman state remained mired in feudal structures, fundamentally unable to change and frustrated by the obvious growing power of its enemies in Europe.

Figure 43. The Ottoman Empire in 1600, with Modern-day Borders

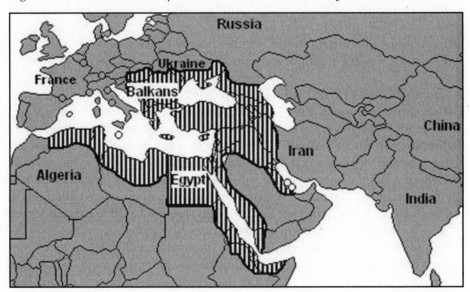

The whole mirage of Ottoman invincibility came crashing down in 1683, when Sultan Mehmed IV launched a massive invasion of Central Europe, a repeat of 1526–29, aiming to take Vienna and crush the Holy Roman Empire. (Ironically, the Turks were unaware that the Thirty Years' War of 1618–48 had devastated the Holy Roman Empire, and that it was no longer counted among the great powers in Europe.) Although most modern-day historians agree that the Ottomans were overreaching themselves, they still packed a powerful punch, and the Habsburg Holy Roman Emperor Leopold I fled the city before the Turks arrived.

This is why, in terms of feudal political protocol, Jan III Sobieski, as king of the Polish-Lithuanian Commonwealth, took over leadership of the allied armies at Vienna in the absence of the Emperor. In any event, the crushing defeat the poorly led Ottoman forces suffered at Vienna severely shook the Empire, but worse was yet to come. The victorious allies were not content to save Vienna. A long-standing project of many popes came to life, and allies lined up in 1684 to help drive the Ottoman Empire out of Christian Europe forever. Turkish defenses quickly crumbled in Hungary and Serbia under Allied assault, but over a few years' time the Ottoman forces recovered and reconquered most of Serbia, while repulsing Venetian advances in Greece. Still, by 1699 the Ottoman Empire was exhausted and forced to admit in the Treaty of Karlowitz that it had to cede territory—all of historic Hungary, conquered in 1526–40, as well as Transylvania and parts of southern Ukraine. For the first time, the Ottoman Empire had to accept the alienation of substantial parts of its empire to Christian *infidels*.

USELESS TRIVIA: WHEN FAILURE IS REALLY A BAD IDEA!

The Ottoman armies at the gates of Vienna in 1683 were led by the Sultan's Grand Vizier (sort of like a prime minister)—named, in this case, Kara Mustafa Pasha. Kara Mustafa had fought many battles in his career and dreamed of one day finally toppling that symbolic bastion of Christendom, the Holy Roman Empire. It was he who convinced Sultan Mehmed IV to launch the invasion in 1683 aimed at Vienna.

Kara Mustafa was overconfident, however. He thought Vienna would be an easy target for the mighty Ottoman forces, and in his arrogance he left his besieging armies woefully exposed. Commonwealth king Jan III Sobieski immediately saw the Ottoman force's vulnerability outside Vienna in September 1683, and he attacked, with decisive results.

Kara Mustafa himself was to pay the cost. After the defeat at Vienna and further defeats in northern Ottoman Hungary, Kara Mustafa fled to Ottoman Belgrade, where he set out scraping together another army. The Sultan did not suffer humiliation well, however. On December 25, 1683, three months after he had led the Sultan's armies to defeat and ignominy, Kara Mustafa was confronted by the Janissary leader in Belgrade with a green cord: the Sultan's pronouncement of the death penalty. Kara Mustafa quietly submitted to his own strangulation with that green cord, and his severed head was presented to the Sultan as proof the sentence had been carried out. He was buried quietly in Belgrade, though his tombstone was later moved to Edirne (in modern-day European Turkey), where you can still see it today.

Thus began a long era of self-examination in the Ottoman Empire, with many different voices arguing about why the Empire seemed to be in decline, and how to revive its fortunes (and its sacred mission as the beacon of the Islamic world). It had become apparent that the Sultan's armies were less and less a match for the infidels'. The advice fell into two general categories: those who advocated mimicking the West's technologies and military advances, and those who looked for answers in the other direction, backward to the distant past of either the early Ottoman state of the 14th century, or even the Classical era of 7th-12th century Arab empire(s).

These debates were not academic; the salvation of the Empire was at stake, and men from both camps were frequently imprisoned, ostracized, or murdered over the next two centuries. Strong-willed ministers began to eclipse the Sultan as the real power brokers in the Empire, leading to widespread corruption. With decline came frustration, and this was often vented against the Empire's non-Muslim minorities, particularly the Armenians and the Christians in the Balkans, in spasms of violence. But the Empire's problems weren't just military; the crucial East-West trade routes the warrior Ottoman state was just learning to master began to wilt away in the 17th century as Western Europeans had found more direct sea routes to the East. The Ottoman Empire's finances deteriorated as quickly as its military fortunes, adding further immediacy to the modernization debate.

> The Atlantic Ocean became the principal freeway of the trading universe that was fast becoming global in scope. First Spain and Portugal, then the Netherlands, France and England benefitted from easy access to the waters that carried European traders in all directions. The great losers in this geographic repositioning were the Italian city-states, the Turks, and other Muslims who had operated in the complex commercial network of the Indian Ocean.[12]

I. Russia

Russia looms large in modern European (and world) history, but in 1600 it was a relatively minor state. It was seen as exotic to many Europeans at the time, and it was developing trade relationships across Europe, but it did not figure in the great European power struggles of the 17th century. In Eastern Europe, Russia was overshadowed by its neighbors, the Polish-Lithuanian Commonwealth, Sweden, and the Ottoman Empire. The country had been brought to ruin by the disastrous reign of Ivan IV "the Terrible" in the late-16th century and the subsequent "Time of Troubles," leaving Russia weak and vulnerable to external enemies. And though later famous for producing stern autocrats, the first several Romanov tsars were actually fairly timid and weak.

USELESS TRIVIA: HOW MUCH HORSEPOWER HAS THAT THING GOT?

Both Poland and the Ottoman Empire saw a meteoric rise in their fortunes throughout the 16th century, but as their expanding borders and spheres of influence collided in the Balkans and Central Europe, rivalry all too often turned to war. In the midst of these wars the Polish nobility came to appreciate the strength, speed, and stamina of the Arabian horses used by their Turkish adversaries, so much so that they took to seizing them as war prizes from Ottoman forces whenever possible. By the mid-17th century, so many Arabians had in this way been brought to Poland that Poles began breeding their own stocks of Arabians. The Polish Arabian was born. The famous Polish winged hussars that swept the Ukrainian Steppe in the 17th century rode on powerful Polish Arabians. Though almost wiped out in the World Wars, the Polish Arabian bloodline continues still today. Polish Arabians are still carefully bred, raised, and trained in Poland though some strains of the bloodline also survive in Russia, the United States, and elsewhere. Polish Arabians are even exported to the Middle East nowadays.

In the 1590s, the late Tsar Ivan IV's infant son, Dmitry, had died while in the care of his regent, Boris Godunov—some say suspiciously—but during the Time of Troubles (after Godunov's brief reign as Tsar from 1598–1605), both the Polish-Lithuanian Commonwealth and Sweden produced candidates for the empty Tsarist throne whom they claimed were the "missing" Dmitry (called the "False Dmitries"), and both invaded Russia in an effort to support their candidates.

The Commonwealth managed to occupy Moscow from 1610 to 1612, but Russian boyars rallied and drove the Poles out in late 1612. The boyars were led by Mikhail Romanov, who became the next Tsar and whose family would rule Russia until 1918. The first few decades of Romanov rule were focused on rebuilding the country after years of civil war and foreign intervention, although Russia did intervene in the Commonwealth's own period of "troubles" during the Cossack rebellion that erupted in 1648, and managed by war's end in 1667 to walk away with eastern Ukraine, including the key city of Kyiv (Kiev).

USELESS TRIVIA: RUSSIAN AMERICA!

While many Americans are aware that Alaska was once a Russian colony, fewer are aware that the Russians once sparred with the Spanish for much of the Pacific coastline. The Spanish ventured as far north as the southern Alaskan coast, founding the settlement of Valdez (1790) in the process, while in turn, the Russians once staked a claim as far south as the northern outskirts of San Francisco (1812).

In the late summer of 1812, while most of Europe was distracted by Napoleon, and the British and Americans were both mired in a futile war, a small party of twenty-five Russians and some eighty Aleutian natives landed on the Californian Sonoma Coast, about two hours north of Spanish San Francisco, and founded what we today call Fort Ross. It is assumed the name "Ross" is a shortened and Americanized version of "Russia" in Russian (*Россія*; Ros-SEE-yah). The colonists were employed by the Russian-American Company (*Россійско-американская компанія*), founded in 1799 by the Russian government to coordinate commercial and colonial activities in the Russian American territories. The colonists of Fort Ross survived initially through the fur pelt trade, though waning stocks forced them to turn to farming. Relations with the local Native Americans were peaceful enough that soon many Russians opted to live outside the fort, and in 1828 an American traveler reported encountering some sixty Russians and eighty Aleuts living in the settlement. The Russian population at the settlement may have peaked at about a hundred, with another hundred fifty Aleuts and local Native Americans.

Alas, though successful, Fort Ross became increasingly untenable as the rather passive Spanish to the south soon gave way to the more aggressive Mexican Empire, while to the north the British and Americans, having buried the hatchet in 1815, were pressing to the Pacific Coast. In 1839, the colonists were ordered to abandon the settlement and head back to Sitka, the Russian capital of Alaska. The fort itself was sold to Swiss immigrant Johann Sutter—yes, *that* John Sutter, who later founded Sutter's Mill, which kicked off the California Gold Rush. Some of the fort's buildings have been preserved or reconstructed by the California state parks service, awaiting your visit. Alaska, of course, was sold by Russia to the United States in 1867.[13]

A major success story in 17th-century Russian history, little known in the West, is the conquest and settlement of Siberia. Early Novgorod in the 12th century was already pushing into Siberia, but its destruction by Muscovy at the end of the 15th century halted all eastward expansion for a century, until 1580, when Yermak Timofeyevich (YARE-mahk Tee-mo-Fay-yeh-veetch) managed to seize Isker, the capital of the Siberian Qaşlik (KOSH-leek) khanate. Almost immediately Ivan IV dispatched soldiers and settlers, and over the next several centuries Russians streamed into Siberia just as Americans did the American West in the 19th century.

By the mid-17th century there were already Russian settlements on the Pacific Ocean, and over the next several centuries various Russian governments sent scientific and exploratory expeditions throughout Siberia, creating a treasure trove of exotic ethnographic, geological, biological, botanical, topographic, and historical reading materials.

One of the most celebrated and famous of these explorers was the Dane Vitus Bering, who was sent on several expeditions in the early 18th century by the Russian government to explore the northern Siberian Pacific coastline (e.g., the Bering Sea), as well as Alaska and the Aleutian Islands. Of course, while a spectacular Russian success story, the conquest of Siberia was all too often disastrous for Siberia's indigenous peoples.

Peter I "the Great" is the first modern Russian ruler, and the tsar who transformed a regional Muscovite empire into a major power, and began Russia's long painful process of Europeanization. Peter traveled in 1697–98 throughout Europe (Sweden, northern Germany, Britain, Holland, and Austria) to study technologies and military advances, personally studying ship building, though he also hired Western experts along the way to accompany him back to Russia.

These newly acquired skills and expertise served Russia very well in the Great Northern War (1700–21), as initial defeats at the hands of the Swedes were reversed by Peter's reorganization of the army and construction of the first real Russian navy. Of course, having massive expanses of territory to retreat into also was very handy and gave Peter the time to carry out his military reforms, but nonetheless his efforts were rewarded with a decisive victory over the Swedes at the Battle of Poltava in Russian Ukraine in 1709. Sweden's King Karl XII abandoned his shattered army on the Poltava battlefield and fled into Ottoman exile.

Humiliated by the Swedes at Narva in November 1700 during the Great Northern War, Peter defiantly decided to build a new capital city near the battlefield, naming it St. Petersburg. He enlisted a platoon of the most famous architects and engineers in Europe, and conscripted Russian peasants, who died by the thousands from exhaustion, accidents, or disease during construction.

St. Petersburg was also Peter's chance to completely reshape Russian society, as he forced Moscow's old entrenched power elites to relocate to his new capital and adopt Western dress and customs, thereby beginning Russia's "Europeanization." For this reason, St. Petersburg has always been Russia's most cosmopolitan and Western-looking city, and for *that* reason, it has always been distrusted by Moscow as "foreign" and subversive. Construction began in 1703, and by 1712, enough of the government and nobility had moved there for Peter to declare it Russia's new capital, as it would remain until 1918.

USELESS TRIVIA: КУНТА-КИНТЕ!

Abraham Hannibal was born in 1688 in the region of Logon in what is today Cameroon, near Lake Chad in Africa. Hannibal was a prince, but this did not spare him from being captured by Arab pirates and sold into slavery. He was brought to Ottoman Constantinople, where he was sold to a Russian diplomat who took him home. In St. Petersburg, however, Tsar Peter came to like *Avram Petrovich Gannibal* (as he was known in Russian) and the Tsar even became his godfather, as Hannibal converted to Christianity. Peter sent Hannibal to France for an education, and when he returned, he became a general in the Russian army. Hannibal married and lived the rest of his life as a Russian nobleman.

More than a century later, Hannibal's great-grandson, still living in Russia, wrote of his African heritage: "'Tis time to quit this weary shore, / So uncongenial to my mind, / To dream upon the sunny strand, / Of Africa, ancestral land, / Of dreary Russia left behind. . . ." This poem was from one of his most famous published works, *Евгений Онегин* (*Eugene Onegin*). Alexander Pushkin wrote often of his African ancestry and frequently decried the cruelty and injustice of the African slave trade.

Peter I died in 1725—after catching pneumonia when he jumped into icy water to save drowning sailors—and thus began the new phase of Russian history, that of the *female* rulers. No less than four male Romanovs—Peter II, Ivan VI, Peter III, and Paul I—ascended the tsarist throne in this period, and all met with "unfortunate accidents"—unfortunately *fatal* accidents—within a couple of years, to be replaced (except for Paul I) by female members of the household who all had long, healthy reigns.

First came Anna (*Анна* I, 1730–40), then Elizabeth (*Элзбета* I, 1741–62), and finally Catherine (*Екатерина* II, 1762–96). These three tsarinas expanded Russia's borders and continued Peter's work of "Europeanizing" Russia while inserting Russia increasingly into European affairs, ultimately achieving for Russia a permanent seat at any discussion of the Great Powers in Europe.

Overwhelmingly, the most influential of these imperial ladies was Catherine II, who is known to history as Catherine the Great. She was actually born a German princess in the Brandenburg port city of Stettin (modern-day Szczecin, Poland), but went on to marry Russian prince Peter (who became Tsar Peter III in 1762). She became ruler herself when Peter was murdered by his own officers in July 1762 because he'd halted a successful campaign against Prussia to save his idol, Frederick the Great. Catherine immediately set about reforming the Russian legal code and modernized the military.

The Great Powers respected Russian military might, and Catherine ensured Russia's military kept abreast of the latest military technologies, strategies, and tactics. Russia's exploding population added to that might by allowing Catherine to field enormous armies, and the Russian "steamroller" legend was born. Catherine put those armies to use by grabbing Ottoman territory, crushing the Tartar khanate in Crimea in 1783, and carving up the ailing Polish-Lithuanian Commonwealth into three partitions with Prussia and Austria in 1772, 1793, and 1795. She also, rather like the 15th-century Hungarian king Mátyás Hunyadi who also had a weak legal claim to his throne, spent lavishly on public art, architecture, and universities, founding the Hermitage.

Catherine was also responsible for many of the spectacles modern-day tourists flock to St. Petersburg to see, such as the Winter Palace and the famous statue of Tsar Peter on a horse. Peter I built St. Petersburg, but it can be said that Catherine II in turn decorated and beautified it.

But Catherine's latter years were filled with a certain dread. Though she was considered by some French *philosophes*[14] as the ideal ruler and an enlightened despot, Catherine relied just as heavily as Peter I had on her absolute and unrestrained rule. In 1789, another monarch elsewhere in Europe, who also tried to rely on absolute rule, met with a nasty popular revolution that spread throughout the country and managed to overthrow the king.

The French Revolution scared the heebee-jeebies out of Catherine, because, well, if *French* peasants thought they had something to complain about, what would *Russian* peasants say about the brutal Russian serf system? Russia already had a long tradition of Russian peasant uprisings, and indeed Catherine had even faced one of the worst of them, the Pugachev Rebellion of 1773–74, but the French Revolution was better organized, reached down to the deepest levels of French society, and worst of all—it had *succeeded*. Catherine died in 1796 before she was able to more effectively deal with the French revolutionaries, but she set the tone for Russia's hardcore reactionary role in Europe over the next century.

USELESS TRIVIA: NOT THE CALYPSO . . .

Catherine, following in the steps of Peter I, built up the Russian navy, and her efforts bore fruit in her wars against the Ottoman Empire on the Black Sea. However, this new navy, combined with her astute diplomatic skills, also helped establish a concept readily accepted in international law today. In the late-18th century, Britain was the star of the Great Powers, and its navy was considered unbeatable. The problem was Britain's irritating habit of seizing neutral vessels trying to trade or enter the ports of Britain's enemies, so in 1780, during the American Revolution, Catherine took the opportunity to form the *League of Armed Neutrality* with Denmark, Sweden, the Netherlands, Prussia, the Holy Roman Empire, the Kingdom of the Two Sicilies, and the Ottoman Empire. The League demanded that Britain respect the rights of neutral ships in times of war (so long as they carried no contraband), and threatened to retaliate together if any one member country's ships were attacked by the British. London grudgingly accepted the League's tenets, and over time, and with some tinkering, the basic rights laid down by Catherine have become embedded in modern-day international law.

J. Of Habsburgs and Austrians

The history of Austria is a bit confusing because it is so strongly associated with the Habsburgs, a powerful medieval family dynasty who eventually came to rule Austria. Austria, as we saw in Chapter 1, started out as an eastern outpost for Charlemagne's Frankish Empire and came under the control of the Babenberg dynasty in the 10th century, which died out in the mid-13th century. After a brief period of Bohemian control, Austria was taken over by the rising Habsburg family as Rudolf I (Habsburg) became Holy Roman Emperor in 1278. Still, for most of the next several centuries, Austria was not a significant player in European affairs, at least not until the late-17th century.

Figure 44. Eastern Europe in 1750

The Habsburgs originated from a small region called Aargau along the modern-day Swiss-German frontier, and made the big time when Rudolf succeeded to the Holy Roman Empire's highest throne in the 13th century. After that, the Habsburgs rapidly gained both lands and power. The largest aristocratic family dynasties in medieval Europe like the Luxembourgs, Hohenstauffens, Anjous, and Habsburgs were often more powerful than countries, and in fact they often *owned* several countries, ruling far-flung empires they gained control of through marriage, conquest, back-room deals, or laberynthine contracts based on very foggy medieval succession laws.

Using these methods, the Habsburgs managed by the early-16th century to briefly amass a vast European empire under the control of their greatest leader, Emperor Charles V: the Holy Roman Empire (including Austria), Bohemia, (Royal) Hungary, Croatia, Spain, the Netherlands (which included Belgium), Lombardy, Sicily and southern Italy, Luxembourg, and parts of eastern France.

For forty years Charles ruled over all these lands but when he retired in 1556, he—by previous agreement—divided his empire in two, giving half to his son Philip and half to his brother Ferdinand. Philip got Spain, the Netherlands, and the Italian and eastern French lands, while Ferdinand became Holy Roman Emperor and retained Austria, Bohemia, and Royal Hungary. From that point on there were *two* Habsburg empires, one centered on Spain and one centered on Austria (creating the *Spanish Habsburg* and the *Austrian Habsburg* lines), though the two cooperated closely. Philip—known as King Philip II—later managed to add Portugal to his empire, though his attempt to subdue England in 1588 didn't go so well. Ferdinand meanwhile made some changes to the Holy Roman Empire to make sure the Habsburgs kept it in the family *indefinitely*.

Figure 45. Charles V's Habsburg Empire, c. 1550

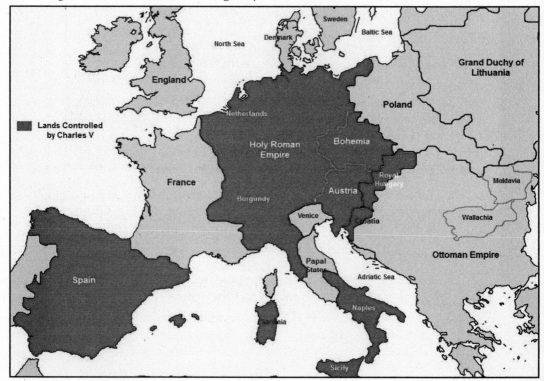

Austria initially posed a problem for the Habsburgs. When they made Vienna the seat for the growing Habsburg empire in the 15th century, Austria was only an *archduchy*—a rank above a regular duchy—which meant that Austria was a fairly low-ranking state with no voting rights in the Holy Roman Empire. The problem was solved when the Habsburgs inherited Bohemia and Hungary in 1526; Bohemia was already a full kingdom in the Holy Roman Empire with all attendant voting rights. The Austrian Habsburgs may have been humbled in the Thirty Years' War (1618–1648), but afterward Austria's wealth and population flourished, while Bohemia and Hungary, once wealthy and powerful medieval kingdoms, sank into poverty and isolation.

Lowly ranked though it was, Austria became the Habsburg's star possession and its star rose even higher when the Spanish Habsburg line went extinct with no heirs in 1700 (giving Spain to the French Bourbon dynasty). In 1740–48 a Habsburg succession crisis led to a worldwide war (the War of the Austrian Succession) the Habsburgs just barely survived,[15] kicking off a century-long Austro-Prussian rivalry. In the 18th century the Habsburgs spoke vaguely of an "Austrian empire," but that name only became official after Napoleon dissolved the Holy Roman Empire in 1806 and Habsburg emperor Franz II suddenly needed an empire—hence, the Austrian Empire. The *Ausgleich* (Compromise) of 1867 with Hungary's aristocrats then gave birth to the "Austro-Hungarian Monarchy," as it was officially known.

K. Prussia, Brandenburg, and the Holy Roman Empire

Do you remember that quote I used from the 19th-century Austrian foreign minister Metternich in the FAQ, about Asia beginning at the *Landstraße* (Provincial Road) at Vienna's eastern gate? (See the question, "What is Eastern Europe?") That one gets tossed around Eastern European histories quite a bit and is well known, but there's another one that shows that even some western Germans considered their eastern brethren to lean a bit toward the side of the Asiatic barbarian hordes. Konrad Adenauer, the West German chancellor of the 1950s who rebuilt West Germany from the ashes of World War II, was in the 1920s a deputy in the Prussian territorial legislature, a provincial legislature. Though Adenauer was a native Rheinlander, his home region had long been incorporated into the Prussian-Brandenburg state and remained so under the German Weimar republic. During infrequent but necessary trips to Berlin, Adenauer supposedly muttered each time the train crossed the Elbe River eastward, *Und hier beginnt Asien* (And here begins Asia).[16]

In 1594, decades after the Teutonic Knights had fled Prussia, Anna Marie of Brunswick-Lüneburg, (whose father was the regent duke of

Polish-ruled Ducal Prussia), married her cousin—blech!—Johann Sigismund of the Hohenzollern family. Johann was already the Elector (ruler) of Brandenburg, and so when in 1618 Anna's father died, Johann Sigismund suddenly found himself the ruler of both (Polish) Ducal Prussia and Brandenburg. From 1618 until obliteration in 1945, the fortunes of Prussia and Brandenburg were united, until 1918 under the Hohenzollern dynasty.

In the 17th century this united state was called "Brandenburg-Prussia" but after Prussia achieved its independence from the Polish-Lithuanian Commonwealth in 1657 (which Prussia negotiated in exchange for its loyalty to Warsaw in the 1654–60 Swedish invasion of the Commonwealth), it became known simply as "Prussia," though the Hohenzollerns were from Brandenburg and the united lands' capital, Berlin, was Brandenburg's capital. (Prussia's—later East Prussia's—capital was at Königsberg.)

Despite being the senior partner in the union, Brandenburg was in the Holy Roman Empire, which meant that its ruling family, the Hohenzollerns, could never achieve a status higher than Electors. However, Friedrich (Frederick) I of Hohenzollern was upgraded from Duke of Prussia to King in 1701; by emphasizing the Prussian side of their state, the Hohenzollerns managed to get themselves upgraded to royalty.

Prussia in the 18th century began to grow, especially under *Friedrich II die Große* (Frederick II "the Great"), who seized Silesia from the Habsburgs in the Silesian War (1740–42) and the War of the Austrian Succession (1740–48) but faced disaster in the Seven Years' War (1756–63)[17], only to emerge as a major European power.

Though ruled by kings, Prussia strangely remained a duchy until 1772, when it finally caught up to its rulers and became a full-fledged kingdom. One of its first acts in its new incarnation was to turn the tables on Prussia's old master, the Polish-Lithuanian Commonwealth, participating in the three Partitions (1772, 1793, 1795) of the Commonwealth with Russia and the Habsburgs. This gained Prussia old "Royal Prussia" (as well as a lot of other Polish territory) on the Baltic shore, finally linking Prussia directly by land to Brandenburg. This in turn led to the creation of *East Prussia*— all of Prussia to the east of Elbing (modern-day Elbląg, Poland) and the Nogath River—and *West Prussia* wedged between eastern Pomerania and East Prussia.

Prussia's fortunes in the coming Napoleonic Wars would reach disastrous lows with several major battlefield defeats and humiliating treaties with Napoleon, but would ultimately see Prussian armies taking part in the occupation of Paris in 1814 and the defeat of Napoleon at Waterloo in 1815—in the process giving birth to modern-day German nationalism.

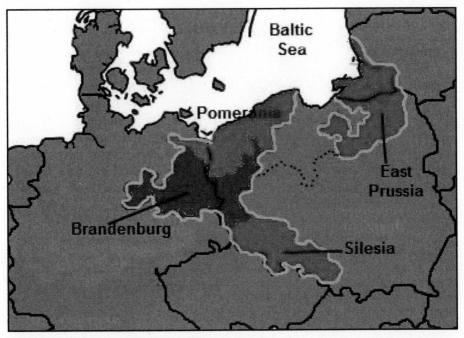

Figure 46. Prussia and Brandenburg in 1750

One last note on Prussia, however: the emphasis in histories is usually on Frederick the Great's military feats, and indeed they are central to Prussian history. An early-19th century East Prussian Minister, Friedrich von Schrötter, once quipped, "Prussia was not a country with an army, but an army with a country." However, Frederick II ("the Great") was actually surprisingly liberal on many social issues of his day. He provided a refuge for French Protestants fleeing persecution in Catholic France. Indeed, he welcomed immigrants from all across Europe. (A century later, Otto von Bismark would try to reverse Frederick's generous immigration policies by "purifying" and *Germanizing*—albeit via bureaucracy rather than force—Prussia's many ethnic and religious minorities.)

Frederick also abolished the use of torture, established an independent judiciary, and created one of the first universal education systems. In the Seven Years' War, at the Battle of Kolin (modern-day Kolín, Czech Republic) in June 1757, a dismayed Frederick infamously shouted at his routed and fleeing soldiers, "Wollt ihr denn ewig leben?" (Do you want to live forever?), earning Frederick the reputation of a warmonger—but he ran one of 18th-century Europe's most liberal and, in many ways, most humane governments.

USELESS TRIVIA: LUNCH IN THE HALLS OF MORIA?

In May 2009 the Japanese survey firm Tokyo Shoko Research Ltd. (TSR) compiled a list of the oldest companies in the world and found after reviewing some 1,975,620 companies that 21,666 of them in 2009 were at least a hundred years old. The oldest continuously operating company in the world in TSR's survey was Kongō Gumi, a 1,433-year-old Japanese construction company founded in 578 CE.

Eastern Europe, with its turbulent history, makes a weak showing in the TSR list but it is not completely unrepresented. Ranking as the world's 14th-oldest company is *Kopalnia Soli "Wieliczka" S.A.*, the Wieliczka (Vyeh-LEETCH-kah) Salt Mines,[18] located just south of Kraków, Poland. Before refrigeration, salt was the only way to preserve meat and fish, so it was a prized (and expensive) commodity in medieval Europe; Wieliczka made its owners rich. The mine had already been known for centuries as (in Latin) *Magnum Sal*, "the Great Salt," by the time a management company was formed in the 1290s. Salt mining halted in 2007, but the Wieliczka mines are famous for another reason, as miners—trapped miles below the surface—took to carving in the soft salt, and over time they carved a plethora of historical and religious figures, and even whole rooms: chapels, banquet halls—and, all told, some thirty-two chambers. Modern-day sculptors continue the tradition still today and Wieliczka hosts tourists, concerts, and weddings in its elegant halls.

Great Hall of the Wieliczka Salt Mine (Image © Vlad Ageshin / Shutterstock)

PEOPLES OF EASTERN EUROPE: THE GYPSIES

Kana e gadje mukhle penge vurdona te traden mobilia, progreso akharde les. Kana e Rroma vi kerde kodo, bari mila akharde les.

("When the *gadje*[1] replaced their wagons with automobiles, they called it progress. When the Roma did the same thing, they called it a pity.")[2]

—Dr. Ian F. Hancock[3]

Gypsies are certainly one of the most misunderstood and marginalized peoples of Eastern European history, in part because of their persistence in living a nomadic lifestyle that leaves them largely outside of settled Europe's established political and economic structures. Their lack of association with any state also left them vulnerable and easy victims of the many historical waves of social/class, economic, or religious violence that have periodically swept Europe. These days Gypsies are becoming more politically savvy and organizing more effectively to represent their interests to the various governments of Europe, and the EU's rules on minority rights have also fostered a sort of Gypsy cultural renaissance, but to say the Gypsies' problems of discrimination are over is to be jumping the gun indeed.

To confuse matters, there are some groups who are sometimes called Gypsies but that actually have very different origins than the Gypsies of Central and Eastern Europe. For instance, the Tinkers or Travellers of the British Isles are sometimes called Gypsies but their origins are believed to be more local. Many Gypsies across Europe today call themselves "Roma" or "Romany," and a language related to the ancient Sanskrit of northern India—also called "Roma"—is increasingly becoming recognized as the language of Gypsies. There are actually many different groups of Gypsies, though, some with their own languages—for instance, the *Béás* (BAY-osh) of eastern Hungary or the *Sinti* in Germany and Austria—but increasingly Gypsies are organizing to have one voice in Europe.

It is believed (i.e., we're not exactly sure) that Gypsies originally entered Europe sometime in the Dark Ages, perhaps closer to 800 CE, after a journey from northern India through Persia (Iran) and Anatolia. The Roma language, many cultural traits of Gypsies, and their darker skin complexions lead most historians to assume they derived from northern India, though why they migrated to Europe is not known. One theory is that they were once lower-class Hindus who were pressed into military service during the Muslim era of military expansion (c. 615–1200) in India and ended up on the doorstep of the Byzantine Empire in that way. The English name "Gypsy" likely derives from the mistaken medieval belief that they had originated in Egypt. The Byzantines applied the Greek term

Ατσιγγάνοι (Ah-TSEE-gahn-oy; meaning traveling entertainers) to the Gypsies, and this term stuck for most Eastern Europeans: in Hungarian–*Cigány* (TSEE-gahn), in Polish–*Cygan* (TSIH-gahn), German–*Zigeuner* (TSEE-goy-ner), Russian–*Цыган* (TSIH-gahn), and so on.

Though Gypsies came to be known in every country of Europe, medieval xenophobia pushed many of them out of Western Europe (like Jews) and so, to this day, the majority of Europe's 8-10 million Gypsies—their exact numbers are always in doubt—are in Eastern Europe. Bulgaria, Romania, Hungary and Slovakia in particular have the largest populations. Numbers are hard to nail down exactly, in part because the relatively nomadic lifestyle of some Gypsies makes it hard for governments to keep track of them, even in those cases when a government actually makes much effort to do so; indeed, the fact that some governments don't go out of their way to this end also hinders accounting for Gypsy populations. A third factor is that, because of traditional (and sometimes well-founded) distrust of governments, many Gypsy communities have become experts at circumventing authority and operating beneath official state radar.

Like the Celts and early Nordic Scandinavians, Gypsy culture is often highly romanticized today in the West, and indeed a visit to certain restaurants in Hungary or Romania will help feed those romanticizations with a burly and dark-skinned Gypsy wearing a black leather vest and playing his violin for enraptured tourists. The 1993 pseudo-documentary (and music-video–like) film *Latcho Drom* helped perpetuate that romantic sense of Gypsy culture, but the ugly reality for the overwhelming majority of Gypsies today is grinding poverty with all its trappings—endemic crime, low life-expectancy, rampant drug abuse, widespread teenage pregnancies, and shockingly low levels of education.

The challenge, of course, is how to aid an outcast community like the Gypsies, many of whose members prefer an existence outside of established state institutions. The answer is coming increasingly from within the Gypsy communities themselves, as community leaders are recognizing the need for education and political engagement with governments, national as well as the EU, to do something about their plight. Still, there is much to do, and stories of police mistreatment of Gypsies or local community-Gypsy tensions throughout Europe are sadly still common even in more developed countries like Slovenia and the Czech Republic.

Gypsy history is difficult to relate because, again, Gypsies have usually existed outside of established political and social orders. Of course, no group of people can live completely separate from a surrounding community, and intermarriage has been a fact of life in Europe for centuries; and so there are many people across Europe and North America today—including artists, actors, politicians, and scientists—who have at least a partial Gypsy heritage, acknowledged or not. Still, the Gypsies have been along for the ride as Europe, and particularly Eastern Europe, has wandered down its twisted and jagged historical path.

Perhaps the most salient and powerful term in modern Gypsy history is *Porjamos* (The Devouring), referring to the not so well known Nazi genocide against the Gypsies in 1939–45. Again, exact numbers are lacking, but an estimated one million Gypsies were murdered by the Nazis, often with even less resistance or aid from their host communities than Jewish deaths evoked. Scholarship on this attempt to liquidate the Gypsy peoples in Europe is still today only sporadic and in its infant stages.

After the war, most of the communist governments in Eastern Europe attempted to "solve" the "Gypsy problem" by forcing Gypsies to settle in fixed communities and attempting to forcibly assimilate them into mainstream society. Their children were forced to attend school, while the parents had to take up "normal" residences and jobs. Perhaps predictably, these housing centers quickly became impoverished and dilapidated nuclei for crime and segregation.

On the other hand, one has to wonder if at least some of the leaders of today's Gypsy communities, who are leading the charge to organize political parties and interest groups to lobby for Gypsy interests, may not have been born of these attempts at forced assimilation. They can move in and understand both worlds, and their communities are benefiting for the first time from such experience and knowledge. Their impact is being felt across Eastern Europe; in Hungary, for example, the Hungarian Academy of Sciences—which since the 19th century has had several ethnography specialists dedicated to the study of Native American cultures and histories—only established its first Gypsy studies programs in the early 1990s, though Gypsies comprise almost 10% of Hungary's population. Change is coming, if slowly.

5. THE VERY, VERY LONG 19TH CENTURY 1800–1914

"When we condemn those mistakes and consider ourselves released from them, then we have not overcome the fact that we are derived from them."
—Friedrich Nietzsche, *The Use and Abuse of History*

SO THIS IS WHAT ROCK BOTTOM IS LIKE

PROLOGUE

Historians call this period the "long 19th century," because Europe had developed (after the French Revolution and Napoleonic wars) a view of the world that would last, albeit somewhat changed, well into the 20th century, until they met a very different reality—a reality we call "World War I." But while World War I seemed shocking and out-of-the-blue to people at the time, we can now look back and see that 19th century Europe was like a red-hot pressure cooker on simmer for a century, ready to blow. The 19th century was about how Europeans reacted to that building pressure.

The century for Europe can be broken into two parts, the first being 1815–48, when Europe was still reeling from the Napoleonic wars. The second would be the rest, from the revolutionary year of 1848 to the disaster of 1914. In the first half of the 19th century, the great European powers were obsessed with preventing another continent-wide war. In the second half, European governments were as much focused on whether their own peoples would rise up against them as what other countries did.

In 1800, Eastern Europe was ruled for the most part by four empires: the Prussian (later German), Russian, Austrian, and Ottoman. The latter two were just struggling to survive. The Balkans would be the first in Eastern Europe to emerge with independent nation states, but only partially fulfilled territorial aspirations gave birth to a plethora of terrorist groups in the late-19th and early-20th century. They cut a bloody swath of assassinations and violence across the Balkans, threatening the Great Power order in Europe. Central Europe, denied what the Balkans had already achieved, also began to simmer. The 19th century was a century of *change*, for Eastern Europeans no less than for the rest of Europe.

A. Introduction 203
B. The Ottoman Empire as Doorstop 208
C. Serbia's Front Row Seat 213
D. Montenegro Hits the 19th Century 218
E. Romania is Born 218
F. Bulgaria's Raw Deal 222
G. Albania as Accident 225

H. *The Italian Risorgimento and Irridentism* 227
I. *Pan-Germanism and How Fritz (and Helga) Got Their Mojo* . . 228
J. *Pan-Slavism and Pie in the Sky* 231
K. *The Austrian Dilemma and Hungary* 233
L. *Russia, the Hope and Prison of Nations* 240
M. *Dawn of the Dead: The Poland That Just Won't Go Away* . . 247

A. Introduction

The 19th century was a revolutionary century in many ways, and was very different from its predecessors. In the 21st century we are used to constant change, but in the 19th century average people across Europe, who were essentially living the same way their ancestors had for centuries, began to feel the social and economic rugs pulled from beneath their feet.

Figure 47. Eastern Europe in 1800

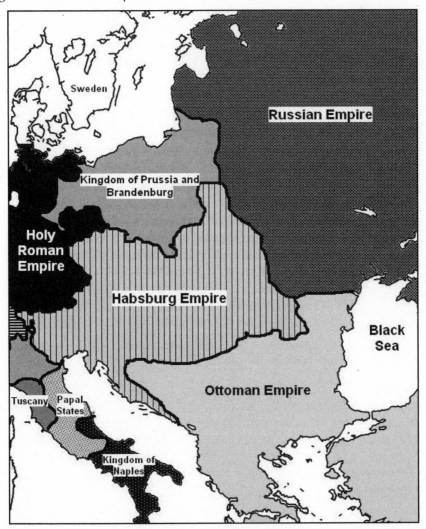

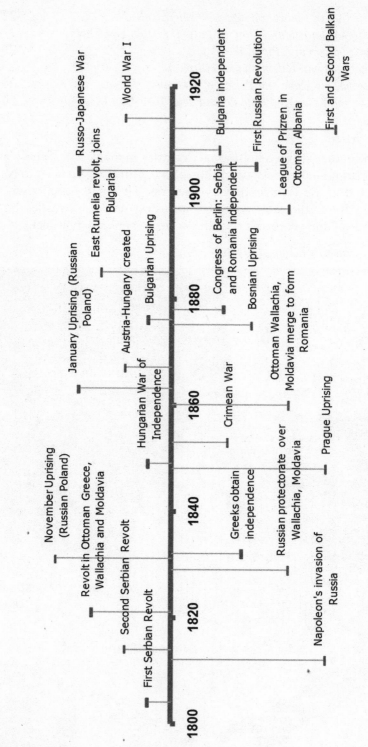

Figure 48. Eastern Europe Timeline, 1800–1914

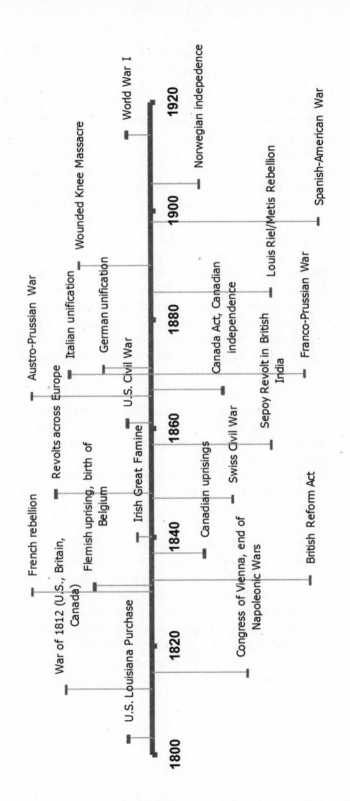

Figure 49. Comparative Western Europe Timeline, 1800–1914

It all started with the French Revolution of 1789–92, and the stubby little Corsican artillery officer who managed to hijack it and have himself proclaimed emperor. The Revolution and Napoleon shook Europe to its core as both strove not just to replace kings but completely reorganize Europe's society from the bottom up. When Napoleon finally met his Waterloo at, well, Waterloo in 1815, Europe's rulers—all looking like deer in the headlights—sat down to a meeting in Vienna to redraw borders and ensure that never again would popular revolt threaten their regimes. They succeeded in creating a system that more or less kept the peace among the Great Powers for a century, until 1914—and that's a pretty good record, as far as peace efforts go. But they failed to address the *reasons* Europe's peoples were becoming increasingly restless, and the result was a plethora of extremist movements (e.g., anarchism, socialism, and nationalism) as well as a growing tide of terrorism and anger with the slow pace of change. It was a century, unlike any other, of peoples pitted against their governments.

The 19th century was all about change—whether it was embraced or resisted. These changes were primarily driven by such new phenomena as romanticism, nationalism, and the industrial revolution. With entrenched ruling elites refusing to acknowledge the plight of common people, revolutionary furor spread rapidly. The big year came in 1848, as we'll see in more detail later, when revolutions broke out simultaneously all across the continent, nearly toppling some governments and leading to lots of bloodshed. Most of these were suppressed quickly, but the rest of the 19th century was filled with political assassinations, terrorist bombings, and revolutionary agitation in almost every country. As *The Economist* once noted, though many people today see *our* age as one of unprecedented uncertainty and violence, folks in the later 19th century would have been right at home in this atmosphere:

> BOMBS, beards and backpacks: these are the distinguishing marks, at least in the popular imagination, of the terror-mongers who either incite or carry out the explosions that periodically rock the cities of the western world. A century or so ago it was not so different: bombs, beards and fizzing fuses. The worries generated by the two waves of terror, the responses to them and some of their other characteristics are also similar. The spasm of anarchist violence that was at its most convulsive in the 1880s and 1890s was felt, if indirectly, in every continent. It claimed hundreds of lives, including those of several heads of government, aroused widespread fear and prompted quantities of new laws and restrictions.[1]

USELESS TRIVIA: MARRIAGES OF CONVENIENCE!

The 19th and 20th centuries saw the rise of nation states in Eastern Europe, but they tended to be small and weak. To counter this, leaders inside and outside the region have from time to time created local blocs or alliances to stand up to bullies and provide regional stability.

Many 19th-century nationalists in Central Europe hoped a reformed Habsburg empire would facilitate their national goals, but as it proved unwilling or unable to do so, they turned elsewhere. In 1848–49, during the Hungarian War for Independence, a Danubian Confederation comprising Hungary, Croatia, Serbia, Wallachia, and Moldavia was proposed as a replacement for the Habsburg empire, but the idea was scuttled by border disagreements and nationalist rivalries. The leader of the failed Hungarian revolt, Lajos Kossuth (LOY-osh KOSH-shoot), kept proposing increasingly democratic versions of this idea for years afterward from his exile in Italy, though few listened. Meanwhile, Serbs and Bulgarians contemplated a Balkan Federation in the 1860s, and kept coming back to the idea in 1896, the 1910s, the 1920s, and again in 1947, despite mutual distrust. Something always got in the way, though.

During World War I the Germans envisioned a bloc of German-controlled puppet states (Poland, Belarus, Lithuania, Latvia, Estonia, Ukraine) that, along with their Habsburg allies, would control Eastern Europe and keep Russia at bay. The idea died with Germany's defeat in 1918, but others had their dreams as well; Poles dreamed of a massive Eastern European confederation called *Międzymorze* ("Between the [Baltic and Black] Seas") with its capital in Warsaw, but this idea died in bloody border wars between Poles and their neighbors in 1918–22. At the Paris Peace Conference in 1919 the victorious West tried (unsuccessfully) to create a bloc of anti-German states in the region, and France also tried with the unsuccessful *La Petit* Enténte alliance. Stalin succeeded in 1945 where others had failed with his (involuntary) empire of 1944–92, though it was never very reliable or stable. Nowadays the EU and NATO continue the tradition.

Eastern Europe, though ruled by foreign empires, was not left out. Revolutions and conspiracies continuously rocked the region, factories opened in the cities sucking peasants from the countryside, and all the while romanticists began laying the foundation for modern ethnic identity in the region.

With the spread of universal education and literacy, the 19th century saw an explosion in literature across the region, and indeed schoolchildren in Eastern Europe today still have to read works from this "classical era" of Eastern European literature, just like English-speaking children have to read Dickens or Emerson. And this literature was written in local languages, not in Latin (the language of the Western European medieval world), French (the *lingua franca* of Enlightenment-era Western Europe), or Greek (the language of the Ottoman Balkans). Linguists sprang up all across the region and began creating the first dictionaries and grammars, standardizing spellings, adapting alphabets, declaring official dialects, and, in the most radical cases, virtually inventing languages.

"National" languages became at once the vehicles for beautiful literature and national expression, as well as—as we'll see in this chapter and the next—weapons in a growing *kulturkampf* (cultural struggle) with rival nationalities. "National" museums became the rage across the region, showcasing "national" paintings, sculptures, "folk" art, and so on, while musicians joined the fray as well with composers like Dvořák, Smetana, Moniuszko, Liszt, and Tchaikovsky falling all over themselves to incorporate national folk themes into contemporary "classical" musical pieces—not unlike Wagner or Puccini.

The region was waking up to a new sense of self-awareness and identity, but it lived in a political environment that did not yet understand or accept these changes, and that indeed considered them hostile and dangerous. Eastern Europeans voted with their feet, flooding Western Europe and beyond in the 19th century, reversing a long historical tradition of *importing* farmers, craftsmen, and technical experts from elsewhere in Europe to becoming a net *exporter* of people. Between 1870 and 1914, an estimated *seven million* Eastern Europeans emigrated from the region to somewhere else, mostly Western Europe, the Americas, or European colonies. And yet, despite this massive wave of emigration, Eastern Europe's population in this same time frame still managed to grow by 50%.[2] Change, indeed!

B. The Ottoman Empire as Doorstop

The 19th century found the Ottoman Empire on the defensive, and both baffled and frustrated by its new role as the Sick Man of Europe. Part of the problem derived from a gradual breakdown in the Sultan's authority and his control over the provinces; the medieval Ottoman state had been expert at conquering territories but not so good at administering them afterward. Part of the reason behind the Ottoman state's growing impotence was external; Europe in the 18th and 19th centuries began to undergo rapid social, economic, and political changes on a scale unprecedented in history, with the pace only accelerating throughout the 19th century.

The Ottoman Empire's enemies were creating a new era in science, finance, and technology to rival any before, while the Ottoman Empire was focused on struggling to maintain a 16th or 17th century status quo. Reformists and antireformists battled it out in Constantinople throughout the 19th century, while the Empire was continuously forced to cede rights and lands to its Christian rivals and watched in frustration as the European great powers increasingly ignored the *Sublime Porte*[3] as irrelevant.

The Empire still managed to eke out a few victories—one of its greatest, the victory at Gallipoli in 1915, occurred just a couple of years before the Empire itself dissolved—and despite the great powers' dismissal of the "sick Man of Europe," the Empire was still seen by Muslims worldwide as a guardian and guarantor of Muslim rights and values. Even some non-Muslims saw the Empire as a bulwark against growing European colonialism and imperialism. In some ways, the modern-day West is still today grappling with the full implications of the post-Ottoman world.

It began with Sultan Selim III, who attempted to introduce Western-style military reforms. The feudally organized Ottoman military, particularly the Janissaries, were so impressed with these reforms that undercut their influence and prestige that they rewarded Selim in 1807 by sending him to meet Allah somewhat sooner than expected. Nonetheless, it was apparent that the Ottoman military was less and less able to defend the empire, and a new reformer, Mahmud II, took note of his predecessor's fate and proceeded more cautiously. When the time came again to challenge the old feudal military establishment, Mahmud was ready.

When the Janissaries came charging toward his palace in the summer of 1826, just as they had against Selim III in 1807, Mahmud had waiting for them a poignant display that illustrated exactly why the military reforms were necessary: he lined the streets to his palace with modern-day Western-style artillery. The Janissaries were literally blasted back to their barracks. Not sure that they had quite gotten the point yet, Mahmud moved his artillery to their barracks and proceeded to blow them into oblivion. The Janissaries, the feudal slave-soldiers whose conquests had helped build the Ottoman Empire since the 14th century, were no more.

USELESS TRIVIA: EASTERN EUROPEAN EGYPT!

In 1769, Muhammad Ali Pasha was born to a Muslim Albanian family in northern Ottoman Greece, and as an adult he entered Ottoman state service. In 1798, when Napoleon invaded Egypt, Muhammad Ali was sent to Egypt by the Ottoman authorities with an army of Albanians and Bosnians to fight against the French, and though he was (like all the Ottoman forces) defeated, Ali took note of the efficiency of the French army, and he began conscripting and training an Egyptian army based on the Napoleonic model. This army proved its worth in 1820–21 when Ali easily defeated and occupied neighboring Sudan.

When ordered by Ottoman authorities to help suppress the Greek uprising in 1827, Ali rebelled, and after crushing an Ottoman army sent to arrest him at Konya in 1832, Ali effectively broke Egypt from Ottoman control. Though he would always nominally claim to still recognize the Sultan as ruler, Ali ruled Egypt as his own kingdom, and Egypt effectively became an independent country ruled by an Albanian dynasty, with Albanians in many key positions. He began to modernize Egypt's economy, introducing cotton to Egypt as a "cash crop." This would have an important impact on Egyptian, European, and even American history, as Jefferson Davis's attempts in the 1861–65 American Civil War to leverage Britain's dependence on Confederate cotton to win British recognition for the Southern cause failed when Britain was able to turn to the Egyptian cotton market instead.

Ali's sons and descendants would continue to rule Egypt as their own nominal kingdom for decades to come, overseeing the construction of the Suez Canal in the 1860s, surviving British seizure in 1882, and even outlasting the Ottoman Empire—to which they technically still belonged—when in 1914 Britain forced Ali's great grandson to break Egypt formally from Constantinople at the beginning of World War I. Though less Albanian with each generation, Ali's descendents continued to rule the now truly independent Egypt for another forty years until the last of the Albanian dynasty, Farouk I, was overthrown in 1952 by the Egyptian military and replaced by the modern-day Egyptian Republic.

Still, even these reforms were not enough, and the Empire continued its slide into decline. In 1804, and again in 1814–15, Serbia revolted and was granted autonomy. In the 1820s, Egypt effectively broke from the Empire (though still officially recognizing the Sultan as ruler). More seriously, however, in 1821 a Greek revolt broke out that would spread and would last most of the following decade. Aside from providing a convenient background for British poets to romantically die in disease-ridden Greek swamps, it began a tradition of massacres and counter-massacres that would haunt the Balkans well into our own age. Aided by an Anglo-French naval intervention in 1827, the Greek rebels drove the last Ottoman forces out of southern and central Greece by 1829, and the Great Powers negotiated full Greek independence in 1832.

Though successful, the Greek War of Independence fed revolutionary chaos throughout the Ottoman Balkans for years since two-thirds of all ethnic Greeks in the Balkans and Anatolia still lived outside the new Greek kingdom. In 1853, the Russians seized Ottoman Wallachia and Moldavia, provoking the Crimean War (1853–56), and though Anglo-French intervention saved the Turks, they realized the extent to which they were now beholden to the great powers.

Throughout the mid-19th century, Britain and Russia were engaged in what we today might call a Cold War of sorts. Russia was seeking access to warm-water ports for its navy in the Indian Ocean as a midway point between its Baltic Sea fleet in Europe and its Pacific Ocean fleet, but the territories it wanted—India, Persia, and Afghanistan—were controlled to varying degrees by Britain. This led to what modern-day historians call "the Great Game," a fierce decades-long contest between Britain and Russia for control of Central Asia and the Indian Ocean basin that played out through espionage, local proxy agents, and wars.

The upshot for the Ottoman Empire was that Britain (and France) viewed the Turks as a helpful obstacle against further Russian penetration into Central Asia, and therefore London and Paris supported and defended the Ottoman Empire, at least when it suited their interests to do so. In this way, Britain and France helped perpetuate Ottoman rule in the Balkans for decades.

In 1875, a Bosnian revolt spread across the Ottoman Balkans, culminating the following year in a Bulgarian Uprising. Frustrated, the Turks vented through widespread reprisals against Christian civilians, particularly the Bulgarians, leading to the Russo-Turkish War of 1877. At one point Russian forces advanced within a few miles of Constantinople, stopped only by a show of force from the British Royal Navy.

The victorious Russians imposed the Treaty of San Stefano on the Ottomans in 1878, which created a massive (Russian-controlled) Bulgarian state encompassing most of the southern Balkans. Alarmed by Russian inroads into the Balkans, the great powers (led by Germany's Chancellor Otto von Bismark) held a conference in Berlin months later in 1878 and forced Russia to make concessions. However, the Ottoman Empire was also compelled to swallow the complete independence of Wallachia and Moldavia (united as Romania) and Serbia. Worse, Bosnia-Herzegovina, while remaining technically Ottoman territory, became an Austro-Hungarian protectorate occupied by Habsburg troops.

The Congress of Berlin, while saving the Ottoman Empire from rival Russia, nonetheless forced the Empire to give up some of its most cherished lands in Europe—many held for centuries. The Ottomans now understood that even their "allies" did not have their best interests at heart, but worse was to come. The formula that had kept Britain as guarantor of the Ottoman Empire was London's desire to use the Ottomans to block Russian Central Asian ambitions, but in 1890 there was a major geopolitical shift in Europe as Britain, alarmed by growing German economic and military might, reacted by gradually realigning itself with the new (anti-German) Franco-Russian alliance.

The Ottomans watched in horror as their main European sponsor gravitated toward an alliance with the Ottoman Empire's arch enemy, and so after 1900 the Ottoman Turks looked increasingly to Germany, which took an interest in the Turks as allies who could now counter British imperial advantages in the eastern Mediterranean and Central Asia. German investments and advisors flooded the Empire.

Across the Ottoman Empire, these events (as well as local alarm at the growing influence of European military and administrative advisors) sparked furious reactions such as the Hamidian massacres of Armenians in 1894–96, carried out by Ottoman forces as well as Kurds and Anatolian Muslims. By the 1870s the empire was bankrupt, and the huge debts owed to *infidel* (European) banks fueled a Europeanized opposition called the Young Turks who were able to temporarily force a constitutional monarchy on the Sultan in 1876.

Driven by a budding Turkish nationalism but as well by a desire to modernize the Empire, the Young Turks forced a parliament on the Sultan in 1908 but quickly lost interest in party politics and overthrew the Ottoman government in a 1913 coup. Led by İsmail Enver Efendi—better known as *Enver Paşa* (Pasha)—the Young Turks ruled the Empire as a dictatorship for its last few years, with the Sultan reduced to the status of a figurehead.

The event that pushed the Young Turks over the edge to stage the coup of 1913 was the Balkan Wars (1912–13), during which several former Balkan Ottoman states launched a coordinated invasion to drive the Turks out of Europe. They nearly succeeded, and the Empire was only saved by squabbling between the Balkan victors over their newly conquered territorial spoils. Four tiny states, all of them former Balkan subjects of the empire and all with tiny conscript armies, had managed to defeat and humiliate the Ottoman Empire. In the 19th century, Ottoman Sultans had had to fear Russian expansionism, but now, in the early-20th century, the Ottoman Empire had to fear *everyone*. The end was near.

> ## USELESS TRIVIA: WHERE TO DATE A TURKISH GIRL . . .
>
> Constantinople had been the capital of Eastern Rome and the Byzantine Empire for more than 1,100 years when Mehmed II conquered it in 1453 and made it his imperial capital—but what was its name? Western histories seem confused on this point. When it was still the Byzantine capital, the Turks called it *Kostantiniye*, but when it became the Ottoman Empire's capital over time they began calling it *Istanbul*, apparently from the Greek phrase εις την πόλιν (Eis-tin-polin), meaning "into the city." The Turks only got around to officially changing the name to Istanbul in 1930, however, by which time it was a moot point anyway because the Turkish republican authorities had moved their capital to Ankara in 1920. Since then, for the first time in 1,600 years, the ancient imperial city has had no emperor.

C. Serbia's Front Row Seat

For much of the past 500 years, Serbia had been on the front line between the ever-warring Muslim and Christian worlds, and Stefan Dušan's neo-Byzantine imperial Serbia had long since been reduced to an impoverished and brutalized peasantry. By the 1790s the Janissaries, Muslim slave-soldiers once fanatically loyal to the Ottoman Sultan (but who had long since lapsed into corruption and mafia-style cronyism) had carved out a virtually independent state for themselves in Serbia, terrorizing the local Christian (Serb) population. Pushed to the edge, Serbs revolted in 1804, but their aim was simply to end the Janissaries' persecution so they sent representatives to Sultan Selim III asking for his help. At first the Sultan was sympathetic but conservatives in Constantinople balked at the idea of the Sultan aiding Christian subjects against Muslims. Selim caved in and declared the Serbs rebels, and the full weight of Ottoman military might came down on Serbian heads. The result, through the Serbian revolts of 1804 and 1814, was a reawakening of Serbian identity and the birth of modern-day Serbia, as well as the beginning of a nightmare for the Ottomans largely of their own making in the Balkans.

Led by the charismatic Djordje Petrović (GEORGE-eh Peh-TRO-veetch)—known better by his Turkish moniker "Black George": Kapaђopђe (Car-ah-GEORGE-eh; written in English often as "Karageorge")—the Serbs managed (with Russian diplomatic assistance) to drive the Turks out of

Serbia, including Belgrade, by 1806. In 1812, however, with the Napoleonic Wars then raging throughout Europe and the French *Grande Armée* invading Russia, Russia's political support for the Serbs lapsed and the Ottomans quickly reinvaded. In 1813 Karageorge fled to the Austrian Empire while Ottoman forces inflicted brutal reprisals against the defeated Serbian peasantry.

Peace did not last long, however, as in 1814 a small regional uprising broke out that quickly spread throughout the country, this time led by Miloš Obrenović (MEE-losh [as in "lotion"] Oh-bren-O-veetch), and now the Russians were back again, browbeating the Ottoman authorities into recognizing limited Serbian autonomy and self-rule. Unimpressed with Obrenović's diplomatic victories, Karageorge returned to Serbia in 1817 to foment a revolt for independence, but Obrenović had him murdered. This was only the first act in a century-long rivalry between the two dynasties, the Obrenovićes and Karađorđevićes, as both struggled for control of Serbia. It would end in 1903 as bloodily as it began.

As the dust settled from the uprisings, Serbia's rulers got down to the business of building a modern state. After centuries of constant war and social dislocation, Serbia in the early-19th century was one of Europe's poorest regions, and the vast majority of Serbs were illiterate. At first, a solution seemed to present itself in the form of Serbs living in the neighboring Austrian Empire who were well-educated and eager for teaching jobs in the newly rising Serbia. However, resentment and cultural bias between the Habsburg-educated Serbs and the peasants of Serbia crippled efforts at universal education, leaving Serbia with one of the poorest education records in Europe well into the early-20th century.

Nonetheless, this period of autonomy quickly generated a cultural renaissance. One of the most prominent figures was Vuk Karadžić (Vook, like "Luke," Kah-RAH-djeetch), who fought in the 1813 battles but fled to Vienna after the initial defeat. Karadžić (whose first name means "wolf") became the literary father of modern-day Serbian, collecting folk tales and standardizing a specifically Serbian form of the Cyrillic alphabet. He was a sort of a combined Shakespeare and Noah Webster for Serbians.

USELESS TRIVIA: SING, SING OUT LOUD!

Remember having to read *Beowulf* in English class? Imagine having to sing it. Actually, Beowulf was probably originally meant to be sung, as a sort of epic poem in song verse. That's how preliterate societies remembered their folklore and histories; they put them to verse and assigned some poor slob with a good memory the job of memorizing dozens of these ballads and belting them out on cue, usually when everyone was drunk around a campfire. Good times.

Well, the ancient Angles and Saxons were not the only ones with folk ballads. Finns and Estonians have their *Kalevala* (KAH-leh-vah-lah), a 23,000-verse poem about the exploits of heroic *Väinämöinen*. South Slavs too have a unique form of epic ballad, called the *bugarštica* (boo-gar-SHTEE-tsah). In the 19th and 20th centuries, Western anthropologists discovered *bugar*šticas being sung in remote parts of Serbia, Croatia, and Macedonia, and so they (along with Vuk Karadžić) preserved as many as they could, ensuring that modern-day Balkan children have to read this stuff in school, too:

Ter mu nače, bolan junaku, Ugrin
     junak govoriti:
"Bog ubio, Ugrin Janko, Ognjena
despot Vuka, Ognjevita Vuka,
Koji uze vojsku redit, a ne umije je
     razredit—
Slavna kralja naredi na istoga silna
     cara, Kralja ugarskoga,
     A Miojla i Sekula na bašu
Romanije, Ognjevite Vuka,
Tu mi ti su sva gospoda u Kosovu
     poginuli!"
*Ruka kralja Vladislav*a

(To the [ill] hero the Hungarian said:
     "May God strike Vuk the Despot[4]
     dead, Fiery Vuk,
Who marshaled troops and knew
     not how—
Against the Sultan sent the king,
     the Hungarian king,
     Against the Anatolian pasha
Sent Mihovil and Sekula, against
Romanian pasha he went, Did Fiery Vuk,
And all the nobles perished there
     [at Kosovo]!")
The Hand of King Vladislav[5]

Despite progress in Serbia's political situation—such as in 1830, when the Ottomans granted Serbia much more autonomy under Russian pressure and evacuated all Turkish troops from Serbia—Serbia focused on expansion, engaging in 1875 in a disastrous war with the Ottoman Empire that almost ended with Belgrade being occupied.

These events, which began with the 1875 Bosnian Uprising and ended with the 1877–78 Russo-Turkish War, led to the Congress of Berlin of 1878, at which the Ottoman Turks were forced to recognize Serbia's independence. This was a major victory, but it created other problems for Serbia. Serbia wanted to rule all lands inhabited by Serbs or historically belonging to medieval Serbia, and prior to 1878, those lands were primarily ruled by the Turks. Few in Christian Europe would defend Ottoman rule over Christian lands so no one openly objected to Serbian land claims against the Turks, but after 1878 many of those lands coveted by Belgrade were now ruled by neighboring Christian states. Although initially aligned with them, Serbia's expansionist desires soon undermined relations with neighboring Bulgaria and the Habsburg empire.

Serbia became a full kingdom in 1882, but the last act of the Obrenović-Karađorđević rivalry played out in June 1903, when a group of Serbian officers broke into the royal palace and murdered King Alexander Obrenović, his wife, several government ministers, and the rest of the royal family. Though never proven, some assume that Russia played a role in instigating this violent coup to reassert its influence in Serbia and regain a foothold in the Balkans. In any event, since Alexander's entire family was killed, it meant the end of the Obrenović dynasty, and the throne passed to the sixty-year-old Petar Karageorgević, who became King Petar I.

When in 1908 Vienna formally annexed Bosnia-Herzegovina, Serbian nationalists were outraged, and terrorist groups bloomed like flowers. The best known was Црна рука (TSER-nah ROO-kah), the "Black Hand," which was secretly run by Serbian army colonel Dragutin Dimitrejević (Drah-GOO-teen Dee-mee-TRAY-yeh-veetch), also known by his codename Apis (AH-peess; "the Bull").

Serbian nationalists were somewhat mollified when the country gained part of Ottoman Macedonia in the two Balkan Wars of 1912–13, but the drive for a Greater Serbia kept the nationalist fires burning, and when the Habsburgs announced that Archduke (and heir) Franz Ferdinand would review imperial troops in Sarajevo on June 28, 1914—the 525th anniversary of the disastrous battle at Kosovo Polje—five young Serbian terrorists-in-training were dispatched to Austrian Bosnia by Dimitrejević. One of them, eighteen-year-old Gavrilo Princip (Gahv-REE-lo PREEN-tseep), changed history.

Figure 50. Eastern Europe in 1900

D. Montenegro Hits the 19th Century

Montenegro achieved independence in 1789 but almost immediately was besieged by both revolutionary French forces in the Napoleonic Wars and Ottoman armies eager for revenge. The country was fought over because of its strategic position on the Adriatic, and the fighting resulted in a significant drop in the population. Montenegro emerged from the Napoleonic Wars intact largely because of Russian military and diplomatic intervention, though it had been devastated by the fighting, and Vladika Petar II began to continue his uncle's work of creating modern state institutions in Montenegro.

This led over time to a secularization of Montenegrin society, and by 1860, the next in line to be vladika, Nikola (Nicholas) Petrović, ruled the country as *Prince* of Montenegro, not vladika. During the wars sparked by the 1875 Bosnian Uprising against the Turks, Montenegrin forces led by Nikola performed well and scored several impressive victories against Ottoman armies, earning the little country wide prestige throughout Europe. Nikola was proclaimed King Nikola I of Montenegro in 1910 by the country's parliament, and once again in the First Balkan War (1912), Montenegro's little armies outperformed their allies against the Ottoman Turks. As the country teetered on the verge of World War I, however, it faced a growing identity crisis as young Montengrins returning from studying abroad in universities in Serbia and Russia brought back ideas of Pan-Slavism and "reunification" with Serbia, and a small but growing intelligentsia in Cetinje began to identify themselves as Serbs.

E. Romania is Born

The story of modern-day Romania is a strange tale of East meeting West. It begins in 1687 when, in the midst of the War of the Holy League, the Habsburgs overran Ottoman Transylvania. Transylvania was ruled by its Hungarian aristocracy, and its cities were a mixture of primarily Germans, Hungarians, Jews, Gypsies, and others, while the mysterious Székely (Szeklers), a notable subgroup of Hungarians, kept to the eastern mountains. In the countryside, Vlachs—Romanians—had been filtering down from the southern mountains since the 12th century, and by 1700 they comprised—this point is hotly debated by Romanians and Hungarians today—at least a sizeable portion (if not a majority) of the rural population. The Habsburgs, keen to weaken the grip of the fickle Hungarian aristocracy on power, convinced Transylvania's Romanian Orthodox Church in 1700 to defect to the Western church and recognize the Pope in Rome in exchange for keeping their Orthodox rites.

Thus was born the Romanian Greek Catholic (or "Uniate") Church, and the autonomy granted this church inadvertently kicked off a Romanian cultural revival. The official Romanian Orthodox Church of Wallachia and Moldavia answered to Constantinople and still functioned largely in Greek, while its masses were performed in Old Church Slavonic inherited from the Bulgarians. Indeed, the Romanian language was written in the Cyrillic alphabet. The Romanian Greek Catholic Church, however, was controlled by Romanians and functioned in Romanian. Its clergy soon adapted the Latin alphabet to Romanian and began a renaissance of Romanian literature. By the 1780s, Romanian Uniate clergy were petitioning Vienna for recognition of Romanian cultural rights.

While a Romanian cultural awakening was flowering in Habsburg Transylvania, a different kind of revolution was brewing in Ottoman-ruled Wallachia and Moldavia. The revolutions that erupted in early-19th century Ottoman Greece and Serbia were fueled from the bottom up, led by long-suffering peasants. In Romania, however, things started on the opposite end, with the noble landowner class (the boyars) leading the charge. The boyars resented the rule of the Greek *Phanariots* imposed by the Turks and by 1800, Wallachia and Moldavia were beginning to feel the ill effects of the erosion of the Sultan's power.

When the Greek War of Independence broke out in 1821, a band of Greek revolutionaries led by Alexander Ypsilantis (Υψηλάντης; the son of a well-known Phanariot family in Wallachia), crossed in to Wallachia from Russia to spread revolution across the Ottoman Balkans, but the young rebels were inexperienced, and cooperation with native revolutionaries such as Tudor Vladimirescu (TOO-door Vlahd-ee-meer-EHSS-koo) was haphazard.

A hoped-for Russian intervention did not materialize, and after a series of battlefield defeats Vladimirescu was seized and executed by his own officers when he turned to negotiation with Ottoman authorities. Ypsilantis fled to Austria where he was interned, and the Romanian revolution fizzled. It was almost a decade later before Russia finally did intervene in Wallachia and Moldavia, ushering in a new era.

USELESS TRIVIA: BOTANICAL BALKANS!

One of the sure signs that spring has finally arrived is the sight—and smell—of fragrant purple lilacs blooming. Lilacs are exceptionally durable, and indeed, the common purple lilac is the state flower of New Hampshire, a state not known for its shy winters. Perhaps then it shouldn't be so surprising that this spring shrub is from Eastern Europe.

Lilacs are believed to have first entered the United States via New Hampshire Govenor Benning Wentworth at Portsmouth in the 1750s,6 when he imported them from England. However, two centuries earlier the Holy Roman imperial ambassador to the Ottoman Empire in the mid-16th century, Ogier Ghislain de Busbeque, a noted horticulturalist, brought *Syringa vulgaris*, the common purple lilac, to the West during his duties in Ottoman Constantinople. The lilac is native to the southern Balkan mountains of modern-day Romania, Moldova, Bulgaria, Serbia, and Bosnia, thriving in the higher, rockier elevations. Other species of lilacs exist as far eastward as Iran and China, particularly in the Himalayas, but the common purple lilacs familiar to most Western Europeans and North Americans came from the Balkans. Botanical enthusiasts today book exclusive wildflower tours to the Balkans timed for the seasons.

The 1829 Russian protectorate was initially welcomed by Romanians, but as time wore on and the Russians proved more overbearing in Romanian affairs than their Phanariot predecessors, resentment grew. This resentment finally spilled over in the revolutionary year of 1848. Hungary next door exploded into revolution against the Habsburgs, and initially Transylvanian Romanians supported them until Kossuth rejected the rights of minorities in the new revolutionary state. The harsh Hungarian suppression of an uprising by Transylvanian Romanians in support of their own rights embittered relations between Hungarians and Romanians, echoing well into our own times. In Moldavia, a group of Romanian nationalists congregated in a main square in the capital, Iaşi (YAH-shee), and read some proclamations before dispersing, but in Wallachia the nationalists managed to seize the capital, Bucharest, for a few months before the Russians reoccupied it in September 1848.

USELESS TRIVIA: SAVE THE WHALES!

Ignacy Łukasiewicz (Eeg-NAH-tsih Woo-ka SHEH-veetch) was just an average, ordinary pharmacist living in Austrian-occupied Poland in the mid-19th century, in Lemberg (modern-day Lviv, Ukraine). Łukasiewicz had higher ambitions than prescriptions, however. Lamps across the Western world in the mid-19th century were lit primarily by whale oil, which was expensive because it required shiploads of brave men to risk their lives hunting one of the huge beasts at sea and dragging it back to shore for processing. Łukasiewicz, however, who lived near the Carpathian Mountains, had discovered in 1851 a chemical process—pharmacists are chemists—to refine the black, gooey stuff that kept bubbling up out of the ground in the mountains into something called kerosene. By 1853 he had invented a lamp to go along with his kerosene invention, making lighting very affordable (and making the whaling industry largely, though not completely obsolete). Łukasiewicz founded the world's first oil well, in Bóbrka (in modern-day southeastern Poland) in 1854, and two years later the world's first oil refinery nearby in Ulaszowice. Soon Vienna began ordering Łukasiewicz's lamps for hospitals and train stations; Łukasiewicz quickly became a rich man.

Łukasiewicz had given birth to the modern-day oil refining industry, but while his oil refineries made him rich they were small scale. Prospectors further south in the Carpathians realized they too had black, gooey stuff coming out of the ground and so, with American funding, the world's first large-scale oil refinery was built in Ploieşti (PLOY-esh-tee), in Wallachia, in 1857, the largest in Europe until the early 20th century. Romania's oil refineries would play a major role also in World War II.

After this defeat, many wealthy Wallachian families sent their sons abroad to study—France was a favorite destination—and soon young Romanians streamed home with revolutionary new ideas from the West. The hard work of the Romanian Uniate clergy in Habsburg Transylvania in establishing a Romanian cultural identity also began to penetrate into Wallachia and Moldavia by the 1850s. The Crimean War broke out over Russian interference in Ottoman Wallachia and Moldavia in 1853, but at war's end in 1856 Russian influence ended and Wallachia and Moldavia were united to form the autonomous (Ottoman) province of Romania in late 1861 under the controversial leadership of *Domnitor* (Dom-NEE-tore; "home ruler") Alexandru Ioan Cuza (COO-zah). Russia also ceded southern Bessarabia (including the Danube River delta on the Black Sea) to Romania.

The Franco-Prussian War (1870–71) removed Romania's staunchest ally, French emperor Napoleon III, and led from 1866 by its colorlful new German prince, Carol I (Karl, Charles) Hohenzollern, the country turned to Austria-Hungary as a natural ally against the Turks. However, as we've seen, Romanian nationalists dreamed of one day annexing Transylvania—especially since Hungary, which once again ruled Transylvania after the 1867 "Compromise" with the Habsburgs, was aggressively suppressing Romanian culture in the province—and so the pro-Austrian orientation never quite sat well in Bucharest. As we'll see in the next chapter, this led to some tough decisions in 1914.

Carol scored a series of victories; by helping the stalled Russians overcome stubborn Ottoman defenses in the 1877 Russo-Turkish War, he obtained independence for Romania from the Ottoman Empire at the Congress of Berlin in 1878. He then also got Romania upgraded to full kingdom status (and himself to king) in 1881, while also negotiating the independence of the Romanian Orthodox Church from Constantinople's control in 1885, to general jubilation.

Finally, by intervening in the Second Balkan War of 1913 against Bulgaria, Carol grabbed southern Dobrudja (DO-broo-jah) from his southern neighbor, in the process creating a new enemy for his country. This all led to an explosion in Romanian patriotism, but also fostered a rabid strain of anti-Semitism. Growing French and Russian anti-Semitism fed Romanian intolerance, but anti-Semitism had deep local roots as well.

F. Bulgaria's Raw Deal

Bulgarian national consciousness developed slower than elsewhere in the Christian Balkans, and was a result of events further afield. As Greece went into meltdown in the 1820s, the Ottoman army needed a constant flow of food supplies, and the Ottoman Bulgarian countryside became the primary provider of those supplies. This led to an economic boom in Bulgaria that, given the almost constant state of crisis the Ottoman Empire found itself in throughout the 19th century, continued steadily for several decades. This boom financed the spread of Bulgarian schools, newspapers, and literature, and a growing awareness of Bulgarian culture. Ottoman Bulgaria's cities in the 19th century were largely inhabited by Turks, Greeks, Armenians, and Jews, so Bulgarian cultural awareness arose initially in rural areas.

The re-establishment of a separate Bulgarian Orthodox church in 1870 was a watershed. The original church had been suppressed and absorbed into the Ottoman millet system,[7] so that by 1800 the Orthodox Church in the Bulgarian lands operated in Greek and answered to Constantinople. The reborn Bulgarian Orthodox Church quickly became the nucleus of a renewed Bulgarian national identity.

Unfortunately, the re-establishment of a national church in 1870 was the last peaceful act in the story of Bulgaria's rebirth. Anti-Ottoman agitation in neighboring Serbia spread to Bulgaria, and by the 1860s, Bulgarian radicals were preparing for a confrontation with Ottoman authorities. Romania's capital, Bucharest, became a headquarters for Bulgarian revolutionaries such as Lyuben Karavelov, Vasil Levski, and the poet Christo Botev. Revolt in Bulgaria finally broke out in 1876 but quickly waned; Botev tried to revive it by leading a band of revolutionaries into Bulgaria's mountains, but he was hunted down by Ottoman forces. Although this revolt fizzled quickly, with their hands full in Bosnia and Serbia, the frustrated Turks carried out horrific massacres all across Bulgaria, most infamously in the village of Batak.

This provoked the Russo-Turkish War of 1877, as the Russians invaded to halt the massacres. After some initial setbacks, with Romanian help the Russians overcame Ottoman defenses and by early 1878 the allies' armies were just outside Constantinople. The Russians imposed the Treaty of San Stefano on the Sultan, creating a huge, independent Bulgaria—under Russian control, of course—that ruled much of the southern Balkans. The Great Powers rejected this large Russian client state in the Balkans, however, and convened the Congress of Berlin in the summer of 1878, dismantling San Stefano Bulgaria and cutting Bulgaria in two: the northern half became an autonomous Ottoman province while the southern half was directly ruled by the Sultan, named "Eastern Rumelia."[8]

USELESS TRIVIA: *REALLY* OLD EUROPE! ·

When the legendary Romulus killed his brother Remus and founded the city of Rome in 753 BCE, Plovdiv—today the second-largest city in Bulgaria—was already *thousands* of years old. London, Paris, Berlin, Vienna, Madrid, Brussels, Amsterdam: all are mere infants compared to Plovdiv. Indeed, Plovdiv is one of the oldest continuously inhabited cities in Europe. With a past that stretches back some 8,000 years, Plovdiv—known to Thracians as *Eumolpia*, to Philip of Macedon as *Philippopolis*, to Romans as *Trimontium*, to the Byzantines as *Paldin*, to the early Slavs as *Plavdiv*, and to the Ottoman Turks as *Filibe*—is one of the few European cities comparable in age to ancient Athens. The earliest cities in Europe began along the Aegean coast and urbanization slowly spread northward along the Danube, so that the Balkans harbor most of Europe's oldest continuously inhabited cities.

The great powers had divided Bulgaria in half because they knew that even an autonomous Ottoman Bulgaria would be dominated by Russia, and they were keen to limit Russia's influence in the Balkans. A German prince,

Alexander of Battenburg, was imposed by the Great Powers as ruler, but when in 1885 Eastern Rumelia revolted against Ottoman rule and joined (northern) Bulgaria, the Russians withdrew their officers and advisors in protest because they (incorrectly) believed Alexander had engineered the uprising behind their backs. Nonetheless, northern and southern Bulgaria were united once again, which moreover whetted some Bulgarians' appetites, as they looked westward to Ottoman-ruled Macedonia and its large Slavic population, some of whom sought union with Bulgaria.

Macedonia is a true crossroads land with a history that includes many peoples. By the 1880s Greek, Serbian, and now Bulgarian nationalists all laid exclusive claim to Ottoman Macedonia, and terrorism began to stalk that sad land. In 1897, a group of Bulgarians in the Ottoman port of Thessaloniki[9] founded the International Macedonian Revolutionary Organization, or the IMRO (Внатрешна Македонска Револуционерна Организација, ВМРО).

The IMRO splintered into competing sects, but each waged war through assassinations and terrorism against pro-Serbian and pro-Greek groups in Ottoman Macedonia, as well of course against the Turks and weak-kneed Bulgarian politicians. In 1903, the IMRO ambitiously seized control of eastern Macedonia and Thrace in the Illenden-Preobrazhenye Uprising (Ee-LEN-den Preh-oh-brah-ZHEN-yeh) for a few months before Ottoman authorities reestablished control.

At the time, Macedonia's Slavs tended to side with either Serbs or Bulgarians, but after World War II a separate and independent (Slavic) Macedonian identity began to arise, ominously at about the same time that Macedonia's large Albanian minority was also discovering Albanian nationalism.

In 1886, Prince Alexander of Battenburg was given the boot by both the Bulgarians (who felt Alexander was too passive) and St. Petersburg (who mistakenly saw Alexander as too aggressive), and replaced by another German prince, Prince Ferdinand of Saxe-Coburg and Gotha, who made brownie points with Bulgarians when he baptized his infant son, Boris, in the Bulgarian Orthodox Church. Ironically, Ferdinand had the qualities the Russians feared Alexander had had, and he secretly plotted behind St. Petersburg's back with Vienna to coordinate the declaration in October 1908 of Bulgaria's independence from the Ottoman Empire with Austria-Hungary's annexation of Bosnia-Herzegovina.

Ferdinand became Tsar of the newly independent Bulgaria, to Russia's chagrin. This success convinced the Balkan countries that they could arrange their affairs without the great powers, so they banded together in 1912 to form the Balkan League, comprising Bulgaria, Serbia, Montenegro, and Greece, with a plan to push the Turks out of Europe. They attacked the Ottoman Balkans in September 1912, beginning the First Balkan War. After great successes—with Bulgarian (and Serbian) troops taking Ottoman Edirne (old Byzantine Adrianople) and only being stopped in desperate fighting on the very outskirts of Ottoman Constantinople at Çatalca

(JAH-tahl-cah) Fortress—the war ended in May 1913 with the Turks barely clinging to the tip of Thrace.

However, the tiny but tenacious Greek army got to the Ottoman Macedonian capital, Thessaloniki, before the Bulgarians, and in any event, the alarmed great powers began to act. To block Serbian ambitions on the Adriatic they created an independent Albania, which prompted Serbia and Greece to form an anti-Bulgaria alliance to carve up Macedonia for themselves. Nonplussed, the Bulgarians attacked their former allies in June 1913, starting the Second Balkan War. However, the already exhausted and depleted Bulgarian armies were routed within weeks, while the Turks re-entered the war and recovered Edirne.

Romania then entered the war unexpectedly and its armies marched unopposed toward Sofia, ending the war. By the Treaty of Bucharest in 1913, Bulgaria lost most of the territories it had won in the First Balkan War, as well as southern Dobrudja (DO-broo-jah) to Romania, while some 50,000 ethnic Bulgarians were expelled from the former Ottoman Macedonian lands now ruled by Greece. Bulgaria seethed with resentment.

USELESS TRIVIA: EXACTLY WHO IS THE MINORITY HERE?

When the Congress of Berlin in 1878 struck down San Stefano Bulgaria, putting Bulgaria back in the Ottoman Empire (with northern Bulgaria enjoying some limited political autonomy), Bulgarians were dismayed and outraged. However, the conciliatory Sultan did allow a Christian governor for Eastern Rumelia (southern Bulgaria). One group that refused to stomach even this very limited concession was a group of Muslim Bulgarians called *Pomaks*, descendants of Bulgarians who had converted to Islam over the centuries of Ottoman rule. Twenty Pomak villages in Eastern Rumelia's Rodope Mountain region rejected the Christian governor and seceded to form the Pomak Republic. The Pomaks enthusiastically sent volunteers to fight the (Christian) Bulgarian rebels when Eastern Rumelia revolted in 1885. The Pomaks held out until 1886 when Bulgaria and the Sultan negotiated new borders.

G. *Albania as Accident*

National identity was slowest to develop in Albania, though with all its neighbors aboil, Albania could not long remain unaffected. The genesis of Albanian national identity was that its neighbors wanted its real estate. Albanian society in the 1870s was still organized on a tribal basis, but the Ottoman defeat in the 1877–78 Russo-Turkish War had led to the stripping of nearly all available Ottoman forces from the rest of the Balkans in the effort to save Constantinople. This in turn meant that Ottoman Macedonia and Albania were almost completely undefended. The fear that Greece, Serbia, or Montenegro might take the opportunity to partition Albania convinced feuding Albanian clans to meet in Prizren, Kosovo, in June 1878, to come up with a common, united program for Albanian autonomy to present to the Ottoman authorities.

Led by a group of (literate) religious leaders and intellectuals, this group became known as the League of Prizren, and their demands were political—for the Ottoman Albanian lands to be united into one—and cultural—that Albanians be given cultural autonomy. They didn't want to leave the Ottoman Empire, just have greater control over their own affairs.

At first Ottoman authorities were sympathetic but could do little. The Albanians then presented their demands to the Congress of Berlin in 1878 only to be dismissed disdainfully by Bismark. When the Congress ceded some Ottoman Albanian lands to Montenegro, Greece, and Serbia (as the Albanians feared), they organized armed guerrilla bands in the ceded lands and waged very bloody insurgent warfare.

The Ottoman authorities, of course, weren't unhappy about this and probably even provided some arms and support to the guerrillas, but the Great Powers began to grumble, so in 1881 the Ottoman army was forced to suppress the Albanian rebels. The League of Prizren was forcibly disbanded, though it did rise again (with new leadership) unsuccessfully in 1897. After 1897, a low-level but fairly steady partisan war raged throughout the Albanian mountains for the next decade and a half, with guerrilla bands fighting the Turks, Serbs, Greeks, Montenegrins, and each other.

The struggle for Albanian identity was not just taking place in the mountains, it was also taking place culturally in the lowlands. The Albanian language was actually written in several different alphabets in the 1870s and 80s; in the Greek alphabet near the Greek border and in Orthodox Christian regions, in the Serbian Cyrillic alphabet near Serbia and Montenegro, in the Arabic alphabet in major Muslim centers, and the Latin alphabet in Albanian Roman Catholic Christian centers.

Albanian intellectuals made two important decisions, first selecting the Latin alphabet (to tie Albania closer to the West) and secondly, choosing the southern lowland Tosk dialect as the official Albanian language instead of the northern dialect, Gheg (commonly spoken by Albanians in Kosovo and western Macedonia). The first books in Albanian were published and schools teaching in Albanian began to open in this period. Ottoman authorities tried several times to stamp out these nascent steps toward Albanian identity, especially after the 1897 uprising and again in 1908 when the Young Turks came to power, but each time Albanians just took to the hills and bloody guerrilla warfare ensued.

In 1912, the First Balkan War broke out and, sure enough, Albania was seen as a prize to be split up after the war. Realizing it was now or never, the Albanian clans once again revolted and declared their independence. Since the Turks were severely distracted by events elsewhere in 1912, the Albanians were successful but they lucked out with the Great Powers' determination to prevent Serbian access to the Adriatic. By war's end in 1913, the Great Powers recognized Albanian independence and set the new state's borders.

As the Balkan states fell into war against each other over Macedonia in the Second Balkan War, the Albanians negotiated a German prince for their new country, Wilhelm (VEEL-helm) of Wied (VEED). He took his throne in February 1914, but as we'll see in the next chapter, 1914 just wasn't going to be a good year and Wilhelm's reign in Albania already only had a few months left in it.

H. The Italian Risorgimento and Irridentism

We need to briefly examine the rise of Italy and Germany in the 19th century because these two countries were early examples in Europe of the belief that a country should represent an ethnic group—or, in Eastern European parlance, a *nation*.

The creation of Italy and Germany in the 19th century had an electric impact on Eastern Europe, with many naturally asking, "Why not us too?" Prior to the 19th century, "Italy" and "Germany" were just vague regional concepts like "New England" or "Central America," which just about no one believed would one day become countries. The Italian wars of unification attracted thousands of volunteers from Eastern Europe, with young Polish and Hungarian revolutionaries hoping to some day bring this new nation-state revolution back home. Indeed, that simple question, "Why not us too?" was a powerful driver of events in Eastern Europe for the 19th and 20th centuries. The Polish national anthem still today bears echoes of the Italian wars.[10]

It all started in the 1790s, with revolutionary France's conquest of Italy, and the spread of French revolutionary ideas in the ancient fossilized Italian states. Napoleon's defeat in 1815 brought the old kings back, and the French reforms were jettisoned, but the kings couldn't put the genie back in the bottle and the Italian states simmered with discontent.

At first, nobody was talking about a united Italy, instead wanting to simply break the stodgy old feudal order, but soon Italian radicals were cooperating across borders. The first to truly articulate a vision of a united Italy was Giuseppe Mazzini (Gee-oo-SEP-pay Mod-ZEE-nee) in the 1830s, and he helped kick off the *Risorgimento* (Ree-sor-gee-MEN-to), the *Resurgence* of Italian identity that would eventually result in the founding of modern-day Italy.

The main obstacles on the road to Italian unification were the Austrians (Habsburgs), who ruled several northern Italian states; the Roman Catholic Pope, who still ruled the large Papal States that covered much of central and eastern Italy; and the French Bourbon dynasty, which ruled the Kingdom of the Two Sicilies comprising most of southern Italy and Sicily. There were a few early revolts in the 1820s and 30s in Sicily and later in the Pope's northern Italian territories, but these were squelched quickly.

In 1848, as elsewhere in Europe that year, revolutions broke out across Italy, achieving surprising successes at first before Austrian and French troops restored Habsburg and Papal rule. In 1859, however, the Italian kingdom of Piedmont-Sardinia, in cahoots with France, provoked a war with the Austrians in northern Italy that ended in an Italian victory, and this is the beginning of the unification of Italy. Successful insurrections broke out across much of northern and central Italy, leading to the founding of *Province Unite del Centroitalia* (United Provinces of Central Italy), which quickly asked to join the Kingdom of Piedmont-Sardinia, the nucleus around which Italy was built.

In the spring of 1860, rebellions broke out across the Bourbon dynasty–ruled Kingdom of Naples (Sicily and southern Italy) so the famous Italian revolutionary Giuseppe Garibaldi (Gahr-ee-BALD-ee) led his *Camicie rosse* (Red Shirts) on a fantastic mission to conquer the old feudal kingdom. Garibaldi landed in western Sicily and took Palermo before crossing the Straits of Messina to the mainland, much of which also quickly fell.

When Garibaldi failed to destroy the main Neapolitan army at Volturno in September 1860, the Piedmontese army came to his rescue and soon all that remained of the Papal state was the city of Rome. France had stationed troops in the city to protect this last outpost of Papal authority but in 1870 France was distracted by the Franco-Prussian War, and Garibaldi and the Italian revolutionaries took the opportunity to seize Rome, to local jubilation. The Piedmont-Sardinian/Italian government officially moved its capital to Rome the next year, completing the unification of Italy.

These victories sent Italians into spasms of euphoria, of course, but they also had a sinister side, the side of *irridenta Italia*, "unredeemed Italy." Having finally accomplished the decades-long struggle for a united Italy, now Italian nationalists wanted *more*. First and foremost, they started looking hungrily at territories once associated with historic Italian states like the Venetian Republic, or even the Roman Empire. *Irridentism* became a watchword for modern-day imperial expansion both for historical lands and new colonies, and very soon Croats, Slovenes, Serbs, Montenegrins, Albanians, Turks, Greeks, and others all found the soil beneath their feet claimed in distant Rome by Italian nationalists.

I. Pan-Germanism, and How Fritz (and Helga) Got Their Mojo

While the Napoleonic experience inspired many Italians, for Germans it was like a cold shower. The ease with which the French revolutionary armies plowed through the German states, dissolving the antiquated Holy Roman Empire in 1806, stunned Germans. Even mighty Austria and Prussia were repeatedly humbled by Napoleon. Despite the Habsburgs renaming the Empire *Sacrum Romanum Imperium Nationis Germanicæ* (Holy Roman Empire of the German Nation) in the 16th century, Germans still thought of themselves as Saxons,

Rheinlanders, or Prussians before "Germans," but years of French intervention in German affairs going back to the Thirty Years' War were changing this.

At first, many Germans—such as Ludwig van Beethoven, who originally named his *Eroica Symphony* after Napoleon—welcomed Napoleon as a rebel breaking the stale old order, but as it became clear Napoleon had his own imperial dreams, Germans turned against him. Prussia gained immense prestige among Germans as General Gebhard von Blücher's army played a role in Napoleon's final defeat at Waterloo, though most understood that Prussia's successes ultimately depended on Russia's victories.

After Napoleon's final defeat in 1815, the Habsburgs formed the *Deutscher Bund* (German Confederation) as a means of maintaining some modicum of control over the literally hundreds of German states and city states. However, a rising German nationalism, coupled with the insolent and insubordinate Prussia, challenged the Habsburgs' grip on the German states. Inspired by the Italian *Risorgimento* and infuriated by renewed French claims for the lands west of the Rhine River,[11] German nationalism slowly crystallized into something called *Pan-Germanism*. Some Pan-Germanists merely viewed German culture as superior and looked at German history as one big, long crusade to civilize Eastern Europe—this view was popular with Austro-Germans—but some took things further and began to dream of a single, united Greater Germany (*Grossdeutschland*).

There were two important differences between Pan-Germanism and the Italian *Risorgimento*, however: First, the Italians had a state, Piedmont-Sardinia, which drove their cause, but Germans had *two* states, Austria and Prussia, both with very different visions for themselves and Europe, and both further divided by religion, Protestant Prussia versus Roman Catholic Austria. Secondly, with the exception of some Italians scattered in Tyrolia, Istria, and Dalmatia, most Italians were concentrated in the "boot" of Italy.

Germans, however, were splattered across Europe from Strasbourg to Moscow like a Jackson Pollock painting. Any attempt to create a single, united German state that included a majority of Germans was going by necessity to include *a lot* of non-German minorities as well, likely generating tense relations with all neighboring states and peoples. Pan-Germanists accepted this as a necessary price.

In 1864, the Austrian Empire and Prussia ganged up to swipe two provinces, *Slesvig* (German: Schleswig) and *Holsten* (German: Holstein) from Denmark. This success emboldened Prussia and its new Chancellor, Otto von Bismark,[12] to use a disagreement over rulership of the new provinces to provoke a war with Vienna, leading to the Austro-Prussian War of 1866. Despite having a larger army, the Habsburgs' forces were stunningly routed at Königgrätz (modern-day Hradec Králové [KHRAH-dets KRAH-lo-veh], in the northern Czech Republic).[13]

This defeat at Königgrätz effectively ended the Habsburgs' domination of the German states, something Prussia sealed with the creation of the *Norddeutsche Bund* (Northern German Confederation")—which pointedly included most German states *except* Austria. Berlin was now the heart and darling of Pan-Germanists, and even some Austrian Germans expressed a desire to ditch their empire and join the Prussian confederation. With the Franco-Prussian War (1870–71), Bismark transformed his boss, Wilhelm I (VILL-helm; "William"), from *König* (king) of Prussia to *Kaiser* (Emperor) of a united Germany. Italy's unification arose from a hundred local revolutions that coalesced around Piedmont-Sardinia, but Germany's unification was a Prussian state project, directed in nearly every degree and detail from Berlin by Bismark:

> The new Reich of 1871—whatever the theory—was in practice a Prussian Reich, shaped to accord with Prussian interests, constructed in conformity to Prussian traditions, ruled by the dynasty of Hohenzollern, and dominated by the Prussian Junker class.[14]

USELESS TRIVIA: THOSE CRAZY ARYANS!

In the summer of 2006, Latvia was proudly hosting a summit of its new NATO allies, and as token gifts for its guests it had arranged for local craftsmen to create traditional Latvian wares. There was one stipulation, however; the Latvian government requested that the craftsmen purposely exclude a traditional Latvian symbol that could cause some misunderstandings. How would NATO's ministers react if they looked at their handmade gifts from their hosts and saw swastikas on them?

The swastika—from *su* meaning "good" and *asti* "to be" in the ancient Aryan Sanskrit language—was born in India some 3,000 years ago and spread all over southern Asia, from China to the Middle East. Modern-day Buddhism and Hinduism still use the swastika, and some ancestors of Native Americans even brought it from Siberia to the Americas. The Nazis hijacked the swastika and forever gave it an evil connotation, but they were not the ones who brought it to Europe. The many Indo-European speaking peoples who migrated into Europe brought this symbol with them, and it can be found in the art and rituals of many early premodern European cultures from Spain to Russia. In the 19th century, Pan-Germanists claimed the swastika as an "ancient German" symbol and used it on postcards, Bibles, and ephemera, even in German-American communities in the Americas. However, the swastika is in reality an ancient symbol born somewhere in southern Eurasia and was shared by many peoples across vast distances.

Bismark waged a *Kulturkampf* (cultural struggle) in the 1880s—against Catholicism, socialists, and "polluting" foreign elements in Germany—that led the policy of *Germanization*, the attempt to force German language and culture on non-Germans. As Pan-Germanists in the early-20th century came increasingly to believe in Germany's imperial destiny, Germanization was applied with ever more vigor to ethnic minorities. School instruction was limited to the German language, certain public displays of non-German culture were banned, and German colonization of non-German areas was heavily encouraged. Special commissions were empowered with forcing minorities to sell their homes to ethnic Germans, and in some extreme cases (mostly with Poles, Danes, and Lithuanians), minorities were deported from regions deemed strategic such as Silesia and Pomerania. Pan-Germanists also created the idea of *Mitteleuropa* (Central Europe), which was that part of Europe (according to Pan-Germanists) where true German *völkisch* (national folk) culture still reigned since the days of Charlemagne, sandwiched between the liberal West and the barbaric, Slavic East. Central Europe was the true repository of the quintessential values of Christian European (read: "German") civilization.[15]

J. Pan-Slavism and Pie in the Sky

The crucial difference between Pan-Slavists on the one hand and the Italian Irridentists and Pan-Germanists on the other is that whereas both the Italian Irridentists and Pan-Germanists were successful, the Pan-Slavists failed, for a bunch of reasons we'll explore shortly. This is an important point because while Italian and German unification are often portrayed today as inevitable, the Pan-Slavist movement is just as often portrayed as unrealistic and utopian. Those silly Slavs.

> It is one of those quirks of history that a German was one of the most influential figures in the development of Slavic historiography. Herder[16] popularized the idea of peace-loving and protodemocratic Slavs as the victims of the aggressive, warlike, and autocratic Germans.
>
> Consequently, he played an essential role in the way the Slavs came to view their own history, as a national struggle against German aggression that culminated in the loss of ancient Slavic freedoms, and he envisioned a day when these "submerged peoples that were once happy and industrious" would rise from their "long, languid slumber" and be "delivered from their chains of bondage."[17]

With the meteoric rise of Italian and German nationalism, it was quite natural that Slavs would eventually catch on. Pan-Slavism was born of growing disappointment with the post–Congress of Vienna (1815) status quo, although there were multiple strains of Pan-Slavism. There was a Czech strain that sought cultural and political autonomy for the Slavic peoples within the context of the larger empires (first Austrian, and later

Russian);[18] there was a South Slavic strain that evolved the furthest toward demands for political solutions; and there was a Russian strain that was, quite naturally, more statist and paternal, seeing Russia as having a mystical destiny to protect Eastern Europe's Slavs from the heathen Turks and brutal Germans.

Pan-Slavists' goals ranged from mere cultural autonomy to outright political independence, though all were inspired by the romanticist movement and growing awareness of local "folk" cultures (and cultural identity) across Europe.

Pan-Slavism during the nineteenth century was an incoherent set of sentimental and often vague pronouncements about cultural affinities and political sympathies among Slav peoples. It was not an ideology with any clear-cut political goals (except when it was used by Russian imperialism), nor did it exert any decisive influence on any major political movement. Few Pan-Slavists envisioned any future 'melting' of all Slavs into one supernation; Pan-Slavism presupposed the existence of individual Slav nations.[19]

USELESS TRIVIA: BRING OUT THAT OL' RED, WHITE, AND BLUE!

If you crack open a book on flags of the world, you may notice that many of the Slavic countries (Russia, Czech Republic, Slovakia, Slovenia, Croatia, and Serbia) have red, white, and blue flags. A coincidence? Nope. Like many nations of Europe, Pan-Slavists were inspired by the French revolutionary cause of 1789 and adopted the French Revolutionary red, white, and blue tricolor flag as the symbol for their movement, though some attribute the Pan-Slavist colors to the Russian flag, to the Americans, or even to the 16th century revolutionary Dutch flag. Pan-Slavism fizzled in the early-20th century but many Slavic countries still retained the old red, white, and blue as their national colors.

The real heart of the Pan-Slavist movement was in the Habsburg Empire, which had large Slavic minorities. The Czechs, led by the Czech historian František Palacký (Fran-TEE-shek Pah-LOTS-kee), organized a Pan-Slavism conference in Prague during the troubles of 1848, which ended disastrously with the Austrians violently suppressing the conference.

The *Ausgleich* (Compromise) of 1867 that formed the dual monarchy encouraged Pan-Slavists to seek a *three-way* solution, with Austro-German, Hungarian, and Slavic governments all answering to the Emperor. This idea, called *Trialism* (an extension of Austro-Hungarian *Dualism*), was quickly shot down by the Hungarians, who knew competition when they saw it. Embittered Czech Pan-Slavists then began to look outside the Habsburg domains to Russia for a solution.

In the Habsburg's southern lands, the Southern Slavs, while seeing Russia as a protector, preferred more local solutions. Croatian romanticists launched the "Illyrianist" movement in the 1840s, which sought recognition for Southern Slavic cultural rights, but Austrian (and Hungarian) alarm at the spread of nationalism in the Empire's Slavic lands thwarted the Illyrianists' modest demands.

The result was a plethora of more aggressive groups seeking political autonomy for some sort of Southern Slavic or *Yugoslav* (*Yugo* in the Southern Slavic languages = "Southern") state. This brand of Pan-Slavism was particularly popular among Croats and Slovenes, while most Serbs looked instead to the nearby newly rising Serbian Kingdom. (Serbian-Bulgarian enmity after a brief war over Bulgarian unification in 1885 also undermined pro-Yugoslav or Pan-Slavist support in either country.) Still, Pan-Slavism endured as a major force in Eastern Europe well into the 1920s and 30s, sometimes encouraging cooperation between erstwhile rivals such as Yugoslavia and Bulgaria, while other times provoking hysterical racist fears in Berlin, Vienna, Rome, and Budapest.

K. The Austrian Dilemma and Hungary

The Austrian Empire was created because the Habsburgs' traditional political vehicle, the Holy Roman Empire, had finally been destroyed in 1806 by Napoleon. The Habsburgs tried to retain their leadership of the German peoples through the Austrian-led *Deutscher Bund* (German Confederation), but while in many ways the transfer of Habsburg power from the Holy Roman Empire to the Austrian Empire was merely a legal detail—the Holy Roman Empire had been moribund since the Thirty Years' War, and Austria had long since become the real seat of Habsburg power—still, the move was essentially a defensive one, a desperate leap by a powerful medieval dynasty into the modern era.

The Austrian Empire was "Plan B" for the Habsburgs, and once they were pushed into creating it, they became stubborn in their defense of its quintessentially feudal political structure. Unfortunately, the coming century was to be one of change that would challenge the very underlying basis of the Austrian Empire, and the Habsburgs' story for the 19th century is basically their struggle to come to grips with those changes. One of my favorite Hungarian writers, Kálmán Mikszáth (KAHL-mahn MEEK-saht), posed the question in a late-19th century story called *Beszterce ostroma* (The Siege of Beszterce) that while everyone admires men who were born before their time, what is to be done with a man who is born centuries *after* his time? He was writing about Franz Josef I, the Austrian emperor who would define most of the Empire's last century.

USELESS TRIVIA: TWO PEAS IN A POD

Gregor Mendel had a weird hobby. He liked peas, and enjoyed culti-vating them in his garden, though not for his salads—just to observe. Born Johann Mendel in Austrian-ruled Silesia (modern-day Hynčice [Hin-CHEE tseh], Czech Republic) in 1822, he went on to attend university and join a monastery, where, as a friar, he labored in the Augustinian Abbey of St. Thomas in Brüno (modern-day Brno, Czech Republic), which is where he had his pea garden. Taking the name "Gregor" upon entering monastic life, he was particularly fascinated by why pea pods were different from one another, and how they passed those different traits on to their offspring. It was only in the 20th century, decades after Mendel's death, that he was recognized as the father of modern genetics.

As the Austrian Empire emerged from the Napoleonic Wars, it enjoyed a certain level of prestige, having aided in the efforts to defeat Napoleon. The postwar peace conference was held in Vienna and presided over by the Austrian foreign minister, Prince Klemens Wenzel von Metternich. He's the gent quoted in the FAQ in the front of this book. At the Congress of Vienna (1815), he helped create the *Deutscher Bund*, the German Confedera-tion (which had as its technical head the Emperor of Austria), and together with Prussia, Russia, and Britain—Britain bolted in 1822—Metternich cre-ated the Concert of Europe, a conservative union designed to resist revolu-tionary political change. He set the tone for Austria's stern conservatism for the rest of the century, but a problem for Metternich was that Europe was changing right beneath his feet.

Indeed, change was happening whether the Habsburgs wanted it or not, and Europe's failure to address that change resulted in a social and politi-cal explosion in the summer of 1848, when revolutions broke out all across the continent. They were caused by a number of factors—e.g., demands for political rights and reform, nationalism, and economic unrest—but all were united in rejecting the imposition of 18th-century politics-as-usual from above onto a rapidly changing 19th-century world. Though they var-ied in degree of ferocity from country to country, none were as intense or as widespread as the uprisings in the Austrian Empire. Demonstrations broke out in March 1848 in Vienna and quickly turned violent, and spread to Milan, Budapest, Prague, and beyond. Both the Habsburg royal family and Metternich fled Vienna—Metternich never to return—and by year's end, Emperor Ferdinand I abdicated the throne in favor of his nineteen-year-old nephew, Franz Josef. Vienna was quickly subdued but revolts raged across the Empire over the summer.

While Austrian authorities eventually overcame the uprisings in Milan, Piedmont, and Venice, Prague defiantly organized self-rule under the *Národní výbor* (Nah-ROAD-nee VIH-bor; "National Committee"), led by the Czech historian František Palacký (Frahn-TEE-shek Pah-LAHTS-kee), and hosted the Pan-Slavic Congress in June. The Habsburgs[20] reacted by unleashing their powerful artillery on the city, followed by Austrian forces fighting pitched street battles with Pan-Slavists, students, and workers. Within a week the Austrians controlled Prague.

If Prague was "pacified" so quickly, the Habsburgs would find themselves paying the difference in Hungary. Early-19th century Hungary had seen aristocratic reformers like István Széchenyi (EESHT-von SAY-chen-yee), who emphasized economic development, but by 1848, a new generation of more radical reformers (with a more nationalist bent) led by Lajos (Louis) Kossuth (LOY-oesh KOESH-shoot) had taken over. With Vienna in chaos in early 1848, Kossuth unilaterally declared Hungarian autonomy within the empire (in what are called the March and April Laws).

The Habsburgs, up to their armpits with revolutionaries everywhere, initially accepted them. However, when it became clear that the Hungarian aristocrats had no intention of respecting *their* minorities, the Serbs of Vajdaság (modern-day Vojvodina in northern Serbia) and the Romanians in Transylvania revolted, while the pro-Habsburg Croatian *Ban*, Josip Jellačić (YO-seep Yel-LAH-cheetch), invaded Hungary in September. Jellačić was defeated, but the Hungarians realized they needed a real army and created the famous brown-uniformed *Honvéd* (HONE-vayd; "National Defense") army—just in time for the Austrians to invade Hungary in December 1848.

Initially Austrian forces did well, plowing through the country and taking Buda, but Hungarian *Honvéd* forces in Transylvania, led by a Polish refugee from the 1831 Polish revolt against the Russians, Józef Bem (YOO-zef Bem), suppressed the Serbian and Romanian uprisings and drove Austrian forces back westward across the Tisza (TEE-suh) River, saving the revolution. A Hungarian counteroffensive in the spring of 1849, with famous victories at Hatvan (HUTT-vun) and Isaszeg (EE-shuh-seg), liberated the entire country by June 1849. However, Kossuth's declaration of independence drove the Austrians to request aid from the Russians, and both reinvaded rebel Hungary in July. After a series of crushing defeats, the Hungarian revolutionary armies surrendered to the Russians in August 1849. The Hungarian War for Independence was over.[21]

USELESS TRIVIA: THAT HAD BETTER BE WINE

On the morning of October 6, 1849, soldiers of the victorious Austrian army brought thirteen generals of the Hungarian revolutionary army to the scaffolds in Arad (now located in northwestern Romania). Per their sentences, nine were hung while four were lined up and shot. The executions were part of a brutal campaign of pacification meted out to the leaders of the 1848–49 Hungarian War of Independence by the Austrian general Baron Julius Jakob von Haynau (HIGH-now). Indeed, so brutal was Haynau's rule in defeated Hungary that he became a PR problem for the Habsburgs and was quietly replaced in 1850.

Today a monument from 1890 marks the grave of the "Thirteen Martyrs of Arad," as Hungarians call them. The thirteen martyrs of Arad are remembered in another way by modern-day Hungarians, however; a legend sprang forth that the Austrian officers who carried out Haynau's orders to execute the thirteen enjoyed a self-congratulatory beer afterward, clinking their glasses in celebration. Because of this legend, Hungarians today refrain from clinking their beer glasses, especially on March 15, the modern-day Hungarian national holiday commemorating the March Laws of 1848. Well, in reality, Hungarians are not scrupulous in observing this ritual–after 1989, many began ignoring it altogether–but they all know of it and as a foreigner in a Hungarian pub, you may find yourself being lectured about this if you're not careful.

The Austrian Empire entered the 1850s as an absolutist empire and something akin to what we would call a police state, but for all that, the Habsburgs saw themselves as being on the defensive. Meanwhile, culture in Vienna flourished with famous artists from all over the empire who would one day be remembered for their contributions to their native German, Hungarian, Czech, Italian, Croatian, Romanian, Serbian, Polish, Ukrainian, and Jewish cultures all converging on Vienna.

Despite this cultural explosion, the Empire's ethnic minorities were becoming more self-aware and demanding political recognition and autonomy, if not outright independence. To some extent the Habsburgs genuinely tried to accommodate at least some of these demands as best they could, but they had their own interests to tend to, and in any event, various groups' claims were often contradictory.

Disaster came in 1859 when Piedmont-Sardinia provoked and won a war with the Austrian Empire, opening the floodgates of Italian nationalism.

The rise of Prussia in the *Deutscher Bund* also weakened the Habsburgs' support across the German lands, but rivalry turned to open confrontation in 1866 in the Austro-Prussian War, which ended with ignoble Austrian defeat at Königgrätz.

The Prussians abandoned the Austrian-led *Deutscher Bund* (German Confederation) and formed the rival *Norddeutsche Bund*, (Northern German Confederation), which all but three German states immediately joined. To boot, Prussia managed to get Austria kicked out of the German *Zollverein* (Tsoll-fare-INE; "customs union," a kind of pan-German free trade zone).

Politically weakened and militarily humiliated, Austrian Emperor Franz Josef quietly turned to the second largest nation in his empire, the Hungarians, and began negotiations via aristocrat Ferenc Deák (FEH-rents DEH-ock). The result was *Das Ausgleich* (Dahss Owss-glikhe; "The Compromise") of 1867. The Empire was divided in two—hence the "Dual Monarchy": (imperial) Austria and (royal) Hungary, each with their own government (complete with prime ministers, parliaments, and administrations), but both ruled by Franz Josef, who was Emperor in Austrian-ruled *Cisleithania* and King in Hungarian-ruled *Transleithania*.[22] The imperial government retained control over military and foreign affairs.

You might think that by finally settling matters with Hungary, Franz Josef and the Habsburgs had sorted out the empire's problems. Well, by striking a deal with the Hungarians, the Habsburgs only encouraged the Empire's other minorities to ask, "Why not us too?," leading to much political strife over the next several decades and further destabilizing the Empire. To boot, Hungary's ruling aristocrats became increasingly nationalistic and began a program of *Magyarization*, whereby they tried to force the non-Hungarians of Transleithania to assimilate into Hungarian culture. Hungary had signed the *Nagodba* (Compromise) with Croatia in 1868 granting Croatia considerable political autonomy, but Hungarian governments felt only loosely bound by this agreement.

While Magyarization was not nearly as coercive as its peer Germanization and Russification programs in the neighboring empires, it still infuriated the Serbs, Slovaks, and Romanians living in Hungary who were trying to achieve recognition for their own cultural rights—earning Hungary the enmity of these peoples for decades and adding more instability to the Habsburgs' already dicey realm. Still, Hungarians today remember the dual-monarchy era very fondly as a sort of second golden age. After Buda and Pest were united in 1873 to form modern-day *Budapest*, the government lavished money on the city, building stately parks and monuments for the millennial celebrations of 1896 and (very intentionally) giving the city a Victorian air.

USELESS TRIVIA: *DER FÜNFTE MAI!*

Somehow the German *der Fünfte Mai* just doesn't quite have the romantic "oomph!" factor that *Cinco de Mayo* has, but they both mean the same thing: May 5th. Moreover, at least one person connected to the events of *Cinco de Mayo* would have used the German version: Maximilian von Habsburg. Maximilian was the brother to the Austrian Emperor, Franz Josef I. How did he end up in Mexico?

Well, in 1857 Mexico slid into civil war—again—and when it emerged from that war in 1861, its economy was in a shambles and its president, Benito Juárez, had to suspend payments on the piles of loans previous Mexican governments had taken from several European countries. Britain, France, and Spain reacted to this Mexican default on its loans by signing the Treaty of London in October 1861, by which they decided to send the repo man to collect on their loans. The collateral? Mexico itself.

In early 1862, French troops landed in Veracruz and began their invasion of Mexico. Actually, they were defeated in one of their first battles with the Mexican army at the Battle of Puebla on May 5—which is what *Cinco* de Mayo is all about—but they quickly brushed that defeat aside and plowed through Mexican defenses to conquer the country by June 1863. Now, normally the European powers would not have even considered meddling in Mexico because of the United States' Monroe Doctrine, which forbade European colonial adventures in the Americas, but since 1861 the U.S. was distracted by its own civil war. Victorious, the European allies decided (through a long story of political considerations) to offer the crown of their new Mexican Empire to Maximilian, the Austrian Emperor's younger brother. In May 1864, Maximilian was crowned Emperor of Mexico in Mexico City.

Unfortunately, Maximilian just ticked everyone off. The peasants, led by former president Juárez, hated Maximilian simply on principle since they wanted a republic—his high taxes to repay the loans didn't help—and Maximilian's feeble attempts at social reform only alienated the wealthy Mexican landowning classes. This lack of friends became an acute problem when the American Civil War ended, and the United States threatened to drive French forces out of Mexico a year later, in February 1866. France withdrew its forces within months, leaving Maximilian very, very alone. By early 1867, the Mexican republicans had driven Maximilian and his tiny group of supporters to the fortified city of Querétaro, which fell in May. Maximilian faced a firing squad in June 1867. His imperial brother blamed the United States for Maximilian's death, and loathed the U.S. until his dying day.

The Habsburgs teamed up with erstwhile foe Germany in 1878 at the Congress of Berlin to keep Russia out of the Balkans, and this led to a reconciliation between the two German powers. The two created a system of alliances with Italy and several Balkan states throughout the 1880s to counter Russian attempts to penetrate the Balkans.

While Austria-Hungary had a decent number of skilled diplomats and a surprisingly good cache of spies, it fell very desperately short in the most important category among the great powers, its armies. Partially because of the conservatism of its massive bureaucracy, partially because of internal politics and other budget-related reasons, the Austro-Hungarian empire was the least prepared for the colossal war that came in 1914. Its military was the smallest of the Great Powers, its arms were the least modern, its strategies and tactics the most dated, and perhaps worst of all, its population the least loyal.

USELESS TRIVIA: THINGS TO NAME A HEAVY METAL BAND AFTER!

Nikola Tesla was born in 1856 in the Habsburg *Militärgrenze* (Military Border) enclave in Croatia established for Serbs in the early-18th century. Indeed, Nikola's father was a Serbian Orthodox priest. At his father's behest he enrolled in university twice (in Graz, Austria and Prague) but dropped out both times, eventually apprenticing as an electrical engineer with a phone company in Budapest. However, it was with this job that Nikola found his calling—no pun intended—and soon Nikola was working for one of Thomas Edison's companies in Paris as an electrical engineer, where he impressed his bosses enough that he was sent to the U.S. to work with the great inventor himself in 1884.

Edison regarded Nikola as brilliant, but the two inventors' collaboration fell apart a few years later over a philosophical difference: should Edison's electrical inventions be powered by Edison's favored direct current (DC) or Tesla's newly perfected alternating current (AC)? The disagreement drove Edison and Tesla apart, but in 1888 Tesla demonstrated the superiority of AC motors to the American Institute of Electrical Engineers, which led to AC becoming the standard for household appliances—kicking off the electrification of the world. Patents for inventions like the Tesla coil piled up, and in 1895 Tesla's AC generator design was used to build what was then the world's largest hydroelectrical generator, at Niagara Falls. By the time of his death in 1943 in New York, Tesla had revolutionized electricity, the radio, and even astronomy. And his birthplace in Croatia, opened as a museum in 2006, has served since to facilitate reconciliation between Serbs and Croats after the 1990s Yugoslav implosion wars.

The eminent German historian Holger Herwig describes the state of the Austro-Hungarian military before World War I thus:

> In terms of per-capita expenditures on the defence budget of 1906 in Austrian *Kronen*,[23] Britain spent 36, France 23.8, Germany 22, Italy 11.6, Russia 9.8, and Austria-Hungary 9.6. Despite a dramatic 64 percent rise in defence spending between 1906 and 1914, the 16 corps commands of the Dual Monarchy in 1914 fielded fewer battalions of infantry (703) than in 1866—notwithstanding a twofold increase in population over that half century. In fact, Austria-Hungary annually trained a smaller percentage of its population (0.29 per cent) than either its ally, Germany (0.47 per cent), or its potential adversaries, Russia (0.35 per cent), Italy (0.37 per cent), and France (0.75 per cent.)
>
> Put differently, the Habsburg Monarchy each year trained only between 22 and 29 per cent of draft-eligible males; the corresponding figures were 40 per cent for Germany and 86 per cent for France. And while the peacetime Army consisted of 415,000 officers and men, the imperial bureaucracy boasted 550,000 servants.[24]

Clearly, 1900s Austria-Hungary could hardly be accused of militarism, and despite the annexation of Bosnia-Herzegovina in 1908, its foreign policy goals were overwhelmingly conservative: keep the status quo. The dual-monarchy's problem was that nearly all its foreign policy challenges were essentially military in nature, in the sense that most of its neighbors (in collusion with some of its own population) wanted Habsburg real estate or influence in Austria-Hungary's eastern lands.

Franz Josef, prone by this period to episodes of dementia, still understood the need for his empire to cling to the status quo. Some of his ministers—chief among them the chief of staff for the army, Count Conrad von Hötzendorf, who repeatedly called in the empire's last two decades for punitive wars against Serbia—did not quite understound that change, *any* change, was the empire's enemy.

L. Russia as both the Hope and Prison of Nations

When Russia's new tsar, Alexander I, took over the helm in 1801, Russia faced a very grave and immediate problem, in the form of Napoleon. Alexander had just taken over from his father, Pavel (Paul) I, who had ruled a mere five years and was murdered, ostensibly because he was very erratic and was often described as mentally unstable, though the fact that he had tried to root corruption out of the Russian government may have also contributed to his early demise; reformers in Russia traditionally have very short life spans. In any event, Pavel died just as Europe again teetered on the brink of war, so Alexander joined the Third Coalition (with Austria and Britain) against Napoleon in 1805—which was then soundly defeated at Austerlitz (near modern-day Brno, Czech Republic); and then the Fourth Coalition (Britain, Russia, Prussia, Sweden, and Saxony), which fared no better, with a Prussian defeat at Jena in October 1806, followed by the Russians at Friedland in June 1807, forcing Alexander to sign the Peace of Tilsit with Napoleon.

Russia effectively became a French ally. After a few years on the sidelines—though Russia seized Finland from the Swedes in 1809—Alexander tried his luck again in 1812 by switching sides (back) to France's enemy, Britain, provoking Napoleon into invading Russia with the *Grande Armée*, a massive army of some 600,000 soldiers. Alexander reacted by just retreating deeper into the Russian interior, only giving battle at Borodino in September 1812. After this inconclusive battle, Napoleon occupied Moscow, expecting that this would end the war. But Alexander just kept retreating. As Napoleon spent his first night in the Kremlin, Russian agents sneaked back into the city and lit multiple fires, so that by dawn most of Moscow was reduced to smoldering ashes.

With no supplies in sight, Napoleon's army was forced to retreat in the fall of 1812 and began to perish under the dual burden of lightning raids by Cossacks and the bitter Russian winter. Russians forces harassed the French as they retreated, nearly destroying Napoleon's army as it attempted to cross the River Berezina (in modern-day eastern Belarus) in November 1812.

When the remnants of the *Grande Armée* straggled into Vilnius at the end of 1812, only about 40,000 of the original 600,000 remained. Napoleon abandoned his army and fled back to France, while Alexander joined another coalition (Russia, Britain, Spain, Portugal, Austria, Sweden, and Prussia), which defeated Napoleon at the Battle of the Nations at Leipzig in October 1813.

By March 1814, Russian and Prussian troops entered Paris, and Napoleon surrendered a few days later with Tsar Alexander I himself waiting patiently in Versailles Palace for Napoleon's surrender. Alexander's role in Napoleon's defeat greatly increased Russian prestige throughout Europe, and Alexander himself was seen as something of a rock star. (*Alexanderplatz*/Alexander Square in Berlin is named after him.) He attended the Congress of Vienna himself in 1815, and played a major role in establishing the postwar order in Europe. Despite all the adulation however, Alexander's Russia had a fundamental problem.

For its part, Western Europe was beginning to feel the earliest effects of the industrial revolution, which would fundamentally change Europe's basic social and economic fabric, causing great tensions but also leading to an exponential expansion in economic growth and technological development. Russia would only begin to experience these effects belatedly, at the *end* of the 19th century. Russia was increasingly being left behind by changes elsewhere in Europe, and St. Petersburg constantly feared for its membership in the Great Power club.

USELESS TRIVIA: LOST AND FOUND!

In the spring of 2002, municipal workers were removing an old Soviet barracks building on the outskirts of Vilnius, Lithuania, when a bull-dozer uncovered what turned out to be thousands of skeletons in a series of mass graves. Now, this is Eastern Europe, so as shocking as such a find might be, authorities have a whole catalogue of possible historical explanations to choose from: Jewish victims of the Nazi Holocaust? Medieval plague victims? KGB victims? Tartar victims?

After some careful examination, it was determined that these were remnants of Napoleon's *Grande Armée*, which had used Vilnius as both a launching pad before and rallying point after his 1812 invasion of Rus-sia. When the French soldiers first entered Vilnius in June 1812, they were met with jubiliation as liberators, but when they straggled back in December from a burning Moscow they were a starving, diseased ghost army. To quote an eyewitness, the French Count Philippe-Paul de Ségur, describing the French re-entry into Russian Lithuania in December:

> Even greater horrors were seen in the spacious barns and sheds dotted here and there along the way. Soldiers and officers alike poured into them until they were filled to bursting. There, like so many cattle, they crowded together around two or three fires. The living, unable to drag the dead away from the circle, lay down on them and died in their turn, and served as deathbeds for still other victims.[25]

And Vilnius itself:

> The capital of Lithuania was still totally ignorant of our disasters, when suddenly these forty thousand starving men filled its streets with groans and lamentations. At this unexpected sight the inhabitants became alarmed and closed their doors.[26]

Thousands died while in Vilnius, and Russian accounts tell of find-ing huge piles of French corpses when they re-entered the city. With its rich history, Eastern Europe often turns up reminders of its long and painful past when modern bulldozers ply the earth in the name of development.

Alexander I died in 1825, leaving the throne to his younger brother, Nicholas (*Николай*; Nyee-KO-lie), who became Tsar Nicholas I. Nicholas was almost immediately confronted with a rebellion by his own officer corps; many Russian army officers who had participated in the Napoleonic wars had seen with their own eyes a better living standard and more importantly, people living in Europe who did not fear their monarchs.

This exposure to life under nonabsolutist rulers radicalized the Russian army officer corps, and they demanded from Nicholas a constitution guaranteeing rights. Unimpressed, Nicholas turned his artillery on the rebel officers, in what became known as the Decembrist Revolt. Indeed, Nicholas I became Russia's most conservative tsar, convinced that democracy, constitutions, and representative parliaments were evil. Further revolts elsewhere in Europe throughout the 1820s and 30s hardened his belief in absolutism, and he founded the infamous Okhrana (*Охрана*) secret police, which became notorious for its widespread spies among the population, brutality, and political arrests.

Ever since the Mongol invasion and the subsequent centuries of Tartar rule and terror, Russians looked with fear toward Asia and the southeast. Peter the Great managed to score some successes in this area, and Catherine the Great finally subdued the Crimean Tartars, but it was Alexander I who really pushed the Russian borders into Asia.

Alexander and his successors pushed further and further into Central Asia—Nicholas founded the city of Vladivostok (*Владивосток*, literally "Conquerer of the East") in 1859 to assert Russian primacy in Asia—but Russia soon bumped up against the British Empire with its colony in India. This led to a decades-long struggle for control over the lands north of the Indian subcontinent between St. Petersburg and London, turning Iran and Afghanistan into bloody proxy battlefields.

This Anglo-Russian confrontation—often referred to as "The Great Game"—culminated in the Crimean War of 1853–56, as Britain (with France) came to the Ottoman Empire's aid after the Turks were soundly defeat by the Russians. The war ended with a humiliating Russian defeat on home soil as Anglo-French forces captured the Black Sea port of Sevastopol, though the Russian navy fared better in fending off British naval attacks in the eastern Baltic. Nicholas died before the war finished, but the need for military reforms was clear to his son and successor, Alexander II.

As a reforming tsar, Alexander II instituted reforms only reluctantly because he saw change, rather like Gorbachev 130 years later, as crucial to the survival of the empire. Also like Gorbachev, Alexander II found himself up against a rusting, entrenched state and social structure that adamantly resisted change. His most famous reform is the emancipation of Russian serfs in 1864, though he still believed passionately in tsarist absolutism, having no problem with shooting Poles or Lithuanians down in their streets if they got a little too rambunctious.

Unfortunately, the extreme oppressiveness and intransigence of his father, Nicholas I, had bred great hostility in Russia's nascent middle class and lower nobility, creating a generation of terrorists who came to see violence as the only means of change in Russia. The most famous revolutionary was the anarchist Mikhail Bakunin, but mid-19th century Russia became a breeding ground for violent revolutionaries espousing anarchism, communism, nihilism, nationalism, constitutionalism, kitchen-sinkism, and so on.

The slow pace of Alexander's reforms infuriated revolutionaries, and he eventually paid with his life when National Will (*Народная воля*; Nah-RODE-nah-yah VOL-yah) anarchist revolutionaries pitched a bomb at his carriage and blew him to imperial smithereens in March 1881.

USELESS TRIVIA: REACH OUT AND TOUCH SOMEONE . . . ELSE . . .

Late-19th century Russia was a breeding ground of discontent, and spawned hordes of revolutionaries who spread out from Russia. Industrializing Europe as a whole seethed with extremists, but nothing compared to the revolutionary anger festering in absolutist Russia. One such person was Emma Goldman, who was born to a Jewish family in Russian-occupied Lithuania in 1869, and who was radicalized by waves of pogroms and Russian oppression in Lithuania. When she was seventeen, she migrated to the United States and joined a group of underground anarchists in New York. Eventually, in 1919, she was deported back to Russia, but not before she befriended a young man who had been born in the American Midwest but whose parents were also refugees from the Russian Empire, from Russian-occupied Poland. Emma became a mentor to this young man, Leon Czolgosz (CHOLL-gawsh), nurturing him on anarchist rhetoric and teaching him the revolutionary arts.

Although a police investigation later cleared Emma of any direct involvement in Czolgosz's crime, there can be no doubt that she laid the spiritual tracks that led Czolgosz to pull out a revolver and shoot U.S. President William McKinley twice in the stomach on September 6, 1901, at the Pan-American Exposition in Buffalo, New York. McKinley died of his wounds eight days later (making Vice President Theodore Roosevelt the new president), while Czolgosz met his fate in the world's first electric chair at a New York state prison in Auburn on October 29.[27]

Alexander's death portended major changes for Russia. It kicked off anti-Jewish pogroms that rocked the Empire for decades.[28] But Russia had been humiliated, *twice*: first by the assassination of its tsar, and secondly by the reversal of a great Russian victory—the defeat of the Ottoman Empire in the Russo-Turkish War of 1877–78 and the creation of a huge Bulgarian client state in the Balkans—by Russia's erstwhile allies at the Congress of Berlin in 1878. The new tsar, Alexander III, reasserted the principle of absolutism (reversing many of his father's reforms), abolished nearly all non-Russian language education, suppressed non-Russian Orthodox religions, and put further restrictions on Jews. On the foreign affairs front, when Germany's new *Kaiser*, Wilhelm II, allowed the Russo-German "Reinsurance Treaty" to lapse in 1890, Alexander negotiated a new alliance with France in 1894, fundamentally reorganizing the great power alignments in Europe. The stage for 1914 was set.

Alexander died shortly after signing the new alliance, and was succeeded by his son, who became Tsar Nicholas II. Poor Nicholas was reputedly a loving father and husband to his family, but he inherited an Empire bursting at the seams with problems, and Nicholas just didn't have the temperament or skills to solve them. His father's reign had been relatively peaceful, but deceptively so: the Okhrana and army swiftly crushed any dissent. Nicholas reacted to these challenges the only way he knew how, by adopting his father's uncompromising and intransigent attitude. It doomed both him and his empire.

Nicholas's slide toward doom began with his continuation of his ancestors' drive into Asia. Since Vladivostok still froze part of the year, Nicholas seized a slice of Chinese Manchuria a few hundred miles south, where the waters were open year round, and by 1898 the Russians had a major naval base at Port Arthur.

Unfortunately, much of the real estate they'd swiped from the Chinese was also claimed by a newly rising power, Japan, and after Nicholas ignored Japanese invitations to negotiate—Make deals with short, yellow Asian peoples?[29]—the Japanese attacked in early 1904. As the historian Nicholas Riasanovsky put it, "Japan proved to be the more skillful aggressor."[30]

The Russo-Japanese War started badly for the Russians, then just went downhill. The Japanese bottled up the Russian fleet in Port Arthur and surrounded the port by land, fending off Russian attempts to relieve it. After driving the Russians from Korea and overrunning Manchuria, the Japanese destroyed the last remaining Russian naval fleet, the Baltic Fleet (which had steamed halfway around the world to relieve Port Arthur), at the Battle of Tsushima Straits in May 1905. With the homefront in open revolt, no fleets left, and the army's confidence seriously shaken, the Russians accepted an American offer to mediate, and a humiliating (albeit reasonable) peace treaty was signed between Russia and Japan in

Portsmouth, New Hampshire in September 1905, presided over by a grinning U.S. president, Teddy Roosevelt.

This defeat brought two major consequences for Russia. First, in July 1905, in the midst of war, a peaceful demonstration of workers with demands for food and labor law reform approached the tsar's Winter Palace in St. Petersburg, but the palace's imperial guard opened fire and Cossacks charged the crowd with sabres drawn, killing at least a hundred. The war had caused serious food and supply shortages, so when news of the "Bloody Sunday" massacre at the Winter Palace spread, open revolt broke out and the Revolution of 1905 was swiftly underway.

With fierce fighting spreading across the empire, Nicholas was forced in October 1905 to issue the October Manifesto, which granted specific concessions, including freedom of speech and assembly, the release of political prisoners, and the creation of a pseudo-parliamentary "consultative body" called the *Дума* (Duma). This manifesto did the trick and the revolution subsided, but over time Nicholas came to ignore its terms.

The second and more serious consequence of the Russo-Japanese defeat for Russia was international humiliation. It wasn't just the sheer embarrassment of having been defeated by an upstart Asian power, it was that the world had seen how poorly organized and led the Russian military was. In the great powers era of the early-20th century, this was like limping among wolves. The disastrous performance of the Russian army and navy threatened Russia's standing as a great power, and though the Empire was finally entering the early stages of industrialization, Russia's feudal state and social structures strangled many of the positive economic effects. Nicholas did what anyone in Russia's position would do, but his timing could not have been worse. When the Russian government finally straightened out its finances from the war, it embarked on a major rearmament program in 1910 to both technologically and organizationally upgrade the Russian armed forces.

The problem was that this rearmament program scared the heebie-jeebies out of neighboring Germany and Austria-Hungary, and quickly provoked a Europe-wide arms race. Already spooked by the 1894 Franco-Russian alliance, the Germans began to develop military plans for dealing with what they saw as a rising Russia, and the German *Reichswehr's* (army) goal was to put those plans to use before Russia became too strong. These plans came in handy just a few years later, in 1914, when an eighteen-year-old kid assassinated a senior member of the Habsburg family in some far-off backwater called Sarajevo, sparking crisis in Europe.

M. Dawn of the Dead: The Poland That Just Won't Go Away

As we saw in the last chapter, the Polish-Lithuanian Commonwealth died a violent (though not unexpected) death in 1795 when Russia and Prussia suppressed the Kościuszko Rebellion and partitioned the Commonwealth with Austria. With this act, the three empires wiped the Commonwealth off the map, and although some were shocked by the destruction of such a large and historical political player, most in Europe—including those who sympathized with the Poles—accepted that Poland was as irretrievably lost as the dodo.

It might have turned out that way if an opportunity for a revived Poland hadn't shown up so soon afterward; Poles flocked to revolutionary France immediately after the events of 1795 and enthusiastically embraced both the revolution and, later, Napoleon as their (political) savior. A guy who had both the desire and, as he quickly demonstrated, the ability to overthrow Europe's entrenched imperial order was just the ticket as far as Poles in 1796 were concerned. Napoleon rewarded their devotion by creating in 1806 the *Duché de Varsovie*, the "Duchy of Warsaw." This was, admittedly, a French puppet state, and its territory covered only a fraction of the old Commonwealth's, but it was Poland nonetheless with its own administration and army. It even managed to grab back some of its old territory from the Austrians in a short war in 1809. Most importantly, however, it was *not* Russian; Tsar Alexander I was forced to recognize the independence of the Duchy of Warsaw when he signed the Treaty of Tilsit with Napoleon in 1807.

Sadly, the Duchy was obviously tied to the fortunes of Napoleon, whose disastrous invasion of Russia in 1812 pretty much sealed the Duchy's fate. As soon as the straggling French troops retreated through the Duchy westward, they were followed by Tsar Alexander's Russian army, on its way to Paris to return the favor to Napoleon. Thus died the first Polish state of 19th century. The Russians could not completely make the Poland issue at the Congress of Vienna in 1815 go away, however, and so Poland v2.0 was born.

Poland—within the small borders of the Duchy of Warsaw—was recreated as an independent state (well, sort of)—tied to Russia through a royal personal union. In other words, Poland was resurrected with the Russian tsar holding the Polish crown as King of Poland. Otherwise, it was to have its own administration and army, and function as an independent country. This Poland was officially known as the Kingdom of Poland, but both then and still today most Poles refer to it as *Kongresówka Polska*, "Congress Poland," because of its creation at the Congress of Vienna.

USELESS TRIVIA: WERE THEY UPSET ABOUT SOMETHING?

Napoleon is often portrayed in the English-speaking world as a tyrant and despot, but it might surprise many to learn that in parts of Eastern Europe, Napoleon is still revered as a hero and liberator.

With the destruction of the Polish-Lithuanian Commonwealth in 1795, Poles flocked to revolutionary France, where a Polish Legion was formed in 1796 to fight in Italy, helping Napoleon capture Rome in 1798. In 1802 Napoleon sent 4,000 Poles (with some Germans and Swiss) to suppress and recapture Haiti for France, but the Poles came to sympathize with the former slaves and were severely depleted by disease (yellow fever) and desertions. Renewed fighting in Europe in 1806 brought Napoleon's armies to the Polish lands, and the ranks of the Legion swelled again with Polish volunteers. At the Battle of Somosierra in Spain in November 1808, *uhlans* (hussars) of the Polish Legion—some 6,000 strong—led a spectacular charge against four cannon battery positions uphill in a gorge that routed the defending Spanish army and opened the way clear to Madrid for the French. When Napoleon invaded Russia in 1812, nearly one-sixth of the French Grand Armée was composed of enthusiastic Polish volunteers.

After his defeat at the Battle of the Nations at Leipzig in October 1813, and his eventual surrender in April 1814, Napoleon was exiled to the tiny island of Elba off the Italian coast. The Polish Legion joined him in exile, and when Napoleon escaped his exile and reappeared in France in March 1815, he had his trusted Polish Legion by his side, fighting loyally alongside him all the way up to his final defeat at Waterloo.

Unfortunately, Congress Poland had a fatal design flaw. As a legacy of both its Commonwealth and Napoleonic heritages, it became a constitutional monarchy—meaning that Poland's king had serious restrictions on his power. The medieval Polish *Sejm* (SAYM; parliament) was revived, and it had considerable authority to challenge any royal prerogative.

This, conceptually, was just not how the Russian tsars were used to doing things. The Russian tsar's power *was* absolute, with minimal limits, meaning his word was effectively law. Even for such a liberal-minded tsar as Alexander I, the idea that there was a part of his realm in which someone could challenge his decisions was inconceivable. It wasn't long before the Russians simply began ignoring Polish laws and authority, replacing most Polish officials with Russians, and seizing control of the Polish army.

Alexander died in 1825 and was succeeded by his younger brother, Nicholas. Tsar Nicholas I already had a very conservative bent, which was exacerbated by the Decembrist Revolt in 1825; and he shortly made it very clear that he would tolerate no nonsense from the Poles. Nicholas didn't even bother being crowned king of Poland. Most Polish administrative structures were dismantled, and the constitution ignored.

Poland was a puppet state again. European maps of the day rarely bothered to include Poland, instead showing Russian territory as extending westward to Prussia. In July 1830 France exploded in revolution, followed shortly by the southern Netherlands. Conservative Nicholas decided to intervene directly but when he ordered Polish army cadets to mobilize, they revolted in November 1830. Soon all of Poland (and Lithuania) was swept up in revolution. After some initial embarrassing defeats, Russian General Ivan Paskievich (Pass-KYEH-veech) quickly rolled up the rebel forces, took back Warsaw in September 1831, and crushed the rebellion weeks later, in early October.

Tsar Nicholas dismantled the last relics of Polish statehood, and Poland was simply absorbed into the Russian state system. Paskievich was appointed governor of the Polish lands, and he set about looting Poland of its national historical treasures and shipping them off to Russia. Discontent only grew in Russian Poland throughout the middle of the century, and though Tsar Alexander II is known for his reforms, he responded forcefully to minority unrest.

Poland broke into open insurrection again in January 1863, with— just as in 1830—a revolutionary government established in Warsaw, and though this uprising was more widespread than in 1830, spreading across Lithuania, Belarus, and western Ukraine, it was less organized. By early 1864 the Russians had regained control over the rebellious lands. This time, the Russians had *really* had it with Polish uprisings, and Alexander II imposed a much harsher form of martial law. Polish was outlawed in public, members of the revolutionary government were executed, and some 18,000 Poles, Lithuanians, and Belarussians were deported to Siberia. Poland was broken up into several Russian administrative units.

USELESS TRIVIA: *APOCALYPSE THEN!*

Many know that Francis Ford Coppola based his 1979 film *Apocalypse Now!* on Joseph Conrad's novel *The Heart of Darkness*. Fewer, however, are aware of Conrad's ties to Eastern Europe.

Joseph Conrad was born Józef Teodor Konrad Korzeniowski (Ko-zheh-NYOF-skee) in Berdyczów (Bare-DIH-choof; now Бердичів [Bare-DEE-chiff] in modern-day western Ukraine) in 1857. His parents, both literary Poles, were exiled for political activities, and Józef (YOO-zef) himself fled Russian-occupied Poland in 1873. After a few years abroad Józef joined the British merchant marine, and by 1886 he had achieved British citizenship—and changed his name to "Joseph Conrad."

In 1889 Conrad sailed up the Congo River (like the lead character Marlow in *The Heart of Darkness*) into the heart of the hellish slave state then operated by the Belgian government in the Congo, where he personally witnessed the horrific living conditions of Africans in the Belgian mines and the atrocities committed against them. Conrad was stricken by malarial fever while in Congo but was also traumatized by the horrors he witnessed there. *The Heart of Darkness* emerged as a novel ten years later. Conrad probably agreed strongly with the famous lines from the 1914 Vachel Lindsay poem, "The Congo": *Listen to the yell of Leopold's*[31] *ghost, / Burning in Hell for his hand-maimed host.*

The impact of that Congo trip on Conrad had an obvious literary result. Few have bothered to further explore, however, Conrad's own sense of exile and alienation from his Polish homeland and the early death of his parents in harsh Russian exile as undercurrent themes in his works.

And as if political oppression wasn't enough, late-19th century Russian Poland also succumbed to industrialization. Poland's cities began to swell as peasants, freed by Tsar Alexander II's 1864 emancipation of Russia's serfs, filed into the cities to fill jobs in the new textile mills and factories. Warsaw grew from about 63,000 in 1800 to 686,000 in 1900, making it the Russian Empire's second largest city.

The 1863–64 uprising was followed by a smaller one in 1905 in Russian Poland in conjunction with the larger Russian Revolution that year, but this "uprising" was minor and driven more by events in St. Petersburg than Warsaw. A small underground revolutionary tradition continued well into the 20th century in Poland but most Poles resigned themselves to their occupied fate. Poles in Prussia faced growing pressure from Germanization but were distracted by industrialization there as well, while Austrian Poland, centered on Kraków, seemed stuck in the 18th century. Kraków had actually been designated an independent city by the 1815 Congress of Vienna, but an uprising by Polish aristocrats in nearby Austrian Galicia in 1846 was countered by a (very nasty) Ukrainian peasant uprising orchestrated by Vienna against the aristocrats, and Kraków fell under Habsburg rule.

With the huge influx of rural labor into Russian and Prussian/German Polish cities, social tensions rose, and a small but rising Jewish middle class became the target of growing anti-Semitism. Catherine II "the Great" had, when she absorbed much of the old Polish-Lithuanian Commonwealth in the Partitions of 1772–95, restricted most of the Commonwealth's large Jewish population to the "Pale of Settlement," essentially the lands of the old Commonwealth (i.e., in Russian Poland, Belarus, and Ukraine). Jews of the Russian Pale had few legal rights and were subjected to periodic fits of social violence both from the Tsarist authorities and local Christian populations, particularly after the assassination of Tsar Alexander II in 1881.

As poor rural Poles and poor rural Jews filled Poland's growing cities and competed for factory jobs and living quarters in what were often old medieval urban centers, two very different worlds collided—worlds that had coexisted for centuries during the old Commonwealth years but that were now forced to compete with one another.

Anti-Semitism was rising across 19th century Europe, particularly in both neighboring Russia and Germany, but tensions between Poles and Jews had an important native Polish dimension as Poles increasingly identified Polish national identity with Roman Catholicism, and the religious diversity of the medieval Commonwealth gave way to a more narrow association of Polskość (Polishness) with Roman Catholicism. This was in part driven by 19th-century Poles suffering cultural discrimination and oppression under the rule of Lutheran (Protestant) Prussians and Orthodox Russians. The Roman Catholic Church became associated with the defense of Polish culture and heritage in occupied Poland. Some Polish intelligentsia attempted to fight anti-Semitism by equating Polish and Jewish suffering under Russian rule, but to no avail. Ironically, Polish Jews were assimilating into Polish culture and society in droves at the time, but most Christian Poles still saw them as alien.

USELESS TRIVIA: TEMPURA PIEROGIS?

When the Japanese fleet fired the first salvoes of the Russo-Japanese War on the night of February 8, 1904 in Port Arthur harbor, the thought of a new and upstart power, Japan, challenging the Goliath Russia stunned the world. The Polish revolutionary Józef Piłsudski (YOO-zef Piw-SOOD-skee) immediately contacted Japanese envoys in the capitals across Europe, offering to form a Polish Legion to fight for Japan, as well as to collect intelligence in Russia for Tokyo in exchange for Japanese support and recognition for Polish independence after the war. Intrigued, the Japanese invited Piłsudski and a Polish delegation to Tokyo via Western Europe and the United States. Piłsudski arrived by ship in Yokohama from Honolulu in July. He offered to provoke uprisings among oppressed non-Russians for the Japanese, setting the Russian Empire aflame.

Unfortunately, the Japanese ultimately decided to decline Piłsudski's offers, though they did send several secret shipments of arms and ammunition to the Poles via diplomatic channels. Though he left Tokyo empty handed, Piłsudski admired Japanese efficiency and discipline, and went home to write a glowing account of the Japanese war effort.

PEOPLES OF EASTERN EUROPE: MUSLIMS

"We made you a nation of moderation and justice." (Quran 2:143)

The Muslim presence in Eastern Europe has been primarily defined by the ongoing rivalry between Christianity and Islam, and further aggravated by local rivalries within both camps. With the astounding impact Christian European civilization has had in recent centuries on the world, it is often difficult for modern-day peoples to imagine that there was a time when Islam was ascendant, and Europe, then the lesser civilization, was on the defensive. In those days, the border between the Christian and Islamic worlds, the "front line" in their conflict, as it were, moved from the Middle East into Europe, to the very gates of Vienna—and remained there for centuries.

This meant that Eastern Europe became the battleground on which countless crusades and jihads were waged, with enough bloodshed and destruction to fill a thousand and one nights' tales. But Islam hasn't only made an impression on Eastern Europe through its soldiers. Traders, diplomats, architects, and scholars from the Arab lands, North Africa, the Cordoba Caliphate, the Volga Bulgars, Persia, and Central Asia have crisscrossed the region. And the cultural flow was not one way; it was said in the 18th century that so many Balkan natives worked in Ottoman administrative positions in Constantinople that the Sultan's court functioned as much in Greek, Albanian, and Serbian as Turkish or Classical Arabic.

For the most part, the Ottoman Turks did not coerce Balkan Christians into converting to Islam. As the historian John Stoye put it: "They did not proselytize because they wanted subjects, not Muslims."[1] Then why, if they weren't coerced, did so many European Christians in the Balkans convert? Some did for financial advantage, to escape special taxes laid on non-Muslims. Many converted simply because Islam seemed to be ascendant; with the Turks decisively and repeatedly defeating the best warriors Christian Europe could throw at them, might it not suggest that Islam really *was* the true religion? The Ottoman Empire of the 14th–16th centuries was a wealthy civilization, plugged into the booming Asian trade network that stretched from Eastern Africa to India to the Far East—that same trade network Europeans were just becoming aware of, with its exotic spices, porcelains, fabrics, and foods. It is also helpful to remember that much of the Balkans spent five centuries under Ottoman rule; perhaps it isn't so much surprising that some converted as that more *didn't*. It may be as simple as access; it seems that Islam may have followed the ancient north-south Roman roads, which were more plentiful in the western Balkans, into Bosnian and Albanian towns and villages. Meanwhile, in the less urbanized eastern Balkans, the vast countryside was more remote and isolated from events in the cities and therefore better able to preserve older local (Christian) traditions. The western Balkans' relative cosmopolitanism made exposure to Islam more widespread, and the potential economic and social advantages of converting more apparent.[2]

USELESS TRIVIA: قضهنلا رصع, A MUSLIM RENAISSANCE!

In the late-19th century, a theological revolt arose among Muslim scholars in Russian-ruled Tartarstan (Crimea and the southern Volga). Led by İsmail Gaspıralı ("Gasprinsky" in Russian), the *Jadids* (from the Arabic *usul-i jaded*, "the new method") preached the pursuit of knowledge for Muslims. Early Islam had embraced science and scholarship, but in the 11th century a scholar named Al-Ghazali rejected inquisitiveness in favor of *taqlid*: blind faith in official religious edicts. The 19th-century Jadids, however, revived the Quranic notion of *ijtihad*, of independent study and verification. As Kazan historian Rafael Khakimov notes, Muslim fundamentalists tend to treat the Quran as a criminal code but Jadids saw the Quran as a living text that might say different things to different people—in other words, as encouraging exactly the diversity the fundamentalists deny. For instance, the Jadids downplayed some aspects of Muslim Shari'a law as "Arabisms," products of Arab culture and tradition rather than the Quran. The Jadids encouraged Muslims to learn about the wider world. The *Qadimists* (Old-Timers) rejected the Jadids but Jadidism spread throughout the Tartar lands and to Russian Central Asia. Sadly, the Russian Tsarist, and later Soviet, authorities feared the Jadids and so Stalin targeted them in his 1930s purges.[3]

Today there are an estimated 35 million Muslims in Eastern Europe—mostly Bosniaks, Albanians, Turks, and Tartars. What distinguishes Eastern Europe's Muslim community from Western Europe's is that Western Europe's Muslims are mostly relative newcomers, immigrants; most

Muslims in Eastern Europe are natives whose families have lived there for *centuries*. The Muslims living in Western Europe have brought with them the very recent cultural traditions and social beliefs of their native lands—usually the poorest and most rural regions of Pakistan, Algeria, or Somalia—which is causing considerable social friction in our post-9/11 urbanized Western world. Eastern Europe's Muslims, on the other hand, are native *Europeans* with long-standing local roots.

All of this is to say that there is a uniquely European brand of Islam, with deep cultural roots in both European and Islamic history and tradition. Despite the recent attempts of Muslim fundamentalists from Saudi Arabia, Egypt, and elsewhere in the Middle East to plant the seeds of militant fundamentalist Islam in Bosnia and Albania, indications are that their call to violent jihad has largely fallen on deaf ears in the Muslim Balkans.

The European Union, as it struggles with Western-Islamic relations, should consider looking to Europe's native Muslims for help in both understanding better the Muslim worldview, as well as holding up the example of Eastern European Muslims who do not see conflict between their Muslim faith and a modern secular republic or free markets. Modern-day Islam does not have to be defined exclusively by militantly xenophobic Saudi clerics or rural Pakistani tribal elders; there is an alternative *modern-day* model for Islam in Eastern Europe. To quote the Grand Mufti of Bosnia-Herzegovina, Mustafa Cerić (TSAIR-eetch):

> We are at the beginning of the debate about Shari'a. I am very glad that many authors now are writing about Shari'a from all perspectives. By this activity Shari'a has a chance to survive, I believe. The understanding of Shari'a will be modified. It will be put into the context of our experience of modern times, I believe.
>
> But Shari'a is not a privilege of Muslim law. You have a Shari'a of Moses and a Shari'a of Jesus and a Shari'a of Muhammad. The Koran says that if God wanted you to be one nation, he could make it. But he made many Shari'a for you and many ways to approach the truth. But you have to [take part] in good deeds. So no one has a monopoly on truth. And no one has a monopoly on the Shari'a.[4]

Figure 51. Eastern Europe Timeline, 1914–39

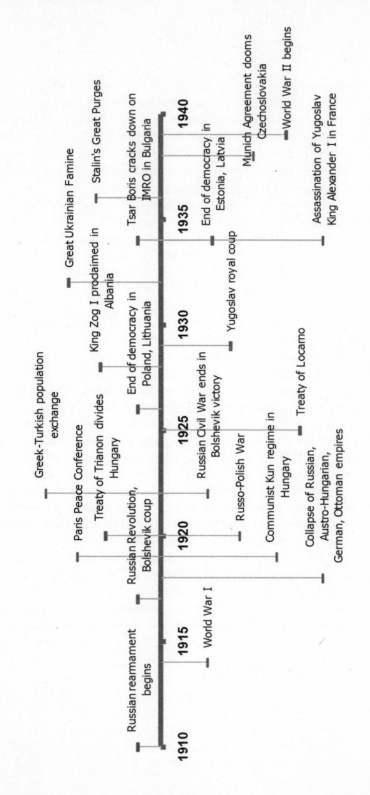

6. THE GREAT WAR, AND A MAGIC YEAR 1914-1939

THEN THE HONEYMOON IS OVER

"Strong, healthy, and flourishing nations increase in numbers. From a given moment they require a continual expansion of their frontiers, they require new territory for the accommodation of their surplus population. Since almost every part of the globe is inhabited, new territory must, as a rule be obtained at the cost of its possessors—that is today, by conquest, which thus becomes a law of necessity. The right of conquest is universally acknowledged."

—General Friedrich von Bernhardi,
Deutschland und der Nächste Krieg
(Germany and the Next War), 1911

"Who rules East Europe commands the Heartland; Who rules the heartland commands the World Island; Who rules the World Island commands the World."

—Sir Halford Mackinder,
Democratic Ideals and Reality, 1919

CHAPTER SUMMARY

When most folks today think of World War I, they think of old black-and-white silent films with jerky movements, and guys wearing ridiculous handlebar moustaches. For its time, though, hiding behind the poor quality film and peacocklike uniforms was a shockingly violent war unlike any that had ever come before. It was the first great war of the industrial age, with factory-made death machines spewing out dead and maimed soldiers at a rate never seen before. 19th-century Napoleonic tactics came up against 20th-century technology, and the result over four years was some 12 million dead,[1] four collapsed empires, and a world shaken to its core. The global economy was mauled, limping on for a decade until ultimately collapsing in 1929. The world of 1918 is almost unrecognizable to that of 1914.

Eastern Europe had widely varying experiences of the war, ranging from Bohemia's and Hungary's relative seclusion from most of the fighting to the horrors the war inflicted on Serbia, Poland, and Ukraine. But its most tangible and lasting effect was the destruction of the four empires that had ruled Eastern Europe for centuries. The collapse of these empires in 1918 enabled the (re-)birth of countries across East Central Europe, belatedly ushering in the age of the nation state in the region.

New nation states led by politically inexperienced elites can be problematic, however. Border disputes poisoned relations in the region and disrupted economic development as rivals refused all cooperation. Trade on the Danube River in the 1920s, for example, was one-sixth its prewar volume. As living standards fell, antidemocratic extremist parties gained ground in elections. By the early 1930s, nearly all the Eastern European states had devolved into right-wing authoritarian dictatorships, with the single exception of Czechoslovakia. As the Great Depression in the 1930s squeezed the life out of the region's already backward and stunted economies, most states turned to either the West or Nazi Germany for Great Power security and aid. It is important to remember, especially in the English-speaking world, that Hitler wasn't yet seen as the madman of World War II in the 1930s, and that many Eastern Europeans feared Stalin's Soviet Union *far more* than Hitler's Germany. Horror stories of collectivization, Siberian gulags, and the Great Purges sent chills down Eastern European spines.

From the beginning, the victorious Western Entente powers tried to control the process of state creation in Eastern Europe through the post-war 1919 Paris Peace Conference, hoping to mold the region into an anti-German and anti-Russian (Bolshevik) bloc, but the West was neither willing nor able to invest the kinds of military and economic resources necessary to have real influence in the region. And as Germany and (Bolshevik) Russia slowly recovered, both sought once again to dominate the region. Despite the euphoria of 1918, it was an extraordinarily dangerous time for Eastern Europe.

A. The War 258
B. Paris, 1919 263
C. The Ottoman Empire Goes Out in Style 265
D. Austria-Hungary as a Bug on the Windshield 268
E. Serbia and History 272
F. Montenegro is Pushed Off the Cliff 274
G. The Failed Superstates I: Yugoslavia 274
H. Bulgaria Tries 1913 Over Again 277
I. The Failed Superstates II: Romania 280
J. Albania: Let's Try That Again 283
K. Hungary Loses the War . . . Again 285
L. The Failed Superstates III: Czechoslovakia 289
M. Ukraine: With Friends Like These 294
N. Belarus Gets Its 15 Minutes . . . Literally 298
O. Libre Baltica: Lithuania, Latvia, and Estonia 299
P. Russia and How Russians Do Change 303
Q. The Failed Superstates IV: Poland 310

A. The War

Let's begin with a general outline of World War I as it unfolded so you have some background for each country's own experience of the war, as described in more detail in each section of this chapter.

In the summer of 1914, the leaders of the great powers decided that they had no choice but to fight. Some of them may have actively sought a European war, but no one wanted the war they got, a war in which Europeans employed their extraordinary ability to mobilize human and material resources to destroy one another. This was a democratic war that reached into the lives of virtually every European; it was also an industrial war, in which death and devastation became the principal purpose of economic production. The war consumed millions of lives, most of them young, and vast resources, all of them wasted. It uprooted ancient institutions, disrupted newly created economic bonds, and shattered the delicate arrangements that had helped to restrain the great powers since 1815.[2]

Ever since the defeat of Napoleon in 1815, the (shaken) European Powers were obsessed with ensuring a continent-wide war did not happen again. Unfortunately, by the early-20th century these efforts had been reduced to what could best be described as a Mexican standoff between two blocs of great powers. This was the state of Europe on June 28, 1914, when an eighteen-year-old Bosnian Serbian nationalist, Gavrilo Princip (Gahv-REE-lo PREEN-tseep), fired three fateful shots in Bosnia's capital, Sarajevo (Sah-rah-YAY-vo), killing the visiting Habsburg archduke Franz Ferdinand and his wife, Sofie.

This assassination did not mean war was inevitable, however. The average well-read person sitting at home on the morning of June 29, reading the previous day's news, would probably not have guessed that in a month's time most of Europe's great armies would be marching against one another. The path that led from a political murder in a Balkan backwater to a worldwide war involving millions of Europeans, North Americans, Asians, and Africans fighting each other is called the July Crisis of 1914. It's a tricky and complicated path, but we'll sort it out very briefly here.

As soon as news of the Archduke's murder spread, sympathetic telegrams rolled in from all the great powers urging the Habsburgs to decisive action. At this early stage in the crisis, Europe's great powers were united in their desire for Vienna to resolve its "Serbia problem" before it became a larger European issue. However, Austria-Hungary's leadership was divided over the wisdom of war with Serbia.

While ministers in Vienna and Budapest bickered and the infamous Habsburg bureaucracy began its slow grind towards war, in St. Petersburg panic set in. Russia certainly did not appreciate radicals assassinating their rulers—remember that Tsar Nicholas II's grandfather had died in such a manner back in 1881—but Serbia was the last outpost of Russian influence in the Balkans, so if Russia was to remain a Great Power (after the Russo-Japanese War of 1904–05), she had to defend her interests. In a crucial step of the July Crisis, Russia declared her support for Serbia if Austria-Hungary attacked it. This complicated everything. The Austro-Hungarian military definitely could not handle both Serbia and Russia at the same time, so Vienna turned to *its* ally, Germany.

There is a long story of fumbling over mobilization of conscripts between Russia and Germany during the July Crisis but in essence, Germany—fearful of growing Russian power—gave its ally, Austria-Hungary, the infamous *carte blanche* (blank check) to do whatever it wanted with Serbia; Germany would deal with Russia.

But Germany had a problem, too: the Franco-Russian alliance of 1894. This alliance meant that Germany was surrounded by its enemies and would have to fight a two-front war, as indeed France declared that it would stick by Russia. However, the Germans had realized in 1894 that this day would come, and had planned for it. Their famous "Schlieffen Plan" essentially said, attack France first and knock it out of the war just like in 1870,3 then turn Germany's full attention to Russia—the bigger threat, according to Berlin—and sort the Ruskies out.

There was still a major variable in these plans, however: What would Britain do? Britain only had very vague agreements with France; would London go to war for France and Russia? The answer came when Germany announced its plans to bypass French fortifications on the Franco-German border by going through Belgium, and the plight of "poor little Belgium" swiftly turned wavering British public opinion. Britain would indeed fight. And so there you have it; exactly a month after the assassination in Sarajevo, on July 28, 1914, Vienna declared war on Serbia, Russia declared war on Austria-Hungary, Germany on Russia, France on Germany (and vice-versa), and when the first Fritz soldier crossed the Belgian border on August 3, Britain declared war on Germany.

You've now got yourself a world war. Why a "world" war when we're only talking about five countries (plus Serbia)? Well, keep in mind that in 1914, these five countries ruled most of the world through vast colonial empires. Literally millions of Indians, Estonians, South Africans, Egyptians, Canadians, Australians, Arabs, Poles, Congoese, Tartars, Vietnamese, Slovenians, etc. etc. etc, eventually marched off to war for these imperial states or in affiliation with them. Both sides mobilized some 65 million soldiers during the war.[4]

So, how did the war itself go? Put bluntly, not well. There had been an explosion (no pun intended) in new military technologies over the previous century, and few in 1914 understood the new technologies well or how to use them (or defend against them) effectively. Most of these new technologies, like the machine gun, had been used in many smaller, local conflicts already, but they hadn't been tried against another army of similar armament and abilities to see how they fared *when the other guys had the same kinds of weapons and training.*

If you think this is odd, consider that we are in a similar situation today, where we have a huge number of very sophisticated legacy weapons and weapon systems developed in the Cold War that have been used in countless minor regional wars but never (thank goodness) in the grand-scale confrontation for which they were designed. We really don't know how the American and Soviet air forces, for example, would have fared against one another head-to head, and we are forced to rely on Tom Clancy–style fictionalized accounts to imagine. Well, in 1914, they found out.

Figure 52. Eastern Europe in May 1914

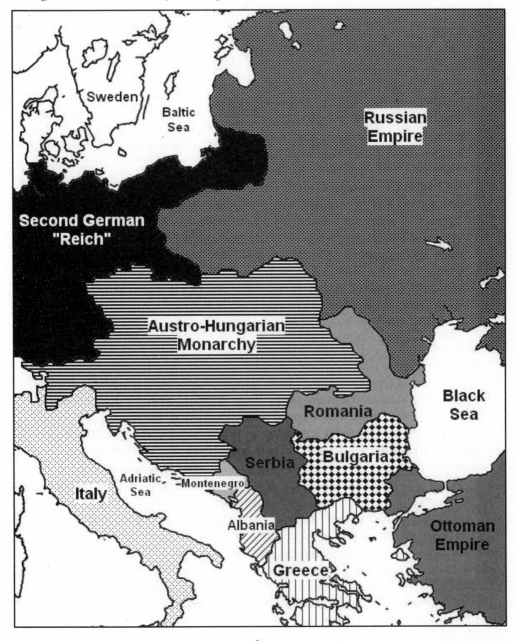

On the Western Front, following the Schlieffen Plan, the Germans immediately invaded Belgium in August 1914, and pushed into France, where they met hard resistance as they slammed up against the French, British, and Belgian armies. In some extremely bitter fighting in September, the Allies managed to halt the German advance on the Marne River, saving Paris. However, while they had stopped the Germans, they were too weak to push them out of France. By November 1914, unable to defeat one another and exhausted, both sides settled in and began building defensive works—the infamous trenches everyone associates with World War I—that stretched some 400 miles from the North Sea to the Swiss border, and that essentially is the story of the Western Front.

Over the next three years, each side tried to penetrate the others' trench systems in massive battles involving hundreds of thousands of men each, for minimal gain. Some of the most horrific battles of human history were fought in these three years on the stagnant Western Front, such as the battles of the Marne, Ypres, Verdun, and Somme. In the first four months of the war alone, almost a million soldiers were lost.[5]

The problem for Germany was that by failing to conquer France in the opening months, the Schlieffen Plan became useless. Germany now had to fight on two main fronts, and its allies turned out to be more liabilities than help. The Germans repulsed a Russian invasion of East Prussia in September 1914, but the Russians were more successful against Austro-Hungarian forces, so that the Germans continuously had to help stabilize the Russo-Austrian front in Galicia. In 1915, the Germans and Habsburgs finally managed to conquer Serbia, leaving the Balkans quiet for most of the rest of the war. After a huge scare in late 1916 when the Russian Brusilov Offensive in Galicia nearly destroyed the Habsburg army, Russia collapsed into revolution in March 1917 and the Germans were able to press eastward deep into Ukraine and the Baltics with minimal resistance. This also meant that Germany was finally able to switch most of its armies to the Western Front.

The Russian Revolution was a boon for Germany but it was more than counterbalanced in advantage by Berlin provoking the United States into the war on the Allied side in 1917. This changed everything, as the Americans could pump millions of fresh soldiers into the Western Front, so in desperation the Germans launched a last-ditch desperate attempt in the spring of 1918 to break through the Allied lines on the Western Front before the Americans could arrive in large numbers.

After months of brutal battles, by August the German armies just gave out. And so the Allies—France, Britain, the U.S., and others—launched coordinated counteroffensives that by the autumn of 1918 drove the Germans from much of France. In early November 1918, Kaiser Wilhelm II abdicated the German throne and fled into exile to neutral Netherlands,[6] while his armies were in full retreat and disintegrating. The armistice of November 11 ended the war.

B. Paris, 1919; the West (Re-)Discovers Eastern Europe

The Peace conference that ended World War I was essentially an Anglo-French show, with the U.S. playing a high-profile but limited role. Russia, which had collapsed into revolution and withdrawn from the war, was not included. The U.S. delegation did want to use the conference to fundamentally reshape international politics to avoid future wars, but the visionary who came up with these ideas, President Woodrow Wilson, was too stubborn and inflexible to negotiate their practical realization. Germany envisioned the conference as a roundtable where all the issues that led to the war would be discussed (perhaps as they should have been in 1914), but was shocked to discover that Britain and France were only interested in revenge. The French in particular, with 1.4 million Frenchmen dead and the whole of eastern France in ruins, were not in a conciliatory mood.

The Germans were not actually included in the conference, but rather simply informed of its decisions, and they were stunned to learn of the terms reached: enormous reparations to the Allies, territorial concessions to France, Poland, Czechoslovakia, and Lithuania, and worse yet, Article 231 of the Treaty of Versailles, which blamed Germany (and its allies) *exclusively* for the war:

> The Allied and Associated Governments affirm and Germany accepts the responsibility of Germany and her allies for causing all the loss and damage to which the Allied and Associated Governments and their nationals have been subjected as a consequence of the war imposed upon them by the aggression of Germany and her allies.

Throughout the 1920s Weimar German leaders like Gustav Stresemann managed to soften or circumvent most of the treaty's harshest provisions, but that clause blaming Germany for the war, coupled with the territorial losses—to *Eastern Europeans!*—infuriated most Germans and fed nationalist and political extremism across Germany, destabilizing the Weimar Republic. There *were* some Germans who, particularly after the Treaty of Brest-Litovsk was imposed on Bolshevik Russia in March, 1918, felt unease at what had seemed like naked German imperialism in the east, as Hitler later complained:

> At the very first sentence containing a criticism of Versailles, you had the stereo-typed cry flung at you, "What about Brest-Litovsk?," "And Brest-Litovsk?" The masses roared this again and again, until gradually they grew hoarse or the speaker finally gave up in his attempt to convince them. You felt like dashing your head against the wall in despair over such people![7]

Nevertheless, most Germans rejected the Treaty of Versailles and sought to revise it, and those revisions more often than not targeted Eastern Europe. Indeed, the victorious West recognized that Germany's defeat had left a power vacuum in Eastern Europe, and they were also concerned about the rise of Bolshevism in Russia, Hungary, and Bavaria8 in 1919. A solution was devised: a (Western-supervised) bloc of allied Eastern European states that would keep both Russian communism and revived German expansionism at bay. This was one of the principal goals of the Paris Peace Conference—to establish a strong string of countries in Eastern Europe to counter Russia and Germany. To this end, the West tried to micromanage the birth of the new states in Eastern Europe, finding itself bogged down at the Paris Peace Conference in intensive negotiations, arguments, and counterarguments by various national delegations fighting over borders for historic and strategic land claims. A pantomime of Eastern European nationalism and absurd petty bickering paraded through the Versailles palace halls, poisoning (and paralyzing) relations in the region for decades.

Still, for all the drama at Versailles, there was a fatal flaw in the West's plan: it could not afford the necessary kinds of military and economic investment that its vision for Eastern Europe required. Large tracts of Eastern Europe had served as battlegrounds in the World War and lay in ruins. Moreover, the collapse of the four empires that had ruled the region until 1918 also meant the collapse of laws and court systems, postal and communications systems, currencies, trade networks, and so on. Eastern Europe in 1918 required massive infusions of cash just to reachieve the economic levels of 1914, much less to develop into countries capable of confronting German and Russian aggression. Britain and France, economically exhausted by the World War, just couldn't afford that in 1919, and the U.S. just wanted to sort out the European map equitably and go home. France halfheartedly created an anti-German alliance in the region called *La Petit Entente* (Little Entente), but it had little support and rusted into irrelevance by 1929. By 1925, Britain and France realized (after a series of European crises) that:

- The Versailles system policies of 1919 were not working.
- The Eastern European states were not going to solve the West's eastern strategic problems.

Therefore, Britain and France reached out to Germany in a spirit of reconciliation and tried to patch up relations. Berlin responded positively, and the three countries (plus Belgium and Italy) signed the Treaty of Locarno in October 1925, which pledged the Germans to accept their current borders—their current *western* borders, that is. The treaty said nothing of Germany's *eastern* borders. The West also arranged nonaggression treaties between Germany and Poland and Czechoslovakia, but the message for Eastern Europe at Locarno was clear: You're on your own.

The Locarno Treaty was a devastating blow for Eastern Europe, and still haunts the region to this day, undermining state legitimacy and leaving the region's countries vulnerable to both internal and external enemies. Germany realized the West was abandoning Eastern Europe, and Soviet Russia took note as well.

C. The Ottoman Empire Goes Out in Style

Having just barely survived the Balkan Wars of 1912–13, about the last thing the Ottoman Empire needed in 1914 was another major conflict. It entered the war, however, in the mistaken belief that with its new German ally, it could recover some of its territory and imperial stamina. That said, Ottoman military forces were often underestimated by the Allied military leaders, with bloody consequences. Still, the Ottoman Empire was simply not ready for World War I, and the experience proved fatal.

In 1914 and 1915, the war went fairly well. Two modern German battle-ships in the Ottoman navy (with German crews wearing fezes), the *Goeben* and the *Breslau*, shelled Russian ports in the Black Sea while a British inva-sion of Mesopotamia (modern-day Iraq) in 1915 was halted in its tracks by the Ottomans at Kut (about sixty miles south of Baghdad). Then of course came the ill-planned Anglo-French (with Australian and New Zea-lander "ANZACs") invasion of Gallipoli in April 1915, which was bloodily repulsed by Ottoman forces by December, at the cost of some 140,000 Allied and 250,000 Ottoman lives. The defense of Gallipoli was a heroic moment for the Ottoman Empire, but one of its last.

The victories of 1915–16 were impressive, but the failures were fatal. Hoping to regain old lost territories, Ottoman forces invaded the Russian Caucasus in 1915 only to be resoundingly repulsed. This provoked one of the war's worst atrocities, as Ottoman forces vented their anger on the (Orthodox Christian) Armenians, killing 1.5 million unarmed Armenian civilians in horrific massacres. Still, the principal danger for the Ottoman Empire came from within. The British secretly inserted a young officer with a background in Middle Eastern archaeology, Thomas Edward Lawrence (or "T.E. Lawrence," the famous "Lawrence of Arabia"), who spoke flu-ent Arabic, into Ottoman Arabia in 1915 to organize rebellious Arab tribes against the Turks. Lawrence's mission proved a spectacular success, and by late 1917 Lawrence's Arab forces were invading Ottoman Syria while a Brit-ish army invaded from Egypt. To boot, a second British invasion of Meso-potamia (Iraq) in 1917 was a success. Finally, the Allies launched a lightning offensive in the Balkans in September 1918 from Greece, forcing Bulgaria to the peace table two weeks later, before advancing to Constantinople's outskirts. The Ottoman Sultan requested an armistice on October 30, 1918.

The Allies intended to continue using the Ottoman Empire in its tradi-tional role as a doorstop in Central Asia and the Caucasus to hold back Rus-sian imperial ambitions, particularly since Russia was now controlled by Lenin and the Bolsheviks. However, the Allies' actions repeatedly under-mined the Sultan's authority. First, the British occupied Constantinople in March 1920 after extensive rioting, making the Sultan appear powerless. Then the Allies forced the Sultan to sign the extremely unpopular Treaty of Sèvres in Paris in August 1920, which—in accordance with the secret Sykes-Picot Agreement between Britain and France in 1916—divided most of the Ottoman Empire between the British and French colonial empires, including ethnic Turkish regions. This treaty gave impetus to an already-growing Turkish nationalist opposition movement led by General Mustafa Kemal—a hero of the Battle of Gallipoli—who gained immense prestige when his Turkish nationalist forces repulsed an Allied-sanctioned Greek invasion of Anatolia and drove Greek forces out of Turkey.

USELESS TRIVIA: FADING MEMORIES . . .

When the leader of the new Turkish Republic, Mustafa Kemal, buried the Ottoman Empire, he initially only stripped Mehmed VI of his title as *Sultan*, leaving him the religious title of "Caliph." Mehmed couldn't bare the insult and fled into exile on a British destroyer, so Mehmed's cousin became Caliph Abdulmecid II. As the republican Turkish authorities quickly discovered, however, the Muslim world still deferred to the caliph's authority, and Muslims as far afield as Persia, Arabia, and Africa still sought the Caliph's guidance. This lingering deference to religious authority was too much of a threat to the Turkish Republic, so in April 1924 the caliphate was abolished and Abdulmecid was forced into exile. The last remnants of the Ottoman Empire were gone.

In its heyday, the Ottoman Empire was seen by most Muslims as the heir to the classical-era Arab Islamic empire(s), but as it slid into decline, coupled with the rise of 19th-century Arab, Persian (Iranian), and Turkish nationalism, the Turks came to be seen by many Arabs as mere barbarian usurpers. This was most pointedly illustrated in January 2002, when Saudi Arabia demolished a 222-year-old Ottoman fortress, Eçyad Castle (EDGE-yahd; in Arabic *Ajyad*) to build a shopping mall and hotel, despite vigorous protests from the Turkish government and United Nations. Overlooking the holy sites of Mecca, Eçyad Castle was built by the Ottomans in 1780 to protect Muslim pilgrims on their *hajj*. Some Arab states have systematically eradicated historical remnants of the centuries-long Ottoman era in their countries, attempting to erase a part of their history they now find distasteful—although, as the republican Turkish authorities discovered in the early 1920s, most Muslims then viewed the death of the Ottoman state as a calamity for Islam.

The Ottoman dynasty itself went extinct only recently when Ertugrul Osman—the last surviving member of the Osman family, and would-be Sultan—passed away at ninety-seven years old in September 2009 in Istanbul. He spent most of his life living in an inconspicuous apartment over a grocery story in New York before being invited back to Turkey by the Turkish government in 1991.

The Greeks had occupied primarily Greek-inhabited coastal Anatolia in 1919 but pushed further inland in 1920 (with Allied blessing), only to be halted in 1921 by Kemal's Turkish forces, and driven back by a counteroffensive a year later, in August 1922, which sent the Greek army in full retreat toward the coast. In a grim precedent to Dunkirk, 1.5 million Greek troops and civilian refugees fled the Turks in panic across the Aegean Sea in a makeshift flotilla of civilian and military ships, while Turkish forces rampaged through ancient Greek cities all along the Anatolian coast. Allied naval forces off the coast watched but did nothing. By October 1922, the Nationalists controlled most of Turkey.

USELESS TRIVIA: A BAD PRECEDENT . . .

With the rise of nationalism in 19th- and 20th-century Europe, ethnic minorities, often coexisting peacefully for centuries, suddenly became seen as liabilities and traitors. Nationalist zealots looked for ways to make ethnic boundaries—often centuries old—fit new state borders.

One of the first large-scale incidents of ethnic cleansing was actually organized by mutual agreement between the two parties involved, the Greeks and Turks, in 1923. The Treaty of Lausanne, which formally ended hostilities between Turkey (in place of the collapsed Ottoman Empire) and the Allies of World War I, also ended a war between Greece and Turkey after the failed Greek invasion of Anatolia in 1919–22. Some 1.5 million Greeks had already fled Turkish Anatolia, and so, to find room for them, the Greeks negotiated the expulsion of 500,000 Turks from Greek Thrace and Macedonia. The Greeks had forced a similar arrangement on Bulgaria the year prior, though on a far smaller scale.

This Greco-Turkish agreement meant the destruction of Greek communities along Anatolia's Aegean coastline and the southern Black Sea coastline dating 3,000 years back to the days of Troy—and, indeed, including the ancient ruins of Troy itself. This "population exchange" created large pools of impoverished and displaced populations that were radicalized by their experiences, serving as powerful agents of destabilization in both countries for decades to come.

Kemal founded the Turkish Republic and moved the capital to Ankara. The basic problem for the Turkish nationalists was that there was no precedent for an Islamic republic; throughout all of Islamic history, the ruler's power derived from his role as leader for the *umma*, the Islamic religious community, but a republic's ruler derives his (or her) power from the people being ruled. Still, Mustafa Kemal, now widely known as *Kemal Atatürk* (Kemal, Father of the Turks), forged ahead with a new constitution and a modern secular republic. In July 1923, the Allies finally caved in and recognized the Turkish Republic, renegotiating the Treaty of Sèvres for the more equitable Treaty of Lausanne.

D. Austria-Hungary as a Bug on the Windshield

The Austrian empire had the great opportunity of making Central Europe into a strong, unified state. But the Austrians, alas, were divided between an arrogant Pan-German nationalism and their own Central European mission. They did not succeed in building a federation of equal nations, and their failure has been the misfortune of the whole of Europe. Dissatisfied, the other nations of Central Europe blew apart their empire in 1918, without realizing that, in spite of its inadequacies, it was irreplaceable. After the First World War, Central Europe was therefore transformed into a region of small, weak states, whose vulnerability ensured first Hitler's conquest and ultimately Stalin's triumph.

—Czech writer Milan Kundera, "The Tragedy of Central Europe"[9]

The Czech historian František Palacký once famously said in the mid-19th century, "If Austria did not exist, it would be necessary to invent it." He was referring to Austria's role as a buffer and placeholder between the other great powers in Eastern Europe. The Austrian, and later Austro-Hungarian, empire served both to keep the very ethnically messy Eastern Europe under wraps, while at the same time serving to minimize Russian influence in Europe. Though counted among the Great Powers in the 19th century, the Habsburg military machine had nearly faded into irrelevance by 1900, seemingly oblivious to the fast pace of technological development elsewhere in Europe. Still, even as late as 1914, for all the political and ethnic strife of the preceding decades, the Austro-Hungarian army, with its myriad nationalities, obediently marched off to war. Desertions among the minority nationalities only became common when it became obvious the war was lost, by 1917–18.

Austria-Hungary's aims in the war were to punish Serbia—meaning, invade the country and install a puppet regime in Belgrade that would not support Serbian nationalism—while at the same time holding off the Russian armies in the east until such time as the Germans were finally able to deal effectively with them. Austria-Hungary's army proved unable to accomplish either goal very well. The first invasion of Serbia was thoroughly repulsed over the summer of 1914, while a second one in the autumn managed to capture Belgrade briefly in December before again being driven out by the tiny but tenacious Serbian Army. Ten months later, after convincing Bulgaria to join—Bulgaria was still seeking revenge for the Second Balkan War of 1913—a joint German, Austro-Hungarian, and Bulgarian invasion in October 1915 overwhelmed Serb defenses and successfully occupied the country. Habsburg forces meted out a brutal campaign of revenge against Serbian civilians both for the embarrassing defeats of 1914 and for guerrilla activity throughout the Serbian hill country.

Figure 53. Eastern Europe in 1924

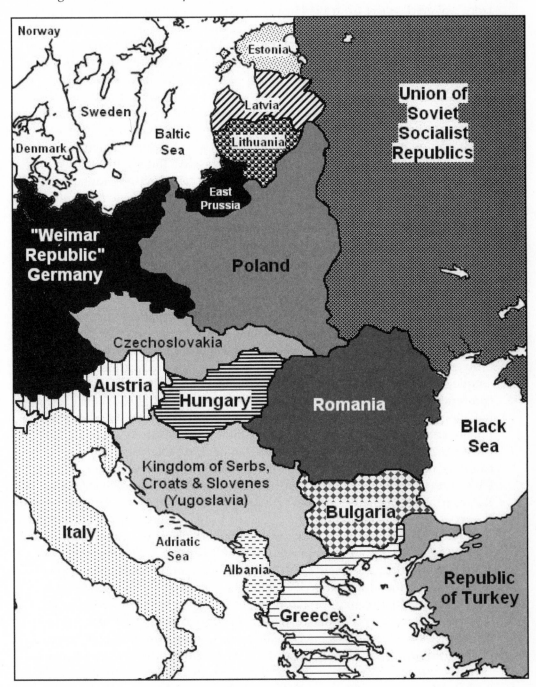

Things didn't go as planned on the Russian front, either. The eastern front wavered wildly from 1914 to 1916 as Russian fortunes rose or fell, but Habsburg forces suffered repeated embarrassing defeats at Russian hands, requiring constant German interventions to hold Austria-Hungary's eastern flank. The largest battle came in the summer of 1916, when the Russians launched in June a massive offensive led by General Aleksei Brusilov (hence, the "Brusilov Offensive"), which, over four months, brought Russian forces back to the Carpathian Mountains and removed more than a million Austro-Hungarian soldiers from the war, nearly destroying the Austro-Hungarian army as a fighting force. Once again, German forces came to the rescue and managed to halt the Russians, though just barely.

The Dual Monarchy also found itself fighting on two more fronts, both with erstwhile allies, as Romania coveted Transylvania and Italy wanted Tyrolia and the Dalmatian coast. With the Russian Brusilov Offensive in full swing, Romania renounced its treaty with Austria-Hungary and entered the war on the Allied side, invading Habsburg Transylvania in August 1916. Anticipating such a move, a joint German and Austro-Hungarian force repulsed the Romanian invasion and quickly overran most of Romania itself, occupying Bucharest in December 1916.

Romania, with its government exiled to Iași, in Moldavia, held out until 1918. Italy declared war against the Austro-Hungarian Monarchy in April 1915, but for all the ineptitude of the Habsburg forces, the Italian army was even more woefully unprepared for modern warfare. After a couple years of fighting avalanche-provoking artillery duels in the Alps, a combined German-Austro-Hungarian force nearly took Italy out of the war in October-November 1917 at the Battle of Caporetto, when the panicked Italian Army retreated in disarray. It surrendered almost two whole Italian provinces in three weeks, as well as 280,000 Italian POWs and some 3,100 cannons, nearly all of the Italian Army's artillery. Ernest Hemingway, the later famous American writer, was a volunteer ambulance driver for the Italian army in this battle and later wrote his novel *A Farewell to Arms* about his experiences at Caporetto.

Habsburg Emperor Franz Josef I, who had ruled the Empire since the revolutions of 1848, died peacefully in November 1916. He was succeeded by his grand-nephew Karl (Charles), who sought to secretly negotiate an exit from the war in 1917 but was rebuffed by the Allies. The Italians got their revenge for Caporetto in October 1918 in the Battle of Vittorio Veneto, in the midst of which the fragile Habsburg army simply imploded. Vienna was open to an Italian occupation and was saved only by an armistice. This was just as well, because by early November 1918, the empire itself had also ceased to exist. In October, 1918, Emperor Karl I offered a version of Franz Ferdinand's popular federated model of empire as a concession to the empire's minorities, but it was forty years too late. They voted with their feet: on October 28, Czechoslovakia declared its independence; on October 29, the Kingdom of Slovenes, Croats, and Serbs (Yugoslavia) followed suit; and on October 31, Hungary left. Austria bolted on November 10, and Poland the next day. Six centuries of Habsburg imperial rule were over.

At the Paris Peace Conference in 1919, the Western Allies wanted to keep the Habsburg Empire at its Eastern Europe nanny post, though they had also agreed to recognize several new countries in the region. U.S. president Woodrow Wilson tried to have it both ways in the tenth of his Fourteen Points:[10]

X. The peoples of Austria-Hungary, whose place among the nations we wish to see safeguarded and assured, should be accorded the freest opportunity of autonomous development.

USELESS TRIVIA: MAYBE NOT THE MODEL SOLDIER . . .

A Czech veteran of World War I, Jaroslav Hašek (Yah-RO-slav HA-shek), decided after the war to pen a satire of his life in the Austro-Hungarian army. In an age before television or radio, Hašek began writing *volumes*, and was on volume IV of his effort when he died of tuberculosis in 1923. Friends nonetheless added colorful illustrations to Hašek's unfinished work and published it in a single volume that same year under the title *Osudy dobrého vojáka Švejka za světové války* (*The Adventures of Good Soldier Švejk in the World War*). It soon became a worldwide bestseller, and has since been translated into many languages. Hašek's satirical portrayal of the simpleton Švejk (Shvike) as he struggled with life in the army, with all its bureaucracy and seemingly absurd rules, struck a note in the post–World War I world where millions of conscripted soldiers were re-entering civilian life.

The Austro-Hungarian empire had ceased to exist by early November 1918, but much to the chagrin of Western politicians and cartographers, the Paris Peace Conference of 1919 reluctantly found itself dealing instead with haughty delegates from more than a half dozen new countries, each determined to secure their own cut of the imperial Habsburg corpse. Karl von Habsburg, recently unemployed, accepted the dissolution of his empire surprisingly gracefully, though he attempted twice in 1921 to force his way back onto the Hungarian throne. This in turn forced both Austria and Hungary—under considerable pressure from the Allies—to permanently renounce the Habsburg dynasty. He lived the rest of his life in exile on the island of Madeira, off the coast of Portugal.

Karl's son and heir, Otto von Habsburg, served in the 1980s and 90s in the European Union Parliament, and was a major advocate for bringing the Eastern European states into the European Union. Upon his death in July 2011 the city of Vienna indulged in some imperial nostalgia by hosting with great pomp and ceremony his funeral, with the streets bedecked in Habsburg imperial black-and-gold flags (instead of modern-day Austria's red and white). Otto's son Karl works with the United Nations and private philanthropic organizations.

E. Serbia and History

History is all about perspective. It isn't usually that the facts change, it's how they're *interpreted* that changes. Gavrilo Princip was and still is worshipped as a hero in Serbia and among Bosnian Serbs, and during the Yugoslav years the exact spot where he stood while committing his murders in Sarajevo was marked by painted feet on the pavement for tourists. One man's act of war is another's act of terrorism. But without getting bogged down in that argument, from the historical perspective over the 20th century most Serbs rejected the cautious approach taken by prime minister Pašić in 1914 in favor of Princip's bold act. They took comfort in the belief that for all the suffering the assassination at Sarajevo brought on Serbia, at least in the end Serbia's national territorial goals were achieved. Keep in mind the scale of suffering we're talking here: an estimated 16% of Serbia's prewar population of 4.5 million died in the war—one in every six Serbs—including nearly half of all soldiers who served in the Serbian army during the war.

With the 1990s implosion of Yugoslavia, Serbia—through the fumbling leadership of Slobodan Milošević (Meel-OSH-eh-veetch)—was reduced nearly to its mid-19th century borders. Remembering the historical suffering and sacrifices of the 20th century has therefore become a somewhat more bitter exercise for modern-day Serbs.

As soon as Vienna's ultimatum expired on July 28, 1914, Austro-Hungarian gunships steamed down the Danube River and began shelling Belgrade after midnight. Historians still argue about how much Nikola Pašić's government knew about the assassination in Sarajevo, but that was a moot point in the summer of 1914 as the Habsburg military machine bore down on Serbia. The small Serbian Army, led by the very competent General Radomir Putnik (a veteran of the 1912–13 Balkan Wars), repulsed the first Habsburg invasion in August, then, after losing ground to a second invasion in November—even losing Belgrade briefly—managed to defeat Austro-Hungarian forces at the Battle of Kolubara River in December and once again drive Habsburg armies from Serbian soil. However, nine months later, in September 1915, rival Bulgaria joined the Central Powers (i.e., Germany and Austria-Hungary), and a month later a joint Austro-Hungarian-German-Bulgarian invasion hit Serbia.

By early December, the reeling Serbian Army, accompanied by hundreds of thousands of civilian refugees, began a long and arduous retreat through southern Serbia, Kosovo, and into the Albanian mountains toward the Adriatic coast. During this retreat, unknown thousands of soldiers and civilians died of exposure, starvation, disease, and attacks from bands of Albanian tribesmen. The French navy rescued the survivors, who then joined British and French forces stationed in Greece. Serbia began a long three-year occupation by its enemies, during which its population suffered brutal reprisals from occupation forces. Food supply disruptions and rampant disease further turned the years of occupation into a living nightmare for Serbs. Again, one in every six Serbians did not survive to see the end of the war.

At the Allied camp at Thessaloniki, Greece, the Serbian government-in-exile spent most of the rest of the war rebuilding the Serbian Army with the help of Allied (particularly French) training and equipment. In 1916, Pašić had the leaders of *Crna Ruka* (Black Hand), the terrorist group that had carried out the assassinations in Sarajevo, arrested and tried. The ringleader, Dragutin Dimitrejević, faced a firing squad in May 1917 for treason.

In 1914, Serbia dismissed the South Slavists in favor of its own nationalist goals but after the disasters of 1915, Pašić needed all the help he could get. When Serbia's primary sponsor, Russia, collapsed into revolution in March 1917, Pašić felt that the only way to secure Allied recognition for Serbian territorial goals was to work with the Croatian-dominated *Jugoslavenski odbor* ("South Slav" or "*Yugoslav* Committee"), so in June 1917 he signed the Corfu Declaration with them, laying the foundations for a postwar Yugoslav state.

The end of the war in the Balkans came swiftly, if somewhat belatedly. With German forces losing ground on the Western front, on September 14, 1918, the Allied armies (French, British, Serbian, Greek) launched their offensive from the Thessaloniki salient, and within days had the dispirited Bulgarians, Germans, and Austro-Hungarian forces in full retreat. Bulgaria sought an armistice on September 29 and the Ottoman Empire on October 30, by which point the Austro-Hungarian empire had begun to crumble. Serbian and French forces surged northward, liberating Belgrade on November 1, and by war's end ten days later held Bosnia, Vojvodina, the Banat, Croatia, and Macedonia, as well as southern Hungary.

With the collapse of Habsburg authority in October 1918, a National Council of Slovenes and Croats took power in Zagreb, and on December 1, 1918, it transferred its authority to Belgrade with the creation of the Kingdom Of Serbs, Croats, and Slovenes. With that act, the Kingdom of Serbia ceased to exist, and the Yugoslav era began.

F. Montenegro is Pushed Off the Cliff

As World War I dawned Montenegro immediately allied with Serbia, resulting by 1916 in the country being occupied by Austro-Hungarian forces, which meted out brutal treatment to Montenegrin citizens as guerrillas retreated into the country's mountains. During the war, Serbia's prime minister, Nikola Pašić, called for Montenegro to be annexed by Serbia, while Montenegro's King Nikola spoke of a broader postwar Yugoslav confederation. Serbian troops liberated the country in late 1918 and were greeted as heroes by the population. However, when pro-Serb politicians met in the city of Podgorica (Pawd-GORE-ee-tsah; "Foot of the the Mountain") in November 1918 and declared both the king dethroned and immediate union with Serbia, some dismayed Montenegrins rebelled.

The rebels were no match for the regular Serbian army forces, however, and the revolt was quickly quelled, though sporadic fighting continued for a couple of years. Montenegro was absorbed into the new Kingdom of Serbs, Croats, and Slovenes (Yugoslavia) and renamed Zeta (*Zetska Banovina*; "the Zeta Banate") by Belgrade, while in 1920 the Montenegrin Autocephalous Orthodox Church was dismantled and absorbed into the Serbian Orthodox Church.

G. The Failed Superstates I: Yugoslavia

Common wisdom today has it that Yugoslavia was a doomed experiment. In the 1990s, ill-informed Western journalists reporting on the Yugoslav implosion wars wrote of the "centuries-old conflict between Serbs and Croats"—when the real genesis of Serb-Croat hostility really only reached back to the rise of nationalism in the 19th and 20th centuries.

So what went wrong in Yugoslavia? For the first Yugoslavia in 1918, the Serbian Kingdom effectively annexed the surrounding Southern Slav territories and took on the clothing of the Southern Slav movement, imposing its king, bureaucracy, and army on its new conationals.

The Second Yugoslavia of 1945–2006 was a more ethnically balanced state, but a fatal flaw in this Yugoslavia was Tito's militant socialist ideology, which rejected and suppressed regional patriotism, leaving ethnic identity in the hands of extremists. When Tito died in 1980, those extremists seized control and destabilized the country, leading to the bloody 1990s.

The desire for Southern Slavic unity harkened back to the 1830s, when Ljudevit Gaj (LYOO-deh-veet Guy), a Croat, founded the *Ilirski Pokret* (Illyrian Movement"), which sought recognition for Southern Slavic cultural rights within the Austrian Empire as Croats, Slovenes, and Serbs felt the earliest stirrings of nationalism and "national awakening."

The failure of the Habsburgs to accommodate these demands spawned more aggressive political movements, however, especially after the Compromise with Hungary in 1867 and the rejection by both Vienna and Budapest of *Trialism* (a proposed three-way imperial arrangement with Austrian, Hungarian, and Slavic components, based on the 1867 Compromise's two-way or *dualist* Austro-Hungarian power-sharing arrangement). Serbs and Bulgarians, each with their own statehood aspirations, showed little interest in South Slavism, so Southern or *Yugo*-Slavist groups tended to be dominated by Croats.

Only during World War I, however, did any of these groups openly call for secession from Austria-Hungary. The *Jugoslavenski odbor* (Yugoslav Committee") was formed in Italy in April 1915 by Croatian lawyer Ante Trumbić (AHN –teh TROOM-beetch), and it quickly got the Allies' attention through its lobbying and fundraising capabilities. Anton Korešec (KOR-eh-shets) led similar efforts in Habsburg Slovenia. Trumbić secured an agreement with Serbia for a postwar Yugoslav state in June 1917 at Corfu (Greece).

As Habsburg administration collapsed in October 1918, Trumbić and Korešec formed a Yugoslav government in Zagreb, which then moved to Belgrade as Serbian and French forces surged northward. On December 1, 1918 the Kingdom of Serbs, Croats, and Slovenes was proclaimed in Belgrade, with former Serbian king Petar I Karageorgević serving as king. The so-called "Triune Kingdom" was born.

It wasn't long after the euphoria died down, however, that the country's government became mired in hopeless party strife. Slovenes envisioned a loose federation, while Croats were divided between Yugoslavists and those who wanted outright independence. Worse, the power vacuum left by the collapse of the Austro-Hungarian empire, coupled with the territorial ambitions of neighbors Italy, Bulgaria, and Hungary required the rapid development of new state institutions.

In short order, the functioning machinery of the former Serbian Kingdom simply became by necessity Yugoslav institutions, to the dismay of Croats. The new Yugoslavia appeared to some to be a Greater Serbia. In the Habsburg years the Croatian Peasant Party (*Hrvatska seljačka stranka*, or HSS), led by Stjepan Radić (STYEH-pahn RAH-deech), had been radicalized by Hungarian intransigence and was very practiced in the art of political obstruction.

In Austria-Hungary, in which Croatia was fairly small, these tactics were mostly symbolic and had little impact on the Hungarian or the Imperial governments, but in Yugoslavia Croats comprised a quarter of the population, so Radić's continuation of these tactics (with the HSS) in opposition to the Serb-centered Yugoslav state[11] had a devastating effect. That, coupled with a poorly designed proportional representation electoral system (which kept governments weak and divided) and lingering wartime distrust[12] ground politics in Belgrade to a halt for years, leaving the country adrift in its most formative period. Just when a compromise finally seemed close, a Serbian nationalist shot Radić dead in June 1928 in the *Skupština* (SKOOP-shtee-nah; national parliament), leading to a national crisis. With the country on the verge of civil war, King Alexander declared a royal dictatorship in January 1929 and, trying to foster unity, changed the name of the country to simply "Yugoslavia."

Alexander attempted to build truly Yugoslav institutions, but these efforts were cut short when he was assassinated while on a state visit to France in October 1934 by an agent of the Bulgaro-Macedonian terrorist organization IMRO, with *Ustaša* (OO-stah-shah) cosponsorship. The *Ustaša* had been founded in April 1929 by Ante Pavelić (AHN-the PAH-veh-leetch) in Sofia, Bulgaria (in an anti-Yugoslav alliance with IMRO, with funding from Mussolini's Italy) to fight for the creation of a Greater Croatia. Alexander's assassination was only the first step in a long campaign of bombings and murders by Ustaše agents[13] across Yugoslavia throughout the 1930s.

Alexander's eleven-year-old son Petar was declared king, with his uncle Pavle (PAV-leh; Paul) to serve as prince-regent. In August 1939, a month before World War II began, the *Sporazum* (Spore-ah-ZOOM, "Agreement") was negotiated, giving Croatia its own government and restoring the *Sabor* (SAH-bore; Croatia's historic parliament); and, most importantly, making Croatian institutions answerable to the king himself—i.e., not to Yugoslav authorities in Belgrade. This was unfortunately seen as too little too late, and it inflamed Serbian nationalists.

With few friends, beset on all sides,[14] Yugoslavia entered the World War II period viciously divided against itself, with a future about as uncertain as a country can have.

USELESS TRIVIA: NO NEED FOR THE RED CARPET. REALLY.

Fame isn't all it's cracked up to be. Just ask Christo Toprakchiev. Toprakchiev attended a military high school in his native Bulgaria, then went on in early 1912 to the Louis Blériot school of aviation in Etampes, France. When the First Balkan War broke out, Toprakchiev rushed home and flew reconnaissance missions over Turkish lines—planes in 1912 didn't carry weapons yet—but on October 19, 1912 his Bleriot-XI plane crashed near his airfield, killing Lt. Toprakchiev. Toprakchiev was declared the first military pilot in history killed in the line of duty. In the 1920s and 30s he was honored as a national hero in Bulgaria and during the Soviet years Toprakchiev, who had been a socialist, was lauded as a martyr for the communist homeland.

Unfortunately, years later historians discovered that another airman, Pietro Manzini, had been killed months before Toprakchiev in Libya during the 1911–12 Tripolitan War between Italy and the Ottoman Empire. Well, if it's any consolation, Toprakchiev is still honored today across Bulgaria with streets and schools named after him.

H. Bulgaria Tries 1913 Over Again

When war broke out in 1914, Bulgaria remained initially neutral. It had just lost a war the previous year in which 60,000 of its sons had died, and its economy was exhausted, so Bulgaria was in no hurry to repeat the experience. Still, there was a powerful belief in the country that it had been swindled by its former allies from the First Balkan War, and that eastern Macedonia (as well as Southern Dobrudja; DO-broo-jah) rightfully belonged to Bulgaria. Both the Allies and Central Powers[15] immediately began courting Bulgaria in 1914, but the Central Powers had the advantage as at least two of Bulgaria's enemies, Serbia and Greece, were in the Allied camp. The Allies just couldn't offer Bulgaria the territories it really wanted. Still, the country was sharply divided on the wisdom of joining the war or not, and so it waited.

USELESS TRIVIA: BLAST FROM THE PAST!

The Macedonian city of Bitola shook with each explosion, as the artillery of World War I wrought terrible havoc. Residents fled in panic as shells—Bulgarian? Greek? British? French? Serbian? German?—exploded around them. Despite the carnage World War I is famous for, almost miraculously on this sweltering July day nobody was seriously injured.

Actually, the day we're talking about was in July 2007, not 1918. The summer of 2007 in Europe was one of the hottest on record, with temperatures soaring up to 107 degrees Fahrenheit (42 degrees Celsius) in regions where 90 degrees Fahrenheit (32 degrees Celsius) was considered hot, and wildfires raged out of control. One such fire entered the outskirts of Bitola (BEE-to-lah), Macedonia's second largest city, destroying homes. While firefighters were trying to bring the situation under control, several large explosions rocked the neighborhood, and residents fled in panic. The fires were setting off unexploded shells from World War I, which lay buried undetected beneath the houses.

During the war, production of munitions was understandably rushed and, quite frankly, did not produce some of the best quality stuff. Some studies have suggested that as much as a third of British artillery shells fired on the Western Front did not explode. Much of Europe, east and west, therefore, is littered with dangerous unexploded munitions (e.g., shells, hand grenades, and aerial bombs) from both World Wars, which modern-day new construction—and, apparently, wildfires—occasionally turn up.

The Central Powers' enticements did eventually win out, and so in September 1915 Bulgaria officially joined the Central Powers. The next month, October, Bulgaria invaded southern Serbia and Macedonia in concert with an Austro-German invasion under way in the north, quickly overwhelming the Serbs. For most of the rest of the war, Bulgarian soldiers merely put in occupation duty in both Serbian and Greek Macedonia, though this meant occasionally meting out nasty reprisals because of some diehard resisters.

The large Allied camp in nearby Thessaloniki, Greece was jokingly referred to by Bulgarians as their largest POW camp. However, the British, French, Italian, Serbian, Montenegrin, and Greek armies in the camp were training and stockpiling supplies, and finally in September 1918, twenty-eight Allied divisions launched an invasion of the Balkans from Thessaloniki. Dispirited Bulgarian forces almost immediately broke and ran. In a sign of the savagery of World War I, disorganized and routed Bulgarian units fleeing back to the pre-1915 Bulgarian borders were hunted down mercilessly by British planes in the steep Macedonian valleys, and mobs of clearly panicked and retreating men were mowed down. Bulgaria officially requested an armistice on September 29, 1918.

To put it mildly, Bulgarians were not happy with the war's outcome. It wasn't just that they'd lost—again—but that the country's politicians had really screwed up—again—and had proved they had no clue how to achieve Bulgaria's aims. A rebellion broke out among peasants and soldiers in the vicinity of the city of Radomir in late September 1918, and though it fizzled out quickly, it did manage to change three things:

- It forced the disgraced king, Ferdinand, to abdicate and flee. He was despised by the Allies anyway and would likely have gotten the boot soon. His popular son, Boris, became tsar.

- It panicked the Bulgarian government into signing the armistice of September 29, ending the war sooner for Bulgaria. In fact, Bulgaria was the first of the Central Powers to jump ship.

- That same panicked Bulgarian government released a radical from jail in hopes that he would quell the Radomir Rebellion. It soon fizzled, but Alexandr Stamboliyski was a free man.

Alexandr Stamboliyski was a radical peasant leader who believed militantly in the rural life. When he became prime minister in October 1919, he declared war on cities and urbanites, whom he considered mere parasites living off the countryside. Stamboliyski's rule was harsh but not without some successes, creating a national labor service and carrying out a land reform designed to safeguard peasants against (urban) land speculators. He defied conventional political definition and was despised by both the political right and left. His government was forced to sign the Treaty of Neuilly-sur-Seine by the Allies in November 1919, in which Bulgaria lost not only the Greek and Serbian regions it occupied in the war but also its access to the Aegean Sea. Greece then forced Bulgaria to accept a population exchange, purging Bulgarians from the lost territories.

Still, instead of pursuing revenge, Stamboliyski opted for a proposed Balkan federation with erstwhile enemies Yugoslavia and Romania, which infuriated Bulgarian nationalists. In June 1923, a group of army officers, working with the Tsar and IMRO, overthrew the Stamboliyski government in a coup. He was arrested, mutilated, and tortured—having "the hands that signed the Treaty of Neuilly" sawed off—and finally executed.

USELESS TRIVIA: THE AMERICAN HEARTLAND . . . IN THE BALKANS!

The Balkans for many Americans may seem obscure, but in 1863 Methodist missionary and philanthropist Christopher Robert of New York founded a secondary school, Robert College, in Constantinople for the Ottoman Empire's Christians (though later it also admitted Muslims). Robert College did not support the independence movements that shook the Ottoman Balkans at the time, but for several decades it educated so many Bulgarians and Macedonians who later went on to prominence that Bulgarian King Ferdinand claimed that Robert College had virtually created the entire Bulgarian state civil service. Robert College also helped facilitate contacts for Bulgaria with private American organizations, so that in World War I, Bulgaria refused to declare war on the United States despite pressure from Vienna and Berlin. When the end came in September 1918, the Bulgarian Finance Minister, Andrei Lyapchev, rode through the Allied lines to seek an armistice under American protection in the American consul's car.

Robert College still exists today, though it now only teaches high school grades 9-12. It is one of the most exclusive high schools in the world, however, and has educated many of the modern-day Turkish Republic's cultural and political leaders, including some prime ministers. Still American-financed and -operated, Robert College is the oldest American high school outside the United States.

Stamboliyski was succeeded as prime minister by Alexandur Tsankov, an exceedingly brutal thug who is most famous for using the communist bombing of the Bulgarian Orthodox St. Nedelya Cathedral (*църква Света Неделя*) in Sofia in April 1925, which killed 128 parishioners, as a pretext for unleashing a police state on Bulgaria. Tsankov also brought IMRO into the inner sanctum of Bulgarian government, making it a powerful force in Bulgarian politics and life, carrying out regular assassinations of public figures, as well as committing terrorist acts in Yugoslav Macedonia, Yugoslavia itself, and Greece. IMRO's reign of terror in Bulgaria and the Balkans continued as it deteriorated from being a terrorist organization with political goals into a common mafia extorting money from Bulgarian businesses, fighting factional turf wars, and running a narcotics black market.[16]

However, when IMRO was implicated (with the Croatian Ustaša) in the 1934 assassination of Yugoslavia's King Alexander in France, several European Great Powers (and Balkan neighbors) threatened to ostracize Bulgaria, labeling it a terrorist state. Fearing the economic impact of isolation, Tsar Boris took matters into his own hands and staged a coup, installing a puppet government and more importantly, forcefully cracking down on IMRO. Its leadership was arrested and its weapons seized. This proved popular with Bulgarians fed up with corruption. For the rest of the 1930s, Bulgaria under Tsar Boris drifted into the pro-Axis camp as much because of Bulgaria's territorial aspirations as because Hitler's Germany had come to play an increasingly important role in the Bulgarian economy, softening the impact of the Great Depression.

I. The Failed Superstates II: Romania

The Allied goal in 1919 of creating Eastern European states strong enough to resist Bolshevik and German expansionism failed, but it did not leave the region untouched. The Allies favored larger, multiethnic "super states" with territorial and economic advantages that, at least on paper, made them formidable local powers. In reality, this attempt to artificially create powerful new states, often ignoring local ethnic and historical realities, fueled tensions in the region and hindered regional political and economic cooperation. This is the story of postwar Romania. In 1914, Romania was about 50,000 square miles (130,000 km²) but by the end of 1920, it had grown to almost 116,000 square miles (300,000 km²), encompassing all ethnically Romanian regions—and much more.

Thus was born *România Mare* (Greater Romania), the realization of every Romanian national goal of the previous century. This success had a price, however; Romania spent the first half of the 20th century jealously guarding those territorial gains from previous owners, as well as against local minority aspirations (about 30% of Romania's population in 1920–40).

Relations with neighboring Bulgaria, Hungary, Yugoslavia, and the Soviet Union were strained at best in the interwar years, leaving the country (and region) vulnerable later to meddling by Hitler's Germany. Like other superstates in the region—neighboring Yugoslavia, Czechoslovakia, and

Poland—Romania's successes after World War I only encouraged enemies within and without to plot against it. The reality is that history has haunted the so-called "winners" of the 20th century in Eastern Europe as much as the losers.

USELESS TRIVIA: OF CHICKENS AND POTS

Herbert Clark Hoover was born a Quaker in Iowa in 1874, eventually becaming a renowned expert on mining engineering. He traveled the world helping governments and private companies build or fix their mines. By 1914, Herbert Hoover was a very wealthy and worldly man.

When World War I broke out in Europe in 1914, Hoover proved adept at helping trapped Americans escape the war zones. By the fall of 1914, it was clear that famine loomed in German-occupied Belgium, so Hoover helped organize the Belgian National Relief and Food Committee, which delivered aid to 9 million European refugees over the next two years.

Impressed, U.S. president Woodrow Wilson put Hoover in charge of American relief efforts in 1917 when the U.S. entered the war. After the war, Hoover returned to a devastated Europe as head of the American Relief Administration, again organizing food shipments—including to former enemy countries, much to the outrage of some Allied peoples. Hoover recognized there was also a desperate need for technical aid in the newer countries of Eastern Europe, so he organized teams of technical experts in railroads, electrical engineering, agriculture, economics, and more to work in Poland, Czechoslovakia, Yugoslavia, and Bulgaria in particular. One of Hoover's most controversial projects was the Soviet famine of 1921, which was caused by Lenin's disastrous policies. Hoover negotiated with Lenin and delivered some 768,000 metric tons of food to Bolshevik Russia. Critics claimed Hoover had helped stabilize Lenin's regime, to which Hoover responded: "Twenty million people are starving. Whatever their politics, they shall be fed!"

Americans remember Herbert Hoover for his presidency of 1929–33, which fizzled in the face of the Great Depression, but in 1914–23, he managed to collect, organize, and deliver millions of tons of food to millions of desperate victims of World War I. That's not a bad legacy.[17]

As Romania entered the summer of 1914, it faced a choice. Since the 1880s, it had belonged to an Austro-Hungarian alliance system that limited Russian influence in the Balkans, because Romania feared Russian intervention and also wanted the rest of Russian Moldavia (Bessarabia). However, Romania also wanted Transylvania, which then belonged to its Habsburg allies. For these reasons the country remained neutral for the first several years of World War I, though there was strong pro-Allied (particularly pro-French) sentiment in the country.

By early 1916, though, the Balkans had fallen to almost complete Central Powers control, leaving Romania nearly surrounded. Still, when the Russians launched the Brusilov Offensive in June 1916, Romania's pro-Allied prime minister, Ion I. C. Brătianu (EE-ohn Brah-TYAH-noo), managed to convince the country to join the Allies. Romania declared war on the Central Powers and invaded Habsburg Transylvania in August 1916.

Unfortunately, by then the Brusilov Offensive had stalled, and within weeks, by mid-September, the ill-prepared Romanian Army was reeling from a fierce, German-led counteroffensive. In November the Germans crossed the Carpathians, and weeks later, in December, they occupied Bucharest. The Romanian government retreated (with Russian aid) to the Moldavian city of Iaşi (YAH-shee). With most of Romania occupied, it held out in Iaşi throughout 1917 with Russian help. But the Russian revolutions and Lenin's Treaty of Brest-Litovsk with the Germans in March 1918 left Romania isolated. The country surrendered to Germany in May 1918. However, Romania renounced this treaty six months later, in November, as the Central Powers collapsed, and it re-entered the war.

On December 1, 1918, with the Austro-Hungarian Empire now history, the leaders of Transylvania's Romanians gathered in *Gyulafehérvár* (DYOO-luh-feh-heer-var[18]) and declared their intention of seceding from Hungary and joining Transylvania to Romania. This is known as the Alba Iulia (ALL-bah YOO-lee-yah) Declaration, and *Ziua Unirii* (Union Day) on December 1 is still Romania's national day. Brătianu himself went to Paris for the 1919 peace conferences, though he alienated the Allies with his intransigence and huge land claims. He redeemed himself in the summer, however, when Romania's army (at the West's behest) crushed the communist Kun regime in neighboring Hungary. In 1920, Transylvania, as well as other territories (e.g., Partium, Bukovina) were taken from Hungary, Bessarabia separated from the defunct Russian Empire, and southern Dobrudja was returned by Bulgaria.

With these territories, Romania inherited a huge minority population, some 28% of the country's population in 1920. And social tensions similar to those caused by educated Habsburg Serbs teaching in 19th-century Serbia arose as Transylvanian Romanians came into contact with the feudal and entrenched Wallachian bureaucracy. Still, *România Mare* (Greater Romania) was now a reality.

As one of the largest territorial winners of World War I, Romania became an arch-supporter of the Versailles Treaty system against any changes sought by the losers. When France began organizing *La Petit Entente* (Little Entente) alliance in 1920 Romania eagerly joined, and its foreign policy orientation was strongly pro-Western.

However, by the late 1920s the West had largely withdrawn from Eastern Europe, and during the Great Depression Romania became very dependent on the German economy, as Hitler sought Romanian foodstuffs and oil. In July 1927, King Ferdinand I died,[19] leaving the throne to his grandson, Mihai (MEE-high; "Michael") but Mihai's father, Carol (Charles), returned unexpectedly from abroad in 1930 and declared himself King Carol II.

Carol manipulated Romania's politics by constantly invoking Hungarian, Bulgarian, or Soviet territorial conspiracies, and in particular he supported a paramilitary nationalist organization called the *Garda de Fier*, the Iron Guard. Led by the hypernationalist Corneliu Codreanu (Co-dray-AH-noo), the Iron Guard was a pseudofascist organization dedicated to preserving *România Mare*, and it cut a bloody swath of assassinations and terrorism across Romanian politics in the 1930s. However, Carol overthrew the Romanian government and turned against the Guard in 1938, imprisoning its leadership and members in a swift national operation.[20] Still, though now an unchallenged royal dictator, Carol couldn't so easily put the nationalist genie back in the bottle, and the country drifted closer to Hitler's Germany.

J. Albania: Let's Try That Again

When the Second Balkan War ended in the summer of 1913, the Great Powers had agreed to recognize an independent Albania with a German prince, Wilhelm of Wied (VEED), as king. They were motivated less by sympathy for the Albanian cause—they had to rummage through history to the 13th century for the last time some kingdom called "Albania" had existed, under Charles I of Anjou—than by a desire to ensure rogue pro-Russian Serbia did not achieve access to the Adriatic Sea.

However, the choice of prince was unfortunate, not for his own sake—he wasn't such a bad guy—but simply because he was German. When World War I broke out, the extremely new and fragile Albanian state simply imploded, so Wilhelm decamped back to Germany in September 1914, never to return. Throughout the war, Albania remained a no-man's land ruled by different feuding clans. It was through this civil war that the defeated Serbian Army marched in the winter of 1915–16, fending off vicious local clan attacks along their whole route as local Albanian leaders tried to seize arms, ammunition, and what little provisions the Serb army carried on its long retreat toward the Adriatic.

The situation remained little changed in Albania after the war ended, until January 1920, when Britain and France announced their willingness to partition Albania between Italy, Greece, and Yugoslavia. Finally moved to action, a truce in the tribal civil war was arranged and a national assembly met weeks later at Lushnjë (LOOSH-nyuh), and a government was cobbled together quickly, moving itself to larger Tiranë (Tee-rah-nuh; often spelled "Tirana" in English). Britain and France ignored these moves by the Albanians but U.S. President Woodrow Wilson pulled the rug from beneath their feet by recognizing Albania and immediately establishing diplomatic contacts. Albania was back, though it took further League of Nations action to get Italian and (Serb) Yugoslav troops off Albanian territory.

In the early 1920s Albanian parliamentary politics became bogged down in vicious infighting until an obscure character named Ahmed Zogu[21], who—with the aid of Yugoslav forces, Albanian exiles, and even exiled White Russian forces—invaded and conquered Albania in 1924. Zogu was "elected" president in January 1925, but he dispensed with the political charade and had himself declared King Zog I in September 1928. He ruled with an iron fist, but also worked hard to create a united Albanian identity as well as transform Albania's archaic tribal social and economic order. He tried to secularize Albanian political and social life to minimize the Muslim-Christian divide in the country (about a 70%-30% ratio), as well as creating a universal education system and an Albanian army.

King Zog's success in fostering Albanian nationalism created headaches, and Albanian nationalists strained relations with neighboring states by demanding part or all of Macedonia, Kosovo, Montenegro, and Epirus.

Despite all Zog's success, his Albania was a desperately poor and underdeveloped country—about as desperately poor and underdeveloped as Europe got, in fact—so when soon after Zog's seizure of power the Italian government (under Mussolini) offered to fund the Albanian National Bank, Zog had no choice but to accept. This marked the beginning of growing Italian influence in the country, with Italian "advisors" soon instructing the nascent Albanian army, and Italian merchants with special rights dominating Albanian ports. In 1934, Zog finally attempted to defy growing Italian control of his country by signing a pact with Greece and Yugoslavia, but this was too little, too late. In April 1939, Zog's son, Leka, was born, which panicked Mussolini into action. Threatened by the prospect of a royal successor to the Albanian throne, two days later Italian troops invaded Albania and overthrew Zog. The king and his family fled to London, and Italian king Victor Emanuelle III had himself crowned King of Albania. Albania was now an Italian puppet state.[22]

K. Hungary Loses the War . . . Again

Despite more than 170 years of Hungarian resistance to Habsburg rule—including at least two major revolts in 1703–11 and 1848–49—the Hungarians really embraced the dynasty after the 1867 *Ausgleich* with Austria.[23] The Compromise with Vienna allowed Hungary to restore much of its old grandeur, to an extent it would not have been able to have done on its own. The Habsburgs had also, ironically, helped preserve Hungary's basic feudal social order, even resisting industrialization in favor of the aristocrats' beloved rural, agrarian estates. This loyalty to the Habsburgs and a feudal social order, coupled with the prewar policy of *Magyarization*,[24] came to haunt Hungary in 1918, however.

USELESS TRIVIA: MEMORIES OF THE WAY THINGS WERE . . .

Ópusztaszer is located in modern-day southeastern Hungary. The original village was known simply as *Szer* (Sare), but later *Puszta* (POOS-tuh), meaning "Plains," was added. The *Ó* means "ancient." Szer had long since vanished by the time someone rummaging around the Vienna National Archives in the late-18th century discovered a lost Hungarian chronicle from the early-13th century, in which King Béla (BAY-luh) IV fingered Szer as the place where the "conquering" Hungarian tribal chiefs, led by Árpád, had stopped and held their first meeting in 895 CE to sort out plans for their new homeland.

This newfound knowledge about Szer captured the emerging Hungarian national imagination, and in 1896 a column was erected on the site and archaeological exploration began. In the 1930s a gazebo replaced the column, but plans for a larger historical museum were interrupted by World War II. Only in the 1970s did the Hungarian communist government finally get around to building an open-air ethnographic museum portraying the lifestyle of the 9th-century Magyars as well as Hungarian village life on the Great Plains (complete with live performances by skilled Hungarian horsemen). There is also an archaeological museum and a huge, 394-foot-long (120 meter) 19th-century panorama painted by Árpád Feszty (FESS-tee) that romantically portrays the 9th-century Hungarian Conquest. The history of the *Ópusztaszer Nemzeti Történeti Emlékpark* (Ópusztaszer National Historical Memorial Park)[25] as a historical theme park is itself an interesting story about the rise of national identity in Eastern Europe.

Hungary, as the lesser half of the Austro-Hungarian empire, had only reluctantly agreed to war against Serbia in 1914, as it feared a victory would bring more Slavic peoples—Serbs—into the already-creaky empire. The Austro-Hungarian army, though surprisingly faithful, proved unprepared for the war, suffering humiliating defeats at the hands of Serbia, Russia, and Italy. Its few victories were usually the result of significant aid from German forces. Hungarians fought faithfully for their emperor, but to little avail.

Ironically, because of its relatively backward and agrarian economy, the Hungarian half of the empire suffered less food rationing than the Austrian half. While battles raged in nearby Galicia, the Balkans, Russian Poland, and Alpine Italy, Hungary itself was little directly touched by the war, with Budapest's famously elegant cafes, restaurants, and theaters functioning undisturbed each evening throughout the war. Hungary's fun only started *after* the war.

With the war clearly lost and the empire just as clearly doomed, mass demonstrations in Budapest on October 31, 1918 demanded independence. Fearing a democratic, or, worse, communist revolt, Hungary's aristocrats chose one of their own, the moderate Mihály ("Michael") Károlyi (MEE-high KAH-ro-yee), to be the country's first prime minister.

Károlyi was a blue-blooded aristocrat but believed that Hungary could only survive if it became a democracy and made peace with its minorities and neighbors. He cultivated closer ties with France and the West and began democratizing the country, but these efforts were for naught: In March 1919 Károlyi received the Vyx Note,[26] which informed Budapest that the Paris Peace Conference intended to give large stretches of eastern Hungary up to the Tisza River—which would include about a third of modern-day Hungary—to rival Romania. His pro-Western policies utterly discredited, Károlyi resigned and eventually fled to France. Panicked, the Paris Peace Conference offered to renegotiate the borders but it was too late; the Hungarian communists, led by Béla Kun (BAY-luh Koon), seized power.

Thus was born the *Magyar Tanácsköztársaság* (Hungarian Republic of Councils"[27]) in late March 1919. An enthusiastic fan (and friend) of Lenin's, Béla Kun immediately set out building a Bolshevik state in Hungary on Lenin's model, including implementing a Red Terror in the Hungarian countryside with his *Lenin-fiúk*.[28] Still, because he defied the Western Allies his regime was initially popular at home. Kun organized an army in defiance of the ACC and invaded Czechoslovakia to recapture Slovakia, eventually provoking a (Western-sanctioned) Romanian intervention from which Kun fled (to Moscow[29]) in August 1919 as Romanian troops overran the country and occupied Budapest (at the Allies' behest). Hungary's 133-day communist experiment was over.

USELESS TRIVIA:
A MAN, HIS PIECE OF TAPE, AND HISTORY!

With the collapse of the Hungarian Soviet Republic in August 1919, the Versailles Treaty administrators known as the Allied Control Commission (ACC) re-entered Hungary to supervise the imposition of defeated Hungary's terms of surrender. The ACC in Hungary was composed of generals from four of the victorious Allied armies—British, French, American, and Italian—and their support staff. The American representative was General Harry "Hill" Bandholtz. Bandholtz had no interest in the historic Hungarian-Romanian rivalry, but he reported with distaste personally witnessed scenes of Romanian soldiers looting during their occupation of Budapest.

On one occasion on the evening of October 5, General Bandholtz was eating dinner when he was informed by an orderly that the Romanian Army had posted guards around the Hungarian *Nemzeti Múzeum* ("National Museum," sort of a Hungarian Smithsonian Museum), and were rounding up trucks all over the city. Bandholtz ran at breakneck speed across the city to the museum, where he threatened his way past Romanian guards with a horse-riding whip. Bandholtz seized the museum's keys and, lacking much else, placed a wide piece of tape across the museum door, writing on it:

This door sealed by Order Inter Allied Military Mission.

H.H.Bandholtz, Pres. Of the day. 5 October 1919

Bandholtz took the only rubber stamp he had on him, an American army mail-censor stamp, and stamped the tape repeatedly. The Romanian soldiers argued but would not break Gen. Bandholtz's "seal." The ruse worked and the museum collection was saved. Today you can still see General Bandholtz's seal in the museum. In the 1930s Hungary erected a statue of Gen. Bandholtz on *Szabadság Tér* (Freedom Square), where the American Embassy is located, but during World War II (when the U.S. and Hungary were at war) the statue was removed. The communists were in no hurry to replace it, but in 1989 Hungary restored the statue.[30]

Shaken by the presence of a Bolshevik state in the heart of Europe, the West teamed up with aristocrats of the *ancien régime* to pick a new leader. He turned out to be a former admiral in the Austro-Hungarian navy, Miklós (Nicholas) Horthy (MEE-kloesh HOR-tee). Hungary began to stabilize and return to normal, but a bombshell was coming: in June, 1920 Hungary was forced by the Allies to sign the Treaty of Trianon in Paris, which gave away 67% of Hungary's prewar territory, as well as 58% of its prewar population, including 3.2 million ethnic Hungarians. It was largely the product of French and Italian efforts to create a friendly bloc in Eastern Europe, using Hungary as the pantry to reward their new allies. Because of prewar Hungary's treatment of *its* minorities, there was little sympathy in the West for the Hungarians trapped in hostile foreign countries after the war, but even the staunchly anti-Hungarian British historian Robert W. Seton-Watson, who was an advisor at the peace conference in Paris and a strong critic of Austria-Hungary, described the Treaty of Trianon as "immoderate."

The country lost territory to Romania,[31] Yugoslavia, Czechoslovakia, and even former (senior) partner Austria. The Treaty of Trianon radicalized the country, making Hungary one of the strongest critics of the Versailles Treaty system along with Germany.[32] The treaty also had huge economic consequences for Hungary, as centuries' old regional markets and trade routes were suddenly severed.[33]

At the time, some compared Trianon—the destruction of the historic Hungarian kingdom—to the Partitions of the Polish-Lithuanian Commonwealth in 1772–95, but in the age of nation states when empires were on the way out, Hungary was bound in 1919 to lose at least *some* of the "St. Stephen Crown lands," as the kingdom's historic territory was called. Hungary's own censuses in 1900 and 1910 showed ethnic Hungarians before the war as making up barely 50% of the population.

Clearly, some territories in 1919 were going to be lost. Still, the extreme punitive nature of the Treaty of Trianon, which severely penalized a country that was, in the larger context of World War I in Eastern Europe, a relatively minor player, only served to fuel tensions in the region. The Treaty of Trianon played a key role in undermining the West's goal of creating a united and cooperative bloc of Eastern European states.

For their part, Hungarians undermined their own efforts to undo Trianon by insisting on a full return to the 1914 borders, rather than just seeking minor revisions that would return Hungarian-majority regions. This unrealistic insistence on the old "St. Stephen" borders spanned the political spectrum, uniting aristocrats with leftist radicals such as Béla Kun. Under the Horthy regency,[34] Hungary staunchly advocated revising the Versailles Treaty system and had hostile relations with most of its neighbors, while developing warm ties with fellow revisionists Germany and Italy.

Horthy restrained some of the worst excesses of the Hungarian nationalists in the 1930s, particularly as the fascist *Nyilaskereszt* (Arrow Cross") party formed, but the country nonetheless drifted closer to Hitler and began to emulate his policies. With the First Vienna Award of November 1938, Hitler forced a prostrate Czechoslovakia to return parts of southern Slovakia to Hungary. Most Hungarians were jubilant, but some wondered about the cost.

L. The Failed Superstates III: Czechoslovakia

Many Westerners admire Czechoslovakia because it seemed to be the one country in Eastern and Central Europe that kept its head, that didn't collapse into dictatorship when even neighboring Germany succumbed. Czechoslovakia maintained a functional democracy throughout the 1920s and 30s, right up until the country's destruction by Hitler. By inheriting much of the Habsburg's industrial lands, it had by far the most advanced economy in Eastern Europe as well as the strongest native middle class.

The Czech lands' native nobility had been systematically destroyed in the 17th century by the Habsburgs, so Czechoslovakia in 1918—unlike Poland, Hungary, or Romania—did not have to contend with aristocratic resistance to reform; the Czech middle class was solidly in control. Still, for all these advantages, Czechs and Slovaks were as new to statehood as their fellow Eastern Europeans and they were not exempt from fits of national chauvinism. The country also shared a problem with Romania and Poland: territorial expansion at its neighbors' expense meant hostile relations with them and it also meant large minorities, 34.5% (i.e., more than a third) of the population in 1921. Add the growth of Slovak national consciousness, and Czechoslovakia was a country on the defensive.

USELESS TRIVIA: FROM VIENNA TO PRAGUE VIA SIBERIA!

When World War I broke out, a few Czech and Slovak nationalists volunteered to form a legion to fight for Russia. Interest was scarce until the Russian Brusilov Offensive mauled the Austro-Hungarian army in the summer of 1916, and ethnic minorities began to desert from the Habsburg forces in droves. By early 1917, the *Československé legie* (Czechoslovak Legion) boasted some 38,000 soldiers.

Unfortunately, the Czechoslovak Legion was born at just about the time its sponsor country, Russia, started coming apart at the seams. As Russia slid into revolutionary chaos in 1917, the Czechoslovak Legion looked for an exit. The war closed all European exit routes, however, so the Legion headed eastward along the Trans-Siberian Railway toward Vladivostok, where it hoped to find shipping transit back to Europe. Because the Legion got in the way of German and Hungarian POWs returning home westward per the Treaty of Brest-Litovsk, the nervous Bolsheviks tried to intern the Legion in May 1918 into camps. This provoked the Legion into seizing all of southern Siberia between the Volga River and Vladivostok. Indeed, it was the approach of the Czechoslovak Legion to Yekaterinburg in July 1918 that prompted the panicked Bolsheviks to murder the captive Romanov tsar and his family.

Tomáš Masaryk and Edvard Beneš helped convince the Allies to recognize the Czechoslovak Legion as an Allied belligerent force before the war ended in November 1918, and the Allies even used the need to rescue the Czechoslovak Legion after the war as an excuse to intervene in the Russian Civil War in 1919–20. In order to disengage from the Civil War, the Czechoslovak Legion cut a deal with Lenin in 1920, handing over to him tons of tsarist gold that had fallen into their hands as well as the White Russian general Alexander Kolchak, for which Lenin (happily) allowed the Czechoslovak Legion to depart on American Red Cross ships. Some 70,000 Czechoslovak Legionnaires left Russia in 1920.

As the Austro-Hungarian Empire entered World War I, most Czechs and Slovaks hoped mainly for greater autonomy after the war, regardless of the outcome. Indeed, the fear was that if the Habsburg empire imploded, then the Czech and Slovak lands might be absorbed by Germany, a country far less hospitable to its minorities.

Both Czechs and Slovaks marched obediently (if unenthusiastically) off to war in 1914, though Pan-Slavist agitation gave hope to many that Russian armies would soon come to their rescue. The repeated Russian defeats, and ultimately the Russian revolution of 1917, squashed those hopes, however, and so as the Habsburg empire began to unravel in 1917–18, Czechs and Slovaks turned to a small but dedicated band of Czech activists led by Tomáš Masaryk[35] (TOE-mosh Mah-SAH-reek) in Paris and London who lobbied constantly for Czech and Slovak rights.

In 1916, Masaryk, along with two other activists, Edvard Beneš (ED-vard BEH-nesh) and Milan Štefánik (MEE-lon Shteh-FAH-neek) founded the *Československa národní rada* (Czechoslovak National Council), which served as a government-in-exile for the yet-unborn country. All three activists traveled Europe and North America to solicit funds and volunteers from Czech and Slovak emigré communities. In May 1918, with Masaryk present, the highly organized Czech and Slovak communities in the United States declared in a public statement at a convention in Pittsburgh their desire for an independent and united Czechoslovak state, which made a major impression on the Allies. Clearly a gifted PR man, Masaryk then read Czechoslovakia's declaration of independence on October 18, 1918, while standing on the steps of Independence Hall in Philadelphia, the building where American independence had been debated and declared some 142 years earlier. Woodrow Wilson was impressed enough to endorse the independence of Czechoslovakia, his first step away from his attempts to salvage the Habsburg empire. Czechoslovakia now existed, though it had no defined borders yet.

For the Czech lands, Masaryk simply claimed all of historic Bohemia and Moravia. Several German communities in western Bohemia (Sudetenland) tried to join Austria in 1918, but the Western Allies didn't buy it. The Slovak lands turned out to be more problematic. Masaryk claimed all of the historic northern Hungarian territories, (literally *Felvidék*, or "Upper Territories"), which were primarily Slovak-populated but still had 745,000 Hungarians, or about 27% of Slovakia's total population of 2.7 million.[36] Czechoslovakia and Hungary fought a couple of wars over these lands in 1918–19, but the Paris Peace Conference forced Hungary to give them to Czechoslovakia. Masaryk also laid claim to an eastern Hungarian territory populated mostly by Ruthenians—soon to be called "Ukrainians"—known to Hungarians as *Kárpátalja*, *Zakarpatsko* to Czechs: "Transcarpathia." The Paris Peace Conference granted Transcarpathia to Czechoslovakia, generating friction with Moscow. Finally, the tiny mining town of *Teschen* (German name; Czech name = *Těšín* [TYEH-sheen],

Polish name = *Cieszyn* [CHEH-shin]), nestled in a strategic Carpathian mountain pass, became a major source of tension for Czechoslovakia and Poland as the Czechoslovak army seized the disputed town in January 1919.

Most European languages' origins are shrouded in some primordial medieval mist, but Slovaks know what day their language was born: February 14, 1843. Okay, this is a bit exaggerated, but not much.

Anton Bernolák had published a treatise on Slovak in 1787, but it didn't really catch on. The Slovaks were descendants of ancient *Moravia Magna* who had been cut off from their western Slavic brethren by the Magyar conquest in 895 CE, and were seen by many as essentially eastern Czechs. With the rise of nationalism and Pan-Slavism in the 19th century, the question arose: are Slovaks simply eastern Czechs, or a separate people?

Driven by concerns with both the Hungarians and Czechs, a Slovak scholar, Ľudovít Štúr (Lyoo-DO-veet SHTOOR) met with some colleagues in February 1843 and decided that Slovak was indeed a separate language from Czech, and (borrowing from Bernolák) they adopted the central Slovak dialect spoken in the Tatry region of the Carpathians as the official Slovak language. Though local acceptance was slow and prominent Czechs such as Palacký were infuriated, Štúr managed to kick off a Slovak literary revolution. Resistance to Magyarization in the post-1867 Habsburg empire hardened Slovak resolve, and Slovaks joined their Czech compatriots during World War I to fight for a homeland after the war.

Slovak euphoria at Czechoslovakia's birth in 1918 slowly turned to dismay, however, as Czechs built a highly centralized state based around Prague, largely ignoring Slovaks. To make matters worse, when local Hungarian civil servants fled after the Habsburg empire's collapse, Prague replaced them with Czechs (in part because there were so few educated Slovaks). Worse, a popular Habsburg subsidy paid to Slovak farmers by Budapest was discontinued by a cash-strapped Prague. Slovaks fumed, prompting anti-Habsburg activist Andrej Hlinka (AN-dray HLEEN-kah) to revive his prewar political party, the *Slovenská ľudová strana* (Slovak People's Party), pressing Prague for Slovak autonomy. From the start, Czechoslovakia was a house divided.

USELESS TRIVIA: THE SAME WORLD, BUT SOMEHOW SO DIFFERENT . . .

Franz Kafka was born into a Jewish middle class family in Habsburg Prague in 1883, his parents owning a successful garment factory. Kafka attended Prague's Charles University and received a law degree, afterward working for a state-owned insurance company. Kafka wrote extensively but didn't see much value in his work, and upon his death in 1924, bequeathed his entire collected works to his friend, Max Brod, with orders to burn it all. Brod disregarded his friend's request and published many of Kafka's novels, making Kafka (posthumously) world famous. Brod fled Nazi-occupied Prague in 1939 with Kafka's collection for British Palestine, where he lived (in Israel) until his death in 1968.

An interesting point about Kafka's life in early-20th century Prague is that his native language was German; Kafka was born into a German cultural realm in his native Prague that coexisted side-by-side with a Czech-speaking world. These two realms were distinct but interacted, compelling local civil servants to learn both languages. Charles University for instance had two faculties, one that taught in German and the other in Czech. A German-speaking elite was common in Austria-Hungary's cities, but German had also become an important language in global science, literature, and business by 1900. (American inventor Thomas Edison even reportedly learned German to be able to read the latest German chemistry books.) The growing middle class of 19th-century Central Europe—whether local, German, or Jewish—often functioned in German,[37] but the rise of nationalism and the birth of nation states across the region in 1918 led to the rapid eclipse of German by local languages like Czech—especially after 1945.

Czechoslovakia was seemingly one of the calmest countries in interwar Eastern Europe, but in reality the country spent much of these decades in almost constant parliamentary and government crisis. The end came as a chilling shock not only to Czechoslovakia but also to all of Eastern Europe, even Prague's enemies.

After absorbing Austria in his *Anschluß* of March 1938, Hitler then turned to Czechoslovakia and demanded the Sudetenland. Hitler was not interested in border revisions; his goal was the destruction of Czechoslovakia, an illegitimate creation of the Versailles Treaty (in his eyes). But he was caught off guard by British attempts to mediate the crisis. Britain believed that Hitler really only wanted minor border changes, but London's concern was that France's treaty with Prague might lead to a repeat of 1914 and another major war.

On September 27, 1938, British Prime Minister Neville Chamberlain made his aims clear in a radio-broadcasted speech to the House of Commons in London:

> How horrible, fantastic, incredible it is that we should be digging trenches and trying on gas masks here because of a quarrel in a far-away country between people of whom we know nothing.

The full implications of the 1925 Treaty of Locarno became clear, and Eastern Europeans were put on notice: they were not worth fighting for, and what's more, they were expendable for European security. Two days later on September 29, 1938, Britain, France, and Nazi Germany signed the Munich Agreement (*Mnichovský Diktát*, "The Munich Dictate" to Czechs), giving the disputed Sudetenland to Germany. Prague was merely informed of the decision and advised to comply. Nazi German troops immediately occupied the disputed regions.[38]

A month later, in November 1938, Nazi Germany and Italy browbeat Czechoslovakia into giving parts of southern Slovakia back to Hungary in the First Vienna Award, with no peep from the West. Six months later, in March 1939, Hitler broke the Munich Agreement, invading and occupying the rest of Czechoslovakia. He created a Slovak puppet state under the Slovak priest Father Jozef Tiso, and Beneš fled to the West. World War II was officially still six months away.

M. Ukraine: With Friends Like These . . .

Many histories of this period rarely mention Ukraine, lumping it as a footnote in with Russian and Soviet history. However, this is when a separate Ukrainian national identity first began to assert itself, and while the independent Ukraine of 1918–21 was short-lived, its history certainly was action-packed.

Part of the problem was Ukrainians themselves, who were divided into *Ukrainophiles* (those who believed in Ukrainian culture) and *Russophiles* (those who saw Ukraine as merely an extension of Russia). Many Ukrain-ophiles lived in Austrian Galicia, whose stubborn Polish aristocrats held only contempt for Ukrainian peasantry, breeding Ukrainophiles. However, in Russian Kiev local intellectuals such as historian Mikhailo Hrushchevs-kiy (*Михайло Грушевський*) had also been laying the cultural foundations for a separate Ukrainian identity before the war.

Ukrainians had a front-row seat to World War I, with Galicia and west-ern Ukraine spending much of the war hosting the front lines and numer-ous bloody battles. Millions of Ukrainians fought in both the Russian Tsarist and Austro-Hungarian armies. Relief came only in early 1917, when Russia exploded into revolution in March and the tsarist administration collapsed. All across the empire local revolutionary provisional governments formed, mirroring the provisional government in Petrograd, but parallel to this in Kiev, the Ukrainian Central Council (*Українска Центральна Рада*), led by Mikhailo Hrushevskiy, declared Ukraine "autonomous" within the Rus-sian Empire. Russia reluctantly consented. Unfortunately, the Council had little influence outside of Kiev, and when in mid-December 1917 the Bol-sheviks invaded Ukraine, its members had to flee.

Working in exile in rural western Ukraine, the Council approached the Allies but discovered that the only Western state interested in East-ern Europe, France, wanted to restore the Russian Empire as a coun-terweight to Germany, and therefore rejected Ukrainian "separatists." The Council had better luck with the Germans, who included Ukrainian independence in the Treaty of Brest-Litovsk they imposed on Lenin in March 1918. By "independent," the Germans of course meant "German puppet state"; Ukraine was freed from Russia in exchange for vital food-stuffs to feed the German war effort. When it became apparent that the Ukrainian Central Council couldn't deliver those foodstuffs, the Ger-mans overthrew it, in April 1918.

Having neither the time nor the patience to form a replacement, the Germans turned to a wealthy local landowner, Pavlo (Paul) Skoropadsky, who had the support of Ukraine's conservative groups and landowners including ethnic Russians. Skoropadsky held the old Cossack title *het-man*,[39] so his government became known as the *Hetmanate*. The Hetmanate quickly managed to form the necessary bureaucratic structures that had eluded the Central Council, and in short order Ukrainian wheat was flow-ing to Germany.

Unfortunately, the Hetmanate (a government run by landowners) ran roughshod over peasants, making itself very unpopular, which became a problem in November 1918, when Germany lost World War I and had to withdraw its forces from Ukraine. Within weeks the Bolsheviks reinvaded Ukraine and tried to establish a Ukrainian Soviet Republic.

Ukraine dissolved into an ugly civil war involving peasants, landowners, Tsarist Russians, Bolshevik Russians, and Ukrainian nationalists, with Jewish settlements all too often attacked by all sides. Embattled Kiev changed hands several times throughout 1919. In the meantime, a Western Ukrainian Republic was founded in Galicia by Simon Petlyura (SEE-mon Pet-LYOO-rah) that immediately fell into conflict with the Poles, who by mid-July 1919 had managed to overrun most of Galicia (including its capital, Lviv/Lvov/Lwów).

USELESS TRIVIA: TICKETS, PLEASE!

In early May 1920, invading Polish forces had fought their way to the outskirts of Kiev against determined Bolshevik Russian resistance. A small unit of Polish hussars were about to continue their advance into the city one morning when they were stunned to see a trolley approaching. War-ravaged Kiev had changed hands six times in bitter fighting over the previous three years between Ukrainians, Germans, and (Red and White) Russians, so a working trolley was an unexpected sight. Shocked, they boarded the trolley and rode toward downtown Kiev. At one stop, a high-ranking Bolshevik officer boarded the trolley. They arrested him and returned to their lines, and Polish forces occupied the city.

With the Bolsheviks gaining the upper hand in the civil war by late 1919, a desperate Petlyura turned to his enemies, the Poles, and cut a deal: Galicia given to Poland in exchange for help in re-establishing an independent Ukraine. Thus began the Russo-Polish War, which started in April 1920 with Polish and Western Ukrainian forces invading Bolshevik Ukraine, successfully liberating Kiev in early May 1920. However, Bolshevik forces led by the brilliant Red Army General Mikhail Tukhachevsky managed to turn the tide and drive the allies from Ukraine, even reaching the outskirts of Warsaw by late August 1920.

The Poles were able to save Warsaw and partially reverse their fortunes, but with both sides exhausted, the Poles abandoned Petlyura[40] and divided Ukraine and Belarus with Moscow in the Treaty of Riga in March 1921. With this treaty, the dream of an independent Ukraine died.

USELESS TRIVIA: THESE NEW INVENTIONS
ARE GETTING OUT OF HAND

In the Boer War (1899–1902) in South Africa, British authorities, frustrated by the guerrilla tactics of the Boers (descendants of Dutch colonists), rounded up Boer civilians (mostly women and children) and imprisoned them in camps. Thus was born the *concentration camp*, with horrific results: some 3,600 Boer soldiers died fighting but 28,000 Boer civilians died of starvation and disease in the British camps. However, the camps proved very effective in controlling the Boer population, and the concentration camp quickly became a staple of 20th-century conflicts.

One such example comes from a seemingly unlikely place, Canada. With the onset of World War I in August, 1914 Canada passed the War Measures Act, which gave the government in Ottawa sweeping wartime powers, including wide authority to deal with "enemies of the state." Immediately Ottawa required immigrants from enemy countries to report regularly. The end result was that of the 80,000 people affected, most were not Germans but *Ukrainians*, some living in Canada for decades.

This process was soon declared inadequate for Canada's security, however, and by mid-1915, twenty-four concentration camps were built across the country in which 8,579 people—5,000 of them Ukrainians from the Habsburg lands—were held. Their money and property were seized, their access to news restricted, and their mail censored. In all, 109 people died in the camps during the war, including some who were shot trying to escape. Many were also forced to work, maintaining roads and rail lines or for war-related private industries such as mines. Indeed, though the war ended in 1918, some companies had become so dependent on camp labor that they convinced the government to prolong the internment until 1920. Internees did not receive their property back and were never compensated. In the 1980s Ukrainian-Canadian groups began agitating for an official acknowledgment of the camps, and finally in 2005 the Canadian government formally apologized and established a fund for education about the camps.[41]

Soviet rule in eastern Ukraine began with a famine, the famine of 1921–22 that resulted in an estimated 5 million Russian and Ukrainian deaths and that was caused in part by Lenin's overzealous agents, a severe winter, and the collapse of the Tsarist economy. Indeed, after the famine, life improved as Lenin realized the idiocy of "war communism"[42] and enacted the New Economic Policy, which essentially allowed a semifree market to develop in the Soviet countryside. Throughout the 1920s Ukrainophiles came out of hiding and Ukrainian culture thrived in Soviet Kiev. Stalin hated the N.E.P., however, and as he gained control of the USSR in the late 1920s, he made his move against both the N.E.P. and Ukraine. In 1929 he ordered collectivization[43] to begin in Ukraine, and took the first steps toward the artificial manmade famine in Ukraine called by Ukrainians the Голодомор (Hol-od-O-more; "the Hunger").

In 1932–33, an estimated 5-7 million Ukrainians died of starvation (some estimates range up to 10 million) as Stalin sealed Ukraine's borders, preventing all entry or exit from the country, while Soviet troops and NKVD agents seized nearly all grain produced, guarding it in special regional depots to be transported to ports *for export*. Meanwhile, horrific stories of cannibalism began to emerge from what had been for centuries one of Europe's most bountiful grain-producing lands. A broken Soviet Ukraine submissively reverted to ethnic Russian rule and Soviet economic integration.

N. Belarus Gets Its 15 Minutes . . . Literally

Belarus was very slow to develop its own national identity, though it had its proponents as early as the 1860s with the likes of Kastus Kalinousky (Кастусь Каліноўскі).[44] Unlike fellow Ruthenian Ukraine, Belarus has deep, dark forests with small isolated villages[45] instead of Ukraine's wide-open plains. Heavy-handed Russification programs in the 1890s generated resentment, however, and interest in an exclusively Belarussian culture—previously associated more with Polish or Lithuanian culture—began to grow. Throughout World War I the front wavered back and forth across Belarus, sending refugees fleeing, but by early 1917 the country found itself occupied by German forces.

As part and parcel of Germany's efforts to create a string of subservient puppet states in Eastern Europe through the March 1918 Treaty of Brest-Litovsk with Lenin's Russia, the Germans helped create the Belarussian National Republic (Беларуская Народная Рэспубліка). Though bound to Germany, Belarussians took this new circumstance seriously and began to organize a Belarussian Council (Беларуская Рада) and form state institutions in Myensk.[46]

The German defeat in November 1918, however, put a damper on these plans, and it wasn't long—December, in fact—before Bolshevik forces were pouring over the border. Belarus was soon overrun by Bolshevik, White Russian, Polish, and Lithuanian armies. Eventually, after the Russo-Polish War of 1920, Belarus was divided between Poland and Bolshevik Russia. Belarus's short period of (semi-) independence was over, but it was never quite forgotten.

Though the Belarussian National Republic did not last long in Belarus, it fled in 1918 and formed a government-in-exile that stood throughout the Soviet era for Belarussian rights and indeed still exists today, based in Canada, in opposition to the dictatorship of Aleksander Lukashenko. The present-day political opposition in Belarus still celebrates the BNR's anniversary, March 25, with rallies.[47]

O. Libre Baltica: Lithuania, Latvia, and Estonia

The Baltic countries are perhaps the quintessential Eastern European countries in microcosm. Of the three, only Lithuania had any tradition of statehood and that was long in the past by 1918. Indeed, Estonian and Latvian national identity had arisen fairly late to the Eastern European scene, as products of intense 19th-century Russification campaigns.

The rise of all three countries at the end of World War I was an indicator of just how far Russian and German imperial fortunes had fallen, as these tiny little countries strode out onto the European stage and confronted befuddled diplomats at the Paris Peace Conference in 1919 with new geographic names in languages that made the Slavic languages look *easy*.

Despite their tiny populations, however, all three countries had—true to their Eastern European pedigree—large ethnic minorities: Russians and Germans stranded by imperial collapse, Poles left over from the Commonwealth days, and Jews. All three started out in 1918 as enthusiastic democracies, and yet by the early 1930s, they had all devolved into authoritarian nationalist dictatorships. And just as all three Baltic states owed their independence in 1918 to the collapse of Russian and German imperialism, the revival of Russia and Germany in the 1930s spelled their doom.

In April 1917, both Finland and Estonia were granted autonomous status by the Russian provisional government after the Russian February Revolution, but later that year the Bolsheviks seized control of Tallinn. An ill-conceived Bolshevik walk-out from the negotiations at Brest-Litovsk in early 1918 brought German armies surging into the Russian Baltics (on their way to Petrograd), and on the day the Bolsheviks fled Tallinn (February 24, 1918), Konstantin Päts (CON-stan-teen Pets) declared Estonia's independence. This is Estonia's national day still today.

The Germans occupied Tallinn the next day, but with German defeat in the World War in November 1918, Päts and the *Maapäev* (temporary Estonian ruling council) took over Tallinn again. The Bolsheviks pounced within days, however, kicking off the *Vabadussõda*, the Estonian War of Independence. Though initially much of the country was overrun by the Bolsheviks, the Estonians recovered, and by February 1919 they managed to liberate all of Estonia.

In July 1919 the Estonians repulsed another Soviet invasion, and this time—freshly equipped with new British and French weapons—they launched a counterattack and headed for Petrograd. Soviet resistance stiffened, however, and by early February 1920 both sides buried the hatchet and signed the Treaty of Tartu, recognizing Estonia's independence.

Estonia in the 1920s was blessed with good leadership that implemented many crucial economic and social reforms, particularly in education. With the Soviet Union looming nearby, the country developed very good relations with neighboring Latvia and Finland, though relations with Lithuania were cooler.

Nothing could prepare the country for the crushing effects of the Great Depression, however, and extremist movements began to arise. Particularly, the Union of Veterans of the Estonian Freedom War (EVKL or "Vaps"; *Eesti Vabadussõjalaste Keskliit*) demanded a more nationalist and authoritarian government in the early 1930s. When Vaps failed to decisively win the elections in early 1934, President Konstantin Päts pre-empted a probable coup with one of his own in March, declaring a state of emergency, dissolving the *Riigikogu* (parliament) and banning Vaps. From 1934 on, Estonia was a mild authoritarian dictatorship, and sought defensive alliances with nearby Scandinavia.

At some point between 1918 and 1920, just about *everybody* invaded Latvia. It began with disillusioned Latvian veterans of the Tsarist armies who, after the German occupation in 1918, formed the pro-Soviet *Latviešu sarkanie strēlnieki*, the "Latvian Red Riflemen," and seized Latvia. Before they reached Riga, a council of underground parties called the *Tautas Padome* (People's Council) led by Kārlis Ulmanis (KARL-eess Ool-MAHN-eess) declared the independence of the Republic of Latvia on November 18, before fleeing to the coastal city of Liepaja (LYEH-pah-yah).

The Latvian Red Riflemen, led by Jakums Vācietis (YAH-kooms Vah-TSEE-tis), declared the Latvian Soviet Republic in Riga, but the Germans reinvaded Lithuania and Latvia with *Freikorps*[48] and *Baltische Landwehr*[49] units in January 1919. As Ulmanis was forming a Latvian army to drive the Germans out, *another* threat to Latvia appeared as former Russian POWs, led by pro-Tsarist General Pavel Bermondt-Avalov, allied with the Germans to subjugate Latvia. The Bolsheviks also reinvaded, so in December

1919, Ulmanis signed an alliance with Poland, which quickly drove all the invaders from Latvian soil. The Russo-Polish War of 1920 brought the Bolsheviks back, but by the autumn the Poles returned and in the Treaty of Riga in 1921, Lenin was forced to recognize Latvian independence.[50]

Finally fully independent and recognized by the West, Ulmanis formed a Latvian government and was elected its first prime minister. Latvia was fortunate in that it had a long coastline with several well-developed ports that allowed the country to quickly reorient its economy from Russia to the rest of Europe. However, like northern neighbor Estonia, this dependence on an export economy left the country exposed to the effects of the Great Depression, which again led to the rise of nationalist parties.

For almost exactly the same reasons, two months after Päts's state of emergency in Estonia, Ulmanis seized power in May 1934 in a bloodless coup to forestall a similar coup by the small but highly vocal Latvian nationalist organization *Pērkonkrust* (PARE-koon-Kroost; "ThunderCross," the Latvian name for the swastika). Latvia devolved into a nationalist rightwing dictatorship. Latvia and Estonia together tried to sign alliances with Sweden and Denmark, but while sympathetic, the Scandinavians feared binding themselves to a region known to be coveted by both Berlin and Moscow.

Lithuania was different from its two fellow Baltic states. It was overwhelmingly Roman Catholic, a consequence of its long ties to neighboring Poland, while Latvia and Estonia—both deeply influenced by Germany and Scandinavia—were primarily Lutheran. It had a long history of self-rule, and was even once a powerful state on the European stage, while neither Latvia nor Estonia had existed as independent countries before the 20th century. Because of this, Lithuania already had well-established national institutions and a clear sense of national identity.

However, Lithuania had committed grave sins in the eyes of its Russian rulers; it was an accomplice to the Poles in the Polish-Lithuanian Commonwealth, and Lithuanians had proven just as rebellious as their former Polish comrades in the Russian Empire. The tsars made Lithuania pay by devastating the Lithuanian lands repeatedly throughout the 19th century, leaving Lithuania a feudal backwater at the onset of the 20th century.

With the Treaty of Brest-Litovsk in March 1918, the Germans created a puppet Kingdom of Lithuania complete with the German Count of Württemberg, who was to be crowned "King Mindaugas II." The German defeat in November 1918, however, nixed those plans and the Lithuanians instead declared their independence under Augustinas Voldemaras (Ow-goo-STEE-nooss Vold-eh-MAR-ahs). The Bolsheviks invaded in January 1919, proclaiming the Lithuanian-Belarussian Soviet Socialist Republic (*Литовско-Белорусская Совецкая Социалистическая Рэспублика*). Throughout 1919,

Lithuania was also invaded by Poles, Freikorps German units, and Bermondt-Avalov's White Russians. By December 1919 the Lithuanians had driven most of the invaders out, but Vilnius (VEEL-nyooss) was still occupied by the Poles. Vilnius's ethnic composition at the time was messy:

> In 1897 a thorough and scientific census of the entire Russian Empire was carried out, the first and only of its kind before the Soviet era. According to this census, no one ethnic group dominated in Vilnius. But we need to tease the ethnic figures out of statistics that specify only religion or native tongue. By religion the city's population broke down into 23.6% Orthodox Christians, 36.9% Catholics, and 41.3% Jews (with assorted Muslims, Karaites, Lutherans, and even two Mennonites as well). By native tongue, Yiddish enjoyed a strong plurality with 40.0% of all inhabitants, followed by Polish (30.9%), Russian (20.0%), Belarusian (4.2%), and Lithuanian (2.1%).
>
> To be sure, these figures are far from unimpeachable. When in doubt, census-takers often erred in favor of Russian over other ethnicities. More fundamentally, into what category should one place, for example, an individual born into a Lithuanian family but educated at the (Polish-dominated) Catholic seminary to become a priest? Lithuanians would consistently argue—with some justification—that their numbers were considerably greater than these statistics would suggest. On another point, the seemingly impressive Russian minority of 20% almost certainly did not reflect the face of the city. Many of these Russians were soldiers and bureaucrats who called Vilna home only for a short period of time, as the dominance of males in this group (almost double the number of women) shows. Still, the 1897 census gives us a general picture of the ethnic makeup of this medium-sized provincial town.[51]

Indeed, Poland's leader, Józef Piłsudski, was a native of Vilnius. Still, Vilnius was the historic capital of Lithuania. This was a common dilemma in Eastern Europe at the time, and as usual it was resolved not by calm negotiation but by force of arms. The Poles briefly lost Vilnius during the Russo-Polish War of 1920 but were back, and in 1922 annexed the city. Lithuania set up a "temporary" capital in Kaunas (COW-nahss), and broke relations with Poland. Lithuania fared better in 1923 when it seized the German-populated free city of Memel (Klaipėda; CLY-pay-dah), giving Lithuania a modern-day industrial port.

Thus did Lithuania, free for the first time in more than a century, enter the 20th century with poisoned relations with neighbors Poland and Germany. Lithuania established a democratic government in 1922 but the Lithuanian parliament was unruly and fractuous, and eleven different governments came and went between 1922 and 1926.

In December 1926 Lithuanian nationalists and the army joined forces to overthrow the government and establish an authoritarian nationalist dictatorship under the "presidency" of Antanas Smetona (Ahn-TAH-nahss Smeh-TO-nah), with the country's early founder, Augustinas Voldemaras, serving as prime minister. Two years later Smetona dissolved the Lithuanian parliament, and a year after that, in 1929, he got rid of Voldemaras. An incident on the Polish-Lithuanian border in March 1938 led to the Polish government demanding that Lithuania resume normal diplomatic relations, *or else*. Lithuania complied. A year later in March 1939, Nazi Germany demanded the return of Klaipėda/Memel. Lithuania, isolated, again had no choice, and a day later—fresh from his visit to Prague after having just destroyed Czechoslovakia—Hitler himself paraded through Klaipėda's (Memel's; MAY-mel) streets.

All of these events in the three Baltic countries took place in the vacuum left from the defunct Russian and German empires. Their revival in the 1930s was an extremely dangerous development for the Baltic states, and the alliance of these two powers in 1939 was positively fatal for the Baltics.

The world was stunned to wake up on the morning of August 23, 1939, to the news that Hitler's Germany and Stalin's Russia had signed the Molotov-Ribbentrop Pact, but those in Kaunas, Riga, and Tallinn understood the implications. A secret clause in that pact divided Eastern Europe between the two expansionist empires, with the Baltics—outside of some German interests—falling under Soviet control.

After the joint Nazi-Soviet partition of Poland in September, the next to feel the Soviet axe was Finland, when in November 1939 it rejected Stalin's request for territorial revisions and the Soviets concocted a border incident as an excuse to invade. The resulting Winter War of November 1939–March 1940 ended in a Finnish defeat (with the country losing a small portion of its territory) but not before a very public humiliation of Soviet forces. The Baltic countries would pay for this Finnish insolence, as Stalin sought to shore up his humbled ego by seizing the Baltics and incorporating them into a larger western Soviet defense zone.

P. Russia and How Russians Do Change

Tsarist misrule and oppression practically ensured revolution in early-20th century Russia, but what might emerge out of that revolution was a variable, an unknown. The provisional governments of Prince Lvov and Alexander Kerensky showed some initial promise, but they could not deliver the peace and provisions that Russia's brutalized peasantry so desired, and when a tiny group of radicals seized power in November 1917, no one could be found to defend the provisional government.

So began the monstrous regime of Vladimir Illyich Ulyanov, better known to the world as N. Lenin. Modern-day Russians struggle with the Soviet legacy both for its achievements and its crimes at home and abroad. There can be no doubt that the Soviet Union did achieve much, but the question for any objective observer is this: was a totalitarian dictatorship that practiced slavery, mass terror, and mass murder the *only way* for Russia to advance in the 20th century? Lenin's and Stalin's mass terror, collectivization, purges, and gulags amounted to what the Polish theoretician Leszek Kołakowski called "probably the most massive warlike operation ever conducted by a state against its own citizens."[52] Was there another way, less bloody and less wasteful, or is the KGB Russia's only route to progress?

When World War I began in 1914, Russians, like almost everyone else in Europe, were seized with patriotic ferver. One of the Tsarist government's first acts, in the same spirit as "liberty cabbage" and "liberty fries," was to change the name of the Russian capital from the German "St. Petersburg" to the more Russian "Petrograd" (Петроград). An initial invasion of East Prussia in the autumn of 1914 went horribly awry, but the Russian army found more success against Austro-Hungarian forces in Galicia and the Ottoman Turks in the Caucasus. With the Brusilov Offensive in Galicia in 1916, Tsarist forces nearly destroyed the Habsburg armies, though successes such as these were often quickly reversed by German forces.

Russian forces struggled against another enemy, however, one within: inefficiency, corruption, and an antiquated economy unable to provide its fighting forces with everything they required. Russian soldiers often went into battle without weapons, boots, or food rations. Civilians also suffered from chronic privations of food and basic necessities. Add in the unnecessary wasting of soldiers' lives by incompetent Russian generals for little or no gain, and by 1916, the Tsarist government had squandered the enormous reservoir of patriotism and good will the war had inspired in 1914. When the Brusilov Offensive petered out in September 1916, the exhausted and hungry country was in an ugly mood. When in March 1917,[53] after several days of food riots in Petrograd, Tsar Nicholas II ordered the army to restore order, he was unpleasantly surprised to see his soldiers instead join the street demonstrations. After some weeks, Tsar Nicholas bowed to the inevitable and abdicated the throne on March 15, 1917. The Romanov dynasty's 300-year reign in Russia had ended.

USELESS TRIVIA: NO, *I'M* SPARTACUS!

On a cold February night in Berlin in 1920, passersby were horrified to see a young woman jump into the Landwehr Canal. A policeman jumped in and saved the suicidal woman and brought her to a mental hospital. For months she was silent until suddenly, one day she informed a startled nurse that she was none other than Grand Duchess Anastasia Romanov, daughter of the murdered Russian Tsar Nicholas II. Ever since the cowardly murder of the tsarist family by the Bolsheviks in July 1918, there had been rumors that some of the children may have escaped. The young woman claimed that one of the Bolshevik soldiers noticed she was still alive among the bodies of her slain family and secreted her off to Romania to recover. She became a worldwide sensation, and many in the Russian émigré community in Western Europe fêted her.

So, was she Anastasia Romanov? When she was taken to the hospital in 1920, the doctors noted that she had vicious bullet and knife (or bayonet) scars all over her body, and she spoke German haltingly with a clearly Slavic accent. She also resembled Anastasia very closely when compared to known photos of Anastasia. As she tried to claim the Romanov fortune, however, courts declared the evidence inconclusive.

That was then. Today we know her real name was Franciszka Szankowska (Fran-CHEESH-kah Shan-KOFF-skah), from Prussian Poland. She had disappeared from her job at a German munitions factory shortly before the mystery woman jumped into the canal in Berlin. A dropped grenade had exploded at her feet in 1916 in her factory, explaining the scars all over her body the German doctors noticed. She died and was cremated in 1984, but samples of her tissue from a biopsy were discovered in 1995 and submitted to DNA testing. The outcome was conclusive: the woman was not even remotely related to the Romanovs, while she was directly related to Franciszka's surviving great nephew. In the meantime, the remains of the royal family were discovered in 1991 and 2007 near Yekaterinburg, Russia, and subsequent DNA tests have conclusively identified them. There is now no doubt that all five of the Tsar's children were murdered that sad day along with their parents in July 1918, including poor Anastasia.

The tsar was gone, but nobody quite knew what to do without him. A provisional government was formed under Prince Georgi Lvov but parallel workers and soldiers' councils (soviets) were formed as well, and Lvov had little authority. The provisional government insisted on remaining in the war. In the meantime, socialist revolutionary Lenin, living in Switzerland, approached the Germans with an offer: grant him access to Russia and funds, and he would take Russia out of the war. The Germans agreed, and in April 1917 Lenin traveled in a sealed train across Germany, then across the Baltic and Scandinavia, finally arriving with the core of the Bolshevik party in Petrograd. By the autumn of 1917 support for the provisional government was disintegrating, so on the morning of November 7, 1917 the Bolsheviks were able to seize strategic buildings around Petrograd. Helpless, Kerensky had to flee.[54]

Once he had power, Lenin had every intention of keeping it. He ruthlessly suppressed all political parties, including the workers and soldiers soviets (which later Soviet history books would romanticize). The Bolsheviks were initially popular, their slogan of "Peace, Land, and Free Bread!" (*Мира, земли и бесплатного хлеба*) striking a strong chord with starved and war-weary Russians, but Lenin quickly unleashed the Cheka and the Red Terror, terrorizing Russia into submission.

Lenin's first priority was indeed to the end the war, signing in March 1918 the Treaty of Brest-Litovsk with Germany, sacrificing much of the western Russian Empire to German imperial interests.[55] His assumption was that Germany and the West would slide into communist revolution shortly, anyway, so this loss was just temporary. Lenin's next problem was civil war, which quickly broke out and involved "White" (i.e., pro-Tsarist or democratic, at least anti-Bolshevik) Russians led by Piotr Wrangel, Admiral Alexander Kolchak, and General Anton Denikin, as well as Finns, the Baltic peoples, Poles, Ukrainians, Germans, Georgians, Armenians, and Azeris, among others. The Western Allies, in the form of the British, French, American, and Japanese armies also intervened inconclusively in 1919–20, occupying Murmansk, Archangelsk, and Vladivostok briefly before evacuating. At one point in 1919, as White Russian forces came dangerously close to taking Petrograd, Lenin moved the Soviet capital to Moscow.

Finally, in 1922, as Wrangel's forces fled Crimea, Russia was firmly in the hands of Lenin's regime, at the cost of some 15 million dead. With all of Russia at his feet, Lenin still had little time for celebration. Between the World War, the civil war, and the Bolshevik policy of "War Communism"—an economic principal that amounted to Bolshevik forces seizing whatever they needed from merchants and farmers—the country's economy was in a state of collapse. Lenin enacted the New Economic Policy (N.E.P.), which allowed for basic capitalist exchange and markets in the Russian countryside. It worked, and soon Russia began to recover from its long nightmare.

USELESS TRIVIA: THE BEST LAID PLANS OF MICE AND MEN

By the summer of 1918, Lenin had ruled Russia for six months, but life in his Russia was grim with civil war, food shortages, travel restrictions, and the terror of the ЧК (Che-Kah; "Cheka"), the early KGB. Later Soviet histories glorified this era, but in truth Lenin's regime hung by a thread.

Sidney Reilly (an alias) was an exceptionally talented (and, on occasion, murderous) Russian-born conman whose résumé made him ideal for espionage, so in the late 1890s he was recruited by the British to perform amazing feats of intelligence gathering and skullduggery around the world. Ian Fleming, the author of the James Bond books, claims to have modeled James Bond in part on Reilly. In that summer of 1918, Reilly was in Russia arranging a stunning plan. Reilly bribed Latvian soldiers guarding the Kremlin as well as some disgruntled army generals and arranged (with funding from London) to arrest and overthrow the Bolsheviks. All Reilly needed was for both Lenin and Trotsky—the two real leaders of the Bolshevik cause—to be in Petrograd. They were scheduled to attend a party congress in early September, so Reilly's plan was set to go, but on the evening of August 30, Fanya Kaplan, a young revolutionary, shot Lenin as he exited a meeting hall. He survived, but the Cheka went into a murderous frenzy, arresting (and torturing and executing) thousands. Eventually Reilly's plan was discovered. Reilly fled to Finland, but many of his friends and co-conspirators met a grim fate.

Lenin was seriously wounded but eventually recovered, though he was never quite the same afterward, dying in 1924 at only fifty-four years of age. One can only wonder what Russia might have been like if Lenin had been arrested and executed, and Bolshevism nipped in the bud. In any event, Reilly himself was caught and executed by the Bolsheviks in 1925 when he was lured back to Russia by a GPU (reorganized Cheka) front organization pretending to want to overthrow the Soviets.

However, Lenin had another basic problem in 1922: namely, Western Europe had failed to collapse into communist revolution as he'd predicted, which left Lenin with a vast, economically underdeveloped and decrepit feudal empire to create the world's most advanced society in. To coordinate (i.e., control) the world's communist parties and spread the Revolution, Lenin created the Communist International (Comintern) in 1919. After a series of strokes in 1923, Lenin—increasingly erratic and paranoid—finally died in 1924.

USELESS TRIVIA: TAXIDERMY!

(Disclaimer: Some squeamish readers may want to skip this one. Really.)

When Lenin was dying, he asked in his will that he be buried in Petrograd. However, the ideological dictatorship he'd built in Russia was weak and vulnerable, and wasn't quite ready to let go of its founder. So the Soviet leadership put together a team of scientists to permanently preserve Lenin's body in 1924, and they began work on the Lenin Mausoleum in Red Square in Moscow. The scientists developed a method of dabbing his skin twice weekly with embalming agents, then bathing his entire body every eighteen months in a chemical solution to keep it hydrated. During World War II his corpse was removed to Siberia until Moscow was safe. This method still continues today, and despite urban legends of Lenin being replaced by a mannequin, his embalmers insist that it's (still) the real McCoy after nine decades.

When Stalin died in 1953, he was laid alongside Lenin until political winds changed, and in 1961 his body was quietly removed from the mausoleum and buried. Lenin's corpse had already started the trend of pickling your deceased communist dictator for display, however, so Georgi Dimitrov's mummified body was put on display in a mausoleum in downtown Sofia after he died in 1949. As soon as the communist regime fell in Bulgaria in 1989, he was removed and quietly cremated. Similarly, the Czechoslovak communist ruler Klement Gottwald was initially prepped and put on display in his own mausoleum in Prague after he died in 1953, but alcoholism and syphilis had ravaged his body, and the Czechs had to use wax and strategic lights to try to keep Gottwald on display, until by 1962 it was apparent he was just too far gone and he was cremated. Others have joined this bizarre communist cult of the dead, like Vietnamese communist Ho Chi Minh and North Korean dictators Kim Il-Sung and Kim Jong-Il, as well as China's Mao Tse-Tung and Angola's former communist ruler Agostino Neto.

After Lenin's death a power struggle raged between Trotsky, the brilliant strategist who had created the Red Army, and Stalin, an undereducated but politically astute thug. By 1927 Trotsky had lost, and Stalin consolidated his power. Recognizing like Lenin in 1922 that the world revolution had stalled, Stalin decided he needed to transform Russia into a beacon for the revolution and so he initiated the first of many Five Year Plans designed to very rapidly industrialize the Soviet Union. Connected to this realization about the stalled world revolution was Stalin's second (paranoid) belief that since the noncommunist world was inherently hostile, any territory, therefore, controlled by the Soviet Union was "liberated" territory. This formula meant that Soviet territorial expansion was in essence an advance of the (stalled) world revolution. To Stalin, "world revolution" meant simply "empire." His foreign minister, Vyacheslav Molotov, saw territorial expansion as crucial:

> It's good that the Russian tsars took so much land for us in war. This makes our struggle with capitalism easier.
> [and . . .]
> My task as minister of foreign affairs was to expand the borders of our Fatherland. And it seems that Stalin and I coped with this task quite well.[56]

Empire, given Russia's condition in 1930, was a tall order. To quickly achieve industrialization, Stalin enacted a few "programs" to get things moving. First, he developed what the writer (and former inmate) Aleksandr Solzhenitsyn called the *Gulags*, a massive prison system stretching across Siberia housing criminals, political prisoners, and others amounting to (from 1929 until the system's dissolution in the 1950s) 7-15 million prisoners (about 3-5 million of whom died).[57] These prisoners weren't just criminals or enemies of the state; Stalin needed slave labor for massive infrastructure projects such as roads, bridges, and canals across Russia's vast expanses. Regional GPU and NKVD[58] offices were issued arbitrary arrest quotas designed to keep the gulag labor pool filled. Next, Stalin needed to break any potential resistance to his policies, so he launched in 1936–39 the Great Terror (known in Russia as "the Yezhov Time," after NKVD head Nikolai Yezhov; *Ежовщина*), in which Stalin essentially went on a wild killing spree (via the NKVD). Peasants and *kulaks*,[59] the Party, the intelligentsia, the armed forces; *everyone* was subjected to arbitrary arrests and imprisonment (i.e., gulags) or execution.

Indeed, in these few years Comrade Stalin was the only person in the Soviet Union who could sleep soundly at night. Between 1934 and 1941, 7 million Soviets were arrested, with 720,000 executed in 1937–38[60] (or 1.7 million between 1937–39[61]). It is estimated that between the gulag system, the Great Purges, collectivization, and the artificial Ukrainian Famine, some 15-20 million Soviet citizens[62] were murdered by their own government from 1930 to 1953. After 1932, official Soviet censuses became a state secret because of the dramatic fall in Soviet population they revealed.

On the foreign relations front, the United States was the first to normalize relations with the USSR, in 1933, followed shortly by Britain, France, and other nations. Stalin's intentions toward Eastern Europe were nakedly clear: expansion. Stalin coveted former Russian imperial territories such as the Baltic states, western Ukraine, and Belarus from Poland, Bessarabia from Romania, and Transcarpathia from Czechoslovakia. He aggressively used the Comintern for espionage and political agitation against each of these countries. The threat of Soviet subversion or military intervention was taken very seriously in the region.

As both Moscow and the West awoke to the dangers posed by Hitler's Germany in 1939, they negotiated toward an alliance, but many in the West were wary of Stalin and Stalin himself distrusted the West after its abandonment of Czechoslovakia—the poster-child pro-Western state in Eastern Europe—in 1938. Negotiations stumbled over Soviet demands for transit rights of the Soviet army through neighboring Poland, Romania, and the Baltic states, something the region's Sovietophobic countries refused. In some respects the Molotov-Ribbentrop Pact of August 1939 between Hitler's Germany and Stalin's Soviet Union made sense as two predatory and expansionist totalitarian empires warily made a truce, pragmatically accommodating one another's imperial ambitions in Eastern Europe. What is clear is that the Soviet Union was woefully unprepared when war came in 1941.

Q. The Failed Superstates IV: Poland

Interwar Poland had, outside of the Soviet Union, Eastern Europe's largest population, and its most formidable army. However, its messy birth in 1918–22 alienated many of its neighbors, and Western attempts to construct a monolithic alliance in the region foundered on the reluctance of some states—Czechoslovakia in particular—to ally with a country known to be on both Berlin's and Moscow's hit list. Poland did have positive relations with *some* neighboring countries, particularly Hungary and Romania, both of whom shared with Poland a semifeudal heritage of lingering aristocratic control (and minimal historic border disputes). However, Poland's foreign relations in the interwar years were defined largely by its need to balance between the reviving German and Soviet threats. Added to the external danger was an internal threat: Poland's success in reclaiming many historical territories of the old Commonwealth left Poland in 1922 with about a third—34%—of its population being (hostile) ethnic minorities.

Some two million Poles fought in the World War I, serving in the Russian, Austro-Hungarian, German, and French armies, and of course the World War came to visit a few times, sending Polish refugees scurrying in all directions. There were two rival revolutionary traditions in occupied Poland by this time, one led by Roman Dmowski (RO-man Duh-MAWFF-skee) and another led by Józef Piłsudski (YOO-zef Pil-SOOD-skee). Where Dmowski was a nationalist who wanted an ethnically "pure" Poland,[63] Piłsudski wanted to recreate the old (multicultural) Commonwealth.

When war broke out in 1914, Dmowski negotiated Polish autonomy with St. Petersburg. He set up a council in Warsaw that was to become a Polish government after the war and created the *Puławy* (Poo-WAH-vih) *Legion* to fight for Russia. However, after Russia's military disasters in

1914–15, the Russians abandoned any pretense of autonomy for Poland, and soon Dmowski left for London. Throughout 1916 Dmowski traveled the Western world raising funds and giving speeches in support of Polish independence. In 1917 in Paris he formed the Polish National Committee (*Komitet Narodowy Polski*), which by 1918 was recognized as a Polish government-in-exile by the Allies. He also recruited some 25,000 Polish émigrés for the Blue Army (*Błękitna Armia*; named after their powder-blue French uniforms), which fought under General Józef Haller on the Western Front in 1918. By the summer of 1918, it looked as if Dmowski was in control of Poland's fate.

USELESS TRIVIA: ONE MAN'S TRASH . . .

In the spring of 2012, members of Poland's NATO contingent in Afghanistan were hunting a tank, one that had eluded them for some time. They had recently received intelligence about its whereabouts, however, and so they closed in on their prey. Finally, in an old warehouse belonging to the Afghan defense ministry, they found it: a ninety-four-year-old French Renault FT-17 light tank.

In 1918 France asked Polish General Józef Haller to organize a Polish army for use on the Western Front, which became known to Poles as *Błękitna Arm*ia (Blue Army," because they wore French blue uniforms). This army was equipped with 120 French Renault FT-17s, which Haller brought with his army to Poland after the war. A couple of these tanks were engaged against the Soviets in a battle in the village of Równe (ROOV-neh; modern-day Rivne, Ukraine) in July 1920 when, having been fighting for hours, they ran out of gas and had to be abandoned. The Soviets seized them and tried copying them but Bolshevik industry was at the time too primitive, and so in 1923 Lenin gifted both tanks to an emir in Afghanistan. By chance, the arid Afghan climate preserved the tanks well. An American discovery in 2003 suggested the tanks might still be around, and so Polish forces hunted until they found one of them in 2012. Polish president Bronisław Komorowski (Bron-YEE-swaff Ko-mor-OFF-skee)—a historian—personally requested the tank from the Afghan government, which Kabul gave (back) to Poland in September 2012. The 6.5-ton tank was immediately shipped home and is set for restoration.

That's not how things worked out, however. In November 1916 the Germans decided (in tandem with Vienna) to create a Polish puppet kingdom in the Russian-Polish lands called the Polish Regency Kingdom (*Polskie Królestwo Regencyjne*). Short of manpower in the war, the Germans tried recruiting a Polish army (*Polnische Wehrmacht*) in 1917, but with minimal success. Berlin then noticed that Dmowski's rival, Piłsudski, had organized a nascent army in Austrian Poland disguised as shooting clubs—Piłsudski had already led a few small raids against Russia—so the Germans decided to simply absorb Piłsudski's force into their army. However, Piłsudski refused to swear an oath to the Kaiser, so in July 1917 he was arrested and the Legion interned in POW camps. Two things had already happened that would impact Poland's fate, though: in March 1917 Russia collapsed into revolution, while a month later the United States entered the war. U.S. President Woodrow Wilson singled out Poland in his Fourteen Points in 1918:

> XIII. An independent Polish state should be erected which should include the territories inhabited by indisputably Polish populations, which should be assured a free and secure access to the sea, and whose political and economic independence and territorial integrity should be guaranteed by international covenant.

The Fourteen Points gave the Polish cause immense prestige across Europe. When the war ended in November 1918, the Germans recognized the inevitable and simply released Piłsudski and put him on a train back to Warsaw. This meant that though Dmowski had an army and official Allied recognition, Piłsudski and his Legion controlled Warsaw.

The two rivals eventually negotiated a cooperation arrangement whereby Dmowski remained in Paris to represent Poland at the 1919 peace conference. Dmowski thought this gave him the advantage as Paris was where all the big decisions were being made by the Allies, but throughout 1919 Piłsudski set out building Polish state institutions. By the time Dmowski returned home months later, he discovered that he was politically marginalized. Piłsudski had already created Poland.

Although Poland now existed, neither it nor its neighbors had clearly defined borders yet, and fighting broke out all over almost immediately. The Poles had the advantage of a multitude of trained and experienced soldiers returning home, including the Blue Army (now 68,000 strong) in early 1919. The main theaters of war from 1918 to 1922 were:

- **Galicia,** where Poles and Ukrainians began fighting over control of the region and its capital, Lvov/Lwów/Lviv/Lemberg. Initially the Ukrainians had the upper hand but Poland was able to organize a professional army from veterans and successfully seize the region.

- **Silesia:** Germany and Poland both claimed Silesia, for ethnic and economic reasons. Both had mixed populations but Northern (Lower) Silesia was primarily German, while southern (Upper) Silesia had a larger Polish minority. The League of Nations organized a plebiscite for Upper

Silesia in 1921, but an overwhelming vote in favor of union with Germany led to a Polish uprising, which was fought bitterly by German Freikorps units. The Western Allies intervened and gave Poland much of Upper Silesia. Germans never accepted this border, however, and politicians in both Weimar and later, Nazi Germany made it a central point of their foreign policy to regain all "historically German" lands.

USELESS TRIVIA: OVER THERE!

Legend has it that when the United States entered World War I in 1917, American General John J. Pershing visited the tomb of American Revolutionary War hero Lafayette shortly after arriving in France, where his aid uttered the phrase *"Lafayette, Nous sommes ici!"* ("Lafayette, We are here!").

Another small group of Americans carried this symbolism to Eastern Europe. Twenty-one American aviators (along with four Poles and a Canadian), lingering in Paris in 1918 as World War I ended, joined the Polish army's new air wing, forming the 7th Polish Air Force Squadron, which became the Kościuszko Squadron. One of its most famous American leaders, Maj. Merian C. Cooper, claimed he was repaying a 150 year-old debt to Poland, referring to Kościuszko's contributions to the American Revolution. In the Russo-Polish War, the Kościuszko Squadron—since Lenin had no air force—helped the Polish Army by bombing and strafing the much-feared Bolshevik cavalry forces. Flying some 400 sorties, the Squadron played a role in saving Warsaw in August 1920 and in the defense of Lwów (modern-day Lviv, Ukraine).

Cooper was decorated with Poland's highest military honor, the *Virtuti Militari*. He went on to fly in the U.S. Army Air Corps in World War II, winning a place of honor on the deck of the USS Missouri as Japan surrendered. In between the wars he also had a "side" career in Hollywood making, among other notable films, *King* Kong. Three American airmen were killed in 1920 in the battle for Lwów, and they were buried with military honors and a monument in the city after the war. Polish Lwów became Soviet Lvov in 1944, however, and Soviet authorities bulldozed the graves in 1969. Modern-day Poland has sought to restore that monument in modern-day Ukrainian Lviv. After the Russo-Polish War, the American volunteers were gradually replaced by Poles, and the Kościuszko Squadron, reformed by members who had escaped from Poland in September 1939, played an important role in the Battle of Britain during World War II.

"Poland's existence is intolerable and incompatible with the essential conditions of Germany's life. Poland must go and will go [. . .] The restoration of the border between Germany and Russia is the precondition for regaining strength of both sides. Germany and Russia within the borders of 1914 should be the basis for an agreement between us."
—Hans von Seeckt, Commander of the German *Reichswehr* (army), 1922[64]

- **Danzig/Gdańsk**—The League of Nations made the city of Danzig/Gdańsk, whose population in 1919 was overwhelmingly German (but surrounded by Poles) a free city. However, to provide Poland with access to the Baltic (per Wilson's Fourteen Points) a slice of territory just west of the city was given to Warsaw. This thin slice of Baltic territory (formerly of East Prussia) became known as the Polish Corridor, and even moderate Germans were enraged as it cut East Prussia off from the rest of Germany.

- **Wilno/Vilnius**—Claimed by Lithuania as its historic capital, but with a large Polish population (though surrounded by Lithuanians), the Poles occupied and eventually annexed the city in 1922, poisoning relations with Lithuania for decades.

- **Russo-Polish War**—Belatedly Piłsudski realized the value of having independent "buffer" states between Poland and Bolshevik Russia, so in 1920 he signed an alliance with the Western Ukrainian leader, Simon Petlyura, and invaded Bolshevik-ruled Ukraine in May to help it achieve independence. After some success, Polish forces overextended themselves and were pushed back to Warsaw itself by August, only to launch a surprise counterattack that shattered Soviet forces, saving both Warsaw and Poland. With the Treaty of Riga in 1921, Piłsudski abandoned Petlyura and divided Ukraine and Belarus with Lenin.

"And now Piłsudski will have to make peace on terms that are worse for him and better for us than under our first offer. But nevertheless we have suffered an enormous defeat; a collosal army of a hundred thousand is either prisoner of war[65] or interned in Germany. In a word, a gigantic, unheard-of-defeat."
—V. I. Lenin, September 20, 1920[66]

Piłsudski initially stepped aside gracefully after the border wars came to a close, and a democratic government was organized with the help of émigrés such as the pianist Ignacy Jan Paderewski (Eeg-NOTS-ih Pah-deh-REV-skee)—who had lived in the West and experienced democracy. All should have boded well for Polish democracy, but Poland in 1922 was still an impoverished and fragmented country struggling with its heritage of more than a century of having been divided between three empires. Very quickly Polish politics became polarized—Poland's first elected president, Gabriel Narutowicz (GAH-bryel Nah-roo-TOE-veetch), was assassinated in December 1922 after only two weeks in office—and the *Sejm* was reduced to chaos.

As Polish politics edged the country toward the abyss, Piłsudski took action in May 1926 and staged a military coup. Poland's first democratic experiment was over. Piłsudski effectively became Poland's dictator, though the Sejm continued to function in a limited capacity. Because he spoke of needing to clean out and sanitize Polish political life, his regime became known as the Sanitation, or *Sanacja* (Sah-NAHTS-yah), regime.

After Piłsudski's death in 1935, a group of veterans of the 1918–22 wars assumed control of the country, forming what became known as the colonels' regime. Piłsudski's foreign minister, Col. Józef Beck (YOO-zef Bek) retained control over foreign affairs and he quickly became the face of the new Polish regime for the West. Contrary to Piłsudski's approach, the colonels favored more nationalist policies—alienating minorities and angering the West, for instance, by taking the opportunity of Czechoslovakia's destruction by Hitler to seize disputed *Cieszyn* in March 1939.

While Beck in particular has been more heavily criticized for the colonels' seeming intransigence throughout 1939 as the West tried to create an anti-German alliance with the Soviets, recent scholarship is coming to better appreciate Poland's "between a rock and a hard place" position; that is, between Nazi Germany and the Soviet Union. As events would shortly prove, Warsaw had correctly sized up the Soviets to be as much a threat as Germany, something the West at the time did not appreciate. And while Hitler's betrayal of the Munich Agreement in 1939 scared Britain and France into signing mutual defense treaties with Warsaw, Poles would soon learn that the West had signed those treaties out of larger geopolitical concerns rather than out of any urgent desire to save Poland.

USELESS TRIVIA: ALL ROADS LEAD TO MADRID!

After decades of almost constant political crises between monarchists, the Catholic church and wealthy landowners on the one hand, and republicans, liberals and socialists on the other, war exploded in Spain in July 1936 when the pro-royalist Spanish Army launched a coup to overthrow the democratically elected Spanish government. For three agonizing years Spain writhed in bloody civil war, with both sides committing gross atrocities against civilians. Hitler provided support to the conservative nationalists, while Stalin supported the republicans.

Much like Italy in the mid-19th century, Spain's plight in the late 1930s attracted volunteers from all over the world. Overwhelmingly, the *republicanos* attracted the more volunteers, with volunteer fighting units coming from as far as the United States and Eastern Europe: 3,000 Poles, 2,500 Russians, 1,500 Czechs or Slovaks, 1,500 Yugoslavs, and 1,500 Hungarians volunteered and fought in the Spanish Civil War. These volunteers gained crucial practical military and networking experience in the war, and they put this knowledge to critical use in resistance movements during World War II.

Despite widespread international support, the *republicanos* lost the war in April 1939 when their last stronghold fell, and nationalist general Francisco Franco formed the Spanish fascist government that ruled Spain as a dictatorship until his death in 1975. Not a particularly good loser, Stalin lashed out at Spanish Civil War veterans after World War II across Soviet-occupied Eastern Europe, packing them off to Siberian exile or, worse, many never to be seen again.

7. WAR!
1939-1945

THE **** HITS THE FAN

Blended photos of the steps of Germany's Reichstag (parliament building) in Berlin; one from 1945 showing Soviet General Georgi Zhukov and staff surveying the conquered city, the other showing tourists in 2012. (Photo: by kind permission of Sergey Larenkov: www.sergey-larenkov.livejournal.com)

Dwie Ojczyzny
To twoja wolność - śmierdzący samogon
i byle dziwka w trykotowej bieliźnie,
a moja wolność - czysty nieba ogrom.
Dlatego mamy dwie różne Ojczyzny.
Tobie Ojczyzną - transakcja giełdowa
i worki mąki schowane po kryjomu,
a mnie Ojczyzną - komora gazowa
i oświęcimski płomień.
Tobie Ojczyzną - Tryumfalny Łuk,
defiladowa muzyczka zwycięska,
a mnie Ojczyzną - parszywy grób
w lasku pod Smoleńskiem!
Tobie Ojczyzną - spokojny kąt
i kark, który posłusznie się gnie,
a mnie Ojczyzną - spalony dom
i rejestracja w NKWD
—Tadeusz Borowski, 1945

Two Countries
To you, freedom is a pungent home brew
and any girl in lacy underwear;
To me, freedom is the pure vastness of the sky.
This is because we have two different countries.
Your country has stock market transactions
and burlap bags of flour tucked in the corner;
My country has gas chambers
and the flames of Auschwitz.
Your country has the Arc de Triomphe
and strident marching bands;
My country can offer a shabby grave
in a forest near Smolensk.
Your country offers a peaceful corner and
Things worth risking your neck over;
Mine—a home burned to the ground
And an arrest warrant from the NKVD.[1]

"Close your hearts to pity! Act brutally! Eighty million people must obtain what is their right. . . . The stronger man is right. . . . Be harsh and remorseless! Be steeled against all signs of compassion! . . . Whoever has pondered over this world order knows that its meaning lies in the success of the best by means of force."

—*Adolf Hitler, in an address to the Wehrmacht on the eve of the invasion of Poland, August 1939*

Figure 54. Eastern Europe Timeline, 1939–1945

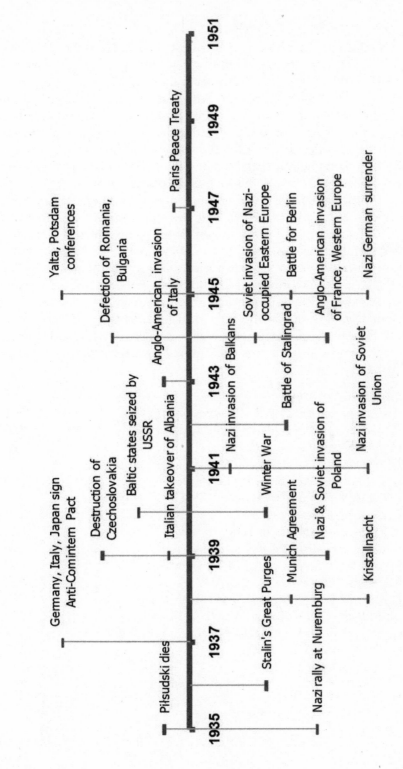

CHAPTER SUMMARY

What civilization, after having nearly destroyed itself in the most destructive war in human history, would be tempted just a generation later to try it *again*? World War II—to Russians the Great Patriotic War (*Великая Отечественная война*)—is often glorified as the "good" war, and indeed most today agree that the world is a better place for the defeat of Hitler and fascism. However, in Europe at least, the war was really a final breakdown of civility and order; it was the final shootout at the OK Corral between rival countries, a gigantic gangland brawl in which all civility broke down.

For Eastern Europeans, this was a war of the Great Powers, and while some countries entered the war enthusiastically as an opportunity to right the wrongs of Versailles (1919), their inescapable fate was to be either pawns or battlefields, or all too often, both. Some realized (too late) that their economic deals with Hitler in the 1930s had been Faustian bargains, while others discovered to their horror that prewar treaties and alliances with the West were worthless. Most had real estate someone else wanted.

To this day Eastern Europeans argue whether their leaders (or their neighbor's leaders) made the right decisions. In the end, though, every Eastern European country lost the war, regardless of which side they chose or what their leaders did. This war haunts Eastern Europe as no other historical event does.

CHAPTER GUIDE

A. The War as You Probably Don't Know It 321
B. About the Numbers Used in this Chapter 326
C. An Overview of the War 328
D. Poland and The Art of Not Being 331
E. The Baltics and a Bad Neighborhood 336
F. The Czech Lands Revert to the 17th Century 339
G. Slovakia Is Born, Sort of 342
H. Hungary Embraces Its Inner Tar Baby 343
I. Romania Guesses Wrong 346
J. Yugoslavia, Serbia, and 1914 All Over Again 349
K. Croatia's Dark Side 351
L. Albania Tries to Keep Its Head Above Water 353
M. Bulgaria: Third Time a Charm? 355
N. The Soviet Union Wins by Knockout in the 9th Round 357
O. The Holocaust 362

A. The War as You Probably Don't Know It

I know you think you know World War II. It's one of the most popular historical subjects in the world, as a visit to most bookstore History sections will prove. However, in this chapter, you're going to get to know World War II from a different angle, from the Eastern European perspective. Even those who are well versed in the events of Operation Barbarossa, Hitler's invasion of the USSR, will get some surprises. The war looks very different through Eastern European eyes.

For the next several figures, we're going to examine a macabre subject, fatalities in World War II. It's not a pleasant subject, I know, but there's an important story to be told here. Let's begin with Figure 55.

Figure 55. Allied and Axis Deaths in World War II

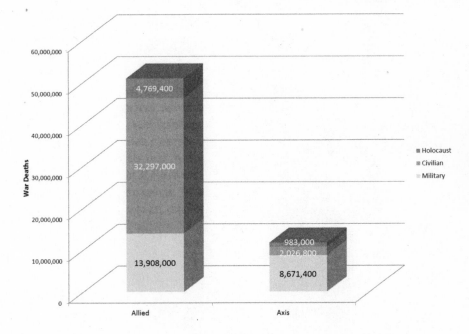

In Figure 55, we see that the Allies lost many more people in the war than the Axis powers, approximately 47.9 million compared to the Axis's 11.7 million. Indeed, the Allies lost *more than four times as many people* to the war as the Axis. Even more important, however, is the fact that 74% of the Axis deaths were military personnel—in other words, soldiers fighting the war—while only 29% of the Allies's dead were soldiers. This reflects the general flow of World War II, which involved Axis aggression against Allied countries and Axis control over large captive Allied civilian populations, coupled with the Axis powers' policies of terrorization, extermination, and slave labor. This includes such horrors as the aerial bombing of defenseless Chinese Nanking by the Japanese and the Nazi Holocaust. The Holocaust, in which some 5-6 million Jews were murdered, accounted for 8% of the Axis powers' own fatalities. Most of the Axis's civilian deaths were inflicted remotely by the Allies, through the Allied use of strategic aerial bombing of Axis industrial cities and targets, including, in the Japanese case, the two atomic bombs dropped on Hiroshima and Nagasaki.[2] Now let's take a look at how the war's fatalities shake out by region.

Figure 56. World War II Fatalities by Global Region

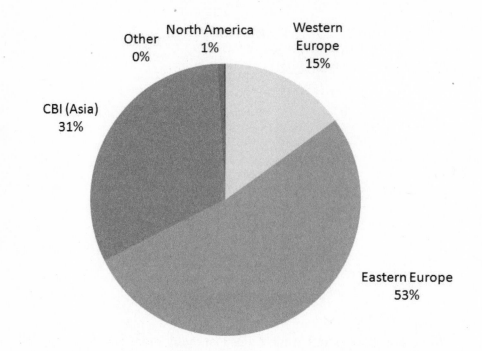

As we can see in Figure 56, more than half of all the people who were killed in World War II were from Eastern Europe. And, to be frank, even these numbers are a bit skewed toward Western Europe; I defined "Western Europe" in the broadest sense, meaning in today's terms—which includes modern-day Germany and Austria, which in 1939–45 contributed 6.5 million (or almost 70%) of Western Europe's 9.4 million war fatalities. But let's take a closer look at Europe by itself (Figures 57 and 58).

Figure 57. Total World War II Fatalities and Total Civilian World War II Fatalities in Europe

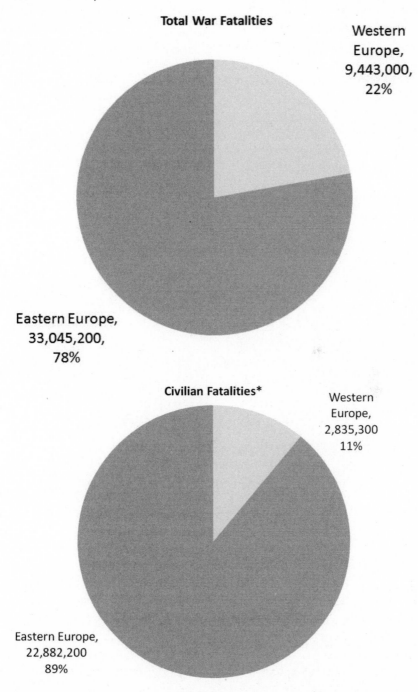

Total War Fatalities

Western Europe, 9,443,000, 22%

Eastern Europe, 33,045,200, 78%

Civilian Fatalities*

Western Europe, 2,835,300 11%

Eastern Europe, 22,882,200 89%

* Includes civilian dead as well as Holocaust victims

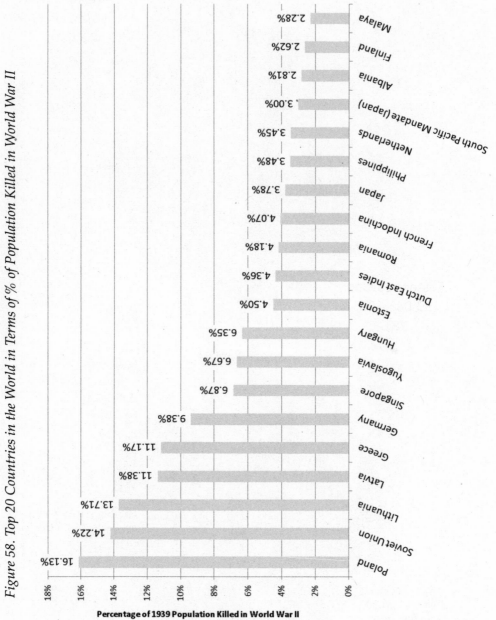

Figure 58. Top 20 Countries in the World in Terms of % of Population Killed in World War II

Figure 59. Eastern Europe Under Nazi Rule, 1942

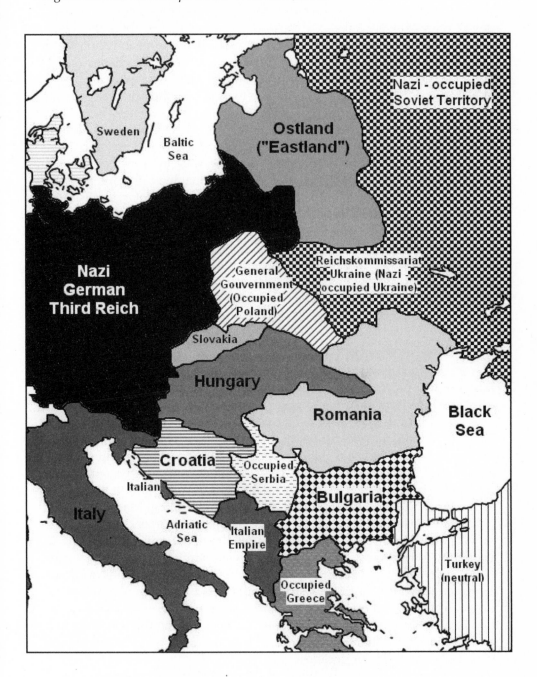

What can we see in this morbid section? Aside from the sheer human cost of the war in which for instance one in every six Poles (about 3,000 each day of the war) were killed, we are also seeing a message about the legitimacy of Eastern Europe, about the right of Eastern European countries to exist. When Hitler invaded Western Europe, he didn't really change much. True, the occupied Western European countries were reduced to the status of Nazi puppet states, but they continued to exist with their prewar political and social structures for the most part intact and functioning. There were never any Nazi plans for a "Westland" province. In Nazi-occupied Eastern Europe, however, Hitler *did* create an "Ostland" (Eastland) province, and countries and institutions alike across the region were mercilessly uprooted and demolished by the Nazis. Hitler couldn't imagine a Europe without Denmark or Belgium, but he *did* create a Europe without Poland or Estonia.

Worse, Hitler also envisioned a Europe without some of its peoples. The Jews were first on Hitler's hit list, but some Eastern Europeans discovered they were also slated for liquidation along with their countries. The atrocities committed in Eastern Europe weren't just the result of Germans behaving badly; they were carefully planned steps in calculated mass murder. This attempt to erase whole peoples and countries has left an indelible mark on the region, one that still today haunts its fledgling democracies.

B. About the Numbers Used in this Chapter

You might think that calculating casualty figures for World War II is easy. Just compare prewar and postwar censuses, right? It's not that easy, however, and here is an example of why: In August 1939, according to the figures I used for this book—more on that later—Poland had a population of about 35 million. By 1945, however, this was Poland: about one in every six Poles had been killed, and there were about 5 million Poles scattered outside Poland in slave labor camps, concentration camps, in foreign armies fighting, or as refugees abroad. The Soviets arrested hundreds of thousands of pro-Western Poles, prompting many to go into hiding. Many returning Polish Jews instead fled to Israel. Poland's borders, courtesy of Stalin, had moved a hundred miles westward, compelling 8-10 million Germans to flee (or be forced) westward, while the Soviets similarly deported 2.1 million Poles from the old eastern territories. Hundreds of thousands of Ukrainians would soon join them. Warsaw, which had a prewar population of over 1 million, was almost completely destroyed by 1945 and had a population of roughly 140,000. Within Poland, millions during the war had been forced from or fled their home regions.[3] Accounting for all these people has kept historians busy for decades.

But it gets even more complicated. When did World War II begin? Most say September 1, 1939, but Czechoslovakia was destroyed in March 1939 and Japan invaded China in 1931. And when did the war end, at least as far as casualties are concerned? The Japanese buried secret caches of chemical weapons across China before the war ended which still today, decades after the war, are killing rural Chinese civilians. Do they count as World War II casualties? What about epidemics or famines caused by the war, or Soviet ethnic cleansing and executions during the war? Because of all this confusion, estimates today of the total human cost of World War II range anywhere from 48 million to 78 million.

I used the online Wikipedia article entitled "World War II Casualties" for this section. I know many wince at the use of Wikipedia for serious academic efforts, but after scanning relevant published materials and scholarly articles, I could find no better aggregation of the most recent estimates of global casualty figures anywhere. The article discusses the nuances of estimating the war's casualties, and includes extensive notes and references. Here is a sample fragment note for Poland:

> In August 2009 the Polish Institute of National Remembrance (IPN) researchers put the figure of Poland's dead at between 5.62 million and 5.82 million. The IPN report estimated, between 5.47 million and 5.67 million Polish citizens died at the hands of the Nazis. Some 150,000 perished under the Soviets. The IPN's figures include 3 million Polish Jews, who perished in Nazi Germany's Holocaust, as well as non-Jewish Poles and other ethnic groups (Ukrainians and Belarussians).

The official estimate made in 1947 of 6.0 million war dead has been disputed by Polish scholars since the end of communist rule in 1989. They maintain that the official statistics include those persons who were listed as missing in 1945, but remained abroad in the west and the USSR after the war. Czesław Łuczak estimated the actual total of war dead to be 4.9 to 5.0 million, including 2.9 to 3.0 million Jews. He estimated the number of ethnic Poles who perished at 2.0 million, including 1.5 million, due to the German occupation of the territory of modern day Poland and the balance of 500,000 in the former eastern Polish regions under both Soviet and German occupation. Łuczak did not include in his figures an estimate for the war dead of Polish citizens from the ethnic Ukrainian and Belarusian groups which comprised about 20% of the 1939 Polish population.

This note continues in the Wikipedia article for another twenty-six lines. This level of thoroughness gives me confidence that these estimates are about as comprehensive and accurate as any available anywhere. To stay on the conservative side, I defaulted to the low-end figures in those (frequent) cases where the article provided ranges. The total war fatality figure in Wikipedia's estimates (given my favoring of the low ends of ranged figures) was 59.8 million dead. For those cases in this chapter where other sources were used, I provide a citation in a footnote.

COLLAGE OF THE EASTERN FRONT

Clockwise from top left: Soviet Il-2 ground attack aircraft in Berlin sky; German Tiger I tanks during the Battle of Kursk; German Stuka dive bombers on the Eastern Front, winter 1943–1944; executions of Jews by German Einsatzgruppen in Ukraine; Wilhelm Keitel signing the German instrument of surrender; Soviet troops in the Battle of Stalingrad. (created by Paul Siebert from images at Wikimedia Commons)

C. An Overview of the War

The causes behind World War I are complicated and can read like the fine print on an insurance policy, but the causes behind World War II—at least in Europe—are easy: Adolf Hitler. Now, there were many peripheral issues that played a role as well but all of them hinged on what Germany and its Charlie Chaplin–esque dictator did. Hitler and the Nazis (along with most Germans) believed Germany was being denied its rightful place among the Great Powers, and they deeply resented the restrictions of the 1919 Versailles Treaty.

Eastern Europe was a major sore point for the Nazis because while German armies had been decisively beaten on the Western Front in 1918—though some German nationalists denied even that—the German *Reichswehr* (army) had been victorious on the Eastern Front, but had been forced to give up its spoils after the war by the West. Germany even lost some pre-1914 German territories to the new Eastern European states! Hitler planned to rectify this "injustice" through *empire*: The *Drittes Reich* (Third Reich)[4] was to be a colossal empire stretching from the French border to the Ural Mountains encompassing Poland, Czechoslovakia, Belarus, Ukraine, the Baltics, and western Russia. This vast swath of territory was to be ruthlessly depopulated through expulsions, mass murder, and slavery, and its native populations replaced by German colonists.

USELESS TRIVIA: A NEED-TO-KNOW BASIS

As ordered, at 4:30 a.m. Lieutenant Hans-Albrecht Herzner led his group of some seventy *Abwehr* (Nazi German military intelligence) agents across the Polish-Slovak border in the lonely Jabłonkow Pass high in the Carpathian Mountains. Herzner's group was the spearpoint of the German invasion of Poland, and their mission was to seize a nearby strategic railway tunnel and bridge near the Polish town of Mosty and hold it until the *Wehrmacht* (army) 7th Infantry division arrived later that morning. Herzner's men seized the railway station next to the tunnel before dawn, but a station worker managed to alert local Polish forces. In the ensuing firefight Herzner extracted his men from the town and eluded Polish soldiers and policemen to retreat safely back to Slovakia.

What Herzner learned only after returning to Slovakia (because of poor radio communications in the Slovak mountains) was that his failed mission had been postponed. The date was August 26, 1939, the original date Hitler had assigned for *Operation Fallweiß* (Operation Case White), the invasion of Poland. However, hours earlier, on August 25, Britain had signed a mutual defense treaty with Poland and France, shaking Hitler's confidence and causing him to delay the invasion. Word of that delay had never reached Herzner's unit already deployed in Slovakia, however, and Herzner—per orders—set out on his mission in the early morning hours of August 26. Germany apologized to Poland for the "incident" and claimed Herzner was a lone madman acting without orders. Tipped off to the German interest in the tunnel, Polish engineers dynamited it days later when the real Nazi German invasion got underway on September 1. It wasn't until February 1940 that German engineers were able to reopen the tunnel. Herzner went on to command the infamous Nachtigall Battalion in Nazi-occupied Ukraine.

The dark year of 1939 began with Western Europe scrambling to deal with Hitler's betrayal of the 1938 Munich Agreement (destroying Czechoslovakia in March), leading to Western guarantees for Hitler's next victim, Poland. The war began formally in September when Hitler (later joined by Stalin) invaded Poland, and Britain and France declared war on Germany. In 1940, Hitler launched an invasion of Western Europe, quickly overrunning the Low Countries, France, Denmark, and Norway. A year later, in 1941, Hitler's plans to betray the USSR were delayed several months by the defection of Yugoslavia and by an Italian fiasco in Greece, prompting Hitler to invade the Balkans. With the Balkans subdued, Hitler finally launched his massive invasion of the Soviet Union, in late June 1941. At first things went spectacularly well, with Soviet forces quickly succumbing in complete confusion. However, the first signs of a Soviet recovery from the shock of the invasion came during the heroic defense of Moscow from October 1941 to January 1942, which effectively halted the Nazi advance for the winter.

In the meantime, the United States entered the war on the Allies' side in December 1941, which threatened Hitler's blockade of Britain and hold on Western Europe, leading to a bitter struggle in the Atlantic Ocean between the Anglo-American navies and Nazi submarines. Popular resistance movements against the Nazis also sprang up across Europe—particularly in Eastern Europe, where the Nazis' brutal policies inspired the war's largest resistance movements.

In 1942–43, Anglo-American forces drove Axis forces from North Africa while Hitler's southern armies in the USSR pushed to the Volga River city of Stalingrad, where a horrific struggle between Nazi and Soviet forces ended in February 1943 with the Soviets capturing an entire German army. This is considered by most historians to be the turning point in the war in Europe. In 1943, an Anglo-American invasion forced Italy out of the war (though German forces in Italy fought on) while the Soviets began a slow but sure westward advance, fighting the largest tank battle in history at Kursk in July.

In 1944, Anglo-American forces launched their invasion of France at Normandy in June, liberating most of the country and Belgium by year's end. Meanwhile, the Soviets in 1944 managed to liberate most of their territory and launched two invasions of Nazi-occupied Eastern Europe, a northern wing aimed at Poland and Czechoslovakia, and a southern wing aimed at Bulgaria, Romania, and Hungary.

By 1945, Germany was in ruins from constant Anglo-American air bombardment, while Allied armies invaded Germany from west and east. Bulgaria and Romania switched sides, but when Hungary tried to do the same Hitler overthrew its government and installed a loyal puppet regime. By April, Berlin was all that remained of the Reich, and the Soviets laid bloody siege. Hitler committed suicide at the end of April as street battles raged throughout his capital, and the Soviet flag was raised over the Reichstag. Admiral Karl Dönitz, Hitler's successor, surrendered to the Allies on May 8–9, 1945.

D. Poland and the Art of Not Being

"I have issued a command—and I will have everyone who utters even a single criticism shot—that the aim of the war lies not in reaching particular lines but in the physical annihilation of the enemy. Thus, so far only in the east, I have put my [SS] Death's Head formations at the ready with the command to send [every] man, woman and child of Polish descent and language to their deaths, pitilessly and remorselessly. . . . Poland will be depopulated and settled with Germans."
—Adolf Hitler, in a meeting with top Wehrmacht generals shortly before the imminent invasion of Poland, August 22, 1939[5]

"Der Blitzkrieg in Polen hat die unerträglichste der noch nicht liquidierten Folgen von Versailles beseitigt. Er hat bedrücktes Deutschtum befreit."[6]
("The Blitzkrieg in Poland has disposed of the most unbearable of the last remaining consequences of Versailles. It has liberated oppressed Germandom.")

Nazi Germany's attitude toward Poland in the 1930s was driven by two contradictory motives. The first was a vicious desire for revenge against Poland for the "humiliations" of 1918–21 and the recovery of lost territory. Even moderate Weimar German politicians in the 1920s often publicly called for Poland's destruction. However, Hitler also recognized that his chief eastern concern was Russia, not Poland, so in 1934 he signed a nonaggression pact with Poland, and even offered Warsaw in early 1939 part in an anti-Soviet pact. However, Poles knew that even a subservient Poland was not a Nazi goal.

Shortly after the destruction of Czechoslovakia in March 1939, Hitler demanded the free city of Gdańsk (Danzig) and unlimited German access across the Polish Corridor. Beck refused. Both Britain and France finally realized that Hitler was not seeking justice but empire, and signed mutual defense treaties with Poland. Both also opened negotiations with Stalin, but mutual distrust stalled talks until the world woke up to the stunning news on August 23, 1939, that Nazi Germany and the Soviet Union had signed a nonaggression pact. While the pact's division of Eastern Europe was a secret, it did not take a professional geopolitical strategist to figure out that Poland was in serious danger.

After the fabricated Gleiwitz (GLY-veets) incident,[7] Nazi German forces invaded Poland in the early hours of September 1, 1939, from the west (Germany), south (Slovakia), and north (East Prussia). Britain and France declared war on Germany on September 3. Poland's forces were hopelessly outnumbered and outclassed. By the end of the first week of September, Kraków had fallen and the Germans had achieved a break-through on the northern front shielding Warsaw. Based on assurances from France of an imminent French invasion of the German Rhineland (per treaty obligations), the Poles launched a series of counterattacks in the middle of the second week known as the Battles of the Bzura River (BZOO-rah) to delay the German advance, but the French invasion never materialized, and within days the battle turned into a Polish bloodbath. Despite heroic resistance, Poland's army began to unravel after that defeat. Worse, this defeat convinced Hitler's ally, Stalin, to enter the fray so that on September 17, Soviet forces invaded Poland. On September 27, Warsaw finally fell to the Germans, and on October 5, the last major Polish army group surrendered. Both London and Paris were stunned by the rapid Polish defeat, inspiring much criticism still today of antiquated Polish tactics and strategy, but as the historians Steven Zaloga and Victor Madej remind us:

> The roots of the Polish defeat are not particularly difficult to trace, though they have often been distorted. The outcome of the campaign was a foregone conclusion before it began—so long as France and Britain had no serious intention of directly intervening on the Western Front. Without Allied military intervention, the Wehrmacht could take the risk of committing the vast bulk of its strength against its much smaller Polish adversary. Although Western historians have been especially critical of Polish strategic deployment, the fact remains that the Polish Army could not have resisted the Wehrmacht single-handedly even under the most favorable circumstances. The task was even more hopeless after the inter-vention of the Red Army on 17 September. Correcting the shortcomings in Polish command decisions, troop dispositions, and tactical doctrine might have caused higher German casualties or prolonged the fighting by a few days or weeks, but it could not have substantially altered the outcome.[8]

USELESS TRIVIA: TRULY UNBEARABLE!

In a 2011 documentary,[9] a British army veteran recounted how in the spring of 1944 in the final stages of the Battle of Monte Cassino in Italy, he was standing on the slope leading to the abbey when he suddenly found himself confronted by a six-foot tall (1.82m), 485-pound (220 kg) bear, and this bear was carrying a large artillery round. This British soldier had just met Corporal Wojtek (VOY-tek).

Corporal Wojtek was a Syrian bear cub adopted as a mascot by Polish soldiers in General Anders' army as they transitted the Middle East from the Soviet Union to North Africa. He was formally inducted into the Polish Army in Egypt when a British officer refused to allow any pets aboard the troop ship as Allied forces embarked to invade Italy in 1943. So Corporal Wojtek accompanied the Polish Army's 22nd Artillery Supply Company to Italy, where the bear was trained to transport mortar and artillery shells to crews on the front. After the war there was a tug-of-war for Wojtek between communist Poland and Polish veterans in the West, but Wojtek ended up living the rest of his life in the Edinburgh Zoo, where he died in 1963. In November 2011 Scotland held a parade of Polish veterans and bagpipe players in Wojtek's honor in Edinburgh, and a bronze statue of Wojtek was unveiled in a local city park.

Once defeated, Poland was divided into German and Soviet zones. Polish administration across the country was dismantled; Hitler and Stalin intended to *destroy* Poland, not occupy it. The Soviet NKVD and Nazi Gestapo cooperated closely, holding several high-level meetings over 1939–41 to coordinate efforts to crush Polish resistance. By late 1940, hundreds of thousands of Poles identified as capable of organizing resistance (e.g., people with college degrees, politicians, sports and cultural icons, and priests) were herded into concentration camps and executed, while hundreds of thousands more were sent to Siberian gulags. The Polish Corridor, Pomerania, and Silesia were annexed by the Reich while the core Polish territories became the *Generalgouvernement für die besetzten polnischen Gebiete* (General Government for the Occupied Polish Territories); the "General Governate."

About 800,000 Poles were expelled from the annexed German territories into the General Governate. The Polish government escaped to Romania (where it was interned), while a Polish government-in-exile formed in Paris. Polish military and civilian refugees were also quietly welcomed into Hungary, to Hitler's ire.

Within Poland, elements of the defeated army coalesced to eventually form the *Armia Krajowa* (Ar-MEE-yah Cry-O-vah; "the National Army"), Nazi-occupied Europe's second largest resistance group after Yugoslavia. In close coordination with the Allies and Polish government-in-exile (which escaped to London after the fall of France in 1940), the AK carried out acts of sabotage, assassination of Nazi officers, intelligence-gathering, and even smuggled a V2 rocket to London from a secret Nazi testing ground near Warsaw.

USELESS TRIVIA: PEEK-A-BOO, WE HEAR YOU

Marian Rejewski (Mah-REE-ahn Reh-YEV-skee) was a star mathematics student at Poznań University when he was inducted into a secret government program on codes and encryptions in 1932, afterward joining the army's *Biuro Szyfrów* (Bureau of Ciphers) for decrypting secret enemy codes. Working with Henryk Zygalski (HINE-rick Tsih-GAL-skee) and Jerzy Różycki (YEH-zhih Roo-ZHITS-kee), he managed to break the official German military code generated by a machine called *Enigma*. In fact, the trio developed a mathematical model called *Bomba* (bomb), which kept up with German updates to Enigma, so that Poland could read Germany's most secret military communications.

As war clearly loomed on the horizon, Warsaw in July 1939 turned Bomba over to Britain and France. Henceforth Alan Turing advanced the Poles' accomplishments to great effect for the Allies during the war in the context of the "Ultra" (as in, "ultra-secret") signals intelligence program that unfolded at Britain's codebreaking center, Bletchley Park. For decades after the war the British remained completely silent about Ultra and Enigma, but finally in 2002, Britain unveiled a plaque at Bletchley Park dedicated to Rejewski, Zygalski, and Różycki for the foundations they laid for the Anglo-American intelligence services being able to read German Enigma-encrypted codes. All three Poles have since received posthumous medals for their work from several Allied governments.

Aside from the AK forces in Poland, approximately 275,000 Poles fought on the Allied side in the war, most in the West. In April 1940 four Polish battalions took part in the unsuccessful Allied defense of

Norway, particularly the Battle of Narvik, while Polish ships supported the British Royal Navy. Some 35,000 Poles fought for France in 1940, while 145 Polish pilots defended Britain during the Battle of Britain (almost 5% of all Allied pilots in the battle). After Hitler's betrayal of Stalin in 1941, the Soviets allowed the Poles to collect POWs from the 1939 campaign and form an army under General Władysław Anders (Vwah-DIH-swaff ON-dairs), which was shipped via Persia (Iran) to Egypt and then equipped and retrained by the Allies. It fought in North Africa and Italy, playing a crucial role in the Battle of Monte Cassino in 1944. The Polish 1st armored division took part in the June 1944 Allied invasion of France at Normandy, fighting in the Falais Pocket battle before going on to liberate, among others, the cities of Ghent in Belgium and Breda in the Netherlands. By war's end it had fought its way to Wilhelmshaven, Germany. Meanwhile, the Polish 1st Parachute Brigade took part in the ill-planned Allied Operation Market Garden in Arnhem, Netherlands.

Some 30,000 Poles also fought in the *Armia Ludowa* (People's Army), a communist force organized by Moscow that accompanied the Soviet army into Poland. By war's end, some 228,000 Polish soldiers were serving in the British, American, and Canadian armies, as well as some 14,000 Polish pilots and 3,000 sailors.[10]

Warsaw suffered two major uprisings during the war, both of which took a staggering toll in terms of both population killed and structural damage. The first came in January 1943, when the Nazis began rounding up Polish Jews concentrated into sealed ghettos for deportation to Auschwitz. Aware of their imminent fate, two Jewish underground forces, the *Żydowski Związek Wojskowy* (Jewish Military Union," ŻZW) and the *Żydowska Organizacja Bojowa* (Jewish Fighting Organization," ŻOB), rose up and held on to the Ghetto for months until resistance collapsed in early May.

A year later the AK launched *Plan Burza* (Plahn BOO-zhah; "Operation Tempest") on August 1, 1944 to liberate Warsaw before the Soviets arrived, but again, after months of bitter fighting, on October 2, AK leader General Tadeusz "Bór" Komorowski was forced to surrender to the Germans. The Soviet Red Army overran German-occupied Poland throughout the summer and autumn of 1944, clearing the country of Germans by January 1945.

USELESS TRIVIA: BUT IT WAS BLOCKING OUR VIEW!

On the night of August 24, 1944, Adolf Hitler demanded to know from his Army chief of staff, Alfred Jodl, "Is Paris burning?" The Allies were on the verge of liberating the city, and so Hitler—nice guy that he was— had ordered that Paris's famous monuments and historic structures should all be destroyed. Dynamite was dutifully placed on everything from bridges across the Seine to the Eiffel Tower, among other famous Parisian sites. Fortunately for France, the *Wehrmacht* commandant in charge of occupied Paris, General Dietrich von Choltitz, disobeyed his orders and did not detonate the explosives. He purposely allowed the Allies to take Paris intact the next day, much to Hitler's fury. Warsaw was not so lucky. After the Warsaw Uprising, Himmler declared:

> Then we will have destroyed Warsaw, the capital, the heart, the flower of the intelligentsia...of the Polish nation; this nation that for 700 years has blocked our road to the East and stood always in our way since the first battle at Tannenberg. [...] The city must completely disappear from the face of the Earth and serve only as a transport station for the Wehrmacht. No stone can remain standing. Every building is to be razed to its foundation.[11]

The Nazi commander of Warsaw, General Erich von dem Bach-Zelewski,[12] carried out Berlin's orders ruthlessly. The remaining population of Warsaw was expelled to concentration camps, and engineers moved in with dynamite and flamethrowers to systematically destroy every building. Libraries, historical buildings, and churches were especially targeted, burning books and artwork. By the time Soviet forces entered Warsaw months later, 80-90% of the city's buildings had been leveled. Warsaw was just a sea of rubble and debris, with few discernible streets or landmarks left. The city's historic downtown area was rebuilt after the war using surviving old maps, paintings, and photos, though the communists also imposed Stalinist architecture on parts of the city.

E. The Baltics and a Bad Neighborhood

The Baltics were doomed the moment Molotov and Ribbentrop inked their infamous pact on August 23, 1939 and everyone knew it. Unlike Poland, however, the Baltic states couldn't attract the attention of either London or Paris. If Neville Chamberlain didn't know anything about Czechs or Slovaks, where did that leave the Balts? The only British or French acknowledgement of the Baltics' plight came in the summer of 1939 in the form of a request for the Baltic states to allow the Soviet army transit rights, which Tallinn, Riga, and Kaunas all rejected just as Warsaw and Bucharest had done.

With that, the West effectively wrote the Baltic states off as goners. All three countries tried to remain neutral when the Germans invaded Poland in September, but Stalin got the excuse he needed when the Polish submarine *Orzeł* (O-zhel; "Eagle") evaded German capture and sailed into neutral Tallinn harbor on September 15. Adhering properly to the law of neutrals, the Estonians seized the ship and interned the crew, but the crew escaped and fled Tallinn westward[13] with their submarine three days later (September 18)—by which point the Soviet Union and Poland were at war.

Using this technicality, a week later, on September 24, the Soviets informed the Estonians that they could not be trusted to maintain security on the Baltic and gave them an ultimatum: accept permanent Soviet military bases in Estonia. Tallinn had no choice but to comply, and a week later Latvia got the same treatment. Lithuania was given the same ultimatum, but to sweeten the deal the Soviets handed Vilnius back to Lithuania from the defeated Poles.

Initially, despite the Soviet bases, all three Baltic states were still left relatively intact. However, the Winter War that the Soviets provoked with Finland from November 1939 to March 1940 severely rattled Moscow, and that, coupled with Hitler's Danish and Norwegian campaigns in April–May 1940—which left the entire western Baltic Sea region under German control—prompted Stalin to secure his northwestern flank in May 1940. The Soviets invented false incidents in all three Baltic countries to justify overthrowing their governments.

By mid-July, each of the Baltic countries saw rigged elections in which Soviet-friendly parties won sweeping victories, and each new (Soviet puppet) government immediately requested admittance to the Soviet Union. By the end of the first week of August 1940, all three Baltic countries were absorbed into the USSR, and their former leaders (those who as yet hadn't escaped) were arrested.[14] Throughout 1940–41, the Soviets began mass arrests and deportations in the former Baltic republics, sending tens of thousands of Balts to the gulags in Siberia.

Not surprisingly, the German invasion of the Soviet Union in June 1941 was welcomed as a liberation by the Baltic peoples. Indeed, some cities, like Estonia's Tartu, rose up in jubilant rebellion against the Soviets as Nazi forces approached. However, after the initial euphoria died down, it became apparent that the Germans had no interest in restoring Baltic independence. Instead they created a large puppet province called *Ostland* (Eastland) encompassing the Baltic countries and Belarus. Still, the Nazi occupation was far less odious than the brutal Soviet rule, so most Balts reluctantly accepted the German order.

One ugly aspect of the Nazi "liberation" was the widespread local belief that all Jews were Soviet sympathizers or collaborators; almost immediately nationalists in all three Baltic countries began attacking and murdering Jews *by the tens of thousands,* and aiding Nazi SS death squads. Ironically, the Soviets had also targeted Jews during the deportations of 1940–41. Estonia became one of Nazi-occupied Europe's first self-proclaimed *Judenfrei*[15] countries.

The Nazis had allowed small defense forces in Estonia and Latvia but interest in these was low, at least until the Soviets finally managed to break the Nazi siege of Leningrad in January 1944, which brought Soviet forces (back) to the Narva River, the eastern gateway to the Baltics. Suddenly Estonians, Latvians, and Lithuanians volunteered in droves to defend their homelands from another Soviet occupation.

The Soviet offensive began in earnest in June 1944, and over the summer and autumn, bitter fighting raged throughout the Baltics as the Germans and local armies fought desperate but futile battles against overwhelming Soviet forces; in June, Vilnius[16] and Kaunas fell, in July Riga, and by the end of September, Tallinn was in Soviet hands. For two days in September 1944, after the Germans evacuated Tallinn but before the Soviets occupied the city, the Estonian flag flew again—briefly—in the country's capital before Jüri Uluots (YOO-ree Oo-LOO-awts) fled to Sweden and formed an Estonian government-in-exile there.[17]

By the time Tallinn fell, most of the Baltics were under Soviet control again with the exception of Courland in western Latvia, where a combined German-Latvian force held out, holding off the Soviets until the end of the war in May 1945. The Courland salient bulged with refugees fleeing the Soviet advance, many of whom tried their luck at sea in makeshift boats to reach Sweden. Throughout the war, but particularly in its final year, the Baltic region's deep, dark forests played host to dozens of different underground partisan groups waging a low-grade but bloody war against the Germans, the Soviets, and each other. Local Baltic nationalists, Jews, trapped Nazi units, Soviet partisans, local ethnic Germans, Russians, Belarussians, and Poles all fought and terrorized one another's civilians through horrific atrocities. Partisan fighting raged throughout the region well into the 1950s as the three Baltic countries were once again forcibly annexed by the Soviet Union, and a new era of NKVD terror and deportations to Siberia began.

"The problem of the Baltic states, western Ukraine, western Belorussia, and Bessarabia we solved with Ribbentrop in 1939. [. . .] They [the Baltic states] found themselves between two great powers, fascist Germany, and Soviet Russia. The situation was complicated. That's why they wavered, but finally made up their minds. And we needed the Baltic states."

—Soviet foreign minister Vyacheslav Molotov[18]

"We were all very glad that the Lithuanians, Latvians and Estonians would again be part of the Soviet state. This meant the expansion of our territory, the augmentation of our population, the fortification of our borders, and the acquisition of an extensive coastal frontier on the Baltic Sea. [. . .] We were absolutely certain that the annexation was a great triumph for the Baltic peoples as well as for the Soviet Union."

—Nikita Khrushchev, Soviet leader[19]

F. The Czech Lands Revert to the 17th Century

"Věrni zůstaneme!"[20]

—Declaration of Czech democrats and leftist intellectuals to the
Czechoslovak government-in-exile, 1939

USELESS TRIVIA: TEUTONIC SUPERIORITY —BORROWED FROM ELSEWHERE!

The stunningly quick Nazi German victories over Poland in 1939, then Western Europe (Denmark, Norway, Netherlands, Luxembourg, Belgium, France, Britain) in 1940 gave the Germans a mythical aura of invincibility. In reality, however, Hitler's military machine wasn't quite ready when war came in 1939, and in some important respects Germany lagged behind the Allies: French heavy and medium tanks had superior firepower and thicker armor than Germany's early Panzer models, for instance, and France *had more* tanks (and planes) than Nazi Germany in 1940. So how did Hitler win?

In part, the German victories derived from superior tactics and strategies: the Germans simply knew how to use their weapons better than their enemies did. But they still needed numbers, numbers of tanks that they just didn't have in 1939. Where did they get them? When the Nazis occupied Bohemia and Moravia in March 1939, they inherited an advanced Czech arms industry, particularly two major tank manufacturers, *Česko-moravská Kolben Daněk* (ČKD) and *Škoda;* ČKD produced a medium tank designated the TNHP, and Škoda built a medium tank called the LTM-35, both of which were more sturdy, capable of traveling farther and easier to maintain than their Panzer peers. Impressed, the Germans simply continued production of these two tanks, renaming the TNHP the PzKpfw38(t) and the LTM-35 the PzKpfw 35(t). The (t) stood for Tscheche, German for "Czech." 150 of the PzKpfw 35(t) models saw German service, along with 1,168 of the PzKpfw 38(t) models. These tanks played a pivotal role in the German campaigns in Poland, Western Europe, North Africa, the Balkans, and, early on, the Soviet Union before being replaced by improved German Panzer models.

The Czechs are often criticized because they were relatively passive under Nazi rule, and indeed occupied Bohemia and Moravia required surprisingly few German troops throughout the war compared to Poland or Belgium. However, the Czechs began the war with a stunning series of betrayals beginning with Munich in September 1938, which paralyzed Czech society: Britain and France cut a "peace-for-land" deal with Hitler despite France's mutual defense treaty with Prague (and the Soviets also ignored their own treaty with Prague). Czechoslovak president Edvard Beneš fled the country to exile in London shortly after the Munich Agreement, leaving the country in the well-intentioned but inexperienced hands of Emil Hácha. Within weeks, in November, Hácha was confronted with Nazi and Italian demands that Czechoslovakia give southern Slovakia to Hungary (the First Vienna Award). Hungary then also seized Transcarpathia. Hácha tried to appease Slovak sensitivity by federalizing the country, but four months later, in March 1939, Hitler forced Father Jozef Tiso to declare Slovak independence while Nazi forces invaded the Czech lands, creating the *Reichsprotektorat Böhmen und Mähren* (The Reich Protectorate of Bohemia and Moravia).

Hácha was now a Nazi puppet. When the war began in September, the Allies recognized Beneš's government-in-exile (with which Hácha secretly cooperated) but in September 1941 Hitler decided to tighten the screws on Czechs and appointed his trusted friend Reinhard Heydrich as military governor.

The brutality of Heydrich's administration finally prompted Czechs to organize in 1941, resulting in an umbrella resistance organization called *Ústřední vedení odboje domácího* (Central Leadership of Home Resistance), comprised of Czechs loyal to the London government-in-exile. In May 1942 Czechoslovak agents inserted by the British managed to assassinate Heydrich, provoking the Nazi massacre of the inhabitants of two Czech towns, Lidice (LEE-dee-tseh) and Ležáky (LEH-zhah-kee). With Heydrich's death, any shred of Czech autonomy evaporated. ÚVOD cooperated closely with Czech communists to collect intelligence, and indeed in 1943 Beneš—still wary of the West after the Munich Agreement—cultivated closer relations with the Soviet Union.

Like the Poles, Czechs and Slovaks were well-represented in the Allied lines throughout the war. About 2,000 Czechoslovak pilots served in the Czechoslovak Free Air Force in Britain throughout the war, including eighty-nine who fought in the Battle of Britain in 1940. The Czechoslovak Free Air Force was led by General Karel Janoušek (KAH-rel Yahn-OW-shek), the first Czech to achieve the rank of Marshal, bestowed by Britain's King George VI in 1945.

When Hitler destroyed Czechoslovakia in March 1939 some 2,200 Czechoslovak soldiers fled to Poland, although Western fears of provoking Hitler denied Poland their use. After the fall of Poland, these and other Czechoslovak soldiers escaped either to the Soviet Union or through Romania to French Syria, where they were formed into three Czechoslovak armies by the Allies: *1. československého armádního sboru* (1st Free Czechoslovak Army, numbering 13,000 by 1944[21]), which fought on the Soviet front and helped liberate Czechoslovakia; the Free Czechoslovak Army[22] (numbering about 10,000), which escaped from France in June 1940 and was reformed in Britain; and a Czechoslovak infantry battalion and an anti-aircraft regiment that served with the British in North Africa. During the Allied invasion of France in 1944, the Czechoslovak Independent Armoured Brigade Group (C.I.A.B.G.) under General Alois Liška (Ah-LO-eess LEESH-kah) played a crucial role in clearing the French coast of German fortifications.

USELESS TRIVIA: THINGS YOU SHOULDN'T BRAG ABOUT

On the morning of May 27, 1942, Reinhard Heydrich, Nazi governor of the Czech lands and a personal friend of Hitler's, was being chauffeured from his palace residence to downtown Prague when two resistance fighters stepped onto the road. One tried to shoot Heydrich but his gun jammed so the other threw a grenade into the car. It detonated, mortally wounding Heydrich, who died days later.

Devastated, Hitler ordered immediate revenge. The Germans chose the village of Lidice (LEE-dee-tseh) to pay for Heydrich's death. In early June 1942, Lidice woke up to find itself surrounded by the SS. The Germans immediately separated the women and children from the men, then gunned down the 172 men. The women were deported to the Ravensbrück concentration camp to become slave laborers. Most died before 1945. The children were initially sent to a factory in Łódź (Woodzh) in Nazi-occupied Poland, but were exterminated weeks later in the Chełmno death camp. Lidice was burned to the ground, and even its cemetery defaced. The Nazi media defiantly described Lidice's fate in detail as a deterrent to further resistance, much to the chagrin later of Nazis at the Nuremburg Trials in 1945.

The end for German rule in Czechoslovakia came in April and May 1945, as American forces sped toward Prague from the West while Soviet (and Czechoslovak) forces fought through Slovakia from the east. U.S. General George Patton's 3rd Army (and the Czech resistance) liberated Plzeň in western Bohemia in April but was halted from taking Prague by General Eisenhower, the commander-in-chief of (Western) Allied forces, to allow the Soviets to take the city. This decision caused great suffering, as the Czech resistance led a revolt in Prague that the Nazis suppressed bloodily before Soviet forces were able to reach the city days later, on May 8, 1945. Beneš returned triumphantly to a reborn Czechoslovakia.

G. Slovakia Is Born, Sort of

After the First Vienna Award, Slovakia was aboil with nationalist resentment. Hitler leveraged this resentment by ordering the Slovak priest and former prime minister Father Jozef Tiso (YO-zef TEE-so) to proclaim an independent Slovakia on March 14, 1939 while German forces occupied Bohemia and Moravia the next day. The *prvá Slovenská republika* (First Slovak Republic) was born. Just months later, though the Slovak army was still being created, Hitler demanded the Slovaks participate in the German invasion of Poland, and obediently Tiso dispatched two infantry divisions (although some Slovak soldiers refused). This was just the beginning, however. In June 1941 Hitler demanded Slovak participation in Operation Barbarossa, and so for the rest of the war the Slovak Republic's very meager military resources were committed to the war against the Soviet Union.

Slovakia was, predictably given its situation, one of the most compliant Nazi-puppet states in Nazi Europe. A paramilitary organization grew out of the deceased Father Hlinka's *Slovenská ľudová strana* (Slovak People's Party) called *Hlinkova garda* (Hlinka Guard), which (in close cooperation with the German SS) began to terrorize Slovak society, particularly Jews, Gypsies, and anyone suspected of treason. Despite his loyalty to Hitler, Tiso had to struggle with even more radical profascist elements in his government as well as growing doubt and unease among Slovaks about the Nazi alliance. Tiso was forced in late 1942 to halt the deportation of Slovak Jews to Auschwitz due to popular outrage and demonstrations, for instance.

While Slovak dismay at the alliance with Hitler grew, Slovak dissidents were equally put off by Edvard Beneš's continued refusal to recognize even the limited Slovak autonomy recognized by Emil Hácha in 1938. With no alterantive in sight, however, the nascent Slovak resistance gave in to Beneš's demands in 1944 and recognized the Czechoslovak government-in-exile in London. Beneš helped organize rebel Slovak army officers, moderate politicians, clergy, and communists into a coalition that in late August 1944 (with help from the Polish AK) launched the *Slovenské národné povstanie* (Slovak National Uprising) against Tiso and the Nazis.

Initially the resistance was surprisingly successful, but within weeks the Hlinka Guard and German forces were able to overcome the Slovak rebels in brutal mountain battles. By the end of October the Germans had suppressed the uprising, and began exacting their revenge—for example, resuming the deportation of Jews from Slovakia. Soviet forces invaded months later, and by April 1945 Bratislava was in Soviet hands. Tiso was later caught and arrested in Austria by American forces, and was hanged for treason in a restored Czechoslovakia in 1947.

H. Hungary Embraces Its Inner Tar Baby

Hungary had been severely radicalized by the 1920 Treaty of Trianon, which deprived the historic Hungarian kingdom of not only non-Hungarian regions—an inevitability in 1920—but also took away several Hungarian-majority regions, leaving *millions* of Hungarians outside the country. The march for justice for prewar Hungary's oppressed minority peoples turned into a gross Allied land grab in 1920 that horrified even some of Hungary's staunchest critics, and—according to some at the time—only ensured future war in the region. Fearing exactly that, Hungary's neighbors in the 1920s and 30s militantly monitored Hungary's adherence to the Trianon treaty terms, fearing Hungarian armies would some day march forth to reclaim the 1914 borders. France's *La Petit Entente* alliance system foundered on the fact that Czechoslovakia, Romania, and Yugoslavia feared Hungarian revisionism more than German. They were right to be concerned, as Budapest aggressively sought revenge.

Hungary's ruling aristocracy welcomed Germany's support but like their Prussian *Junker* aristocratic counterparts in Germany, Hungary's aristocratic elites did not particularly like Hitler, the eccentric upstart commoner born lowly in Austria.

However, Hitler's role in helping Hungary recover some territories in the November 1938 and August 1940 Vienna Awards (which gave southern Slovakia and northern Transylvania back to Hungary) made him a star in the Hungarian public's eyes, and strengthened Hungary's small but growing neofascist extreme right wing. Distrusting Hitler, Horthy tried to balance the growing influence of this radical right wing in Hungarian politics with pro-Allied political appointments, but the guiding mantra behind all Hungarian policies at the time was territorial revision, and the Allies simply couldn't give Hungary what it most wanted. Worse, Hitler notwithstanding, the Vienna Awards were actually about as fair a deal as Hungary could reasonably have expected, but they only whetted the country's appetite for *more*: the aristocrats—who had owned estates in the lost territories—would not be satisfied until Hungary recovered *all* of its 1914 territories (instead of just the Hungarian-majority regions), and the right-wing extremists heartily agreed.

USELESS TRIVIA: IS IT OVER YET?

In the early spring of 2000, a young Slovak doctor interning in a Russian mental hospital in the small town of Kotelnich (*Котельнич*) about 300 miles (500 km) northeast of Moscow was surprised to learn that an elderly patient at the hospital did not understand Russian. Records were vague and did not specify the man's nationality but he recognized that the man spoke Hungarian. The records only said he had been brought to the hospital in 1947 suffering from mental illness. Armed with this new clue, the hospital reached out to Hungary, and in time a Hungarian psychiatrist arrived to interview the patient.

Thus began the final chapter in András Toma's odyssey. Born in 1925 in a Hungarian region of Slovakia, Toma joined the Hungarian army during World War II and was captured in January 1945 by Soviet forces and ended up in a POW camp. Toma's mental condition quickly deteriorated, however, and by 1947 he was transferred to the mental hospital near Kotelnich. Unable to communicate with his doctors and suffering from mental illness, Toma's nationality was gradually forgotten as other Hungarian POWs either were released to go home or died in the 1950s. Only by chance in 2000 was he discovered by that Slovak doctor. Toma—dubbed in the international press "the last POW of World War II"—was taken back to Hungary in August 2000. His mental illness had ravaged his memory, but DNA tests soon identified his remaining relatives, and he lived his last few years with family until his death in 2004. The Hungarian government agreed to pay his soldier's pension, with full back pay.

The inevitable came to pass, however. At first Horthy resisted Hitler's pressures, declining Hitler the use of Hungary's railway network for the Wehrmacht during its invasion of Poland in September 1939. Horthy even annoyed the *Führer* further by allowing Polish military and civilian refugees safe haven. However, Hungary's descent into the abyss began when Hitler offered Horthy the chance to recover the Vajdaság/Vojvodina region from Yugoslavia in April 1941 after the pro-German Yugoslav government was overthrown in a coup by the pro-Allied Yugoslav army. Hungarian forces eagerly joined the Germans and Italians in dismembering Yugoslavia, only weeks after Hungary had signed a treaty of eternal friendship with Yugoslavia.[23]

Push really came to shove weeks later, however, when Hitler invaded the Soviet Union in June 1941. Berlin pressured Horthy to join the war against Moscow, and the German requests were conveniently punctuated by the aerial bombing of Kassa (KUH-Shuh; modern-day Košice [Ko-SHEE-tseh], Slovakia) on June 26.[24] Hungary declared war on the Soviet Union, but at first Hungary only sent one of its most advanced mechanized army units to join German forces invading Soviet Ukraine. After the German failure to take Moscow, however, Hitler strong-armed Horthy in 1942 into committing the bulk of Hungary's military forces to the war.

This proved disastrous in January 1943, as Soviet forces fending off a German attempt to relieve besieged Stalingrad utterly destroyed the Hungarian Second Army at the Battle of Voronyezh on the Don River; only 40,000 of the original 200,000 soldiers returned home. In that single stroke, Hungary ceased to be a major military factor in the war. Horthy secretly opened negotiations with the Western Allies.

Actually, Horthy and several pro-Western Hungarian aristocrats had been in almost constant communication with the West. While there was a hardcore pro-German wing in the Hungarian government, after Voronyezh Horthy and others hoped to negotiate an end to the war with the West. Their plans had two fatal flaws, however: first, the Hungarians believed Western armies were coming, but unbeknownst to Budapest, Churchill's plans for a Balkan invasion had been dismissed by the Americans.[25] Indeed, Horthy underestimated the West's commitment to the Soviet alliance—and *all* Hungarians were united in their terror at the thought of a Soviet occupation. Secondly, Hungarian overtures to the West all included stipulations allowing Hungary to keep the regained territories of the 1938 and 1940 Vienna Awards. The West could never ask other Allied countries to give up prewar territory to a defeated Axis country.

Hitler was aware of these Hungarian overtures to the West, and in March 1944 occupied the country and placed Horthy under house arrest. Regaining his stature somewhat after the assassination attempt on Hitler in July (and the defection of Romania in early September to the Allied camp), Horthy recognized the inevitability that Soviet, not Western armies were coming and he negotiated an armistice with Stalin, which he announced on national radio on October 15, 1944. Hitler reacted swiftly, deposing Horthy and installing the fascist *Nyilaskeresztpárt* (NYEE-lush CARE-est Part; "Arrow Cross party"), and its leader, Ferenc Szálasi (FARE-ents SAH-luh-shee) in power.

Szálasi—who styled himself *Nemzetvezető* (National Leader, e.g., *Der Führer)*—immediately began terrorizing the country into complete submission, and also used his few months in power to restart the deportation of Hungarian Jews to Auschwitz, which Horthy had repeatedly stalled or stopped. Hungary was now all that stood between the Soviet armies and Germany, so Hitler had no intention of letting Hungary get away as Romania and Bulgaria had just done.

The Germans began fortifying Budapest and several corridors throughout the country, forcing the Soviets to slog mercilessly throughout the autumn of 1944 through brutal battles across Hungary. Meanwhile, the Anglo-American air forces began round-the-clock bombing raids on Budapest and military targets across the country.

In December 1944, the Soviets began their all-out assault on Budapest, by now a Nazi German megafortress, and for a hundred days—three months—the city endured devastating aerial and artillery bombardment and brutal house-to-house fighting. Budapest fell to the Soviets in February 1945 and Hungary was largely clear of German forces by April, though some pro-Szálasi fanatics retreated with the Germans, earning Hungary the technical distinction of being Hitler's last loyal ally.[26]

I. Romania Guesses Wrong

Romania entered the war years as a staunchly pro-Versailles system country opposed to any border revisions. When the war began, like neighboring Hungary, Romania helped Poles escape the destruction of their country. The Nazi-Soviet Molotov-Ribbentrop Pact of August 1939 was received with horror in Bucharest, and the Romanian government turned to the West, particularly Paris, for security. Romania did have significant pro-German elements, especially among the younger nationalists who admired Hitler, but Romania's intelligentsia remained steadfastly loyal to France, the power that had most helped Romania achieve independence in the 1870s and *România Mare* (Greater Romania) in 1919–20. The security Romania felt with its Western alliance in 1939 gave way, however, to the *annus horribilis* of 1940: in the spring, France was conquered by the Nazis and British forces were driven from Continental Europe, then in June the Soviet Union demanded Bessarabia, followed in August by Hitler forcing Romania to cede northern Transylvania back to Hungary. Then Bulgaria took the opportunity to demand Southern Dobrudja back.

Isolated, Romania was forced to accede to each of these demands, losing much of its post–World War I gains. King Carol II's popularity in Romania flat-lined, and on September 6, 1940, the remnants of the Iron Guard teamed up with the Romanian Army to overthrow Carol, forcing him to abdicate in favor of his nineteen-year-old son, Mihai.

USELESS TRIVIA: WHEN THE PAST IS STILL THE PRESENT

In April 2001 German Chancellor Gerhard Schroeder was preparing for a state visit to Romania, which was not unusual given that Romania was a friendly country seeking at the time to join both NATO and the European Union. What was unusual was that Romanian authorities had prepared a surprise for the German chancellor; they were going to arrange for him to meet his father.

Corporal Fritz Schroeder had been a Wehrmacht soldier posted in October 1944 on guard duty in the Hungarian Transylvanian village of *Pusztacsány* (POOS-tuh-chahn)—now Romanian *Ceanu* Mic (Chay-AH-noo meek). Soviet forces soon overran the village, however, and Schroeder's father was killed and buried in a mass grave. The future chancellor was only six months old, and had never known his father. Though it wasn't clear in which mass grave his father had been buried, the chancellor was able to kneel solemnly close to his father's grave for the first time during that visit in 2001.

The September coup brought army General Ion Antonescu (EE-own ON-toe-nes-koo) to power, initially in a power-sharing arrangement with the Iron Guard. However, the Guard went on a killing spree across the country against Jews, Gyspies, foreigners, and political enemies that disrupted the Romanian economy to such an extent that, with German approval, the Romanian Army suppressed the Guard in January 1941.

Though Antonescu resisted immense pressure from Hitler to have Romania's Jews shipped to Auschwitz, he staged his own pogroms across the country leading to the deaths of some 400,000 Romanian Jews.[27] Antonescu, styling himself the *Conducător* (The Leader), officially joined the Axis Powers, and seven months later Romania eagerly joined Hitler in invading the Soviet Union in June 1941. The Romanian Army quickly recovered Bessarabia and Bukovina, then, alongside Hitler's Wehrmacht, pushed on into Ukraine and Crimea. Happy with Romania's enthusiastic support for the Soviet war, Hitler granted Romania all of the lands between the Dniester and Bug (Book; rhymes with *Luke*) rivers in southern Ukraine as compensation for the lands lost in 1940. Romania called this new territory *Transnistria*, and the Romanian Army celebrated its triumphs with a bloody anti-Jewish pogrom in occupied Odessa in October 1941.

However, after the Battle of Stalingrad in 1943 Romanian forces suffered catastrophic defeat and began a long retreat. Worse, the Anglo-American air forces, now based in Italy, began to bomb Romanian economic and military targets regularly. Finally, Germany, which had become a great consumer of Romanian oil, bread, and meats, was importing these commodities in greater numbers than ever—but wasn't paying for them, instead ensuring their continued delivery via German troops stationed in Romania. The Romanian economy slid into ruin as the dreaded and seemingly unstoppable Soviet armies approached from the east.

By May 1944, Soviet forces had reached the Moldavian city of Iaşi and were poised to strike into the heart of the country. On August 23, 1944, the king, Mihai I—long seen as a weakwilled figurehead—stunned everyone by leading a royal coup supported by pro-Allied elements of the Army, arresting Antonescu and ejecting German forces from the country. In September Romania signed an armistice and the Romanian Army joined the Soviets as they fought their way toward Germany. Mihai's coup and defection restored some national dignity, but the country did not avoid Soviet occupation.

USELESS TRIVIA: THEY CAN GET HERE FROM THERE?

One of the Western Allies' chief weapons in the war was strategic bombing, a concept that was and still is controversial both from a military perspective and because it caused so much "collateral damage" (i.e., civilian deaths). It seemed the ultimate realization of aerial combat, however, being able to drop tons of bombs from the sky on the enemy's factories, shipyards, rail lines, and troops below.

Though most documentaries on the strategic bombing campaigns focus on Germany, economic and military targets in Eastern Europe were also heavily bombed. As the Western armies advanced, their airfields drew closer to Eastern Europe and Nazi targets in Poland, Czechoslovakia, Hungary, and the Balkans were all targeted by American B-24s, B-29s, and British Lancasters. One of the most famous Allied air raids on Eastern Europe was Operation Tidal Wave against Romania in early August 1943.

Romania had a large stock of oil, and one of its largest refineries was in the city of Ploieşti (PLOY-esh-tee). The Nazi war machine depended heavily on the Ploieşti oil fields to fuel its tanks, planes, and trucks—so on August 1, 1943, 178 American and British B-24 bombers took off from Benghazi in Libya and flew 2,400 miles northward across the Mediterranean, then across the Adriatic over the Balkans, finally reaching Romanian territory while flying at a very low altitude to avoid radar. Unfortunately, there was confusion among the bombers and the attacks on the refinery were haphazard and uncoordinated. The Germans were able to repair the refinery and have it back up to full capacity within weeks. Only 88 bombers of the original 178 managed to return to their base, but more raids followed later.

J. Yugoslavia, Serbia, and 1914 All Over Again

In March 1941, Prime Minister Dragiša Cvetković (Drah-GEE-shah Tsvet-KO-veetch) signed the Tripartite Pact with Germany and Italy, allying his country with the Axis Powers. King Pavel (Paul) I was not pro-German but the country was surrounded, and the treaty only obliged Yugoslavia to allow the Germans "non-military" use of Yugoslavia's rail network. By the spring of 1941, the Allies had been either decidedly defeated or driven from Europe, so a frail and creaky kingdom like Yugoslavia—which had a thousand internal cultural fault lines—would do well to make peace with the neighborhood bullies.

However, as Cvetković returned from Vienna two days later, on March 27, 1941, the Yugoslav military led by General Dušan Simović (DOO-shahn See-MO-veetch) staged a military coup and overthrew the government. King Paul's son Petar II was installed on the throne, and the new German alliance was renounced.

Hitler, being the good-humored guy he was, immediately ordered the invasion of Yugoslavia. On April 6 at 5:15 a.m., Nazi German Ju-87 Stuka dive-bombers attacked Belgrade as German, Hungarian, and Italian forces invaded the country. The Yugoslav Army couldn't last long against such odds, and on April 17 signed an armistice. Croatia declared its independence (under German auspicies) and was given Bosnia-Herzegovina; Slovenia was partitioned by Germany, Italy, and Hungary; and Hungary annexed Vojvodina as well. Italy added Kosovo and Montenegro to its Adriatic empire. Bulgaria later occupied Macedonia, leaving Serbia as a German protectorate.

The first (of several) resistance movements to arise was led by Draža Mihailović (DRAH-zhah Mee-HIGH-lo-veetch), an officer in the Yugoslav army loyal to the king and Yugoslav government-in-exile then forming in London. Mihailović began to organize underground military cells based on the Balkan *chetnik* model,[28] composed overwhelmingly of Serbs. Mihailović sought to fight the Germans (and Italians, Bulgarians, and Croatian collaborationists) by sabotage and assassination, but was cautious because of the German tendancy to take reprisals out on civilians. After the German attack on the Soviet Union in June 1941 Yugoslav communists led by Josip Broz[29] (YO-seep Brawz; famously known by his pseudonym "Tito"), sprang into action and organized a pan-Yugoslav resistance, leading a very bloody guerrilla campaign in the Bosnian and Montenegrin hills.

In November 1942 Tito pulled many noncommunist resistance groups into a single umbrella resistance group, the *Antifašističko Vijeće Narodnog Oslobođenja Jugoslavije* (Anti-Fascist Council for the Liberation of Yugoslavia), known commonly by its Serbo-Croat acronym, AVNOJ

(AHV-noy). Despite the war, the Yugoslav countryside collapsed into civil war as Serbs, Bosnians, and Croats waged bloody guerrilla wars against one another, and Mihailović's Chetniks fought pitched battles against Tito's communist partisans. Bosnia in particular became a battleground.

Impressed with AVNOJ's more aggressive approach, in 1943 the Western Allies switched their support from Mihailović's Chetniks[30] to Tito's AVNOJ partisans, with permanent British and American intelligence agents (and supplies) assigned to Tito. Tito and his partisans seemed better organized and more willing to take risks in fighting the Germans— even if those risks resulted in harm to civilians. About a million Yugoslavs died in the war, as many from ethnic strife and local partisan civil wars as Axis atrocities.

With substantial British (and American) supplies and technical aid, Tito's Yugoslav partisans throughout 1944 developed into a major force numbering some 800,000. Belgrade was liberated in a closely coordinated effort between Tito's partisans and Soviet and Bulgarian forces in October.

Although German forces were in the autumn of 1944 rapidly pulling out of the Balkans to support sagging fronts against the Soviets closer to home, Tito's partisans played a crucial role in harassing and forcing them out of the remaining parts of Yugoslavia throughout the winter and spring of 1945. In this way, Yugoslavia was unique among the European states in having at least in part liberated itself from Nazi control, and, more importantly for the next chapter, being one of the few Eastern European states without Soviet forces on its soil at war's end. Tito's partisans have been both romanticized and criticized, but as historian R.J. Crampton observes, they were crucial to the survival of Yugoslavia:

> Tito's partisans claimed to be one of the most successful of European resistance forces. Until at least the middle of 1943, however, the Germans still regarded the četniks as their main enemy, particularly in Serbia and long the Belgrade-Zagreb route which was the Germans' chief strategic concern. The Germans continued to dominate the cities and to extract from the country the mineral resources they coveted, and the German forces tied down in Yugoslavia were never their élite; in military terms the partisans were little more than an irritant. Their most important

achievement was to create a force which stepped rapidly and ruthlessly into the political vacuum left when the Germans departed. Also, and more importantly, the partisans kept alive and rehabilitated a sense of Yugoslav nationality and recognition of the value of the concept of Yugoslavdom at a time when both were under attack from without and from within.[31]

K. Croatia's Dark Side

With the destruction of Yugoslavia in April 1941 by Germany and its allies, the Ustaša (OO-stah-shah) immediately declared an independent Croatia (under close German supervision) on April 10. The Ustaša leader, Ante Pavelić (AHN-teh PAH-veh-leetch), returned from exile in Italy and declared the birth of *Nezavisna Država Hrvatska* (Independent State of Croatia, or *NDH* for short) with himself as its *Poglavnik* (Croatian for *Führer*).

Thus was born one of the most infamous and murderous regimes in Nazi Europe. The NDH was initially very popular among Croats, who resented Serb-dominated Yugoslavia. However, the sheer brutality of the Ustaša regime, coupled with the corruption and incompetence of its administration, soon alienated many Croats. Indeed, Pavelić's band of thugs and hooligans created many headaches for his mentor in Berlin, Hitler, and it became quickly clear that the NDH was a German puppet state on a short leash. Pavelić's popularity among Croats was further dented when he was forced to give Dalmatia and Istria to Italy and Germany (while both maintained large occupation forces in Croatia itself as well), though Croatia did gain Bosnia and Herzegovina.

A fundamental issue driving Ustaše conduct was the fact that the (pseudo-)independent Croatian state they created was only about 51% ethnically Croatian; the Ustaša had a minority problem. Ante Pavelić's answer to this problem was mass expulsion, mass conversion, and mass murder. He immediately deported a couple hundred thousand Serbs to German-occupied Serbia, but the economic disruptions this caused—not to mention the heightened Chetnik guerrilla activity—brought immediate rebuke from Berlin, so the Ustaše established a series of concentration camps into which NDH's Serbs, Jews, and Gyspies (as well as Croatian dissidents) were rounded up and subjected to starvation, systematic beatings, rapes, torture, and ultimately murder.

USELESS TRIVIA: NO, REALLY, WHOSE SIDE ARE YOU ON?

Lingering regional ethnic hostility, coupled with modern-day political factors, often makes exploration of Yugoslavia's 20th-century history difficult even for scholars. One famous figure to emerge from fascist Croatia during the war with particular controversy was the Roman Catholic Archbishop Cardinal Alojzije (Aloysius) Stepinac (Ah-LOY-zee-yeh Steh-PEE-nots). He still inspires heated debate today.

On the one hand, Cardinal Stepinac denounced Yugoslavia and welcomed its demise in 1941. He publicly blessed Ante Pavelić and Pavelić's mentor, Hitler, for "freeing" Croatia. He often met with Pavelić, and publicly celebrated the NDH's birthday each April 10. In the past he had condemned "schismatic" Serbs and the Serbian Ortho-dox Church. He also created and oversaw the Catholic chaplin corps for the fascist Croatian army, some of whose priests committed bone-chilling atrocities against Serbs and Jews during the war, with a few even managing Ustaša concentration camps. Stepinac endorsed the forced conversion of Serbs and Jews.

On the other hand, Cardinal Stepinac became disillusioned with the Pavelić regime and he repeatedly publicly condemned—at his own great risk—the regime's mistreatment of Jews, helping to organize the transfer of Croatian Jews to safer regions of the Balkans. He is believed to be responsible for saving hundreds, possibly thousands of Jews from deportation to Auschwitz. Stepinac also eventually came to deplore the violent persecution of Serbs and the Orthodox Church in Croatia, using weekly sermons to publicly condemn the mistreatment and murder of Serbs and Gyspies, to Pavelić's extreme irritation.

Stepinac was convicted of collaboration after the war by Tito, though after five years in prison he was transferred to house arrest in his home town, dying of a blood disorder in 1960. In 1998 Pope John Paul II, a fel-low anticommunist crusader, declared Cardinal Stepinac a martyr and had him beatified, the first step for Roman Catholics in making Stepinac a saint. Today, many Croats and Catholics see Stepinac as a hero who stood up to both fascist and communist regimes, and many Jews see Stepinac as a hero who saved hundreds of Jewish lives. To some Serbs, however, Stepinac was (initially) a seemingly approving witness, if not an outright accomplice to forced conversions and mass murder.

One of the most infamous of these camps was at Jasenovac (Yah-SEN-o-vahts), about 60 miles (100 km) southeast of Zagreb, where between 56,000 and 97,000 people were killed.[32] Italian generals and hardened German

SS veterans were reportedly sickened by the atrocities they witnessed at Jasenovac. Both (Orthodox Christian) Serbs and Jews were often forced to convert to Roman Catholicism, though the "converted" were often murdered by Ustaše thugs, anyway, such as the infamous killing in August 1941 at Glina of 500 Serbs who were locked in a church and beaten to death after agreeing to convert. In all, it is (conservatively) believed that some 330,000-390,000 Serbs, 30,000 Jews, 30,000 Gypsies, and 12,000 Croatians were murdered by the Pavelić regime, though the exact body count of fascist Croatia's victims has been a source of long historical dispute, as noted by the United States Holocaust Memorial Museum:

> Determining the number of victims for Yugoslavia, for Croatia, and for Jasenovac is highly problematic, due to the destruction of many relevant documents, the long-term inaccessibility to independent scholars of those documents that survived, and the ideological agendas of postwar partisan scholarship and journalism, which has been and remains influenced by ethnic tension, religious prejudice, and ideological conflict.

With Italy's fall to the Allies in 1943, the Ustaše state's days were numbered. Very soon American and British bombers filled the Croatian skies, targeting ports, rail lines, and industrial sites, as well as dropping supplies to the increasingly active AVNOJ partisans. By 1944, with their control over the Balkans disintegrating, the Germans saw Pavelić as a major liability and seized control of the country. As the year passed it became clear the Germans could no longer hold the Balkans, however, so they withdrew their forces into Hungary, effectively ceding most of the NDH to Tito and the AVNOJ partisans, who spent the winter of 1944 and the first half of 1945 driving the Ustaše from Croatia and Slovenia. Ustaše forces retreated into (Western-occupied) Austria to surrender.

L. Albania Tries to Keep Its Head Above Water
When war came to Albania in 1939, it reverted to its decades-old standard of collapsing into anarchy, with Italy effectively controlling the cities while tribal bands took to the mountains and waged sporadic guerrilla war against the invaders and each other. When Italy invaded and overthrew the Albanian government in April 1939, sending King Zog fleeing, the West barely took notice and at no point during World War II did the West entertain the idea of recognizing Zog's Albanian government-in-exile. Italy created a puppet fascist administration in Albania but when Italy launched its invasion of Greece from its Albanian bases on October 28, 1940, Greek troops not only repulsed the Italian invasion but also overran southern Italian-occupied Albania, holding about a quarter of Albanian territory by December 1940.

As the Italian occupation crumbled, Germany invaded to save its Italian ally, and by April 1941, Albania and Greece were both under German occupation.

USELESS TRIVIA: THE ONES WE DON'T WANT TO BRAG ABOUT

South America has been a favorite destination for generations of Eastern European émigrés. From 1870 to the 1930s, hundreds of thousands of them crossed the Atlantic and made new homes in the growing countries of South America, from Colombia and Peru to Brazil, Chile, and Argentina. Unfortunately, that tradition continued when the war ended in 1945, as many connected to the defeated Axis regimes fled prosecution. Some were merely bureaucrats in the wartime regimes, but many were high-ranking officials or soldiers guilty of war crimes. By 1945 sympathetic elements within the Vatican began to organize secret escape routes (known as "rat lines") to help German, Italian, Vichy French, Croatian, Hungarian, Baltic, Bulgarian, and Albanian fascists flee Allied-occupied Europe. Initially they fled to (then fascist) Spain or Portugal, but by 1946 several South American countries actively sought to attract these criminal refugees. Argentina, then ruled by dictator Juan Peron (who espoused a neofascism based on nationalism and Catholicism) aggressively worked to bring Catholic German and Croatian war criminals to Argentina by supplying them with false credentials.

As research by Argentine journalists and historians in the 1990s revealed, Peron employed his SS and Ustaša guests to create his own security services, whose bloody legacy would haunt Argentine society for many years. Sadly, dictators in other countries—Chile, Brazil, Paraguay, and others—emulated Peron's use of Nazi collaborators to brutally suppress opposition. Even Ustaša leader Ante Pavelić managed to flee to Buenos Aires on a rat line, though he died in Spain in 1957 after being shot in Argentina. These rat lines were often purposely ignored or even aided by many governments, including the U.S. and Britain, for reasons related to security and Cold War politics.

The Germans gave Albania back to Italy in 1941 (as German forces headed for the Soviet Union), but this time the Italians dispensed with the puppet administration and ruled Albania directly. Albanian resistance so far had been sporadic and uncoordinated, but in October 1941 the Yugoslav AVNOJ communist resistance led by Josip Broz "Tito" helped organize an Albanian communist resistance led by Enver Hoxha (EN-vare HOE-jah), sharing training, supplies, and intelligence with Hoxha's group.

Two other main groups arose, one led by Abaz Kupi (AH-baz KOO-pee) who was royalist and supported King Zog's efforts in London, and another called *Balli Kombëtar* (National Front), which fought against the Italians initially. But after the German takeover and after the Germans combined Yugoslav Kosovo and northern (Greek) Epirus with Albania, *Balli Kombëtar* began to collaborate with the Germans in the hopes of creating a Greater Albania. *Balli Kombëtar* forces, combined with the Albanian-recruited SS Skanderbeg Division created by the Germans in 1944, committed gross atrocities against Serbs and Jews in Kosovo, Macedonia, and Montenegro.

When Italy collapsed with the Allied invasion in 1943, Albanian partisans attempted to seize control of the country but German paratroops beat them to it. Collaboration with Tito's communists earned Hoxha recognition from the Western Allies, which included intelligence-sharing and supplies. With German forces withdrawing from the Balkans in the autumn of 1944, Hoxha's communists were able to fully liberate the country by the end of November, expelling as well the *Balli Kombëtar* and Abaz Kupi's forces.

War's end brought rejoicing in Albania but the country found itself at a dangerous crossroads; like neighbor Yugoslavia, Albania had largely liberated itself (although with much outside help) and had no Soviet troops in the country. However, Tito talked of incorporating Albania into Yugoslavia, and, at least in 1945, nobody in Washington, London, or Moscow objected to the idea.

M. Bulgaria: Third Time a Charm?

Bulgaria still hoped in 1939 to achieve its territorial ambitions, but wanted to avoid the mistakes of 1913 and 1915. It was one of the few countries in the region that was relatively well-disposed toward both Germany and Russia. Sofia was therefore probably one of the few European capitals to actually welcome the Nazi-Soviet Molotov-Ribbentrop Pact in August 1939, as the Bulgarians believed this saved them from having to choose sides.

When war broke out in September 1939, Bulgaria declared its neutrality, and waited. When neighboring Romania was forced by Moscow and Berlin to cede territory in 1940, Bulgaria took advantage of the moment to demand Southern Dobrudja (DOE-broo-jah), but alarm bells nonetheless went off in Sofia: while Bulgaria had what it considered to be legitimate territorial claims against its neighbors, it did not necessarily want to see them *destroyed*. German and Italian penetration of the Balkans unnerved Bulgaria.

Bulgaria's room for political maneuvering evaporated at the end of 1940, when an Italian invasion of Greece went seriously wrong. King Boris had declined an Italian invitation to join the war, and by December 1940 Greek troops were overrunning Italian Albania. By March 1941 Hitler began massing German troops in Romania along the Bulgarian frontier with an obvious message: these troops were going to invade Greece. The only question was, would they cross Bulgaria peacefully, or would they fight their way across? Bulgaria's Tsar Boris III got the hint, and on March 1 signed the Tri-Partite Pact with Germany and Italy. Bulgaria refused to take part in the invasion of Yugoslavia but with the Greek defeat in April, Germany began to transfer its troops to the upcoming Soviet front, and asked Bulgaria to take on occupation duty in both Greek Thrace and Yugoslav Macedonia. Tsar Boris readily agreed.

Popular elation with the "recovery" of Thrace and Macedonia[33] won the government's pro-German policies some grudging respect from Bulgarians wary of 1918 redux, but that respect turned to horror months later when Hitler betrayed the Molotov-Ribbentrop Pact and invaded the Soviet Union. Tsar Boris refused immense German pressure to join the war against the Soviets, telling Berlin that traditionally Russophile Bulgarians would never fight against Russians. Hitler accepted this argument, but 1941 just went from bad to worse for Bulgaria; resistance to Bulgarian occupation forces in Thrace and Macedonia grew, while in December, Berlin forced a reluctant Bulgaria to declare war against both Britain and the United States. This was inspired by Hitler's awareness of contacts between Bulgaria and the United States (mostly through neutral Turkey). King Boris hoped to switch sides while avoiding a German occupation.

Like Hungary, however, a major sticking point in negotiations was that Bulgaria hoped to keep Thrace and Macedonia, something the Americans could not promise. Hitler was aware of these negotiations, leading some to believe that Hitler had Tsar Boris murdered when he died unexpectedly (at the age of forty-nine) shortly after a visit to Berlin, in August 1943. After his death, a regency was established for his six-year-old son, Simeon, but the new government cracked down on growing anti-Axis dissent. Meanwhile, after Italy folded, Anglo-American bombers pounded Sofia regularly. Washington was done negotiating, and as 1944 dawned, it was clear the Soviets were coming.

The endgame came swiftly. In the early summer of 1944 the Soviets demanded that Bulgaria switch sides, but the Bulgarian government simply crumbled, and it took three long months for a new one to form. In the meantime, in September, Romania *did* switch sides, which quickly brought the Soviet army to Bulgaria's borders. Fed up with dallying Sofia, Stalin invaded Bulgaria on September 5, 1944 despite Bulgaria's earlier refusal to join Hitler in his war against the Soviets. Wisely, the Bulgarian Army did not resist, and a communist-led alliance called the Fatherland Front seized power. On September 9, Bulgaria finally switched sides and declared war on Germany, and the Bulgarian First Army eagerly joined the Soviet drive into Austria, meeting up with British forces there in May 1945.

N. The Soviet Union Wins by Knockout in the 9th Round

"If 10,000 Russian women die of exhaustion in digging an anti-tank ditch, this is of no interest to me except to the extent to which the ditch is readied for Germany."
—Heinrich Himmler, October 4, 1943, Posen (Occupied Poland)[34]

The USSR was one of the key players—and factors—of World War II, without which the Allied victory in Europe likely would not have been possible. But if the Soviet Union's immense sacrifices in the Allied cause helped win the war, so too did the USSR's alliance with Hitler in 1939–41 allow the Germans to invade and conquer Poland, Western Europe, and the Balkans— eventually providing Hitler with the security and resources to eventually attack the Soviet Union itself:

> Germany was able to go to war against the Soviet Union only after taking over most of continental Europe and adapting most of the economic resources thus acquired to the German war effort.[35]

Stalin's accommodation with Hitler in the Molotov-Ribbentrop alliance in August 1939 made sense in many ways, as it allowed two aggressively expansionistic empires to divide a disputed region (i.e., Eastern Europe) peacefully while giving each the security to pursue other imperial goals. The subjugation of Poland in 1939–41 is an interesting study in Soviet-Nazi cooperation, for instance. But what were Stalin's long-term goals for the Pact with Hitler? The division of Eastern Europe provided a territorial buffer zone for Stalin, although that buffer zone may have actually compromised Soviet security by creating a long mutual border with Nazi Germany, removing any third-party countries through which Nazi armies would have to pass in a sneak attack on the USSR.

Others believe that by providing Hitler security in the east, Stalin hoped to encourage the Nazis to invade the West, leading to a World War I–style bloody stalemate, a capitalist civil war, which Stalin could safely watch from the sidelines. If so, imagine then Stalin's horror as Nazi armies steamrolled through Western Europe in the spring of 1940 in little more than a month, only a few days longer than the Polish campaign. Suddenly, besides Churchill's defiant but defeated island nation, Stalin found himself facing Hitler alone. This may explain Stalin's sudden aggressiveness toward the Baltic countries in the summer of 1940.

The truth is, we'll never know Stalin's motives in 1939 for certain. What is clear about Stalin's policies prior to the war is that they left the country woefully unprepared for the war that came in June 1941. The communist ideology that governed the Soviet Union, coupled with traditional Russian xenophobia and Stalin's own personal paranoia, isolated the Soviet regime and distorted the true motives of other powers, driving the Soviet political and military leadership to make crucial mistakes that would cost the lives of *millions* of Soviet citizens and soldiers in the war.

The problem wasn't information. Moscow in the 1930s had the world's largest intelligence-gathering network in the form of multiple state intelligence services, dedicated communist parties around the world, and friendly informants in other countries—all of which provided a steady stream of intelligence flowing into the Kremlin on a scale that would have astonished and thrilled any other government. The problem in Moscow was not the availability of information, but the very fundamentally flawed way that information was interpreted by Stalin and his leadership, guided as they were by undue distrust of the outside world.

During the Great Purges of 1937–39, Stalin—distrusting any potential political rivals—had subjected the Red Army to a virtual massacre of its officer corps, as British historian John Keegan describes:

> By the autumn of 1938 three out of five of the Red Army's Marshalls were dead, thirteen out of fifteen army commanders, 110 out of 195 divisional commanders and 186 out of 406 brigadiers. The massacre of those in administrative and politico-military appointments was even more extensive: all eleven deputy commissars for defence were shot, seventy-five out of eighty members of the Military Soviet, and all military district commanders, together with most of their chiefs of political administration—those party commissars whose function was to ensure that soldiers should not take decisions or commitments which might attract the disfavour of the party.[36]

The damage to the Red Army became evident when in November 1939 Finland refused to negotiate territorial changes Stalin wanted near Leningrad, and the Soviets concocted a border incident to invade Finland in what became known as the Winter War. Finland's tiny but professional army halted the massive Soviet war machine in its tracks throughout the winter of 1939–40, only succumbing as weather conditions improved in March, allowing Soviet forces to make better use of planes and tanks. Estimates of Soviet casualties from this war range from 400,000 to a million,[37] but the greater loss was the prestige of the Soviet army, which appeared incompetent.

In essence, due to Stalin's purges the Soviet army that attacked Finland in November 1939 was a decapitated and ill-equipped rabble led by amateur and inexperienced officers, fighting in extreme arctic conditions. Indeed, Hitler took note of the Red Army's performance and hastened his own plans for the German invasion of the Soviet Union.

This was the condition of Soviet defenses on June 22, 1941 when the Germans did invade the USSR. The results were instantly disastrous;

some 1,200 Soviet planes—a quarter of the Soviet air force—were destroyed *by the end of the first day*, while hundreds of thousands of Soviet soldiers were either killed or captured in these first days, with hundreds of thousands more in full and panicked retreat eastward. The Germans invaded the Soviet Union with 3 million troops—one group aimed at the Baltics and Leningrad, another at Moscow, and the third driving into Soviet Ukraine. The Baltics were quickly overrun, and over the next three months Belarus and Ukraine fell, as did Smolensk and Soviet Crimea.

By September 1941 the Germans were threatening Moscow itself. In the first week Stalin had collapsed into depression, and secluded himself in his private dacha until a delegation of the Politburo led by Molotov summoned him back to his duties on June 29. Stalin reportedly thought his unexpected vistors had come to arrest him for his failures.[38] The visit reinvigorated the chastened dictator, however, and on July 3, Stalin, in his shaky Russian, made his first radio speech in years to the nation as described by the Russian historians Mikhail Heller and Alexander Nekrich:

> At this moment of crisis Stalin, who had deprived millions of their homes, property and rights during collectivization, who had created a system of slave labor camps, who had executed the best military leaders and the cream of the intelligentsia, who had shot or imprisoned millions of Soviet citizens, issued a pleading call to his 'brothers and sisters'.[39]

If the Soviet leadership had failed its people, though, the Soviet people did not fail their leaders. Their ability and willingness to continue fighting and working despite extreme deprivations and hardships—and despite the sometimes criminal incompetence and neglect of their own leaders—played a major role in the eventual Allied victory. But for all the failures of Stalin and the Soviet system, the primary cause of Soviet citizens' misery was the Nazi German policy of treating Russians, Belarussians, and Ukrainians as they had the Poles: as Slavic *Untermenschen*,[40] unworthy of life other than as slaves for the superior Aryans. Hitler specifically issued an order at the beginning of Operation Barbarossa absolving any German soldier who committed atrocities or war crimes in the Soviet Union of any crime under German law. Indeed, the Wehrmacht and the SS did not disappoint their Führer, with wholesale slaughter on an unprecedented scale in modern times against Soviet civilians and POWs.

The first hint of the resistance this German mistreatment was provoking among the Soviet people came as the onion-shaped spires of St. Basil's in the Kremlin were visible to the invaders just outside Moscow in October 1941, when a frantic Soviet defense denied the Germans

Moscow and pushed them sixty miles (100 km) back westward by January 1942. This was the first clear victory in Europe for the Allies in the war.

USELESS TRIVIA: THE MEANING OF RESISTANCE

The northernmost German army group to invade the Soviet Union in 1941 had as its goal the city of Leningrad, the old imperial Tsarist capital. German forces quickly advanced through the Baltics but were halted within a few miles of Leningrad by stubborn Soviet resistance. They quickly besieged the city, setting up a blockade and shelling the city daily with heavy artillery. For 900 days—two and a half years—Soviet forces and the city's population withstood the German siege and bombardment, suffering widespread starvation and disease as well as battle deaths. Only sporadic supply runs across or around Lake Ladoga kept the city supplied throughout the siege. Soviet forces finally managed to break open a small corridor in January 1943, and managed to lift the siege a year later, in January 1944, by which time some 800,000 of Leningrad's original 2.5 million residents had died.

Moreover, despite Stalin's best efforts, some competent military men *did* survive his purges in the late 1930s. While Hitler and much of the world took note of the humiliation handed to Soviet forces by the heroic Finns in the 1939–40 Winter War, few had noticed a battle fought far to the east in the summer of 1939, the Battle of Khalkhin Gol (Mongolian River). This battle was provoked by the Japanese along the Mongolian border with Japanese-occupied Chinese Manchuria, called *Manchukuo*. Perhaps assuming they would dash the Soviet army as quickly as they had the Russian army in the 1904–05 war, the Japanese invaded Soviet-allied Mongolia in May 1939, but by August found their mauled forces in full panicked retreat after decisive defeat at the hands of Soviet General Georgi Zhukov. The battle convinced Tokyo to sign a nonaggression pact with Moscow, crucially sparing the Soviets a two-front war. It was General Zhukov whom Stalin summoned to save Moscow in October 1941.

As soon as German forces invaded the Soviet Union in June 1941, British Prime Minister Winston Churchill immediately offered Stalin an alliance. Then came the Japanese attack on Pearl Harbor in December 1941, and the addition of the Americans to the Anglo-Soviet alliance. Over time the Western Allies supplied the Soviets with 18,700 planes, 10,800 tanks, 9,600 guns, 401,400 motor vehicles, 44,600 machine tools, 2,599,000 tons of petroleum products (e.g., oil, engine grease, gasoline), 517,500 tons of nonferrous (i.e., noniron) metals, 172,000 tons of wire and cable, 1,860 locomotives, and 11,300 railroad flatcars, as well as tons of food, clothing, and medical supplies.[41] After General Mikhail Tukhachevsky's execution in the Great Purges, the Soviet leadership seriously underestimated the need for mechanized transport in modern-day war, and so a great part of the Red Army's mobility in World War II came from American-supplied trucks and trains. Many a Soviet mechanic quickly became adept at fixing Studebaker or Ford engines.

Nonetheless, for all those supplies, Soviet soldiers still had to do the fighting themselves. Though halted at Moscow, German forces continued to surge eastward into Ukraine and southern Russia throughout 1942, until they approached the Volga River and a mid-sized city that straddled the western bank known (since 1925) as Stalingrad. The Soviets made a stand at Stalingrad in July, slowly allowing the Germans to push deeper into the city until, in November, the Soviets encircled the city, trapping the German 6th Army inside. It held out two more months until surrendering in February 1943.

The Battle of Stalingrad is considered the turning point of World War II, and showed the world that the Soviet army was now a force to be reckoned with. Throughout 1943, Soviet forces began finally to advance westward, liberating several crucial cities and fighting in July the largest tank battle in history at Kursk, in which some 2.25 million Soviet and German soldiers, including 6,000 tanks, slogged it out over several weeks' time. The Soviet victory at Kursk broke the back of the Wehrmacht, putting it permanently on the defensive in Eastern Europe.

In January 1944, the Soviets launched their next major offensive, pushing through Crimea and across the Dnieper River by May, and driving the Germans from most of the Baltics over the summer. Also over the summer Soviet forces invaded German-occupied Poland, while throughout the autumn a second major Soviet army group cleared the Balkans of Germans and fought its way through Hungary toward the Reich. By October, all Soviet territory had been liberated from Nazi rule.

By January 1945, Soviet forces were on the Oder River, only some 30 miles (50 km) from Berlin itself. The Battle for Berlin began in earnest on January 12, and for four horrific months the city was fought over in brutal house-to-house combat. Hitler abandoned his defenders on April 30 by suicide, and on that day the Soviets managed to raise the Soviet flag on the Reichstag's roof. The Germans finally surrendered on May 7, 1945—officially May 8 to the West, May 9 to the Soviets—ending the war in Europe.

O. The Holocaust

The Holocaust easily stands out as the most egregious crime in modern history, an attempt to exterminate an entire people by way of a factory death system. In 1939–45 the Germans committed grisly atrocities in Eastern Europe almost unparalleled in modern history, but Europe's Jews endured outright *genocide,* the mass-murder of 5-6 million unarmed civilians. Hitler used traditional anti-Semitism and outrage at the defeat of 1918 to stir German popular opinion against Jews, but the Nazis still felt compelled to deceive Germans about the reality of the Holocaust: the main death camps were built remotely in occupied Poland, and Nazi news outlets spoke only of Jewish *Umsiedlung nach dem Osten* (Resettlement to the East).

Still, the Holocaust wasn't just a bunch of evil SS guards working in secret mass death camps; the Holocaust involved thousands of railway workers, factory workers, delivery people, construction workers, administrators, bureaucrats, healthcare workers, utilities workers, and farmers, as well as banks to finance the system, countless private contractors, and so on. And although the Holocaust was overwhelmingly a German crime, it had far too many willing helpers:

> It's completely undisputed that the Holocaust would never have happened without Hitler, SS Chief Heinrich Himmler and the many, many other Germans. But it's also certain "that the Germans on their own wouldn't have been able to carry out the murder of millions of European Jews," says Hamburg-based historian Michael Wild. [. . .] They [non-Germans] are men who have until now received surprisingly little attention—Ukrainian gendarmes and Latvian auxiliary police, Romanian soldiers or Hungarian railway workers. Polish farmers, Dutch land registry officials, French mayors, Norwegian ministers, Italian soldiers— they all took part in Germany's Holocaust. [. . .] Historian Feliks Tych estimates that some 125,000 Poles rescued Jews without being paid for their services. It's clear that the perpetrators always made up a small minority of their respective population. But the Germans relied on that minority.[42]

The story of the Holocaust is well known, though given the surprising number of Holocaust deniers, perhaps not well enough. Though Jews across Nazi-occupied Europe were beaten, humiliated, had their possessions seized, were herded into sealed-off ghettos, and often murdered since 1939, the real Holocaust began only in early 1942, ironically driven in part by Allied successes. The Soviet repulse of Nazi forces at Moscow in 1941–42 scotched Nazis plans to forcibly resettle Jews in the east, and Allied control of the Atlantic similarly made a plan to expel Europe's Jews to French Madagascar unrealistic.

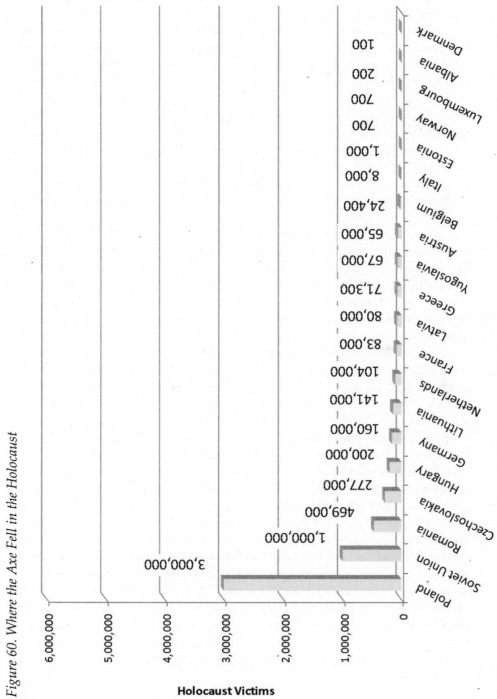

Figure 60. Where the Axe Fell in the Holocaust

Holocaust Victims

The top Nazi leadership (including Hitler) met in January 1942 at the Wannsee Conference near Berlin to come up with a new plan. The result was the *Endlösung der Judenfrage* (Final Solution to the Jewish Question), the mass murder of Europe's Jews. A system of six major death camps was established in Nazi-occupied Poland: Auschwitz-Birkenau,[43] Chełmno, Bełżec, Majdanek, Sobibór, and Treblinka.[44] (Later, in desperation, other concentration camps across Nazi Europe effectively became death camps for Jews as well.)

From early 1942 on the sole purpose for these camps was the mass murder of Jews and the quick disposal—via crematoriums—of their bodies. Trains arrived from across Nazi-occupied Europe packed with Jews speaking dozens of languages from all walks of European life, but nearly all shared a single fatal destiny. Maintaining this massive drain on Nazi resources literally right up until the camps were liberated by Allied armies in 1944 or 1945 showcases the lunacy of extremist ideologies like Nazism. The six death camps in Poland were the workhorses of the Holocaust but they were supported by an intricate system of subcamps stretching across Nazi-occupied Europe—ultimately some 42,500 camps, according to new research by the United States Holocaust Memorial Museum.[45] The Nazis nearly achieved their purpose. Out of a prewar population in Europe of some 9 million Jews, two-thirds, or about 6 million, were murdered in the Holocaust.

Local collaboration is not something Europeans, Eastern or Western, have been enthusiastic to explore, but it is a dark abyss into which modern historians are increasingly peering. Anti-Semitism was rife across 1930s Europe, East and West, and the truth is that the Nazis rarely had problems finding willing collaborators. Still today, Europeans are still coming to grips with this era in their countries' histories.[46] After decades of Soviet dictatorship, Eastern European countries are also emerging from an artificial absolution offered by ideologically driven Soviet historiography and beginning to examine the real legacy of the Holocaust in their respective countries. There are sometimes painful truths to confront. Jan T. Gross's 2001 book *Sąsiedzi* (*Neighbors*), about a pogrom in the Polish village of Jedwabne (Yed-VAHB-neh),[47] stirred a very heated debate in a country used to seeing itself exclusively as a victim in the war. But Poland is not alone with these moral struggles. As the generation that fought and experienced the war slowly passes, many younger European historians are proving more willing to examine the darker corners of their countries' histories than their predecessors.

USELESS TRIVIA: THE FOLKS YOU WANT ON YOUR SIDE!

The story of Oskar Schindler was popularized by the 1993 Steven Spielberg film *Schindler's List*, with the Irish actor Liam Neeson portraying the womanizing, opportunistic German industrialist who finds redemption through saving Jews forced to work in his wartime factory in Nazi-occupied Poland. An almost as widely known figure is Raoul Wallenberg, the son of a large Swedish banking family who, during the war, was a Swedish diplomat in Budapest. With some aid from both other members of the Swedish Embassy and sympathetic Hungarian bureaucrats, Wallenberg managed to issue Swedish passports to Hungarian Jews, saving an estimated 15,000 from Auschwitz. The Soviets arrested Wallenberg in 1945, and Soviet records indicate he died in Lyubyanka Prison in Moscow in 1947.[48]

A much lesser known figure in Eastern Europe was the Japanese Consul to Lithuania, Chiune Sugihara. When Lithuania was annexed by the Soviet Union in 1940, Sugihara was supposed to shut down the Japanese consulate in Kaunas, but as desperate Polish Jews fleeing Nazi-occupied Poland began to flood Lithuania, Sugihara and his wife stalled, creating Japanese transit visas for these Jewish refugees. Soon the Polish underground AK made contact, and Sugihara shared with them the tools and technique of forging Japanese travel documents, and he also negotiated transit for these Jews through the USSR. Sugihara is credited with saving between 6,000-10,000 Polish and Lithuanian Jews. These actions cost Sugihara his career in the Japanese foreign service, but years after the war a Polish AK veteran found him in Japan and lobbied Israel for his recognition as one of the Righteous.

Still, contrary to surprisingly popular belief in the West, Eastern Europe did not only produce collaborators (nor was it the sole source of collaborators). Slovaks and Bulgarians, for instance, protested and successfully stopped their pro-Hitler governments from sending Jews to Auschwitz.[49] The Albanian *besa* tribal code of honor prompted many Muslim Albanians to harbor Jews during the war. In 1963, Israel created the official title מלועה תומוא ידיסח (Righteous Among the Nations) and established a memorial to those Righteous at Yad Vashem.[50] The Israeli Supreme Court uses this title to describe those non-Jews who risked their lives to help Jews escape the Holocaust, and investigates cases before bestowing the title on a deserving Gentile. As of 2009, there were 22,765 Righteous Among the Nations. 11,870—or 52% of them—are from Eastern Europe, and nearly a third of all the confirmed Righteous (6,135) came from one country alone: Poland. It is important to remember that saving Jews in Nazi-occupied Eastern Europe was a far riskier act than in Western Europe; Western Europeans risked imprisonment or execution, but Eastern Europeans also risked the lives of family, friends, and associates.[51] Yad Vashem only recognizes those individuals whose stories can be verified, but as Marek Edelman, a leader of the 1943 Warsaw Ghetto Uprising, observed, not all savers of Jewish lives could be counted:

> In the interview Edelman said, "Twelve thousand Jews survived in Warsaw until the Warsaw Uprising (August, 1944). Those who perished in the Warsaw Uprising, that's another story. In order for 12,000 Jews to survive, 100,000 persons had to be involved. Warsaw had 700,000 inhabitants at that time, thus every seventh Pole was involved."[52]

Holocaust history can be very contentious, and Edelman's numbers are controversial for some. But whether one believes his accounts (as a witness) or not, his testimony underscores the deceptive complexity of Holocaust history for people, nations, and even corporations still today. Historians such as Lucy Dawidowicz helped rescue the Holocaust as a historical topic from obscurity as just another subcategory in a long list of Nazi horrors, and this is important because it is in modern times an almost mind-bogglingly shocking example of human cruelty and callousness. The Holocaust is Exhibit A in any indictment of Nazism and political extremism. In an age uncomfortable with moral absolutes, the Holocaust has spawned an unending discussion about the nature of evil in human affairs. These kinds of discussions are, I think, where history can provide the most value for society, in fostering discussions that explore why people behaved the way they did in circumstances such as the Holocaust, be they Nazi SS soldiers, German housewives, Ukrainian camp guards, Jewish *Ghetto-Polizei* (Ghetto police), or "Polish farmers, Dutch land registry officials, French mayors, Norwegian ministers, Italian soldiers."

USELESS TRIVIA: I'M NOT CRYING WOLF, I'M JUST CRYING.

Jan Karski was an agent for the Polish AK who had himself smuggled into the Warsaw Ghetto to witness living conditions, and then infiltrated the Bełżec death camp disguised as a Ukrainian guard to collect eyewitness accounts of the Nazi mass murder of Jews. (Other AK agents, such as Witold Pilecki [VEE-told Pee-LETS-kee],[53] did the same in Auschwitz.) Karski was captured once and endured Nazi torture, only to escape. In 1943 he smuggled his findings to Britain.

To his bewilderment and frustration, the Western Allies refused to believe his story, though he had also smuggled microfilm containing pictures and first-hand accounts. In the U.K. Churchill refused to see him, while in the U.S., President Roosevelt met Karski, but none he met believed his story. Even some Jewish American leaders dismissed Karski's account as wildly overzealous Polish propaganda. In desperation, Karski published his accounts in 1944 in a book called *Story of a Secret State* that sold well but more for its cloak-and-dagger stories than as an account of Nazi atrocities. As Allied armies began liberating Nazi camps in 1944 and 1945, however, Karski's claims gained credibility and the full horror of Nazi crimes began to come to light. It was only shortly before his death in 2000 that Karski's wartime efforts were recognized and his 1943 report acknowledged as the first credible portrait of the Holocaust.

HOME IS WHERE THE BORDER IS!

World War II was truly a total war, a war in which every aspect of life was subordinated to the war effort—and therefore became a target as well. But World War II was also the result of a century's worth of frustration in Europe with the slow pace of change and the inability of the Great Powers to find satisfactory solutions to national and ethnic conflicts across the Continent. World War II was a total breakdown in civility as countries and peoples jettisoned morals and resorted to violence to impose their own justice, others be damned. These imposed solutions were to be *permanent*, forever more unquestionable. Throughout the war, *50 million* European civilians[1]—most of them Eastern Europeans—were forced from their homes to suit the victorious powers. The Axis Powers got things rolling but the Allies soon retaliated in kind, all at tremendous human cost.

Victims usually received a knock on the door and were given an hour or less to pack whatever they could carry, and were herded down the road or to waiting trains. The flow did not ebb or wait for winter, and death from exposure, starvation, exhaustion, or violence was a common fate. Survivors usually never saw their homes again, and received no compensation. Indeed, the Nazis and Soviets both looted and pillaged their empires in Eastern Europe to the extent that Anne Applebaum notes: "By 1945, the idea that the ruling authorities could simply confiscate private property without providing any compensation whatsoever was an established principle in Eastern Europe."[2]

It all began with the Axis Powers, who sought to mold a conquered Europe to suit their ideology:

- The seizure of the Sudetenland region from Czechoslovakia in September 1938 by Nazi Germany was followed by the immediate expulsion of up to 150,000 Czechs.[3]

- The defeat of Poland in 1939 led in the spring of 1940 to the expulsion of c. 800,000-1,000,000 Poles from the parts of Silesia and Pomerania annexed directly to the Reich.

- *Generalplan Ost* was Hitler's plan, finalized in 1941, for the German colonization of Eastern Europe. It called for the liquidation of Slavs and Balts from the lands between Germany and the Ural Mountains by way of mass murder, expulsion, and enslavement, to be replaced by 8-10 million German colonists. The plan was postponed until after the war, when a test run in 1942 in Polish Lublin and Zamość (renamed "Himmlerstadt") proved too disruptive to the war effort. 100,000 adults were sent to concentration camps, while c. 4,500 young children were sent to Lebensborn orphanages for Germanization. The rest were exterminated. Some 2.5 million Poles[4] were expelled from their home regions by the Nazis during the war, and about 200,000 Eastern European children, most of them Poles, were forced into (or abandoned to) the Nazi Lebensborn program for resettlement with German parents and Germanization.[5]

- The Holocaust, during which (1942–45) the Nazis systematically murdered between 5.5 to 6 million Jews, about two-thirds of Europe's Jewish population. The Nazis dedicated immense resources to the Holocaust, isolating and shipping (by train) Jews from across the Continent to a series of death factories in rural Nazi-occupied Poland right up to the final days of the war. Hostility and large-scale appropriation of Jewish property across Europe (Eastern and Western) compelled hundreds of thousands of Holocaust survivors to opt to emigrate to Israel or the Americas after the war.

- The defeat of Yugoslavia and the subsequent Italian occupation of Albania, Montenegro, and parts of Dalmatia in 1941 led to the immediate expulsion of tens of thousands of Croats and Slovenes from Istria, Dalmatia, and Slovenia to make way for Italian colonists. Fascist Croatia, Italian-Albania, Bulgaria, and Hungary in turn also expelled hundreds of thousands of Serbs.

- When Bulgaria forced Romania to cede southern Dobrudja in 1940, the resulting Treaty of Craiova forced some 80,000 Romanians and 65,000 Bulgarians to leave their homes.

- The Nazis relied heavily on slave labor for industrial production during the war, ultimately using some 8-12 million slaves,[6] most of them Jews, Soviet POWs, Poles, or other Slavs. Some 795,889 to 955,215 died in these camps,[7] in "30,000 slave labor camps; 1,150 Jewish ghettos; 980 concentration camps; 1,000 prisoner-of-war camps; 500 brothels filled with sex slaves; and thousands of other camps used for euthanizing the elderly and infirm, performing forced abortions, 'Germanizing' prisoners or transporting victims to killing centers."[8]

The Soviets form a category all their own in this regard, both when they were allied to Hitler and after he betrayed them. Indeed, the Soviets continued their internal mass deportations well into the 1950s.

- In the 1939–41 Soviet occupation of eastern Poland, some 1.25 million Polish citizens[9] were deported to Siberia and Central Asia, and 388,000 Polish POWs imprisoned in camps.[10]

- In three major deportation waves in the Baltics—in the first occupation of 1939–41, the reoccupation in 1944–45, and again in 1949—the Soviets deported some 120,000-170,000 Estonians, Latvians, and Lithuanians to Siberia, about 10% of the Baltics' adult population.[11]

- After the 1939–40 Winter War with Finland, some 91,000 Finns fled or were expelled by the Soviets from the seized territory between Leningrad and Viipuri (modern-day Russian Vyborg).

- When the USSR seized Bessarabia back from Romania in 1940, the Soviets similarly deported about 45,000-90,000 Romanians from Bessarabia[12] (renamed the Moldavian S.S.R.).

- After Hitler's attack in 1941, 780,000 Volga Germans were deported to Soviet Central Asia.

- In 1943, an estimated 1.1 million ethnic Chechens, Kalmyks, Tartars, Ingush, Balkars, Karachays, and others from Crimea and the Caucasus were deported to Siberia in horrendous conditions, with, for instance, some 20% of all Tartars dying along the way.

- As Soviet forces re-entered eastern Poland in 1944, between 1.5 and 2.1 million more Poles were expelled from the eastern territories beyond the Curzon Line[13] westward into Poland.

The grand finale came after the war, however, as the Allies sought permanent solutions—and revenge. Though implemented largely by the Soviets, the Western Allies readily agreed to most of the following:

- 1944–46 Soviet-liberated Poland and the USSR, from which 7-10 million Germans fled or were expelled westward into Germany by Soviet and Polish armed forces. Victims included some war-era Nazi colonists, but the vast majority were native local civilians.[14]

- An additional 2-3 million Germans[15] were expelled from Czechoslovakia in 1945 (with as many as 250,000 Südeten Germans murdered in the process), as a part of the (President Edvard) Beneš Decrees. Some 42,000 Czechs and Slovaks fled or were forced westward from prewar Transcarpathia in 1945 as it was annexed by the Soviet Union.[16]

- An additional 500,000[17] Germans were deported from Hungary, Yugoslavia, and Romania in 1945, though Hungary did so reluctantly, and only the minimum required by the ACC.

- Per the Beneš Decrees, some 30,000 Hungarians were deported from Czechoslovakia before the Allies halted the expulsions. Prague then tried to arrange a voluntary population transfer with Hungary, but after a few trials, Hungary declined further cooperation. The Beneš Decrees had revoked citizenship for Germans and Hungarians, but Hungarians could reapply if they adopted Slovak names. Some 400,000 did so (about half the Hungarians living in Slovakia) but the law was nullified in 1948, and most then reverted to their Hungarian names.[18]

- Approximately 350,000 Italians were terrorized into fleeing the Yugoslav Dalmatian coast, the city of Fiume (modern-day Rijeka, Croatia) and the Istrian Peninsula by Tito's partisans, as well as tens of thousands of Hungarians from Vojvodina and Bulgarians from Macedonia.

- Hundreds of thousands of ethnic Germans and Hungarians were arrested and deported from Hungary and Romania in 1944–46 to be used as slave labor in mines in Soviet Ukraine.

- Enraged by the wartime "Greater Albania," Greece expelled 20,000-30,000 Albanians in 1944.

- *Akcja Wisła* (Operation Vistula) was launched in 1947 by communist Polish, Soviet, and Czechoslovak forces in response to a fierce guerrilla war being waged in the northern Carpathian mountains (Galicia) by Ukrainian separatists, die-hard Polish AK soldiers, and residual Wehrmacht "Werewolf" units. Some 850,000 Ukrainians and Lemkos living in Poland were deported to Soviet Ukraine, while another 140,000 were forcibly resettled in the "Recovered Territories."[19] In 1990, Poland officially apologized for Akcja Wisła.

- Operation Keelhaul: A series of operations from 1944 to 1948 in which British and American military forces forcibly repatriated Eastern European, especially Soviet citizens in Western Europe back to their respective countries. This included some 2.8 million Soviet POWs, as well as millions of civilian refugees and slave laborers. Though reports streamed in of repatriated peoples being arrested or even executed by Soviet security forces in full view of their Western deliverers, repatriations continued. One infamous case was the Bleiburg Massacre in Austria in which 40,000 fascist NDH Croats and other anticommunist refugees turned over by the British to Tito's partisans were slaughtered, including women and children.

USELESS TRIVIA:
THE QUALITY OF MERCY IS NOT STRAINED . . .

On November 18, 1965, the German Bishops Conference, the governing body for the Roman Catholic church in (West and East) Germany at the time, received an extraordinary letter. It began with the exhortation (in Polish), *Przewielebni Bracia Soborowi!* (Reverend Brother Councilors), and went on to review the history of Polish-German relations. It had been crafted by the leaders of the Polish Roman Catholic church, and concluded with this particularly powerful paragraph (in Polish):

W tym jak najbardziej chrześcijańskim, ale i bardzo ludzkim duchu, wyciągamy do Was, siedzących tu, na ławach kończącego się Soboru, nasze ręce oraz udzielamy wybaczenia i prosimy o nie. A jeśli Wy, niemieccy biskupi i Ojcowie Soboru, po bratersku wyciągnięte ręce ujmiecie, to wtedy dopiero będziemy mogli ze spokojnym sumieniem obchodzić nasze Millenium w sposób jak najbardziej chrześcijański. Zapraszamy Was na te uroczystości jak najserdeczniej do Polski.[20]

And in German:

In diesem allerchristlichsten und zugleich sehr menschlichen Geist strecken wir unsere Hände zu Ihnen hin in den Bänken des zu Ende gehenden Konzils, gewähren Vergebung und bitten um Vergebung. Und wenn Sie, deutsche Bischöfe und Konzilsväter, unsere ausgestreckten Hände brüderlich erfassen, dann erst können wir wohl mit ruhigem Gewissen in Polen auf ganz christliche Art unser Millennium feiern. Wir laden Sie dazu herzlichst nach Polen ein.[21]

Which translated as:

In the most Christian, but as well in the most human spirit, we extend to you our hands as we forgive you, and in turn seek your forgiveness. If you, Bishops of Germany and Council Fathers, would take our outstretched hand in restored brotherhood, only then will we be able to celebrate with peace of mind Poland's upcoming Millennium[22] in the fullest Christian sense. With open hearts, we invite you to come to Poland for these celebrations.[23]

The Polish Roman Catholic church had taken the first step in Polish-German reconciliation, recognizing in the letter both the horrors inflicted on Poles during the war but also acknowledging the suffering of German civilians after the war. The letter was read aloud in Polish churches to the horror of the Polish communist regime, and was condemned by both Warsaw and East Berlin. However, the spirit of the letter could not be undone and its spirit still reverberates today among Poles and Germans.

Rows of star tombstones at Soviet cemetery, Gdynia, Poland (Shutterstock)

8. THE FRYING PAN, THE FIRE, ETC. 1945–1989
THE PAX SOVIETICA

JAŁTA

Written and Performed by Jacek Kaczmarski
From his 1986 album *Litania*

Jak nowa - rezydencja carów
Służba swe obowiązki zna
Precz wysiedlono stąd Tatarów
Gdzie na świat wyrok zapaść ma

Okna już widzą, słyszą ściany
Jak kaszle nad cygarem Lew
Jak skrzypi wózek popychany
Z kalekim demokratą w tle

Lecz nikt nie widzi i nie słyszy
Co robi Góral w krymską noc
Gdy gestem w wiernych towarzyszy
Wpaja swą legendarną moc

Nie miejcie żalu do Stalina
Nie on się za tym wszystkim krył
To w końcu nie jest jego wina
Że Roosevelt w Jałcie nie miał sił
Gdy się Triumwirat wspólnie brał
Za świata historyczne kształty
Wiadomo, kto Cezara grał
I tak rozumieć trzeba Jałtę

W resztce cygara mdłym ogniku
Pływała Lwa Albionu twarz
Nie rozmawiajmy o Bałtyku!
Po co w Europie tyle państw?

Polacy? Chodzi tylko o to
Żeby gdzieś w końcu mogli żyć!
Z tą Polską zawsze są kłopoty
Kaleka troszczy się i drży
Lecz uspokaja ich gospodarz
Pożółkły dłonią głaszcząc wąs
Mój kraj pomocną dłoń im poda
Potem, niech rządzą się, jak chcą

Nie miejcie żalu do Churchilla
Nie on wszak za tym wszytkim stał
Wszak po to tylko był Triumwirat
By Stalin dostał to, co chciał
Komu zależy na pokoju
Ten zawsze cofnie się przed gwałtem
Wygra, kto się nie boi wojen
I tak rozumieć trzeba Jałtę

Ściana pałacu słuch napina
Gdy mówi do Kaleki Lew
Ja wierzę w szczerość słów Stalina
Dba chyba o radziecką krew

I potakuje mu Kaleka
Niezłomny demokracji stróż:
Stalin to ktoś na miarę wieku!
Oto mąż stanu, oto wódz!

Bo sojusz wielkich - to nie zmowa
To przyszłość świata - wolność, ład!
Przy nim i słaby się uchowa
I swoją część otrzyma - strat

Nie miejcie żalu do Roosevelta
Pomyślcie, ile musiał znieść
Fajka, dym cygar i butelka
Churchill, co miał sojusze gdzieś!
Wszakże radziły trzy Imperia
Nad granicami, co zatarte
W szczegółach zaś już siedział Beria
I tak rozumieć trzeba Jałtę

Więc delegacje odleciały
Ucichł na Krymie carski gród
Gdy na zachodzie działa grzmiały
Transporty ludzi szły na wschód

Świat wolny święcił potem tryumf
Opustoszały nagle fronty
W kwiatach już prezydenta grób
A tam transporty i transporty

Czerwony świt się z nocy budzi
Z woli wyborców odszedł Churchill
A tam transporty żywych ludzi
A tam obozy długiej śmierci

Nie miejcie więc do Trójcy żalu
Wyrok historii za nią stał
Opracowany w każdym calu
Każdy z nich chronił, co już miał
Mógł mylić się zwiedziony chwilą
Nie był Polakiem ani Bałtem
Tylko ofiary się nie mylą
I tak rozumieć trzeba Jałtę

YALTA,[1]

by Jacek Kaczmarski[2]

Like a new residence of the Tsars
The Servants all know their duty
From where the Tartars were
   expelled,
Where verdict will be passed on the
   world

Here the windows can see, and the
   walls listen[3]
How the Lion[4] coughs on his cigars
How the wheelchair[5] creaks when
   pushed
With the invalid in the background.

But nobody sees and nobody hears
What the Mountain Man[6] does in
   the Crimean Night[7]
While through his faithful comrades' deeds
He gives voice to his legendary
   power

Don't find fault with Stalin,
His motives were never hidden
And in the end it was not his fault
That Roosevelt had no strength at
   Yalta
As the Triumvirate shaped the his-
   tory of the world together.
It's obvious who played Caesar
And that's how Yalta should be
   understood.

In the embers of the cigar
You could see the face of the Lion
   of Albion[8]
Don't mention the Baltic!
Why do we need so many coun-
   tries in Europe anyway?

Poles? In the end they must settle
For simply having a place to live.
Poland has always been trouble.
The Invalid worries and trembles.

But their host calms them,
As he strokes his yellowed beard
"My country will lend a helping
   hand,
And later they can arrange their
   affairs as they please."

Don't find fault with Churchill,
None of this was his doing.
After all, the Triumvirate only
   existed
For Stalin to get what he wanted.
Those who want peace
Will always bow to the threat of
   violence,
Triumph is only for those who do
   not fear war,
And that is how Yalta should be
   understood.

The walls of the palace listen
  intently
When the Lion whispers with the
  Invalid
I think we can take Stalin at his
  word
That he is concerned only about
  Soviet blood.

The Invalid nods in agreement,
That stubborn guardian of
  Democracy.
Stalin is the man of the century,
The father of the country, the
  leader!

An alliance of Great Men, this is not
  a gang
This is the future of the world:
  peace and order!
Through them the meek shall
  survive
And will get their share . . . of woe.

Don't find fault with Roosevelt,
Think how much he had to
  endure.[9]
A pipe, cigar smoke, and the bottle
Churchill, who distrusted alliances
The three emperors discussed bor-
  ders new and vague,
While hidden in the details was
  Beria[10]
And that's how Yalta should be
  understood.

So the delegates dispersed
And silence fell once again over the
  Tsar's Crimean palace
And while guns still roared in the
  West
People were being herded in the
  East.[11]

The Free World eventually cel-
  ebrated triumph
And all the front lines emptied of
  men
Flowers were already falling on the
  President's grave[12]
While transports upon transports
  continued.[13]

The night gives way to a Red Dawn,
And elections have taken Churchill
  away[14]
And there are transports of live
  people[15]
And there are camps of slow death

So don't find fault with the Big
  Three,
History has reached its verdict
With every detail carefully
  arranged
Each of them guarded what was
  theirs
Anyone there could have made the
  same mistakes
Though it was not a Pole or a Balt—
Only the victims are not fooled.
And that is how Yalta should be
  understood.

"I replied that there was another possibility, that if a workable plan of collective security was set up in Europe and throughout the world the Soviet Union would not have fears of attack from the West and therefore would not have any need to obtain strategic areas on its western frontiers and that since the Soviet Union had no reasonable right to demand additional terri-tory per se, it might be persuaded to drop its claims to these areas of eastern Europe."

—Elbridge Durbrow, Division of European Affairs, U.S. State Department, in a discussion with former
  U.S. Ambassador to the Soviet Union and noted Sovietophile Joseph E. Davies, February 3, 1943[16]

Figure 61. Eastern Europe Timeline, 1944–1991

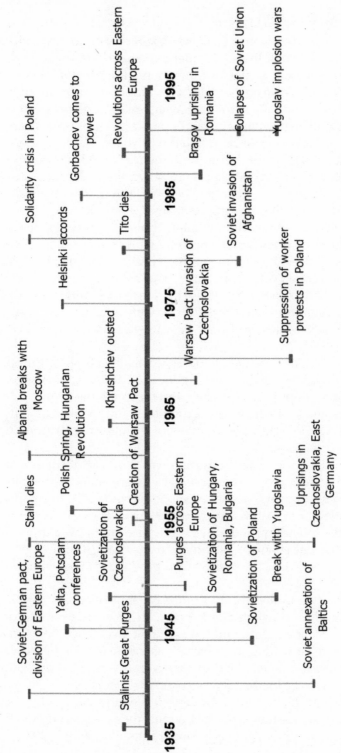

CHAPTER SUMMARY

World War II was the greatest challenge the Soviet Union ever faced in its history, and it survived. In fact, it emerged as a major world power to be reckoned with. Russian armies had surged into the heart of Europe just like in 1814 and had played a crucial role in the war. Some have speculated that the war may have actually *saved* the Soviet Union from its own implosion, so disastrous and disruptive had Stalin's prewar policies been. In any event, before the war Moscow was an isolated backwater, and its leaders looked upon as fanatic ideologues, but in 1945 the Soviet red star held immense respect around the world—a respect unknown since Alexander I in 1815—and diplomats from every country lined up to ingratiate themselves with Stalin, who now had the appearance of an elder statesman.

Problems arose almost immediately, however, between the wartime allies over differing visions of the postwar world, and very soon the Soviet Union found itself embroiled in another conflict, this one global in scope. Stalin set out to build an empire larger and better defended than the one that had failed him during the 1939–41 alliance with Hitler, and the implications for the countries of Eastern Europe were obvious: their security and their independence—restored only in 1918—were to be sacrificed on the altar of Soviet security.

The Soviet Union immediately began shaping Eastern Europe in its own image, hijacking or demolishing local institutions, using the NKVD to terrorize local populations, sealing and fortifying the empire's new borders, and installing obedient puppet regimes. Europe was literally cut in half, and the worst nightmares of many of the interwar Eastern European countries came to pass.

The Stalinist era in Eastern Europe was a period of traumatized and (literally) decimated peoples being subjected once again to a new extremist ideology and militarism that choked economic and social development for years. However, after Stalin's death, Soviet imperial rule in Eastern Europe devolved into something more like a Soviet commonwealth with fraternal communist leaders often as willing to argue, haggle, or stonewall one another and even Moscow as the West, provoking much indigestion for Soviet leaders.

One thing that united this byzantine cabal of rulers across the region, including those who eventually broke with Moscow, was the desire to remain in power at all costs, and it was at that level that all the Soviet Bloc regimes were most willing to cooperate, as much against their own populations as external threats. The puppet-governors installed by Stalin in the 1950s had come to be by the 1980s local petty despots clinging to a discredited ideology and its worn-out symbols, left-wing tyrants who resembled to a surprising degree the right-wing tyrants they'd replaced in 1945. Ironically, the challenge they'd always feared came ultimately in 1989 not from the West, but from Moscow.

CHAPTER GUIDE

A. *Introduction: The Cold War, or This Town Isn't Big Enough* . . 379
B. *The Warsaw Pact: The Farm Animals Unite* 388
C. *Yugoslavia: Exit, Stage Left* 392
D. *Albania as an Island* 395
E. *Bulgaria Finally Gets Something in Return* 398
F. *Romania Goes Off the Deep End* 401
G. *Hungary and Its Food-Based Ideologies* 404
H. *Czechoslovakia, Just East of Eden* 409
I. *East Germany as the Runt of the Litter* 413
J. *Poland, the Perennial Pain in the Butt* 417
K. *The Soviet Union, Keeping Up with the Joneses* 425

A. *Introduction: The Cold War, or This Town Isn't Big Enough*

"Created by a minority coup rather than by exertion of popular will, the Soviet state was always intrinsically insecure. It was the product of momentary confusion during an avoidable war rather than of any insoluable internal crisis of the tsarist regime it replaced. Its founders did not consider it secure unless the revolution they promoted to keep themselves in power would triumph abroad as well. Although they tried their best to spread it, they did not succeed; disunity among their enemies nevertheless allowed their state to survive and grow. All the same, as taught by Marxist doctrine, they continued to insist that the outside world remained implacably hostile. Whether this was true or not, their constant perception of a threat prevented Soviet leaders from ever feeling sufficiently secure. This made them different from other leaders, and Stalin more different than most."
—Historian Vojtěch Mastny[17]

"After establishment of Bolshevist regime, Marxist dogma, rendered even more truculent and intolerant by Lenin's interpretation, became a perfect vehicle for sense of insecurity with which Bolsheviks, even more than previous Russian rulers, were afflicted. In this dogma, with its basic altruism of purpose, they found justification for their instinctive fear of outside world, for the dictatorship without which they did not know how to rule, for cruelties they did not dare not to inflict, for sacrifice they felt bound to demand."[18]
—George F. Kennan, Deputy Chief of the U.S. mission in Moscow, "The Long Telegram," February 22, 1946.

The Cold War was a global confrontation between the West (primarily the United States) and the Soviet Union, framed largely in military terms but, as nuclear weapons made war impractical, it played out primarily in political, economic, and even cultural terms. Its scale was unprecedented, so that relations between any two countries anywhere were forced through the prism of this Soviet-American confrontation, subjecting every cultural exchange or trade agreement to the scrutiny of Washington and Moscow. Both sides supported minor proxy wars by client states in remote locations such as eastern Asia, Central America, and Africa, and the world was awash with spies and counter-spies. For four and a half decades the world stood poised on the brink of global war and, with both sides bristling with nuclear weapons, total annihilation. In the absence of military confrontation, *everything* became a weapon, from ping pong to jazz, from healthcare to lapel pins.

The thing about the Cold War was that originally, neither side planned, expected, or wanted it. It came as a surprise to both Moscow and Washington, and both saw their actions in the Cold War as essentially defensive. As two ideologically driven countries, both seriously misunderstood the intentions and motivations of the other. However, before someone organizes a group hug and choruses of "Koombaya" break out, the root problem wasn't just a case of misunderstood signals; Stalin rejected cooperation with the West in favor of *empire*, disregarding many of the agreements he'd signed with the West at Teheran, Yalta, and Potsdam. Former Soviet foreign minister Maxim Litvinov explained it in 1946 as "a return in Russia to the outmoded concept of security in terms of territory—the more you've got, the safer you are."[19]

To the hyperparanoid ruler of the USSR, any state or territory not directly under his control posed an innate threat to himself and the Soviet Union. The West, particularly the Americans, were sympathetic to Soviet security needs but never fully understood Stalin's mania and reacted with puzzlement and dismay as the Soviets began constructing a fortress-like empire in Eastern Europe, disregarding agreements signed with the West.[20] After the humiliation of 1941 Stalin trusted no one, however, and even Khrushchev later secretly blamed him for being overly paranoid and confrontational with the West, in effect provoking the Cold War.[21] Stalin's paranoia and mania for security ironically undermined Soviet security, as historian John Lewis Gaddis noted:

> The Kremlin leader was slow to recognize that Soviet authority would not be welcomed everywhere beyond Soviet borders; but as he did come to see this he became all the more determined to impose it everywhere. The Eastern Europeans were slow to recognize how confining incorporation within a Soviet sphere was going to be; but as they did come to see this they became all the more determined to resist it, even if only by withholding, in a passive but sullen manner, the consent any regime needs to establish itself by means other than coercion. Stalin's efforts to consolidate his empire therefore made it at once more repressive and less secure.[22]

For Eastern Europe, 1945 was *not* going to be a repeat of 1918. All the Great Powers agreed that the Eastern European states' sovereignty was going to be limited in some way, in the interest of the greater good (i.e., European stability)—but how much? Few in Washington or London likely had a solid idea of exactly what postwar Eastern Europe would look like, but thinkers in both governments secretly echoed the thoughts of British historian E.H.Carr that Eastern Europe needed to be *controlled*:

> "[T]here can be no security in Western Europe unless there is also security in East-ern Europe, and security in Eastern Europe is unattainable unless it is buttressed by the military power of Russia."[23]

USELESS TRIVIA: DEN DANSK FOLKEREPUBLIK!

As World War II wound down to its final days in Europe, trust between the Western powers and their Soviet allies was already showing some cracks. The Soviets had demanded as early as 1943 bases in the west-ern Baltic, including Finland's Åland Islands and a Soviet role in run-ning the Kiel Canal along the German-Danish border. With a growing awareness that Soviet troops were unlikely to vacate any territory they liberated from the Germans, the Western Allies hurriedly launched a series of operations in early May 1945 to save Denmark from a Soviet occupation. First, the British secured the surrender of German forces in the Netherlands and Denmark on paper on May 4. They then sailed two cruisers and destroyers into Copenhagen harbor on May 5 and landed a planeload of British paratroopers in the city. British commandos then seized the Kiel Canal, as well as the German port of Wismar (just east of Lübeck and the Danish border), directly in the path of Soviet forces advancing westward along the Baltic coast. (The Red Army arrived at Wismar only hours later.)

The threat of a Soviet occupation was not theoretical; on May 4, the Soviets demanded that Nazi forces on Denmark's Bornholm Island surrender to them. The Nazis replied that all German forces in Den-mark had already surrendered to the British. Regardless, Soviet forces bombarded the island for several days, then occupied it on May 9. Moscow had earlier demanded a military base on Bornholm Island but returned it to Denmark in April 1946, on condition. Imagine if Den-mark had been subsumed into Eastern Europe, and forced to become a *Dansk Folkere*publik (People's Republic of Denmark). . . .

The West's primary concern about Eastern Europe in 1945 was that it stop inspiring wars among the Great Powers, and this persuaded the West to agree to some pretty radical solutions for the postwar region such as the mass expulsion of millions of ethnic Germans. With the old Austro-Hungarian and Ottoman nanny empires long gone, the U.S. and Britain turned to the Soviet Union to babysit the region, readily accepting that Moscow would establish "governments friendly to the Soviet Union"—whatever that meant—in Eastern Europe after the war. Churchill had some inkling that Soviet military penetration of Eastern Europe was likely going to have permanent strategic consequences, so he proposed to Stalin in Moscow in October 1944 percentages of British vs. Soviet influence in the Balkans: 10% : 90% for Romania, 90% : 10% for Greece, 50% : 50% for Yugoslavia and Hungary each, and 25% : 75% for Bulgaria.

With Soviet armies already overrunning Eastern Europe, however, Stalin brushed aside this belated attempt to forestall Soviet domination of the region. The Roosevelt administration in the U.S. was obsessed with *not* repeating the mistakes of the 1919 Versailles Treaty, and felt that the United Nations was crucial for postwar peace. To this end Roosevelt subordinated all other considerations to preserving the anti-Hitler alliance during and after the war. In practical terms this meant that, while sympathetic to Eastern Europe's plight, Roosevelt nevertheless viewed accommodating Soviet security demands in the region as a necessary evil.

In any event, by 1943 Roosevelt realized that Soviet armies were going to overrun Eastern Europe, anyway, so he thought it practical to recognize Soviet goals in the region in exchange for Soviet cooperation after the war. He did try to bind Stalin to promises of democratic governments and free elections in Eastern Europe, particularly Poland, but when alarming cables streamed in to Washington and London over 1944–45 from Western diplomats in the region describing Soviet brutality and breaches of agreements, these were ignored in the name of Allied unity.

Further, Western military policies led to a tacit Anglo-American acceptance of a Soviet sphere of influence in Eastern Europe. First, the West fended off Soviet demands for military representation in occupied Axis Italy by agreeing to exclusive postwar Soviet military representation in Hungary, Romania, and Bulgaria.

Then, an American insistence on deferring any discussions of postwar borders or political arrangements until after the war allowed the Soviets to create a *fait accompli* in Eastern Europe by masquerading de facto Sovietization of the region under the guise of wartime military necessity. Eastern Europeans pleaded with the West in vain for protection against Soviet imperialism:

"But, General Sikorski[24] went on to say, if no opposition to the imposition on the part of Stalin were evidenced now, he will take it for granted that neither the United States nor Great Britain are going to lift a finger to prevent the domination at the close of the war of eastern and southern Europe by the Soviet Union, and the imperialistic ambitions of the Soviet Union will be greatly accelerated and enhanced as a result of any present failure on the part of the United States to make its views known."

—U.S. Under Secretary of State B. Sumner Welles, noting a conversation with Gen. Władysław Sikorski; January 4, 1943[25]

Figure 62. Eastern Europe in 1960

Figure 62 represents Eastern Europe in 1960, at the height of Soviet imperial rule. The white line that snakes across the divided Germany and around Austria and the eastern Italian border to the Adriatic is the mythical "Iron Curtain," though it was more nuanced than shown here. Until 1955, for instance, eastern Austria was on the Soviet side of the Iron Curtain. Both Yugoslavia and Albania eventually

bolted from the Soviet sphere and fortified their borders against the Soviet satellites as well as the West. This map also excludes the divided city of Berlin. When communist insurrections failed in Greece and Turkey, the Iron Curtain was effectively extended to their borders as well.

Eastern Europe's plight was further aggrevated by confusion in Western polices after the death of Roosevelt in April 1945 and elections in Britain in July that toppled the Churchill government. The new U.S. president, Harry Truman—whom Roosevelt hadn't even told about the atomic bomb, much less Eastern Europe—grappled for months with contradictory internal policy statements and growing evidence that the Soviets were building and fortifying an empire in Eastern Europe. Truman did start raising questions and complaints with Moscow, but received only rebukes from Stalin, who felt that Roosevelt had given him a green light. As even sympathetic former Soviet foreign minister Maxim Litvinov expressed in puzzlement, "Why did you Americans wait till right now to begin opposing us in the Balkans and Eastern Europe? You should have done this three years ago. Now it is too late, and your complaints only arouse suspicion here."[26] Churchill further invoked Eastern Europe's plight in his iconic speech at Westminster College in Fulton, Missouri in March 1946:

A shadow has fallen upon the scenes so lately lighted by the Allied victory. Nobody knows what Soviet Russia and its Communist international organization intends to do in the immediate future, or what are the limits, if any, to their expansive and proselytizing tendencies. I have a strong admiration and regard for the valiant Russian people and for my wartime comrade, Marshal Stalin. There is deep sympathy and goodwill in Britain - and I doubt not here also - towards the peoples of all the Russias and a resolve to persevere through many differences and rebuffs in establishing lasting friendships. We understand the Russian need to be secure on her western frontiers by the removal of all possibility of German aggression. We welcome Russia to her rightful place among the leading nations of the world. We welcome her flag upon the seas. Above all, we welcome constant, frequent and growing contacts between the Russian people and our own people on both sides of the Atlantic. It is my duty however, for I am sure you would wish me to state the facts as I see them to you, to place before you certain facts about the present position in Europe.

From Stettin in the Baltic to Trieste in the Adriatic an iron curtain has descended across the Continent. Behind that line lie all the capitals of the ancient states of

Central and Eastern Europe: Warsaw, Berlin, Prague, Vienna, Budapest, Belgrade, Bucharest, and Sofia; all these famous cities and the populations around them lie in what I must call the Soviet sphere, and all are subject, in one form or another, not only to Soviet influence but to a very high and in some cases increasing measure of control from Moscow. [. . .] Whatever conclusions may be drawn from these facts - and facts they are - this is certainly not the Liberated Europe we fought to build up. Nor is it one which contains the essentials of permanent peace.[27]

Although there was continuous friction between the Soviets and the West over the fate of Poland from 1943 to 1947—both Britain and the U.S. had millions of Polish immigrants, and hundreds of thousands of Poles had fought in Western armies throughout the war—the West was determined not to let Eastern Europe get in the way of cooperation with Moscow. The breaking point in relations came only came when Stalin began to make demands in 1946 against Turkey and Iran, which suggested that he wanted to reach *beyond* Eastern Europe, to expand the Soviet realm *further*. Only then did Truman move aggressively to contain Stalin's ambitions.

With the European Recovery Plan (ERP, or Marshall Plan) in 1947,[28] Truman in effect recognized Soviet domination of Eastern Europe by forcing Stalin to break Eastern Europe's economic ties to the West and create a counter Soviet economic zone. Stalin's attempt to force the Western powers out of West Berlin during the Berlin Blockade of 1948–49 convinced the West to form the North Atlantic Treaty Organization (NATO) in 1949, formalizing the American military commitment to Western Europe. This is the beginning of the Cold War.

From Eastern Europe's perspective, the Soviet occupation meant an abrupt end to the sovereignty regained in 1918. And Stalin's new realm was to be a *Soviet*, not a *communist* empire; Stalin sought neither friends nor utopias, only obedient *subjects*. Eastern Europe was to be a Soviet buffer zone where any future wars were to be contained and fought, safeguarding the Soviet motherland. Little distinction was made between former Axis enemies or Allies; all were (eventually) subjugated with equal ferocity and brutality. Indeed, loyal communists often found themselves arrested and imprisoned alongside former wartime fascist agents. When Czechoslovak foreign minister Jan Masaryk (Yon Mah-SAH-rik), who had pursued Soviet-friendly policies, flew to Moscow in early July 1947 to discuss the American Marshall Plan with Stalin, he said upon return that he had "left for Moscow as Minister of Foreign Affairs for a sovereign state," but that he was "returning as Stalin's stooge."[29]

USELESS TRIVIA:
SOME KRAZY KAT YOU'VE NEVER HEARD OF!

Willis Conover was born in Buffalo, New York in 1920, though because his father was in the Army his family moved around the U.S. a lot. He led an unassuming life, but his one great love was music, and in particular, jazz. Lacking musical talent, however, he instead became a jazz deejay. He was blessed with a deep baritone voice well suited to radio, and spent his entire life as a jazz deejay, working some forty years until his death in 1996 tirelessly promoting jazz albums, musicians, and events.

The twist, of course, is that Willis was a deejay for VOA, the *Voice of America* radio station created by the United States to broadcast American culture behind the Iron Curtain during the Cold War.[30] Willis started working with VOA in 1954, but he was stunned on his first trip to communist Poland in 1959 when he was mobbed at the Warsaw airport by hundreds of fans. During the Stalinist years, jazz was banned by the communist governments as decadent American bourgeois culture but Willis' passion for jazz translated well across cultural and political boundaries, and millions behind the Iron Curtain—by the 1960s, *20-30 million* listeners worldwide—secretly tuned in each week to Conover's show, often at great personal risk.

The Cold War went through several phases, the first phase being dominated by its chief architect, Stalin. He had terrorized Soviet society—including its ruling elites—into complete submission making the Soviet state an extension of his will. But, after his death, his successors never quite commanded the Soviet state as he did. Though the USSR still had some amazing achievements and victories, it began a slow slide into decline.

By 1960, the Cold War had become thoroughly institutionalized in both the U.S. and the Soviet Union—U.S. President Eisenhower warned against exactly this in his farewell address in January 1961—becoming embedded in government policies, feeding a circular logic of massive military spending and national security scares that gave the Cold War a momentum of its own beyond specific threats. This made agreements between the two rival sides far more difficult even when genuine good will existed.

To boot, the West began its process of decolonization after World War II, with the British, Portuguese, Dutch, Belgians, and French all divesting themselves of global colonial empires in excruciating (and often bloody) processes that Moscow often skillfully exploited, adding a Cold War dimension to these conflicts.

USELESS TRIVIA:
A LITTLE FOGGY ON THE DEFINITION OF TREASON

Ryszard Kukliński (RIH-shard Koo-KLEEN-skee) was born to a modest middle class household in Warsaw in 1930, where he grew up with an idyllic early childhood. The war came when he was only nine years old, however, and Ryszard witnessed the full horrors of the Nazi occupation, including seeing his home destroyed and his father—who was active in the resistance—arrested and taken away forever.

In 1947, at seventeen years old, Ryszard joined the Polish Army and over the next decade rose through the ranks, achieving his first command in 1953 and working by the 1960s for the General Staff. Kukliński became a leading expert on military exercises, and throughout the 1970s he regularly met with the leading military brass of all the Soviet Bloc states in his efforts to design increasingly realistic war games for the Warsaw Pact. Also, from 1972 on, Col. Kukliński led a crew of Polish intelligence officers on multiple yachting trips to Western Europe, where—posing as tourists—Kukliński and his crew collected data on NATO port traffic, which was passed on to the eager Soviets.

Kukliński was a crucial asset for the Warsaw Pact, or would have been had he not also been a CIA spy, one uniquely placed with access to the most sensitive military secrets of all the Warsaw Pact armies. Kukliński deeply resented Soviet rule over Poland, and his staunch patriotism led him to his second career as a spy. On his first yachting mission to Western Europe, Kukliński secretly contacted the CIA and simply offered his services, refusing all compensation. Over the next decade, he supplied Washington with tens of thousands of secret documents containing critical data on Soviet strategic war plans and the latest Soviet weapons systems. Information gained from Kukliński played a crucial role in shaping NATO's response to the Soviet threat in the 1970s and 80s. The CIA was forced to wisk Kukliński and his family out of Poland in 1981 as he was on the verge of being discovered. He lived the rest of his life in the U.S., and is now buried in the free Poland he strove for.

The end came when the decades of economic incompetence and misrule took their inevitable toll on Stalin's empire. Mikhail Gorbachev took over in 1985 and immediately initiated reforms to save the sinking Soviet ship. He was idealistic, believing fervently in communism and the Soviet Union, but his naïvité that Stalin's wheezing old war horse could be saved led Gorbachev happily to take the first real steps toward ending the Cold War. Gorbachev tried to break the Stalinist straightjacket that was strangling the Soviet economy and society, never quite realizing that the straightjacket was all that held the Soviet empire together. He proved every bit the imperialist his predecessors had been, sending the army into Lithuania or Azerbaijan when they dared dream of self-determination.

Still, Gorbachev's enduring gift to both Eastern Europe and Russia was his renunciation of the Brezhnev Doctrine in 1989, freeing Russia of this massive imperial drain on its economy, and leaving the satellite dictators suddenly forced to confront their own oppressed and increasingly restless populations on their own.

B. The Warsaw Pact: The Farm Animals Unite

"On the basis of our experience during the past twenty days and prompted by a feeling of responsibility for the common cause, I take the liberty of proposing to use acceptable methods in explaining to the leaders of the Soviet party and Government that the unprofessional, crude, and insulting behavior of certain Soviet military commanders is objectively detrimental to the authority and reputation of the Soviet Union and to the unity of the Warsaw Pact."

—Hungarian Generals István Oláh and Ferenc Szűcs, July 5, 1968[31]

In May 1955, the foreign ministers of the Soviet Union, Poland, East Germany, Czechoslovakia, Hungary, Romania, Bulgaria, and Albania gathered in the *Pałac Namiestnikowski* (Governor's Palace) in Warsaw to sign a military alliance. This alliance, known officially as the "Warsaw Treaty of Friendship, Cooperation and Mutual Assistance"—the "Warsaw Treaty Organization" (WTO) for short, though in the West it became known as the *Warsaw Pact*—was born of several different Soviet objectives. Although the Soviet Union already closely controlled the militaries of its puppet regimes in Eastern Europe through "advisors," Khrushchev wanted to create a more formal structure that could better coordinate Soviet Bloc military actions. Officially, the alliance was created in response to West Germany's induction into NATO only days earlier. However, the Pact also assured the loyal regimes in the region of Moscow's commitment to keeping its imperial dependents in power and served as a convenient strawman for Moscow; the Soviets could masquerade as the peace party by repeatedly offering to disband the Warsaw Pact if Western Europe would in turn abandon NATO.

USELESS TRIVIA: KEEP YOUR FRIENDS CLOSE, AND YOUR ENEMIES CLOSER

On April 24, 1974 West German intelligence officers burst into Günter Guillaume's residence and arrested him for being an East German spy. Guillaume reportedly blurted out that he was an officer in both the East German *Volksarmee* (People's Army) and *Stasi* (East German KGB), and expected proper treatment as such—to his teenage son's astonishment. A native of East Germany, Guillaume had been planted in the West by the Stasi to embed himself in the West German political apparatus, and through his friendship with West German Chancellor Willy Brandt, had succeeded beyond the Stasi's wildest dreams. As a secretary and close friend of Brandt's, Guillaume had access to some of NATO's top secrets as well as communications between Bonn and Washington, which he passed on to the Stasi.

Despite having won a Nobel Peace Prize for easing tensions between West Germany and Eastern Europe with his *Ostpolitik*, Chancellor Brandt was forced by the Guillaume scandal to resign on May 5, 1974, as the highest levels of his administration had been penetrated by the Stasi. East German spy chief Markus Wolf later claimed that the Guillaume affair had actually been a major screw-up on the Stasi's part, because Brandt's policies had been helpful to East Germany and the Stasi did not want to disrupt his political career, and that Guillaume's carelessness undermined his achievements. However, Stasi files indicated that the East German leadership feared Brandt's charm offensive might lull Moscow into acquiescing to German reunification—which would mean certain doom for East Germany and its communist leadership.[32]

The Warsaw Pact started out almost immediately with crises in Poland and Hungary in October and November 1956. After Hungary was resubjugated, the Pact was greatly shaken a few years later, when in October 1962 Khrushchev—recklessly, in the opinion of several Soviet Bloc leaders—gambled with the missiles in Cuba, nearly dragging Moscow's Warsaw Pact allies into an unnecessary war.

Infuriated, the Eastern European puppets began demanding that Moscow allow greater discussion in the Pact, in effect making the Warsaw Pact a *real* alliance rather than just a Soviet control mechanism. The Soviets never fully relinquished control but from the mid-1960s on, the Eastern European states began to have greater voices in the Pact. Its overall strategic direction was still firmly in Moscow's hands, however, and beginning in 1961, the Soviets upgraded Stalin's defensive policies. Stalin assumed that war with the capitalist West was inevitable and so he built as large a massive empire to deflect that war from the Soviet Motherland, but in 1961 Khrushchev—still anticipating war with the West—decided to go Stalin one further and pre-emptively invade Western Europe first. This became the main battle plan for the Warsaw Pact and remained so until 1990; at the slightest hint of trouble, invade Western Europe and overrun it before the Americans can react effectively.

By the late 1960s, the Warsaw Pact had developed into a sort of military commonwealth, designed as much to keep the deeply unpopular communist regimes in power as to defend Soviet interests against the proverbial Western aggression. When Alexander Dubček began to build a more democratic model of communism in Czechoslovakia, it was the frightened Polish and East German regimes that urged a hesitant Brezhnev to lead a Warsaw Pact invasion of that country in August 1968 to suppress the "Prague Spring." Though successful, the invasion of Czechoslovakia led to disruption in the Pact, as Albania left the alliance and Romania openly denounced the intervention.

These events were only symptoms of other internal issues, however. The Six Day War in the Middle East in June 1967 caused panic in Moscow and the satellite capitals as over six days' time, the outnumbered Israeli forces—armed with a hodgepodge of mostly outdated Western equipment—managed to inflict decisive defeat on five Arab armies and air forces, several of them armed and trained very much like Soviet Bloc forces. How might the Warsaw Pact fare against a better armed and trained NATO?

A further problem within the Pact was the surprising candor with which Moscow acknowledged that in a war with the West, NATO would likely use nuclear weapons in Central Europe to counter huge Warsaw Pact advantages in ground forces. The Soviets' open willingness to sacrifice parts of Eastern Europe in a war unnerved even Moscow's strongest allies in the region.

Another challenge vexing Moscow was tied to its core strategy of the Warsaw Pact invading Western Europe in the event of a crisis with the West; the Soviets had assigned each Pact military a role in that invasion, but just how reliable were the Pact's conscript armies? Worse, the Soviet satellite armies struggled to keep up with Western technology.

Figure 63. A Divided Europe: NATO vs. the Warsaw Pact in 1980

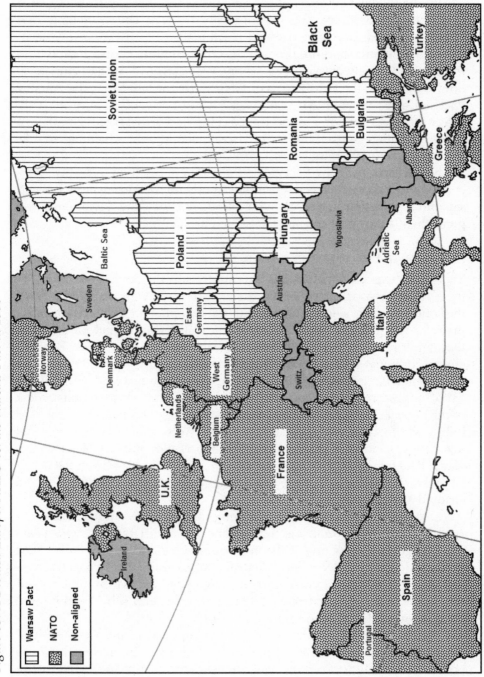

By the Gorbachev years of the late 1980s, the Warsaw Pact had crystalized into two camps: the reform-inclined Soviet Union, Poland, and Hungary on one side, and stalwart reactionaries East Germany, Czechoslovakia, Romania, and Bulgaria on the other. Military cooperation within the Pact had largely disappeared, having crumbled over disagreements on how to deal with the Polish crisis of 1980–81. By the late 1980s, the Warsaw Pact had, according to NATO estimates,[33] a 3-to-1 advantage over NATO in heavy tanks, 3.1 million ground troops compared to NATO's 2.2 million, a 2-to-1 advantage in front line strike aircraft, and a slight advantage in submarines armed with missiles and torpedoes.

By 1989, the Warsaw Pact existed more on paper than in reality, however, and served merely as a consultative body for the increasingly isolated satellite regimes. In July 1991, with its *raison d'être*—the Soviet empire—gone, the Warsaw Pact officially dissolved itself.

C. Yugoslavia: Exit, Stage Left

Yugoslavia was unusual among the countries in the Soviet realm in 1944 for a couple reasons. First of all, there were no Soviet forces occupying the country at war's end. Indeed, with the exception of Belgrade, the Germans had largely abandoned Yugoslavia to the communist partisans as they withdrew from the Balkans. Secondly, Yugoslavia nonetheless still embraced Soviet-style communism on its own. The communist partisans were somewhat popular as liberators and the communist leader, Josip Broz "Tito," was seen as a dashing war hero and charismatic leader, unlike most of the other Eastern European communist leaders who had spent the war hiding in Moscow. With pressure from the West, there were some initial democratic window-dressing measures such as allowing Ivan Šubašić (EE-van SHOO-bah-sheetch) into the government in June 1944 (from the royalist prewar leadership), but the heavily rigged elections of November 1945 ensured a communist victory.

Later in the Cold War, many Westerners came to see Yugoslavia as the "good" communist country, as the humane one, but in its first several years Tito's Yugoslavia was one of the most oppressive and fanatic Soviet Bloc states. Indeed, the OZNA (early Yugoslav KGB) immediately began arresting any anticommunist enemies, real or imagined, so that by 1947 tens of thousands of Yugoslav citizens had been arrested, and some even imprisoned in former Ustaša concentration camps.

The Stalinist state terror started early in Yugoslavia, and like the Soviet Union in the 1930s, it was all-pervasive. But Tito's aggressiveness was not just internally focused; he sent Yugoslav forces into southern Austria in 1945 to claim *Kärnten* (Carinthia) province (with its Slovene minority) for Yugoslavia, withdrawing only in the face of blunt British (and Soviet) opposition. Tito also seized the Italian cities of Fiume and Trieste in April 1945, evacuating them only after Stalin bowed to Western protests.[34] He also tried to incorporate Albania into the Yugoslav federation, and vigorously supported the Greek communist rebels in their uprising against the British-supported government in Athens. Tito's forces twice shot down American planes overflying Yugoslav territory in 1946, to Stalin's fury and horror.

USELESS TRIVIA:
EXACTLY WHOSE SIDE ARE YOU ON, PART II?

Milovan Djilas (MEE-lo-vahn JEE-lahss) was born in Montenegro in 1911, and went to Belgrade University in the early 1930s, where he became a communist activist. During World War II, he joined Tito's underground communist resistance, and saw active fighting while also helping to write and distribute the communist newpaper, *Borba* (The Battle). He finished the war a member of the Yugoslav communist party central committee, serving as the liaison between Tito and Stalin in 1944 and again in 1948. Djilas became vice president, second only to Tito in the postwar government.

Djilas was in charge of propaganda and founded several new periodicals, while also publishing his own articles. By the early 1950s, however, Djilas became disillusioned with Tito's Yugoslavia and began to publish critical articles, culminating in his 1955 book, *The New Class and an Analysis of the Communist System* (*Нова класа и анализа комунистичког система*). Djilas condemned the existing communist states of the Soviet Union and Eastern Europe—including Yugoslavia—for simply replacing one set of privileged elite ruling classes with another, while perpetuating social and economic inequalities via police states even more corrupt and oppressive than the ones they'd replaced.

This book earned Djilas a long prison sentence but he continued to write in prison, publishing several more books that kept him in prison much of his adult life. Though he became a hero to Eastern European dissidents and Western anticommunist intellectuals, he remained a committed communist. He died peacefully in his native Montenegro in 1995, mourning the death of his beloved Yugoslavia.

In August 1947 Tito signed the Bled[35] Agreement with Bulgaria's Georgi Dimitrov, uniting the two countries in a Balkan federation. Initially, Stalin supported the idea but then his usual paranoia kicked in and he squelched it and scolded both leaders, creating the first public cracks in the Yugoslav-Soviet relationship. Tito learned that Moscow did not want brotherly communist states in Eastern Europe, only obedient puppets. Stalin reacted strongly again a year later when Tito complained about the behavior of Soviet forces liberating Belgrade in 1944, as they had committed widespread looting and raping. Tito also discovered that the Soviets had infiltrated the highest levels of the Yugoslav government and army with NKVD spies. The breaking point came when Tito disobeyed Stalin's orders to stop supporting the Greek communist rebels; in March 1948 the Soviets pulled their technical advisors out of Yugoslavia. Then, at the June 1948 Cominform meeting in Bucharest—which the Yugoslavs boycotted— the Soviets officially labelled Tito a heretic and booted Yugoslavia from the club.

The loyal Soviet Bloc states blockaded their borders with Yugoslavia, extending the Iron Curtain. For any other communist leader in Eastern Europe, such condemnation from Stalin would have been the kiss of death, but Tito was popular enough in Yugoslavia to survive the crisis, and he purged Yugoslavia of pro-Moscow communists. Stalin's paranoid handling of Yugoslavia had created a disaster for the Soviet Union in the form of an independent and alternative vision of communism outside of Moscow's control. Indeed, Tito loudly proclaimed in the world press that Stalin and the USSR were merely red imperialists.

After Stalin's death, Tito began to warm up to the Soviet Union again—he urged Khrushchev to crush the Hungarian Revolution in 1956—and in general relations between Moscow and Belgrade normalized. However, Tito had no intention of resubmitting to Soviet overlordship, and in September 1961 he hosted in Belgrade a summit attended by the leaders of India, Egypt, Indonesia, and Ghana for a movement started by India's Jawaharlal Nehru in the mid-1950s called the Non-Aligned Movement, which sought to create an alternative to either the American or Soviet sides in the Cold War. Tito also built up the Yugoslav army to be the world's fourth largest in the 1960s, after the Soviet, American, and British armies, and the Yugoslav army trained vigorously in anticipation of a Soviet invasion.

For all the talk of a third way, however, Tito was a committed communist and Yugoslavia was a dictatorship with all the usual trappings. Tito's Yugoslavia was generally less oppressive than its Soviet Bloc neighbors, and by opening its borders to the West it attracted enough investment and tourists to prop up the straightjacketed economy. In the 1970s and 80s, Yugoslav citizens enjoyed a higher standard of living than neighboring Soviet Bloc states (though still significantly lower than Western Europe's), making Yugoslavia a crucial stop on the Eastern European black market circuit. Still, this just masked a decrepit, corrupt, and often brutal police state whose economy was mired in bureaucratic malaise.

The country itself was reorganized along federal lines, with five republics: Serbia, Croatia, Slovenia, Bosnia-Herzegovina, and Macedonia. Each republic was equal, ending Serbian dominance of the country but also suppressing all ethnic expression. With a resurgence in regional nationalism (and even some terrorism) in the 1970s, particularly in Croatia, Tito responded with increasing brutality to any regional or national expression at home. He also allegedly targeted antiregime Croatian dissidents living abroad in the West for assassination.[36] When he died in 1980, it was only a matter of time before opportunists like Slobodan Milošević and Franjo Tudjman came to power, destabilizing the delicate balance that had held Yugoslavia together and leading to the fratricidical wars of the 1990s.

D. Albania as an Island

Item number one on Albania's postwar agenda was its very existence. Like neighbor Yugoslavia, Albania had no Soviet or foreign troops occupying it at war's end but its largest resistance group during the war, the communists led by Enver Hoxha (EN-vair HOEDZH-ah), were tied to Tito's Yugoslav partisans. Tito wanted to annex Albania, an idea that Stalin initially went along with until relations soured between Moscow and Belgrade in 1946–48. Stalin then supported Albanian independence. By 1947, Hoxha managed to consolidate his power and purge pro-Yugoslav rivals. The borders with Greece and Yugoslavia were heavily fortified, and Soviet naval bases were built on the country's Adriatic coast.

Hoxha's dictatorship was predictably a brutal and oppressive one, with unknown thousands imprisoned or executed—in a country with a population of barely over a million in 1950. So severely underdeveloped was Albania in 1947, however, a society still organized largely on tribal principals, that just about any development was an improvement. Hoxha began an extensive modernization program that built paved roads, schools, hospitals, utilities, and emphasized self-reliance as Hoxha modernized the country's medieval agricultural system. Indeed, Albania was the only country in Eastern Europe to consistently see its living standard rise throughout the entire period of the Cold War, though when the communists fell from power in 1990, Albania was still easily the poorest country in Europe.

USELESS TRIVIA: A BAD START

In 1947, U.S. president Truman declared the Truman Doctrine, pledging active U.S. support for any peoples resisting communist aggression. This in effect committed the U.S. to a policy of containing the Soviet Union like a contagious disease. In 1947, however, American policy-makers jumped at a British proposal to try an experiment on communist Albania, attempting to overthrow the communists.

Operation Valuable, as the British called it—Operation Fiend to the Americans—recruited and trained Albanian refugees living in camps in Italy and Greece as paramilitaries to be inserted covertly into Albania to foment an anticommunist uprising. Why Albania? It was easily accessible for the Anglo-Americans, just across the Adriatic from Italy, but more importantly Albania was geographically isolated, surrounded by rival Yugoslavia to the north and east, and pro-Western Greece to the south. Recruitment began immediately among many different exiled Albanian political groups.

In 1947–52, some 300 Albanian commandos were trained and infiltrated into Albania—and almost all of them were captured or killed, with only a handful successfully escaping to Greece. The captured commandos were put on public trials in Tiranë and executed. For years, Washington and London wondered what went wrong, with subsequent reviews focusing on the competence of the British and American secret service personnel who designed the operation. However, as embittered Albanian survivors of the operation long suspected, it was revealed years later that the liaison between the British SIS and American CIA, a British agent named Kim Philby, was in fact a Soviet spy who kept Moscow informed about the operation. With each insertion, Albanian communist forces were ready and waiting.

When Stalin died in 1953, Hoxha became increasingly disturbed by Khrushchev's anti-Stalinist reforms. Albania joined the Warsaw Pact when it was formed in 1955, but Hoxha was worried whether the Pact would really protect Albania from a Yugoslav invasion, and indeed Khrushchev's charm offensive in Belgrade in the mid-1950s sent chills down Hoxha's spine. Khrushchev's anti-Stalinist rhetoric rankled the Albanian communists but Soviet plans to defer Albanian industrialization in favor of turning the country into an agricultural export economy for the Warsaw Pact proved the last straw.

In 1960 Albania sided openly with China against the Soviets as Sino-Soviet relations collapsed into open argument at a global communist conference in Moscow attended by eighty-one communist parties from around the world. Khrushchev withdrew Soviet advisors from Albania, halted aid shipments, and abandoned the Soviet naval bases on the Albanian coast.

Ironically, erstwhile enemy Yugoslavia became a benefit for Hoxha as it insulated Albania from any direct Soviet military intervention. Khrushchev did try to foment revolt in Albania against Hoxha, but Hoxha unleashed the *Sigurimit të Shtetit* (Albanian KGB, the *Sigurimi*) on pro-Moscow communists. Meanwhile, China stepped in to fill the economic void left by the Soviets, and Chinese advisors flooded the country.

Hoxha admired Mao and he happily followed his new mentor's lead when Mao launched the Cultural Revolution in 1966. Hoxha unleashed a massive Maoist wave of repression in 1967, closing all churches, mosques, or synagogues in a bid to create the world's first fully atheist state, banning any public or private religious expression and even beards for Muslims. Military ranks were abolished, intellecuals and teachers were arrested and sent to remote rural farms as forced labor, and remaining clan chiefs—crucial to the Albanian resistance movements of the late-19th and early-20th centuries—were arrested, imprisoned, or executed.

Albania became the ultimate closed state, with no official contact with either the United States or the Soviet Union, and virtually no cultural or economic contact with the rest of Europe. Private citizens were allowed only limited access to telephones and radios. Hoxha built half a million bunkers and gun emplacements all along Albania's borders and coastline, and numbers were taken off all houses and buildings to confuse any would-be invaders. When Brezhnev invaded Czechoslovakia in 1968, Albania officially left the Warsaw Pact.

When Mao died in 1976 and was succeeded by the reformer Deng Xiaopeng, Hoxha cut all ties with China and expelled the Chinese advisors, completely isolating Albania from the outside world. About this time Amnesty International described Albania's human rights record as possibly the worst in the world. Like Stalin, Hoxha became hyperparanoid in his waning years, launching a series of deadly purges in the early 1980s among even his most loyal communist colleagues.

Just as the bloodbath was reaching its height, however, Hoxha's health began to fail and he turned the reins of government over to a long-time loyalist, Ramiz Alia (RAH-meez AH-lee-yah). Hoxha died in 1985. Oddly enough, just before his death Hoxha uncharacteristically made a public speech calling for Kosovo's "reunification" with Albania. In any event, few could guess when Alia took over in 1985 that this colorless communist bureaucrat would lead Albania out of its self-imposed darkness to embrace the outside world.

E. Bulgaria Finally Gets Something in Return

The communists faced some unusual challenges in Bulgaria. On the surface, Bulgaria looked slam-dunk for them; its population was traditionally pro-Russian, there was a strong history of leftist politics in the country, and the conservative ruling elites had thoroughly discredited themselves in the war. To boot, Bulgaria did not have strong ties to the West—well, besides Germany, and in 1945 that didn't count for much.

However, for all that, Bulgaria stumped the Soviets. Late in the war an effective and popular underground opposition had developed that would easily cream the communists in elections. Secondly, thanks to the Ottoman Turks, Bulgaria had no native reactionary nobility or aristocracy, and unlike in Poland, Hungary, or Romania, rural land was already distributed relatively fairly in Bulgaria so that the peasantry—the bulk of Bulgaria's population—were satisfied. The communists' problem in Bulgaria was that Bulgarians were too content, with little interest in revolutionary change.

Of course, the communists had a trump card in the form of the Soviet army that occupied Bulgaria in 1945. Immediately the communists, using the Soviet army and NKVD, began to terrorize the Bulgarian population into submission, and the country was racked with arrests, executions, and absurd conspiracies. In the decade of the rightwing authoritarian regime in the country, the pro-Hitler government had managed to murder some 5,632 political prisoners, and during the war another 357 Bulgarians were executed for political activities, but in just 1945–48 the communists in Bulgaria managed to murder 30,000-40,000 Bulgarians.[37]

The surviving wartime opposition, led by the brave Nikola Petkov, tried to slow down the Sovietization of the country by astutely using every legal technicality from the inter-Allied agreements at Yalta and Potsdam to shine an international light on the illegality of the communists' activities. Petkov did catch the Western Allies' attention, and they consequently used what little leverage they had in Soviet-occupied Bulgaria to press Moscow successfully on elections and other issues.

Unfortunately, the Paris Peace Treaty[38] in 1947 that formally ended World War II between the Allies and Bulgaria also brought an end to the last shreds of Western influence in the country, and with it, the last charade of Soviet tolerance for any opposition:

On June 4, the United States Senate ratified the treaty, on June 5, Petkov was arrested; on September 20 the peace treaty came into force, on September 23 Petkov was executed.[39]

The Sovietization of Bulgaria was led by Georgi Dimitrov, a longtime communist and former head of the Comintern who had spent the war in Moscow at Stalin's side. Dimitrov was a committed Stalinist who had no trouble terrorizing his native land into servile obedience, ignoring international pleas for Petkov's life. Dimitrov signed the Bled Agreement with Tito in August 1947 and even bragged to the press that soon Bulgaria, Yugoslavia, Albania, Romania, and even Greece would be united into a communist Balkan federation.

However, whereas Tito reacted with indignation when Stalin intervened and publicly reprimanded Tito and Dimitrov, Dimitrov obediently reversed himself and blamed Western agents for the whole affair. A year later, as Tito broke from Stalin's grip, Moscow further tightened its hold on Bulgaria. Dimitrov died suddenly during a trip to Moscow in July 1949—leading to rumors that he was murdered by Stalin—and was eventually succeeded by Vulko Chervenkov, another Stalinist in Dimitrov's mold. Chervenkov continued to terrorize Bulgaria, and indeed the Bulgarian gulags bulged with slave labor in the early 1950s. Chervenkov was booted out of the leadership shortly after Stalin's death in 1953, and eventually replaced by Todor Zhivkov.

Zhivkov was a mixed bag for Bulgaria. On the one hand, he was a dictator, a committed communist who was slovenly loyal to Moscow. Indeed, in the late 1960s Zhivkov even offered for Bulgaria to be willingly absorbed into the Soviet Union, an offer Moscow politely declined. His loyalty to Moscow isolated Bulgaria, with enemies Turkey, Greece, and Yugoslavia, coupled with renegade Ceauşescu's Romania, leaving Zhivkov's Bulgaria a neo-Stalinist island.

Still, for all his unwavering faithfulness to Moscow, Zhivkov was not quite the monster that Dimitrov and Chervenkov had been; while there were still political prisoners, he quietly closed down the infamous Lovech and Skravena gulag slave labor colonies, and soft-pedalled the Stalinist-era collectivization campaigns. He also, perhaps through his lap dog–like loyalty, managed to squeeze considerable economic largess out of the Soviet Union, to the extent that Bulgaria was able to develop substantial economic infrastructure during the 1960s and 70s, almost all of it bankrolled by Moscow. No other satellite received proportionately as much Soviet aid. This was no mean feat. Bulgaria had suffered relatively little during the war, but postwar communist policies had been ruinous, causing a huge drop in already low Bulgarian living standards. Zhivkov's milking of the Soviet cash cow helped considerably improve living conditions for Bulgarians.

USELESS TRIVIA: BUT IT'S NOT RAINING . . .

Georgi Markov was running a bit late. He darted up a flight of steps at Waterloo Bridge to catch a bus across the bridge to Bush House in London, world headquarters for the BBC, where Markov worked. As he reached the top of the stairs he felt a sharp stinging pain in his right thigh, and he turned to see a heavy-set man in his forties picking up an umbrella. The man apologized with a foreign accent, and hurried to catch a taxi. Markov boarded the bus and went to work though the stinging sensation grew into a throbbing pain. That evening at home Markov developed a high fever, and was rushed to a local hospital accompanied by his wife and a colleague from the BBC. The initial diagnosis was blood poisoning, but he did not respond to any treatments. The next day Markov went into shock, and after a few more agonizing days, on September 11, 1978, Georgi Markov died.

Georgi Markov was born in Sofia, Bulgaria in 1929, and became a prominent writer and playwright in his homeland. However, Markov had become disenchanted with the corruption and brutality of the communist regime, so he defected to the West in June 1969 and shortly thereafter began covering Bulgarian affairs as a journalist for the BBC, Deutsche Welle, and Radio Free Europe. He received over the next several years warnings from Sofia to shut up, but he refused. Learning of Markov's plans to write a book on Bulgaria's communists, Zhivkov in June 1977 gave the order to the DS (*държавна сигурност*; Bulgarian KGB) to "silence" Markov. With some technical assistance from the Soviet KGB, the operation was carried out successfully on Todor Zhivkov's birthday, September 7, 1978.

Markov's death was front-page news in London and around the world, and an autopsy turned up a tiny round metal pellet in the wound on Markov's thigh. British and American germ warfare specialists found two .34 mm holes in the pellet and traces of ricin, which is more deadly than rattlesnake venom and has no known antidote. Markov was declared a homicide victim. Just before the communists lost power in Bulgaria, however, the security forces destroyed all files on Markov and murdered the archivist. A handful of Soviet KGB defectors have acknowledged Moscow's role in the murder, but Russia still refuses to allow British investigators access to either the files or former agents. The nearly microscopic pellet is on display in Scotland Yard today. Thirty years later Scotland yard continues to actively investigate Markov's murder, now with cooperation from EU and NATO ally Bulgaria.[40]

There is a darker side to Zhivkov's reign, however, above and beyond his willingness to imprison or even kill dissidents; the anti-Turk campaigns of the 1980s. There were hints of what was to come in the 1970s, when Zhivkov began to allow discrimination against ethnic Turks in Bulgaria who did not "go native." In 1984, however, he openly mandated that all ethnic Turks must change their names to ethnically Bulgarian names, and the DS (*държавна сигурност*; Duhr-ZHAHV-nah SEE-goor-nost; Bulgarian KGB) began to actively attack Turks or encourage Bulgarians to do so.

As anti-Turk pogroms became more widespread, Zhivkov cynically opened the border with Turkey, effectively ethnically cleansing Bulgaria of some 300,000 Turks. Postcommunist Bulgaria has redemptively welcomed these victims back from Turkey and instated minority protection laws. Such were the circumstances by the late 1980s as an increasingly elderly and corrupt Zhivkov watched with bafflement as the communist regimes elsewhere in Eastern Europe creaked and teetered on the verge of doom, while Zhivkov struggled to understand Gorbachev and the need for reforms.

F. Romania Goes Off the Deep End

King Mihai's dramatic coup in August 1944 was an attempt to forestall Soviet influence in the country, and the king installed a pro-Western government in an effort to attract Western, particularly American sympathy for Romania's fate. Unfortunately, Soviet occupation forces trumped what little sympathy Washington could muster for faraway Romania, and in March 1945 the Soviets instead installed Dr. Petru Groza (PEH-troo GROW-zah) as prime minister. Groza—strictly speaking not a communist, but a politically astute opportunist—began the Sovietization of Romania. King Mihai fought Groza tooth and nail but since Groza had Stalin's blessing, the king's actions counted for little. The communists began the usual mass arrests, and under the pretense of war reparations, the Soviets began the looting of Romanian raw materials. The Soviets also seized back Bessarabia, making it the Moldavian Soviet Socialist Republic, though with Groza's appointment Romania gained back Northern Transylvania from Hungary. Romania's incorporation into the Soviet realm was completed in December 1947, when Groza forced the king to abdicate and flee into exile.

Groza remained in power officially until 1952—at which point he was "kicked upstairs" through an empty promotion—but in reality after 1947 he was eclipsed in terms of real power in the country by his foreign minister, Ana Pauker (AH-nah POW-ker). Pauker was a committed Stalinist and an early veteran of the tiny prewar Romanian communist party who had spent the war in Moscow, but she had two fatal flaws in Stalin's eyes: she was a *she*, and she was Jewish.

A long-time colleague in the party, Gheorghe Gheorghiu-Dej (Geh-ORG –eh Geh-ORG-yoo desh), conspired with Stalin to oust Pauker and other Jews from the Romanian communist party in 1952, and Gheorghiu-Dej emerged as the ruler. Gheorghiu-Dej continued such Stalinesque policies as the building of the *Canalul Dunăre—Marea Neagră* (Danube–Black Sea Canal) in the early 1950s,[41] but he wasn't a cookie-cutter Stalinist. He had a nationalist streak, and soon after Stalin's death he began distancing Romania from Moscow. Khrushchev rewarded Gheorghiu-Dej for his cooperation during the 1956 Hungarian Revolution by withdrawing Soviet troops from Romania, but this provided Gheorghiu-Dej with the breathing room to begin developing a more independent foreign policy, including opening Romania up to some limited Western economic aid and development.

USELESS TRIVIA: IS THIS THE WAY TO SAN JOSE?

On the morning of March 5, 1953—the day Stalin died, though that wouldn't be publicized for several more days—Lt. Franciszek Jarecki (Fran-CHEE-shek Yar-ETS-kee), a twenty-two-year-old star pilot in the Polish People's Republic air force, was gearing up for a training flight. Jarecki had attended Poland's top flight schools and was one of only a handful of Polish pilots allowed to fly the newest Soviet fighter aircraft, the Mig-15. On this morning, Jarecki took off with his squadron from his base on the Baltic and began training exercises. Suddenly, Jarecki's plane broke formation and bolted due north; his colleagues set after him in attack formation. Within ten minutes he was over his destination, however, and landed at Rønne airport on Bornholm Island in the northern Baltic, on Danish territory. Lt. Jarecki was defecting, and what's more, he was giving the West its first up-close look at a Mig-15.

The Cold War inspired some on both sides to forsake their own countries and defect to the other side. Some did so out of political or ideological conviction, some for money, others for personal reasons. At the end of the Korean War twenty-two American POWs refused to return to the U.S., while turncoat intelligence agents like Kim Philby did great damage to the West. However, overall the democratic and prosperous West had a huge advantage in attracting enemy defectors. Eastern Europeans felt little loyalty to the Soviet puppet regimes ruling their countries and they defected in droves, by the hundreds of thousands, in fact. These Eastern European defectors provided valuable intelligence on Soviet weapons, training, plans, and economic conditions, and very often at great personal risk to themselves and their families.

When Gheorghiu-Dej died in March 1965, he was replaced by a younger and less-known colleague who would become one of Eastern Europe's legendary monsters: Nicolae Ceauşescu (Nee-KO-lye Chay-oo-SHESS-koo). At first, Ceauşescu eased oppression a bit, and continued Gheorghiu-Dej's policy of independence from Moscow, making him quite popular at home. This was most dramatically shown in 1968 when Ceauşescu refused to participate in the Warsaw Pact invasion of Czechoslovakia, and went so far as to publically condemn it. Why didn't Moscow rein in Ceauşescu? Indeed, Vladimir Rezun, a Soviet military intelligence analyst who defected to the West in the 1970s, reported in his book *Inside the Soviet Army*[42] that while preparing for the August 1968 invasion of Czechoslovakia, many Soviet soldiers, not briefed on their mission yet, assumed they were on their way to crush Ceauşescu's insolent Romania, not Dubček's Czechoslovakia. However, for all his annoying bluster, Ceauşescu remained essentially loyal to Moscow and there was no danger of the Soviet system falling in Ceauşescu's Romania. Moscow feared that Dubček's reforms might ultimately lead Czechoslovakia out of the Soviet orbit, however, and in any case unlike Romania, Czechoslovakia bordered the West.

Ceauşescu was mistakenly viewed by the West in the 1970s as a second Tito who was breaking from Moscow, and he was rewarded with presidential visits from Richard Nixon, Gerald Ford, and Jimmy Carter, as well as a hefty credit line from Western banks. In reality, however, Ceauşescu was actually retrenching Stalinism in Romania. He visited North Korea and China in 1971 and came back with stars in his eyes, stars that did not bode well for his countrymen. One result was Ceauşescu's program of *Sistematizarea* (Systematization), which led to the destruction of traditional and historic towns across the country and replacing them with antlike Stalinist concrete-slab building block hives whose grid layout was designed for maximum crowd control.

West Germany and even communist Hungary howled about the destruction of historic German and Hungarian towns in Transylvania, but Romania's own beautiful historical architectural treasures were not spared either, particularly in Moldavia. Worse, Ceauşescu came up with a plan to boost the country's population from 23 million to 30 million by the year 2000 by outlawing abortions, banning all forms of contraception, and leveling a tax on women who did not have children, up to 10% of their monthly salaries.

The *Securitate* (Romanian KGB) routinely harassed childless women. This *did* result initially in a bumper crop of Romanian children, but often their families could not afford them, and without adequate healthcare infrastructure, hundreds of thousands of Romanian children were abandoned to state orphanages where they were often severely underfed, underclothed, diseased, not provided with even the most rudimentary education, and frequently subjected to abuse from underpaid and under-trained staff.

Postcommunist Romania immediately repealed these barbaric laws, and major improvements have since been made.[43]

As for the easy credit from Western banks, that came to haunt Roma-nians. Ceaușescu piled up some $13 billion (USD) in debt by the late 1970s, and so he took drastic action; he banned any further borrowing and then focused the economy almost exclusively on repaying the debts. Romania's entire industrial and consumer output was exported abroad for Western "hard" currency while oil, gas, and food were severely rationed, electricity was cut to a few hours each day, and many basic commodities such as milk, soap, and gasoline became available only on the black market. Food and department stores stood empty.

Romania's living standard plummeted in the 1980s, while Ceaușescu himself and his family lived in ridiculously opulent luxury that would have embarrassed France's Louis XIV. Romania's foreign debt was paid off by the summer of 1989, but the extreme poverty and oppression had come with a price. In November 1987, some 30,000 workers at a tractor factory in Brașov (BRAH-shoff) exploded into protests and stormed the offices of the city's mayor and the local communist party, both of which as they discovered were well-stocked with meats, cheeses, and choco-lates, all unavailable to ordinary Romanians. The *Securitate* (Romanian KGB) and army suppressed this uprising but oppression only works for so long: as 1989 drew to a close in Romania, few in the country or outside of it understood how close this artificially impoverished and terrorized nation was to revolution.

G. Hungary and Its Food-Based Ideologies

From the Soviet perspective, Central Europe was more complicated than the Balkans; it bordered the West directly, had strong cultural ties to the West, and it had political and cultural institutions that more closely resem-bled the West's. For these reasons, Poland, East Germany, Czechoslovakia, and Hungary were handled differently by Moscow than the Balkan states. As a defeated Axis country, Hungary had the Trianon borders[44] reimposed and an Allied Control Commission ran its national affairs, but its fate was ultimately defined by Soviet interests, even if initially they were soft-ped-alled to allay Western fears.

Like in Poland, the Soviets installed a communist-dominated pro-visional government in the first major Hungarian city they captured,

Debrecen (DEH-breh-tsen), but after Budapest was taken a more balanced provisional government was established that was more acceptable to the Western powers. Relatively free elections were held in November 1945 that stunned the Hungarian communists with their poor showing, and revealed to them that their primary enemy was the popular peasant-oriented *Független Kisgazdapárt* (Independent Smallholders' Party). A coalition government was formed including members of all the major parties but, ominously, Soviet ACC representative Kliment Voroshilov gave control of the Interior (i.e., the police) and Defense (the army) ministries to the communists. The communists spent the next year quietly penetrating other leftist parties, until with the signing of the Paris Peace Treaty in 1947, the communists felt secure enough to stage a coup and begin arresting members of the Independent Smallholders Party (as well as other centrist or right-leaning parties).

In what future communist dictator Mátyás Rákosi[45] (MAH-tyosh RAH-ko-shee) most famously described as *szalámi taktika* (salami tactics), slicing away the opposition one by one, the communists forced all other left-wing parties into a (communist-controlled) umbrella party called the *Magyar Dolgozók Pártja* (Hungarian Workers' Party), which won rigged elections later that same year. By 1948 the communists jettisoned their fellow left-wing coalition members, and many Social Democrats found themselves with unplanned Siberian vacations. On August 19, 1949 Hungary was proclaimed a People's Republic (*Magyar Népköztársaság*), and the Sovietization of Hungary began.

Hungary's first phase of Sovietization coincided with a particularly nasty spasm of Stalin's paranoia that resulted in a wave of purges across Eastern Europe, inspired by Stalin's failures with both the West and Yugoslavia. Mass arrests and show trials reminiscent of the late 1930s Great Purges swept the Soviet Bloc, each carefully scripted by Moscow and directed by local Soviet "advisors." A gulag system was created, the worst camp being at Recsk (Rechk) in northeastern Hungary. Thousands of innocent people, including loyal communists, suddenly found themselves imprisoned or worse on ridiculous trumped-up charges. The highest profile casualty was László Rajk (LAHSS-lo Rike), the communist interior minister, who was arrested in May 1949 and accused of being a spy for Tito, former Horthyists, and the West. After severe torture he confessed, was found guilty and quickly executed. As the former interior minister and head of the savage ÁVO,[46] Rajk was little missed, but his kangaroo trial and execution would come back to haunt the Stalinists just a few years later.

USELESS TRIVIA: IS BUDAPEST BURNING?

On the night of July 4, 1954, crowds poured into Budapest's streets. The anger and defiance in the air was palpable, and in short order rioting broke out; cars were burning, storefronts were smashed, and angry mobs stalked Pest shouting slogans of betrayal and injustice. The government considered calling in the army, but could a conscript force be trusted? Should Soviet forces be called in? What had provoked this outpouring of outrage in the capital of the Hungarian People's Republic in 1954?

A small black and white ball. Life in Stalinist Hungary was grim, but one of the few outlets in which Hungarians could find fulfillment was sports—and that meant soccer. In the early 1950s Hungary had the *Aranycsapat* (Golden Team), a crack soccer team full of all-stars who plowed through the 1952 Olympics and then piled up victory after victory across Europe, so that by the time of the 1954 FIFA World Cup in Bern, Switzerland, Hungary was heavily favored to win. Indeed, the Hungarians dominated the first half against West Germany, but some injuries and two questionable referee calls later, the Germans won 3-2 in what is called today *Das Wunder von Bern* (The Wonder of Bern).

The victory is said to have played a major role in the beginning of German healing from the guilt of the war and the foundation of a peaceful, democratic (West) German identity, but more than five decades later, the bitterness is still apparent in Hungarians who were alive at the time. Some historians have tried to draw lines between the loss of this last bastion of hope and the national explosion that nearly toppled the Hungarian communist regime two years later, in 1956. When the legendary Hungarian team player Ferenc Puskás (FAIR-ents POOSH-kosh) died in 2006, he was given a state funeral with military honors attended by thousands. He was buried in St. Stephen's Basilica, which houses a holy relic from Hungary's first Christian king. Meanwhile, the city of Szeged (SEH-ged) hosts a monument to the Aranycsapat.

That wasn't a problem yet in 1949, however, and Rákosi set out terrorizing the country into submission, imprisoning some 100,000 Hungarians and forcing collectivization on the countryside. Rákosi was a particularly bad ruler, even by communist standards, and in short order Hungarian living standards deteriorated while the economy tanked. Extensive food rationing and an oppressive police state combined to make early 1950s Hungary a living hell, worse than the war years. Stalin's death and the Berlin Uprising in 1953 spooked the Soviets, so Rákosi was summoned to Moscow and removed from power, replaced by the more gregarious and popular—if somewhat naïve—Imre Nagy (EEM-reh NAWDGE). Nagy was a dedicated communist and an expert on agriculture who had been purged from the Party in 1949. He decried Rákosi's police state and mishandling of the economy, and set out to reform both. Rákosi bided his time however and played the unfolding power struggle in post-Stalinist Moscow well, and managed to oust Nagy in 1955 and get himself reinstated. This was a mistake on Moscow's part. The Soviets had apparently forgotten just how unpopular Rákosi had been, and why. Within months Rákosi pushed the country to the boiling point again. Even the Soviet Politburo could sense something wrong, so they ousted Rákosi again but retained Rákosi's Stalinist cohorts in power, a fatal error. The regime stumbled through 1956 trying to relieve the obvious building pressure in the country by allowing increasingly open discussion about the regime's failures, even admitting that the purges of 1949–52 had been falsified— reburying László Rajk in a lavish state funeral in early October 1956—but all for naught.

A couple of weeks later, on October 23, just as a heated Polish-Soviet confrontation seemed to be resolving peacefully, a crowd of some 200,000 Hungarians demonstrating in Budapest in support of the Poles soon issued their own demands for reform and the return of Nagy. However, agents of the ÁVH[47] opened fire on the crowd, kicking off the Hungarian Revolution. The enraged demonstrators attacked the *Magyar Rádió* (Hungarian Radio) station and a statue of Stalin, while street fighting erupted throughout the city. Soviet forces near Budapest were summoned but within days the whole country was swept up in revolution, with communist party buildings and ÁVH offices ransacked and burned. Hungarian flags with the communist emblem torn from the center became a symbol of the revolution. The Stalinists handed the government over to Imre Nagy and fled, and after several days of street battles, Soviet forces withdrew on October 30, leaving the revolutionaries in control of much of the country. Nagy, a committed communist, initially tried to rein in the crowds—at one point being booed when he addressed them as *Elvtársaim!* (Comrades!)—but he understood that bad governance, not counterrevolution, was the culprit.

Nagy created a new government with noncommunists, disbanded the hated ÁVH, and called for a multiparty system. Hungary was hoping for an Austrian solution and neutrality.[48] Ominously, a day earlier, Israel invaded Egypt's Sinai Peninsula.[49]

Khrushchev is known to have wavered in his consideration of how to deal with Hungary, but legend has it that he was convinced to crush the revolution by Chinese leader Mao Tse-tung, who reasoned that while the Poles were just anti-Russian, the Hungarians were truly anti-communist and needed to be dealt with. On November 1, the day Hungary withdrew from the Warsaw Pact, Soviet forces invaded the country although Moscow initially denied an invasion was underway. On November 3, the Soviets requested a meeting with revolutionary Hungary's top military leaders, and promptly arrested them.

The next day, on November 4, the Soviet Army attacked Budapest, and after days of Soviet tank assaults, artillery fire, and air raids, the revolutionary Hungarian forces finally folded on November 10, and Soviet control of Hungary was restored. One of the last rebel radio broadcasts famously pleaded simply "*Segítsetek! . . . Segítsetek! . . . Segítsetek!*" (SHEG-eet-cheh-tek; "Help us! Help us! Help us!") before going off the air forever. Nagy and his government fled to the Yugoslav embassy, but were tricked into leaving and were arrested. They were imprisoned in Romania for a year before being brought back secretly and tried, found guilty, and, in 1958, executed and buried in unmarked graves.

One of the rebel leaders wasn't arrested, however. János (John) Kádár (YAH-noesh KAH-dar) was a reform-minded communist in the 1950s and ally of Nagy's, but in the midst of the second Soviet invasion on November 1 he switched sides. Khrushchev installed Kádár as Nagy's replacement after the revolution, and predictably the ÁVH was allowed to wreak its revenge; tens of thousands were arrested and hundreds executed. The Hungarian army—which for the most part had sided with the rebels—was purged, and the Soviets built more military bases for an expanded presence in Hungary. However, despite his public rhetoric about counter-revolution, Kádár understood that the country had been pushed to the brink by bad government, and he made this statement in December 1961:

Aki nincs a Magyar Népköztársaság ellen, az vele van; aki nincs az MSzMP ellen, az vele van; és aki nincs a Népfront ellen, az vele van.

(Those who are not against the Hungarian People's Republic are with us; those who are not against the MSzMP [*Magyar Szocialista Munkáspárt*; Hungarian Socialist Workers Party] are with us, and those who are not against the People's Front [postrevolution government] are with us.)

The message was clear: don't criticize or undermine the regime, and we'll leave you alone. In what the West termed "Goulash Communism," Kádár relaxed many state controls and restrained the worst aspects of the police state, allowing Hungarians a degree of political freedom unknown elsewhere in the Soviet Bloc. He also increased the production of consumer goods in the country, and used both Soviet economic aid and, later, Western bank credits to improve the standard of living in the country to the extent that by the 1970s Hungarians enjoyed relative freedoms and a lifestyle enviable elsewhere in the communist world.

Mind you, Hungary was still a dictatorship and police state, loyal to Moscow—Hungary participated in the Warsaw Pact suppression of Dubček's Czechoslovakia in 1968—but Kádár's regime was less intrusive than other communist dictatorships in Eastern Europe, and though dissident groups existed in Hungary as elsewhere, Kádár—who ruled Hungary until 1988—never faced another revolutionary challenge like that of 1956, or like those that continuously shook Poland in the 1970s and 80s.

Still, this increased living standard was achieved artificially through foreign aid and loans, and when both ran out in the late 1970s the country's economy plunged. Hungarians saw their living standard gains begin to disappear as Hungary's economy was dragged down along with the rest of the Soviet empire. This is what ultimately led to Kádár's ouster in 1988 by a group of young reformers, and a series of amazing events shortly thereafter, involving some more food analogies.

H. Czechoslovakia, Just East of Eden

Czechoslovakia was supposed to be different. It had strong democratic traditions that resumed after the war. It did *not* have its neighbors' historical *Russophobia*, and indeed with memories of the Munich betrayal of 1938 fresh in their memories, Czechs and Slovaks—with a nostalgic tinge of Pan-Slavism—largely welcomed the idea of a Soviet alliance. The communist party in Czechoslovakia had some genuine support, and with the region's most industrialized economy, Czechoslovakia actually *had* a sizeable working class for socialists to get excited about. So what went wrong? The answer, once again, is to be found in one man's megalomania; Stalin did not trust the Czechoslovaks because for all their Russophilia, they had the deepest cultural and historical ties to the West in the region.

As soon as Czechoslovakia was liberated in 1945, the Czechoslovak government-in-exile, led by Edvard Beneš, returned home from London and resumed control. While favoring closer ties with the Soviets, Beneš had few illusions about Stalin and wanted to try to balance the country between Moscow and the West. The first postwar government included communists, with Beneš retaining the presidency but with the communist Klement Gottwald (CLEH-ment GOAT-valt) as prime minister. In early 1946, elections were held and the communists won a sizeable number of votes, and while not enough to form their own government, it was enough for them to grab the critical ministries—e.g., defense, interior, and finance—in the new coalition.

At a time when the rest of Eastern Europe was mired in medieval-style witch hunts for class enemies, Czechoslovakia remained an oasis of peace and democratic stability. Indeed, postwar Czechoslovakia became a prime refuge for those fleeing other Soviet Bloc states—including Tito's Yugoslavia. Unfortunately, Czechoslovakia was far too strategic for Moscow to contemplate "letting go," and in June 1947 Stalin took the occasion of the United States' Marshall Plan[50] to begin tightening Czechoslovakia's leash. Initially Stalin gave his blessing to Prague to accept the American invitation but two days later foreign minister Jan Masaryk (Yon Mah-SAH-rick), son of the founder of Czechoslovakia, was summoned to Moscow and ordered to refuse. Within weeks, arrests of opposition politicians and cultural leaders across the country began.

USELESS TRIVIA: WELCOME HOME! WELL, MAYBE NOT.

At slightly past 9:00 p.m. on June 13, 1948, an American-made Dakota DC-3 suddenly came to life on the grass of Kbely airfield in northeastern Prague, and it taxied down the runway in the darkness. As it lifted into the air, its pilot—Josef Bernát, and copilot Karel Šťastný (SHTAHST-nee)—contacted a stunned American airfield in Frankfurt, Germany that helped guide them out of Czechoslovakia and across Germany into France. They then contacted a British RAF airfield in Manston, on the southeastern tip of Britain, and arranged to land. Their fuel ran out over the English Channel but they amazingly nursed the engines to the British airfield, where an RAF officer awaited them.

Thus culminated a daring plan conceived by fifteen former Czechoslovak Free Air Force veterans of World War II to escape to Britain and seek asylum. The communists were consolidating power in their homeland and were hunting down and imprisoning veterans who had fought in the West during the war. Even a hero like Marshal Karel Janoušek (Yan-OW-shek) was arrested, stripped of his wartime honors[51] by the communists, and imprisoned. By May 1948 for instance, over a thousand Free Czech air and army veterans had fled across the border to the American zone of Germany. Marshal Janoušek died in abject poverty in 1971 in Prague, though his full honors were restored after 1989.

The communists then organized armed militias—in effect, brownshirts just like Hitler's in 1920s Weimar Germany—who went around throughout the autumn of 1947 attacking opposition leaders (those not yet arrested) and causing chaos. In early 1948, Stalin threatened to take matters into his own hands if "order was not restored," prompting exasperated noncommunist members of government to resign in February 1948, followed by Beneš in June. The noncommunist foreign minister, Jan Masaryk, was found dead below his open bedroom window, and Gottwald became president.

Czechoslovakia started down the road of Sovietization. Having gotten started later than neighboring satellite states, Gottwald only belatedly got around to the show-trial purges. In 1952 Rudolf Slánský, first secretary of the Czechoslovak communist party, was arrested. Just like Rajk in Hungary, Slánský was made to admit to a long list of incredible crimes before being executed in December 1952. Like a scene from a mafia movie, several of the purge victims were secretly cremated and their ashes poured into asphalt mix and used to pave some of the new roads being built outside Prague.

Most of the Soviet Bloc states underwent some form of de-Stalinization after Stalin died in 1953, but Czechoslovakia continued on with its brutal social and economic policies throughout the 1950s. The crises in neighboring Poland and Hungary in 1956 only stiffened the militant resolve of the Stalinists in Prague, and Czechoslovakia remained one of the most repressive regimes in 1950s Eastern Europe.

By 1963, however, as elsewhere Stalinism in Czechoslovakia had produced a bumper crop of economic failures and widespread social discontent. Something had to give. The regime in Prague began finally to include reformers in the government and back off from obviously failing policies. Czechoslovakia began to experience the first hints of liberalization.[52] Fearing they'd opened the proverbial can of worms, panicking Stalinists forced a showdown in October 1967 with liberal communists that they lost, and they were forced to give way to a young Slovak communist, Alexander Dubček (DOOB-chek).

At first Moscow supported Dubček's reforms, and with amazing speed nearly all censorship was lifted, freedom of expression and assembly were reaffirmed, the StB[53] was severely restrained, and talks of multiparty elections filled the air. Throughout the spring and summer of 1968, Czechoslovakia embarked on what Dubček called "national communism" or "communism with a human face," while a stunned world press referred to the "Prague Spring."

Dubček did caution against anti-Soviet or anticommunist rhetoric, but two decades of repression generated a torrent of public discussion across the country; the Soviets became increasingly concerned. In June, the Soviets decided to make that point apparent by holding Warsaw Pact exercises on Czechoslovak soil. Taking the hint, Dubček opened talks with Brezhnev in July 1968 and tried to assure Moscow that Czechoslovakia would remain loyal. But neither Brezhnev nor the nervous leaders in neighboring East

Germany or Poland were convinced. A couple of weeks later, a secret Warsaw Pact meeting decided Czechoslovakia's fate.

In the early morning hours of August 21, 1968 the armies of the Soviet Union, Poland, Hungary, East Germany,[54] and Bulgaria crossed the Czechoslovak border while Soviet paratroopers seized Prague airport. As soon as he learned the news, Dubček ordered both the Czechoslovak armed forces and all Czechoslovak citizens *not* to resist the invaders, knowing that resistance was indeed futile. Overall the invasion was successful, though Czechs and Slovaks managed to register their hatred of the occupiers through passive means; refusing to provide directions or provisions and painting swastikas on tanks. Dubček and his government were arrested and flown to Moscow, and while his popularity probably saved his life, Dubček was replaced in early 1969 by the hardliner Gustav Husák (Goo-STAV HOO-sock). Dubček's reforms were reversed, and Czechoslovakia sank back into a neo-Stalinist mold.

USELESS TRIVIA: SPORTS AS ALLEGORY, PART II

On March 21, 1969, in Stockholm, Sweden sports fans from around the world hunkered down to watch the annual Ice Hockey World Championships. Playing that day were the Soviet and Czechoslovak teams, and after a brutal and bruising game the Czechoslovaks were victorious. Czechoslovak fans in the stands began chanting loud and clear for the world's media: "Dub-ček! Dub-ček! Dub-ček!"

The previous summer, Soviet and Warsaw Pact armies had crushed Alexander Dubček's reformist experiment in fellow communist Czechoslovakia. Czechoslovak hockey fans took their uncomfortably candid protests even further on March 28, when the Czechoslovak team again trounced the Soviet team, 4-3, and Prague exploded into spontaneous street celebrations that rapidly turned into protests against the Soviet occupation forces. The Soviet Aeroflot airlines office was ransacked, and Soviet military units out in the streets were accosted. Eventually Czechoslovak security services restored order, and in any event the Soviet team went on to win the gold in Stockholm that year—the Czechoslovak team won the bronze medal—but the world had seen Czechoslovaks' true feelings.

Husák continued on as Czechoslovakia's leader for the last two decades of communist rule, overseeing the country's continued economic decline and hyperrepressive policies. Under Husák, Czechoslovakia joined the conservative wing of the Warsaw Pact, resisting any and all reforms and constantly urging Moscow to deal decisively with the constant rumbles for change in Poland and Hungary. Ironically, because of the 1968 invasion Western banks refused to extend any credit to Czechoslovakia so long as Husák remained in power, leaving postcommunist Czechoslovakia with an unexpected gift: no foreign debt.

Access to West German, Austrian, and *Voice of America* or *Radio Free Europe* TV and radio transmissions made Czechoslovaks painfully aware of their lack of freedom and declining living standard throughout the 1970s and 80s. This gave a strong impetus to dissident groups, most famously the *Karta 77* (Charter 77) Helsinki Accords[55] human rights monitoring organization, which Husák hounded mercilessly with the StB. Husák could not insulate his country from his economic failures forever, however, and as 1989 dawned on Czechoslovakia, few could guess that a surprising figure would end up greeting enthusiastic crowds from the balcony of Prague Castle by year's end.

I. East Germany as the Runt of the Litter

In many ways, East Germany was the most Eastern European of all the Soviet satellite states. It was the eastern part of a Central European country and it had a proud history, but it also knew the bitterness of defeat and foreign occupation, and worst of all, it spent much of its history trying to convince other European countries that it had a right to exist. Because of these factors, East Germany developed an extreme inferiority complex that manifested as goose-stepping militarism and an incredibly paranoid regime, even by Soviet standards.

It was bad enough that fellow Soviet satellite states secretly distrusted East Germany—declining the East German *Volksarmee's* (People's Army) assistance at the last minute during the Czechoslovak crisis of 1968—or that the West often behaved as if West Germany was the *only* legitimate German state. But Moscow kept German unification—which would mean the end of East Germany—on the bargaining table with the West well into the 1960s, and happily did business with Bonn in the 1970s and 80s, to East Berlin's utter dismay and fury.

East Germany's birth was completely accidental and largely unwelcomed. At the Yalta Conference in February 1945, the wartime Allies agreed to split occupation duties in the soon-to-be-defeated Third Reich, with the United States, Britain, France, and the Soviet Union each assigned a zone. Berlin was similarly divided between the four Allies. The ultimate goal was to reunify Germany at some point—confirmed at the Potsdam Conference in the summer of 1945—after the war. The occupation zones were only for temporary military purposes, and indeed Austria got the exact same treatment, with Vienna also split between the Allied powers. As cooperation between the Soviets and Western Allies ground to a halt in 1946–47 with the onset of the Cold War, however, the prospect of German reunification faded. Stalin tried to force the Western Allies out of Berlin through the Berlin Blockade of 1948, but that only strengthened the West's resolve to hang on.

Moved to action by the failed Soviet blockade (as well as a British budgetary crisis), the West formalized the division in 1949 when they combined their three zones into one to form *Bundesrepublik Deutschland* (Federal Republic of Germany), or "West Germany." Although not giving up on its plan for a united (and neutral) Germany, Stalin reluctantly allowed an East German government to form in 1949, and thus was born the *Deutsche Demokratische Republik* (German Democratic Republic).

In 1950, the Sovietization of East Germany began in earnest under Walter Ulbricht (VA-tair OOL-brikht), with the usual widespread arrests, collectivization of the agricultural sector, and closing of the borders. Ulbricht ruffled military feathers across Europe in mid-1950 when he bragged publically that Germany would soon be reunited just like Korea, referring to the North Korean invasion of South Korea then underway.

However, a problem for Ulbricht and the East German communists was that the Soviets, while officially absolving the communist GDR of any connection to the Nazis, still insisted in the name of war reparations on dismantling and stripping away every factory and every piece of heavy machinery, electrical appliance, or raw material its soldiers could lay their hands on in the country, severely undermining East Germany's economic recovery. This ongoing Soviet looting did not endear the communists to the population, and rather like in neighboring Poland, the average East German saw the communists as merely the pawns of a foreign power. This resentment against the Soviets and the communists and their failed economic policies boiled over in June 1953 as more than a hundred thousand East Berlin workers stormed into the streets in protest at a government measure raising productivity quotas without increasing salaries. Ulbricht reacted by immediately requesting Soviet intervention, and Soviet tanks stormed East Berlin, killing hundreds and crushing the uprising.

West Germany's entry into NATO in 1955 led to the creation of the Warsaw Pact, and with it Moscow's consent for East Germany to form its own army (*Volksarmee*, or "People's Army") and join the Warsaw Pact. Despite this success, East Germany had a unique problem among its Soviet Bloc peers, which was that Germany (as a whole) was still technically subject to the four Allies agreements at Yalta and Potsdam in 1945—in other words, it was still technically a defeated and occupied country—and there were provisions about the free movement of people and goods between the Allies' occupation zones. Berlin in particular, though divided, was an open city in the 1950s so that anyone could (and did) pass between the West and East Berlin zones relatively unhindered. Many Berliners worked in one zone and lived in another, or did their shopping in the opposite zone, and most had family spanning the zones.

The problem for East Germany was the rapid decline in its standard of living compared to West Germany coupled with the Ulbricht regime's increasing oppressiveness, which led to an exodus: Hundreds of thousands of young, educated or skilled East Germans fled East Germany through Berlin each year, some 2.6 million by 1961 out of a total population of 17 million.[56] No country can survive very long losing 15% of its population, and so Ulbricht took drastic action: with Soviet approval, on the morning of August 13, 1961, East Germany began construction of the infamous Berlin Wall to isolate the East German (i.e., Soviet) zone of the city from West Berlin, cutting off streets, sewers, subway lines, and even buildings. Over time the Berlin Wall became increasingly sophisticated, with land mines, guard dogs, a "no man's land," barbed wire, watch towers, and security cameras. East Berlin, and by extension East Germany, became a prison.

The Wall did its job and East Germany's population stabilized, though the same cannot be said for the East German economy. Despite tinkering with some minor economic reforms in the 1960s, East Germany's economy slid deeper and deeper into oblivion. Nobody outside of the Soviet Bloc would offer East Germany any credit lines, but a surprising knight in shining armor came to East Berlin's rescue: East Germany's nemesis, West Germany. West German chancellor Willy Brandt, who was very aware that any Soviet-American confrontation would be fought on German soil first and foremost, embarked in the late 1960s on a new policy of engagement with Eastern Europe in a bid to ease East-West tensions. Called *Ostpolitik* (Eastern Politics), Brandt's primary focus was East Germany, which earlier West German politicians shunned, and he worked with a wary Ulbricht to open economic and family exchanges between the two Germanies. The ultimate prize for East Germany was the *Grundlagenvertrag* (Basic Treaty) in 1972 by which West Germany agreed to treat East Germany as an equal partner, including welcoming East Germany into the United Nations as a full member state.

USELESS TRIVIA: I GUESS THEY MEAN IT . . .

On the evening of August 17, 1962, Peter Fechter and his close friend Helmut Kulbeik (COOL-bike) were hiding in a carpenter's workshop on *Zimmerstraße* (Zimmer Street) in East Berlin. Both men—eighteen years old each—were observing intently the East German border guards, known in East German slang as *Grepos* (from *Grenzpolizei*, "Border Police"), as they made their usual rounds. Seeing a moment's opportunity, both slithered through a narrow window in the shop that deposited them squarely onto the wide gap of land between the barriers of the Berlin Wall known as the Death Strip, and dashed madly for the western side. Reaching the western side of the gap, both flung themselves at the 6.5-foot-high (2 meter) wall crowned with barbed wire, and scrambled to get over it as shouts of "Halt!" pierced the night air. By now, a crowd had gathered on the West Berlin side, and they helped Kulbeik disentangle himself from the barbed wire as he climbed down on the Western side. But as Fechter still struggled, shots rang out. Fechter grimaced, then collapsed backward onto the Eastern side of the wall.

By now the crowd on the West Berlin side had grown to sizeable proportions and included journalists and tourists with cameras. With the Cold War at its height, the Westerners dared not try to climb the wall to help Fechter, who wailed in pain, nor would the East German border guards come to his aid. The crowd in West Berlin watched in horror over the next hour as Fechter slowly bled to death, and when his pleas for help finally ceased, the infuriated West German crowds shouted *Mörder!* (Murderers!) while the East German guards fetched Fechter's body.

Fechter was one of the first to die attempting to escape East Berlin, one of 133 confirmed deaths by the time the Wall came down in 1989. Fechter was a victim of the East German regime's "shoot to kill" orders, whereby the East German border guards on the wall had standing orders to shoot any escapees—men, women, or children—without hesitation. A picture taken of the dying, crumpled body of Fechter at the foot of the Wall made newspapers all over the world and proved a PR nightmare for East Germany and the Soviet Union. But the Wall stood nonetheless, though increasingly as an indictment of the Soviet system. For years after Fechter's death, West Berliners left flowers and held vigils at the site, and today in a reunited Berlin a memorial stands on the spot.

Despite his successes with Brandt, Ulbricht was seen as an aging Stalinist, and in 1971 Brezhnev replaced him with a rival, Erich Honecker.

Honecker did implement a more consumer-friendly economy, but he rejected Ulbricht's policy of German reunification—knowing that any East-West union would be fatal to East Germany and its system. Instead he touted *Abgrenzung* (Separation"), a sort of "Separate but Equal" theory of the two Germanies. Honecker was perfectly suited to the Brezhnev era, attending perfectly orchestrated party functions and parades while living largely in denial about conditions in East Germany.

When Gorbachev took over the Soviet Union in 1985, Honecker entered a foggy reality where Moscow talked of the need for great reforms, reforms that Honecker neither understood nor wanted. Tensions rose steadily between East Berlin and Moscow, and Honecker even banned Soviet publications—which espoused *glasnost*[57] and *perestroika*[58] — in East Germany just like Western publications. Honecker huddled with Czechoslovakia's Husák and Romania's Ceauşescu in defiance of the Gorbachev reforms, but as events would show, at his peril.

USELESS TRIVIA: EVERYBODY LOVES GATED COMMUNITIES!

After a long, hard day's work of oppressing the masses, East Germany's dictatorial elite liked to retreat to their own exclusive gated community known as *Waldseidlung* (Forest Settlement) in the small scenic town of Wandlitz, just north of East Berlin. Wandlitz was more than gated; it was cordoned off to ordinary citizens by machine-gun–toting *Stasi* guards, and had exclusive shops stocked with luxuries unimaginable elsewhere in East Germany. Wandlitz was an oasis of luxury where the top political brass lived in delightful and scenic ignorance of what conditions in the rest of the country were really like. The opulence of Wandlitz after the fall of the East German regime scandalized East Germans.

J. Poland, the Perennial Pain in the Butt

"What would be the harm if as a result of the rout of Poland we were to extend the socialist system into new territories and populations?"

—Iosif Stalin, September 7, 1939[59]

There is probably nothing on this planet as lonely and unappreciated as a Polish communist. The dawn of communist rule in Poland was viewed by most Poles as merely a resumption of Russian imperialism. Conversely, no matter how loyal the Polish communist party and its leadership were to Moscow, the Soviets always viewed Poles with suspicion, a suspicion born of a long history of Russians ruling Poles, and largely regretting it. The communists in Warsaw bent slavishly to Moscow's every whim in a constant bid to win Soviet trust, but it was never completely forthcoming, while this lap dog mentality only confirmed for Poles their belief that a Polish communist was just a Russian agent.[60] As communist (mis-)rule in Poland generated intolerable living conditions, this in turn generated civil unrest and the occasional open rebellion, which Moscow saw as confirmation that Poles were just a bunch of ingrates and troublemakers. Being a Polish communist, one got it from all sides.

There had been a tiny native communist party in prewar Poland, but in a fit of paranoia Stalin summoned its entire membership to Moscow in 1938 and had most of them executed. Ironically, those who survived were lower-level cadres sitting in Polish jails, doing time for illegal communist activities. Communists were also seen by many Poles as Nazi collaborators because of the 1939–41 period of Soviet-Nazi cooperation, during which the communists closely worked with occupation forces. After Hitler's betrayal of Stalin in 1941 the Soviets and Poles suddenly found themselves allies, but relations were always tense between the "London Poles" (Polish government-in-exile in London) and Moscow. The Western Allies, whose only focus was preserving the anti-Hitler alliance, constantly pressured the London Poles to forget September 1939 and work with the Soviets, but in April 1943 Stalin reacted to the Nazi discovery of the Katyń (KAH-tin) graves[61] by breaking relations with the London Poles. Having demanded at Yalta (and received) the eastern Polish territories seized in cooperation with Hitler in 1939–41, Stalin then created a communist provisional government and installed them in the first Polish city (in the new borders) to fall into Soviet hands—Lublin (LOO-bleen)—in July 1944.

The Sovietization of Poland began the moment the first Soviet boot hit Polish soil in 1944, with AK units who had fought alongside Soviet forces in the liberation of Poland suddenly finding themselves disarmed and arrested by their "allies." After some Western pressure the Soviets relented and allowed elections in 1947, with the Polish president-in-exile in London, Stanisław Mikołajczyk (Stah-NYEE-swaff Meeko-WHY-chik), taking part. However, terror carried out by the UB (*Urząd bezpieczeństwa*; "Office of Security"; the early Polish KGB) combined with vote rigging ensured a communist victory; soon Mikołajczyk had to flee Poland for his life.[62]

Meanwhile, a civil war raged throughout eastern and southern parts of the country as Ukrainian UPA insurgents[63] and trapped AK forces battled the communists and each other. By 1946 some 60,000 AK soldiers had been arrested—most of them were deported to Siberian gulags—while a 1947 amnesty offered by the communists netted a further 70,000 AK veterans. Fighting continued into the early 1950s, while the UB arrested some 2,000,000 Poles in 1944–48.

Poland's fate after the war was dictated by its strategic position between the Soviet Union and Germany. Communist rule in Poland began with Władysław Gomułka (Vwah-DIH-swaff Go-MOO-kah), who had spent the war in Poland, but Gomułka was purged in 1948 and replaced by Stalin's favorite, Bolesław Bierut (Bole-EH-swaff BYARE-oot). In 1949, Soviet general Konstantin Rokossovsky was appointed Polish defense minister, while senior-level positions in the Polish army were staffed with Soviet officers; the Poles were clearly not to be trusted.

As elsewhere, the Soviet Union seized Polish industries and raw materials as reparations,[64] for instance seizing between 1944–55 millions of tons of Silesian coal at a time when the country's coal mining production was running at less than half of prewar capacity, condemning many Poles to freezing winters without heat.[65] Bierut's rule over Poland was predictably disastrous, with forced collectivization severely disrupting food production and Soviet-driven subversion of Polish national institutions causing great discontent. Stalinist rule in Poland began to unravel slowly after the Soviet dictator's death in 1953, to the extent that when Khrushchev made his famous "secret" speech in February 1956, denouncing Stalin and his crimes, the dam burst. Bierut died of a heart attack days after the speech, and the fumbling Polish communist leadership managed in June 1956 to provoke a mass worker uprising in the western city of Poznań (POZE-non) in June 1956. In the Poznań unrest, an angry mob of demonstrating workers seized control of Poland's fourth largest city for three days before being bloodily suppressed by the army.

The Poznań Uprising severely rattled the Polish leadership, and Władysław Gomułka—who had been imprisoned in 1949—was once again asked to take over the leadership. Moscow reacted with alarm at this breach in Stalinist protocol (i.e., not consulting Moscow) and on October 19, 1956, as the party officially elected Gomułka leader, Soviet paratroops seized a runway at Warsaw's airport and a surprise delegation from the Soviet Politburo—headed by Khrushchev himself—arrived.

Soviet troops throughout Poland began seizing strategic transportation points, the Soviet navy closed in on Gdańsk harbor, and a column of Soviet tanks advanced on Warsaw as Khrushchev demanded the Poles reinstate the old Stalinist leadership.

The Poles, headed by Gomułka, stood their ground, however, and for two long days both sides argued while Polish workers in Warsaw erected barricades. At one point in the crisis, Defense Minister Rokossovsky informed Khrushchev that the Polish armed forces would likely fight the Soviets. On October 22, Khrushchev gave way and allowed Gomułka to stay in exchange for promises of loyalty to Moscow. Soviet forces would likely have defeated the Poles, but at the price of giving the world a spectacle of the brotherly Soviet Union pummeling a supposed ally. As it turned out, Khrushchev averted crisis in Poland only to face it the next day in Hungary.

USELESS TRIVIA: DID HE JUST TRIP?

It was December 7, 1970, and West German chancellor Willy Brandt was in Warsaw to sign the Treaty of Warsaw, by which West Germany recognized the postwar "Oder-Neisse line" borders with Poland. This was a part of Chancellor Brandt's *Ostpolitik* policies aimed at easing Cold War tensions in Europe. Still, this was the first time a West German chancellor had visited Poland—only twenty-five years after the war—and his reception in Warsaw was proper, but icy. While on a planned stop to the 1943 Warsaw Ghetto Uprising memorial, however, Brandt astonished his hosts, the press corps and his own entourage by suddenly dropping to his knees and bowing his head. The crowd watched in stunned silence for several minutes as Brandt knelt confessional-style at the foot of the monument, with Polish army honor guards towering over him. In what became known as the *Kniefall in Warschau* (Act of Penance in Warsaw), Brandt, in a single dramatic gesture of contrition that still reverberates today, helped move forward the dialogue between Poles and Germans about their long mutual history. Asked later why he did it, Brandt said: *"Unter der Last der jüngsten Geschichte tat ich, was Menschen tun, wenn die Worte versagen. So gedachte ich Millionen Ermordeter."* (Under the weight of recent history, I did what people do when words fail. Thus did I acknowledge the millions murdered.)[66] A grateful modern-day Warsaw has erected a monument to Brandt's gesture, in a square named after him.

Poland under Gomułka became the new model Soviet Bloc state, completely loyal but with some measure of independence. The Soviet "advisors" who controlled Poland's police and army were withdrawn—including Rokossovsky—though of course Soviet troops remained. Gomułka was seen as a hero to Poles, but his star faded over the 1960s as Poles came to realize that he intended to keep his promise of loyalty to Moscow. Gomułka's Poland was less repressive than the Stalinist years, but few meaningful economic or political reforms were undertaken.

By the end of the 1960s Gomułka was isolated and quite unpopular, horrifying Poles with his participation in the 1968 Warsaw Pact invasion of Czechoslovakia and his violent suppression of student protests at the University of Warsaw that summer. The last straw came in December 1970, when Gomułka raised prices on a score of basic food items just weeks before Christmas—the major Polish culinary holiday—predictably provoking worker demonstrations. Gomułka ordered the army to open fire on the unarmed workers, and the infamous iconic picture of a somber procession of workers carrying a dead comrade on a door doomed Gomułka. Days later Moscow replaced him with Edward Gierek (ED-vard GYAIR-ek).

The unrest in 1968 across Poland had been led primarily by students and the intelligentsia,[67] but the protests in 1970 were by workers, which unsettled both Warsaw and Moscow. Gierek, who had once been a coal miner, was seen as an ideal leader for the times and he immediately moved to alleviate some of the worst economic complaints. At first, his reforms seemed to work, and for a few years in the early 1970s Poles began to see a real improvement in their living standards. However, communist Poland's economic ills were rooted in its basic ideological foundations and required far more comprehensive changes. Worse, much of Gierek's economic growth was funded through foreign (Western) loans, and soon external global circumstances and the Party's own corrupt spending led to an exhaustion of Western credit lines and $40 billion in debt.[68] By 1974, living conditions began to deteriorate again. Gierek tried to raise prices and introduce rationing in 1976 but he provoked a workers uprising in Gdańsk. It was suppressed, but the founding afterward of *Komitet Obrony Robotników* (Committee for the Defense of Workers," KOR) was a very bad sign for the communists: the intelligentsia and workers were beginning to cooperate in their mutual struggle against the regime.

USELESS TRIVIA: LET'S GO SHOPPING!

The Soviet satellite states had a basic economic problem, one that worsened dramatically as their economies crumbled throughout the 1970s and 80s. Marxist-Leninist dogma rejected any notion of capitalist economics, and one consequence was that their currencies weren't *convertible*, meaning there was no way to determine how many Polish złoties or Soviet rubles equaled a Japanese yen or U.S. dollar. The Soviet Bloc countries took care of this problem by simply imposing an arbitrary rate of exchange—one extremely advantageous to themselves—on anyone who crossed the Iron Curtain.

Western tourists in the Eastern Bloc were stuck with that solution, but the Eastern Bloc governments often needed to import food, goods, and technologies from abroad. Since their currencies were not convertible, they were forced to use *foreign* convertible (or "hard") currencies, known as *valuta*.

Initially the communist regimes just tried exporting and selling their industrial goods abroad, but poor quality made it difficult for these wares to compete in foreign markets. Desperate, in the 1970s, several Eastern Bloc states began to sell these locally produced "for export" consumer goods in their home markets—calling the practice "internal export"—but the catch was they were available only in special shops (alongside imported Western luxury goods) *that only accepted Western "hard" currencies.* Imagine having shops in your country that do not accept your country's own currency! It was technically illegal for ordinary citizens to own foreign "hard" currencies, but the desperate governments just looked the other way as their citizens unloaded their secret stashes of dollars, francs, and deutschmarks in these shops. In Poland these shops were known as *Pewex*, in East Germany *Intershop*, in Czechoslovakia *Tuzex*, in Bulgaria Corecom. Few survived the collapse of the communist regimes in 1989–92.

The anticommunist resistance in Poland received a powerful boost in the form of the election in October 1978 of Kraków's Roman Catholic archbishop Karol Wojtyła (KAH-rol Voy-TIH-wah) to the papacy as Pope John Paul II. The symbolic significance of the first Polish pope strengthened the Church in Poland as a bastion of resistance to the regime, but the regime unwittingly helped the opposition when it allowed Pope John Paul II to pay an official Papal visit to the country in 1979—but at the same time refused to help organize his visit. Gierek effectively gave the Church and its antiregime allies a license to develop nationwide organizations and networks, which came back to haunt the regime a year later when local protests at the Lenin Shipyards in Gdańsk over the termination of a crane operator quickly transformed into nationwide protests over living conditions and state oppression.

Within weeks those networks that developed from the Papal visit sprang to life to form an independent trade union, *Solidarność* (Solidarity), with 10 million of Poland's 15 million workers—half of all Polish adults—as members. In the face of such a determined and effective challenge the regime in Warsaw unraveled, to the horror of neighboring Soviet Bloc rulers. Gierek was ousted, but nothing could stop the regime's free fall. East Germany and Czechoslovakia pushed hard for a Warsaw Pact intervention but Brezhnev dithered, worried that an intervention might resemble 1956 (Hungary) rather than 1968 (Czechoslovakia):

"We cannot rely on the present [Polish] leadership, but see presently no real possibility to replace it."
—Soviet leader Leonid Brezhnev in a Soviet Politburo session, April 30, 1981[69]

In the end, the communist party and regime were saved from collapse by a military coup led by army General Wojciech Jaruzelski (VOY-chekh Yah-roo-ZEL-skee),[70] who seized power and imposed martial law in December 1981. Martial Law lasted until 1983, with the country's borders sealed, phone lines between cities cut, mail and internal travel restricted, and a national curfew imposed. About a hundred Poles were killed, and 10,000 Solidarność activists like leader Lech Wałęsa (Lekh Va-WEN-sah) were arrested in sweeping national raids.

Jaruzelski, however, ignored the economy and somewhere in the mid-1980s it collapsed. The złoty became worthless, and the country was essentially reduced to a black market–driven barter system. Corruption, tapped phone lines, and long lines outside empty shops became the norm. The regime's authority derived exclusively from its ability to impose itself by force. In the meantime, like its AK predecessor, Solidarność re-organized itself and operated underground, secretly distributing news and support for members' families. Jaruzelski was forced to raise basic food prices 40% in early 1988, provoking strikes that the SB (*Służba Bezpieczeństwa*, "Security Service," the successor to the 1950s UB) failed to break. But worse was to come when he asked Moscow for help. 1988 was not going to be like 1981, as Jaruzelski soon discovered.

USELESS TRIVIA: KHMYELNITSKY IS DEAD, RIGHT?

When Poland achieved independence in 1918, it pledged to respect minority rights, but nationalists soon began to exclude minorities from government and suppress their newspapers and schools. In response, a group of disgruntled Polish Ukrainians met in Vienna in 1929 and formed the Organization of Ukrainian Nationalists (OUN; *Організація Українских Націоналістів*). Throughout the 1930s OUN grew more and more radical and began assassinating local Polish officials, provoking reprisals from Polish police. When war came in 1939, OUN welcomed the German invasion as a liberation and it waged a bloody campaign against the Polish AK, as well as Polish and Jewish civilians in Galicia.

However, as the war progressed some of the OUN leadership realized that Poland was no longer the main enemy, so in October 1943 the Ukrainian Insurgent Army (UPA; *Українська Повстанська Армія*) was formed. Led by Roman Shukhevych and Stepan Bandera, UPA rejected OUN's anti-Semitism and concentrated its efforts against the Germans and Soviets, fighting several battles against each. UPA's activities did not stop at war's end, and from 1947 to 1953 Soviet, Polish, and Czechoslovak forces mounted a series of campaigns to root UPA out of their Carpathian Mountain bases. In Poland, this resulted in *Akcja* Wisła (Operation Vistula), the forced expulsion of most Ukrainians from southeastern Poland. Shukhevych was killed by Soviet forces in a battle near Kiev in 1950, while Bandera was assassinated by the KGB in Munich, West Germany in 1959, after which the UPA insurgency fizzled. Some UPA insurgents did eventually manage to escape across the Iron Curtain to Austria and the West, however.

K. The Soviet Union, Keeping Up with the Joneses

"Stalin used to say, 'Truth is protected by battalions of lies.'"
—Vyacheslav Molotov, Soviet Foreign Minister (1939–52)[71]

"But the possibility remains (and in the opinion of this writer it is a strong one) that Soviet power, like the capitalist world of its conception, bears within it the seeds of its own decay, and that the sprouting of these seeds is well advanced."
—George F. Kennan, American diplomat, 1947[72]

USELESS TRIVIA: WHOSE SIDE ARE YOU ON?, PART III

Trofim Lysenko (Tro-feem Lih-SEN-ko) was born in Tsarist Ukraine in 1898, and went to university to become a biologist. Lysenko wanted to be noticed, and his first break came in 1927 when he announced to a stunned Soviet government that he had managed to grow peas in the winter in Soviet Azerbaijan outdoors without using fertilizers. No one could repeat Lysenko's amazing feat, but no matter, his star was on the rise and over the next several years Lysenko turned out a number of stunning agricultural "discoveries" that seemingly defied conventional scientific wisdom. Those discoveries, coupled with a practiced willingness to denounce his fellow scientists for their slavish adherence to apparently discredited Western bourgeois science, resulted in a trail of destroyed careers and prison sentences. But Lysenko was appointed the head of the Soviet Academy of Agricultural Sciences in 1935.

One of Lysenko's most famous acts was to denounce the science of genetics as Western propaganda, suppressing Soviet genetic research for decades. Of course, Lysenko was a crackpot who played the system well, becoming Stalin's pet by ratting out colleagues who imitated "Western science" instead of Soviet science. Lysenko terrorized Soviet academia from 1935 until being quietly removed in 1965. In the process, Lysenko did great damage to Soviet science, leaving the Soviets decades behind the West and also contributing through his often fabricated achievements to the destruction of Soviet agriculture.

The period of 1945–65 is often seen as the golden age of the Soviet Union, when its prestige from having played a leading role in the defeat of Hitler was highest, and its military and scientific prowess seemed to match that of the West. The Soviets had quickly caught up to the U.S. by building their own atomic, then hydrogen bombs,[73] and had launched Sputnik, the first manmade satellite, into space; followed by sending

Yuri Gagarin and Valentina Tereshkova, the first man and woman (respectively), into space. Each year the May Day parades through Red Square were pageants of Soviet military might, with row after row of seemingly invincible armored vehicles and missiles flowing in between platoons of stern-faced goose-stepping Soviet soldiers and sailors, all emblazoned with that universally recognized symbol of Soviet power, the red star.

The Polish writer Czesław Miłosz (CHESS-wahv MEE-woesh) wrote about this stuff in his 1953 book *The Captive Mind*, in which he describes how dictatorships attract young and impressionable youth with this kind of militaristic pageantry, using romantic slogans, uniforms, and brightly colored posters and flags. Indeed, at its core the Soviet Union was an empire, a dictatorship with a ruling elite and its imperial domains to protect and exploit. A crucial component of the USSR was its official state ideology, which envisioned world revolution through which all countries would eventually succumb to a Soviet-style socioeconomic system (and, therefore, political system). "We will bury you! (*Мы вас похороним!*), Khrushchev had insisted to the West.

But through the years, Soviet policies became less revolutionary and more conservative, designed to protect and keep what Moscow already had. The postwar Soviet Union had two key areas of weakness that dogged it through most of the Cold War: its economy and its ability to match (if not surpass) Western technology. Stalin defined the West as an innate enemy of the Soviet Union, and through his megalomaniac paranoia, created the very confrontation with the West that he believed already existed. In the absence of war, this confrontation committed Moscow to a global competition in precisely those areas in which it was weakest, economy and technology; and despite some surprising successes and amazing achievements, the Cold War proved for the Soviets a vast (and ultimately fatal) waste of talent and resources.

The Soviet Union's main concern in 1945 was the fact that much of its European territory lay in ruins, with the country's most productive regions reduced to rubble, farm fields torn up, rail lines and bridges destroyed, and basic sanitation, irrigation, and utility systems laid to ruin. Meanwhile more than 20 million of the country's citizens—e.g., peasants, doctors, engineers, skilled machinists, party cadré—lay dead.

USELESS TRIVIA: PAY NO ATTENTION TO THAT MAN BEHIND THE CURTAIN!

One of the first military confrontations of the Cold War took place over the ancient Hermit Kingdom, Korea. A technical decision in 1945 to divide occupation duties between U.S. and Soviet forces on the Japanese-occupied Korean peninsula led to the eventual creation of opposing Korean states, one communist and the other pro-Western. Soviet-sponsored North Korea attacked and invaded pro-Western South Korea in June 1950, provoking an American-led United Nations military effort to defend South Korea. However, the U.S./U.N. counterinvasion of North Korea provoked a communist Chinese intervention, which prolonged the war for several years, until 1953.

In June 1951 Lt. Col. Bruce Hinton of the U.S. 336th squadron was flying in North Korean skies when his squadron encountered Chinese Mig-15s. Until this point, American F-86 Sabre jets had easily dominated the Korean skies, piling up a kill ratio against the North Korean and Chinese air forces of 13:1. However, Hinton was stunned to see how skillfully the Mig-15s engaged his Sabres. Though it would not be confirmed for decades, the Soviet and American air forces had met for the first time.[74]

Though worried about sparking World War III, Stalin ordered several Soviet air force units (totaling some 20,000-26,000 personnel) to aid his allies along a narrow stretch of the North Korean-Chinese border on the Yalu River—later famously coined by American pilots "Mig Alley." The Mig-15 and F-86 jets were roughly equal in capability, so pilot skills were crucial. Because Americans and Soviets counted "kills" differently, historians are still quibbling over the score. For secrecy's sake, Soviet pilots' jets and uniforms had Chinese or North Korean markings, and in one reported case Migs strafed a downed Mig pilot in the Yellow Sea rather than allow him to be captured (and confirm the presence of Soviet pilots). Only in the 1990s did Moscow confirm that Soviet pilots had fought in the war.[75]

Indeed, some theorize that it was this incredible and almost insurmountable level of destruction that drove Stalin to forsake his promises at Yalta and Potsdam—and instead build yet another Russian empire in Eastern Europe, so as to requisition the region's industrial and natural resources to restore the badly mauled Soviet economy. In 1950, while Western Europe united to create the European Coal and Steel Community (ECSC)[76] to share its resources as it recovered from the war, the Soviet Union created a parallel but involuntary community in Eastern Europe whose resources Moscow appropriated for its own reconstruction.

The price for Eastern Europe's Soviet liberation from Nazi tyranny was to be the plundering of its economic assets.[77] But another crucial driving factor in Stalin's decision to repeat the traditional Russian imperial experience in Eastern Europe in 1944–46 was to try again what had failed in 1939–41, this time with much more territory. In 1939–41, eastern Poland and the Baltics had proven inadequate; now *all* of Eastern Europe would have to put in buffer zone duty for the Soviet Union.

In his waning years, Stalin's paranoia only increased. Particularly from 1949 onward, he became increasingly erratic and distrusted everyone around him, including longtime devotees like Vyacheslav Molotov.

Soviet citizens had sacrificed much and felt empowered by their contribution to the war effort, and there was widespread hope that the worst excesses of the prewar years would give way to a more liberal Soviet state. Stalin saw this as a challenge to his absolute power, and initiated a series of sweeping purges and show trials in the USSR and across the Eastern European satellites to terrorize them into subservience, with Soviet "advisors" carefully choreographing trials. Soviet war veterans, though touted and glorified in public, actually came under particular scrutiny because they had experienced the world beyond Soviet borders; Stalin feared a repeat of the 1825 Decembrist Revolt.

Stalin's paranoia and need to control everything directly fractured the communist world. His refusal to allow his most devoted disciple in Eastern Europe, Josip Broz "Tito," any level of autonomy led to the rupture with Yugoslavia in 1948, and his refusal to take the Chinese communists seriously even after their stunning victory over Chiang Kai-shek's nationalists in 1949—giving Mao Tse-Tung a frosty reception on his first visit to Moscow, and ignoring tremendous Chinese casualty rates to prolong the 1950–53 Korean War—ultimately convinced Mao that Moscow was not worthy to lead the communist world. This breach, though usually described in ideological terms, really had its origins in Stalin's paranoia, requiring not agreement but submission.

Stalin's death in March 1953 left the Soviet empire rudderless, and for some time confusion reigned. His successors began easing some of Stalin's worst excesses, closing the gulags and slave labor camps, allowing for greater production of consumer goods, and restraining the KGB. This easing of oppression in Eastern Europe had consequences, provoking explosions in East Germany and Czechoslovakia in 1953. All the Eastern European satellites shuddered and squirmed as post-Stalinist Moscow decompressed, but the crises that rocked Poland and Hungary in 1956 finally solidified the rise of Stalin's successor, Nikita Khrushchev.

Khrushchev was a bundle of contradictions, a man who genuinely wanted peaceful coexistance with the capitalist West but who also believed passionately in the inevitability of communist economic (and, if need be, military) victory. The good news was that Khrushchev was a reformer, a guy who believed in the need for change; and, indeed, many Soviet people began to see a real improvement in their lives during the Khrushchev era. The bad news was that some of Khrushchev's reforms, while well-intentioned, actually just made things worse. In the end, Khrushchev's own lack of diplomatic skills, coupled with his often ill-conceived reforms, proved his undoing, as he discovered when the Soviet military, KGB, and key elements of his own party teamed up to oust him.

Two areas Khrushchev's reforms focused on were the Soviet economy and the military. For the economy, Khrushchev tried to address the Soviet Union's notorious food production inefficiencies, but the end result of all his efforts was a disastrous downward spiral in critical grains output, requiring the Soviet government to import tens of thousands of tons of wheat and other grains from 1962 on. On the military side, Khrushchev believed—not without some validity—that the Soviet Union could not win a long-term arms race with the West, so he emphasized the Soviet nuclear missile threat as a deterrent to a Western attack. In some ways this presaged the MADD strategy, but the wisdom of a nuclear-based defense came into doubt when Khrushchev placed Soviet nuclear missiles in Cuba, just ninety miles from the American coast—seriously undermining any American ability to respond to a Soviet attack—leading to a white-knuckling, nail-biting thirteen-day-long confrontation with the U.S. in late October 1962.

USELESS TRIVIA:
THE PEN REALLY IS MIGHTIER THAN THE SWORD

On August 1, 1975, Soviet leader Leonid Brezhnev met with European leaders as well as U.S. President Gerald Ford and Canadian Prime Minister Pierre Trudeau in Helsinki to sign the Final Act of the Conference on Security and Cooperation in Europe—the Helsinki Accords—which in the spirit of détente recognized the Soviet sphere in Eastern Europe. Eastern European exile groups howled in dismay, and the *Wall Street Journal* implored the President, "Jerry, Don't Go!"[78]

The Helsinki Accords seemingly achieved several long-standing Soviet goals in Europe, but was it a victory? As a sop to the West for its cooperation, Moscow had included under Article VII a section on respect for human rights and fundamental freedoms, while Article VIII guaranteed the self-determination of peoples. The Soviets never gave this window-dressing a second thought.

They should have. Dissidents in Eastern Europe seized upon these two articles to form Helsinki committees dedicated to monitoring the observance of the Helsinki Accords, much to the extreme annoyance of Moscow and and the Soviet Bloc dictatorships. The world press reported widely on these dissident groups who risked police beatings and arrest, official harassment, exile, job loss, or even death to report gross human rights violations by the communist regimes. Even in Moscow itself a Helsinki Watch group formed, despite vigorous KGB harassment. The Helsinki Accords, in tandem with the United Nations Human Rights Charter, legitimized opposition to the Soviet Bloc regimes.

Khrushchev's reforms and his gamble in Cuba had terrified Soviet *apparatchiks*—a class of dull, witless bureaucrats who ran things and enjoyed a privileged lifestyle compared to that of most Soviet citizens. Several segments of the Soviet establishment teamed up in October 1964 to oust Khrushchev and replace him with Leonid Brezhnev. By 1970 the Soviet Union had achieved a rough military parity with the West, but its economy had already begun to slump. Worse, the West began to widen its technological advantage beyond Moscow's grasp, as historian Vojtěch Mastny noted:

In the purely military sense, at issue was no longer matching its Western rival in building useless nuclear weapons but rather keeping up with the West's rising preponderance in technologically advanced conventional armaments—a battle the Soviet system was not equipped to win.[79]

USELESS TRIVIA: THE OPPOSITE OF GREEN?

Soviet disregard and mismanagement of natural resources and the environment in the name of development was infamous, and while all industrializing countries have a noted tendency to ignore pollution until it becomes a major health issue—the very polluted Cuyahoga River in northern Ohio caught fire *ten times* between 1868 and 1969—the Soviet Union was exceptional in its willingness to ignore the environmental impact of its economic policies. A stark example is the Aral Sea, which entered the 20th century as the world's fourth largest freshwater sea (or technically, lake), larger than Lake Michigan. In the 1950s Stalin diverted the two rivers feeding the Aral Sea, the Syr Darya and Amu Darya, to help develop agriculture in Soviet Central Asia. This amazing engineering feat was accomplished, but with predictable results: by 2008, the Aral Sea had shrunk to just 26% of its 1950 size, destroying centuries-old fishing communities. Aral is also the sole source of fresh water for a very thirsty region. Worse, the Soviets had built one of their main germ warfare research (and weapons storage) facilities on Vozrozhdenie Island in the middle of the Aral Sea. The island was remote and inaccessible, but today it is no longer an island.[80]

Brezhnev had three major policy drives: first, halt all reforms. Secondly, rein in the satellite states (most famously invading Czechoslovakia in 1968 to suppress Dubček's reforms). Finally, ease the Cold War confrontation that was putting such a massive drain on an increasingly creaky Soviet economy. For his third goal, Brezhnev found the West equally interested in détente with the waning Vietnam War and the OPEC oil embargo wreaking havoc on the West's economies. A series of treaties were signed ranging from the SALT[81] treaties to the 1975 Helsinki Accords. However, a series of foreign policy defeats unnerved Moscow, undermining cooperation: China's defection, the decisive defeat of Soviet-armed and trained Arab armies in 1967 and 1973, the 1979–89 Afghanistan War quagmire, and the 1980–81 *Solidarność* crisis in Poland. The rise of a Polish Pope, John Paul II, in 1978, and Ronald Reagan as U.S. president in 1980 put Brezhnev on the defensive.

By the time of Brezhnev's death in 1982, the Soviet economy was circling the drain and the status quo was no longer an option. After a couple of octogenarians rulers, the Soviets chose in 1985 the young Mikhail

Gorbachev, who idolized Yuri Andropov[82] and understood the need for reforms. Gorbachev was a dedicated communist and a patriotic Soviet citizen who believed the Soviet Union could be reformed and made to be economically viable, without changing its fundamental nature. He was wrong, but we have Gorbachev's naiveté to thank for bringing an end to the Cold War. Over time it dawned on the suspicious Americans that Gorbachev was sincere, and wanted to make some serious agreements about arms control and easing the global military confrontation. In 1987, emboldened, U.S. president Ronald Reagan demanded at the Brandenburg Gate in West Berlin, in front of the Berlin Wall:

> General Secretary Gorbachev, if you seek peace, if you seek prosperity for the Soviet Union and Eastern Europe, if you seek liberalization: Come here to this gate! Mr. Gorbachev, open this gate! Mr. Gorbachev, tear down this wall![83]

Little did Reagan or anyone else understand at the time that Gorbachev apparently intended to do exactly that. As is often the case with empires, colonial domains are expensive and can be a big drain on the state treasury. Simply put, the Soviet Union couldn't afford Eastern Europe anymore, with its deeply unpopular regimes that required huge subsidies and elaborate (and expensive) military and police apparatuses to keep them in power. The old *apparatchiks* and the military establishment began to bleet in earnest at Gorbachev's reforms as they saw the Soviet state itself threatened, while Gorbachev insisted he was saving it. They were right—and thank heavens Gorbachev ignored them.

9. EASY COME, EASY GO, 1989-92

YET ANOTHER AGE OF EMPIRES IN EASTERN EUROPE COMES TO AN END

"None of us know all the potentialities that slumber in the spirit of the population, or all the ways in which that population can surprise us when there is the right interplay of events."

—Czech dissident Václav Havel

CHAPTER SUMMARY

By sheer force of will Stalin created a mighty empire in the lands where Europe and Asia meet, but with his passing in 1953, none of his successors were ever able to master his imperial domains as he did. In Stalin's time, contradictions were literally air-brushed from history—owners of the Большая советская энциклопедия, the "Great Soviet Encyclopedia," sometimes received updates they were supposed to paste in over prescribed pages in their books as facts changed to suit Stalin—but his successors could not so easily ignore the growing contradictions in the Soviet economy or political life. Historians may argue over exactly when the USSR's decline began but it was clear to many by the Brezhnev era of the 1970s that the Soviet Union had passed its prime.

The Cold War no doubt hastened the Soviet demise, but one man in particular deserves more credit than most for ending the Cold War *peacefully*: Mikhail Gorbachev. Indeed, Gorbachev inadvertently helped push the decaying Soviet empire to its inevitable collapse. 1989 will long be remembered in Eastern Europe like 1918, as a euphoric year of renewed freedom and opportunity, but collapsing empires often leave chaos and uncertainty in their wake, even "evil" ones. Few would argue that the past twenty years have not seen much progress, or that Eastern Europe isn't a better place to live with the passing of the stodgy old ideological dictatorships, but even the West has had trouble grappling with the full implications of a post-Soviet world, and Eastern Europe for once has had to start learning how to define *itself*.

CHAPTER GUIDE

A. Introduction: Ashes to Ashes, We All Fall Down 436
B. Poland and the Ghosts of 1980: The First Steps 438
C. The Hungarian "Refolution" 440
D. East Germany Goosesteps into Oblivion 441
E. Elvis is Dead, but Czechoslovakia Goes Velvet Anyway 443
F. Bulgaria Knows Peer Pressure When It Sees It 445
G. Asking for a Light in the Romanian Powderkeg 446
H. Albania and Frost in Hell 447
I. Playing Fiddle on the Deck of the Titanic: the Soviet Union . . 450
J. Libre Baltica, Part II 452
K. Agonia: The Many Deaths of Yugoslavia 452

Figure 64. Eastern Europe Timeline, 1988–92

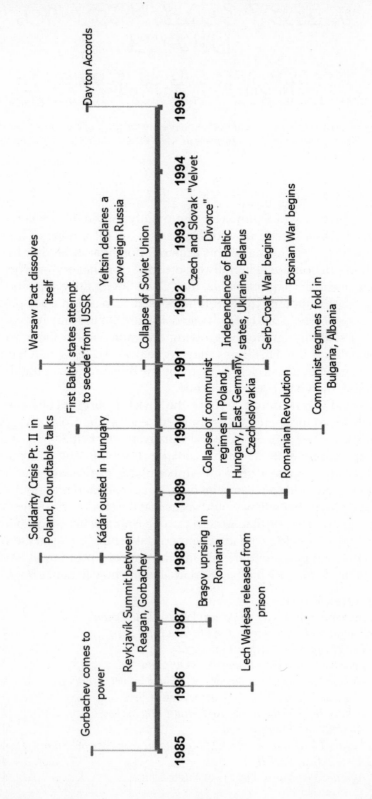

Figure 65. Comparative Global Changes Timeline, 1970–2000

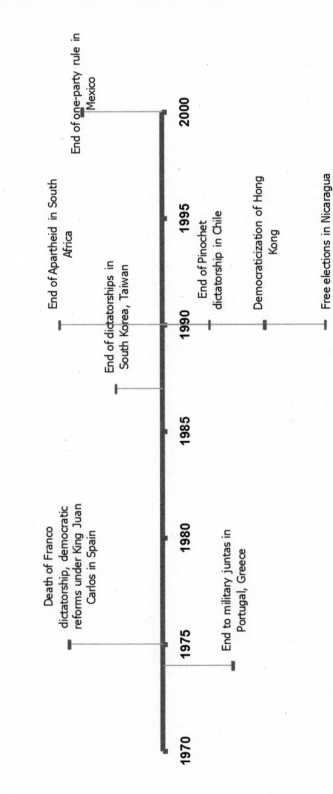

A. Introduction: Ashes to Ashes, We All Fall Down

"The collapse of the Soviet Union was the greatest geopolitical catastrophe of the century."

—Russian Federation President Vladimir Putin, in his annual State of the Nation speech to the Russian parliament, April 2005

Whatever uncertainty or chaos was wrought by the collapse of the Soviet Union, the price was well worth it. The geostrategic benefit for Moscow (and Europe) of keeping trouble-prone Eastern Europe under wraps for half a century was far outweighed by the costs to both Russia and Eastern Europe, and, by proxy, to all of Europe. Soviet rule in the region actually did bring an unusual measure of peace to Eastern Europe for half a century, but it was peace bought at the expense of crucial economic, social, and political progress. While Western Europe underwent a fundamental transformation during the postwar years, eschewing militarism and colonial empires for more democratic societies and greater transnational cooperation, Eastern Europe was effectively frozen in time.

Moscow did Eastern Europe a favor by shattering the region's old feudal elites in 1944–46, but the region benefitted little otherwise from Soviet rule; Eastern Europe never decompressed from Europe's 20th-century era of dictatorships, never underwent the self-examination that Germany or Italy had to undergo as they transformed from dictatorships into democratic societies. The price Eastern Europe—and by extension, the European Union—is paying today for the long era of Soviet isolation and insulation against change is decaying and outdated economic infrastructure, inexperienced political elites, and societies well-schooled in corruption and the evasion of authorities. The collapse of the Soviet Union was *vital* for the region's social, economic, and political development, and did not come a moment too soon, even for Russia.

Just about *nobody*—from people on the street to learned *Sovietology* scholars—expected the collapse when it came. There were a few lonely souls in the 1980s who, studying the calcified Soviet economy, made the obvious observation that this couldn't go on forever, and Western statesmen routinely claimed that by their very nature repressive regimes were doomed, but everyone back then thought it would happen sometime in the distant future—and then came 1989.

In retrospect, despite what a few nostalgic former servants of the *ancien régime* say today, it is clear that the Soviet collapse was both inevitable and desirable. Gorbachev's reforms no doubt hastened it, but what made 1989 the tipping point for the Soviet collapse? Was it Gorbachev's address to the parliamentary assembly of the Council of Europe in Brussels in July 1989, when he declared to the stunned audience:

The social and political order in some particular countries did change in the past, and it can change in the future as well. But this is exclusively a matter for the peoples themselves and of their choice.

Any interference in internal affairs, any attempts to limit the sovereignty of states—whether of friends and allies or anybody else—are inadmissible.

—Mikhail Gorbachev, July 6, 1989,
to the Parliamentary Assembly
of the Council of Europe

STALIN'S EMPTY BOOTS

In this photo, we see a modern-day reconstruction of the remnants of the Stalin statue in Budapest that was torn apart by the furious mob on the first night of the Hungarian Revolution on October 23, 1956. While a copy, the platform (including the boots) are life-size reproductions of the original and are displayed in an outdoor museum in present-day Budapest called Memento Park[1] that has preserved many communist-era statues, plaques, and sculptures with descriptions of their original settings. The site of the original Stalin statue is now home to a monument dedicated to the 1956 Revolution. (Photo used with the kind permission of Memento Park [www.mementopark.hu], Budapest, Hungary.)

This meant a renunciation of the Brezhnev Doctrine, or in simpler terms, it meant the communist regimes of Eastern Europe were on their own and could not count on Moscow for help. The world found this hard to believe and so Gorbachev was forced to repeat it often, as in October, 1989 when—after the communist regimes in Poland and Hungary had already fallen without a peep from Moscow—Gorbachev proclaimed on a visit to

Helsinki, in reference to demonstrations then shaking East Germany, that "the Soviet Union had no right, moral or political, to interfere in the events in Eastern Europe."[2]

The Brezhnev Doctrine was over. But Gorbachev's public renunciations of the Brezhnev Doctrine, while dramatic, were just a public admission of what he had already been practicing for more than a year. Indeed, the full implications of Gorbachev's new policies were already frantically playing out in the satellite capitals as panicking politburos reacted to the new winds from Moscow.

B. Poland and the Ghosts of 1980: The First Steps

"Solidarity has never had a vision of an ideal society. It wants to live and let live. Its ideals are closer to the American Revolution than the French."
—Writer & Solidarity activist Adam Michnik[3]

The story begins in April 1988, when a desperately broke Polish communist government raised food prices a staggering 40%, provoking protests and strikes. This time, however, the SB (Polish KGB) was unable to quell or contain the unrest, and the strikes spread across the country. In the seven years since Martial Law had been declared, Jaruzelski's regime had failed to implement any meaningful reforms, and the Polish economy sank into oblivion. The country effectively functioned on Dollars and Deutschmarks, shops were empty, and though martial law had ended in 1983, police and soldiers were still omnipresent.

Indeed it was widely understood that those policemen and soldiers were *all* that kept the communists in power. By August 1988 the country once again stood on the verge of chaos while the Solidarity trade union re-emerged from the shadows. Jaruzelski once again pondered martial law, but 1988 was not 1981, as Jaruzelski discovered when he phoned Moscow for instructions and support from Gorbachev—and was told he could expect neither. Soon the panicked and cornered regime was forced to do exactly what its predecessor had done in 1980: negotiate with Solidarity.

Thus began the Roundtable Talks in December 1988 between the Polish communists, Solidarity, representatives of the Catholic Church, and smaller opposition groups. By April 1989, the Roundtable negotiations bore fruit in the form of a compromise. Jaruzelski would become president (a title not used in Poland since the *Sanacja* days), but semifree elections would be held for the Polish parliament, with one-third of the seats in the *Sejm* reserved exclusively for the communists while all of the seats in the upper house (*Senat*) would be contested. The elections were held in June, with resounding results: Solidarity won 160 of the 161 seats of the Sejm that it could contest, and 92 of the 100 seats available in the Senat. Stunned by this defeat, Jaruzelski tried for months to entice Wałęsa into a communist-led coalition government, but Wałęsa refused. Finally, in August 1989, Jaruzelski caved in, and on August 23, 1989, Solidarity activist Tadeusz Mazowiecki (Tah-DAY-oosh Mah-zo-VYETS-kee) became the first noncommunist prime minister in Eastern Europe since 1948.

In December 1989, the old PRL (*Polska Rzeczpospolita Ludowa*; People's Republic of Poland) finally died as the name reverted to *Rzeczpospolita Polska*, the Republic of Poland. Meanwhile any mention of the communists was purged from the Constitution and the communist party's assets—mostly in the form of buildings and bank accounts—were seized across the country. The *Polska Zjednoczona Partia Robotnicza* / PZPR (Polish United Workers Party, as the communists were known) itself imploded in January 1990.

But Poland still had a communist president, General Jaruzelski, a holdover from the April 1989 Roundtable Agreement. What was radical in 1989 was stale by 1990, so Jaruzelski resigned as President in September 1990 and Solidarity leader Lech Wałęsa won the presidential elections held in December. At Wałęsa's inauguration, Ryszard Kaczorowski[4] (RIH-shard Catch-or-OFF-skee), the president of the Polish government-in-exile that had persisted in London since World War II, turned over to Wałęsa, as the first freely elected Polish president since 1926, his official seals of office.

USELESS TRIVIA: FREEDOM'S JUST ANOTHER WORD!

On October 26, 1989, Frank M., a native of Bad Freienwalde in East Germany, quietly lowered himself into the frigid water and began to swim quietly for the other side, a considerable distance. However, the shoreline was watched intently and soon East Germany's infamous *Grepos* (border guards) were on the shore demanding Frank return. Frank ignored them, however, and soon a fusillade of bullets followed. Frank M. sank beneath the waves. His body was recovered hours later.

Frank M. is notable for a couple reasons. An estimated 1,200 East Germans were killed by their own government as they tried to flee their prisonlike homeland, and Frank M. is thought to be *the last* of them, killed only about a week before the fall of the Berlin Wall on November 4, 1989. Another notable point about Frank M.'s tragic death is that he was not trying to flee westward; he was shot dead as he tried to swim *eastward* across the Oder River, to Poland. Since early 1989, Poland had begun dismantling its communist police state, and East German authorities closed their border with Poland. Frank M. was the last of a number of East Germans caught (and killed) trying to flee to Poland.

C. The Hungarian "Refolution"

British journalist and historian Timothy Garton Ash described the dramatic collapse of the communist regimes throughout Eastern Europe as a *Refolution* (i.e., Reform + Revolution) because despite the revolutionary nature of the changes in the region, it was largely (though not completely) accomplished without violence. Nearly everywhere, however, it began with some sort of confrontation, whether it was Solidarity strikers confronting government SB forces in Poland, or the student protestors who rocked Prague, Dresden, and Sofia. Hungary is the exception, however, where change came from above, and largely peacefully.

In Poland, the communist regime collapsed dramatically, but in Hungary the communist state was simply dismantled like a tent at the end of a camping trip. This isn't to undercut the bravery of those Hungarians who undertook the changes of 1988–90, but only to point out that while the Polish revolution was driven by a coalition of shipyard workers, coal miners, and intellectuals, the Hungarian revolution was carried out primarily by bureaucrats.

In May 1988, while Jaruzelski was trying to stamp out wildcat strikes across Poland, something else was stirring in Budapest. During the 1970s and 80s, the Hungarian regime had quietly sent young scholars abroad to study economics in the West. These scholars returned fully aware that Hungary's economic woes needed more than the bandaid reforms the communists were enacting, and they coalesced to form a reformist wing of the communist party. The regime of János Kádár, which had been in power in Hungary since the suppression of the 1956 Revolution, was keenly aware of the country's growing economic plight but was hogtied by its own ideology and could not offer any effective solutions. In May 1988 the moderate reformists, led by Károly Grósz (KAH-roy Gross), ousted Kádár by promoting him to a powerless figurehead position and began very cautiously enacting economic reforms while easing oppressive measures.

Piqued by the slow pace, in November more radical reformists led by Miklos Németh (MEE-klosh NAY-met) and Imre Pozsgay (EEM-reh POZH-guy) nudged Grósz aside. Within months, in early 1989, they forced the *Magyar Szociálista Munkáspárt* (Hungarian Socialist Workers Party) to agree to open and free elections, and political parties began to form in Hungary for the first time since 1947.[5] Over the summer of 1989, the reformists maintained their momentum over Party conservatives by holding a lavish and nationally televised state funeral for Imre Nagy, the executed leader of the 1956 Revolution, in a replay of the 1956 reburial of László Rajk.

Admitting that the Revolution of 1956 was legitimate proved fatal to the communist cause, and in October 1956—on the 33rd anniversary of the 1956 Revolution—the *Magyar Népköztársaság* (People's Republic of Hungary) gave way officially to the Republic of Hungary, and the Hungarian communist party imploded. Elections held in March 1990 were the first free elections in the country since 1945, and brought Eastern Europe's first fully noncommunist government to power.

D. East Germany Goosesteps into Oblivion

The ease with which the communist dictatorships in Poland and Hungary relinquished power amazed the world, but the greatest impression was made on neighboring East Germany and Czechoslovakia, both of which pushed for a Warsaw Pact intervention but found the Pact too divided to act. East Germans had an interest in Hungary in particular, as over the summer of 1989, tens of thousands of East Germans visited Hungary (still technically a fellow Soviet Bloc state, after all), only to demand free exit to Austria. At first the Hungarians, not wanting to provoke a fellow Warsaw Pact member, hesitated, but as the "Iron Curtain" along the Austro-Hungarian border was being dismantled, anyway, they relented and the East German refugees flooded westward to freedom. Infuriated, East Berlin immediately halted all travel to Hungary, but hundreds of East German refugees in Czechoslovakia—which was still staunchly procommunist and antireform—laid siege to the West German Embassy, demanding political asylum in the West. Both East Berlin and Prague were forced, to their extreme embarrassment, to negotiate an agreement that allowed the refugees to flee to West Germany.

Undaunted, the aging Erich Honecker, East Germany's dictator, planned elaborate celebrations for the 40th anniversary of the German Democratic Republic to be held in early October 1989. Soviet leader Gorbachev attended the celebrations, but as hand-selected East German "Party loyalists" marched by Gorbachev's stand, they chanted *Hilf uns, Gorby!* (Help us, Gorby!), to Honecker's extreme displeasure.

Inspired by the Poles, small-scale demonstrations had been sprouting up across East Germany since 1988 led mostly by university students, but after the October 1989 celebrations these demonstrations grew, particularly in Dresden and Leipzig, and were joined by both blue- and white-collar workers. After a particularly large protest in the third week of October, Honecker ordered a Tiananmen Square–style[6] attack on the crowds. But other elements of the regime, who could see the writing on the wall, reversed Honecker's orders and ousted him from power on October 18. Egon Krenz (AY-gon Krents) became East Germany's new ruler.

USELESS TRIVIA: THEY DON'T BUILD ICONS LIKE THEY USED TO!

"Die Mauer wird in fünfzig und auch in ein hundert Jahren noch bestehen bleiben, wenn die dazu vorhandenen Gründe noch nicht beseitigt sind!" (The Wall will still be standing in fifty or even a hundred years if conditions still warrant it!) So declared East German dictator Erich Honecker defiantly in January 1989. At the time, most believed him. However, 1989 was to be a year of surprises.

The end began in November 1989, as crowds of demonstrators surged in East Germany's largest cities demanding change. The stubborn Honecker had been ousted weeks earlier, and his replacement, Egon Krenz, tried futilely to manage events that were spinning swiftly out of his control. On November 9, Krenz decided to allow symbolic limited border crossings to ease tensions, and Günter Schabowski (GOON-tair Shah-BOFF-skee), the Minister of Propaganda, was tasked with announcing this new policy on live television that night at a press conference. Strangely, Schabowski wasn't fully briefed on the new rules and he declared that night to startled reporters that the borders would simply be opened. Asked when, he replied blankly on live television that as far as he knew, they were open now.

The obvious result was a massive crush of East Berliners at the Berlin Wall that night, and a bunch of very scared and confused border guards making frantic phone calls for orders. None were issued; no one wanted to take responsibility for the mess. The frazzled guards, without orders, finally just stepped aside and the jubilant East German crowds surged through the crossings to freedom in West Berlin. Astounded West Berliners responded with flowers and champagne, and soon the historic images that flashed across televisions around the world that night began to materialize—of deliriously happy Germans, Easterners and Westerners, dancing together on the Wall and attacking it with sledgehammers. The Berlin Wall had fallen, and the city began its long process of reunification.

A comedy of miscommunications and errors within the East German regime led in early November 1989 to the collapse of the Berlin Wall, which was televised worldwide. Despite the symbolic significance of the fall of the Berlin Wall, much more was to come. Krenz tried unsuccessfully to slow the pace of change, but in December 1989, East Germany found itself in step with Poland as both removed any mention of the communist party from their constitutions.

Unable to preserve the regime, Krenz and the entire East German communist government resigned, and the country's first free elections ever, in March 1990, showed that most East Germans favored (re-)union with West Germany. Negotiations began immediately between Bonn and East Berlin, leading to the Treaty on the Final Settlement With Respect to Germany ("2 + 4 Agreement") signed between East and West Germany on the one hand (i.e., the "2"), and the four World War II occupying allies (U.S., Britain, France, USSR) in Moscow, ending the Allied occupation of Germany from the war and paving the way for German (re-) unification. After tidying up loose ends with other countries such as Poland, the union took place on October 3, 1990, at which point East Germany ceased to exist and a reunited Germany was reborn.

USELESS TRIVIA: ARE YOU SURE YOU WANT TO THROW THE BABY OUT WITH THAT BATHWATER?

As (re-)unification approached in the summer of 1990 in Germany, West German Federal authorities busily studied East Germany's legal system to determine what to integrate into the unified German law code and what to discard. Clearly, with its Soviet legal pedigree, many East German laws were going to be scrapped. Beyond the obvious ones that violated individual rights and international norms, West German authorties had one that irked them and had to go: East Germany's "socialist" right on red law.

This was a traffic law that allowed East German motorists to turn right at a red light. Designed to relieve traffic pressures in urban areas, West German authorities saw it as typical of socialist countries, undermining respect for the rule of law by allowing exceptions, leading to chaos. The fact that the "right on red" law also existed in other Western European countries and even the United States did not deter West German authorities. The law was struck down when unification came on October 3, 1990—but protests in the East convinced Bonn to relent, and it even spread across the rest of Germany.

E. Elvis is Dead, but Czechoslovakia Goes Velvet Anyway

In Czechoslovakia, Gustav Husák had been adamant about rejecting Gorbachev's reforms, and he allied with Honecker's East Germany and Ceaușescu's Romania as a conservative antireform bloc within the Warsaw Pact. The fall of the communist regimes in Poland and Hungary, while distressing, were not wholly unexpected, but the swift fall of Honecker's regime in East German really rattled Husák.

Weeks later, when thousands of students commemorating International Student Day on November 17, 1989 in Prague began to call for reform and democratization, Husák sicced the *StB* (*Státní bezpečnost*, "State Security," Czechoslovak KGB) on them with clubs and truncheons. Students and dissidents met in theaters across the country over the next several days to plan a response, ultimately organizing the *Občanské forum* (Civic Forum), led by *Karta 77* dissident Václav Havel. (In Slovakia, a parallel organization called *Verejnosť proti násiliu*, "Citizens Against Violence," formed.) For weeks, each night students and workers gathered in growing demonstrations or staged strikes that paralyzed Czechoslovak society.

USELESS TRIVIA: WHAT TO CALL THOSE PEOPLE ABOUT WHOM WE KNOW NOTHING?

When Czechoslovakia peacefully went through its "Velvet Divorce" in 1992 and split apart, English speakers suddenly had a problem. The smaller of the two, Slovakia, presented little difficulty, but English-speakers had no term for the new Czech country. Historically, the Czech lands had been known as Bohemia—no problem there—but Bohemia was a medieval kingdom; modern-day Czechs call their country something else: Čechy (Cheh-khih). The issue has been only clumsily resolved in English: "The Czech Republic." Simply said, English is alone in having no equivalent like "Czechia" or "Czechland" to more elegantly describe the Czech lands. Somebody should get on this right away.

At about this time, Poland and the Soviet Union issued an official apology for their 1968 invasion of Czechoslovakia, evoking angry (and ironic) denunciations from the Husák government. Gorbachev was very active behind the scenes during the November 1989 crisis, keeping contact with Havel and the Civic Forum while pressuring Husák to accept peaceful change. Czechoslovak citizens massed on the night of November 26 some 750,000-strong in Prague and organized a massive nationwide strike on November 27 that finally brought the communists to their knees, forcing them to open negotiations with the Civic Forum.

On November 29, the national assembly struck down government censorship, released all political prisoners, and removed all references in the constitution to the communist party. The borders were opened, fortifications along the West German border were dismantled, and on December

10, 1989, Gustav Husák named the first noncommunist government in Czechoslovakia since 1948. Husák then promptly resigned.

Weeks later, on December 28, former dissident Václav Havel was chosen by the Federal Assembly to replace Husák as president, and the next day, the assembly elected none other than Alexander Dubček as its speaker, and both were received by rapturous crowds on a balcony overlooking Václav (Wencelas) Square in Prague. Thus ended what Czechs would later call the *sametová revoluce*, the Velvet Revolution.

F. Bulgaria Knows Peer Pressure When It Sees It

The ripples of the changes shaking Eastern Europe in 1989 spread out and reached into the most unlikely places, spooking one of the Soviet Bloc's staunchest pro-Soviet regimes so much that it crumbled like a house of cards at the slightest challenge. Sofia has a park, Southern Park (Южен парк; YOO-zhen Park)—the city's second largest—which the communists for years treated sort of like Speakers' Corner in Hyde Park in London. Any polemicist or nutcase could stand on their proverbial soapbox in the park and let loose on almost any subject, within reason, with minimal fear of repercussions from the regime. Since few people heard the rants, anyway, it was an allowable vent for antiregime resentment and of course the DS (Bulgarian KGB) could keep track of dissidents.

As the West watched in awe at the events unfolding in East Germany and Czechoslovakia, in early November 1989 a group of activists, Eko-glasnost, managed to muster some 5,000 people for an environmental protest in Southern Park. Eko-glasnost was, on the surface, merely an environmental group founded by Lyubomir Ivanov, a mathematician, explorer, and political activist, but Ivanov's intent was to develop an effective challenge to the communist regime. It turned out he didn't have to. Bulgaria in 1989 was very similar to Hungary in that its communist party had a very organized and determined reformist wing. These reformists, claiming to want to head off East German and Czechoslovak-style mass protests, used the excuse of the Eko-glasnost demonstration to oust longtime communist dictator Todor Zhivkov on November 10, replacing him with his foreign minister, Petar Mladenov.

At first, the West assumed Mladenov was just window-dressing, an attempt on the communists' part to avoid real change, but within months Mladenov shocked the critics by relinquishing the communist party's monopoly on power in February 1990, and holding free and open elections in June 1990, the first such since 1931 in Bulgaria. The communist reformers had the momentum in Bulgaria (again, like Hungary) but the opposition was splintered and poorly organized, allowing the communists—reformed into the Bulgarian Socialist Party (*Българска социалистическа партия*)—to win the elections. But later the opposition became better organized and succeeded in winning elections. In July 1991 Lyubomir Ivanov led the effort to rewrite the Bulgarian constitution.

G. Asking for a Light in the Romanian Powderkeg

By early December 1989, the world stood amazed as communist regimes had fallen like dominoes across Eastern Europe and the Berlin Wall had fallen—and all relatively peacefully. That was about to change. On the night of December 16, the Romanian *Securitate* (the Romanian KGB) tried to arrest an ethnic Hungarian Reformist priest, László Tőkés (LAHSS-low TEWK-aysh) in Timişoara (Tee-mee SHOW-ah-rah), but a crowd of his parishioners—soon joined by ethnic Romanians—surrounded the house in an act of stunning bravery and defiance, refusing to give way.

Encouraged as the Securitate withdrew in confusion, the crowd grew and moved downtown where they attacked communist party buildings. Rioting spread in the city and the crowds chanted anticommunist slogans throughout the next day until the army was called in and carried out a bloody massacre, killing hundreds of unarmed civilians. Ceauşescu held a mass rally in Bucharest (televised live) on December 21 to bolster support for his regime, but was stunned when the crowd began to heckle him, and shooting broke out. Ceauşescu fled into the Central Committee building while Bucharest erupted into anticommunist riots.

At first, the army and *Securitate* attacked the rioting protestors (with horrific consequences) but overnight and on December 22, while workers from surrounding towns streamed into the capital to join the protests, the army switched sides and attacked *Securitate* forces. Ceauşescu and his wife Elena fled the capital in a helicopter but the pilot landed unexpectedly, claiming the army was threatening to shoot him down, and abandoned the dictator and his wife by the side of a rural road.

They were arrested later that day by local police while hitchhiking. Meanwhile fierce fighting raged all across Romania between the army and the Securitate, but eventually the army gained the upper hand and the battles turned into hunting expeditions as soldiers sought out secret Securitate arms caches and safehouses.

On Christmas Day, December 25, stunned Romanians watched video footage on their TVs of Nicolae and Elena Ceauşescu being put on an improvised trial for crimes against humanity, and immediately after being found guilty, led into a nearby courtyard and gunned down. The *Conducător*[7] was dead, and Securitate resistance waned as their cause died with Ceauşescu.

The Romanian Revolution of 1989 filled the world's living rooms with images of open warfare in the heart of Europe for the first time since World War II. An estimated 1,000 were killed in the fighting, and for months afterward diehard Securitate stragglers sniped at crowds or kidnapped citizens for torture and execution. The Romanian Revolution was a genuine popular revolt against tyranny, and like the Hungarian Revolution of 1956, Romanians cut the communist symbol out of the center of their flag. However, some observers have come to view the Romanian Revolution more as a coup, with communist party colleagues throwing Ceauşescu to the lions to save their own skins.

Indeed, the impromptu court that convicted and executed Ceauşescu on December 24, 1989 was comprised of Romanian officials who knew of Ceauşescu's crimes in detail *because they had helped him commit them*. These same officials formed an umbrella group of mostly former communists, the *Frontul Salvării Naţionale* (National Salvation Front) that held power in the country for years to come, and while discarding the worst elements of communist rule, still resisted meaningful economic reforms.

The Front still did Romania a great favor in getting rid of the psychopath Ceauşescu, and if Romania remained corrupt and relatively undeveloped, it was far less oppressive under the Front and allowed Romanians hitherto unheard of freedoms. Also, by creating the façade of democracy in Romania, it unintentionally planted the seeds of democratic institutions that later empowered Romanians to oust the Front in free elections and replace it with more democratic-minded politicians. The Front may have succeeded in slowing reform for some time, but it helped give birth to a modern-day democratic Romania.

H. Albania and Frost in Hell

As 1989 closed, Albania seemed as hermetically sealed as ever, and uncompromisingly entrenched in its hyper-Stalinist ways. However, despite extremely tight controls on information, news of the collapse of the Soviet Bloc in Eastern Europe seeped in, and began to foment disruptions in the Land of the Eagles.[8] In January 1990, demonstrations by workers broke out in Shkodër (SHKO-der), and the Albanian communists under Ramiz Alia declared a state of emergency, all the while loudly denouncing the reforms elsewhere in Eastern Europe.

More worker demonstrations erupted in Berat (BAY-rat) in May, and in July students in Tiranë held protests while thousands—some estimate about 5,000—sought refuge in foreign embassies in Tiranë. The *Sigurimi*

447

(SEE-goor-ee-mee; Albanian KGB) carried out brutal beatings and murdered hundreds of citizens unlucky enough to get caught outside the safety of the foreign embassy compounds, but living conditions in the country were so terrible that many Albanians still thought it worth the risk. With the country's economy stuck in the usual Stalinist quagmire, Alia was forced to seek economic assistance abroad, which meant agreeing to a few "ground rules." In September 1990, he agreed to respect the requirements of the Conference on Security and Cooperation in Europe (CSCE), guaranteeing human rights. This was put to the test just months later, in December, when massive student protests again rocked Tiranë, and after an unsuccessful attempt by the Sigurimi to break up the demonstration. Alia gave in and conceded many of the students' demands.

In response to the students, in December 1990 Alia granted an end to the dictatorship, the formation of a pluralistic multiparty political system, and an end to censorship and political prisoners. It was an astounding victory. Within weeks the first opposition newspapers and political parties in Albania since the 1920s sprang up, and free elections were held just months later, in March and April 1991. Alia was chosen president by the new parliament, and the formulation of a new constitution began, but economic conditions continued to deteriorate and tens of thousands of Albanians tried to escape the country in what amounted to a boat exodus throughout 1991 across the Adriatic to Italy—which, at its closest point, is only about 60 miles (100 km) from Albania—prompting a major joint operation by the Italian and Albanian navies to turn these boats back.

Still, while some hard years of economic change lay ahead, Albania was a free land as religious institutions closed by the communists opened again and Albanians developed a functioning democracy in what was probably one of the last places in Europe one would expect it. In April 1992, Sali Berisha (SAH-lee Bare-EE-shah) became Albania's first noncommunist and first freely elected president since the 1920s.

USELESS TRIVIA: WASH YOUR HANDS!

In ancient Rome, pollution wasn't just an environmental problem but a spiritual one as well. Things like a death or a crime required that the community be spiritually cleansed and repurified through ceremonies conducted by priests, to get rid of bad mojo. This process was called *lustration*.

In modern-day Eastern Europe, this process of lustration lives on, but in a different guise: "lustration" describes the processes by which the modern-day governments are coming clean about the long-suppressed secret deeds and crimes of the pre-1989 dictatorships. Instead of priests, these modern-day lustration processes are conducted by courts and parliaments. The exercise is not just for the history books; many of these crimes were committed within living memory, which means that often the victims as well as the perpetrators are still alive, and potentially subject to either compensation or criminal charges.

The communist regimes' secret police services all spied extensively on their own citizens, relying heavily on citizen informants, some voluntary, others not. In 1990 some countries such as Germany and Romania simply threw their archives open, allowing citizens access to all their own records, but this brought traumatic revelations of personal betrayals by close friends and family members. Other countries such as Poland have been more cautious in releasing records, provoking accusations that elements of the former regime were protecting themselves. After all, the lead archivist for the DS (Bulgarian KGB) in Sofia was outright murdered in 1990.

Further complicating matters has been the fact that some of the communist regimes, seeing the coming collapse in 1989, planted falsified records to discredit dissidents and enemies, forcing current governments to subject records to extensive verification processes. When the Polish communist party Central Committee building was transformed into the Warsaw Stock Exchange in April 1991, Polish Cardinal Józef Glemp walked through the exchange on its first day and blessed the facilities, "driving the communist demons out," as he quipped. It is not quite so easy, however. After the horrors of the Nazi regime, Germans created a special word for this kind of national self-examination: *Vergangenheitsbewältigung*, literally "confrontation with your past." Eastern Europeans have a century's worth of the history of right- and left-wing dictatorships to confront. Still, though painful and fraught with unpleasant discoveries, it is not for naught:

> "If twenty years ago, lustration had been carried out [by the first post-Soviet government], today [Russians] would not be living in a corrupt, authoritarian state."

—*Yuly Nisnevich, Professor at the Moscow Higher School of Economics*

I. Playing Fiddle on the Deck of the Titanic: the Soviet Union

With the collapse of the Soviet imperial realm in Eastern Europe, many non-Russian groups in the Soviet Union itself began to wonder how far this end-of-empire thing could be taken. Soon Gorbachev found himself fighting a rearguard action to keep individual Soviet republics from bolting, with particularly strong secessionist movements in the Baltics, the Caucasus, and Russia itself. Gorbachev tried to shore up his position with a national referendum on the continued existence of the Soviet Union in March 1991 and the results came back generally positive. However, when Gorbachev used these results to negotiate a new union treaty with the republics, the result was a far weaker union that devolved much power from Moscow onto the individual republics, in effect reducing the Soviet Union to a confederation. Fearing things were spinning out of his control, Gorbachev resorted to force in April 1991, with Soviet security forces killing 177 unarmed civilians in Lithuania, Georgia, and Azerbaijan. But as his own puppets in Eastern Europe had already discovered, the time for military solutions had long since passed. Gorbachev reluctantly decided to sign the new treaty.

Soviet hardliners panicked. A week or so before the signing ceremony in August 1991, Gorbachev took off to the small Crimean resort of Foros for a vacation. On the evening of August 18, a surprise delegation of military and KGB officers showed up at Gorbachev's dacha and demanded he institute a state of emergency to forstall the new union treaty. Gorbachev flatly refused. He was then put under KGB arrest (with all phone lines to his dacha cut), and the next day the conspirators announced on Soviet television the formation of something called "The State Committee on the State of Emergency," which took over power in the country as Gorbachev was "unwell." Soviet army and KGB troops flooded Soviet cities.

However, Russians knew a coup when they saw one and an opposition began to coalesce around Russia's parliamentary building called the White House. In an amazing lapse of judgment the coup conspirators allowed Russia's radical president, Boris Yeltsin, to enter the White House from where he directed countermeasures, even holding dramatic press conferences for the world's media from atop a Soviet tank while urging Soviet soldiers not to attack the large civilian crowds that had formed around the building. The weak-kneed coup-plotters launched several probing attacks against the crowd resulting in several civilian deaths but did not have the stomach to order the all-out assault required, and the embarrassing stand-off endured for days, with each passing hour chipping away at the coup's credibility. Over time several military units declared they would not attack the crowds if ordered, and finally, on August 21, the coup folded.

When Gorbachev arrived back in Moscow he was greeted as a hero, but with muted applause. The real hero who had saved everyone from a neo-Stalinist relapse was Boris Yeltsin. Yeltsin had been a protégé of Gorbachev's but his reformist zeal got him booted out of the Supreme Soviet in the late 1980s. Undeterred, Yeltsin built up his own populist power base within Russia and pushed through radical reforms in the Russian Federation despite Gorbachev, even managing in June 1991 to get himself elected president of Russia in the first free elections in Russia since possibly 1917. Russia was still just one of sixteen "republics" (provinces) in the Soviet Union, but Yeltsin had effectively put Russia's growing autonomy on a collision course with Gorbachev's Soviet authority, and during the events of the August 1991 coup attempt, Yeltsin was able to leverage his power as president of Russia ("president" meaning "governor") to override and counter many orders being issued to the Soviet military.

When Gorbachev returned after the coup, he was returning to a Soviet state whose authority had seriously eroded and whose government had been crippled by the bumbling (and frequently drunk) conspirators. Yeltsin simply began behaving like Russia was a sovereign state, and with each day more and more people believed him, ignoring Gorbachev and the Soviet Union in favor of Yeltsin's Russian Federation. Within days Yeltsin ordered the seizure of the communist party's assets across Russia, and the administrators, police, and courts complied.

In November, Yeltsin met with the leaders of Ukraine and Belarus (ignoring Gorbachev altogether) and created the Commonwealth of Independent States (CIS) to coordinate economic and security policies, in effect dissolving the USSR. Gorbachev tried to continue as if nothing had happened but Ukraine declared its independence on December 1, followed shortly by other Soviet republics. Gorbachev recognized the inevitable and resigned his post on Christmas Day, 1991, and the Soviet flag was replaced over the Kremlin by the Russian national flag.

Stalin had organized the Soviet Union into "republics" based on the fiction that these countries—many of which had tried to declare their independence in 1918 but were reconquered by Bolshevik armies—were enthusiastic voluntary members of the Soviet Union, with the added bonus that he was able to get the United Nations in 1945 to recognize both Soviet Ukraine and Belarus as full voting members of the UN, in effect giving the Soviet Union three votes (against just one each for Britain and the U.S., for example).

This created headaches in 1991, however, as these bogus republics suddenly became real ones and tried to bolt the crumbling Soviet Union with all the assets Stalin had assigned to them, not intending that they would ever actually leave. This indeed still generates tensions today between Russia and what Russians call the "near abroad" (ближнее зарубежье, meaning lands once ruled by the former Soviet Union).

J. Libre Baltica, Take II

The earliest and starkest declarations, however, came from the Baltic states—Lithuania, Latvia, and Estonia—which, as early as May 1989, declared illegal their incorporation into the Soviet Union in 1940 (and 1944). In August 1989, as Tadeusz Mazowiecki in neighboring Poland was taking up his historic post, Baltic activists organized the *Baltijos kelias* (Lithuanian) / *Baltijas ceļš* (Latvian) / *Balti kett* (Estonian)—"the Baltic Way"—on the 50th anniversary of the Molotov-Ribbentrop Pact, forming a 400-mile (600 km) long human chain stretching from northern Estonia to southern Lithuania to call attention to the Balts' plight. In Estonia, a continuous series of rock concerts by Estonian musicians, coupled with demonstrations, called for Estonian independence, while in Latvia and Lithuania local congresses were formed to organize national resistance.

In early 1990 the three states moved to declare their independence but Gorbachev blockaded them into submission, forcing them to back down temporarily. But a year later, in January 1991, events again began to spin out of control and Gorbachev ordered Soviet military forces into Vilnius, Riga, and Tallinn. Barackades were erected in the streets and Soviet forces killed several civilians in Riga and Vilnius—tarnishing Gorbachev's image around the world—but all for nought. As soon as the Soviet coup collapsed in Moscow in August 1991, all three Baltic states declared their independence. Gorbachev still stalled, but Yeltsin forced the issue by recognizing their independence regardless. In September 1991 Lithuania, Latvia, and Estonia were welcomed into the United Nations as full members.

K: Agonia: The Many Deaths of Yugoslavia

Every day (in the 1970s) along the barbedwire fence dividing the Yugoslav-Romanian border, border guards from both countries passed one another as they went about their respective rounds. One day, the Romanian border guard broke the protocol of silence and shouted across the fence to his Yugoslav colleague, "Hey Ivo, what are you going to do if Tito dies?" With that, he erupted into laughter and continued on his rounds. The next day, as the two approached each other again, it was the Yugoslav guard's turn as he shouted across to his Romanian colleague, "Hey Ioncu, what will you do if Ceauşescu *doesn't* die?" and he roared with laughter as he walked on.

—Popular joke circulating throughout Eastern Europe in the 1970s

Ironically, Yugoslavia's demise had little to do with the question of communism or the deposition of dictators. Gorbachev's renunciation of the Brezhnev Doctrine meant nothing in Yugoslavia, as it had never really applied to Tito's realm, and the changes sweeping late 1980s Moscow that proved so devastating to the Eastern European dictatorships had little effect in Belgrade. Indeed, after 1991 Yugoslavia stood out as the sore thumb of

Eastern Europe, the final holdout of the postwar communist dictatorships. There was trouble brewing in the country, but it was not so much anticommunist in nature as *anti-Yugoslav*. The liberation movements of 1989 that freed Eastern Europe of the Soviet-installed dictatorships unleashed very different forces in Yugoslavia.

The story begins in April 1987 with a young, up-and-coming member of the Serbian communist party, Slobodan Milošević (Slo-BO-dan Meel-AW-sheh-veetch), being sent to Kosovo to calm local tensions after some interethnic violence. Instead, Milošević inflamed local tensions by giving a fire-and-brimstone Serbian nationalist speech, making him the darling of Serbian nationalists on whose backs he rode to supreme power in the country over the next two years. He began dismantling the Tito-legacy Yugoslav state machinery and taking over regional governments across Yugoslavia. It was Milošević's attempt to change the Yugoslav constitution in 1989 to allow him to do the same to the Federal republics that stirred trouble in Slovenia and Croatia.

Throughout 1990 Milošević weakened Yugoslav national institutions by continuously provoking political crises, further concentrating power in his hands and causing Slovenia and Croatia to distance themselves from Belgrade. Both finally held referendums and declared their independence in June 1991, provoking Milošević to declare a national emergency and order the JNA (*Jugoslovenska Narodna Armija*; Yugoslav People's Army) to seize control of the breakway republics. After only ten days of fighting, the JNA abandoned Slovenia—which had few Serbs—instead concentrating on neighboring Croatia, which had significant Serbian minorities dating from the days of the Ottoman-Habsburg wars. Croatia was led at this point by Franjo Tuđman (FRAN-yo TOODJ-man), a Croat nationalist as ardent as Milošević; Milošević was determined that the Croat Serbs would be ruled by Belgrade, and Tuđman was just as determined that his reborn Croatia would keep every inch of its Yugoslav-era borders. From 1991 to 1995, the JNA and Croatian armed forces (aided in part by a sympathetic Hungary) fought one another across Croatia, with the JNA initially holding the upper hand, seizing eastern Slavonia and large parts of Serb-populated southern Croatia, but with revived Croat forces launching a spectacular counteroffensive in 1995 that not only drove JNA forces from much of Croat soil but also effectively ethnically cleansed Croatia of most of its Serbian minority. Both sides committed gross atrocities against each others' civilians, the details of which the EU and United Nations are still sorting out today.

Meanwhile, in the midst of the Serb-Croat War, the various ethnic groups of Bosnia-Herzegovina began to stir. Milošević declared his intention of retaining Bosnia-Herzegovina, which convinced Muslims (Bosniaks) and Croats to band together while Bosnian Serbs simultaneously established their own state (*Republika Srpska*).

When, after a referendum, Bosnia-Herzegovina declared its independence in March 1992, the Serbian enclaves—with JNA army units wearing Republika Srpska uniforms—attacked, quickly overrunning some 70% of the republic and laying bloody siege to its capital, Sarajevo. The Bosnian Serb leader, Radovan Karadžić (Rah-DO-van Kar-AH-djeetch), waged a genocidal war against Muslim Bosniaks, ethnically cleansing Bosnia through terror and mass murder, the most infamous example being the massacre of some 8,000 Bosniak refugees at Srebrenica by Republika Srpska forces in July 1995.

Just months into the conflict, Bosnian Croats suddenly turned on their erstwhile Bosniak allies in August 1992, transforming the conflict into a three-way war. But under Western pressure the Bosnian Croats settled with the Muslim Bosniaks in 1994.

A series of Bosnian Serb massacres of Bosniak civilians during the summer provoked a sustained NATO aerial bombing campaign against Republika Srpska forces across Bosnia in September and October 1995. This campaign helped reverse Bosnian Serb military gains. Washington then heavily pressured Milošević, Tuđman, and Bosniak leader Alija Izetbegović (Ah-LEE-yah Ee-zet-beg-O-veetch) to negotiate, resulting in the Dayton Peace Accords in November 1995, ending the Bosnian War.

Just as the Bosnian War was finally winding down, things exploded in Kosovo. Over the 1990s, Milošević had been dismantling the Kosovo republic's administration and replacing it with his own, excluding Albanians from any positions of authority. Some Kosovo Albanians responded by founding underground groups, some of which began attacking Serbian authorities and civilians. The main group to emerge was *Ushtria Çlirimtare e Kosovës* (UÇK; Kosovo Liberation Army, or KLA) whose attacks provoked major Serbian (JNA) military reprisals in 1996. These operations turned into a massive campaign of ethnic cleansing against Kosovo Albanians, which in turn prompted Western (as well as Russian) attempts at mediation in late 1998. The failure of these talks led to another NATO bombing campaign, from March until June 1999, this time targeting all of (remaining) Yugoslavia, ending in a Serbian capitulation and Kosovo's occupation by NATO forces.

With the Ten Day War in June 1991, Slovenia secured its independence, and Macedonia followed in September 1991. (With Milošević then focused on Croatia, Macedonia's exit was ignored by Belgrade.) In November 1995, Yugoslavia (Serbia), Croatia, and Bosnia-Herzegovina signed the Dayton Peace Accords, ending both the Serb-Croat War and the Bosnian War and recognizing Croatia's and Bosnia-Herzegovina's independence.

The NATO air campaign in 1999 brought an end to the Kosovo War, too, but left Kosovo as (a NATO-administered) part of Yugoslavia. Milošević lost an election in October 2000, and after attempting to falsify the results, was ousted by a popular revolt in Belgrade and was eventually turned over the International War Crimes Tribunal in the Hague. After a series of minor revisions in the 1990s, Belgrade ditched the Yugoslav name in favor of *Заједница Србија и Црна Гора* (Union of Serbia and Montenegro) in February 2003. However, in May 2006 Montenegro voted to secede, and in February 2008 Kosovo also voted for its independence.

Collectively known as the Yugoslav Implosion Wars, an estimated 125,500 people were killed in them and some 3.4 million were driven from their homes as refugees. The suffering inflicted through ethnic cleansing, mass rapes, and other war crimes, as well as destruction to Bosniak, Kosovo Albanian, Serbian, and Croatian homes and historic cultural sites throughout the region is incalculable.

USELESS TRIVIA: WARS AREN'T JUST FUN FOR PEOPLE!

Zoos are fun places where people can see and learn about exotic animals from all over the world. For armies, however, zoos are also wonderful places with lots of reinforced concrete and defensible positions. Throughout late 1991, Yugoslav and Serb militia forces laid bloody siege to the Croatian city of Vukovar (VOO-ko-var) in eastern Slavonia. About 34 km (21 miles) northwest of Vukovar, upstream on the Drava River, lays the city of Osijek (O-see-yek), which Yugoslav and Serb forces also attacked while they besieged nearby Vukovar. Osijek also happened to be home to Croatia's largest zoo, whose natural defenses Croatian forces utilized to help repel Yugoslav and Serb attacks against Osijek.

Many animals—captive in their cages—were killed by crossfire, mortars, artillery, and strafing by JNA jets, while survivors were often driven insane by the incessant explosions and gunfire around them. The zoo's staff refused to abandon them, however, staying behind to continue to feed and (try to) protect their animal charges amid the fighting. Some paid with their lives. The zookeepers had a helper in their midst, Zoltán Takács (ZOL-tahn TUH-kotch), a fellow zookeeper from neighboring Hungary.[9] The zoo staff arranged with Takács to make repeated trips from the Osijek Zoo to Hungary, each time bringing with him as many animals from Osijek as possible. This included animals as large as an elephant, as well as lions and tigers, and many smaller ones. Takács had much help, for instance from local Croatian ferrymen who risked Serb mortar fire to bring Takács and his animal charges across the Drava River as they made their 35 km (21 mile) trip northward to Hungary and from there to zoos in Hungary, western Croatia, or Slovenia. Some animals, including a giraffe, had to be abandoned as too large to safely smuggle, but hundreds of other animals were saved. After the war, the animals were eventually returned to their home zoo in Osijek.

The Yugoslav Implosion Wars were the largest-scale military operations in Europe since World War II, and they shattered many myths (and hopes) about the post–Cold War world. They opened political rifts between the West and post-Soviet Russia, as well as within the West itself. The two American-led NATO campaigns proved controversial (though many Eastern Europeans outside Yugoslavia appreciated the decisive NATO military intervention). A decade after the wars ended, Slovenia is increasingly prosperous while both Serbia and Croatia are more democratic, and in 2013 Croatia joined Slovenia as a member of the EU; Slovenia had joined in 2004. Croatia's years of reluctance to investigate and prosecute war crimes suspects had—alongside its unresolved border issues with Slovenia—slowed its accession. As for Serbia, with its arrest of top war crimes suspects sought by the International Criminal Tribunal for the former Yugoslavia (including Bosnian Serb leaders Radovan Karadžić and Ratko Mladić) now out of the way, as of this writing it likewise appears destined to join the EU ranks, though not before 2014.

Macedonia is mired in an absurd political feud abroad (with neighboring Greece) and corruption at home. Bosnia-Herzegovina and Kosovo, both nominally independent, are still sharply divided by ethnic conflict and have so far failed to develop truly national institutions.

Despite clearly contradictory goals, nationalists in all warring regions often colluded in the dismantling of the Yugoslav state and indeed today relations between Belgrade, Zagreb, Ljubljana, and Sarajevo are actually surprisingly cordial, with cooperation on important issues common. But their collective legacy of war, war crimes, and ethnic cleansing has left an indelible and divisive mark on modern-day Europe.

A Romanian Army T-72 (Soviet-manufacture) tank guards a key entrance road into the city of Arad in northwestern Romania in 1989, near the River Mureş (MOO-resh), in the closing stages of the Romanian Revolution.

(Photo by the author)

**Written and performed by Hungarians Tamás Cseh[10] and
Géza Bereményi, originally on their 1990 album *Új Dalak***

Kelet-Európa,
Európa lichthofja,
kidobált szemetek, a fal ridegen
    mered.
Kelet-Európa,
vagy Kelet-Közép-Európa,
sor került rád is, Káin,
    mostohagyerek.
Édes szivem, te,
vak, süket nóta,
ócska a verkliéneked.

56-Európa,
68-Európa,
debillé pofozott, ősz, eltorzult
    gyerek.
Kelet-Európa,
ott ülnek a boltba
tiranno- marxo- geronto- és
    trabantfejesek.
Kényszeres nóta,
vak zongorista,
hallgatom tompa éneked.

Félszeg Európa,
részeg Európa,
rokona embernek, így hát
    majomrokon.
Nem is Európa,
igenis Európa,
szemüveged kapd le, tán jár még
    egy pofon.
Nem is Európa,
igenis Európa,
mit álmodsz, én továbbgondolom.

Prága-Európa,
Varsó-Európa,
szőrszálat hasogatsz, csűrsz és
    csavarsz.

Remény-Európa,
röhej-Európa,
jópofa hatalmi játék e tavasz.
Édes szivem, te,
reszli-Európa,
álmom, hogy másmilyen maradsz.

Na mi van Európa,
Kelet-Európa,
hol a bal, hol a jobb, már nincs itt
    irány.
Reszli-Európa,
köztes-Európa,
feketepiacon vett engem anyám!
Hájas az élet,
részeg kis népek,
sok egymást vádoló talány.

Most te jössz, Kelet-Európa,
mindennek tudója,
bakancsban ugrálod hős
    tojástáncodat.
Valaha-Európa,
csak volt-Európa,
adtál te ezért már vért, szégyent
    sokat.
Járd, Kelet-Európa,
tánc van, Kelet-Európa,
táncolj, mert éppen most szabad.

Lóden-Európa,
kübli-Európa,
hol a tömegbe szállt, leszállt az ész.
Gyerünk, Európa,
Kelet-Európa,
sunyítva képzelegsz és röhögsz, ha
    remélsz.
Édes szivem, te,
szóljon a nóta,
énekeld azt, hogy semmi vész.

Szeretlek, Európa,
földnek sója,
vén gazemberek játéka, szivem.
És ismét Európa,
Kelet-Európa,
mondd azt már megintcsak kérlek,
    hogy igen!

Szűk, boros szájjal
énfölém hajolva
dúdold még ezt kicsit nekem:

Igen - Kelet-Európa.
Igen - Kelet-Európa.

Eastern Europe[11]
by Tamás Cseh and Géza Bereményi (1990)

Eastern Europe,
Europe's atrium,
The outcasts,
The wall still stands starkly.
Eastern Europe, or East Central
Europe,
Now it's your turn, you stepchild,
Cain.
My dearest, you, a blind and deaf
song,
you're sung to the accompaniment
of an old street organ.

1956 Europe,[12] 1968 Europe,[13]
Slapped till you're silly,
Gray, disfigured child.
Eastern Europe,
Sitting in your shops are tyrannical,
Marxist, bitter old Trabant[14] faces.
A compulsory song, a blind pianist,
I heard you softly singing.

Clumsy Europe, drunken Europe,
Related to humans
And thereby to monkeys, too.
You're not even Europe, but yes,
you are Europe,
Take off your glasses because
there's another blow coming.
No, you're not even Europe, but
yes you are Europe,
Your dreams are now my thoughts.

Prague Europe, Warsaw Europe
You cut your own hair and bend
your words.
The Europe of Hope, Europe of the
Absurd,
This spring is a pretty little power
    game.[15]
My dearest, raspy Europe,
I hope you will always be different.

So how are you, Europe? Eastern
    Europe,
Where's the left, where's the right?
There's no direction here
    anymore.[16]
Raspy Europe, in-between Europe,
My mother bought me on the black
    market.
A fat lifestyle, drunk little peoples
Posing each other accusatory
    riddles.

Now it's your turn, Eastern Europe,
All-knowing,
Wearing heavy boots you jump
    about in heroic dances.
Once-upon-a-time Europe, the
    once-was Europe,
You've shed enough blood, shamed
    yourself plenty.
It's your turn, Eastern Europe.

The dance has begun, Eastern Europe.
Dance now, because now you finally can![17]

Trenchcoat Europe, trough Europe,
When you form into crowds you lose your mind.
Let's be off, Europe,
Eastern Europe.
You quietly daydream and then laugh at your hope.
My dearest, please call the tune,
Sing aloud and show me you're not afraid anymore.

I love you, Europe, Salt of the Earth,
The games of old scoundrels, my dear.
And once again, Europe, Eastern Europe,
Please do say "yes" for me once again!
Lean over me with your wine-breath
And hum to me a little again, that

Yes, Eastern Europe;
Yes, Eastern Europe.

USELESS TRIVIA: FROM DEATH COMES LIFE!

It was the Nazi propaganda machine that first used the expression "iron curtain" to describe what would happen to Europe in the event of an Allied victory in the war, predicting an inevitable postwar fall-out between the Western democracies and the Soviet regime. That was a rare moment of prescience on the part of the Nazi rulers, so much so that Winston Churchill borrowed the expression when he made his famous description of the 4,400 mile-long (7,000 km) heavily-militarized border separating Soviet Europe from Western Europe during his speech at Westminster College in Fulton, Missouri in 1946. In creating the Iron Curtain, the Soviets and their puppet states applied the "defense in depth" principle, creating multiple layers of defensive works with wide buffer zones between them, using several different kinds of barbed, electrified, and razor wire fence, and placing trip wires and booby traps, minefields, watchtowers, and in some extreme cases manned machinegun pillboxes, while patrolling the border areas intensively with guards and military dogs. For some Soviet Bloc citizens, merely being within fifteen miles of the border without official permission was a crime resulting in a long prison sentence. Many who tried to cross were shot by their country's own border guards. The Iron Curtain transformed Eastern Europe into a prison, and its many defensive positions into a collective zone of death. That is, it was a zone of death for humans. A strange phenomenon developed over time whereby the "no-man's land" between the Iron Curtain's many defense zones became a de facto nature preserve where wildlife, some threatened by industrialization and the destruction of their natural habitats, found refuge.

The Iron Curtain became a beacon of life and a sanctuary for many Central and Eastern European animal and plant species endangered elsewhere in the industrializing Bloc. This status was secure so long as the Cold War continued and the Iron Curtain stood, but in 1989 the Soviet empire imploded and the Iron Curtain was dismantled. A Europe divided for two generations was once again united.

The collapse of the Soviet empire, while an occasion for rejoicing throughout Europe, nevertheless brought chaos and new political and economic challenges, but even amid all these changes some politicians across the newly united Europe recognized the Iron Curtain's role as an unplanned nature preserve, and began enacting legislation to formally protect these animal refuges. This culminated ultimately in the mid-2000s in the Iron Curtain Green Belt and Trail. Now Europe is crossed from north to south not by an artificial militarized border but by a long green nature preserve and hiking trail stetching from the Finnish-Russian border down through the Baltics, through Poland and Germany (along the old East-West German border) and further through Central Europe and into the Balkans, terminating on the Bulgarian-Turkish border on the Black Sea. The Iron Curtain Trail[18]—the brainchild of European Parliament MP Michael Cramer—hosts a series of nature preserves and also includes hiking and bicycle trails, as well as monuments and historical stops along the way relevant to the Cold War and the nearby countries, and it is still under development.

Painting of an iconic kiss between Brezhnev and Honecker, on Berlin Wall at East Side Gallery; February 20, 2013 (Image © badahos / Shutterstock.com)

EPILOGUE

Q: *A szocializmusban mitől félnek legjobban az emberek?*
A: *Attól, hogy nem lehet tudni, mit hoz a múlt.*
(**Q: What are people afraid of the most in socialism?**
A: You never know what the past will bring.") [1]

It has now been more than twenty years since the events of 1989–92, and an entire generation of Eastern Europeans has been born and raised to adulthood who have no memories of Soviet tanks or secret underground dissident *samizdat* newspapers. This generation thinks of the communist past as exactly that—the past, something that happened long ago, and while the past has a way of hanging around in Eastern Europe, these younger Eastern Europeans think of themselves as *Europeans* first and worry about things like Smartphones and the Eurovision song contest. Indeed, even the world's stereotypes of Eastern Europeans as stern commissars or steroid-infused Olympic athletes has been updated to images of skeletal supermodels and cheap immigrant plumbers. Throughout the 1970s and 80s, world news outlets provided a daily reminder that the region still suffered under conditions that for most Western Europeans were a relic of the war years but nowadays, if Eastern Europe makes the news, it's because a company is opening an office there, or someone in Romania makes a UFO video that goes viral. Travel shows have started featuring Eastern European destinations, and cities like Prague have become important stops on the European tour circuit. A strange but welcome sense of *normalcy* has descended upon the region. Let's now take a (brief) look, in FAQ format, at how Eastern Europe has come along over the past twenty (+) years and balances its past with its new present.

Q: Does Eastern Europe still exist?
A: I was on the phone not long ago with the CEO of a major German company, and I asked him about his company's operations in Eastern Europe. He began describing things they were doing in Russia and Ukraine, when I interrupted him to ask about Poland. "Poland?" he asked, astonished. "That's not Eastern Europe, that's *Central Europe.*"

Most Poles would be very pleased to have heard that answer and would heartily agree. Eastern Europe is a concept invented by others, by the West, and it has always carried the connotation of a backward, underdeveloped, superstitious, and remote region isolated from the modern ideas and life-styles of Western Europe. To be Eastern European implies that one is poor, undereducated, and provincial, and prone to occasional irrational fits of horrendous violence inspired by ethnic or religious fanaticism. But these and other stereotypes are beginning to fade.

In the early 2000s, French newspapers complained about cheap immigrant labor from Eastern Europe—with images of the Polish plumber—but when in 2011 the EU began to ease certain work permit categories that restricted how many Eastern Europeans could work in Western Europe, Germans in particular were astonished when so few Eastern Europeans took advantage of the opportunity. A subtle shift is underway, perhaps driven by a new generation which has lived its entire life without an East-West divide, without Soviet tanks or heroic underground dissidents. My generation assumed that the Iron Curtain was a more or less permenant feature of our world, but the average twenty-three-year-old European today, whether in Antwerp or Zagreb, sees the Soviet empire in the same terms as the Holy Roman or the Ottoman empires: history.

Still, the "Eastern Europe" label isn't going away quite so easily. Most global businesses, for instance, still include an Eastern European or CEE (Central & Eastern Europe) region. The Eastern Europe label was never a rational concept; Vienna is a "Western" city while Prague is an "Eastern" city, but Prague is actually about 100 miles (160 km) *west* of Vienna. For many Europeans 40+ years old, the memories of Soviet Eastern Europe continue to inform what they see today, but that ignores many of the political and economic gains countries in the region have made, closing many of the developmental gaps between Western and Eastern Europe and even, in a few categories, surpassing their Western peers.

There are still some hurdles to overcome. Do Dutch or Spanish students learn about Poland or Romania in their European history classes? Still, the imaginary line that once so starkly separated a continent *is* fading in many people's minds, and for once the Western European states are thinking of the countries of Eastern Europe in terms of their ability to contribute to European prosperity rather than their potential roles as threats to Western security. Eastern Europe is slowly becoming eastern Europe, and its inhabitants are getting on with the daily business of being *Europeans*.

Q: How does Eastern Europe fit into the world today?

A: In the 1970s, the American political scientist Immanuel Wallerstein came up with the *World Systems* theory, which classified the world's countries as either core or periphery countries. In his theory, core countries are the developed countries that consume the world's resources, while the periphery countries are doomed to supplying the core countries with raw materials, making their economies in the process forever dependent on the core countries (and thereby stunted in development). Wallerstein classified Eastern Europe as a periphery region, but he later (1990s) refined his theory to include a "semi-periphery" category of "in-between" economies, into which most of Eastern Europe was moved. This fits with Cold War terminology which described the advanced Western countries as the "First World," the Soviet Bloc (i.e., Eastern Europe) as "Second World," and the rest of the world as the "Third World." Still, in a world today where nine of the twenty largest economies (by GDP) in the world are in Asia or Latin America and the world's manufacturing base has largely relocated to so-called periphery countries, Wallerstein's theory is on thin theoretical ice.

Indeed, as the European Union struggles to find a solution to its debt crisis, some of the better-performing economies in Eastern Europe have brought these countries into a surprisingly prominent role in the EU's internal power struggles. As a British EU-watcher noted in late 2012:

> Forty years ago Europe was being shaped by those who had survived World War II on the Western Front. Today, more and more, it is being driven by those who lived through the brutality of the Eastern Front, and who endured 40 years of communism.[2]

This new role for some Eastern European countries is reshaping the EU's political structures, and may breathe hope into broken EU policies and practices increasingly seen as undemocratic or ineffective. The EU and NATO are still viewed by a majority of Eastern Europeans as crucial for European prosperity and security, whereas many Western Europeans have become disillusioned or see the EU as an unfulfilled promise. All Eastern European countries still have some important economic and political challenges, and the region is still classified by investors as an "emerging markets" region (and as such it is still attracting many investment $$$s from Western Europe nowadays), but Eastern Europe may have an important, if unexpected role in helping revitalize Europe and the European Union project.

Q: Are ethnic tensions and anti-Semitism still problems in Eastern Europe?
A: In a word, yup. In 2011, Slovakia passed a language law targeting its Hungarian minority, sparking mutual acrimony. A 2010 school funding law in Lithuania generated tensions with Poland, with radical nationlists on both sides inflaming the issue, impacting relations between Vilnius and Warsaw still in 2012. A series of random murders in the spring of 2012

in Macedonia has threatened the delicate balance between Slavic Macedonians and Albanians as radical Islamicists have taken credit for the murders. Hungary has spawned a shameful neofascist movement called *Jobbik*—a pun in Hungarian meaning "the Rightists," from the full name *Jobbik Magyarországért Mozgalom*; "Movement for a Better Hungary"— which has a paramilitary wing like Hitler's 1920s S.A. Brownshirts and which has been involved in violent confrontations with Gypsies. Jobbik parliamentary supporters have also publicly made shockingly anti-Semitic statements. And stories of abuse of Gypsy rights have also emerged with saddening regularity from the Czech Republic, Slovenia, and other countries in the region.

In Germany, the *Bund der Vertriebenen* (Federation of Expellees—an influential organization representing those Germans expelled from Eastern Europe after World War II), under its controversial leader Erika Steinbach, is building a museum called *Zentrum gegen Vertreibungen* (Center Against Expulsions), which lavishly details the plight and suffering of German expellees, while largely ignoring the similar plights of non-Germans expelled or worse by the Nazis or Soviets during and after the war. Violence against foreigners has been rising in Germany recently, particularly in the former GDR regions.

In Russia, violent attacks against non-Russians have been rising steadily, especially in the country's main urban centers, with 57 killed and 196 injured in racist-motivated attacks in Moscow alone in 2009, according to a report by the Immigration and Refugee Board of Canada.[3] Meanwhile, in Latvia a referendum on making Russian a second language of the country was struck down in voting results, causing yet more frictions between majority Latvians and the country's large Russian minority.

Clearly, minority and ethnic issues remain divisive in Eastern Europe, but there has been some progress and there have been some bright spots. Some of the region's governments have somehow managed to find ways to cooperate despite long histories of animosity, and these examples have had an important impact on people's views in the region. Old habits do indeed die hard, and nationalist or religious populist demagogues will always exist in every country—think of the xenophobic Jean-Marie le Pen in France— but modern-day Eastern Europe is far removed from the nationalist demagoguery of the 1930s.

Q: What's happening with Russia? What went wrong?
A: With all the Eastern European countries, there was always—and still is—the danger of recidivism, the danger that the region's considerable non-democratic past will reassert itself and that these countries will succumb to

nationalist authoritarian governments promising to restore some glorious past golden age. The transformation that Eastern Europe has undergone since 1989 has been a series of economic, social, and political revolutions, all of them radically altering how Eastern Europeans live—and for some, not all those changes have been welcome or beneficial.

The closing of unprofitable industries subsidized by the communists but unable to compete on open markets has meant large-scale unemployment in some areas. Reforms have also pushed many bureaucrats and state employees who had thrived under the communists out of not only their jobs, but out of positions of power and prestige in society. In nearly all the former Soviet Bloc countries, more responsible fiscal policies have meant painful cuts to long-cherished government services—impacting healthcare, education, retirement pensions, and so on.

The temptation on the part of ruling elites or nationalists to try to legislate a new golden age is a danger everywhere in Eastern Europe. The self-pitying *Jobbik* neofascist movement in Hungary is attracting a surprising number of adherents. Poland, Bulgaria, and Estonia all struggle with corruption. In Romania, petty political rivalries threaten to tear the country's nascent democratic experiment apart. The post-1989 reforms across Eastern Europe were necessary and have overwhelmingly improved the lives of most Eastern Europeans, but they've not come without pain, and some question the price.

The reforms were most necessary in Russia, a state that at the Soviet collapse in 1991 was most mired in corruption, bureaucratic lethargy, a brutal and oppressive police system, and a ruling elite more akin to medieval aristocracy than a modern-day republic. However, the depth of Russia's desperate need to change in 1991 meant that the required reforms would be more painful and more far-reaching than those in its former satellite states in Eastern Europe. Russians had to endure many years of misery as the artificially propped Soviet economy collapsed and the Russian government fundamentally reorganized itself.

This already excruciating process was made worse by the rise of parasitic former agents of the regime who leveraged their connections and access to funds and contacts to transform themselves into economic warlords, or as Russians soon called them, *Oligarchs*. They seized and exploited the assets of the former Soviet economy and made billions in the process. For most Russians, the 1990s were a new time of troubles with collapsing living standards, mass unemployment, rising crime rates, an alternately hostile or ineffective government, and all this in the midst of the humiliating collapse of the Soviet empire—defeat in the Cold War.

Boris Yeltsin had started very promisingly down the road of reform in the early 1990s, but the Soviet economy went into a tailspin and Yeltsin fumbled in dealing with corruption and rampant crime. He resigned suddenly in December 1999 and appointed a former sycophant from St. Petersburg, Vladimir Putin, as his successor.

Initially Putin talked democracy, but within a couple of years he began to dismantle Yeltsin's democratic reforms and recentralize state power in his own hands. He also undid most of Yeltsin's economic reforms, though the real consequences of this did not become immediately apparent because of global surging oil prices—Russia has the world's second largest oil deposits, after Saudi Arabia—which allowed Putin to artificially stimulate the Russian economy.

The economic crisis of 2008–09 and subsequent weak global oil prices have taken this ability away from the Russian government, however, and the Russian economy has been devastated. Putin is a former colonel in the KGB who relies on *Siloviki* (*Силовики*—See-LO-vee-kee; former KGB or state security apparatus agents) to rule modern-day Russia, appointing them as ministers, governors, mayors, and so on.

Putin's Russia has not sunk to Soviet levels of oppression or brutality—though it does rival the Soviet years in terms of corruption—but it has held back Russian economic and political development as its leaders try to squeeze every ounce of nostalgia for the imperial Soviet past they can. Indeed, at least some modern-day Russian commentators have claimed that Putin and his henchmen have, by delaying crucial reforms to modernize Russia's economy and society, in effect kept the Soviet legacy alive in Russian society on artificial life support, so that Russians in 2013 still live in the era of Soviet disintegration. The pain Russians experienced in the much-derided Yeltsin era of the 1990s is not finished, only delayed.

Many scions of the *ancién regime* in Moscow see the ascension of Eastern European countries to NATO as a threat, as Western military expansion into traditional Russian spheres of influence. But this is a 19th century view. NATO's chief attraction for Eastern Europeans is its stabilizing effect on security in the region, not just from external threats but from internal destabilizing forces as well. Indeed, because of NATO, Russia now has a far more stable and secure western frontier. If anything, Moscow should welcome cooperation with NATO in Eastern Europe as helping to provide a level of security for Russia that seven decades of Soviet rule did not—and unlike the old Soviet empire, NATO doesn't cost the Kremlin a cent (or kopek). NATO has a proven record in fostering regional cooperation and professionalizing the civilian-controlled militaries of its members, which is its strongest legacy in Eastern Europe. Since 1991, there have been a few half-hearted attempts at cooperation between Russia and NATO, with Russian officers present now stationed in NATO's headquarters and a joint exercise held in 2012. Russia has even been offered membership in NATO a couple times, but Moscow continues to see NATO as a Cold War foe rather than a modern organization for European security. Russia's envoy to NATO, Dmitry Rogozin, summed up Moscow's basic problem with NATO in 2009, "Great powers don't join coalitions, they create coalitions. Russia considers itself a great power."[4] Sooner or later, however, the reality is that Russia and Europe have much in common in terms of their security concerns and challenges, and these will be met only through very close and detailed cooperation between Russia and the outside world.

Despite Stalin's intentions in 1945, the reality is that the Soviet empire in Eastern Europe compromised and weakened Soviet security by forcing Moscow to divert immense resources to prop up deeply unpopular regimes over a large geography. In NATO, Russia gains the security that eluded it during the Cold war. Russia has benefitted from NATO as much as Poland, and Moscow needs to recognize this.

Q: Yikes! Are there any bright spots in the region's future?

A: At British football (read: soccer) matches, it is common for the crowds to sing the medley "You'll Never Walk Alone." Within about fifteen years of 1918, most of the democratic governments in Eastern Europe had collapsed into nationalist authoritarian dictatorships, but more than twenty years after 1989, (relatively) secure and stable democracies are flourishing throughout the region.

What made the difference? The most crucial element has been Western Europe's embrace of the region via the European Union and NATO. While some in the West balk at the cost of including Eastern Europe in these institutions, the history of the 20th century has shown that *not* doing so can be far costlier. Other international institutions like the International Monetary Fund and the World Bank also proved crucial in helping several Eastern European countries stabilize their economies during the 2008–09 global economic crisis (and avoid the fate of other EU members like Greece, Spain, or Italy), showing once again the value of embracing the East. (Many Western banks were heavily exposed to the crisis in Eastern Europe, which could have had catastrophic results for the Western economies had not the IMF and World Bank intervened in the East.) The West is finally learning that ensuring security and prosperity in Paris,

London, and Berlin requires promoting the same in Warsaw, Budapest, and Sofia.

Furthermore, Eastern Europe is not alone in other ways as well. There are precedents for what the region is going through today. In his 1991 book *The Third Wave*, the American political scientist Samuel P. Huntington described his theory of the spread of democracy (and its attendant free market economics) as happening in three historical waves—the first hitting the core Western countries in the 19th century; the second Germany, Italy, and Japan after World War II; and the third wave beginning in the 1970s with the collapse of dictatorships in Portugal, Spain, and Greece and spreading by 1989 to include South Africa, South Korea, the Philippines, Brazil, Taiwan, and yes, finally, Eastern Europe.

Considering how most of these countries are faring today, this is a pretty good club for Eastern Europe to belong to, but it also means that other countries are also struggling with similar historical legacies of dictatorships, some of them with considerably less exposure to democratic principles and values than some Eastern European countries have. Indeed, Transparency International's 2012 Corruption Perception Index rated Romania and Bulgaria higher than Greece.[5]

Ultimately, one of the most important factors about democracy in Eastern Europe is that unlike in Germany or Japan, it arose in Poland, Estonia, and Romania from native elements and largely unassisted. Democracy in the region, while clearly trying in many ways to emulate the successful democracies of the West, is homegrown.

Q: What does the future hold for Eastern Europe?
A: For all its challenges, Eastern Europe's future has never been brighter. Security threats to the region are relatively minor, and more importantly, the burden of facing them is being shared through common regional, European, and trans-Atlantic mechanisms. The European Union, while not without its own flaws and growing pains, has played a crucial role in shaping the reforms in the region and continues to drive change. Ultimately, the quest for normalcy, once fought for in the streets against security forces, has moved into parliamentary chambers, courtrooms, and business boardrooms. The enemies before 1989 were the agents of dictators, but the enemy today is simply inertia.

REFERENCE

This is where it all becomes clear—with pierogis thrown in for good measure

1. MUSICAL CHAIRS, OR PLACE NAMES IN EASTERN EUROPE

Eastern Europe is a wondrous place where you can visit many countries—without ever leaving home! Borders and even populations change sometimes, so here's a quick field guide to the different (changing) geographic names in the region. They are alphabetized by their current name (or its common English version), with historic variations following. It is important to remember that history and ethnic borders overlap in Eastern Europe, and for whatever country these places are in now they have often played an important role in the histories of many peoples or countries. As the historian Max Egremont noted, "This is a part of Europe where boundaries are vague, where names deceive."[1]

Alba Iulia, Romania—*Gyulafehérvár* (Hungarian), *Weißenburg* (German)

Antakya, Turkey—*Antioch* (Greek)

Belgrade, Serbia—*Beograd* (*Београд*; Serbian), *Nándorfehérvár* (Hungarian), *Singidunum* (Roman)

Braşov, Romania—*Brassó* (Hungarian), *Kronstadt* (German)

Bratislava, Slovakia—*Pozsony* (Hungarian), *Preßburg* (German)

Brest, Belarus—*Берасьце* (BEAR-ahst-yeh; Belarussian), *Brześć* (Polish), *Brestas* (Lithuanian), *Брест-Литовск* (Brest-Litovsk; Russian). Now known simply as *Brest*, formerly "Lithuanian Brest."

Brno, Czech Rep.—*Brüno* (German)

Bucharest, Romania—*Bucureşti* (Romanian), *Bukarest* (German)

Budapest, Hungary—*Buda* (Royal half of city prior to 1873), *Pest* or *Pesth* (Commercial half prior to 1873), *Aquincum* (Roman), *Budin* (Turkish)

Bydgoszcz, Poland—*Bromberg* (German)

Cetinje, Montenegro—*Цетиње* (Serbian), *Cettigne* (Italian)

Chełmno, Poland—*Kulm* (German)

Chişinau, Moldova—*Kishinyev* (*Кишинев*; Russian)

Cluj Napoca, Romania—*Kolozsvár* (Hungarian), *Klausenburg* (German)

Cracow, Poland—*Kraków* (Polish), *Krakau* (German), *Krakov* (*Краков*; Russian)

Danube River—*Donau* (German), *Duna* (Hungarian), *Dunaj* (Slovak), *Dunăre* (Romanian), *Dunav* (*Дунав*; Bulgarian & Serbian), *Istros* (*Ιστρος*; Greek)

Daugava River—*Dvina* (*Двина*; Russian), *Dzvina* (*Дзвіна*; Belarussian), *Dźwina* (Polish)

Daugavpils, Latvia—*Dyneburg* (German), *Dźwinów* (Polish), *Dvinsk* (*Двинск*; Russian)

Dubrovnik, Croatia—*Ragusa*—or—*Ragusium* (medieval Latin)

Edirne, Turkey—*Adrianople* (Byzantine Greek)

Elbe River—*Labe* (Czech)

Gdańsk, Poland—*Danzig* (German)

Gniezno, Poland—*Gnesen* (German)

Hrodno, Belarus—*Гродно* (*Hrodno*; Belarussian), *Grodno* (Polish)

Iaşi, Romania—*Jassy* (as written frequently in English or German)

Istanbul, Turkey—*Constantinople* (Roman)

Izmir, Turkey—*Smyrna* (Greek)

Jarosław, Poland—*Yaroslav* (*Ярослав*; Ukrainian)

Kaliningrad, Russia—*Königsberg* (German), *Karaliaučius* (Lithuanian), *Królewiec* (Polish)

Kaunas, Lithuania—*Kowno* (Polish), *Kovno* (*Ковно*; Russian), *Kovno* (עגװאָק; Yiddish)

Klaipėda, Lithuania—*Memel* (German)

Košice, Slovakia—*Kassa* (Hungarian), *Kaschau* (German)

Kosovo—*Kosova* (Albanian)

Kyiv, Ukraine—*Kiev* (*Киев*; Russian), *Kijów* (Polish), *Sambat* (Khazar)

Liepaja, Latvia—*Libau* (German)

Ljubljana, Slovenia—*Aemona* (Roman), *Laibach* (German)

Łódź, Poland—*Lodz* or *Lodsch* (German), *Lodzh* (שזדאל; Yiddish)

Lviv, Ukraine—*Lvov* (*Львов*; Russian), *Lwów* (Polish), *Lemberg* (German)

Malbork, Poland—*Marienburg* (German)

Minsk, Belarus—*Myensk* (*Менск*; Belarussian[2]), *Mińsk* (Polish), *Минск* (Russian)

Montenegro—*Crna Gora* (*Црна Гора*; Serbian)

Moscow, Russia—*Moskva* (*Москва*; Russian), *Moskau* (German), *Moskwa* (Polish)

Narew River—*Naura* (Lithuanian), *Narai* (*Нараў*; Belarussian)

Neisse River—*Nysa* (Polish)

Niemen River—*Nemunas* (Lithuanian), *Memel* (German)

Niš, Serbia—*Naissos* (Byzantine Greek)

Novi Sad, Serbia—*Újvidék* (Hungarian)

Oder River—*Odra* (Polish)

Osijek, Croatia—*Eszék* (Hungarian)

Pécs, Hungary—*Fünfkirchen* (German), *Sophianae* (Roman), *Beş* (Ottoman Turkish)

Plovdiv, Bulgaria—*Philippopoulus* (Greek), *Filibe* (Ottoman Turkish)

Podgorica, Montenegro—*Подгорица* (Pawd-GOR-ee-tsah; Serbian)

Poznań, Poland—*Posen* (German)

Prague, Czech Rep.—*Praha* (Czech), *Prag* (German)

Pristina, Albania—*Prishtinë* (Albanian), *Prishtina* (*Приштина*; Serbian), *Priştine* (Turkish)

Rijeka, Croatia—*Fiume* (Italian)

Skopje, Macedonia—*Üsküb* (Ottoman Turkish)

Sofia, Bulgaria—*Serdica* (Roman)

St. Petersburg, Russia—*Leningrad* (*Ленинград*; Soviet Russian 1924–92), *Petrograd* (*Петроград*; Tsarist Russian, 1914–24)

Szczecin, Poland—*Stettin* (German)

Tallinn, Estonia—*Reval* (medieval German), *Lyndanisse* (Danish)

Tartu, Estonia—*Dorpat* (German)

Thessaloniki, Greece—*Salonika* (short form, Greek), *Solun* (*Солун*, Bulgarian), *Selanik* (Ott. Turkish)

Tirana—*Tiranë* (Albanian)

Tisza River—*Theiss* (German), *Tisa* (Slovak & Romanian), *Tuca* (Tee-sah; Serbian)

Toruń, Poland—*Thorn* (German)

Ventspils, Latvia—*Windau* (German), *Windawa* (Polish)

Vienna, Austria—*Wien* (German), *Bécs* (Hungarian), *Vídeň* (Czech)

Vilnius, Lithuania—*Wilno* (Polish), *Wilna* (German), *Vilna* (*Вилна*; Russian), *Vilna* (ענליוו; Yiddish)

Vistula River, Poland—*Wisła* (Polish), *Weichsel* (German)

Vltava River, Czech Rep.—*Moldau* (German)

Volgagrad, Russia—*Stalingrad* (*Сталинград*; Soviet, 1925–61), *Tsaritsyn* (*Царицын*; 1595–1925)

Warsaw, Poland—*Warszawa* (Polish), *Warschau* (German), *Varshava* (*Варшава*; Russian)

Wrocław, Poland—*Breslau* (German), *Vratislav* (Czech)

Yekaterinburg, Russia—*Екатеринбург* (Russian), *Sverdlovsk* (*Свердловск*; Soviet, 1924–92)

Zagreb, Croatia—*Andautonia* (Roman), *Agram* (German), *Zágráb* (Hungarian)

2. Eastern Europe in Numbers

This is the section where we take a look at Eastern Europe by numbers, to give you a feel for how the region shapes up in comparison to the rest of the world.

Population

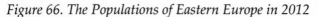

Figure 66. The Populations of Eastern Europe in 2012

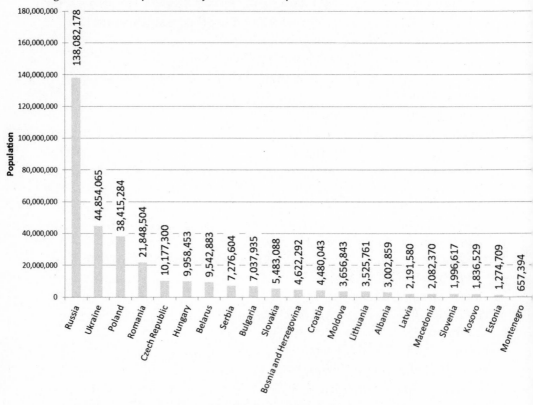

Source: CIA World Factbook, estimated as of July 2012

As of July 2012 there are about 322 million Eastern Europeans, which is 39% of Europe's 816 million people and just shy of 5% of the world's 7 billion people. As you can see in Figure 66, they are not distributed evenly across the region. Three-quarters of all Eastern Europeans live in just four countries: Russia, Ukraine, Poland, and Romania.

Figure 67. Comparing Populations: Western vs. Eastern Europe (2012)

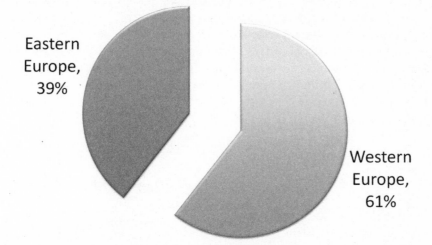

Source: CIA World Factbook, estimated as of July 2012

As we take a look at the population of Europe as a whole, we can see that Western Europe has about three-fifths of Europe's population, though it is more evenly distributed than Eastern Europe's.

Figure 68. Eastern Europe's Population by Region (2012)

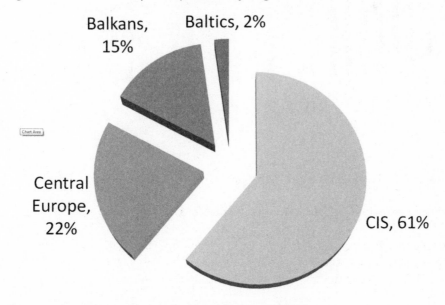

(Source: CIA World Factbook, estimated as of July 2012)

Figure 68 shows the distribution of population by region in Eastern Europe. The CIS (Commonwealth of Independent States) countries are represented here by Belarus, Moldova, Russia, and Ukraine. The Balkans refers to Albania, Bosnia, Bulgaria, Kosovo, Macedonia, Montenegro, Romania, and Serbia. The Baltic countries are represented by Estonia, Latvia, and Lithuania. Central Europe refers to Croatia, the Czech Republic, Hungary, Poland, Slovakia, and Slovenia. Moving Croatia and Slovenia over to the "Balkans" group only involves about 6.5 million people, not changing the balance significantly.

Figure 69. Europe's Top 30 Countries by Population (2012)

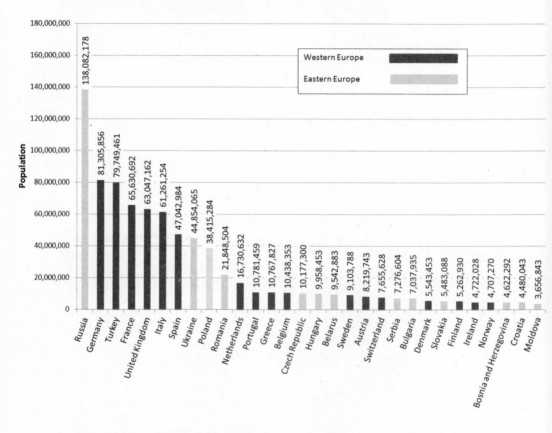

Source: CIA World Factbook, estimated as of July 2012

Figure 69 shows Europe's top thirty countries by population. I did this because of a common belief that the countries of Eastern Europe are all "small countries" without any real significance for Europe.

Figure 70 examines Europe's thirty-five largest cities, by urban population. Now, Figure 70 is an approximation for a few reasons. First, it is based on urban populations, which is to say only the amount of people living within city limits, but of course nowadays cities' populations often spill over their borders into suburbs or what are often called "metropolitan areas," so that for instance the city of New York had a population of about 8.2 million in 2010 but the larger New York (city) metropolitan area had almost 19 million inhabitants. Also, the populations provided in Figure 70 are based on census estimates ranging from 2008 to 2011. And as well, census methodologies are different from country to country. This is all to say that you shouldn't get too hung up on any city being in 25th versus 26th place.

However, what we can infer from Figure 70 is that Eastern European urban centers are not insignificant and play an important role in modern-day Europe. An interesting trait that Figure 70 reveals about Eastern European cities, however, is that they tend to be huge concentrations of people (and presumably resources) within their countries, often accounting for 10% or more of the national population. (Russia's huge population hides this element but it is true there too.) This speaks to the less even distribution of populations in Eastern Europe, a common situation in emerging markets economies.

Figure 70. 35 Largest European Cities by Population (c. 2010)

Country	Population (c. 2010)	European Rank by Population	% of National Population
Moscow, Russia	11,503,501	1	8.3%
Istanbul, Turkey	8,803,468	2	11.0%
London, UK	7,825,200	3	12.4%
St. Petersburg, Russia	4,879,566	4	3.5%
Berlin, Germany	3,490,445	5	4.3%
Madrid, Spain	3,273,049	6	7.0%
Kyiv, Ukraine	2,797,553	7	6.2%
Rome, Italy	2,761,477	8	4.5%
Paris, France	2,211,297	9	3.4%
Minsk, Belarus	1,836,808	10	19.2%
Hamburg, Germany	1,794,453	11	2.2%
Budapest, Hungary	1,733,685	12	17.4%
Warsaw, Poland	1,716,855	13	4.5%
Vienna, Austria	1,714,142	14	20.9%
Bucharest, Romania	1,677,985	15	7.7%
Barcelona, Spain	1,621,537	16	3.4%

Figure 70. 35 Largest European Cities by Population (c. 2010) [continued]

Novosibirsk, Russia	1,473,737	17	1.1%
Kharkiv, Ukraine	1,449,000	18	3.2%
Munich, Germany	1,353,186	19	1.7%
Yekaterinburg, Russia	1,350,136	20	1.0%
Milan, Italy	1,337,178	21	2.2%
Sofia, Bulgaria	1,270,284	22	18.0%
Prague, Czech Republic	1,262,106	23	12.4%
Nizhny Novgorod, Russia	1,250,615	24	0.9%
Samara, Russia	1,164,896	25	0.8%
Belgrade, Serbia	1,154,589	26	15.9%
Omsk, Russia	1,153,971	27	0.8%
Kazan, Russia	1,143,546	28	0.8%
Chelyabinsk, Russia	1,130,273	29	0.8%
Ufa, Russia	1,062,300	30	0.8%
Brussels, Belgium	1,048,491	31	10.0%
Birmingham, UK	1,016,800	32	1.6%
Dnepropetrovsk, Ukraine	1,001,612	33	2.2%
Volgograd, Russia	1,021,244	34	0.7%
Cologne, Germany	1,000,298	35	1.2%

Source: Wikipedia, most estimated as of 2010 (Note: Populations are of municipalities only, and exclude larger metropolitan areas. Estimates, based on censuses, range from 2008 to 2011.)

Figure 71. Minorities as a % of Population Across Eastern Europe (2010)

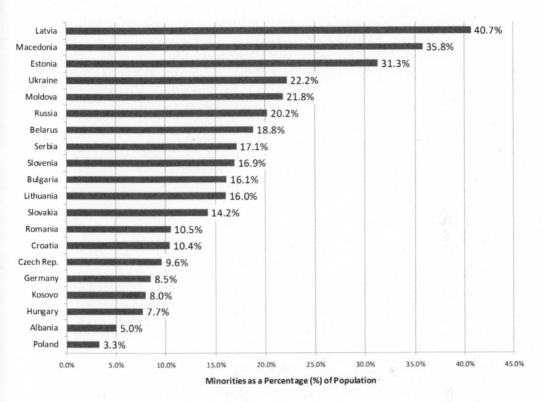

Minorities as a Percentage (%) of Population

Source: CIA World Factbook, estimated as of July 2010

In Figure 71, we're taking a look at a major source of tension in Eastern Europe. This figure is compiled (by the CIA World Factbook) from a range of sources—e.g., censuses, government estimates, and NGOs—spanning the past decade, but it makes the point. This point is not only relevant in 2010, but clearly has been an important factor in the region since the 19th century. Minority rights are crucial for maintaining peace and friendly relations in the region. Western Europe has its minority issues as well; from Basques in Spain and France to Germans in Italy's Tyrol region, from Turks in Germany to North Africans in France. However, minorities have played a key role in the savagery of Eastern Europe's wars and failed diplomacy in the 20th century, so recognizing and accommodating their rights while respecting their resident country's needs as well is critical.

Much progress has been made in this regard since 1989, but the region is still rife with disaffection. The Soviets in the 1950s and 60s made a concerted effort to colonize the Baltics; should modern-day ethnic Russians living in Latvia and Estonia—where they form a significant portion of the population—be made to pay for historic Soviet imperialism? Slovakia in 2009 enacted a controversial law forcing its minorities, primarily ethnic Hungarians, to deal with Slovak administration exclusively in Slovak. Is that just? Meanwhile, Lithuania in 2011 enacted a similar law that may impact schools for the country's Polish minority, sparking tensions. Serbs in Kosovo, Poles in Belarus, Turks in Bulgaria, Chechens or Tartars in Russia, Albanians in Macedonia—these and other ethnic minority issues will continue to test the region and the EU for the foreseeable future.

Both Bosnia & Herzegovina and Montenegro were excluded from Figure 71 because neither is based on ethnicity. In other words, there is no such thing as a majority population in either country. Figure 72 below examines how the citizens of both countries identified themselves in recent censuses:

Figure 72. The Ethnic Breakdowns of Bosnia-Herzegovina and Montenegro, 2010

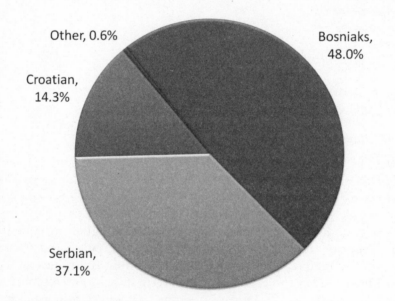

Source: CIA World Factbook (estimated July, 2010)

USELESS TRIVIA: BRING OUT YOUR DEAD!

One of Warsaw's most beautiful art collections is not in any museum; it is the city's oldest functioning cemetery, Powązki (Po-VONZ-kee). Started in what in 1790 was a village outside of Warsaw, Powązki was just another cemetery until it became the last resting place for heroes of the 1830–31 Uprising against the Russian Empire. As Polish autonomy in Russian Poland evaporated throughout the 19th century and the tsars banned public displays of Polish culture or patriotism, Poles turned to Powązki as an outlet for national expression.

The 19th century was for Russian-occupied Poland, as well as for much of Eastern Europe, a period of national awakening that found expression in literature, music, and art, so as famous Poles died— beginning with the death of the famed national composer Stanisław Moniuszko (Mon-YOOSH-ko) in 1872—renowned sculptors created beautiful stone, metal, and wooden monuments to memorialize the deceased, but also embedded national symbols and themes into their art. In this way, over the next several decades of the 19th and 20th centuries, Powązki grew into a massive necropolis of stunning sculpture art like a huge outdoor museum that, as a primarily Roman Catholic cemetery, the Orthodox Russians rarely bothered to intrude upon. The cemetery was severely damaged during World War II but afterward hosted a new military section for the fallen of the Warsaw Uprising of 1944. Postwar Poland's new Russian masters allowed Powązki to fall into disrepair, but in the 1970s and 80s famous Polish antiquarian (and patriot) Jerzy Waldorff (YEH-zhih VAHL-dorff) led restoration efforts.

To visit the tombs of Poland's medieval historical figures, one must venture primarily to Wawel Castle in Kraków, but Powązki Cemetery picks up where Wawel left off, and is the final resting place for some 75,000 Polish cultural, academic, political, and military figures including, since 1999, Jerzy Waldorff himself. Powązki is often compared to Paris's Cimetière du Père-Lachaise.[1]

Figure 73. Languages in Eastern Europe at Home and Abroad (2009)

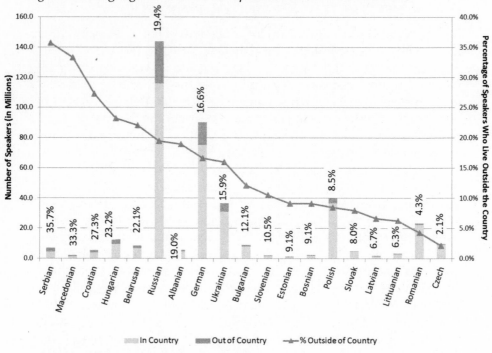

Source: Ethnologue (www.ethnologue.com)

Figure 73 is a busy chart showing us a lot of things, so let's break it down. The vertical bars as a whole represent the numbers of speakers for each language, so we can see for instance that Russian currently has over 140 million speakers. The top portion of each bar represents the percentage of speakers who live *outside* the native country, so using our Russian example again, we can see that 19.4% of all Russian speakers live outside of Russia. (This top portion is also represented by the percentage at the end of the bar.) If we do some quick math, we can deduce that of some 140 million native Russian speakers in this world, about 27 million—or 19.4% of them—live outside Russia's borders. I have arranged all the languages according to this percentage, from largest to smallest, with Serbian at the top (35.7% of speakers living outside Serbia) to Czech at the bottom (with only 2.1% of Czech-speakers living outside of the Czech Republic). I inserted the line to more dramatically illustrate that slope. This line helps you see, for instance, that of the nineteen languages portrayed in this chart, only eight have less than 10% of their native speakers living outside the home country. It's important to keep in mind that we're talking languages here, so that for instance a certain portion of those Serbian speakers who live outside of Serbia live in nearby Bosnia or Montenegro, where they are not considered minorities, per se.

Education

Figure 74. Literacy Levels Across Europe in 2011

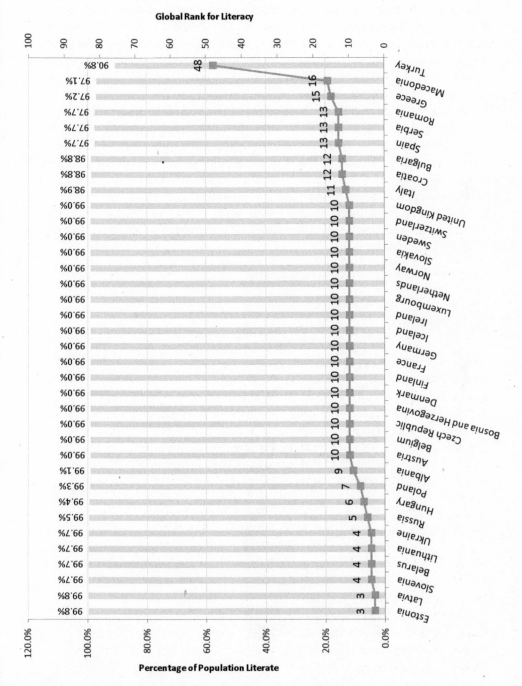

Source: UNESCO, "United Nations Development Programme (UNDP) Report 2011"

One of the few benefits accrued during the communist years in Eastern Europe was the aggressive education systems. Now, there were sometimes great gaps in the quality of certain kinds of education, and of course there was also a certain level of ideological penetration and control in education (though this differed over time and in different countries), but nevertheless, one of the positive benefits can be seen in Figure 75, which lists European countries in order of their level(s) of literacy in 2011. Figure 75 also provides (i.e., the line) each country's global rank for literacy level, though because of rounding, many countries share the same rank, as can be seen most dramatically with seventeen European countries ranking 10th globally. This is one of the few rankings where the former Soviet states (e.g., Russia, Ukraine, Belarus) rank on a par with their Central European and Baltic peers. Although the difference is often only a matter of a few tenths of a degree, the Balkans nevertheless reveal again some important educational challenges to economic development. Just for comparison's sake: Canada, the United States, Japan, and South Korea all ranked 10th at 99.0%, while China ranked 22nd at 95.9%, and Mali brought up the rear with 26.2%, ranking 123rd.

A page of a medieval Russian chronicle dated to the 11th century

(Image © Alexey Fateev / Shutterstock)

Politics

Figure 75. The European Union in Eastern Europe in 2013

Source: European Union website (www.europa.eu)

Figure 75 shows European Union membership in Eastern Europe in 2013, with European Union member states (striped), candidate states (checkered), and the rest. Albania is in the early stages of negotiating to become a candidate country to join the EU. The (mostly positive) influence of the European Union on legal, government, economic and educational development in Eastern Europe would be difficult to underestimate, even with the post-2009 PIIGS (Portugal, Italy, Ireland, Greece, Spain) debt crisis and the strains on the Euro. Moldova is simply far too underdeveloped in political and economic terms to begin the process of joining the EU, and there is also a small residual Soviet-era segment of the Moldovan population that is resistant to joining Western institutions, but oddly enough a large number of Moldovans are by proxy EU citizens through a back-door clause by which neighboring Romania—an EU member state—grants Romanian passports to any Moldovan citizen who requests one, for obvious historic reasons.

The Hungarian Parliament building in Budapest was consciously modeled after the British parliament building, but situated on the Danube within sight of the Habsburg's royal palace (across the river in Buda) to remind the Habsburgs of parliamentary rights. Similarly, the parliament can be seen from the U.S. Embassy in Szabadsag Tér (Freedom Square), but during the Cold War the Soviets erected a statue dedicated to the Red Army in the line of sight between the embassy and parliament, as a reminder to Washington that Hungarian-American relations were filtered through a Soviet prism. (Shutterstock)

Figure 76. NATO in Eastern Europe in 2012

Figure 76 shows the North Atlantic Treaty Organization (NATO) member states (striped) and non-member states in Eastern (and Central) Europe in 2012. NATO also includes several cooperation agreements and partnerships with non-NATO states, including Austria, Bosnia-Herzegovina, Finland, Macedonia, Moldova, Montenegro, Russia, Serbia, Sweden, and Ukraine. (Source: NATO website [www .nato.int])

NATO has played a crucial role in Eastern Europe not just in terms of security—though that alone is a major benefit—but also in terms of helping these countries to truly professionalize their militaries and bring them securely under civilian control. It must be remembered that many of these countries—e.g., Poland, Romania, the Baltics, Hungary, Croatia—have histories in the 20th century alone of either military coups or undue influence over government affairs by the militaries. This in part fed some of the extreme nationalism of the 1930s in the region, which served as a serious destabilizing factor.

Because of this, I maintain that NATO has been an immensely positive force for Eastern Europe, and has even benfitted nonmembers such as Russia, providing Moscow with security along its western frontier unknown throughout the 20th century, including from the Warsaw Pact days.

Hungarian police paramilitary forces deployed along the Yugoslav—soon to be Croatian—border (in Barcs, Hungary) during the 1991 Serb-Croat War. Though it did not make international headlines at the time, the war did spill over into Hungary on a few occasions. (Photo by the author)

Economy

Figure 77. CIA World Factbook Ranking of Eastern European Economies by GDP-PPP in 2011

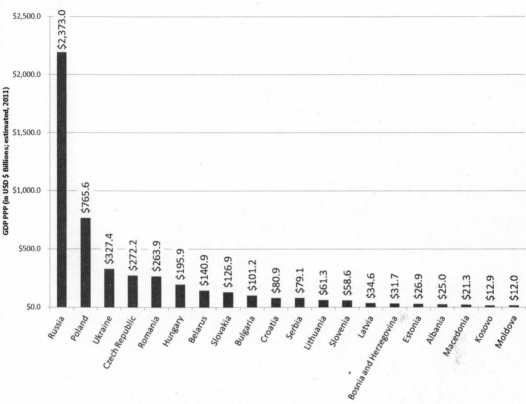

Source: CIA World Factbook, estimated 2011

Figure 77 ranks the region's economies by size out of 226 countries, as measured through GDP (gross domestic product; i.e., how much wealth the economy generates in a year) based on PPP (purchasing power parity, a method of equalizing currency exchange rates for an apples-to-apples comparison). The CIA World Factbook estimates the United States as having the world's largest economy in 2011, clocking in at $15.0 trillion,[2] followed by China at $11.3 trillion. Russia shows up with a respectable 7th-largest economy ranking at about $2.4 trillion, followed here by 21st-ranked Poland at $756.6 billion.

Figure 78, on the next page breaks out GDP-PPP by region in Eastern Europe in 2011. If you compare Figure 78 with Figure 66, you'll find that while the CIS and Baltic countries' GDP-PPP are roughly in line with their population size, the Balkans—with 15% of the region's population but only generating 11% of its GDP-PPP—and Central Europe, which has only 22% of Eastern Europe's population but which generates 30% of its GDP-PPP, are not.

Figure 78. GDP-PPP in Eastern Europe by Region (2011)

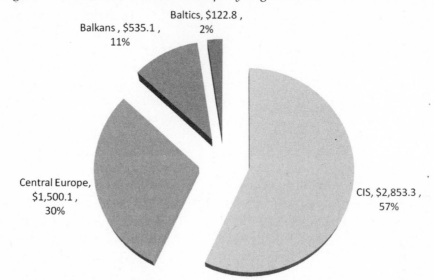

Source: World Bank, CIA World Factbook (estimated, 2011)

Figure 79. GDP-PPP Growth in Eastern Europe (2011, estimated)

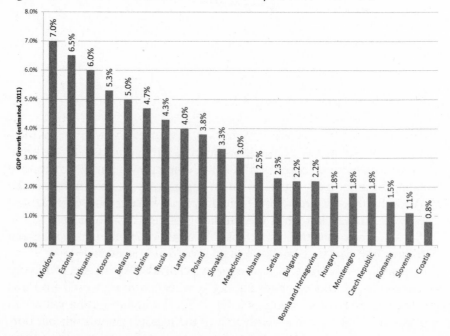

Source: World Bank, CIA World Factbook (estimated, 2011)

Figure 80 examines Eastern Europe according to a few popular economic indices. These are not absolute measures of anything, but show how the countries of the region stack up in the world.

The World Economic Forum's Global Competitiveness Index 2010–2011 examined 139 countries for their institutions, infrastructure, macroeconomic development, health and primary education systems, higher education, market efficiency, labor market efficiency, financial markets, technological development, market size, business sophistication, and innovation. Switzerland was rated the most competitive economy in the world—the U.S. was number 4—while the wartorn African country of Chad ranked the lowest. As can be seen in Figure 78, Estonia, the Czech Republic, and Poland lead Eastern Europe on the index while Bosnia-Herzegovina, Serbia, and Moldova all bring up the rear for the region.

USELESS TRIVIA: INFLATION AS A LIFESTYLE!

Many Westerners know of the catastrophic (and largely self-inflicted) currency disaster of early Weimar Germany's *Reichsmark* in 1923, but not many know the record for currency hyperinflation goes to Hungary in 1945–46. At war's end in 1945, the Hungarian *pengő* began a slide that would ultimately result at one point in 1946 in $.20 U.S. cents being worth 10,000,000,000,000,000,000 pengős, or ten *quintillion* pengős. In August 1946, the Hungarian government introduced a new currency, the forint, which it still uses today. The first forint was valued at 400,000,000,000,000,000,000,000,000,000 pengős, or four hundred octillion pengős.

For the Legatum Institute's Prosperity Index 2010, countries are measured according to their economy, entrepreneurship and opportunity, governance, education, health, safety & security, personal freedom, and social capital. Legatunm only examined 110 countries for its index, which impacts the results. Nonetheless, there are some important nuggets of information here. Norway was judged the most prosperous (by these criteria) while Zimbabwe placed as least prosperous. Ten of twenty Eastern European countries still placed higher than the 50th rank, with Slovenia, the Czech Republic, Poland, Hungary, and Estonia leading the group. The former Soviet republics lag the rest on this index.

The IFC's and World Bank's Ease of Doing Business Index 2011 bases its final rankings on the ease of doing the following in each country: starting a business, dealing with construction permits, registering property, getting credit, protecting investors, paying taxes, trading across borders, enforcing contracts, and closing a business. The IFC and World Bank ambitiously ranked 183 countries for this index. This survey shows us some of the usual suspects, with for instance all three Baltic countries scoring high, and Hungary, Slovakia, and Slovenia all ranking below 50 as well, but a few surprises are in the mix as well. Macedonia ranks 38th, ahead of Hungary, Slovakia, and Slovenia. Quite frankly, I can't explain that one. Meanwhile, the Czech Republic, and Poland—usually among the top-scorers in these indices—show up with middling-level ranks. Lingering state bureaucracy may be to blame for that. There is little surprise in finding that Ukraine, Russia, Kosovo, and Bosnia-Herzegovina bring up the rear again in this survey.

All indices and rankings contain a certain level of built-in bias, no matter how objective or fact-based the organizers try to make them. The criteria are all weighted, and some issues such as ease of paying taxes may have cultural interpretations behind them that skew results. Indeed, some of these indices have been accused of having a pro-American, pro-European, or otherwise bias. Still, these indices all have some value in providing a comparative glimpse of how Eastern Europe shows up on the global political and economic radar.

Figure 80. Eastern Europe Across Various Economic Indices, 2010

Country	World Economic Forum Global Competitive Index 2010-2011	Legatum Institute Prosperity Index 2010	IFC & World Bank Ease of Doing Business Rankings 2011
	Global Rank	Global Rank	Global Rank
Albania	88	-	82
Belarus	-	54	68
Bosnia	102	-	110
Bulgaria	71	46	51
Croatia	77	38	84
Czech Rep.	36	24	63
Estonia	33	35	17
Hungary	52	34	46
Kosovo	-	-	119
Latvia	70	47	24
Lithuania	47	42	23
Macedonia	75	72	38
Moldova	94	86	90
Montenegro	49	-	66
Poland	39	29	70
Romania	67	51	56

Source: World Economic Forum[3], Legatum Institute[4], IFC & World Bank[5]

Figure 80. Eastern Europe Across Various Economic Indices, 2010 [continued]

Russia	63	63	123
Serbia	96	-	89
Slovakia	60	37	41
Slovenia	45	21	42
Ukraine	89	96	145

Trg bana Josipa Jelačića (Ban Josip Jelačić [YO-seep YELL-ah-cheech] Square) in Zagreb, Croatia (Shutterstock)

Technology

Figure 81. Broadband Internet Penetration of European Countries, 2011

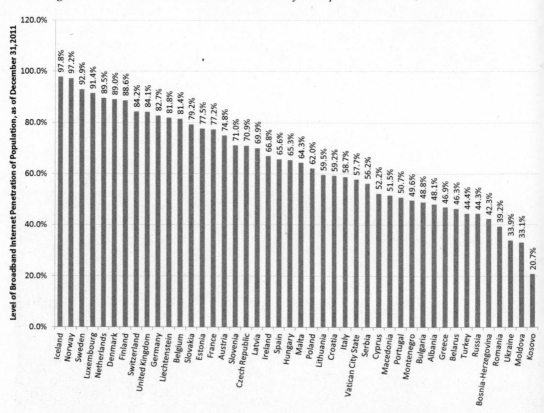

Source: InternetWorld Stats (www.internetworldstats.com); estimated as of December 31, 2011

Figure 81 shows us simply the amount of each country's population that had access to broadband Internet by the end of 2011. Now, this does not necessarily mean that everyone represented in each percentage has broadband Internet in their own homes; some may have access through local schools, libraries, or Internet cafes, for example. It just means that on a fairly regular and reliable basis, they can access the Internet via a broadband connection. Internet World Stats collected these statistics from several sources—the European Union, Nielsen Online, ITU, Facebook, GfK, "and other trustworthy sources." Collecting this kind of information is always a mixture of art and science, but nevertheless these figures give you a sense of how technologically plugged into the global economy each country is.

We get an inkling from Figure 79 of why, for instance, Slovakia, Estonia, Slovenia, the Czech Republic, and Latvia are frequent destinations for off-shored functions by Western European companies. Some Eastern European countries like Poland, Romania, and Russia also rate highly as outsourcing destinations because they have islands of excellent technological connectivity, coupled with large, well-educated populations and other resources. Still, Figure 81 makes clear that for a few Eastern European countries, technology represents a serious challenge to economic development.

Skyline of old town in Vilnius (Vilniaus senamiestis), Lithuania (Image © Birute Vijeikiene / Shutterstock)

Alcohol

Figure 82. Traditional Alcohol Consumption in Eastern Europe

We begin by admitting that Figure 82 is a gross oversimplification. You can purchase just about any kind of locally made alcohol in any Eastern European country, and a few countries are well-known for many different alcoholic drinks. Still, there is some truth to Figure 82, as we'll explore briefly below.

The Vodka belt

Vodka—a diminutive term for "water" (*woda*, *voda* or *вода*) in the Slavic languages—was first invented somewhere between medieval Poland and Ukraine, but its production is now most associated with Poland, Ukraine, Belarus, Russia, the Baltics, Finland, and Sweden. The European Union is mulling the protection of the product name "vodka" as made in these countries, especially as cheaper (price and quality) vodkas from Asia and elsewhere in the world are entering the market in greater numbers.

Beer

Beer is manufactured in every country in Eastern Europe and is a popular alcoholic drink of choice in most, including Poland, Hungary, Romania, and Serbia. However, a few countries belong to particularly strong Central European "beer cultures" where beer is a serious endeavor indeed and comes in many native varieties. The Czech Republic easily stands out as an important beer country comparable in the quality and variety of the local brews with Germany, Belgium, and Ireland. However, Slovakia, Slovenia, and Croatia also get honorable mention. Homebrewing is far less common in Eastern Europe than North America or Britain (in part due to laws), but it is slowly catching on.

Wines

It is believed the first wine grapes were domesticated, squished, and fermented into wine in the Caucasus somewhere between Georgia and Armenia 6,000 years ago, and from there spread southward into Persia and beyond, (re-)entering Europe through the Balkans and spreading, especially by the Phoenecians and Greeks, to southern Europe and by the Romans to northern Europe. Of course, wines from as far north as southern Germany (Bavaria, the Rhineland) have achieved some reknown in the world, but the Balkans are still prime viticultural turf. Indeed, vineyard-covered slopes are a part of the rural Balkan charm. Though universally produced, in the Balkans Bulgaria's wineries are actually making something of a global mark, with Romanian, Serbian, and Macedonian wines close on their heels. Hungary is known for its Tokay (TO-kuy) series white wines, as well as many red wines, many of which were born of Roman and later French and Flemish grape "colonization" due to immigrants.

Brandy

The Balkans in particular but Hungary, and to some extent the Czech Republic, Slovakia, Poland, Belarus, and Ukraine as well—in other words, those countries touched by the Carpathian Mountains—are famous for a variety of fruit brandies, still often homemade with each family boasting its own recipes. Indeed, if you ever find yourself in a Carpathian village, it is an extremely common form of hospitality for the locals to offer you their own plum, apricot, peach, pear, sour cherry, or apple *pálinka* (Hungary), *palincă* (Romania), or slivovitz (as plum brandy is called with slight variations in the name in most of the region's except Hungary, where it is *szilvapálinka).* There are endless varieties of these fruit brandies across the region, even within countries, such as Polish-Czech *śliwowica,* Romanian *ţuică,* or Balkan or Turkish *rakia.* Whatever they call it, if the locals offer you some they are showing you the highest honor so accept it graciously but don't plan on engaging in any intellectually challenging endeavor afterward, especially if it's the homemade stuff. Imbibing these with some solid foods is a good idea. You can also usually find these brandies commercially made in shops, but those often lack the flavor and kick of the homemade stuff. Some may also be surprised to learn Polish *koniak* (cognac) has also achieved some notoriety.

USELESS TRIVIA: HEART OF GOLD!

In the midst of the Warsaw Uprising in late 1944, the Nazi commandant in charge of the city, General Erich von dem Bach-Zelewski, ruthlessly crushed the AK Polish resistance as it tried to liberate the city. After the Uprising was suppressed, von dem Bach-Zelewski—who during the war dropped "Zelewski" from his name to de-emphasize his Polish heritage—infamously obeyed Hitler's orders to obliterate the city, sending in demolition teams to destroy Warsaw's historic buildings block by block. Amid all this destruction, however, von dem Bach-Zelewski did something that many still today find puzzling; he personally saw to it that a Polish cultural icon was saved, one whose music had even been banned by the Nazis once they destroyed Poland in 1939: Chopin's heart.

The famous pianist Fryderyk Chopin was born in Warsaw in 1810 to a Polish mother and an immigrant French father but he fled Russian-occupied Poland to Paris after the failed 1831 uprising, where his brilliant musical career unfolded. Chopin—better known as *Frédéric Chopin*—died at the age of thirty-nine, most likely of tuberculosis, and was buried in Paris's famous *Cimetière du Père-Lachaise* as befitted such a cultural icon. However, his sister returned to Poland from his funeral with his heart encased in a crystal urn, preserved in cognac. Chopin's heart was entombed in a column dedicated to him in Warsaw's *Bazylika Świętego* Krzyża (Holy Cross Church), and it was this crystal urn that von dem Bach-Zelewski saved in 1944. The cognac is credited with preserving Chopin's heart still today.

Others

The Baltic and Slavic peoples are also famous for honey-based alcohols, from wines to brandies to liqueurs such as *krupnik* (Lithuanian *krupnikas*), or Polish *miód pitny* (myood PEET-nih; "drinking honey"), *miodówka* (MYAW-doof-kah; honey vodka), or Russian *медовуха* (myed-o-VOO-khah), whose disarming sweetness can sneak up on you. Many of these are classified as meads.

Figure 83. The Consumption of Pork vs. Beef for Select Countries

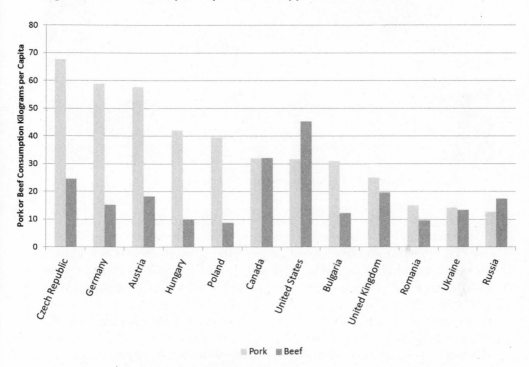

Source: U.S. Department of Agriculture, Foreign Agricultural Service, Livestock and Poultry: World Markets and Trade, annual. (www.fas.usda.gov)

For the final chart in this section, I wanted to just take a random snapshot of some aspect of Eastern Europe in comparison with the rest of the world, and so I chose preference for meat consumption. Figure 83 shows how uniquely the United States stacks up in terms of its beef consumption. Simply said, if you're traveling in Central Europe, I hope you like pork.

The simple but elegant pierogi (Image © Dzinnik Darius / Shutterstock)

3. MRS. JANKOWSKA'S HOMEMADE PIEROGIS

Most people in the West know what a pierogi is, especially if you live near one of the major industrial cities that attracted so many Polish immigrants in the 19th and 20th centuries. You can go to the frozen section of your local foodmarket and, Lo!, there you can find a box or bag of rock-solid frozen little industrial dumplings with the usual bland assortment of cheese, potato, or sauerkraut fillings. First of all, though strongly associated in the West with Poles, pierogi are actually widely known among all the Western and Eastern Slavic peoples. In fact, it's not quite known where they originated. One theory is that they were brought to the Slavs by the invading Mongols from China. (Remember those little Chinese steamed dumplings?) Secondly, in Eastern Europe, pierogis come with a multitude of different fillings—potato, cabbage, mushrooms, various meats, cheeses, fruits, or vegetables—and an equally wide variety of preparation styles: boiled, fried, deep-fried, breaded & baked, covered in a gravy or sauce (sour cream is a Russian favorite!), and more. In short, no two pierogis are alike.

If you're lucky, you live in or near an Eastern European community where you can buy some homemade varieties of the real thing, but if you're one of the millions out there who still think Grandma bought her pierogis in a box, well, Mrs. Jankowska has kindly consented after an arm-wrestling match to share a basic pierogi recipe—imbued with her native sensibilities—for your culinary exploration.

First, the filling

Farmer Cheese
Potatoes
1 large onion
1 stick butter
Pinch o' salt
Pinch o' black pepper

We start with the filling because it has to chill for some time. How much/many potatoes and farmer cheese do you need? It is less important how much than that both are the exact same amount. (So, if 1 pound of potatoes, then 1 pound of farmer cheese, etc.) To be safe, maybe start off with a half pound (225 grams) of each. Boil the potatoes and mash them (without adding any spices). Meanwhile, dice and sauté the onion in butter, adding a pinch of salt and black pepper. Finally, mix the sautéed onion, mashed potatoes, and farmer cheese together in a bowl, and chill for at least two hours.

Now, the dough

2 cups of flour (450 ml)
1 egg yoke
½ cup hot water (c. 64 g)

Add about a half cup of boiling water to the flour and mix (carefully!), then add the separated egg yoke to the mix. Keep kneading until soft and elastic, adding a little water if too hard and dry, or a little flour if too sticky until the dough won't stick to your hands. Do lots of folding and kneading. Lots.

Marrying the two

Roll the dough out until it is about a quarter inch (6mm, or about two-thirds of a centimeter) thick, then take a common drinking glass—it must be made of glass—and turn it upside down. Press it gently into the dough and wiggle until you get a circle cutout, and continue until all the dough is used up. Then, put a dough circle in the palm of your hand and add about a tablespoon-sized dollop (15 ml) of the filling mixture into the center. Fold the dough in half to form a semicircle, and pinch the ends until closed. You got yourself a pierogi there in your hands. Repeat until finished with dough and filling.

Now, you can boil these things in heavily salted water, but take them out about thirty seconds after they start floating, or they'll just disintegrate. When you take them out of the boiling water, have a melted bowl of stick butter waiting to quick baste them with before you pile them together on a plate; this butter coating will prevent them from sticking together. Let them dry a few minutes and then chow down! This is how most Poles enjoy pierogis. If you prefer (as many Westerners do), you can lightly fry them in vegetable oil (both sides), until a light gold color.

There, it was that simple. Experiment on your own with new fillings, and *Smacznego!* (Smotch-NAY-go; "Bon appétit!") Also, don't forget to wash your hands so you don't leave little grease smudges on these pages.

NOTES

FOREWORD

1. See the Bibliography for full book details.

INTRODUCTORY FAQ

1. Davies, 1996: p. 28

2. Johnson, 1996: p. 3. By "Central Europe," Johnson means primarily "East Central Europe"—e.g., Poland, Czech Republic, and Hungary.

3. Sometimes written "Bosniaks" or "Bosnyaks."

4. Walter J. Boyne, "Carbon Copy Bomber," *Air Force Magazine* (www.airforce-magazine.com), June 2009, Vol. 92, No. 6; accessed September 28, 2011

PAGE XXVI

1. Bori, 2005: p. 5

SECTION I

1. Lemberg is modern Lviv, Ukraine. In the 20th century, the city belonged, in order, to Austria-Hungary (Lemberg), Poland (Lwów), then the Soviet Union (Lvov) and now Ukraine.

2. Czernowitz (Chair-NO-veets) is modern-day Chernivtsi, Ukraine. In the 20th century the city belonged, in order, to Austria-Hungary (Czernowitz), Romania (Cernăuţi), the Soviet Union (Chernovtsy), and now Ukraine.

3. Munkács (MOON-kotch) is modern-day Mukachevo, Ukraine. In the 20th century, the city belonged to Austria-Hungary (Munkács), Czechoslovakia (Munkačevo), Hungary (Munkács), the Soviet Union (Mukachevo), and now Ukraine.

4. As quoted in: Eric Hobsbawm, *On History*. New York: The New Press, 1997; pp. 1–2

A FEW WORDS ABOUT A WORD

1. David Kang, *East Asia Before the West, Five Centuries of Trade and Tribute*. New York: Columbia University Press, 2010; p. 82

A WORD (OR TWO) ABOUT TIME

1. If you did the math and are scratching your head because 2012-1431 = 581, it's because Muslims and Jews use a lunar calendar—the Western Gregorian calendar is solar-based—and therefore the length of our years does not always match up.

LANGUAGES

1. University of Texas Linguistics Research Center (www.utexas. edu/cola/centers/lrc/eieol/IEfam.html)

2. An early medieval native Slavic alphabet that was later replaced by the much simpler Cyrillic alphabet.

3. Ondrej Cerny, Jan Kepler Gymnazium student, Prague, the Czech Republic, "A Rotten Language," in a competition sponsored by the Vaclav Havel Library. *Radio Free Europe/Radio Liberty* (www. rferl.org/content/feature/1915747.html), December 28, 2009

GEOGRAPHY

1. Image (in modified form) courtesy of NASA, www.nasa.gov

2. Timothy Garton Ash, "As at Auschwitz, the gates of hell are built and torn down by human hearts," *The Guardian* (www. guardian.co.uk), December 23, 2009. Ash was writing about the peculiar geostrategic realities that have challenged Eastern Europeans, Poles in particular, in the 20th century.

3. "Lech" = "Poles" This derives from the ancient Slavic Lechitic tribes who formed the core of the early Polish population. Yes, "Lech" is a common name among male Poles today, like Lech Wałęsa.

4. The central Polish city Gniezno (GNYEZ-no) gets its name from the Polish word *gniazdo*, "nest." It's not actually clear if Gniezno was ever the capital of early Poland but it was the early base for the church in 10th century Poland, and Poland's first kings (11th century) were crowned in Gniezno.

5. Lipniacka, 2000: p. 5

6. Cunliffe, 1998: p. 3

7. "Magyarország - Ne legyen Balkán!" ("Hungary - Don't be Balkan!") exhorted the 1990 Hobo Blues Band song "Hely a térképen" (Place on the Map).

8. Milan Kundera, (translated by Edmund White), "The Tragedy of Central Europe," *New York Review of Books*, Volume 31, Number 7. April 26, 1984

RELIGION

1. Actually, from the beginning Hus's followers began splintering into increasingly radical groups like the Táborites or the Jednota bratrská (United Brethren), but the blanket term "Hussites" is still applied to the whole lot.

2. "Habsburg" is sometimes written "Hapsburg" in English, though English texts have increasingly utilized the original German spelling, Habsburg.

SECTION ii

1. Sabaliauskas, 1993: p. 115

INTRODUCTION: PREHISTORY

1. Derived with minor changes from Peter Bellwood's map "The earliest Neolithic cultures of Europe," Figure 4.1 (Bellwood, 2005: p. 69).

2. Nick Thorpe, "Europe's oldest prehistoric town unearthed in Bulgaria." *BBC World News* (www.bbc.co.uk), October 31, 2012.

3. From: Merrriam-Webster online etymological dictionary entry for "-ish" (www.merriam-webster.com), as available on April 12, 2010.

4. Still, this may not be so far-fetched. A DNA study in 2000 found that 35.6% of Czech and Slovak males belong to the y-chromosome haplogroup R1b, which is very common among Celts but rare among Slavs. One modern group that hosts a Beltaine Festival each spring is the Czech Bratrstvo Keltů (Celtic Brotherhood), whose website is www.beltine.cz.

5. Biskupin museum website: www.biskupin.pl

INTRODUCTION: HISTORY

1. Independence Chart design by Tomek Jankowski, graphic creation by Sharon Price.

2. Milan Kundera, (translated by Edmund White), "The Tragedy of Central Europe," *New York Review of Books*, Volume 31, Number 7. April 26, 1984.

3. Siddiqui, Dr. Habib, "Letter from America: Humors of Molla Nasreddin Hodja." *The Asian Tribune* (www.asiantribune.com), June 10, 2010.

4. A mullah in Islam is a religious and Shari'a legal scholar.

5. Numbers from: Goble, Paul, "Belarusians Increase Share of Republic's population but Speak National Language Less, Census Shows," *Window on Eurasia* (www.windowoneurasia.blogspot.com), September 9, 2010; accessed same day. The remaining 8% are Poles, Jews, Lithuanians, Ukrainians, Tartars, Armenians, and others: *Национальный статистический комитет Республики Беларусь* (National Statistical Committee of the Republic of Belarus), Press release "Основные демографические и социальные характеристики населения Республики Беларусь по итогам переписи населения 2009 года" ("Basic Demographic and Social Characteristics of the Republic of Belarus Based on the Census of 2009"), September 8, 2010 (www.belstat.gov.by/homep/ru/indicators/pressrel/census.php); accessed on September 9, 2010.

INTRODUCTION: THE CLASSICAL AGE IN THE EAST, OR EASTERN EUROPE - THE PREQUAL

1. Seven emperors were born in Sirmium (modern Sremska Mitrovica, northern Serbia) in Pannonia province, two more were from elsewhere in Pannonia, six were from Moesia province, three were from Thrace, and one each from Greece, Dalmatia, Dacia, and Dardania—a province later absorbed by Moesia and Dacia.

2. Throughout this book I make reference to "barbarians" and "civilization," but I am not making a value judgment about

peoples. "Civilization" here does not mean drinking your tea with your pinky finger sticking up; it refers to peoples who live in permanent year-round settlements with diversified economies and who rely primarily on agriculture and trade for their food, and usually whose societies have adopted some means of written communication. "Barbarians," while originally a pejorative term invented by urban peoples to describe those outside their cultures, here simply means those peoples living a semi-nomadic or nomadic existence whose economies often rely in part on pillaging neighboring peoples and who are illiterate.

CHAPTER 1: SETTING THE STAGE 500–800 CE

1. "Arabian Coins: Unearthed Treasure Proves Early East-West Trade Route," *Der Spiegel* (www.spiegel.de/international), September 7, 2010.

2. It's thought that the modern Hungarian name for Vienna—Bécs (BAYTCH)—may derive from an Avar settlement that had once existed on the site.

3. Ostler, 2005: p. 309

4. Sometimes called in English Salonika.

5. You can check out the company website here, in Romanian: www.dacia.ro

6. Fine, 1994: p. 37

7. The Vistula River begins in the Carpathian Mountains along Poland's southern border and flows northward to the Baltic Sea. The Narew (NAH-rev) is an eastern tributary of the Vistula River. The Niemen (NYEH-men) River originates in modern Belarus and flows through Lithuania to the Baltic Sea. The Daugava (Dow-GAH-vah) River begins in northwestern Russia and flows westward through Belarus and into Latvia and the Baltic Sea.

8. Juodkrantė was once Prussian Schwarzort (SHVARTS-ort).

CHAPTER 2: THE ORIGINS OF STATES 800–1242 CE

1. For more information on the Sorbs, see: www.domowina. sorben.com/index.htm, or: www.ski.sorben.com/site/docs/ english/index.htm

2. For more information on the Kaszubs, see the English-language section on the right of this page: www.republika.pl/modrag-lina/kaszlink.html.

3. Wilson, Derek, *Charlemagne*. New York: Doubleday, 2006; p. 121.

4. According to Hungarian legend, Árpád allegedly gave Svi-atopluk a white stallion as the Magyars entered the Basin, and when Sviatopluk accepted it, Árpád declared it to be payment for the lands of the Carpathian Basin—sort of like the legends of the Dutch purchasing Manhattan from the Delaware Indians for $24. In 1991, as the Hungarian Parliament was debating how best to compensate citizens who had had property seized illegally by the communists, debate turned to earlier political victims as well who had lost property to the fascists during World War II, or to the Horthy regime before the war, and so on, raising the question of how far back in Hungary's history the law should go. A cartoon then appeared in the popular satirical weekly news magazine *Ludas Matyi* showing the ghost of Sviatopluk with his white stallion asking where he should apply for restitution. . . .

5. A "Ban" was Croatia's name for its ruler. A Ban rules a Banate. Christian Europe translated Ban as "duke," though Croat kings still called themselves Ban after the country was elevated to the status of kingdom. Medieval Bosnia also called its ruler a "Ban."

6. "Lechitic" means the northernmost tribes of the early Western Slavic peoples, who would one day form the core element of the Polish people.

7. *Pole* (POLE-leh) or *polye* (POLE-yeh) in the Slavic languages means "field," and *Polanie* = "field-wanderers," or "People of the Fields."

8. The Curonians eventually gave their name to Courland (in modern western Latvia), and the Latgales (or Latgallians) gave their name to Latvians.

9. Known as *Saulės Mūšis* in Lithuanian; "Battle of the Sun," to Germans it is the Battle of Schaulen (SHOW-len). The battle site was in either modern northern Lithuania or southern Latvia; historians aren't sure. Some believe it was fought near the Lithuanian city of Šiauliai (Shee-OW-lee-eye).

10. The Mongol Empire's rulers called themselves Great Khans ("Great Kings") or Khagans ("Emperors"), but the "g" was silent in the Mongol pronunciation, so it is rendered here as "Kha'an." This has misled some to describe Genghis and his successors as 'Khans," or mere kings.

11. Located in what is today Uzbekistan, Turkmenistan, and northern Iran.

12. Barford, 2001: pp. 198–199

13. Modern Szczecin (SHCHEH-cheen), Poland. In 19th- and 20th-century Prussian/German Pomerania, Stettin was the capital, while the Oder River—on which Stettin lies—divided German Pomerania into western Vorpommern (Inner Pomerania) and eastern Hinterpommern (Outer Pomerania).

PEOPLES OF EASTERN EUROPE: THE JEWS

1. Dimont, 1962: p. 226

2. Tony Judt, with Timothy Snyder, *Thinking the Twentieth Century* (New York: The Penguin Press, 2012), p. 17.

3. Many such stories have surfaced in the press since 1989, including the cases of a Polish anti-Semitic skinhead couple (David Gardner, "Meet the Polish neo-Nazi skinhead couple who discovered they are JEWISH - and turned their lives around," The Daily Mail Online [www.dailymail.co.uk], September 27, 2010), and a prominent anti-Semitic leader in Hungary's far-right Jobbik movement, Csanád Szegedi, who was outed by Jobbik researchers ("Anti-semitic leader resigns after he is outed as Jewish," BBC World News [http://www.bbc.co.uk], August 16, 2012).

CHAPTER 3: THE MEDIEVAL YEARS 1242-1600 CE

1. The name "Golden Horde" may have derived from their widespread pillaging (i.e., gold) or the Steppe habit of using colors to denote directions.

2. Malcolm, 1994: p. 12

3. King, 2008: p. 15

4. A "Ban" for some Southern Slavic peoples was the ruler, and a Ban's country was his Banate. Croatia also used this title.

5. The Serbian *Zahumlje* = Hum. "Herzegovina" derives from the German Herzog (HAIR-tsawg), meaning at different times "Duke" or "Prince," so Herzegovina = Slavicized "Duchy" or "Principality." Hum became Herzegovina in the 15th century.

6. Croatian forces did manage to spare most of Croatia an Ottoman occupation, earning the country the title *antemurale Christianitatis* ("Bulwark of Christendom") from Pope Leo X in 1519.

7. No relationship to the Sicilian city of the same name.

8. An ambitious Hungarian gunsmith named either Urbán or Orbán tried to sell his massive cannon to both the Byzantines and Turks, but the Byzantines were broke so he ended up providing some seventy regular cannons to the Turks at Constantinople, as well as three massive artillery pieces, the largest of which was 27 feet long and weighed nearly 19 tons, and shot a stone cannonball weighing 600 pounds. It took so long to load this monster that it could only be fired seven times a day, but that was enough. Urbán (or Orbán) was reportedly killed when one of his cannons exploded.

9. "The Levant" refers to the eastern Mediterranean coastal regions of what is today Turkey, Syria, Lebanon, and Israel/Palestine.

10. National Geographic Society (2012, July 26). "'Basarab' surname may not indicate direct relation to Vlad the Impaler." ScienceDaily. Retrieved November 3, 2012, from www.sciencedaily.com /releases/2012/07/120726121140.htm.

11. It was with this history in mind that the presidents of the newly liberated postcommunist Hungary, Czechoslovakia, and Poland met in 1991 at the ruins of Charles Roberts's old Visegrád fortress to form the Visegrád Triangle–later, the Visegrád Group after Czechoslovakia split and Slovenia also joined–to coordinate their policies and efforts to join NATO and the EU.

12. János Hunyadi was likely of either mixed or full Vlach (Romanian) origin, and he is known to modern Romanians as *Ioncu de Hunedoara*.

13. Original Hungarian from Zsofia Valentin (www.mamalisa. com/?p=332&t=es&c=44). English translation by T. Jankowski.

14. Sometimes in English texts the Brusi are referred to as "Old Prussians."

15. Urban, 2003: p. 277

16. Nogat in Polish, a tributary of the Vistula River in modern northern Poland, and once the historic border between West and East Prussia.

17. Website at: www.zamek.malbork.pl. "Malbork" is Marienburg in Polish.

18. Rusyn was the Eastern Slavic language spoken in Kieven Rus. The language that developed from Rusyn in the western Rus territories after the Lithuanian conquests was called Ruthenian, which had several dialects—e.g., Red Ruthenian, Black Ruthenian, and White Ruthenian. In the 19th and 20th centuries, the Ruthenians living in historic Ukraine became known as "Ukrainians," though some modern Eastern Orthodox Slavic peoples in Polish and Ukrainian Galicia reject any Ukrainian identity and still insist on referring to themselves as Ruthenians.

19. Referring to the early-6th century A.D. Byzantine emperor who dramatically reformed the Eastern Roman (Byzantine) legal system.

20. Under Pope John Paul II, Jadwiga was made a saint in 1997. Polish history is replete with legends about Jadwiga and her generosity.

21. Known to Germans as the Battle of Tannenberg, and to Lithuanians the Battle of Žalgiris (Zhal-GEER-eess).

22. The 1410 battle involved Poles, Lithuanians, and Germans but included Ruthenian, Czech, French, Scottish, Russian, and Tartar mercenaries.

23. A 19th-century German romantic nationalist term that roughly translates as "Twilight of the Gods" but meant something like "national apocalypse."

24. A boyar was a titled noble land-owner in premodern Russia, Ukraine, and the Orthodox Balkans, like Western feudal aristocrats.

25. In 1944, Stalin berated Soviet film director Sergei Eisenstein for his film *Ivan the Terrible*, which depicted the Oprichnina negatively; Stalin believed that Ivan IV's murderous Oprichnina had transformed Russia into a great power. Just as Ivan IV's Oprichnina had weakened Russia and allowed the raiding Crimean Tartars to burn Moscow to the ground in 1572, however, so too did Stalin's terrorization and purging of the Red Army in the 1930s lead to military disaster against the Finns and Germans in the early stages of World War II.

26. Because in Ukrainian the hard "h" sound is spelled with the Cyrillic letter "g" (Г), hence "Halych."

27. The Balkans have a long tradition of peasants taking to the mountains as guerrillas against local overlords, rival clans, and ethnic groups, and, ultimately, the Habsburg and Ottoman empires. A *Kuruc* (KOO-roots) and *Hajduk* (HIGH-dook) were essentially the same thing, just from different eras; kuruc were medieval, while hajduks were 17th–19th century: Slovaks, Hungarians, Ukrainians, Romanians, Bulgarians, Greeks, Albanians, and Serbs at one time or another all formed such mountain guerrilla bands. The Habsburgs often recruited hajduk guerrillas for use in their wars with the Turks. Small bands of Romanian and Hungarian hajduks even continued to fight the Soviets (and each other) well into the 1950s in communist Romania.

PEOPLES OF EASTERN EUROPE: THE GERMANS

1. Bessel, 2009: pp. 211–212

2. The general who led the Russian invasion of East Prussia in 1914 at the beginning of World War I was Gen. Paul von Rennenkampf, a Baltic German who was loyal to the Tsar.

3. The migrations of ethnic Germans from Kazakhstan, Transylvania, and other places in Eastern Europe to Germany after the collapse of the communist regimes generated controversy because many of these immigrants could not speak German and had retained very few German cultural traits beyond a surname and Oma's (Grandma's) strudel recipe. Meanwhile, in Germany itself, Turkish *Gastarbeiter* ("guest workers") imported after World War II to fill in after Germany's losses of young men in the war, still had great difficulty after three generations obtaining German citizenship.

CHAPTER 4: THE DAWN OF A NEW AGE 1600–1800

1. The Palatinate was one of the Electoral Lands (or voting "provinces") of the Holy Roman Empire, based along the northern Rhine River. Friedrich's wife was Elisabeth Stuart, daughter of King James I of England. She became known as the Winter Queen because her reign in Bohemia was so short, and she lived the rest of her life supporting the Protestant cause from the Netherlands.

2. "Defenestration" means to throw someone out a window, likely deriving from "window" in either Latin *fenestra*, or German, *Das Fenster*.

3. Ingria gets its name from the Finnic tribes who once inhabited the area but today the area is the solidly Russian oblast (province) of St. Petersburg.

4. Warsaw was almost completely destroyed by the Swedes in the war. In 2012, a drought in Poland revealed tons of large pieces of marble and other treasures (from nearby palaces suddenly exposed by the unusually low Vistula River) that had been

dumped by looting Swedish forces in 1655. Some historians speculate that this war pointlessly weakened both the Commonwealth and Sweden, leaving them both easy prey for a growing Russia.

5. Jean-Jacques Rousseau, "Considerations on the Government of Poland and its Proposed Reformation" (Composed but never published), April, 1772, Constitution Society, (www.constitution.org/jjr/poland.htm); accessed June 24, 2010.

6. Wolff, 1994: p. 266

7. Szlachta (SHLAH-khtah), a particularly Polish form of nobility that encompassed the aristocracy all the way down to the poorest noble title-holders.

8. Sobieski's daughter, Clementina, would later marry into the Scottish royal Stuart dynasty, and her son Charles ("Bonnie Prince Charlie") tried unsuccessfully to seize the British throne in 1745.

9. The Sejm (same) was the old medieval Polish parliament, expanded after the Union of Lublin in 1569 to include Lithuania's nobility.

10. The Cossacks borrowed the title *Hetman* (meaning supreme military commander) from the Polish-Lithuanian Commonwealth. Some speculate the Poles themselves had borrowed the term from the German military rank *Hauptmann*, "Captain."

11. Snyder, 2003: p. 117

12. Appleby, Joyce, *The Relentless Revolution, A History of Capitalism*. New York: W.W.Norton & Co., 2010; p. 39.

13. Further information about Fort Ross can be found at: www.mcn.org/1/rrparks/fortross

14. French philosophers of the Enlightenment. The Philosophe Voltaire corresponded with Catherine and was a devoted fan for a time.

15. The crisis was over whether a female, Maria Theresa, had the legal right to succeed her father (Holy Roman Emperor Charles VI). As her allies abandoned her, Maria Theresa invoked her

title as Queen of Hungary to appeal to her Hungarian subjects to fight for her, which they did.

16. From MacDonough, 1996: p. 307

17. The Seven Years' War, known in North America as the French and Indian War, was essentially a global confrontation between Britain and France but which played out in Central and Eastern Europe as each side had its allies, Prussia for Britain and the Habsburgs (Austria) and Russia for France. For more information, see: www.kopalnia.pl

PEOPLES OF EASTERN EUROPE: THE GYPSIES

1. Same as goyim in Hebrew; non-Gypsies or Romany.

2. From: www.geocities.com/~patrin/tradition.htm

3. Dr. Ian F. Hancock is a linguist, anthropologist and historian, and is considered the father of modern Romany studies in Europe.

CHAPTER 5: THE VERY, VERY LONG 19TH CENTURY – 1800–1914

1. "For jihadist, read anarchist," *The Economist*, August 18, 2005.

2. Figures taken from Magocsi, 1993: p. 93.

3. A term used by the Turks describing the palaces where the Ottoman Sultan held court; Westerners often used it to refer to the entire Ottoman Empire.

4. Referring to Vuk Branković, who switched to the Turkish side in the 1389 Battle of Kosovo.

5. Original and translation, with minor edits, from: Miletich, 1990: pp. 88–89

6. For more information: www.extension.unh.edu/FHGEC/docs/Lilacs.htm

7. The Ottomans allowed political representation for their non-Muslim subjects by religion through a sort of union known as millets, so that, for example, there was a Jewish millet, an

Orthodox Christian millet, and a Protestant Christian millet. Each millet had its own representatives at the Sultan's court. The Orthodox millet was controlled by Greeks.

8. The name "Rumelia" derived from *Rum*, Turkish for "Rome." The Ottoman Turks saw themselves as the heirs to the Roman and Byzantine empires.

9. Thessaloniki (or Salonika) was the Ottoman capital for both its Macedonia and Thrace provinces, as it still is today for modern-day Greece. In the early-20th century Jews actually comprised the city's largest ethnic group, followed by Greeks, but it also had substantial Bulgarian, Turkish, and other minorities. Greece expelled Bulgarians and Turks from these regions after World War I, and later most of the city's Jews were killed in the Holocaust.

10. *Jeszcze Polska nie zginęła* ("Poland Has Not Yet Perished"), with the stanza: Marsz, marsz, Dąbrowski/ z Ziemi Włoskiej do Polski/ za Twoim przewodem/ złączem się z Narodem! ("March, march Dąbrowski from the Italian lands to Poland, Under your command we will reunite the nation!"). General Jan Henryk Dąbrowski led the Polish Legion during the Napoleonic Wars in Italy and was invoked by Poles fighting in 1860s Italy.

11. Inspiring the famous German nationalist (and anti-French) song, *Wacht am Rhein!* ("The Watch on the Rhine!"): Lieb' Vaterland, magst ruhig sein, fest steht und treu die Wacht, die Wacht am Rhein! (Dear Fatherland, ease your mind, Solid and staunch stands the Watch, the Watch on the Rhine!).

12. His name was originally written "Bismark" but many modern sources add the extra "c" to spell "Bismarck." Me, I'm lazy and saved myself a keystroke.

13. Both Königgrätz and Hradec Králové mean "The King's Castle" in German and Czech, respectively.

14. Barraclough, 1979: pp. 422–23

15. As late as World War II, the war was portrayed (then by the Nazis) as a struggle between Western and Central Europe for domination of the Continent.

16. Johann Gottfried Herder, Prussian romanticist philosopher of the late-18th and early-19th century who viewed Slavs as "noble savages" rather like some Europeans and Americans of the day portrayed Native Americans.

17. Johnson, 1996: p. 132

18. Pan-Slavism held little attraction for Poles, especially those already ruled by Russia. In fact, some 19th-century Polish aristocrats tried to claim they were descended from the ancient (Iranian) Sarmatians, and that non-noble Poles derived from the Slavic masses.

19. Djilas, 1991; p. 27

20. The Austrian army commander, Alfred von Windischgrätz, flooded Prague with soldiers, and when riots broke out—during which his wife was killed by a ricocheting bullet while standing near a window—he pulled his forces from the city and shelled it for hours.

21. Kossuth lived in exile in the Ottoman Empire, then Britain, France, the United States, and finally, until his death in 1894, Italy. He was immensely popular in the 1850s throughout the West, and when he entered the United States in 1852 he was given a hundred-gun salute in New York harbor, was feted at the White House, and he became only the second foreign citizen (after Lafayette) to address both combined houses of the U.S. Congress.

22. "Cisleithania" and "Transleithania" sound complicated but are simple Latin terms. The Leitha River separates Austria and Hungary, so the lands *on this side* of the Leitha River—or Cisleithania—belonged to Austria, while the lands *across* the Leitha—Transleithania—were ruled by Hungary.

23. The Austro-Hungarian empire's currency in 1906, German for "crowns."

24. Herwig, 1997: p. 12

25. de Ségur, 1980: p. 270

26. ibid: p. 272

27. For more information, see: www.buffalohistoryworks.com/pa-namex/assassination/mckinley.htm

28. Several of the *Narodnaya Volya* revolutionaries were Jewish, although (Christian) Russians and Poles were also involved.

29. Russia was also deeply concerned about recent Japanese successes against China, and wasnted to use Port Arthur to block further Japanese ambitions in China.

30. Riasanovsky, 1969: p. 446

31. King Leopold II, king of Belgium 1865–1909, who operated the brutal mines in Belgian Congo that resulted in millions of Africans' deaths, reportedly half the Congo's population at the time. Leopold was so reviled in his later years that he could not travel outside Belgium.

PEOPLES OF EASTERN EUROPE: MUSLIMS

1. Stoye, 1964: p. 34

2. In the early-20th century, a little-known Hungarian painter with the pseudonym "Tivadar Csontváry" (CHONT-var-ee) traveled throughout the Ottoman Balkans and Levant (modern Turkey, Syria, Lebanon, and Israel) and painted daily scenes in amazingly vibrant colors of this now lost Muslim world, including Ottoman Jajce (YIGH-tseh) and Mostar (MOE-star) in Bosnia. His portfolio can be seen online at: www.hung-art.hu

3. Paul Goble, "Tatar Jadids Believe the Koran Encourages the Diversity Fundamentalists Deny, Kazan Historian Argues," *Window on Eurasia* (www.windowoneurasia.blogspot.com/), December 15, 2010; Daniel Kimmage, "Central Asia: Jadidism -- Old Tradition Of Renewal," *Radio Free Europe/Radio Liberty* (www.rferl.org), August 9, 2005.

4. "Interview: Bosnia's Grand Mufti Defends Religious Freedom," *Radio Free Europe/Radio Liberty* (www.rferl.org), July 16, 2009.

CHAPTER 6: THE GREAT WAR, AND A MAGIC YEAR - 1914-1939

1. Compared to the Napoleonic Wars (1795–1815), in which 3.5 million died, most of them from disease, exposure, or starvation (rather than bullets).

2. Sheehan, 2008: p. xix

3. Referring to the Franco-Prussian War of 1870–71, during which Prussia's army easily out-maneuvered Napoleon III's French forces and defeated France. The Versailles palaces outside Paris were humiliatingly used by Bismark to declare a united German empire (under Prussian control) in 1871.

4. Fromkin, 2004: p. 5

5. Keegan, 1999: pp. 135-136

6. His son, Crown Prince Wilhelm, accompanied him into Dutch exile but returned to Germany in the 1920s to try to restore the Hohenzollerns to power. He supported the Nazis until they murdered his close friend, after which he retreated from politics. Several different lines of the Hohenzollern dynasty still survive. Indeed, Wilhelm II's great-great grandson (who would be emperor but is today a business manager), Georg Friedrich (George Frederick), Prince of Prussia, was married quietly in a subdued ceremony at Frederick the Great's summer palace in Potsdam, Sanssouci Palace, in August 2011.

7. Hitler, 1971: p. 464

8. As imperial Germany imploded, a Bavarian Soviet Republic (*Bayerische Räterepublik*) lasted for three weeks in April-May, 1919, inflicting a Red Terror until it was crushed by Freikorps units.

9. Milan Kundera, (translated by Edmund White), "The Tragedy of Central Europe," *New York Review of Books*, Volume 31, Number 7. April 26, 1984.

10. Lenin decried the Allies as imperialists, so in January 1918 the indignant Woodrow Wilson put together a list of the war aims of

the United States, called the Fourteen Points. Some today still see the Fourteen Points as a model for international relations. Remarkably, five of the fourteen points dealt with Eastern Europe.

11. Radić contended that the Allies had pressured for the rushed creation of Yugoslavia in 1918, relying naturally on the Serbian state as the framework for the new country. Radić insisted that only an independent Croatia (with its own government and institutions) could consider joining Yugoslavia, and that therefore Yugoslavia (as it existed) was illegal and illegitimate.

12. Serbs had fought on the Allied side while Croats had served in the Habsburg army and state.

13. *Ustaša* refers to the organization, while *Ustaše* refers to its members.

14. In 1919 Italy inherited much of the Istrian Peninsula. After 1922, Italian fascist "Black Shirt" thugs took to terrorizing Slovenes and Croats in Italian Istria who refused to Italianize their names and speak Italian. They resorted to such tactics as beatings, torture, murder, and the firebombing of homes.

15. In World War I, the 'Central Powers' were Germany, Austria-Hungary, and their allies: the Ottoman Empire and later, Bulgaria.

16. Tsankov himself later became a fascist admirer of Adolf Hitler and even served as prime minister of a Bulgarian government-in-exile in Berlin in 1944 as Soviet forces overran his native country. He eventually escaped to a comfortable retirement-in-exile in Buenos Aires after the war.

17. More information can be found on Herbert Hoover's humanitarian exploits at: www.rememberinghoover.be/Humanitarian_Vision.htm

18. Soon to be renamed Alba Iulia (AHL-bah Yoo-LEE-ah) by the Romanians.

19. Of the Romanian branch of the Hohenzollern dynasty. In May, 2011 the 89-year-old former king Mihai severed all "historic and dynastic links" with the German Hohenzollerns in a bid to emphasize the native Romanian character of the former royal

family. His grandson, Prince Paul, opposed the move.

20. Codreanu himself was strangled by his prison guards later in 1938 on the king's orders, while a story of an escape attempt was circulated in the press.

21. He actually was born with a Turkified Albanian name—Ahmet Zogolli—but later "Albanianized" it to "Ahmed Zogu" for obvious political reasons. This was common for Albanian Muslims in the Ottoman era, so that we today sometimes have trouble discerning historic Turks from Albanians.

22. The next time a member of the Zogu family would set foot on Albanian soil would be 1993, when Crown Prince Leka returned from British exile.

23. Upon his death in July 2011, Otto von Habsburg, heir to the throne, was buried in the Habsburg family crypt in Vienna but per family tradition, his heart was buried separately, in the 10th-century abbey in Pannonhalma, in western Hungary.

24. Trying to force Hungarian language and culture on the country's non-Hungarian ethnic minorities.

25. Homepage: www.opusztaszer.hu

26. A diplomatic note delivered by Lt. Colonel Ferdinand Vyx of the French Army to the Hungarian government concerning imminent border revisions.

27. In Russian, "soviet" (*совет*) actually means "council," so "Soviet Union" (*Советский Союз*) can also be translated as "The Union of Councils." Hungarian (*Szovjetunió*) and German (*Die Sowjetunion*), like English, also used the Russian term, but in 1919 Hungarians translated the Russian word so that Kun's *Tanácsköztársaság* is sometimes rendered in English the "Republic of Councils" and other times the "Soviet Republic." Postwar Poles (*Związek Radziecki*) and Ukrainians (*Радянський Союз*) also translated "soviet," adding to the confusion.

28. "The Lenin Boys," Kun's Cheka (early KGB) used to terrorize Hungary into submission. Miklós Horthy countered in 1920 with an anti-Red "White" Terror. Both devastated the Hungarian countryside.

29. Kun later became an agent for the Comintern in Germany in the 1920s, but was seen by Lenin as ineffective. He was arrested and executed in 1938 during the Stalinist Great Purges in Moscow.

30. The statue can be seen at: www.budapest.usembassy.gov/ statue_of_bandholtz.html

31. Indeed, Hungary lost 103,093 km² (39,804 miles²) to Romania alone (including 1.7 million ethnic Hungarians), leaving post-Trianon Hungary only 92,963 km² (35,893 miles²), or 10% smaller than the lands it lost to Romania alone. (Rothschild, 1998: p. 155)

32. When Kosovo declared its independence from Serbia in February 2008, some Serbian nationalists complained of the "Trianonization" of Serbia.

33. Gábor Putsay, "Nehéz trianoni béklyó: Elcsatolták az iparterületek 50, a vasúthálózat 63, az úthálózat 65 százalékát" (Trianon's Heavy Fetters: 50% of Industrial Markets, 63% of the Rail Network, and 65% of Roads Lost), *Magyar Hírlap* (www. magyarhirlap.hu), June 4, 2011.

34. The West had forced Hungary to renounce the Habsburg dynasty, but Hungary's aristocrats wanted to retain the monarchy, so Horthy was declared a regent to an empty throne—laying the grounds for the joke that Hungary had a regent but no king, the regent being an admiral with no navy.

35. His full name was Tomáš Garrigue Masaryk, and he is often affectionately referred to today by Czechs simply as "TGM."

36. According to the 1921 Czechoslovak census, the total population was 13.6 million, with 51% Czechs, 14.5% Slovaks, 23% Germans, and 5.5% Hungarians, with the remaining 6% being Ruthenians (Ukrainians), Gypsies, Jews, Poles, Russians, and others.

37. Similarly, historian John Lukacs notes that mid-19th-century Buda and Pest had more German and Yiddish speakers than Hungarian speakers, but after unification in 1873 the city underwent a rapid "Magyarization." Lukacs adds that Austrian-

occupied Kraków underwent a similar process of "Polonification" after Polish independence in 1918. (Lukacs, 1988: pp. 100–103).

38. British Foreign Secretary Lord Halifax worried that in resolving a crisis sparked by the alleged mistreatment of German minorities by Prague, London was in turn only giving Hitler a license to mistreat and expel Czechs from the Sudetenland (which he did), but Chamberlain ignored these concerns in the name of European peace. (Reynolds, 2007: p. 78)

39. A *hetman* was the head of Cossack military forces. This title was borrowed from the Polish-Lithuanian Commonwealth, as the leading general of Commonwealth forces was called the Hetman. "Hetman" may have derived from the German (or Austrian) rank *Hauptmann* (captain).

40. Petlyura was assassinated in Paris in May 1926, ostensibly by the Soviet GPU, a KGB predecessor. Ukrainian President Victor Yushchenko laid flowers on Petlyura's grave during an official visit to Paris in 2005.

41. More information can be found at the Canadian First World War Internment Recognition Fund website here: www.internmentcanada.ca

42. War Communism was an economic policy of Lenin's from 1917–21 whereby the (anti-peasant) Bolsheviks simply seized whatever food and materials they needed from the countryside to keep the cities provisioned. Widespread economic collapse in 1921 convinced Lenin to change tactics.

43. Collectivization was a Stalinist practice of uprooting peasant farming communities and forcing them into huge state-owned agricultural collectives controlled by bureaucrats in Moscow. The resulting disruption of traditional food-producing networks led to declining harvest yields and widespread starvation. Stalin told Churchill in 1942 that 10 million Soviet peasants had died from collectivization in the 1930s (Taubman, 2003: p. 37).

44. Kalinousky—known in Russian as "Kalinovsky"—led a parallel rebellion in Belarus to the 1863 uprising in Poland, and was

hanged in 1864.

45. Indeed, for centuries Belarus was a favorite vacation destination for Polish, Lithuanian, German, and Russian aristocrats for big-game hunting.

46. "Myensk" (*Мейск*) is Belarussian for Minsk (*Мінск*), the capital of Belarus, though Russophile Belarussians insist on using "Minsk."

47. The official website of the Belarussian National Republic is: www.radabnr.org. Dictator Alexander Lukashenko blocks this website in present-day Belarus.

48. *Freikorps* ("Free Corps") units were impromptu pseudomilitia units formed after World War I in Germany by returning army veterans. These Freikorps units were hotbeds of nationalism, and because the regular army had collapsed, the German government often used the Freikorps just like the army.

49. *Der Baltische Landwehr* (Baltic Militia) was a militia formed by Baltic German barons to protect their interests after the Tsarist collapse in 1917.

50. Most of the Latvian Red Riflemen veterans fled to exile in Soviet Russia, but ended up being executed in the 1930s Stalinist Great Purges.

51. Weeks, Theodore R., "From 'Russian' to 'Polish': Vilna-Wilno 1905–1925. Washington D.C.: *NCEEER* (National Council for Eurasian and East European Research), June 4, 2004.

52. From John Ballantyne's article, "Counting Stalin's victims 50 years on"; *News Weekly* (www.newsweekly.com.au), March 5, 2003.

53. I use the Gregorian dates, which in 1918 were thirteen days ahead of Julian calendar dates, placing the "February Revolution" in March 1917.

54. Kerensky fled first to France, then eventually to the United States, where he lived the rest of his life in New York, teaching university classes.

55. And in the process, giving many of the Russian Empire's

minorities their first taste of freedom, or at least life outside of Russian rule.

56. Both quotes by Vyacheslav Molotov, the first on January 14, 1975, and the second on November 29, 1974. From: Resis, 1991: p. 8.

57. Numbers taken from: Heller & Nekrich, 1986: p. 306. Estimates of the numbers of gulag victims vary greatly, but conservative estimates show about 1 million executions prior to World War II, with another 2 million deaths by exhaustion, exposure, disease, or starvation in the camps.

58. The Polish Bolshevik Feliks Dzierżyński (Felix Dzerzhinsky) created the Cheka (ВЧК) in 1918 to terrorize Russian society, and it has been reorganized often since: the GPU (ГПУ; 1922–34), the NKVD (НКВД; 1934–46), the MGB (МГБ; 1946–53), the KGB (КГБ; 1953–91) and since 1992 the FSB (ФСБ). However, these organs were always just one of many Soviet security structures.

59. According to the Soviet government in the 1930s, a kulak was a wealthy peasant who resisted collectivization. Soviet authorities never defined what "wealthy" meant—i.e.,who was worth killing—so in practice a kulak was really any peasant the Soviet government wanted out of the way.

60. Courtois et al, 2004: pp. 206–207

61. Heller & Nekrich, 1986: p. 306.

62. Courtois, 2004: p. 4. Stalin claimed to Churchill in Moscow (1942) that collectivization had killed 10 million Soviet kulaks in the 1930s (Taubman, 2003: p. 37).

63. Dmowski damaged the Polish cause abroad (and his own reputation) with frequent blatantly anti-Semitic remarks.

64. Shirer, 1990: p. 212; Gen. von Seeckt was praising in a memorandum to the Weimar government the Treaty of Rapallo between Berlin and Moscow. Von Seeckt strongly advocated a German-Soviet anti-Western alliance, and openly agitated for the destruction of Poland. The Weimar government, which sought coexistence with the West, removed von Seeckt in 1926.

His anti-Versailles and anti-Polish views remained very influential, however.

65. With all the wars in the region from 1914 to 1925, often overlooked is the plight of POWs. One disastrous example were Soviet POWs—combined with leftover Russian POWs from World War I captured by the Germans—held by the Poles in 1921 and totaling 80,000-85,000. They lived in deplorable camp conditions. Disease (typhoid, cholera, dysentery, the influenza epidemic) ripped through the camps. It is estimated that up to 20,000 Polish POWs also died in Soviet and Lithuanian POW camps at around the same time (1919–21). In 2004, an official joint Polish-Russian historical commission estimated that 14,000-20,000 Soviet POWs died in the camps, almost all by disease, repudiating claims by some Russian historians that the POWs had been executed. ("Polish-Russian Findings on the Situation of Red Army Soldiers," *Naczelna Dyrekcja Archiwów Państwowych* / Head Office of the State Archives, www.archiwa. gov.pl / lang-en / exhibitions / 398–polish-russian-findings.html, accessed July 1, 2010.)

66. Pipes, 1996: p. 106

CHAPTER 7: WAR! ~ 1939~1945

1. Tadeusz Borowski (Tah-DAY-oosh Bor-OFF-skee) was a Christian Polish survivor of Auschwitz who initially escaped to France after the war but returned to Poland and became a devout communist (believing communism would stop wars and suffering) until the communists arrested and tortured his best friend. Disillusioned, he committed suicide in 1951 but he left behind a powerful body of poetry and prose about the shattered wartime generation. Translation from Polish by Magda and Tomek Jankowski.

2. Approximately 110,000 died in the two immediate atomic bomb blasts in August 1945 while effects from radiation and other injuries probably amounted to a total of 240,000 deaths by 1950. Source: U.S. Department of Energy Office of History and Heritage Resources. "The Manhattan Project, An Interactive History" (www.cfo.doe.gov / me70 / manhattan / hiroshima.

htm) and (www.cfo.doe.gov / me70 / manhattan / nagasaki.htm); accessed April 27, 2010.

3. Most of the figures for this paragraph were taken from: Kersten, 1991: pp. 163–165.

4. In Nazi historical lore, the Holy Roman Empire (c. 1000–1806) was the first German Reich, and imperial Germany (1871–1918) the second.

5. Evans, 2008: p. 11. Several of the attending generals' diaries confirm Hitler's words, including Franz Halder's. (See Rossino, 2003: p. 10)

6. "The Blitzkrieg in Poland has disposed of the most unbearable of the last remaining consequences of Versailles. It has liberated oppressed Germandom." (Eisenhart Rothe, 1942: p. 298). This is from official Nazi propaganda from 1942, describing the invasion of Poland.

7. Nazi SS units staged a fake attack on a radio station in the German border town of Gleiwitz (modern Gliwice [GLEE-vee-tseh], Poland) on August 31, 1939 and left several bullet-riddled bodies of Dachau inmates dressed in Polish military uniforms strewn outside. Claiming provocation, poised German armies invaded Poland hours later, at 4.15 a.m. on September 1.

8. Zaloga / Madej, 1991: p. 157

9. The website for production company Animal Monday's film Wojtek, the Bear that Went to War, made originally for the BBC: www.wojtekfilm.com.

10. Numbers from: Garliński, 1988 and Koskodian, 2009

11. Wituska & Tomaszewski, 2006: p. xxii. Speech given by Himmler in occupied Poznań (German *Posen*) in October 1944.

12. Gen. Bach-Zelewski, as his name indicates, was mixed Polish-German. Historically, Poles and Germans often intermarried. Friedrich Nietzsche, for instance, was Polish *szlachta* (nobility) on his mother's side. Bach-Zelewski already had a brutal record with civilians on the Eastern Front but some suspect his zealous destruction of Warsaw may have been to prove his "Germanness" to his Nazi superiors.

13. The Orzeł went on to fame in the Allied cause in April 1940 by sinking the German troop transport ship Rio de Janeiro just off the Norwegian coast. The Norwegian government at that point refused to believe British intelligence claims that Hitler intended to invade Norway, but when the Rio de Janeiro sank and hundreds of Wehrmacht soldiers washed up on Norwegian beaches.

14. Kārlis Ulmanis and Augustinas Voldemaras both died in a Soviet prison in 1942, while Konstantin Päts died in a Soviet mental hospital in 1956.

15. *Judenfrei* was a Nazi expression literally meaning "Free of Jews," and meant a territory had expelled or killed its entire Jewish population.

16. The Soviets restored Vilnius to (Soviet) Lithuania but expelled its Polish population to Poland. Most of its Jewish population died in the Holocaust.

17. In 1992, Uluots's successor in Sweden, Heinrich Mark, handed over in a ceremony in Tallinn the official prewar seals of office to the newly elected Estonian president, Lennart Meri, formally ending the Estonian government-in-exile.

18. From an interview Molotov gave to Felix Chuev in November, 1974: Resis, 1993: pp. 8–9.

19. Khrushchev, 1970: p. 148

20. "We remain faithful!"

21. Detailed information on Czechoslovak forces in the Soviet Union available at: www.czechpatriots.com/csmu/intro.php

22. Great webpage on Free Czechoslovak forces at: www.nasenoviny.com

23. Hungarian prime minister Pál (Paul) Teleki (PAHL TEH-leh-kee), who had signed the Yugoslav treaty weeks earlier, signed the invasion orders then went home and committed suicide. Teleki was an ardent revisionist but hoped for a regional confederation that could sort out regional issues. As if to further mock Teleki's idealism, Hungarian forces inflicted gross atroci-

ties in Vojvodina, massacring 4,000 Serbian and Jewish civilians in 1942.

24. Though the Soviets were blamed at the time, many believe the German air force (Luftwaffe) carried out this raid to provoke Hungary into the war.

25. There had been two Western Allied plans for a Balkan intervention; one envisioned an invasion from Greece northward (but was nixed by the Americans as too costly and unlikely to get as far as the Soviets). Another pictured an offensive out of northern Italy (from Venice) to link up with (a turncoat pro-Allied) Hungary to trap German forces in the Balkans, but unexpectedly tough German resistance in Italy slowed the Allied advance, killing this plan.

26. This charge was leveled at Hungary after the war and played a role in Hungary being forced to re-accept the 1920 Trianon borders; but, strangely, although for example the Soviets reported encountering the 33rd Waffen SS "Charlemagne" French volunteer division while fighting in Berlin, few accused Vichy France of being Hitler's last loyal ally. Szálasi fled to Germany, where he was arrested by U.S. forces and sent back to Hungary, where he was executed in 1946.

27. It had long been debated whether this anti-Jewish violence in Romania was spontaneous or whether authorities, local or in Bucharest, ordered it. However, in March 2012 Moldova turned over 15,000 pages of archival material from that era to the United States Holocaust Museum, and these records reportedly show that Antonescu closely directed these attacks in a bid to make Romania *Judenfrei* ("Free of Jews"). Indeed, Romania was the only Axis country besides Germany to maintain death camps for Jews, in Transnistria. Richard Solash, "Archive Reveals New Details Of Holocaust In Moldova." *Radio Liberty-Radio Free Europe* (www.rferl.org) April 6, 2012; Keno Verseck, with additional reporting by Katja und Viktor Schulmann, "Romania's Forgotten Holocaust; Filmmaker Confronts Leaders Over Silence." *Der Spiegel* (www.spiegel.de/international), November 15, 2012.

28. The Chetniks derived from Macedonian irregulars in the 19th century who struggled against Turks, Bulgarians, Serbs, and Albanians—and each other. Known as четовање (CHEH-to-vah-nyeh), meaning self-sufficient guerrillas, the Serbs were impressed by these small fighting units' ferocity and self-reliance, and they organized their own such units, calling them четници (CHET-nee-kee) for use against the Ottomans, Habsburgs, and Germans.

29. Tito was born to a Croat father and Slovenian mother, which may explain his strong pro-Yugoslav inclinations (rather than to Croat nationalism).

30. Mihailović was arrested and executed for treason after the war for wartime massacres of Croat and Muslim civilians in Bosnia. He was posthumously recognized by the United States with a medal, however, for the Chetniks' secret aid in helping downed American airmen reach safety.

31. Crampton, 1994: p. 203

32. Figures in this paragraph taken from the United States Holocaust Memorial Museum (www.ushmm.org) online article, "Jasenovac."

33. Technically, the Germans had merely allowed the Bulgarians to occupy these territories, with their fate to be decided after the war.

34. Sereny, 2002: p. 28. Posen (PO-zen) = modern Poznań (POEZ-non), in western Poland.

35. Heller & Nekrich, 1986: p. 349

36. Keegan, 1989: p. 175

37. Khrushchev claimed a million Soviet soldiers died in the war in his memoirs Khrushchev Remembers (Khrushchev, 1970: p. 155).

38. Lukacs, 2006: pp. 125–126; Pleshakov, 2005: p. 221

39. Heller & Nekrich, 1986: p. 374

40. Usually translated as "subhuman." Its counterpart was Übermenschen, "superior humans" or "supermen."

41. Heller & Nekrich, 1989: pp. 411–412

42. Dark Continent: Hitler's European Holocaust Helpers," *Der Spiegel* (www.spiegel.de), May 20, 2009.

43. "Auschwitz" (OWSH-veets) is the German name for the Polish town *Oświęcim* (Awsh-VYEN-cheem), located about 31 miles (50 km) west of Kraków.

44. Pronunciation: Birkenau (BEER-keh-now), Chełmno (HELM-no; German = Kulm), Bełżec (BEL-zhets), Majdanek (My-DON-ek), Sobibór (So-BEE-boor)

45. Eric Lichtblau, "The Holocaust Just Got More Shocking," *New York Times* (www.nytimes.com), March 1, 2013; accessed March 13, 2013.

46. Lizzy Davies, "France responsible for sending Jews to concentration camps, says court; First legal admission of country's collaboration in Nazi atrocities," *The Guardian* (www.guardian.co.uk), February 17, 2009. Also: "Norway apologises for deporting Jews during Holocaust." *BBC News* (www.bbc.co.uk), January 27, 2012.

47. The question was whether the Germans ordered a pogrom or Jedwabne's Polish population freely carried it out. Similar controversies led to the creation of the *Instytut Pamięci Narodowej* (National Institute of Remembrance; www.ipn.gov.pl), a Polish government entity that investigates crimes from the Nazi and communist eras in Poland. In 2001 Polish president Alexander Kwaśniewski officially apologized for Polish crimes against Jews.

48. Wallenberg's death in 1947 has not been confirmed, and the Wallenberg family has over the years received hints that he may have survived beyond that date, including archival information provided to the family by the Russian government as recently as 2012.

49. Abe Selig, "Bulgarian teacher to be posthumously honored by Yad Vashem," *Jerusalem Post* (www.jpost.com), June 28, 2010.

50. Website: www.yadvashem.org

51. When Ryszard Kukliński's father was discovered by the Nazis to be working for the Polish AK, for instance, they simply showed up at his apartment building mid-day and dynamited the entire building without warning or evacuating neighbors or residents. His mother luckily escaped.

52. Kielen-Rybicka, (requoted from the Polish weekly Tygodnik Powszechny), *Buffalo News* (www.buffalonews.com), May 29, 1993.

53. Pilecki also wrote a report on the Holocaust that later attracted attention in the West. He was executed by the communists in Poland in 1948 as a spy after collecting evidence of Soviet and Polish communist atrocities against Polish civilians. As of 2013, Polish authorities are still searching for Pilecki's unmarked grave.

SPECIAL INSERT: HOME IS WHERE THE BORDER IS!

1. Applebaum, 2012: p. 10

2. Ibid: pp. 12–13

3. From: "Forced displacement of Czech population under Nazis in 1938 and 1943," by Pavla Horáková, *Radio Praha* (www.radio.cz), October 13, 2003.

4. Figure from: Gross, 1988: p. 227

5. Most were seized from their parents but some were orphans whose parents had died in the war, or were the (unwanted) offspring of soldiers and local girls, either through relationships or rape.

6. Aly, 2007: pp. 156–157

7. Figures from: "Concentration Camp System: In Depth" on the United States Holocaust Memorial Museum website (www.ushmm.org).

8. Eric Lichtblau, "The Holocaust Just Got More Shocking," The *New York Times* (www.nytimes.com), March 1, 2013.

9. Gross, 1988: p. 227. "Polish citizens" includes ethnic Ukrainians, Belarussians, Jews, and others as well as ethnic Poles.

10. Ther & Siljak, 2001: p. 51; Courtois et al, 2004: p. 209.

11. Palmer, 2006: p. 347; Courtois et al, 2004: pp. 212–213

12. Ther & Seljak, 2001: p. 213. Romanians estimate that more than a million Romanians were deported by the Soviets between 1940–46. (Pacepa, 1987: p. 144)

13. Applebaum, 2012: p. 129; Ther & Siljak, 2001: p. xii. The Curzon line was proposed by British Foreign Secretary Lord George Curzon in 1919 as the border between Poland and Lenin's Russia, based on the 1797 Russo-Prussian border. Poland and Lenin rejected Curzon's border in 1920 but Stalin resurrected it in 1944, claiming the Curzon Line was an ethnic boundary, despite the Soviet having to deport c. 2 million Poles from the lands east of the Curzon Line in 1939–41 and 1944–45.

14. Bessel, 2009: pp. 211–245

15. Ibid

16. Applebaum, 2012: p. 133

17. Ibid; Ther & Siljak, 201: p. 53

18. Kostya, 1992: pp. 162–168

19. Recovered Territories" (*Ziemie odzyskane*) was the official term used by the Polish Communist government to refer to the lands (Silesia, Pomerania, southern East Prussia) annexed from postwar Nazi Germany. Stalin gave these lands to (communist) Poland in exchange for taking one-third of eastern Poland (called by Poles the *Kresy* lands) in 1939. Still, the annexation of these lands was very popular. The expulsions of 1944–46 artificially purged these lands of their German heritage, and the communists militantly suppressed any references to non-Polish culture(s) in these regions for decades. Post-1989 Poland has made strides toward changing this.

20. Website: www.episkopat.pl/?a=konferencje&doc=2005616_0

21. Website: www.berlin.polemb.net/index.php?document=312

22. Referencing the 1966 celebrations of a thousand years of Polish Christianity and statehood, from Mieszko's conversion of Poland in 966 CE.

23. English translation by the author.

CHAPTER 8: THE FRYING PAN, THE FIRE, ETC. 1945–1989

1. Translation from the Polish by Magda and Tomek Jankowski.

2. Jacek Kaczmarski was a very popular dissident singer-song-writer exiled from communist Poland and strongly associated with Solidarity in the 1980s. The view of the Yalta Conference held in Soviet Crimea in early February 1945 that Kaczmarski portrays here, of a Western abandonment of Eastern Europe to Soviet imperialism, is widely held in present-day Eastern Europe, though historians still argue this point.

3. Refers to Stalin having his guests' rooms thoroughly "bugged."

4. The "Lion" refers to British prime minister Winston Churchill.

5. References to a wheelchair or an invalid refer to U.S. President Franklin D. Roosevelt, who had been handicapped by polio and was wheelchair-bound.

6. Refers to Stalin, who was born in the Georgian mountains.

7. Yalta is in Crimea, hence the earlier reference to the Tartars.

8. "Albion" is an older name for England.

9. Roosevelt's physical condition deteriorated rapidly in early 1945; his appearance at the conference shocked many delegates. He died six weeks after returning home from Yalta. Historians have since argued how much his condition affected his mental state at Yalta.

10. Lavrenti Beria, head of the Soviet NKVD during the 1940s; essentially, Stalin's Torquemada in the 1940s and early 50s.

11. Refers to the NKVD's mass arrests and deportations to Siberian gulags of hundreds of thousands of Eastern Europeans in Stalin's new European empire from 1944–49.

12. Roosevelt's death in April 1945.

13. Again, referring to the mass deportations to the Siberian gulags.

14. Churchill lost an election held in the midst of the Potsdam conference in 1945, and was replaced as prime minister.

15. Again, a reference to the trains taking prisoners to Siberian gulags.

16. *United States Department of State Foreign Relations of the United States diplomatic papers* (FRUS), 1943. The British Commonwealth, Eastern Europe, the Far East: Volume III (1943); "Memorandum of Conversation, by Mr. Elbridge Durbrow of the Division of European Affairs," February 3, 1943; p. 503 (www.digital.library.wisc.edu/1711.dl/FRUS). Former Ambassador Davies had tried to convince Mr. Durbrow that the U.S. should recognize Soviet postwar territorial claims in Eastern Europe for the sake of better relations between Moscow and Washington.

17. Mastny, 1993: p. 11

18. From a 5,500-word telegram sent by Kennan from his post in Moscow to the State Department, fundamentally changing U.S. policy toward the Soviets.

19. From an interview Litvinov gave to CBS correspondent Richard C. Hottelet in London on June 18, 1946; as quoted in Wilson D. Miscamble's From Roosevelt to Truman: Potsdam, Hiroshima and the Cold War. New York: Cambridge University Press, 2006; p. 296

20. That American military spending had dropped from $556.9 billion in 1946 to just $52.4 billion in 1947, and the U.S. military went from 12.1 million personnel in 1945 to just 1.5 million by 1950 had no impact on Stalin's paranoia. Figures from U.S. Department of Defense (www.defense.gov).

21. Fursenko & Naftali, 2006: p. 23

22. Gaddis, 1998: p. 33

23. E.H.Carr, "Security in Europe," (article unattributed in original), *The Times* (archive.timesonline.co.uk), March 10, 1943; p. 5.

24. General Władysław Sikorski (Shee-KOR-skee) was prime minister of the Polish government-in-exile in London. He died in a plane crash in July 1943.

25. *United States Department of State Foreign Relations of the United States diplomatic papers* (FRUS), 1943. The British Common-

wealth, Eastern Europe, the Far East: Volume III (1943); "Interest of the United States in the Polish Government in Exile, and its Relations with the Soviet Union, (Memorandum of Conversation by the Under Secretary of State Welles)," January 4, 1943; p. 317 (www.digital.library.wisc.edu/1711.dl/FRUS).

26. To American journalist Edgar Snow; June, 1945; Geoffrey Roberts, "Litvinov's Lost Peace, 1941–1946," *Journal of Cold War Studies*, Volume 4, Issue 2; Spring 2002.

27. Full text available here: www.hpol.org/churchill; accessed January 17, 2011.

28. The Marshall Plan, named after U.S. Secretary of State George Marshall, was designed to hasten European recovery from the war by pumping tens of billions of dollars into Europe and giving European states special trading advantages with the U.S. Truman offered Moscow and the Soviet Bloc states participation in the ERP—Czechoslovakia initially accepted, but was forced by Stalin to rescind—but he knew they would reject it because the ERP required economic integration with (capitalist) Western Europe. Stalin countered by creating the Communist Information Bureau (Cominform). It is believed that the ERP provoked Stalin into crushing the last facades of independence in Eastern Europe in 1947–48 and tighten his control.

29. Grogin, 2001: p. 117

30. See website: www.voanews.com. See the "About VOA" section for more on Willis Conover.

31. In a report to the Hungarian Politburo describing the widely perceived technical and coordination failures of Warsaw Pact exercises held in Czechoslovakia in June–July 1968 designed to intimidate the Dubček government; quoted in: Mastny & Byrne, 2005: p. 292.

32. Klaus Wiegrefe, "How East Germany Tried to Undermine Willy Brandt," Translated from German by Christopher Sultan, *Der Spiegel* (www.spiegel.de/international/germany/0,1518,705118,00.html), July 8, 2010.

33. Michael Dobbs, "Warsaw Pact Sees Parity With West; Estimates

Differ From NATO Data," *Washington Post* (www.wasgington-post.com), January 31, 1989; accessed June 10, 2010.

34. Both cities had an Italian majority but with substantial Croat and Slovene minorities, and were surrounded by Croat or Slovene populations. In 1947, after Tito had terrorized some 66,000 ethnic Italians into fleeing Fiume, the city was turned over to Yugoslavia by the Paris Peace Treaty and became the Yugoslav (now Croatian) city of Rijeka. In 1954, Yugoslavia signed a treaty with Italy giving Trieste and a thin connecting strip of land to Italy, leaving the rest of the Istrian Peninsula to Yugoslavia. Today the peninsula is divided between Italy, Croatia, and Slovenia.

35. Bled, a medium-sized town in modern northwestern Slovenia, was where the agreement was signed.

36. Andreas Wassermann, "Killing Croatian Exiles: Tito's Murder Squads Operated in West Germany," *Der Spiegel* (www.spiegel.de), December 9, 2010.

37. Stats from: Courtois et al, 2004: pp. 395–396. The murdered were mostly local educated elites, and mass graves are still turning up across Bulgaria.

38. With the Paris Peace Treaty, Bulgaria of course lost Macedonia and Thrace forever, but was allowed to keep Southern Dobrudja.

39. Crampton, 1993: p. 160

40. "Police in fresh 'umbrella assassination' probe," *CNN online*; June 20, 2008 (www.cnn.com).

41. Planning for the Danube-Black Sea Canal project actually began under Pauker but work started under Gheorgiu-Dej. Construction relied heavily on slave laborers from gulag camps in the Danube Delta, so many of whom died from exhaustion, malnutrition, and unsafe working conditions that it became known as the *Canalul Morţii*, the "Canal of Death." Poor design and construction led to a halt in work in 1953 but it was restarted in the late 1970s—now with paid workers—and was completed. Today it is a part of a larger European river-canal network linking the Black Sea to the North Sea.

42. Rezun wrote several books about Soviet military topics, publishing under the pseudonym "Viktor Suvorov"; Suvorov, 1984: pp. 3-13.

43. See: www.ceausescu.org/ceausescu_texts/overplanned_parenthood.htm

44. Referring to the Treaty of Trianon of June 1920. Hungary in 1947 actually lost more territory than the Trianon borders, five small villages to Czechoslovakia, but in the mid-1950s Prague gave them back to Hungary as a goodwill gesture.

45. An old colleague of Béla Kun's and a veteran of the 1919 communist regime in post–World War I Hungary. Like Kun, Rákosi had fled to Moscow, but survived Stalin's purges (unlike Kun).

46. *Államvédelmi Osztálya*, "State Security Department," Hungarian KGB of the late 1940s.

47. *Államvédelmi Hatóság*, "State Security Authority," the renamed ÁVO.

48. In 1955 the Soviets shocked the West by proposing that Austria—which was divided between the World War II Allied powers just like Germany—be given its independence, so long as it remained neutral in the Cold War. This was an unsuccessful Soviet ploy to get the West to agree to the same deal for Germany (to neutralize West Germany) but after this "Austrian Solution," Hungarians hoped that Moscow might accept the same deal for them.

49. The Israeli invasion of Egypt was the first military phase of the Suez Crisis of 1956, and distracted the world's attention from the crisis unfolding in Hungary, giving the Soviets the cover to re-invade the country and violently suppress the revolution with minimal international interference.

50. Officially known as the European Recovery Program (ERP), the Marshall Plan—named after George Marshall, U.S. Secretary of State—was created by the U.S. as a four-year plan in 1947 to stabilize and rebuild Europe's economy after World War II. The plan was offered to the USSR and its Eastern European satellites as well—Czechoslovakia accepted the plan before being forced to reject it by Moscow—but the Soviets rejected it

because it would have required the integration of the Eastern Bloc's economies with the West.

51. And Marshal Janoušek's honors were many; he was a veteran of the 1918–19 Czechoslovak Legion as well as the Free Czechoslovak Air Force.

52. One significant result of this period of relative liberalization was the rise of a large group of very talented film makers—e.g., Miloš Forman, Jiří Menzel, and Jan Němec—who throughout the 1960s created their own film style, the "Czechoslovak New Wave," which achieved global recognition.

53. *Státní bezpečnost*; "State Security Service," Czechoslovak KGB

54. The East German army massed on the Czechoslovak border, but at the last minute the Warsaw Pact decided against allowing East German participation, for fear they might be seen as latter-day Nazis. Only noncombat *Volksarmee* logistics troops were allowed to participate, to East Berlin's fury.

55. In August 1975 the Soviet Union, much of Europe—East and West—and the United States signed the Final Act of the Conference on Security and Cooperation in Europe, or the Helsinki Accords for short. The accords were designed to ease tensions across Cold War Europe.

56. "Why the Berlin Wall was Built," *The Berlin Wall Online* (www. dailysoft.com/berlinwall), accessed July 15, 2010.

57. Гласность, Russian for "Openness."

58. Перестройка, Russian for "Restructuring" or "Reforming."

59. As quoted in an entry in Georgi Dimitrov's private journal (Dimitrov, 2003: p. 116), Stalin declared (*Sanacja*) Poland a fascist state.

60. Indeed, a leading Polish communist who spent the war in Moscow, Wanda Wasilewska (VAHN-dah Vah-seel-EV-skah), even suggested to Stalin in 1944 that Poland be incorporated directly into the Soviet Union. He declined.

61. A Russian village (in Russian, Катынь) near Smolensk around which the Soviets kept, in a few camps, the Polish officer corps

POWs captured during the September 1939 invasion of eastern Poland in cooperation with Hitler. In 1940, Stalin ordered the liquidation of these POW officers, forcing them to dig their own mass graves before the NKVD executed them. Approximately 14,700 Poles—some estimates range up to 25,000—were killed and buried at Katyń. The Nazis uncovered the mass graves later in 1943 and invited the Red Cross to verify the remains, at which point Stalin broke relations with the London-based Polish government-in-exile. After the war Polish communists blamed the Nazis for the massacre but in 1990 Soviet leader Mikhail Gorbachev released documents proving that Stalin himself had ordered the massacre and the NKVD had carried it out. In April 2010 the Russian government made these documents available online: www.rusarchives.ru/publication/katyn/01.shtml

62. Upon Mikołajczyk's return to London in 1947, Churchill is said to have expressed astonishment that he was still alive.

63. *Українська Повстанська Армія* ("Ukrainian Insurgent Army") fought for an independent Ukraine. Some 10,000-15,000 UPA guerrillas fought in the Carpathian Mountains until resistance petered out in the early 1950s. Soviet forces killed UPA leader Roman Shukhevych near Kiev in 1950.

64. Though Poland was recognized as an Allied country, the Soviets justified seizures of critical machinery and raw materials on the grounds that they had belonged to Germans during the Nazi occupation of Poland. Former German territories in Silesia, Pomerania, and Prussia were particularly looted, but no part of Poland was spared.

65. Kaser & Radice, 1986 (Vol. II): pp. 517 and pp. 575–76.

66. From the German-language "Biografie" section at the official Willy Brandt website (www.willy-brandt.org), Dezember (December) 1970, "Kniefall in Warschau"; accessed July 8, 2010. Also the official Warsaw city website: (www.beta. um.warszawa.pl), menu item O Warszawie ("About Warsaw"), article titled "Skwer Willy Brandta" ("Willy Brandt Square"), dated March 2, 2010 (also accessed on July 8, 2010).

67. A particularly Eastern European social class that could be roughly defined as the intellectual elite among educated white-collar workers. As the middle class developed more slowly in Eastern Europe, the intelligentsia played a leading role in the development of a modern civil society.

68. This debt would be paid back only in October 2012. "Poland pays off communist debt," *Thenews.pl* (*Polskie Radio dla Zagranicy*), October 30, 2012.

69. Byrne & Mastny, 2005: p. 52

70. Jaruzelski was already infamous in Poland as the minister of defense who ordered Polish forces to participate in the 1968 Warsaw Pact invasion of Czechoslovakia, and who two years later, per Gomułka's orders, ordered the army to open fire on unarmed protesting workers in December 1970.

71. Resis, 1993: p. 215

72. George F. Kennan, "The Sources of Soviet Conduct," *Foreign Affairs*, 25, no. 4 (1947): pp. 566–582. Published originally as author "X."

73. The largest manmade explosion in history was a Soviet hydrogen bomb test in October 1961 in the Soviet Arctic. This bomb was originally made for 100 megatons but was scaled down to 50 MTs for safety purposes. The largest American nuclear test was a 15 MT bomb on the Bikini Atoll in 1954.

74. Diego Zampini, "Russian Aces over Korea, Mikoyan-Gurevich MiG-15 Fagot pilots," *AcePilots.com* (www.acepilots.com/russian/rus_aces.html); accessed June 24, 2010.

75. Mark O'Neill, "Soviet Involvement in the Korean War: A New View from the Soviet-era Archives," *OAH Magazine of History*, Vol. 14, No. 3, Spring 2000 (www.oah.org/pubs/magazine/korea/oneill.html); accessed June 24, 2010.

76. First proposed by French reconstruction planning commissioner Jean Monnet and French foreign minister Robert Schuman as a coal-sharing arrangement with newly-created West Germany, the ECSC began with six members (France, West Germany, Italy, Netherlands, Belgium, Luxembourg) and formed the kernal out of which the modern European Union developed.

77. Stalin's economic policies toward Eastern Europe essentially amounted to pillaging, but in 1955 Khrushchev began to negotiate more equitable economic relationships with the satellite states. Indeed, over time after 1960 several satellite regimes haggled surprisingly advantageous deals with Moscow.

78. Daniel C. Thomas, "The Helsinki Accords and Political Change in Eastern Europe" in *The Power of Human Rights, International Norms and Domestic Change*. Edited by Thomas Risse, et al (Cambridge, MA: Cambridge University Press, 1999); p. 212.

79. Mastny & Byrne, 2005: p. 55

80. From: "World's 4th-largest lake almost gone," by Chong Wu, *CNN.com* SciTech Blog, October 15, 2008; also Nikanovo & Nazarova, 1997: pp. 9–28.

81. Strategic Arms Limitations Talks, limiting nuclear weapons between the U.S. and the USSR.

82. Yuri Andropov had extensive experience in Eastern Europe—he had been Soviet ambassador in Hungary during the 1956 crisis, and later head of the KGB—which meant he had an accurate picture of the Soviet realm's true condition. He was one of the octogenarians succeeding Brezhnev (Nov. 1982–Feb. 1984). He saw the need for extensive reforms and believed they would save the USSR, but he died before he could implement them.

83. Text of speech from: www.reaganfoundation.org/reagan/speeches/wall.asp

CHAPTER 9: EASY COME, EASY GO ~ 1989~92

1. Website: www.mementopark.hu

2. Beschloss & Talbott, 1994: p. 134

3. Matthew Kaminski, "From Solidarity to Democracy," *Wall Street Journal* (www.wsj.com), November 9, 2009.

4. Sadly, Kaczorowski—along with much of the Polish leadership—died in a tragic plane crash near Smolensk in Russia in April 2010 as they were on their way to attend ceremonies with Russian government officials to mark the 1940 Katyń Massacre.

5. One of these political parties, the *Fiatal Demokraták Szövetsége* ("Young Democrats' Alliance") or FDSz, or, more popularly, *Fidesz* (FEE-dess), kept up the Hungarian tradition of food-based political analogies when it chose as its symbol the Hungarian Orange, derived from a satirical film made by Péter Bacsó in 1969 called *A Tanu* ("The Witness") about a simple dam maintenance worker caught up in the purge show trial hysteria of early 1950s Stalinist Hungary. At one point in the film, an arbitrary communist party decision for Hungary to corner the world's orange market stumbles when an entire orchard manages to produce a single orange—though this single orange prompts a major state celebration as a triumph for socialism anyway. Fidesz named its primary party newspaper the *Magyar Narancs* (The Hungarian Orange), still available (as a liberal publication no longer affiliated with that once liberal, now conservative party) at: www.mancs.hu

6. Only months before, in June, Chinese communist hardliners had ordered the Chinese People's Army to attack peaceful student protestors in Tiananmen Square in Beijing, leading to hundreds or possibly even thousands of deaths, and a new wave of repression throughout the country.

7. Meaning "leader," used by Antonescu during World War II, similar to the Nazi Führer. Ceaușescu liked this term and adopted it as well.

8. "Albania" in Albanian is *Shqipëria*, literally "Land of the Eagles," referring to its mountainous terrain.

9. "Yugoslav War Savages Zoo Animals," *Chicago Tribune* (reprinted from the *Toronto Globe and Mail*; www.chicagotribune.com), October 18, 1991

10. Famous Hungarian singer-songwriter since the 1960s who passed away in August 2009. Home page: www.cseh-tamas.hu.

11. Translated from the Hungarian by Tomek Jankowski.

12. Reference to the 1956 Hungarian Revolution.

13. Reference to Prague Spring and the Soviet invasion of Czechoslovakia in 1968.

14. The Trabant was a communist-era East German 2–cylinder car infamous for its pollution and poor quality, though very affordable.

15. Written during 1989, refers to the changes then shaking the region.

16. Refers to Eastern Europe's having been ravaged by the extremist ideologies of both the political left (communism) and the right (fascism) in the 20th century.

17. This song was written in response to the dramatic changes of 1989, which this line in particular poignantly highlights.

18. Iron Curtain Trail website: www.ironcurtaintrail.eu/en/index.html.

EPILOGUE

1. Popular joke in communist-era Eastern Europe. From: Katona, 1994: p. 147. Translated from Hungarian by Tomek Jankowski.

2. Little, Allan, "Germany, Poland and the shifting centre of European Union power," *BBC World News* (www.bbc.co.uk), December 17, 2012.

3. Immigration and Refugee Board of Canada, Russia: Situation and treatment of visible ethnic minorities; availability of state protection, 1 October 2009, RUS103139.E, available at: www.unhcr.org/refworld/docid/4b7cee862d.html; accessed 6 May 2012.

4. Valentina Pop, "Russia does not rule out future NATO membership," *EUObserver.com* (http://euobserver.com), April 1, 2009

5. See the Transparency International website: cpi.transparency.org/cpi2012/results, accessed December 17, 2012.

REFERENCE

MUSICAL CHAIRS, OR PLACE NAMES IN EASTERN EUROPE

1. Egremont, 2011: p. 220

2. After two centuries of Russian rule, the Russian "Minsk" (Минск, or, in Belarussian Cyrillic, Мінск) is now commonly used among Belarussians.

EASTERN EUROPE IN NUMBERS

1. Website, in Polish: http://www.sowa.website.pl/powazki/index.html

2. Actually, the CIA World Factbook ranks the European Union as the world's largest economy at $15.4 trillion in 2011, but the EU does not have an economy, rather a collection of almost thirty different smaller economies, each with their own regulatory regimes and laws, some even with their own currencies. Despite significant progress toward a single, united economy, there are still important legal impediments to cross-border economic activity in the EU.

3. Website: www.weforum.org

4. Website: www.prosperity.com

5. Website: www.doingbusiness.org. IFC = International Finance Corporation

Bibliography

Why do people make bibliographies? They're a lot of work; this one took weeks. So why did I create this? Why are you reading this? I can't answer the latter question but I can tell you that besides having to properly accredit those whose work I have cited or otherwise relied on to write this book, I also wanted to provide you, the reader, with someplace to turn to if some topic I mentioned piqued your interest and you want to learn more. Although this book seems *really* thick, it covers a big topic and just barely touches very briefly on thousands of little topics, every one of which deserves a book of its own. In fact, many of them already *have* books written about them, which I used to help me put this book together. That's what this bibliography is for you, a collection of little doors, each one leading deeper into some topic that I could only mention in a sentence or two. Dive in.

Ádám, **Magda**, *The Little Entente and Europe (1920–1929)*. Translated from Hungarian by Mátyás Esterházy. Budapest, Hungary: Akadémiai Kaidó, 1993.

Albats, **Yevgenia**, *The KGB and Its Hold on Russia; Past, Present and Future*. Translated from Russian by Catherine A. Fitzpatrick. New York: Farrar-Straus-Giroux, 1994.

Almond, **Mark**, *Decline Without Fall: Romania Under Ceausescu*. London: Alliance Publishers Ltd., 1988.

Anisimov, **Evgenii V.**, *The Reforms of Peter the Great: Progress Through Coercion in Russia*. Translated from Russian by John T. Alexander. Armonk, NY: M.E. Sharpe, 1993.

Applebaum, **Anne**, *Iron Curtain, The Crushing of Eastern Europe 1944–1956*. New York: Doubleday, 2012.

Ascherson, **Neal**, *Black Sea*. New York: Hill & Wang, 1995.

Ascherson, **Neal**, *The Polish August, The Self-Limiting Revolution*. New York: The Viking Press, 1982.

Ash, **Timothy Garton**, *The Polish Revolution*. New Haven, CT: Yale University Press, 2002.

Avrich, **Paul**, *Russian Rebels, 1600–1800*. New York: W.W. Norton & Company, 1972.

Axworthy, **Mark** and **Serbanescu**, **Horia**, *Men-At-Arms Series: The Romanian Army of World War 2*. London: Osprey Publishing, Ltd., 1991.

Bak, János M., editor (et al), *Az 1956-os Magyar Forradalom* [The 1956 Hungarian Revolution]. Budapest, Hungary: Tankönyvkiadó, 1991.

Banac, Ivo, editor, *The Diary of Georgi Dimitrov 1933–1949.* Translated from German by Jane T. Hedges, from Russian by Timothy D. Sergay, and from Bulgarian by Irina Faion. New Haven, CT: Yale University Press, 2003.

Bandholtz, Maj. Gen. Harry Hill, *An Undiplomatic Diary.* Edited by Fritz-Konrad Krüger. New York: Columbia University Press, 1933.

Banescu, N., *Historical Survey of the Romanian People.* Bucharest, Romania: Romanian Cultura Nationala, 1926.

Barford, Paul M., *The Early Slavs.* Ithica, NY: Cornell University Press, 2001.

Barron, John, *KGB, The Secret Work of Soviet Secret Agents.* New York: Bantam Books, 1981.

Bellwood, Peter, *First Farmers, the origins of Agricultural Societies.* Malden, MA: Blackwell Publishing, 2005.

Benda, Kálmán et al, *One Thousand Years, A Concise History of Hungary.* Translated from Hungarian by Zsuzsa Béres. Budapest, Hungary: Corvina, 1988.

Benz, Ernst, *The Eastern Orthodox Church, Its Thought and Life.* Translated from German by Richard and Clara Winston. New York: Anchor Books, 1963.

Berend, Ivan T., *Decades of Crisis, Central and Eastern Europe Before World War II.* Berkley, CA: University of California Press, 1998.

Bernhard, Michael H., *The Origins of Democratization in Poland, Workers, Intellectuals, and Oppositional Politics, 1976–1980.* New York: Columbia University Press, 1993.

Bernstein, Carl and **Politi, Marco,** *His Holiness, John Paul II and the Hidden History of Our Time.* New York: Doubleday, 1996.

Bertényi, Iván et al, *Királyok könyve: Magyarország és Erdély királyi, királynői, fejedelmei és kormányzói* [The Book of Kings: Hungary's and Transylvania's Kings, Queens, Crown Princes and Regents]. Budapest, Hungary: Officina Nova, 1995.

Beschloss, Michael and **Talbott, Strobe,** *At the Highest Levels: The Inside History of the End of the Cold War.* Boston: Backbay Books, 1993.

Bessel, Richard, *Germany, 1945.* New York: HarperCollins Publishers, 2009.

Bobelian, Michael, *Children of Armenia, A Forgotten Genocide and the Century-Long Struggle for Justice.* New York: Simon & Schuster, 2009.

Bobrick, Benson, *Fearful Majesty: The Life and Reign of Ivan the Terrible.* New York: G.P. Putnam's Sons, 1987.

Boll, Michael M., *Cold War in the Balkans, American Foreign Policy and the Emergence of Communist Bulgaria 1943–1947.* Lexington, KY: The University Press of Kentucky, 1984.

Borhi, László, *Hungary in the Cold War 1945–1956, Between the United States and the Soviet Union.* Budapest, Hungary: Central European University Press, 2004.

Bori, István et al, *The Essential Guide to Being Hungarian, 50 Facts & Facets of Nationhood.* Translated from Hungarian by Paul Olchváry. Williamstown, MA: New Europe Books, 2005.

Bortoli, Georges, *The Death of Stalin.* Translated from French by Raymond Rosenthal. New York: Praeger Publishers, 1975.

Bouwsma, William J., *Venice and the Defense of Republican Liberty, Renaissance Values in the Age of the Counter Reformation.* Berkley, CA: University of California Press, 1984.

Bozoki, Andras et al, *Democratic Legitimacy in Post-Communist Societies.* Budapest, Hungary: T-Twins Publishers, 1994.

Bradley, John, *Lidice, Sacrificial Village.* New York: Ballantine Books, 1972.

Breuilly, John, *Nationalism and the State.* Chicago: University of Chicago Press, 1993.

Bridge, F.R. and **Bullen, Robert**, *The Great Powers and the European States System, 1815–1914.* London: Longman, 1991.

Brzezinski, Richard, *Polish Armies 1569–1696, Vol. I-II.* Oxford, UK: Osprey Publishing, Ltd., 1988.

Bujak, Adam, *Nekropolie królów i książąt polskich* [The Burial Places of the Kings and Princes of Poland]. Warsaw, Poland: Wydawnictwo "sport i Turystyka," 1988.

Cate, Curtis, *The Ides of August: The Berlin Wall Crisis, 1961.* New York: M. Evans & Company, 1978.

Chapman, Colin, *August 21st: The Rape of Czechoslovakia.* Philadelphia: J.B. Lippincott Company, 1968.

Chirot, Daniel, editor, *The Origins of Backwardness in Eastern Europe, Economics and Politics from the Middle Ages until the Early Twentieth Century.* Berkley, CA: University of California Press, 1989.

Cohat, Yves, *The Vikings: Lords of the Seas.* Translated from French by Ruth Daniel. New York: Harry N. Abrams Inc., 1987.

Comrie, Bernard, editor, *The Major Languages of Eastern Europe.* London, UK: Routledge, 1987.

Conquest, Robert, *Stalin, Breaker of Nations.* New York: Penguin Books, 1991.

Courtois, Stéphane et al, *The Black Book of Communism: Crimes, Terror, Repression.* Translated from French by Jonathan Murphy and Mark Kramer. Cambridge, MA: Harvard University Press, 2004.

Cowley, Robert, editor, *The Cold War, A Military History*. New York: Random House, 2005.

Crampton, R.J., *A Short History of Modern Bulgaria*. Cambridge, UK: Cambridge University Press, 1993.

Crampton, R.J., *Eastern Europe in the Twentieth Century*. London: Routledge, 1994.

Crankshaw, Edward: *The Fall of the House of Habsburg*; Penguin Books, New York, United States; 1963.

Crozier, Brian, *The Rise and Fall of the Soviet Empire*. Roseville, CA: Forum, 2000.

Crummy, Robert O., *The Formation of Muscovy 1304–1613*. London: Longman Group UK Ltd., 1987.

Cunliffe, Barry, *Prehistoric Europe*. Oxford, UK: Oxford University Press, 1998.

Davies, Norman, *God's Playground, A History of Poland, Vol.1: The Origins to 1795*. New York: Columbia University Press, 1982.

Davies, Norman, *God's Playground, A History of Poland, Vol.2: 1795 to the Present*. New York: Columbia University Press, 1982.

Davies, Norman, *Rising '44: The Battle for Warsaw*. New York: Viking, 2003.

Davies, Norman, *Europe, A History*. Oxford, UK: Oxford University Press, 1996.

Davies, Norman, *White Eagle, Red Star, The Polish-Soviet War 1919–1920*. London: Pimlico, 2003.

Davies, Norman and Moorhouse, Roger, *Microcosm, Portrait of a Central European City*. London: Pimlico, 2003.

Dawidowicz, Lucy S., *The War Against the Jews, 1933–1945*. New York: Bantam Books, 1975.

de Bray, Reginald George Arthur, *Guide to the Slavonic Languages*. New York: E.P. Dutton & Co., Inc., 1963.

de Madariaga, Isabel, *Russia in the Age of Catherine the Great*. London: Phoenix Press, 2002.

de Ségur, Count Philippe-Paul, *Napoleon's Russian Campaign*. Translated from French by J. David Townsend. Arlington, VA: Time-Life Books, Inc. 1980.

de Zayas, Alfred-Maurice, *A Terrible Revenge, The Ethnic Cleansing of the East European Germans, 1944–1950*. Translated from German by John A. Koehler. New York: St. Martin's Press, 1994.

Deák, István, *The Lawful Revolution, Louis Kossuth and the Hungarians 1848–1849*. London: Phoenix Press, 2001.

Deák, István; Gross, Jan T. and **Judt, Tony,** *The Politics of Retribution in Europe: World War II and Its Aftermath.* Princeton, NJ: Princeton University Press, 2000.

Dedijer, Vladimir, *The Battle Stalin Lost, Memoirs of Yugoslavia 1948–53.* New York: Grosset & Dunlap, 1972.

Dedijer, Vladimir, *The Road to Sarajevo.* New York: Simon & Schuster, 1966.

Dehio, Ludwig, *The Precarious Balance, Four Centuries of European Power Struggle.* Translated from German by Charles Fullma. New York: Vintage Books, 1965.

Dekan, Ján, *Moravia Magna: The Great Moravian Empire.* Minneapolis, MN: Control Data Arts, 1981.

Demetz, Peter, *Prague in Black and Gold: Scenes From the Life of a European City.* New York: Hill & Wang, 1997.

Deschner, Gunther, *Warsaw Rising.* New York: Ballantine Books, Inc., 1972.

Deutscher, Isaac, *Stalin, A Political Biography.* New York: Oxford University Press, 1970.

Dimitrov, Bojidar, *Bulgarians, Civilizers of the Slavs.* Translated from Bulgarian by Marjorie Hall Pojarlieva. Sofia, Bulgaria: Borina Publishing House, 1995.

Dimont, Max I., *Jews, God and History.* New York: Signet Books, 1964.

Diocoviciu, Hadrian, et al, *Istoria Romanilor* ["The History of Romanians"]. Bucharest, Romania: Editura Didactica si Pedagogica R.A., 1995.

Diószegi, István, *A Ferenc József-I kor nagyhatalmi politikája* ["Great Power Politics in the Era of Franz Josef I"]. Budapest, Hungary: Kossuth Könyvkiadó, 1987.

Djilas, Aleksa, *The Contested Country: Yugoslav Unity and Communist Revolution 1919–1953.* Cambridge, MA: Harvard University Press, 1991.

Djilas, Milovan, *Conversations with Stalin.* Translated from Serbo-Croat by Michael B. Petrovich. San Diego, CA: Harcourt Brace Jovanovich, Inc., 1962.

Djilas, Milovan, *The New Class: An Analysis of the Communist System.* New York: Frederick A. Praeger, 1957.

Djordjevic, Dimitrije and **Fischer-Galati, Stephen,** *The Balkan Revolutionary Tradition.* New York: Columbia University Press, 1981.

Dobson, David, *Scots in Poland, Russia and the Baltic States, 1550–1850.* Baltimore, MD: Geneological Publishing, 2003.

Dolot, Miron, *Execution by Hunger, The Hidden Holocaust.* New York: W. W. Norton & Company Ltd., 1985.

Dragnich, Alex N., *Serbs and Croats, The Struggle in Yugoslavia*. San Diego, CA: Harcourt Brace & Company, 1992

Dugan, James and **Stewart, Carroll,** *Ploesti*. New York: Bantam Books, 1963.

Dukes, Paul, *The Making of Russian Absolutism, 1613–1801*. London, UK: Longman, 1988.

Dvornik, Francis, *The Slavs in European History and Civilization*. New Brunswick, NJ: Rutgers University Press, 1962.

Eden, Anthony, *The Suez Crisis of 1956*. Boston: Beacon Press, 1960.

Eisenhart Rothe, General Ernst von, editor, *Ehrendenkmal der Deutschen Wehrmacht: Kriegsausgabe vom Ehrendenkmal der Deutschen Armee und Marine* ["Monument to the German Armed Forces: The War Edition of the Monument to the German Army and Navy]. Berlin and Munich: Deutscher National-Verlag (German National Publishing House), Second edition, 1942.

Egremont, Max, *Forgotten Land, Journeys Among the Ghosts of East Prussia*. New York: Farrar, Straus & Giroux, 2011.

Engle, Eloise and **Paananen, Lauri,** *The Winter War. The Soviet Attack on Finland 1939–1940*. Harrisburg, PA: Stackpole Books, 1973.

Evans, Richard J., *The Coming of the Third Reich*. New York: Penguin Books, 2003.

Evans, Richard J., *The Third Reich in Power*. New York: Penguin Books, 2005.

Evans, Richard J., *The Third Reich at War*. New York: Penguin Books, 2008.

Eversley, Lord, *The Partitions of Poland*. New York: Dodd, Mead and Company, 1915.

Fest, Joachim, *Hitler*. Translated from German by Richard and Clara Winston. New York: Harcourt, Brace, Jovanovich, 1973.

Findley, Carter Vaughn, *The Turks in World History*. Oxford, UK: Oxford University Press, 2005.

Fine, John V. A. Jr., *The Early Medieval Balkans: A Critical Survey from the 6th to the Late 12th Century*. Ann Arbor, MI: University of Michigan Press, 1997.

Fine, John V. A. Jr., *The Late Medieval Balkans: A Critical Survey from the Late 12th Century to the Ottoman Conquest*. Ann Arbor, MI: University of Michigan Press, 1996.

Fischer, Fritz, *Germany's Aims in the First World War*. New York: W.W. Norton & Company, 1967.

Fischer-Galati, Stephen, *20th Century Rumania*. New York: Columbia University Press, 1991.

Fletcher, Richard, *The Barbarian Conversion From Paganism to Christianity*. Berkley, CA: University of California Press, 1999.

Fodor, Dr. István, *In Search of a New Homeland, The Prehistory of the Hungarian People and the Conquest*. Translated from Hungarian by Helen Tarnoy. Budapest, Hungary: Corvina Kiadó, 1975.

Fodor, Dr. István, *The Hungarians of the Conquest Period*. Budapest, Hungary: Hungarian National Museum, 1996.

Fol, Aleksander and Marazov, Ivan, *Thrákia és a Thrákok* [Thrace and the Thracians]. Translated from Bulgarian to Hungarian by T. Tedeschi Maria. Budapest, Hungary: Gondolat, 1984.

Franaszek, Antoni and Kuczman, Kazimierz, editors, *Odsiecz wiedeńska 1683, Vol.I-II* ["The Siege of Vienna, 1683; Vol. I-II"]. Kraków, Poland: Państwowe Zbiory Sztuki na Wawelu, 1990.

Franklin, Simon and Shepard, Jonathan, *The Emergence of Rus, 750–1200*. London, UK: Longman, 1996.

Fraser, Angus, *The Gypsies*. Oxford, UK: Blackwell, 1995.

Freely, John, *The Grand Turk, Sultan Mehmet I—Conqueror of Constantinople and Master of an Empire*. New York: The Overlook Press, 2009.

Fromkin, David, *Europe's Last Summer: Who Started the Great War in 1914?* New York: Vintage Books, 2004.

Fursenko, Aleksandr and Naftali, Timothy, *Khrushchev's Cold War, The Inside Story of an American Adversary*. New York: W. W. Norton & Company Ltd., 2006.

Gaddis, John Lewis, *The United States and the Origins of the Cold War, 1941–1947*. New York: Columbia University Press, 1972.

Gaddis, John Lewis, *We Now Know: Rethinking Cold War History*. Oxford, UK: Oxford University Press, 1998.

Galántai, József, *Hungary in the First World War*. Translated from Hungarian by Éva Grusz and Judit Pokoly. Budapest, Hungary: Akadémiai Kiadó, 1989.

Galántai, József, *Trianon és a kisebbségvédelem* ["Trianon and the Protection of Minorities"]. Budapest, Hungary: Mæcenas, 1989.

Garliński, Józef, *Poland in the Second World War*. New York: Hippocrene Books, Inc., 1988.

Geary, Patrick J., *The Myth of Nations; the Medieval Origins of Europe*. Princeton, NJ: Princeton University Press, 2002.

Georgiev, Georgi, *Felkelés Bulgáriában 1923* ["Uprising in Bulgaria, 1923"]. Translated from Bulgarian to Hungarian by Károly Lengyel. Budapest, Hungary: Kossuth Könyvkiadó, 1981.

Gibney, Frank, *The Frozen Revolution, Poland: A Study in Communist Decay*. New York: Farrar, Straus and Cudahy, 1959.

Gieysztorowa, Irena, editor, et al, *Atlas historyczny Polski* ["Historical Atlas of Poland"]. Wrocław, Poland: Państwowe Przedsiębiorstwo Wydawnictw Kartograficzynych, 1967.

Gilbert, Martin, *Atlas of Russian History, From 800 B.C. to the Present Day*. Oxford, UK: Oxford University Press, 1993.

Gilbert, Martin, *The Righteous, The Unsung Heroes of the Holocaust*. London, UK: Black Swan Books, 2002.

Gimbutas, Marija, *The Balts*. London: Thames and Hudson, 1963

Gimbutas, Marija, *The Slavs*. New York: Praeger Publishers, 1971

Glenny, Misha, *The Balkans: Nationalism, War and the Great Powers, 1804–1999*. New York: Viking, 2000.

Glenny, Misha, *The Fall of Yugoslavia, the Third Balkan War*. London, UK: Penguin Books, 1992.

Glenny, Misha, *The Rebirth of History: Eastern Europe in the Age of Democracy*. New York: Penguin Books, 1993.

Gojda, Martin, *The Ancient Slavs*. Edinburgh, Scotland: Edinburgh University Press, 1991.

Grogin, Robert C., *Natural Enemies: The United States and the Soviet Union in the Cold War, 1917–1991*. Lanham, MD: Lexington Books, 2001.

Gross, Jan T., *Revolution from Abroad, The Soviet Conquest of Poland's Western Ukraine and Western Belorussia*. Princeton, NJ: Princeton University Press, 1988.

Grosser, Alfred, *The Western Alliance, European-American Relations Since 1945*. Translated from German by Michael Shaw. New York: Vintage Books, 1980.

Grousset, René, *The Empire of the Steppes, a History of Central Asia*. Translated from French by Naomi Walford. New Brunswick, NJ: Rutgers University Press, 1970.

Gwertzman, Bernard and Kaufman, Michael T., *The Collapse of Communism*. New York: Random House, 1991.

Halperin, Charles J., *Russia and the Golden Horde: The Mongol Impact on Medieval Russian History*. Bloomington, IN: Indiana University Press, 1987.

Hames, Peter, *The Czechoslovak New Wave*. Berkley, CA: University of California Press, 1985.

Hamm, Michael F., *Kiev, A Portrait, 1800–1917*. Princeton, NJ: Princeton University Press, 1995.

Harris, Whitney R., *Tyranny on Trial: The Evidence at Nuremberg*. New York: Barnes & Noble Books, 1995.

Heer, Friedrich, *The Holy Roman Empire.* Translated from German by Janet Sondheimer. London, UK: Phoenix Giants, 1968.

Hegyi, Klára, *Török berendezkedés Magyarországon* [The Turkish Order in Hungary]. Budapest, Hungary: História Könyvtár, 1995.

Hegyi, Klára and **Zimányi, Vera,** *Az oszmán birodalom Európában* [The Ottoman Empire in Europe]. Budapest, Hungary: Corvina, 1986.

Heller, Mikhail and **Nekrich, Aleksandr,** *Utopia in Power, The History of the Soviet Union from 1917 to the Present.* Translated from Russian by Phyllis B. Carlos. New York: Summit Books, 1986.

Herold, Christopher J., *The Age of Napoleon.* Boston: Houghton Mifflin Company, 1991.

Hertz, Aleksander, *The Jews in Polish Culture.* Evanston, IL: Northwestern University Press, 1988.

Herwig, Holger H., *The First World War: Germany and Austria-Hungary, 1914–1918.* London, UK: 1997.

Hitchcock, William I., *The Struggle for Europe.* New York: Anchor Books, 2003.

Hitler, Adolf, *Mein Kampf* [My Struggle]. Translated from German by Ralph Manheim. Boston: Houghton Mifflin Company, 1971.

Hohenberg, Paul, *A Primer on the Economic History of Europe.* New York: Random House, 1968.

Hohenzollern-Sigmaringen, Ileana von, *I Live Again: Ileana, Princess of Romania.* New York: Rinehart & Company, Inc., 1952.

Holmes, George, editor, *The Oxford Illustrated History of Italy.* New York: Oxford University Press, 2001.

Hopkirk, Peter, *The Great Game: The Struggle for Empire in Central Asia.* New York: Kodansha International, 1992.

Horváth, Ándrás Paloczi, *Pechenegs, Cumans, Iasians: Steppe peoples in medieval Hungary;* Translated from Hungarian by Timothy Wilkinson. Budapest, Hungary: Corvina, 1989.

Hourani, Albert, *A History of the Arab Peoples.* Cambridge, MA: Balknap Press of Harvard University Press, 1991.

Hristov, Hristo, *Bulgaria: 1300 Years.* Translated from Bulgarian by Stefan Kostov. Sofia, Bulgaria: Sofia Press, 1980.

Huntington, Samuel P., *The Third Wave, Democratization in the Late 20th Century.* Norman, OK: University of Oklahoma Press, 1993.

James, Edward, *The Franks (The Peoples of Europe).* Cambridge, MA: Basil Blackwell Inc., 1991.

Jędrzejewicz, Wacław, *Piłsudski: A Life for Poland.* New York: Hippocrene Books, Inc., 1982.

Jelavich, Charles and **Barbara,** *A History of East Central Europe, Vol. VIII: The Establishment of the Balkan National States, 1804–1920.* Seattle: University of Washington Press, 1993.

Johnson, Lonnie R., *Central Europe; Enemies, Neighbors, Friends.* New York: Oxford University Press, 1996.

Jones, Gwyn, *A History of the Vikings.* New York: Oxford University Press, 1984.

Kann, Robert A., *A History of the Habsburg Empire 1526–1918.* Berkley, CA: University of California Press, 1977.

Karski, Jan, *The Story of a Secret State.* Boston: Houghton Mifflin Company, 1949.

Kaser, M.C. and **Radice, E.A.,** editors, *The Economic History of Eastern Europe 1919–1975, Vol.I Economic Structure and Performance between the Two Wars.* Oxford, UK: Clarendon Press, 1985.

Kaser, M.C. and **Radice, E.A.,** editors, *The Economic History of Eastern Europe 1919–1975, Vol.II The War and Reconstruction.* Oxford, UK: Clarendon Press, 1986.

Kaser, M.C., editor, *The Economic History of Eastern Europe 1919–1975, Vol.III Institutional Change within a Planned Economy.* Oxford, UK: Clarendon Press, 1986.

Katona, Imre, *A helyzet reménytelen, de nem komoly: Politikai vicceink 1945–től máig* [The Situation is Hopeless, but Not Serious: Our Political Jokes From 1945 to Today]. Budapest, Hungary: Móra Könyvkiadó, 1994.

Keegan, John, *The First World War.* New York: Alfred A. Knopf, 1999.

Keegan, John, *The Second World War.* New York: Penguin Books, 1990.

Keesing's Research Report, *Germany and Eastern Europe Since 1945, From the Potsdam Agreement to "Ostpolitik".* New York: Charles Scribner's Sons, 1973.

Kennedy, Hugh, *The Great Arab Conquests: How the Spread of Islam Changed the World We Live In.* Philadelphia: Da Capo Press, 2007.

Kenney, Padraic, *A Carnival of Revolution, Central Europe 1989.* Princeton, NJ: Princeton University Press, 2002.

Kenrick, Donald and **Puxon, Grattan,** *The Destiny of Europe's Gypsies.* New York: Basic Books, Inc., 1972.

Khrushchev, Nikita, *Khrushchev Remembers.* Translated from Russian and edited by Strobe Talbott. Boston: Little, Brown and Company, 1970.

King, Charles, *The Ghost of Freedom, A History of the Caucasus.* New York: Oxford University Press, 2008.

Kingley, Ronald, *Russia, A Concise History.* .London, UK: Thames and Hudson, 1993.

Kinross, Lord, *The Ottoman Centuries*. New York: Morrow Quill Paperbacks, 1977.

Kirschbaum, Stanislav J., *A History of Slovakia: The Struggle for Survival*. New York: St. Martin's Griffin, 1995.

Klingaman, William K., *1919: The Year Our World Began*. New York: Harper & Row, 1987.

Kliuchevsky, V.O., *A Course in Modern Russian History, The Seventeenth Century*. Translated from Russian by Natalie Duddington. Armonk, NY: M.E. Sharpe, 1994.

Kohn, Hans, *Pan-Slavism, Its History and Ideology*. New York: Vintage Books, 1960.

Kołakowski, Leszek, *Main Currents of Communism, Vol. I-III*. Translated from Polish by P.S. Falla. Oxford, UK: Oxford University Press, 1978.

Koncius, Dr. Joseph B., *History of Lithuania*. Chicago: Lithuanian Catholic Press, 1971.

Koncius, Dr. Joseph B., *Vytautas the Great, Grand Duke of Lithuania*. Miami, FL: The Franklin Press Inc., 1964.

Köpeczi, Béla, editor, et al, *History of Transylvania*. Translated from Hungarian by Adrienne Chambers-Makkai, et al. Budapest, Hungary: Akadémia Kiadó, 1994.

Kostya, Sándor A., *Northern Hungary: A Historical Study of the Czechoslovak Republic*. Translated from Hungarian by Zoltán Leskowsky. Toronto: Associated Hungarian Teachers, 1992.

Kotkin, Stephen, *Armageddon Averted: The Soviet Collapse 1970–2000*. New York: Oxford University Press, 2001.

Kristó, Gyula, *Hungarian History in the Ninth Century*. Translated from Hungarian by György Novák. Szeged, Hungary: Szegedi Középkorász Műhely; 1996.

Kristó, Gyula and Makk, Ferenc, *Az árpád-ház uralkadói* ["Rulers of the House of Árpád"]. Budapest, Hungary: I.P.C. Könyvek Kiadó Kft., 1996.

Kriwaczek, Paul, *In Search of Zarathustra: The Prophet and the Ideas That Changed the World*; New York: Alfred A. Knopf, 2003.

Labuda, Gerard, *Dzieje narodu i państwa polskiego, Pierwsze państwo polskie* ["History of the Polish People and States: The First Polish State"]. Kraków, Poland: Krajowa Agencja Wydawnicza, 1989.

LaFeber, Walter, editor, *The Origins of the Cold War, 1941–1947*. New York: John Wiley & Sons, Inc., 1971.

Lamb, Harold, *Genghis Khan: Emperor of All Men*. New York: Bantam Books, 1963.

Lane, **Arthur Bliss**, *I Saw Poland Betrayed: An American Ambassador Reports to the American People*. Boston: Western Islands, 1948.

Laqueur, **Walter**, *Europe in Our Time*. New York: Penguin Books, 1992.

Lawrence, **John**, *A History of Russia*. New York: Farrar, Straus and Cudahy, 1960.

Lázár, **István**, *Hungary, a Brief History*. Translated from Hungarian by Albert Tezla. Budapest, Hungary: Corvina, 1989.

Lederer, **Ivo**, editor, *Problems in European Civilization: The Versailles Settlement; Was it Doomed to Failure?* Boston: D.C. Heath & Co., 1960.

Lendvai, **Paul**, *The Hungarians, A Thousand Years of Victory in Defeat*. Translated from Hungarian by Ann Major. Princeton, NJ: Princeton University Press, 2003.

Lenin, **V.I.**, *What is to be Done? Burning Questions of our Modern Movement*. Translated from Russian by Joe Fineberg & George Hanna. New York: International Publishers, 1971.

Lewis, **Bernard**, *Islam and the West*. New York: Oxford University Press, 1993.

Lewis, **Bernard**, *The Muslim Discovery of Europe*. New York: W.W. Norton & Co., 1982.

Lieven, **Anatol**, *The Baltic Revolution, Estonia, Latvia, Lithuania, and the Path to Independence*. New Haven, CT: Yale University Press, 1994.

Lincoln, **W. Bruce**, *In War's Dark Shadow, The Russians Before the Great War*. New York: The Dial Press, 1983.

Lincoln, **W. Bruce**, *Red Victory, A History of the Russian Civil War*. New York: Simon & Schuster Inc., 1991.

Lincoln, **W. Bruce**, *The Conquest of a Continent, Siberia and the Russians*. Cornell, NY: Cornell University Press, 2007.

Lipniacka, **Ewa**, *Xenophobe's Guide to the Poles*. London, UK: Oval Books, 2000.

Little, **Robert**, editor, *The Czech Black Book*. New York: Praeger Publishers, 1969.

Lockhart, **R. H. Bruce**, *Retreat From Glory*. New York: G. P. Putnam's Sons, 1934.

Longworth, **Philip**, *The Making of Eastern Europe*. New York: St. Martin's Press, 1994.

Lopez, **Robert S.** and **Raymond, Irving, W.**, *Medieval Trade in the Mediterranean World*. New York: Columbia University Press, 1990.

Lukacs, **John**, *Budapest 1900, A Historical Portrait of a City & Its Culture*. New York: Grove Weidenfeld, 1988.

Lukacs, **John**, *June 1941, Hitler and Stalin*. New Haven, CT: Yale University Press, 2006.

Lukas, **Richard C.**, *Forgotten Holocaust, The Poles under German Occupation 1939–1944*. New York: Hippocrene Books, Inc., 2005.

Lungu, Dov B., *Romania and the Great Powers, 1933–1940.* Durham, NC: Duke University Press; 1989.

MacDonough, Giles, *Prussia: The Perversion of an Idea.* London, UK: Mandarin, 1996.

MacMillan, Margaret, *Paris, 1919: Six Months That Changed the World.* New York: Random House, 2002.

Madden, Ray J., Chairman, *The Katyn Forest Massacre, Hearings before the Select Committee to Conduct an Investigation of the Facts, Evidence, and Circumstances of the Katyn Forest Massacre.* Washington, D.C.: United States Government Printing Office, 1952.

Maenchen-Helfen, Otto J., *The World of the Huns: Studies in their History and Culture.* Berkley, CA: University of California Press, 1971.

Magocsi, Paul Robert, *A History of East Central Europe, Vol. I: Historical Atlas of East Central Europe.* Seattle: University of Washington Press, 1993.

Malcolm, Noel, *Bosnia, A Short History.* New York: New York University Press, 1994.

Malcolm, Noel, *Kosovo, A Short History.* New York: HarperPerennial, 1999.

Mallory, J.P., *In Search of the Indo-Europeans: Language, Archaeology and Myth.* London, UK: Thames and Hudson, 1989.

Marton, Kati, *Wallenberg, Missing Hero.* New York: Arcade Publishing, 1995.

Marx, Karl, *The Revolutions of 1848, Political Writings: Volume 1.* Edited by David Fernbach. New York: Penguin Books, 1993.

Massie, Robert K., *Nicholas and Alexandra.* New York: Dell Publishing Company, 1968.

Massie, Robert K., *Peter the Great, His Life and World.* New York: Ballantine Books, 1980.

Mastny, Vojtech, *The Cold War and Soviet Insecurity: The Stalin Years.* New York: Oxford University Press, 1993.

Mastny, Vojtech and **Byrne, Malcolm,** *A Cardboard Castle? An Inside History of the Warsaw Pact, 1955–1991.* Budapest, Hungary: Central European University Press, 1995.

May, Ferdinand, *A fekete kéz* [The Black Hand]. Translated from German to Hungarian by Dezső Tandori. Budapest, Hungary: Kossuth Könyvkiadó, 1979.

Mierzwiński, Mariusz, *Malbork, Zamek Zakonu Krzyżackiego* [Marienburg, Last Castle of the Teutonic Knights]. Bydgoszcz, Poland: Oficyna Wydawnicza EXCALIBUR, 1998.

Miletich, John S., *The Bugarštica, a Bilingual Anthology of the Earliest Extant South Slavic Folk Narrative Song.* Translated from the old Southern Slavic by John S. Miletich. Urbana, IL: University of Illinois Press, 1990.

Miłosz, Czesław, *The Captive Mind.* Translated from Polish by Jane Zielonko. New York: Vintage Books, 1981.

Mohen, Jean-Marie and **Eluere, Christiane,** *The Bronze Age in Europe.* Translated from French by David & Dorie Baker. New York: Harry N. Abrams Inc., 1999.

Monroe, Will S., *Bulgaria and Her People.* Boston: The Page Company, 1914.

Montgomery, John Flournoy, *Hungary, the Unwilling Satellite.* Morristown, NJ: Vista Books, 1993.

Morgan, David, *The Mongols (The Peoples of Europe).* Oxford, UK: Blackwell, 1994.

Musil, Jiři, editor, *The End of Czechoslovakia.* Budapest, Hungary: Central European University Press, 1995.

Musset, Lucien, *The Germanic Invasions, The Making of Europe 400–600 A.D.* Translated from French by Edward and Columba James. New York: Barnes & Noble Books, 1965.

Nakanishi, Michiko, *Heroes and Friends, Behind the Scenes of the Treaty of Portsmouth.* Portsmouth, NH: Peter E. Randall Publisher LLC, 2005.

Nicholls, A.J., *Weimar and the Rise of Hitler.* New York: St. Martin's Press, 1991.

Nicolson, Harold, *The Congress of Vienna, A Study in Allied Unity: 1812–1822.* San Diego, CA: Harcourt Brace Jovanovich, Inc., 1974.

Nikanova, Svetlana & Nazarova, Tatyana (et al; editors): *Арал, вчера и сегодня: Проблемы и перспективы Аральского кризиса* ["Aral, Yesterday and Today: Problems and Perspectives on the Aral Crisis"]. Alma-Ata, Kazakhstan: Published by the МФСА / *Международный фонд спасения Арала* [IFSA, or International Fund for the Salvation of the Aral], 1997.

Norwich, John Julius, *A Short History of Byzantium.* New York: Alfred A. Knopf, 1997.

Norwich, John Julius, *The Middle Sea, A History of the Mediterranean.* New York: Vintage Books, 2007.

Nove, Alec, *An Economic History of the U.S.S.R.* New York: Penguin Books, 1989.

Obolensky, Dimitri, *Byzantium and the Slavs.* Crestwood, NY: St. Vladimir's Seminary Press, 1994.

Obolensky, Dimitri, *The Byzantine Commonwealth, Eastern Europe, 500–1453.* Credtwood, NY: St. Vladimir's Seminary Press, 1971.

Occleshaw, Michael, *Dances in Deep Shadows, The Clandestine War in Russia 1917–20*. New York: Carroll & Graf Publishers, 2006.

Odom, William F., *The Collapse of the Soviet Military*. New Haven, CT: Yale University Press, 1998.

Opalski, Magdalena and Bartal, Israel, *Poles and Jews, A Failed Brotherhood*. Hanover, NH: Brandeis University Press, 1992.

Ormos, Mária, *From Padua to the Trianon 1918–1920*. Translated from Hungarian by Miklós Uszkay. Budapest, Hungary: Akadémiai Kiadó, 1990.

Ostermann, Christian F., editor, *Uprising in East Germany, 1953: A National Security Archive Cold War Reader*. Budapest, Hungary: Central European University Press, 2001.

Ostler, Nicholas, *Empires of the Word, A Language History of the World*. New York: Harper Perennial, 2005.

Ostrogorsky, George, *History of the Byzantine State*. Translated from German by Joan Hussey. New Brunswick, NJ: Rutgers University Press, 1991.

Owen, Francis, *The Germanic People: Their Origin, Expansion & Culture*. New York: Dorset Press, 1960.

Pacepa, Lt. General Ion Mihai, *Red Horizons, The True Story of Nicolae & Elena Ceausescu's Crimes, Lifestyle and Corruption*. Washington, D.C.: Regnery Gateway, 1987.

Pakstas, Prof. Kazys, Ph.D., *Lithuania and World War II*. Chicago: Publications of the Lithuanian Cultural Institute, 1942.

Palmer, Alan, *The Baltic, A New History of the Region and Its People*. Woodstock, NY: The Overlook Press, 2006.

Palmer, Alan, *The Crimean War*. New York: Dorset Press, 1987.

Palmer, Alan, *The Decline and Fall of the Ottoman Empire*. New York: Barnes & Nobles Books, 1994.

Pauli, Hertha, *The Secret of Sarajevo*. New York: Appleton Century, 1965.

Pease, Neal, *Poland, the United States and the Stabilization of Europe, 1919–1933*. New York: Oxford University Press, 1986.

Phillips, E.D., *The Royal Hordes: Nomad Peoples of the Steppe*. New York: McGraw Hill Book Company, 1965.

Pipes, Richard, editor, *The Unknown Lenin, From the Secret Archive*. Translated from Russian by Catherine A. Fitzpatrick. New Haven, CT: Yale University Press, 1996.

Piwarski, Kazimierz, editor, *Odbudowa ziem odzyskanych* [Rebuilding the Recovered Territories]. Poznań, Poland: Poznań Instytut Zachodni, 1957.

Platonov, S.F., *The Time of Troubles*. Translated from Russian by John T. Alexander. Lawrence, KS: University Press of Kansas, 1985.

Pleshakov, Constantine, *Stalin's Folly, The Tragic First Ten Days of World War II on the Eastern Front.* Boston: Houghton Mifflin Company, 2005.

Polisensky, J.V., *History of Czechoslovakia in Outline.* Prague, Czechoslovakia: Bohemia International, 1991.

Prizel, Illya, *National Identity and Foreign Policy, Nationalism and Leadership in Poland, Russia, and Ukraine.* Cambridge, UK: Cambridge University Press, 1998.

Quimet, Matthew J., *The Rise and Fall of the Brezhnev Doctrine in Soviet Foreign Policy.* Chapel Hill, NC: The University of North Carolina Press, 2003.

Reed, John, *The War on All Fronts: The War in Eastern Europe.* New York: Charles Scribner's Sons, 1919.

Renfrew, Colin, *Archaeology and Language: The Puzzle of Indo-European Origins.* London, UK: Penguin Books, 1989.

Resis, Albert, editor, *Molotov Remembers, Inside Kremlin Politics: Conversations with Felix Chuev.* Chicago: Ivan R. Dee Publishers, 1993.

Reston, James Jr., *The Last Apocalypse, Europe at the Year 1000 A.D.* New York: DoubleDay, 1998.

Reynolds, David, *Summits: Six Meetings That Shaped the Twentieth Century.* New York: Basic Books, 2007.

Riasanovsky, Nicholas V., *A History of Russia.* Oxford, UK: Oxford University Press, 1969.

Rice, Patty C., *Amber, Golden Gem of the Ages.* Bloomington, IN: AuthorHouse, 2006.

Robinson, Francis, editor, *Cambridge Illustrated History of the Islamic World.* Cambridge, UK: Cambridge University Press, 1996.

Rogerson, Barnaby, *The Last Crusades, the Hundred-Year Battle for the Center of the World.* New York: The Overlook Press, 2009.

Rossino, Alexander, *Hitler Strikes Poland, Blitzkrieg, Ideology, and Atrocity.* Lawrence, KS: University Press of Kansas, 2003.

Rothschild, Joseph, *A History of East Central Europe, Vol. IX: East Central Europe Between the World Wars.* Seattle: University of Washington Press, 1998.

Rothschild, Joseph, *Return to Diversity, A Political History of East Central Europe Since World War II.* New York: Oxford University Press, 1993.

Sabaliauskas, Algirdas, *We, the Balts.* Translated from Lithuanian by Milda Bakšytė-Richardson. Vilnius, Lithuania: Science and Encyclopedia Publishers, 1993.

Sachar, Howard M., *The Course of Modern Jewish History.* New York: Vintage Books, 1990.

Salisbury, Harrison E., *The 900 Days, The Siege of Leningrad*. New York: Harper & Row, 1969.

Sayer, Derek, *The Coasts of Bohemia: A Czech History*. Translated from Czech by Alena Sayer. Princeton, NJ: Princeton University Press, 1998.

Schama, Simon, *Landscape and Memory*. New York: Vintage Books, 1996.

Schreiber, Hermann, *Teuton and Slav; the Struggle for Central Europe*. Translated from German by James Cleugh. New York: Alfred A. Knopf, 1965.

Seaton, Albert and **Seaton, Joan**, *The Soviet Army, 1918 to the Present*. New York: Meridian/New American Library, 1986.

Sedlar, Jean W., *A History of East Central Europe, Vol. III: East Central Europe in the Middle Ages, 1000–1500*. Seattle: University of Washington Press, 1994.

Sereny, Gitta, *The Healing Wound, Experiences and Reflections, Germany, 1938–2001*. New York: W. W. Norton & Company, 2002.

Seward, Desmond, *The Monks of War, The Military Religious Orders*. London, UK: Penguin Books, 1995.

Shawcross, William, *Dubček*. New York: Simon & Schuster, Inc., 1990.

Sheehan, James J., *Where Have All the Soldiers Gone? The Transformation of Modern Europe*. Boston: Houghton Mifflin Company, 2008.

Shephard, Ben, *The Long Road Home: The Aftermath of the Second World War*. New York: Alfred A. Knopf, 2011.

Shirer, William L., *The Rise and Fall of the Third Reich: A History of Nazi Germany*. New York: Simon & Schuster, 1990.

Simontsits, Attila L., *The Last Battle for St. Stephen's Crown*. Cleveland, OH: Weller Publishing Co. Ltd., 1983.

Skultety, Joseph, *Sketches From Slovak History*. Translated from Slovak by O.D. Koreff. Middletown, PA: First Catholic Slovak Union, 1930.

Slánska, Josefa, *Report on My Husband*. Translated from Czech by Edith Pargeter. New York: Atheneum, 1969.

Snell, John L., editor, *The Nazi Revolution: Hitler's Dictatorship and the German Nation*. Edited by Allan Mitchell. Lexington, MA: D.C. Heath & Co., 1973.

Snyder, Timothy, *Bloodlands: Europe Between Hitler and Stalin*. New York: Basic Books, 2010.

Snyder, Timothy, *The Reconstruction of Nations: Poland, Ukraine, Lithuania, Belarus, 1569–1999*. New Haven, CT: Yale University Press, 2003.

Stachiw, M. and **Sztendera J.**, *Western Ukraine at the Turning Point of Europe's History 1918–1923 Vol.II*. New York: Shevchenko Scientific Society, 1971.

Steed, Henry Wickham, *The Habsburg Monarchy*. London, UK: Constable and Company Ltd., 1919.

Stetsko, **Yaroslav**, *Ukraine and the Subjugated Nations: Their Struggle for National Liberation*. Edited by John Kolasky. New York: Philosophical Library, 1989.

Stone, **Daniel**, *A History of East Central Europe Vol. IV, The Polish-Lithuanian State, 1386–1795*. Seattle: University of Washington Press, 2001.

Stone, **Norman**, *The Eastern Front, 1914–1918*. New York: Charles Scribner's Sons, 1975.

Stone, **Randall W.**, *Satellites and Commissars, Strategy and Conflict in the Politics of Soviet-Bloc Trade*. Princeton, NJ: Princeton University Press, 1996.

Storozynski, **Alex**, *The Peasant Prince: Thaddeus Kosciuszko and the Age of Revolution*. New York: Thomas Dunne Books (St. Martin's Press), 2009.

Stoye, **John**, *The Siege of Vienna*. New York: Holt, Rinehart and Winston, 1964.

Subtelny, **Orest**, *Ukraine, A History*. Toronto: University of Toronto Press Inc., 1994.

Sugar, **Peter F.**, *A History of East Central Europe, Vol. V: Southeastern Europe Under Ottoman Rule, 1354–1804*. Seattle: University of Washington Press, 1993.

Sugar, **Peter F.** and **Lederer**, **Ivo J.**, *Nationalism in Eastern Europe*. Seattle: University of Washington Press, 1971.

Sumner, **B.H.**, *Peter the Great and the Emergence of Russia*. New York: Collier Books, 1962.

Suvorov, **Viktor**, *Inside the Soviet Army*. New York: Berkley Books, 1984.

Suvorov, **Viktor**, *The Liberators: My Life in the Soviet Army*. New York: Berkley Books, 1988.

Szarski, **Tomasz**, et al, *Biskupin, the Guide to the Archaeological Reservation*. Wrocław, Poland: ZET, Dukarnia TIR, 2001.

Szulc, **Tad**, *Czechoslovakia Since World War II*. New York: The Viking Press, 1971.

Talbott, **Strobe**, *The Great Experiment: The Story of Ancient Empires, Modern States, and the Quest for a Global Nation*. New York: Simon & Schuster, 2008.

Tapié, **Victor-L.**, *The Rise and Fall of the Habsburg Monarchy*. Translated from French by Stephan Hardman. New York: Praeger Publishers, 1971.

Taubman, **William**, *Khrushchev, the Man and his Era*. New York: W.W. Norton & Company, 2003.

Tazbir, **Janusz**, *Poland as the Rampart of Christian Europe, Myths and Historical Reality*. Translated from Polish by A. Kisiel. Warsaw, Poland: Interpress Publishers, 1987.

Ther, **Philipp** and **Siljak**, **Ana**, editors, *Redrawing Nations: Ethnic Cleansing in East-Central Europe, 1944–48*. Lanham, MA: Rowman & Littlefield Publishers, Inc., 2001.

Trotsky, **Leon**, *History of the Russian Revolution, Vol. I–III*. Translated from Russian by Max Eastman. London, UK: Sphere Books Limited, 1967.

Trotsky, Leon, *The Balkan Wars 1912–13*. Translated from Russian by Brian Pearce. New York: Pathfinder, 1991.

Ungváry, Krisztián, *The Siege of Budapest: One Hundred Days in World War II*. New Haven, CT: Yale University Press, 2006.

Urban, William, *The Teutonic Knights: A Military History*. Mechanicsburg, PA: Stackpole Books, 2003.

Vásáry, István, *Az Arany Horda* [The Golden Horde]. Budapest, Hungary: Kossuth Könyvkiadó, 1986.

Völgyes, Iván, editor, *Hungary in Revolution, 1918–19; Nine Essays*. Lincoln, NE: University of Nebraska Press, 1971.

Volkogonov, Dmitry, *Lenin, A New Biography*. Translated from Russian by Harold Shukman. New York: The Free Press, 1994.

Wagner, Wolfgang, *The Genesis of the Oder-Neisse Line*. Stuttgart, (West) Germany: Brentano-Verlag Stuttgart, 1957.

Waldorff, Jerzy, *The Rest is Silence: Powązki Cemetery in Warsaw*. Warsaw, Poland: Interpress Publishers, 1988.

Wandycz, Piotr S., *The History of East Central Europe Vol VII, The Lands of Partitioned Poland, 1795–1918*. Seattle: University of Washington Press, 1993.

Wandycz, Piotr S., *The Price of Freedom, a History of East Central Europe From the Middle Ages to the Present*. London, UK: Routledge, 1993.

Watt, Richard M., *Bitter Glory, Poland and Its Fate 1918–1939*. New York: Simon and Schuster, 1979.

Watt, Richard M., *The Kings Depart: The Tragedy of Germany, Versailles and the German Revolution*. New York: Barnes & Noble Books, 1968.

Wedgwood, C.V., *The Thirty Years War*; New York: Book of the Month Club, 1938.

Weiser, Benjamin, *A Secret Life, The Polish Officer, His Covert Mission, and the Price He Paid to Save His Country*. New York: Public Affairs, 2004.

Werth, Alexander, *Russia at War 1941–1945*. New York: E. P. Dutton & Co. Inc., 1964.

Werth, Alexander, *Russia: The Post-War Years*. New York: Taplinger Publishing Company, 1971.

Wheeler-Bennet, John W., *Brest-Litovsk, The Forgotten Peace, March 1918*. London, UK: MacMillan & Co Ltd., 1963.

Wilson, Andrew, *The Ukrainians, Unexpected Nation*. New Haven, CT: Yale University Press, 2002.

Wiskemann, Elizabeth, *Europe of the Dictators, 1919–1945*. New York: Harper Torchbooks, 1966.

Wituska, Krystyna, *Inside a Gestapo Prison: The Letters of Krystyna Wituska, 1942–1944.* Edited and translated by Irene Tomaszewski. Detroit, MI: Wayne State University Press, 2006.

Wojatsek, Charles, *From Trianon to the First Vienna Arbitral Award, The Hungarian Minority in the First Czechoslovak Republic 1918–1938.* Montreal: Institut des Civilisations Comparées (Institute of Comparative Civilizations), 1981.

Wójcik, Zbigniew, editor, *Dzieje narodu i państwa polskiego: Wojny kozackie w dawnej Polsce* [History of the Polish People and States: The Cossack Wars in Early Poland]. Kraków, Poland: Krajowa Agencja Wydawnicza, 1989.

Wolff, Larry, *Inventing Eastern Europe; The Map of Civilization on the Mind of the Enlightenment.* Stanford, CA: Stanford University Press, 1994.

Zaloga, Steven and **Madej, Victor,** *The Polish Campaign, 1939.* New York: Hippocrene Books, Inc., 1991.

Zaprudnik, Jan, *Belarus, At a Crossroads in History.* Boulder, CO: Westview Press, 1993.

Zawodny, J.K., *Death in the Forest, The Story of the Katyn Forest Massacre.* Notre Dame, IN: University of Notre Dame Press, 1962.

Zbarsky, Ilya and **Hutchinson, Samuel,** *Lenin's Embalmers.* Translated from Russian by Barbara Bray. London, UK: Harvill Press, 1999.

Zeinert, Karen, *The Warsaw Ghetto Uprising.* Brookfield, CT: Millbrook Press, 1993.

INDEX

Abdulmecid II (Caliph), 266
Adalbert, Saint, 107
Adenauer, Konrad, 195
Adolf II von Holstein (Count), 161
Adriatic Sea, 32, 74, 99, 103, 136, 227, 283, 348, 349, 383, 384, 395, 396, 448
  SeaTrade, 124, 130, 131, 150, 177, 186
Aegean Sea, 13, 47, 135, 136, 267, 279
Afghanistan, 243, 311
Africa, 66, 175, 190, 250, 253, 259, 260, 266, 297, 308, 380, 394
  North Africa, 47, 58, 62, 64, 80, 92, 183, 210, 253, 330
Agincourt, Battle of (1415), 152
Alaska, 188, 189
Alba Iulia, 282
  Gyulafehérvár, 282
Albania, 64, 133, 210, 224, 228, 253, 273, 284, 371, 383, 393
  Albanian language, 22, 79, 226
  Balli Kombëtar / National Front, 355
  Communist collapse (1990), 447, 448
  Communist era, 388, 390, 395
  League of Prizren (1878), 226
  Medieval origins, 131, 133
  Modern origins, 225
  Restored (1918), 283
Alcohol. See Food
Aleutian Islands, 189
Alexander, 154
Alexander III (Romanov), Tsar, 245
Alexander II (Romanov), Tsar, 118, 243, 244, 249, 259
Alexander I (Karageorgević), King, 276, 280
Alexander I (Obrenović), King, 216

Alexander I (Romanov), Tsar, 240, 241, 243, 247, 248, 249
Alexander of Battenburg, Prince, 224
Alexander the Great (of Macedon), 59, 60
Algirdas, 148
Alia, Ramiz, 397, 447, 448
Ali, Muhammad Pasha, 210
Allenstein. See Olsztyn
Allied Control Commission (ACC), 287, 370, 404
Amber Road, 72, 83
Anarchism, 118, 206, 244
Anastasia (Romanov), Grand Duchess, 305
Anatolia, 10, 26, 46, 133, 211, 266
Anders, Władysław (General), 335
Andrei I (of Halych-Volhynia), King, 157
Andrusovo, Treaty of (1667), 176, 180, 181, 183
Andruszów, Treaty of (1667). See Andrusovo, Treaty of (1667)
Anjou Dynasty, 133, 140, 151
Ankara, 213, 267
Ankara, Battle of (1402), 135
Anna I (Romanov), Tsarina, 191
Antonescu, Ion (General & Dictator), 347
Antwerp, 150
Apis. See Dimitrejević, Dragutin
Arabian horses (Polish stock), 187
Arabs, 40, 55, 64, 65, 67, 72, 78, 87, 92, 99, 106, 136, 177, 210, 212, 260, 265, 266, 390
  Abbasid Dynasty, 65, 81, 100, 104, 266
  Ajyad Castle, 266
  Arabic language, 19, 226, 265
  Cordoba Caliphate, 65, 117, 253
  Fatimid Dynasty, 65, 104

Umayyad Dynasty, 65, 80, 81, 117
Arad, 236
Aral Sea, 87, 431
Archangelsk, 306
Aristocrats, 129, 140, 156, 158, 165,
    168, 183, 193, 218, 286, 289, 296,
    316, 343, 398
  Boyars, 155, 156, 174, 190, 219
  Junkers, 230, 343
  Szlachta, 175, 178, 180, 295
Armenia, 60
Armenians, 55, 129, 186, 222, 306, 450
  Armenian language, 12
  Hamidian Massacres (1890s), 212
  Massacre (1915), 265
Arnhem, Battle of (1944), 335
Árpád, 101, 285
Árpád Dynasty, 101, 140
Arrow Cross. See Hungary
  - Nyilaskeresztpárt
Aryans, ancient, 10
  Sanskrit language, 10
  Swastika, 230, 301
Asen & Peter, 97
Asparukh, 78
Athens, 58
  Parthenon, 177
Atlantic Ocean, 25, 330, 468
  Trade, 175, 186
Attila, Khan, 73
Augsburg, Battle of (955), 101
Augsburg, Treaty of (1555), 2
Augustus II (Wettin), King, 178
Auschwitz. See Holocaust
Austerlitz, Battle of (1805), 240
Australia, 260, 265
Austria, 62, 114, 143, 145, 159, 189,
    240, 289, 343, 353, 356, 371, 383,
    392, 413, 424, 441
  Anschluss (1938), 294
  Austrian Empire, 131, 178, 191,
    192, 196, 214, 227, 229, 230, 231,
    233, 247, 251

Austro-Hungarian empire, 195,
    211, 216, 222, 224, 237, 239, 240,
    246, 259, 268, 273, 281, 282, 285,
    288, 289, 291, 292, 293, 295, 304,
    310, 343
  Das Ausgleich / Compromise
    (1867). See Hungary
  Interwar, 271, 288
  Origins, 94
  Treaty of 1955, 407
Austrian Solution (1955). See Austria
Austrian Succession, War of (1740-
    48), 195, 196
Austro-Prussian War (1866), 229, 237
Avars, 73, 76, 94, 101
Azerbaijan, 388, 425
Azov, Sea of, 78, 80, 183
Babenberg Dynasty, 143, 192
Bach-Zelewski, Erich von dem
    (General), 336, 496
Baghdad, 65, 78, 99, 104, 265
Bakunin, Mikhail / Michael, 244
Balasita, Battle of (1018), 97
Balkans, 15, 17, 19, 26, 27, 39, 47, 58,
    62, 73, 74, 79, 80, 87, 114, 131,
    135, 138, 139, 140, 142, 174, 176,
    183, 186, 208, 211, 220, 222, 239,
    253, 259, 262, 279, 281, 382
  Balkan Federation, 279, 393
  Balkanization, 26
  Balkan League, 224
  Balkan Mountains, 26, 220
  Balkan Wars (1912-13), 212, 216,
    218, 222, 224, 226, 265, 268, 272,
    277, 283, 355
  Ottoman Conquest, 126, 127, 128,
    130, 131, 133, 135, 137
  Roman Balkans, 62, 74, 79
Baltic Peoples, 93, 105, 107, 109, 110,
    111, 115, 143, 146, 148, 149
  Baltic languages, 17, 146
  Origins, 83

Baltics, 20, 27, 35, 72, 84, 107, 108,
    111, 146, 160, 175, 262, 306, 359,
    450, 452
    Independence (1918), 299
    Independence (1991), 452
    Ostland. *See* World War II
    Soviet annexation (1940), 303, 337,
        357, 428
    Soviet re-conquest (1944), 339
Baltic Sea, 32, 75, 83, 107, 154, 155,
    175, 211, 245, 306, 337, 384, 402
    Trade, 67, 82, 150
Banat, 273
Bandera, Stepan, 424
Bandholtz, Harry, 287
Basarab Dynasty, 137, 139
Basarab I cel Mare, Prince, 137
Basil II Βουλγάροκθονοσ, Emperor,
    97
Batak, Massacres at (1876), 223
Báthory Dynasty, 167, 169
Báthory, Erzsébet/Elizabeth, 167
Báthory, István/Stephen (Prince,
    King), 167, 173
Batory, Stefan/Stephen. *See* Báthory,
    István/Stephen (Prince, King)
Battle of the Nations (1813). *See*
    Leipzig, Battle of (1813)
Batu, Khan, 112, 114, 123, 124, 157
Bavaria, 142
    Bavarian Soviet Republic (1919),
        264
Bayan, Khan, 73
Becket, Thomas (Saint), 106
Beck, Józef/Joseph (Colonel &
    Foreign Minister), 315, 331
Beethoven, Ludwig van, 229
Beijing, 397
Béla IV, King, 102, 112, 114
Belarus, 25, 100, 178, 182, 241, 249,
    296, 309, 314, 338, 359, 451
    Belarussian language, 16, 56
    Belarussian S.S.R., 451
    Independence (1918), 298

Lithuanian-Belarussian Soviet
    Socialist Republic (1919), 301
Belgium, 25, 174, 250, 260, 262, 281,
    330, 335, 339, 386
Belgrade, 97, 105, 185, 214, 216, 268,
    272, 273, 274, 276, 349, 350, 384,
    392, 393, 394, 395
    Nándorfehérvár, 127, 142
    Siege of (1456), 135
    St. Mark's Church, 126
Bem, Józef/Joseph (General), 235
Beneš, Edvard/Edward, 290, 291,
    294, 340, 342, 409, 411
Beowulf, 215
Berat, 131, 447
Berezina River, Battle of (1812), 241
Bergen, 150
Bering Strait, 189
Bering, Vitus, 189
Berisha, Sali, 448
Berlin, 195, 196, 230, 233, 241, 279,
    305, 336, 356, 364, 384, 441, 443
    Berlin Airlift (1948-49), 414
    Berlin Wall (1961-89), 415, 416, 442
    Congress of (1878), 211, 216, 223,
        225, 226, 239, 245
    Division (1945-89), 413, 415, 442
    Reichstag, 331
    Siege of (1945), 331, 361
    Uprising of 1953, 406, 414, 429
    Wandlitz, 417
Bermondt-Avalov, Pavel/Paul
    (General), 300
Bermondtists. *See* Russia
Bernolák, Anton, 292
Bessarabia, 221, 309. *See* Moldavia
Bethlen, Gábor (Prince), 167
Bierut, Bolesław, 419
Bilá hora, Battle of (1620), 165
Biskupin, 51
Bismark, Otto von, 115, 197, 211, 226,
    229
Bitola, 277
Black Death (1348-51), 124, 130, 242

Black Sea, 17, 62, 76, 77, 80, 82, 87, 97,
99, 112, 125, 138, 139, 148, 157,
183, 221, 243, 265, 267, 402
Danuve-Black Sea Canal, 402
Trade, 67, 124, 131, 137
Bled Agreement (1947), 393, 399. *See
also* Balkan Federations
Blitzkrieg, 339
Blücher, Gebhard-Leberecht von
(General), 229
Bocskay, István/Stephen (Prince),
167
Bogdan I, Prince, 137
Bohemia, 35, 49, 93, 95, 96, 101, 105,
106, 107, 140, 142, 160, 167, 192,
194, 195, 291, 340, 341, 444
Bohemian Glass, 165
Founding of, 95
Hussite Bohemia, 162
Medieval, 143
Mongol invasion, 114, 143
Bolesław I, 106, 108
Bolesław III, 151
Bolesław II, King, 106
Bonaparte, Napoleon, 206, 210, 229,
233, 241, 247, 248, 259
Bonn, 389, 443
Boris I Godunov, Regent & Tsar, 187
Boris III, Tsar, 224, 278, 279, 280, 355,
356
Bór-Komorowski, Tadeusz/
Thaddeus (General), 335
Bornholm Island. *See* Denmark
Borodino, Battle of (1812), 241
Bosnia-Herzegovina, 37, 40, 64, 105,
210, 220, 253, 259, 272, 273, 349,
351, 395, 453
Austro-Hungarian annexation
(1908), 216, 224, 240
Austro-Hungarian protectorate
(1878-1908), 211
Bosnian language, 15
Medieval, 129, 130
Uprising (1875), 211, 216, 218, 223

Bosnian War (1992-95), 453, 454
Botev, Christo, 223
Bourbon Dynasty, 195, 227
Brahe, Tycho, 145
Brandenburg, 161, 191, 196
Brandenburg-Prussia, 115, 171, 195
Brandt, Willy, 389, 415, 420
Brandywine, Battle of (1777), 179
Braşov, 404
Brătianu, Ion I.C., 282
Bratislava, 25, 142, 343
Pozsony, 142
Brest
Union of (1596), 181
Brest-Litovsk, Treaty of (1918), 263,
282, 290, 295, 298, 299, 301, 306
Brezhnev Doctrine. *See* Soviet Union
Brezhnev, Leonid, 390, 397, 411, 416,
423
Brîncoveanu, Prince, 168
Britain, 108, 131, 169, 174, 175, 188,
189, 211, 212, 227, 234, 238, 240,
241, 250, 260, 262, 263, 264, 265,
273, 278, 284, 287, 300, 306, 309,
315, 330, 331, 332, 335, 336, 339,
340, 341, 346, 347, 348, 350, 353,
356, 371, 381, 382, 386, 392, 396,
400, 410, 413, 443
British Empire, 123, 243, 265, 297
English language, 12, 15
Jamestown colony, 169
Secret Intelligence Service (SIS),
396
Spanish Armada (1588), 131, 194
Britain, Battle of (1940), 313, 335, 340
Brno, 241
Brüno, 234
Broz, Josip/Joseph, 274, 349, 350,
354, 371, 392, 393, 394, 399,
403, 405, 410, 428
Brugge, 150
Brusilov, Aleksei (General), 270
Brusi/Old Prussians, 107, 110, 146

Bucharest, 161, 220, 222, 270, 282,
   346, 385, 394, 446
Bucharest, Treaty of (1913), 225
Budapest, 101, 102, 107, 233, 234, 239,
   286, 292, 365, 384, 405, 406, 407,
   408, 437, 440
   Romanian occupation (1919), 287
   Siege of (1944-45), 346
   Unification of Buda and Pest
    (1873), 237
Bugarštica, 215
Bug River, 347
Bukovina, 347
Bulgaria, 19, 35, 55, 58, 64, 80, 87, 94,
   95, 100, 110, 126, 131, 207, 216,
   220, 222, 233, 267, 276, 280, 282,
   283, 371, 382
   Anti-Turkish pogroms, 401
   Bulgarian language, 13, 15, 78,
    219, 222
   Bulgarian Orthodox Church, 40,
    97, 222, 224
   Bulgars, ancient, 77, 81
   Communist collapse (1989), 445,
    446
   Communist era, 308, 388, 398, 412,
    422
   Coup of 1923, 279
   Eastern Rumelia, 223, 224
   First & Second empires, 96, 105
   IMRO/VMRO. *See* Terrorism
   Interwar, 277, 281, 346
   Mongol invasion, 114, 126
   National awakening, 222
   Onogur (Great Bulgaria), 78, 80
   Ottoman conquest, 126
   Radomir Rebellion (1918), 278
   San Stefano Bulgaria, 223, 225, 245
   Uprising (1876), 211, 223
   Volga Bulgars, 67, 78, 112, 253
   World War I. *See* World War I
Burebişta, King, 79
Byzantine Empire, 15, 16, 35, 37, 38,
   40, 73, 74, 78, 81, 82, 87, 94, 99,

   100, 101, 104, 110, 126, 127, 130,
   131, 135, 157
   End, 133
Bzura River, Battle of (1939), 332
Caesar, Julius, 62, 73, 79
Caffa, 124
Cairo, 104
Calixtus III, Pope, 142
Canada, 13, 97, 260, 297, 335
Cantemir, Prince, 168
Canterbury, 106
Canute the Great, King, 108
Čapek, Karel/Charles, 13
Caporetto, Battle of (1917), 270
Caribbean, 175, 248
Carol/Charles I (Hohenzollern),
   Prince & King, 222
Carol/Charles II (Hohenzollern),
   King, 283, 346
Carpathian Mountains, 25, 114, 158,
   221, 270, 282, 292, 371
   Carpathian Basin, 73, 74, 76, 92,
    101, 112, 127
Carter, Jimmy (President), 102, 403
Carthaginians, 91
Časlav, Prince, 105
Caspian Sea, 77, 87, 99
Catalun, Battle of (451). *See* Chalons,
   Battle of (451)
Catherine II, 115, 161, 178, 183, 191,
   192, 243
Caucasus, 22, 46, 62, 64, 80, 100, 112,
   129, 265, 359, 370, 425, 450
Ceauşescu, Elena, 446
Ceauşescu, Nicolae/Nicholas, 39,
   139, 399, 403, 417, 443, 446, 452
   Execution, 446
Celts, 49, 73, 94, 127
   Celtic languages, 12
Central Asia, 19, 22, 55, 66, 87, 154,
   180, 243, 254, 265, 369, 370
   Anglo-Russian rivalry, 211, 212,
    243

Central Europe, 15, 27, 47, 49, 72, 101, 106, 136, 139, 142, 144, 165, 174, 184, 231, 289, 384, 404, 413
České Budějovice, 144
Cetinje, 128, 218
Chalons, Battle of (451), 92
Chamberlain, Neville (Prime Minister), 294, 336
Charlemagne, 93, 107, 192, 231
Charles I (Anjou), King, 133, 283
Charles I (Luxembourg), Emperor. *See* Karel/Charles I (Luxembourg), Emperor & King
Charles I Robert (Anjou), King, 23, 140, 151
Charlestown, Battle of (1775), 179
Charles V (Habsburg). *See* Karl V
Chervenkov, Vulko, 399
Chicago, xix
China, 2, 19, 55, 66, 80, 87, 112, 124, 131, 135, 139, 220, 253, 327, 397, 427, 428
    Cultural Revolution, 397, 403
    Manchuria, 87, 245, 360
    Tiananmen Square Massacre (1989), 441
Chopin, Frédéric, 496
Chotek, Sofie (Countess & Duchess), 259
Christianity. *See* Religion
Churchill, Winston (Prime Minister), 357, 360, 382, 384
Cieszyn/ Těšín, 315
Cinco de Mayo, 238
Cluj Napoca, 57
Codreanu, Corneliu, 283
Cold War, xvi, xix, 25, 55, 102, 118, 260, 379, 414, 426, 431, 456
    Cuban Missile Crisis (1962), 429
    Defections, 402, 410, 439
    Détente, 403, 404, 409, 415, 421
    Dissent, 393, 400, 404, 409, 413, 414, 423

End (1989-92), 436
    Espionage, 380, 387, 389, 396, 400
    Helsinki Accords (1975), 413
    Iron Curtain, 383, 384, 386, 394, 403, 416, 424, 441, 459
    Non-Aligned Movement, 394
    Origins, 380
    Refolution, 440
Collectivization, 359
Columbus, Christopher, 88, 134
Comintern. *See* Communist International
Commerce, 59, 65, 66, 71, 72, 81, 83, 97, 99, 124, 130, 134, 137, 147, 149, 150, 152, 154, 159, 160, 168, 175, 177, 178, 188, 210, 222, 253, 257, 264, 306, 380, 408, 413, 419, 422, 438. *See* also Atlantic Ocean, Baltic Sea, Black Sea, Adriatic Sea trade
Commonwealth of Independent States (CIS), 451
Communism, 206, 244, 274, 279, 282, 286, 287, 288, 306, 308, 335, 352, 356, 357, 385, 390, 392, 393, 394, 396, 398, 399, 401, 405, 407, 409, 417, 421, 422, 428, 437, 451, 453
    Communism with a Human Face, 411
    Goulash Communism, 408
Communist Information Bureau (Cominform), 394
Communist International (Comintern), 307, 309, 399
Communist security forces, 358, 412, 441
    ÁVH (Hungary), 407, 408
    ÁVO (Hungary), 405
    Cheka (Bolshevik Russia), 306, 307
    DS (Bulgaria), 400, 445
    GPU (USSR), 309
    KGB (USSR), 156, 242, 304, 400, 429, 450

NKVD (USSR), 298, 309, 333, 338, 394, 398
OZNA (Yugoslavia), 392, 394
SB (Poland), 424, 438
Securitate (Romania), 403, 404, 446
Sigurimi (Albania), 397, 447
Stasi (GDR), 389
StB (Czechoslovakia), 411
UB (Poland), 418
Comnenus, Manuel (Emperor), 105
Comnenus, Michael (Prince), 133
Conference on Security and Cooperation in Europe (CSCE), 448
Conover, Willis, 386
Conrad, Joseph. *See* Korzeniowski, Józef Teodor Konrad
Constantine and Methodius, 13, 94, 95, 96, 100
Constantinople. *See* Istanbul
Constantinus/Constantine I, (Roman) Emperor, 37, 62
Cooper, Merian C. (Major), 313
Copernicus, Nicholas, 145, 182
Cordoba Caliphate. *See* Arabs
Cossacks, 171, 175, 180, 183, 187, 241, 246, 295
Sech/Sich, 180, 183
Subjugation by Russia, 183
Courland, 83, 338
Duchy of, 175
Cracow. *See* Kraków
Craiova, Treaty of (1940), 369
Crimea, 124, 169, 254, 265, 306, 347, 359, 361, 370, 450
Crimean War (1853-56), 182, 211, 221, 243
Khanate of, 125, 191, 243
Crnojević Dynasty, 128
Croatia, 64, 94, 96, 104, 130, 131, 177, 194, 207, 215, 228, 232, 233, 235, 236, 239, 273, 274, 276, 369, 371, 395, 455
Croatian language, 15

Independence (1991), 453, 454
Jasenovac Camp, 352
Militärgrenze (Military Border), 177, 239, 453
Nagodba (Compromise) of 1868, 237
NDH/Fascist Croatia, 349, 351, 352, 353
Origins, 103
Sabor, 104, 276
Sporazum (Agreement) of 1939, 276
Crusades, 65, 135, 253
Albigensian Crusade (1243-44), 41
Baltic Crusades (13th-14th centuries), 83, 108, 111, 146, 160
Confederation of Livonia, 149, 155, 161
Fourth Crusade (1204), 97, 133
Great Northern Crusade (1255), 143
Knights Templar, 113
Livonian Brotherhood of the Sword, 109, 111, 148, 149
Livonian Order, 149, 154
Nicopolis. *See* Nicopolis, Battle of (1396)
Teutonic Knights, 110, 113, 114, 143, 146, 148, 151, 152, 153, 154, 160, 195
Varna Crusade (1444), 135
CSCE. *See* Conference on Security and Cooperation in Europe (CSCE)
Cuban Missile Crisis (1962), 389
Cumanians, 81, 110, 112, 114
Cuza, Alexandru Ion (Domnitor), 221
Cvetković, Dragiša (Prime Minister), 349
Cyril and Methodius. *See* Constantine and Methodius
Cyrus the Great (Achaemenid), 59
Czechoslovakia, 286, 288, 309

Communist era, 308, 370, 371, 385, 388, 392, 404, 409, 417, 422, 423, 441

Czechoslovak Free Air Force. *See* World War II

Czechoslovak Legion. *See* World War I

Czechoslovak National Council (1916), 291

Czechs and Slovaks fighting abroad (WW II), 340

Destruction (1938-39), 289, 294, 303, 330, 331, 336, 339, 340, 368

Interwar, 21, 263, 264, 271, 280, 281, 289, 310, 316, 343

Karta 77/Charter 77, 413, 444

Pittsburgh Declaration (1918), 291

Prague Spring (1968), 390, 397, 403, 409, 411, 412, 413, 421, 444

Uprising of 1953, 429

Velvet Divorce (1991), 444

Velvet Revolution (1989), 443, 445

Czech Republic, 94, 145, 165, 232, 236, 268

Czech language, 13, 159, 293

Independence (1992), 444

Czolgosz, Leon, 244

Dacia (car), 79

Dacians, 78, 79. *See* also Vlachs

Dalmatia, 21, 74, 103, 104, 130, 228, 229, 270, 351, 369, 371

Danube River, 25, 27, 72, 73, 78, 79, 87, 136, 140, 142, 272

Danube Delta, 60, 221

Danzig. *See* Gdańsk

Dark Ages, 73, 88

Daugava River, 83

Davis, Jefferson, 210

Dayton Peace Accords (1995), 454

Deák, Ferenc/Francis, 237

Debrecen, 405

de Busbeque, Ogier Ghislain, 220

Denikin, Anton (General), 306

Denmark, 35, 37, 75, 84, 97, 108, 109, 115, 145, 149, 150, 165, 170, 171, 229, 330, 337, 339, 381

Bornholm Island, 381, 402

Danish language, 12, 48

Union of Kalmar, 170

Deportations. *See* Population Transfers

Dimitrejević, Dragutin, 216, 273

Dimitrov, Georgi/George, 308, 393, 399

Djilas, Milovan, 393

Dmowski, Roman, 310, 312

Dnieper River, 27, 65, 67, 76, 99, 100, 179, 361

Dniester River, 27, 76, 100, 137, 347

Dobrudja, 222, 225, 277, 279, 282, 346, 355, 369, 399

Doja, Gheorghe (George). *See* Dózsa, György (George)

Dönitz, Karl/Charles (Admiral), 331

Don River, 27, 99, 345

Doroshenko, Petro (Cossack Hetman), 181

Dózsa, György (George), 158

Dracula. *See* Vlad III

Dracula (novel), 139

Dragutin, Stefan, 126

Drava River, 103, 455

Dresden, 441

Dušan, Stefan (Tsar), 126, 128, 133, 134, 213

Dubček, Alexander, 390, 403, 409, 411, 412, 445

Dubrovnik, 103

Ragusa, Republic of, 130

Durrës, 131

Dušan, Stefan (Tsar), 126

Dvořák, Antonín, 208

Eastern Europe

Concept of, xvi

Definition, xvi

Film, 67, 411, 441

Folk art, 208, 230

Historical flow, 54
Literature, 22, 55, 182, 190, 208, 215, 219, 226
Neolithic, 46, 72
Populations, 208
Edelman, Marek, 366
Edirne, 185, 224
Edison, Thomas, 293
Egypt, 58, 62, 64, 104, 210, 260, 265, 335, 394
Egyptians, ancient, 91
Suez Canal, 210
Eisenhower, Dwight (General & President), 341, 386
Eko-glasnost, 445
Elbe River, 27, 92, 93, 195
Elzbyeta/Elizabeth I (Romanov), Tsarina, 191
Enlightenment, the, 191
Enver Pasha (İsmail Enver Efendi), 212
Epirus, 80, 284
EpirusDespotate of, 133
Estonia, 37, 72, 109, 149, 160, 170, 171, 215, 299, 301
Eesti, ancient, 83
Estonian language, 17
Independence (1918), 299
Independence (1991), 452
Interwar, 300, 310
Soviet annexation (1940), 337
Soviet re-conquest (1944), 339
Vaps, 300
Esztergom, 102
Ethnic Cleansing. See Population Transfers
European Recovery Plan (1947), 385, 410
European Union, 207, 347, 428, 453
Farouk I, King, 210
Fascism, 289, 301, 343, 355, 385
Fechter, Peter, 416
Ferdinand I (Habsburg), Emperor, 234

Ferdinand II, (Holy Roman) Emperor, 165
Ferdinand of Saxe-Coburg and Gotha, Prince & Tsar, 224, 278, 279
Ferenc/Francis II (Rákóczy), Prince, 168
Feudalism, 180, 282, 285, 307, 436
Finland, 82, 171, 215, 241, 260, 299, 300, 303, 306, 307, 337, 358, 370
Finnish language, 18
Winter War. See Winter War (1939-40)
Finnic Peoples, 82, 99, 109, 149
Karelians, 82
Livonians, 83
Sami, 82
Food, 72, 253, 273, 281, 283, 304, 360, 361, 419
Agriculture, 80, 154, 210, 222, 285, 295, 298, 395, 414, 425
Alcohol, 495
Beer, 144, 236, 495
Bread, 306, 347, 359
Coffee, 177
Eastern European foods, 13, 498
Grains, 154, 298, 397, 429
Political analogies, 236, 405, 440
Rationing, 285, 298, 304, 306, 360, 399, 404, 406, 421, 424, 429, 438
Shopping, 422
Wheat, 295, 429
Ford, Gerald (President), 403
France, 25, 58, 114, 133, 140, 152, 165, 174, 183, 191, 195, 227, 229, 238, 240, 242, 243, 248, 260, 262, 263, 264, 265, 273, 276, 278, 280, 282, 283, 284, 286, 287, 288, 295, 300, 306, 309, 313, 315, 330, 331, 332, 334, 335, 336, 339, 340, 346, 362, 386, 413, 443
Francs, 422
French language, 9, 15, 208
Origins, 94

Revolution (1789-92), 191, 206, 228, 232, 438
Franco, Francisco (General), 316
Franco-Prussian War (1870-71), 222, 228, 230
Frankish Empire, 35, 73, 76, 92, 94, 95, 99, 103, 159, 192
    Merovingians, 92
Franz Ferdinand (Habsburg), Archduke, 216, 259, 270
Franz Josef/Francis Joseph I (Habsburg), Emperor & King, 224, 233, 235, 237, 238, 240, 270
Friedland, Battle of (1807), 241
Friedrich/Frederick I (Hohenzollern), Duke & King, 196
Friedrich/Frederick II, 145, 191, 196, 197
Friedrich/Frederick (V - Elector of Palatinate, I - King of Bohemia), 165
Gagarin, Yuri, 426
Galicia, 262, 286, 295, 296, 304, 312, 371, 424
    GaliciaHalych-Volhynia, 157, 179
Gallipoli, Battle of (1915), 209, 265, 266
Gambia River, 175
Garibaldi, Giuseppe, 228
Gaspıralı, İsmail, 254
Gasprinsky, Ismail. See Gaspıralı, İsmail
Gdańsk, 146, 419, 421, 423
    Danzig, 150, 314, 331
Gediminas, 148
Gellért, Saint, 107
Genghis, Kha'an, 112, 123
Genoa, 124, 137
Geography, 24
George, Saint, 141
Georgia (Caucasus), 129, 306
Germanic Peoples, 50, 73, 83, 92, 115
    Völkerwanderung, 37, 73

Germany, 25, 62, 83, 153, 174, 189, 212, 227, 232, 236, 262, 264, 280, 283, 286, 289, 290, 295, 299, 301, 303, 306, 310, 322, 331, 355, 383, 398, 436
    Abgrenzung/Separation, 417
    Deutscher Bund/German Confederation (1815), 229, 233, 237
    Deutschmarks, 422, 438
    Drang nach Osten, 93, 95, 159
    FRG (West Germany), 347, 388, 389, 403, 406, 413, 414, 415, 441, 443, 444
    GDR (East Germany), 372, 388, 389, 390, 404, 412, 413, 422, 423, 438, 441, 443, 445
    German Empire (1871-1918), 115, 211, 230, 239, 240, 245, 246, 260, 262, 263, 272, 273, 277, 282, 290, 295, 296, 298, 300, 301, 304, 306, 310
    Germanization, 93, 115, 197, 231, 368
    German language, 15, 19, 159, 231, 293
    Germans in Eastern Europe, 84, 218, 299, 300, 302, 313, 338, 370, 371
    German Unification, 228
    Grundlagenvertrag/Basic Treaty (1972), 415
    Medieval. See Frankish Empire, Holy Roman Empire, Austria
    Nazi Germany (1933-45), 147, 153, 230, 280, 283, 289, 294, 310, 315, 326, 328, 332, 336, 337, 338, 339, 340, 341, 342, 345, 346, 347, 348, 349, 351, 354, 355, 356, 357, 358, 359, 361, 364, 368, 369, 370, 387, 414, 418, 428
    Norddeutsche Bund/Northern German Confederation (1866), 230

Origins, 94
Reunification (1990), 413, 414, 417, 443
Volga Germans, 161, 370
Weimar Republic (1919-33), 153, 195, 263, 288, 302, 312, 331, 343, 410
Gestapo, 333
Géza, Crown Prince, 101, 107
Gheorghiu-Dej, Gheorghe/George, 401, 402
Gierek, Edward, 421, 423
Goethe, Johann, 182
Göktürk Empire, 80
Golden Horde, 123, 137, 148, 154, 155, 243. See also Crimea, Khanate of
Goldman, Emma, 244
Gomułka, Władysław, 419, 421
Gorbachev, Mikhail/Michael, 243, 387, 392, 401, 417, 436, 438, 441, 443, 444, 450, 452
Goths, 101
Gottwald, Klement, 308, 409, 411
Great Depression, 280, 281, 283, 300, 301
Great Game. See Central Asia
Great Northern War (1700-21), 171, 178, 183, 189
Great October Revolution. See Soviet Union, 'Bolshevik Coup (1917)'
Great Powers, 26, 186, 191, 206, 211, 212, 223, 226, 227, 239, 241, 246, 259, 268, 280, 283, 328, 357, 368
Concert of Europe (1815-22), 234
Greco-Turkish War (1919-22), 267
Greece, 74, 168, 185, 222, 224, 226, 228, 267, 273, 275, 277, 278, 280, 284, 355, 371, 382, 384, 395, 396, 399, 456
Civil War (1944-49), 393
Greek language, 5, 10, 12, 16, 208, 219

Greeks, ancient, 13, 47, 58, 59, 64, 82, 86, 88, 124, 131, 267
War of Independence (1821-32), 210, 219
Grósz, Károly/Charles, 440
Groza, Dr. Petru, 401
Grunwald, Battle of (1410), xvii, 153, 336
Guillaume, Günter, 389
Gulags. See Stalinism
Gustav II Adolf (Vasa), King, 170
Gustav I (Vasa), King, 170
Gustavus Adolphus. See Gustav II Adolf (Vasa)
Güyük Khan, 123
Gypsies, 218, 342, 347, 351, 352
Habsburg Dynasty, 127, 130, 142, 143, 145, 148, 162, 165, 167, 168, 169, 178, 192, 196, 216, 218, 220, 222, 227, 229, 232, 233, 235, 237, 238, 240, 246, 259, 268, 271, 273, 282, 285
Hácha, Emil, 340, 342
Hašek, Jaroslav, 271
Hajduks, 158
Haller, József/Joseph, General, 311
Halych-Volhynia. See Galicia
Hamburg, 75, 150
Hanseatic League, 147, 149, 150, 154, 161
Hatvan, Battle of (1849), 235
Havel, Václav, 444
Haynau, Julius Jakob von (Baron & General), 236
Hedwig/Jadwiga (Anjou), King, 151
Hemingway, Ernest, 270
Henry II, King (Britain), 106
Henryk II Pobożny (Silesia), Prince, 113
Herder, Johann Gottfried, 231
Herodotus, 61, 86
Heydrich, Reinhard, 340, 341
Himalayan Mountains, 220
Himmler, Heinrich, 336, 357

Hindenburg, Paul von (Field
    Marshal), 153
Hiroshima, 322
Hitler, Adolf, 159, 279, 289, 294, 303,
    315, 316, 328, 330, 331, 335, 336,
    339, 340, 341, 342, 343, 344, 345,
    346, 347, 349, 351, 352, 355, 356,
    357, 360, 362, 410
Hlinka, Andrej, 292
Hohenzollern Dynasty, 196, 197, 230,
    262, 283, 346
Holocaust, 19, 152, 242, 322, 326, 338,
    342, 346, 347, 351, 352, 362, 420
    Auschwitz, 335, 342, 346, 347, 364,
        365
    Bełżec, 364, 367
    Chełmno, 341, 364
    Majdanek, 364
    Nazi Extermination Camps, 118,
        335, 362, 367
    Sobibór, 364
    Treblinka, 364
    Wannsee Conference (1942), 364
    Yad Vashem, 365
Holy League, War of (1684-99), 176,
    177, 218
Holy Roman Empire, 39, 96, 103, 142,
    143, 144, 145, 159, 161, 171, 184,
    185, 192, 220
    Dissolution (1806), 195, 228, 233
    Origins, 101
Honecker, Erich, 416, 441, 442, 443
Hoover, Herbert, 281
Horodło, Union of (1413), 153
Horthy, Miklós/Nicholas (Admiral
    & Regent), 288, 289, 343, 344,
    345, 405
Hötzendorf, Conrad von (Count),
    General, 240
Hoxha, Enver, 354, 395, 397
Hradec Králové
    Königgrätz, 230
Hrushevskiy, Mikhailo/Michael
    (Historian & Leader), 295

Hungary, 35, 37, 57, 64, 87, 94, 104,
    105, 107, 110, 111, 126, 127, 128,
    130, 137, 139, 148, 151, 157, 160,
    166, 167, 195, 218, 220, 227, 236,
    237, 273, 280, 282, 283, 289, 291,
    343, 382, 398, 453, 455
    Communist collapse (1988-90),
        437, 440, 441, 443
    Communist era, 370, 388, 392, 403,
        404, 412
    Das Ausgleich/Compromise
        (1867), 237, 285
    Etelköz, 100, 101
    Great Plain, 114, 285
    Hungarian language, 13, 18, 19,
        100, 103, 118, 159
    Hungarians as minorities, 288,
        291, 343, 370
    Hyper-inflation, 489
    Interwar, 271, 285, 310, 316, 333,
        340, 346
    Liberation (1684-90), 185
    Magyarization, 237, 285, 288
    Magyars, ancient, 15, 22, 77, 81,
        100, 111, 112
    Medieval, 140
    Mongol invasion, 114, 130, 140
    Nyilaskeresztpárt/Arrow Cross
        Party, 289
    Origins, 100, 285
    Ottoman rivalry, 135, 140
    Ottoman rule, 176
    Revolution of 1956, 389, 394, 402,
        407, 411, 420, 429, 440, 447
    Rovás runic script, 22
    Royal Hungary (1526-1690), 142,
        169, 194
    Soviet Republic/Republic of
        Councils (1919), 264, 282, 286,
        287, 405
    Volga Magyars, 112
    War of Independence (1848-49),
        102, 220, 235, 236
Huns, 73, 77, 87, 101, 103

Hunyadi, János/John (Regent, General), 140, 141, 182
Husák, Gustav, 412, 417, 443, 445
Hus, Jan/John, 36, 145
Hussites. *See* Religion
Hussite Wars (1420-34), 35, 36, 145
Iaşi, 220, 270, 282, 348
ibn Abd-al-Wahhab, Muhammad, 177
ibn Iaqub, Ibrahim, 106
Ikškile
    Üxküll, 149
Illenden-Preobrazhenye Uprising (1903), 224
Illyrians, 79, 127, 131
India, 10, 55, 58, 87, 131, 243, 253, 260, 394
Indian Ocean, 211
    Trade, 66, 186
Industrialization, 244, 246, 250, 259, 289, 308, 309, 362, 395, 404, 409, 414, 419, 422
    Industrial Revolution, 206, 241
Intelligentsia, 218, 309, 336, 346, 359, 421
Iran, 55, 64, 135, 220, 243, 253, 266, 335, 385
    Iranian peoples, ancient, 48, 87
    Persian Empire, 40, 59, 61, 66, 74, 87, 91
    Persia, Ottoman, 136
Ireland, 62
Iron Curtain. *See* Cold War
Irridentism, 228, 283, 289
Isaszeg, Battle of (1849), 235
Islam, 2, 32, 37, 42, 43, 60, 64, 65, 66, 74, 78, 82, 99, 106, 112, 124, 139, 142, 169, 177, 186, 210, 213, 225, 226, 253, 267, 279, 284, 397
    Bektashi Dervish Sufists, 43
    Jadidism, 254
    Jihad, 253
    Sharia Law, 266
    Wahhabism, 177

Israel, 58, 118, 365, 390
    War of Independence (1948), 119
Istanbul, 43, 213
    Constantinople, 37, 38, 39, 74, 78, 92, 96, 126, 133, 134, 135, 142, 168, 209, 211, 213, 220, 222, 253, 265, 279
Istrian Peninsula, 103, 229, 351, 371
István/Stephen I, King & Saint, 101, 107, 288
Italy, 38, 40, 58, 73, 76, 131, 133, 142, 145, 194, 231, 236, 240, 248, 270, 286, 287, 288, 330, 371, 382, 383, 393, 396, 436, 448
    Fascist era (1922-45), 284, 289, 294, 330, 340, 344, 347, 349, 351, 353, 355, 362, 369
    Irridenta Italia, 228, 236
    Italian Renaissance, 174
    Lombardy, 92
    Papal States, 227
    Piedmont-Sardinia, 228, 229, 235, 236
    Risorgimento, 227, 229, 231, 316
Ivan/John III, 155
Ivan/John IV, 149, 155, 156, 173, 186, 187, 189
Ivan/John VI (Romanov), Tsar, 190
Ivanov, Lyubomir, 445, 446
Jadwiga. *See* Hedwig/Jadwiga (Anjou)
Jagiellonian Dynasty, 140, 142, 151, 154, 173
Jagiełło, Władysław II (King & Grand Duke). *See* Jogaila
Janissaries. *See* Ottoman Empire
Jan/John III Sobieski, King, 176, 178, 184, 185
Jan Kazimierz/John Casmir II (Vasa), King, 176
Jánošík, Juraj, 158
Janoušek, Karel (General, Marshal), 340, 410
Japan, xix, 66, 245, 252, 306, 322, 360, 365, 427

Jarecki, Franciszek (Lieutenant), 402
Jaruzelski, Wojciech (General), 423,
    438, 439, 440
Jawhar as-Siqilli, General, 104
Jebe, General, 112
Jellačić, Josip / Joseph (Ban &
    General), 235
Jena, Battle of (1806), 241
Jerusalem, 108
Jewish Eastern Europe, 82, 117, 152,
    218, 242, 293, 299, 337, 338, 342,
    346, 351, 352, 397, 420
  Anti-Semitism, 108, 117, 119, 362
  Anti-Zionism, 119
  Aramaic language, 19
  Ashkenazi, 117
  Haskalah and the Sects, 41
  Hebrew language, 19, 117, 119
  Ladino language, 19, 117
  Pogroms, 118, 244, 347, 364, 401
  Sephardim, 117
  Yiddish language, 19, 21, 117
  Żydowska Organizacja Bojowa
    (Jewish Fighting Organization;
    ŻOB), 335
  Żydowski Związek Wojskowy
    (Jewish Military Union; ŻZW),
    335
Jewish Eastren Europe
  Anti-Semtism, 424
Jodl, Alfred (General), 336
Jogaila (Władysław II Jagiełło), King
    & Grand Duke, 148, 152
Johann Sigismund (Hohenzollern),
    Elector & Prince, 196
John I (Luxembourg), King, 144
John Paul II (Pope), 95, 352, 423
Jordanes, 76
Julián, Dominican friar, 112
Juodkrantė, 84
Justinian I, Emperor, 151
Kaczorowski, Ryszard / Richard, 439
Kádár, János / John, 408, 409, 440
Kafka, Franz, 48, 293

Kai-shek, Chiang, 428
Kalevala, 215
Kaliningrad, 83
  Königsberg, 143, 146
Kalinousky, Kastus, 298
Kama River, 78
Kant, Immanuel, 145
Karađorđević. See Karageorgević
Karadžić, Vuk, 214, 215
Karageorge, 214
Karageorgević Dynasty, 214, 216
Karakorum, 114, 123
Karavelov, Lyuben, 223
Karel / Charles I (Luxembourg),
    Emperor & King, 144
Karl / Charles I (Habsburg), Emperor
    & King, 270
Karl / Charles XII (Palatinate-
    Zweibrücken), King, 171, 189
Karlowitz, Treaty of (1699), 168, 177,
    185
Karl V (Habsburg), Holy Roman
    Emperor, 194
Károlyi, Mihály / Michael, 286
Karski, Jan / John, 367
Kastrioti, Gjergj / George
    (Skanderbeg), 133, 182
Kaszubs, 93
Katyń Massacre (1940), 315, 418
Kaunas, 302, 303, 338, 365
Kaup (Ancient port), 83
Kazakhstan, 110, 161, 431
Kazan Khanate, 155
Kazimierz / Casmir III, 117, 151, 152
Kemal Atatürk. See Kemal, Mustafa
Kemal, Mustafa, 266
Kepler, Johannes, 145
Kerensky, Alexander, 303
Kestutis, 148
Kettler, Jacob (Duke), 175
Khalkhin Gol, Battle of (1939), 360
Khazar Empire, 78, 80, 100, 110, 135
Khmyelnitsky, Bohdan, 175, 180, 181

Khmyelnitsky Rebellion, 175, 180, 187
Khrushchev, Nikita, 380, 388, 389, 394, 396, 397, 402, 407, 419, 426, 429
Khwarizmian Empire, 112
Kiel, 150
Kieven Rus, 16, 27, 83, 95, 96, 97, 110, 111, 112, 123, 148
   Mongol invasion, 113, 154, 157, 243
   Successor states, 154, 157, 179
   Varangians, 99
Kingdom of Serbs, Croats and Slovenes. See Yugoslavia
Kipchak Khanate. See Golden Horde
Klaipėda, 146
   Memel, 302
Klushino, Battle of (1610), 174
Kniefall in Warschau. See Brandt, Willy
Košice
   Kassa, 345
Kolchak, Alexander (Admiral & General), 290, 306
Kolin, Battle of (1757), 197
Köln, 150
Kolubara River, Battle of (1914), 272
Königgrätz, Battle of (1866), 229, 237
Königsberg. See Kaliningrad
Konrad Mazowiecki. See Konrad of Mazovia, Duke
Konrad of Mazovia, Duke, 110, 146
Konya, Battle of (1832), 210
Korea, 245, 308, 403, 427
Korean War (1950-53), 402, 414, 427, 428
Korzeniowski, Józef Teodor Konrad, 250
Kościuszko, Tadeusz/Thaddeus (General), 178, 179, 247
Kosiv, Sylvestr (Orthodox Metropolitan), 181

Kosovo, 126, 128, 133, 226, 273, 284, 349, 355, 397, 454
   Independence (2008), 455
Kosovo Polje, Battle of (1389), xvii, 126, 127, 215, 216
Kosovo War (1996-99), 454
Kossuth, Lajos/Louis, 207, 235
Köten, Khan, 112, 114
Kotromanić Dynasty, 130
Kraków, 49, 94, 105, 106, 107, 113, 150, 174, 176, 179, 251, 332, 423
   Kazimierz district, 152
   Lajkonik, 113
   Wawel Castle, 179
Krenz, Egon, 441, 442
Krewo, Union of (1385), 151
Krum, Khan, 96
Kublai, Kha'an, 124
Kubrat, 78, 80
Kukliński, Ryszard (Colonel), 387
Kulin, Ban, 129
Kun, Béla, 282, 286, 289, 405
Kupi, Abaz, 355
Kursk, Battle of (1943), 330, 361
Kurucs, 158
Kyiv, 100, 107, 113, 180
   Kiev, 187, 295, 296
   Kijów, 181
Ladoga, Lake, 100, 360
Lajos/Louis II (Jagiellonian), King, 142, 145
Lake Peipus, Battle of (1242), 154
Languages, 9, 208, 480
   Arabic Alphabet, 22, 226
   Baltic languages, 10, 12, 17, 21, 146, 299
   Celtic languages, 12
   Cyrillic Alphabet, 15, 16, 22, 80, 95, 100, 214, 219, 226
   Eastern European loan words, 13, 35
   Eastern Slavic languages, 16
   Finno-Ugric language family, 17, 82

Germanic languages, 12
Germanic Runic Futharks, 22
Glagolitic alphabet, 22, 95
Greek Alphabet, 22, 226
Indo-European language family,
10, 83
Latin Alphabet, 15, 16, 22, 226
Old Church Slavonic, 96, 219
Pronunciation, 5
Romance languages, 12, 17
Semitic languages, 19, 117, 226
Slavic languages, 12, 13, 48, 78, 305
Southern Slavic languages, 15
Southern Slavic languages
disambiguation, 16
Thraco-Illyrían languages, 12, 79
Turkic language family, 19, 100
Western European Languages, 9
Western Slavic languages, 15
Latin Empire, 97, 133
Latvia, 37, 109, 149, 160, 175, 230,
299, 300, 301. *See* also Baltic
Peoples
Independence (1918), 300
Independence (1991), 452
Interwar, 301
Latvian Soviet Republic (1918),
300
Livonian language, 18
Pērkonkrust/Thundercross
movement, 301
Soviet annexation (1940), 337
Soviet re-conquest (1944), 339
Lausanne, Treaty of (1923), 267, 268
Lawrence, Thomas E. (T.E.), 265
Lazar, Prince, 127
League of Nations, 284, 312
Lebanon, 58
Legnica, Battle of (1241), 113, 114
Leipzig, 441
Leipzig, Battle of (1813), 241, 248
Lemkos, 371
Leningrad. *See* St. Petersburg

Leningrad, Siege of (1941-44), 338,
360
Lenin, V.I., 22, 48, 281, 282, 286, 290,
295, 298, 301, 304, 306, 307, 308,
314
Leo III, Pope, 93
Leopold I (Habsburg), Emperor, 184
Levant, 40, 60, 61, 62, 64, 135
Lev II (of Halych-Volhynia), King,
157
Lev I (of Halych-Volhynia), King, 157
Levski, Vasil, 223
Lidice Massacre (1942), 340, 341
Liepaja, 300
LiepajaLibau, 175
Liška, Alois (General), 341
Lilacs, 220
Lipany, Battle of (1434), 145
Liszt, Franz (Ferenc)/Francis, 208
Lithuania, 83, 109, 146, 151, 152, 153,
171, 182, 231, 243, 244, 249, 299,
300. *See* also Baltic Peoples
Independence (1918), 301
Independence (1991), 452
Interwar, 263, 302, 314
Lithuanian-Belarussian Soviet
Socialist Republic (1919), 301
Lithuanian Empire, 148, 154, 157,
179, 301
Lithuanian language, 22, 148
Napoleonic invasion (1812), 242
Origins, 111
Partitions (1772-95), 178
Polish-Lithuanian
Commonwealth. *See* Poland
Raganų Kalnas (Witches Hill), 84
Soviet annexation (1940), 337
Soviet era, 388
Soviet re-conquest (1944), 339
Litvinov, Maxim (Foreign Minister),
380
Livonia, 149, 161, 170, 171
Livonian Confederation. *See*
Crusades

Livonian War (1558-83), 155, 173, 175
Ljudovit, Duke, 103
Locarno, Treaty of (1925), 264, 294
Łódź, 341
Lombards/Langobards, 73, 92
London, 139, 150, 284, 291, 294, 334, 340, 342, 349, 400, 445
London, Treaty of (1861), 238
Louis IX, King, 114
Lovech, 399
Lübeck, 150, 161, 381
Lublin, 113, 368
Lublin, Treaty of (1569). See Lublin, Union of (1569)
Lublin, Union of (1569), 154
Łukasiewicz, Ignacy/Ignatius, 221
Lusatia, 106, 142
Lushnjë, 284
Luther, Martin, 145
Luxembourg, 339
Luxembourg Dynasty, 140, 144
Lviv, 157, 296
    Lemberg, 21, 221
    Lwów, 21, 312, 313
Lvov, Georgi (Prince), 303, 306
Lysenko, Trofim, 425
Macedonia, 19, 58, 105, 215, 216, 225, 226, 227, 273, 276, 277, 279, 280, 349, 355, 356, 371, 395
    Independence (1991), 454
    Macedonian language, 13, 15
    Rise of Macedonian identity, 224
Madrid, 248
Magdeburg Law, 159
Mahmud II, Sultan, 209
Malbork
    Marienburg, 146, 147, 160
Manzikert, Battle of (1071), 135
Marchfeld, Battle of (1278), 143
Marco Polo, 67
Maria Theresa (Habsburg), Empress & Queen, 195
Marienburg. See Malbork
Markov, Georgi/George, 400

Marne River, 262
Marshall Plan (1947). See European Recovery Plan (1947)
Masaryk, Jan/John (Foreign Minister), 385, 410
Masaryk, Tomáš/Thomas G., 290, 291
Matthias Corvinus, King, 138, 141, 191
Maximilian (Habsburg), Archduke, 238
Mazepa, Ivan (Cossack Hetman), 171, 183
Mazovia, 110
Mazowiecki, Tadeusz/Thaddeus, 439, 452
Mazzini, Giuseppe, 227
McKinley, William (President), 244
Mediterranean Sea, 58, 64, 65, 72, 91, 92, 99, 212, 348
    Mediterranean SeaTrade, 67
Mehmed II, Sultan, 39, 134, 135
Mehmed IV, Sultan, 184, 185, 266
Memel. See Klaipeda, See Klaipėda
Mendel, Gregor, 234
Metternich, Klemens von (Prince), xvi, 195, 234
Mexico, 188, 238
Michael VIII Palaeologus, Emperor, 133
Mickiewicz, Adam, 182
Middle East, 47, 66, 80, 87, 177, 183, 253, 265, 390
Mieszko I (Piast), Duke, 106
Mig-15 (Mikoyan-Gurevich), 402
Mihailović, Draža (General), 349, 350
Mihai/Michael I (Hohenzollern), King, 283, 346, 348, 401
Mihai/Michael I Viteazul, Prince, 139, 167, 168
Mikołajczyk, Stanisław, 418
Milan, 234
Militärgrenze (Military Border). See Croatia

Milošević, Slobodan, 272, 395, 453, 454
Miloš I (Obrenović), Prince, 214
Miłosz, Czesław, 426
Milutin, Stefan Uroš II, 126
Mindaugas, 111, 146, 148
Minorities. *See* also individual peoples
Minsk, 298
Mircea cel Bătrân, Prince, 137
Mladenov, Petar, 445
Mohács, Battle of (1526), 102, 130, 136, 142, 162, 166
Mohi, Battle of (1241), 114
Mohyla, Petro (Orthodox Metropolitan), 181
Mojmir, 94
Moldavia, 138, 139, 168, 207, 211, 282, 348, 403
  Bessarabia, 282, 346, 370, 401
  Moldavian S.S.R., 401
  Origins, 137
  Phanariot rule, 168, 219
  Revolution of 1848, 220
  Russian protectorate, 219
  Union with Wallachia (1861), 221
Moldova, 86, 220
Molotov-Ribbentrop Pact (1939), 303, 310, 332, 336, 338, 346, 355, 356, 357, 418, 452
Molotov, Vyacheslav (Foreign Minister), 309, 359, 425, 428
Mongolia, 87, 360
Mongols, 65, 66, 123, 124. *See* also Golden Horde
  Invasion of Europe, 111
  Quriltai, 114
Moniuszko, Stanisław, 208, 479
Monte Cassino, Battle of (1944), 335
Montenegro, 224, 226, 228, 349, 355, 369, 393, 455
  Absorption into Yugoslavia, 274
  Independence, 169
  Independence (2006), 455

Montenegrin Autocephalous Orthodox Church, 128, 274
  Secularization, 218
Moravia, 291, 340
Moravia Magna, 94, 100, 101, 292
Moscow, 154, 161, 190, 229, 291, 296, 306, 358, 359, 365, 380, 385, 392, 394, 395, 397, 399, 401, 404, 411, 413, 418, 450, 466. *See* also Muscovy
  French occupation (1812), 241, 242
  German Quarter, 160
  Kremlin, 241, 359, 451
  Polish occupation (1610-12), 174, 187
  Red Square, 426
  Soviet capital (1918), 306
Moscow, Battle of (1941-42), 330, 345, 359, 361
Munich Agreement (1938), 315, 330, 340, 409
Murmansk, 306
Muscovy. *See* Russia
Mussolini, Benito, 276, 284, 294
Mustafa, Kara Pasha (Grand Vizier), 185

Nagasaki, 322
Nagy, Imre, 406, 407, 440
Napoleonic Wars, 131, 169, 178, 188, 195, 196, 202, 206, 210, 214, 227, 228, 229, 234, 240, 248, 259
  Grande Armée, 241, 242, 248
  Russian invasion, 248
Narew River, 83
Narutowicz, Gabriel (President), 315
Narva, Battle of (1700), 171, 189
Narva River, 338
Narvik, Battle of (1940), 335
Nasreddin Hodja (Mullah), 55
Nationalism, 118, 196, 206, 224, 231, 237, 244, 259, 264, 266, 267, 276, 279, 289, 296, 298, 299, 301, 338, 342, 346, 368, 395, 402, 453

NATO, 207, 230, 311, 347, 385, 387, 388, 389, 390, 392, 414, 454
Nehru, Jawaharlal, 394
Nemanja, Stefan (Grand Zhupan), 105
Nemanjić Dynasty, 105
Németh, Miklós / Nicholas, 440
Nerodimlje, 126
Netherlands, 174, 175, 189, 194, 262, 330, 335, 339, 362, 386
Neuilly-sur-Seine, Treaty of (1919), 279
Neva, River, 154
New York, 46, 165, 239, 244, 266, 279
New Zealand, 265
Nicholas of Myra (St. Nicholas), 40
Nicopolis, Battle of (1396), 135, 137, 140
Niemen River, 83
Nihilism, 244
Nikolai / Nicholas II (Romanov), Tsar, 245, 246, 259, 304, 305
Nikolai / Nicholas I (Romanov), Tsar, 242, 244, 249
Nikola I (Petrović), King, 218, 274
Niš, 105
Nixon, Richard (President), 403
Nogat River, 147
Normandy Invasion (1944), 330, 335, 341
Normans, 133
Northern European Plain, 25
North Sea, 150, 262
Norway, 97, 108, 171, 330, 335, 337, 339, 362
Novgorod, 100
Nuremburg Trials (1945-46), 341
Obrenović Dynasty, 214, 216
Oder-Neisse Line. *See* Poland
Oder River, 361, 439
Ögedei, Kha'an, 112, 114
Oleg (Founder of Kieven Rus), 100
Oliwa, Treaty of (1660), 171, 176
Olomouc, 114

Olsztyn
    OlsztynAllenstein, 146
Ópusztaszer, 285
Ordensstaat. *See* Prussia
Orzeł (Submarine), 337
Osijek, 455
Osman, 135
Ostland. *See* World War II
Ostpolitik, 389, 415, 420
Oświęcim. *See* Auschwitz under Holocaust
Otto I, Emperor, 101, 106
Ottokar II, King, 144
Ottokar II (Přemyslid), King, 143
Ottoman Empire, 15, 19, 39, 55, 66, 67, 102, 125, 126, 127, 128, 130, 131, 133, 134, 137, 139, 140, 141, 142, 158, 162, 167, 168, 169, 177, 180, 181, 186, 191, 218, 220, 222, 224, 225, 226, 228, 243, 245, 253, 398
    Collapse, 265
    Eçyad Castle, 266
    Janissaries, 43, 136, 183, 185, 209, 213
    Ottoman military superiority, 136, 177, 183
    Peak, 183
    Phanariots, 168
    Reform, 209
    Sick Man of Europe, 208
    Sykes-Picot Agreement (1916), 265
    Young Turk coup (1913), 212
Pacific Ocean, 188, 189, 211
Paderewski, Ignacy, 315
Palacký, František, 232, 235, 268
Palermo, 228
Palestine. *See* also Israel
    British mandate (1918-48), 118, 293
Pan-Germanism, 229, 230, 231
Pan-Slavism, 218, 231, 291, 292
    Illyrianism, 274. *See* also Yugoslavia
    Trialism, 232

Pan-Turkism, 19
Paris, 101, 114, 182, 247, 262, 264, 265, 282, 288, 291, 333, 346, 496
  Liberation (1944), 336
  Peace Conference (1919). See Versailles, Treaty of (1919)
  Siege of (1814), 241
  Versailles Palace, 241
Paris, Peace Treaty of (1947), 398, 405
Pašić, Nikola/Nicholas (Prime Minister), 272, 273, 274
Paskievich, Ivan (General), 249
Päts, Konstantin, 299, 300, 301, 338
Patton, George S. (General), 341
Pauker, Ana/Anna, 401
Pavelić, Ante, 276, 351, 352, 353
Pavel/Paul I (Karageorgević), King, 349
Pavel/Paul I (Romanov), Tsar, 190, 240
Peasants, 180, 190, 191, 219, 238, 278, 295, 296, 398
  Serfdom, 191, 243
Pechenegs, 101, 110
Pécs, 42, 160
Peloponnesian War (431-401 BCE), 58
Pepin, 92
Pereyaslav, Treaty of (1654), 176, 180, 181, 183
Petar/Peter II (Karageorgević), King, 276
Petar/Peter II Njegoš (Petrović), Archbishop & Vladika, 218
Petar/Peter I (Karageorgević, King), 275
Petar/Peter I (Karageorgević), King, 216, 349
Petar/Peter I Njegoš (Petrović), Archbishop & Vladika, 169
Peter I, 160, 168, 171, 189, 191, 243
Peter III (Romanov), Tsar, 190, 191
Peter II (Romanov), Tsar, 190
Petit Entente, la, 264, 283, 343
Petkov, Nikola, 398

Petlyura, Simon, 296, 314
Petőfi, Sándor/Alexander, 182
Petrović, Djordje. See Karageorge
Petrović Dynasty, 169
Phanariots, 219, 220
Philadelphia, 291
Philby, Kim, 396, 402
Philip II (Habsburg), 194
Piast Dynasty, 106, 107, 151
Piłsudski, Józef/Joseph, 252, 302, 310, 312, 314
Piłsudski, Józef/Joseph, 314
Ploiești, 221. See World War II for 1943-44 airraids
Plovdiv, 126
Plzeň, 341
Podgorica, 274
Poitiers, Battle of (732 CE), 65
Poland, 25, 41, 43, 83, 84, 93, 94, 111, 115, 126, 137, 138, 140, 146, 147, 148, 157, 160, 166, 174, 180, 182, 207, 227, 231, 236, 243, 244, 260, 289, 295, 301, 306, 309, 382, 385, 398
  Akcja Wisła (Operation Vistula, 1947), 371, 424
  Armia Krajowa (AK), 334, 335, 338, 342, 365, 419, 424, 496
  Blue Army (1917-19), 311
  Communist collapse (1988-90), 437, 438, 441, 442, 443
  Communist era, 370, 371, 372, 386, 387, 388, 390, 392, 402, 404, 409, 412, 414, 417
  Congress Poland (1815-31), 247
  Coup of 1926, 315
  Destruction (1939), 303, 331, 337, 339, 342, 344, 346, 357, 368, 369, 418, 428
  Duchy of Warsaw (1806-12), 247
  General Gouvernement, 333
  Government-in-exile, 333, 418, 439
  Kościuszko Squadron, 313
  Lajkonik Festival, 113

May 3 Constitution, 178
Medieval, 151
Mongol invasion, 113, 151
Origins, 34, 105
Partitions (1772-95), 117, 178, 191,
    196, 247, 248, 288
Polanie, 105
Poles fighting abroad (WW II),
    334, 340, 342, 385
Polish Corridor. *See* Prussia
Polish-German Reconciliation, 372
Polish language, 15, 22, 119, 159,
    182
Polish Legion (France), 247, 248
Polish-Lithuanian
    Commonwealth, 37, 41, 117,
    125, 149, 154, 155, 167, 170, 171,
    173, 179, 181, 182, 184, 185, 186,
    187, 196, 247, 248, 299, 301, 310
Polonization, 182
Poznań Uprising (1956), 419
Rebirth (1918-22), 310, 331
Sanacja/Interwar, 21, 263, 264,
    271, 281, 292, 296, 301, 302, 310,
    336, 438
Saxon union, 178
Sejm, 178, 248, 315, 438
Solidarność/Solidarity Crisis
    (1980-81), 409, 423, 438
Spring in October (1956), 389, 407,
    411, 419, 429
Uprising (1831), 235, 249, 496
Uprising (1863), 249
Uprising (1970), 421
Ziemie odzyskane/Recovered
    Territories, 371, 420
Polo, Marco, 124
Polovtsy. *See* Cumanians
Poltava, Battle of (1709), 183, 189
Pomaks, 225
Pomerania, 93, 106, 115, 151, 160, 171,
    196, 314, 333, 368, 402
Population Transfers, 20, 115, 129,
    231, 249, 267, 326, 333, 336, 368

Baltic expulsions, 369
Beneš Decrees, 370
German expulsions, 159, 382
Port Arthur, 245, 252
Portsmouth, Treaty of (1905), 246
Portugal, 49, 131, 134, 194, 241, 271,
    386
Poznań, 334, 419
Pozsgay, Imre, 440
Prague, 95, 107, 144, 161, 165, 234,
    239, 291, 292, 293, 303, 341, 365,
    384, 411, 412, 413, 441, 444
    1848 Pan-Slavist Congress, 232,
    235
    Charles University, 144
    St. Vitus Cathedral, 144
Prehistoric Europe, 47
Přemyslid Dynasty, 95, 143, 144
Pribina, 94
Princip, Gavrilo, 216, 259, 272
Prizren, 126, 226
Prussia, 41, 149, 178, 191, 195, 229,
    230, 234, 237, 241, 247, 251, 305,
    343
    Ducal Prussia, 152, 196
    East Prussia, 262, 304, 314, 332
    Independence, 176
    Ordensstaat, 146
    Origins, 84, 145
    Polish Corridor, 314, 333
    Prussian Union, 152
    Rise of, 195
    Royal Prussia, 152, 196
Prusso-Danish War (1864), 229
Prut River, 27, 73
Puccini, Giacomo, 208
Puebla, Battle of (1863), 238
Pułaski, Kazimierz/Casmir, 179
Pushkin, Alexander, 190
Puskás, Ferenc/Francis, 406
Putin, Vladimir, 436
Putnik, Radomir (General), 272
Racławice, Battle of (1794), 178
Radić, Stjepan, 275

Radio Free Europe (RFE), 413
Radomir, 278
Radu, Prince, 139
Ragusa, Republic of. *See* Dubrovnik
Rajk, László, 405, 407, 411, 440
Rákóczy Dynasty, 168
Rákosi, Mátyás/Matthew, 405, 406, 407
Rastislav, 94, 95
Reilly, Sidney, 307
Rejewski, Marian, 334
Religion, 32
  Art, 41
  Bogomils, 40
  Buddhism, 230
  Calvinism, 37, 142
  Cathars, 40
  Christianity, 34, 65, 72, 82, 92, 93, 94, 95, 96, 99, 100, 101, 103, 106, 107, 108, 117, 142, 157, 160, 185, 222, 226, 231, 253, 279, 284, 372, 397
  Crusades. *See* Crusades
  East-West rivalry, 35
  Great Schism, 32, 38
  Greek Catholics. *See* Religion - Uniates
  Hinduism, 230
  Hussites, 35, 145, 162
  Jesuits, 175, 181, 183
  Judaism, 42, 82, 108, 117, 236, 242, 244, 245, 251, 296, 335, 342, 369
  Lutheranism, 37, 175, 301
  Manichaeism, 40
  Nicaea, Council of (325 CE), 38
  Orthodox Christianity, 16, 32, 35, 37, 96, 100, 128, 139, 157, 181, 222, 224, 245, 265, 353
  Pagans, 35, 40, 72, 93, 102, 107, 115
  Papacy, 37, 92, 95, 96, 102, 142, 219, 227, 423
  Protestant Reformation, 2, 36, 145, 162, 165, 173, 197, 229
  Református, 37, 142, 167, 446. *See* also Calvinism
  Religious wars, 32, 35, 41, 82, 94, 95, 106, 108, 127, 133, 135, 136, 141, 145, 157, 160, 165, 167, 181, 185
  Roman Catholicism, 2, 35, 36, 39, 96, 113, 130, 139, 165, 173, 180, 227, 229, 231, 251, 301, 316, 352, 353, 372, 423, 438
  Uniates, 39, 181, 219
  Zoarastrianism, 40
Renaissance, 141
  Renaissance in Eastern Europe, 174
Revolutions of 1848, 206, 220, 232, 234
Rhine River, 229, 329
  Rhineland, 332
Riga, 149, 150, 161, 170, 300, 303, 338, 452
Riga, Treaty of (1921), 296, 301, 314
Rijeka
  Fiume, 21, 371, 393
River Kalka, Battle of (1223), 112
River Yaik, Battle of (1229), 112
Robert College, 279
Rodope Mountains, 225
Rokossovsky, Konstantin (General), 419, 420
Romance languages. *See* Languages
Roman Civilization, 13, 17, 37, 38, 40, 50, 59, 62, 64, 66, 74, 76, 88, 92, 127, 131, 135, 228, 253
  Collapse, 68, 79
  Constantine I. *See* Constantinus I
  Dacia, 64, 79
  Latin, 10, 15, 26, 38, 73, 77, 94, 96, 101, 102, 130, 141, 208
  Pannonia, 64, 94
Romania, 26, 60, 64, 80, 87, 110, 139, 221, 225, 236, 237, 270, 279, 286, 287, 289, 309, 382, 398. *See* also Wallachia and Moldavia

Alba Iulia Declaration (1918), 282
Braşov Uprising (1987), 404
Communist era, 158, 370, 388, 390, 392, 401, 408, 417, 443
Frontul Salvării Naţionale/ National Salvation Front, 447
Independence, 211
Interwar, 21, 305, 310, 337, 343
Revolution of 1989, 446
România Mare/Greater Romania, 280, 346
Romanian language, 22, 79, 80, 219
Romanian Orthodox Church, 39, 219
Romanians, ancient. See Vlachs
Sistematizarea/Systematization, 403
Transnistria, 347
Unification, 218
Roman I, Prince, 157
Romanov Dynasty, 187, 190, 290, 304, 305
Romanticism, 206, 208
Rome (City), 62, 65, 95, 144, 157, 219, 228, 233, 248
Roosevelt, Franklin D. (President), 382, 384
Roosevelt, Theodore (President), 244, 246
Rousseau, Jean-Jacques, 173
Różycki, Jerzy/George, 334
Rudolf I (Habsburg), Emperor, 143, 192
Rum, Sultanate of, 55, 135
Rurik, 99
Rurikid Dynasty, 155, 157
Russia, 19, 82, 84, 100, 102, 136, 148, 168, 170, 176, 180, 181, 182, 211, 218, 230, 232, 234, 240, 247, 252, 263, 264, 283, 294, 299, 303, 355, 388, 400, 450, 466. See also Soviet Union

Decembrist Revolt (1825), 243, 249, 428
Europeanization, 189, 190
Muscovy, 125, 149, 150, 154, 156, 173, 189
Napoleonic invasion (1812), 241, 247
Near Abroad, 451
Novgorod, 147, 150, 154, 155, 189
Okhrana, 156, 243, 245
Oprichnina, 156, 243
Origins, 154
Provisional Government (1917), 295, 303, 306
Pugachev Rebellion (1773-74), 192
Reign of the Tsarinas, 190
Revolutionary unrest, 244
Revolution of 1905, 246, 250
Revolution of 1917, 262, 282, 290, 291, 295, 299, 304, 312, 379
Russian-American Company, 188
Russian Empire, 117, 125, 175, 178, 181, 183, 186, 196, 211, 212, 214, 223, 224, 232, 233, 235, 239, 240, 248, 250, 254, 260, 265, 268, 281, 295, 296, 301, 304, 309, 310, 417
Russian Federation (1991), 451
Russian language, 16, 56, 96
Russian Orthodox Church, 181, 183
Russification, 56, 245, 298, 299, 301
Time of Troubles, 155, 174, 186
White Russians, 290, 296, 300, 302, 306, 371
Russo-German Reinsurance Treaty, 245
Russo-Japanese War (1904-05), 245, 246, 360
Russo-Polish War (1920), 296, 299, 301, 302, 314
Russo-Turkish War (1877-78), 211, 216, 223, 225, 245
Ruthenia, 157, 180, 291, 298. See also Galicia

Ruthenian language, 148
Ryazan, 113
Sajó River, 114
Salonika. *See* Thessaloniki
Samo, 76
Sandomierz, 113
San Francisco, 188
San Stefano, Treaty of (1878), 211, 223, 225
Sarai, 123, 157
Sarajevo, 216, 246, 259, 260, 272
Saratoga, Battle of (1777), 179
Sarmatians, 86, 232
Saule, Battle of (1236), 109, 111, 148, 149
Savannah, Battle of (1779), 179
Sava, Saint, 105
Saxony, 171, 241
Scandinavia, 27, 81, 99, 150, 300, 301
    Vikings, 67, 83, 97, 99, 108. *See* Kieven Rus - Varangians
Schabowski, Günter, 442
Schindler, Oskar, 365
Schroeder, Gerhard, 347
Scotland, 62
Scythians, 86
Selim III, Sultan, 209, 213
Seljuq Empire, 55, 61, 135
Serb-Croat War (1991-95), 453, 454
Serbia, 35, 40, 64, 126, 127, 129, 130, 131, 142, 185, 207, 215, 218, 220, 223, 224, 226, 227, 228, 232, 233, 235, 236, 237, 239, 240, 259, 273, 274, 277, 282, 283, 352, 355, 395, 455
    Black Hand. *See* Terrorism
    Chetniks, 349, 350
    Coup (1903), 214, 216
    Duklja, 105
    Independence (1878), 211, 213
    Mongol invasion, 114
    Origins, 104
    Raška, 105
    Revolt (1804), 210
    Revolt (1814), 210, 219
Serbian Empire, 133, 134, 135
Serbian language, 15, 214
Serbian Orthodox Church, 105, 126, 274, 352
Serbian refugees, 177, 273, 453
    World War I. *See* World War I
    Zeta, 128. *See* also Montenegro
Seton-Watson, Robert W. (Historian), 288
Sevastopol, 347
    Siege of (1854-55), 243
Seven Years War (1756-63), 191, 196
Sèvres, Treaty of (1920), 265, 268
Shkodër, 447
Shukhevych, Roman, 424
Šiauliai, 109
Siberia, 82, 230, 249, 250, 290, 309, 316, 337, 338, 369, 370, 405, 419
    Exploration & Settlement, 189
    Trans-Siberian Railway, 290
Sicily, 58, 104, 227
Sigismund, Emperor & King, 140, 141
Silesia, 83, 106, 113, 114, 143, 160, 165, 196, 234, 312, 333, 368, 372, 419
Silesian War (1740-42), 196
Silk Road, 66
Simeon II, Tsar, 356
Simeon I, Tsar, 96
Simović, Dušan (General), 349
Six Day War (1967), 390
Skanderbeg. *See* Kastrioti, Gjergj
Skopje, 126
Skoropadsky, Pavel/Paul (Hetman), 295
Slánský, Rudolf, 411
Slavery, 79, 99, 104, 175, 250
Slavonia, 103, 453, 455
Slavs, 67, 83, 93, 94, 95, 96, 103, 111, 115, 117, 129, 130, 148, 149, 153, 154, 157, 161, 179, 215, 231, 359
    Early states, 75
    Karantanija, 76

Nitra (state), 94
Pan-Slavism. *See* Pan-Slavism
Polabian Slavs, 93
Samo, 92
Slavic languages. *See* Languages
Slavic Migrations, 74
Slovakia, 167, 232, 237, 286, 289, 291,
    345, 444
  First Republic (1939-44), 294, 340,
    341, 342, 343
  Hlinkova garda/Hlinka Guard,
    342
  Independence (1992), 444
  National Uprising (1944), 342
  Origins, 292
  Slovak language, 15, 292
  Slovak National Uprising (1944),
    342
  Slovenská ľudová strana/Slovak
    Peoples Party, 292
Slovenia, 94, 228, 232, 273, 349, 353,
    369, 395, 455
  Independence (1991), 453, 456
  Origins, 103
  Slovenian language, 15
Smetana, Bedřich, 208
Smetona, Antanas, 303
Smith, John (Captain), 169
Smolensk, 148, 359
  Smolensk War (1632-34), 174
Societatis draconistrarum, 141
Sofia, 126, 276, 308, 355, 356, 385, 445
  Serdica, 96
  St. Nedelya Cathedral, 279
  Южен парк/Southern Park, 445
Solidarność/Solidarity. *See* Poland
Solzhenitsyn, Alexandr, 309
Somosierra, Battle of (1808), 248
Sorbs, 93
Soviet Union, xix, 23, 25, 119, 161,
    261, 264, 280, 281, 283, 294, 300,
    303, 308, 310, 315, 316, 327, 330,
    331, 335, 336, 337, 340, 346, 355,
    365, 369, 370, 371, 379, 380, 386,

    388, 392, 394, 395, 397, 398, 399,
    403, 404, 406, 409, 412, 414, 417,
    418, 419, 422, 425, 443, 444
  Bolshevik Coup (1917), 303, 306
  Bolshevik Russia (1917-22), 263,
    265, 280, 296, 299, 300, 301, 305,
    314
  Brezhnev Doctrine, 388, 437, 452
  Civil War (1918-22), 290, 296, 299,
    306
  Collapse (1989-91), 436, 450
  Founding, 303
  Glasnost, 417
  Great Terror (1936-39), 254, 309,
    359, 361, 405, 418
  Gulags. *See* also Stalinism
  Gulag system, 359
  Khrushchev's Secret 20th
    Congress Speech (1956), 419
  New Economic Policy (NEP), 298,
    306
  Perestroika, 417
  Soviet Bloc, 390, 394, 397, 403, 405,
    408, 410, 413, 415, 421, 422, 423,
    428, 441, 445, 447, 453
  Sovietization, 384, 398, 401, 405,
    411, 414, 418
Spain, 41, 49, 58, 80, 101, 106, 117,
    131, 134, 147, 174, 188, 194, 230,
    241, 248
  American Silver Mines, 32
  Civil War (1936-39), 316
  Reconquista, 19, 65
  Spanish Armada (1588). *See*
    Britain
  Spanish language, 9
Sputnik (satellite), 425
Srebrenica Massacre (1995), 454
Stalingrad, Battle of (1942-43), 330,
    345, 361
Stalin, Iosif/Joseph, 22, 39, 161, 298,
    303, 304, 308, 316, 335, 337, 345,
    356, 357, 359, 360, 379, 385, 386,
    387, 390, 393, 395, 396, 399, 401,

402, 405, 406, 409, 414, 418, 425, 426, 428, 429, 451

Stalinism, 23, 118, 386, 399, 401, 403, 405, 411, 412, 421, 447, 451

Black Market, 424

Collectivization, 298, 304, 309, 399, 406, 414, 419

De-Stalinization, 396, 407, 408, 411, 419, 429

Gulags/Slave colonies, 304, 309, 337, 392, 397, 399, 402, 419

Post-war purges, 385, 395, 397, 398, 399, 401, 405, 410, 411, 419, 428

Stamboliyski, Alexandr, 278

Stanileşti, Battle of (1711), 168

Stanisław, Saint, 106

State

Definition of, 2

Historical development, 2

Ştefan/Stephen III cel Mare, Prince, 138

Stefan Uroš IV, King. *See* Dušan, Stefan (Tsar)

Stefan Uroš V, King, 126

Štefánik, Milan, 291

Stephen II, Pope, 92

Stephen I, King & Saint (Hungary). *See* István/Stephen I

Stepinac, Alojzije (Cardinal), 352

Steppe, 10, 26, 47, 48, 62, 64, 73, 78, 79, 82, 84, 85, 100, 110, 180

Steppe Warfare, 85, 86, 101, 113, 180

Stjepan II, King, 130

Stockholm, 150, 412

Stoker, Bram, 139

St. Petersburg, 160, 170, 178, 182, 191, 241

Founding, 189

Leningrad, 338, 358, 359, 360, 370

Petrograd, 295, 299, 304, 306, 308

Winter Palace, 246

Stresemann, Gustav, 263

Stuart Dynasty, 165, 178

Štúr, Ľudovít, 292

Šubašić, Ivan, 392

Subedei, General, 112

Suceava, 139

Sudetenland, 160, 291, 294, 368

Sugihara, Chiune (Diplomat), 365

Suvorov, Viktor (Author), 403

Suvorov, Viktor (General), 178

Suzdal, 112, 113

Švejk, the Good Soldier, 271

Sven Tveskæg, King, 108

Sviatopluk, 94, 95, 101

Svyatoslav I, Prince, 110

Sweden, 35, 37, 84, 99, 115, 149, 154, 155, 165, 173, 175, 176, 178, 183, 186, 187, 189, 241, 338, 365, 412

Loss of Finland, 241

Swedish Empire, 170, 171

Swedish language, 48

Switzerland, 193, 248, 262, 306, 406

Syria, 58, 265, 341

Szálasi, Ferenc/Francis, 345

Szczecin, 161, 384

Stettin, 115, 150, 191

Széchenyi, István/Stephen (Count), 235

Szeged, 406

Tallinn, 149, 150, 299, 303, 337, 338, 452

Reval, 149

Tannenberg, Battle of (1410). *See* Grunwald, Battle of (1410)

Tannenberg, Battle of (1914), 153, 262

Tartars, 125, 126, 155, 169, 180, 191, 242, 243, 254, 260, 370

Origins, 124

Tartar language, 19

Tartu, 337

Dorpat, 149

Tartu, Treaty of (1920), 300

Tatry, 158, 292

Tchaikovsky, Piotr/Peter, 208

Ten Day War (1991), 453, 454

Tereshkova, Valentina, 426

Terrorism, 206, 244, 259, 279, 315
  Crna Ruka/Black Hand, 216, 273
  IMRO/VMRO, 224, 276, 279, 280
  Iron Guard, 283, 346, 347
  Ustaša, 276, 351, 353, 392
  Ustaša, 280, 353
Tesla, Nikola, 239
Teutonic Knights. *See* Crusades
Thessaloniki, 74, 94
  Allied Camp (1915-18), 265, 273, 278
  Ethnic composition, 224
Thirteen Years War (1454-66), 152
Thirty Years War (1618-48), 37, 115, 145, 165, 167, 170, 184, 195, 229, 233, 289
Thrace, 64, 79, 356
  Thracians, ancient, 26, 79
Tilsit, Treaty of (1807), 241, 247
Timişoara, 446
Timofeyevich, Yermak, 189
Timur (Tamerlane), 124, 135
Tiranë, 284, 396, 447, 448
Tiso, Jozef/Joseph, 294, 342, 343
Tisza River, 235, 286
Tito. *See* Broz, Josip/Joseph
Tőkés, László (Priest), 446
Tokyo, 252
Tomislav I (of Trpimir), King, 103
Toqtamish Khan, 124
Transcarpathia, 291, 309, 340, 370
Transylvania, 26, 110, 139, 140, 160, 169, 173, 218, 220, 235, 270, 282, 343, 346, 347, 403
  Alba Iulia Declaration (1918). *See* Romania
  Independence, 166, 168
Trebinje, 104
Trianon, Treaty of (1920), 288, 343, 404
Trieste, 384, 393
Triune Kingdom. *See* Yugoslavia
Trotsky, Lev/Leon, 308
Troy, 267

Trpimir Dynasty, 103
Truman, Harry (President), 384, 396
Trumbić, Ante, 275
Truso (ancient port), 83
Tsankov, Alexandur, 279
Tse-Tung, Mao, 308, 397, 407, 428
Tsushima Straits, Battle of (1905), 245
Tudjman, Franjo, 395
Tuđman, Franjo/Francis, 453
Tukhachevsky, Mikhail/Michael (General), 296, 361
Turkey, 55, 58, 59, 60, 64, 266, 267, 356, 384, 385, 401
  Founding of the Republic (1918-22), 266, 267
  Pan-Turkism. *See* Pan-Turkism
  Republic, 213, 279, 399
  Turkish language, 19, 22
Turkic Peoples, 78, 80, 87, 100, 110, 123, 124, 370
  Azeris, 306
Tvangste (Port), 143. *See* also Königsberg
Tvrtko, King, 130
Tyrol, 229
Ugra River, Battle of (1480), 155
Ukraine, 19, 41, 60, 87, 100, 136, 157, 185, 236, 243, 249, 250, 251, 262, 291, 297, 306, 309, 312, 314, 326, 338, 359, 425, 451
  Austrian Ukraine. *See* Lviv (Lemberg), Galicia
  Czech/Hungarian Ukraine. *See* Transcarpathia, Galicia
  Early independence (1918-21), 294
  Galicia. *See* Galicia
  Great Famine (1932-33), 298, 309
  Lithuanian Ukraine (1325-1569), 148, 157, 179
  Origins, 179
  OUN/UPA, 371, 418, 424
  Polish Ukraine (1569-1667), 175, 180

Polish Ukraine (1667-1795), 178
Russian rule (1667-1918), 176,
181, 183, 187, 189
Ukrainian Central Council (1917-
18), 295
Ukrainian language, 16
Ukrainian Orthodox Church, 39,
180, 181
Ukrainian S.S.R., 298, 371, 451
Western Ukrainian Republic
(1918-20), 296, 314
Ulbricht, Walter, 414, 415, 416
Ulmanis, Kārlis/Charles, 300, 301,
338
Ulrich von Jungingen, Grand
Master, 152
Uluots, Jüri, 338
United Nations, 266, 415, 427, 451,
452, 453
United States, xix, 13, 55, 102, 169,
188, 220, 221, 239, 244, 245,
261, 262, 263, 264, 279, 281,
284, 287, 291, 306, 309, 312,
316, 330, 335, 341, 343, 346,
347, 348, 350, 353, 356, 371,
379, 386, 389, 392, 394, 400,
405, 410, 413, 425, 427, 443
Central Intelligence Agency
(CIA), 387, 396
Civil War (1861-65), 210, 238
Fort Knox, 102
Native Americans, 46, 165, 230
Revolution (1775-83), xvii, 178,
179, 313, 438
Truman Doctrine, 396
U.S. Constitution, 178
U.S. Dollars, 32, 422, 438
Voice of America (VOA), 386, 413
West Point, 179
Ural Mountains, 17, 82, 100, 329,
368
Üxküll. See Ikšķile
Uzbeg, Khan, 124
Uzbeks

Uzbek language, 19
Vācietis, Jakums, 300
Václav I (Přemyslid), King (13th c.),
114
Václav I (Přemyslid), Prince (10th
c.), 95
Valdemar IV, King, 150
Vampires, 139
Varna, 140
Vasa Dynasty, 170, 173
Vavil, Archbishop & Vladika, 128
Venice, 235
Venetian Republic (Empire), 128,
130, 131, 133, 136, 137, 165,
168, 177, 185, 228
Ventspils
Windau, 149, 175
Versailles, Treaty of (1919), 263, 264,
382
Article 231, 263
Paris Peace Conference (1919),
263, 271, 282, 291, 299
Versailles Treaty System, 264,
265, 279, 280, 283, 287, 288,
289, 343, 346
Victor Emanuelle III, King, 284
Vidin, 126
Vienna, 25, 73, 142, 168, 185, 195,
214, 219, 234, 235, 236, 253,
270, 272, 279, 349, 384
Congress of (1815), 131, 206, 231,
234, 241, 247, 251, 259
Division (1945-55), 414
Ottoman Siege of (1529), 136, 184
Ottoman Siege of (1683), 176, 177,
184, 185
Vienna Awards (1939-40), 289, 294,
340, 342, 343, 345, 346, 355, 401
Vikings. See Scandinavia
Vilnius, 241, 242, 302, 337, 338, 452
Wilno, 21, 314
Visegrád
Visegrád summits, 140, 151
Vistula River, 83, 105, 371

Vittorio Veneto, Battle of (1918). *See* Isonzo, Battles of (1918)

Vlachs, 79, 218

Vlad III, 137, 139

Vlad II, Prince, 141

Vladimirescu, Tudor, 219

Vladimir I, Prince, 100

Vladimir (state), 113

Vladivostok, 243, 245, 290, 306

Vlastimir, 105

Vlastimirović Dynasty, 104

Vlorë, 131

Vojvodina, 235, 273, 344, 349, 371

Voldemaras, Augustinas, 301, 303, 338

Volga Germans, 161

Volga River, 65, 67, 78, 99, 100, 111, 123, 154, 290, 330, 361

Voltaire, 173

Voronyezh, Battle of (1943), 345

Voroshilov, Kliment, 405

Vukovar, 455

Vyborg, 370

Vytautas, Grand Duke, 149, 152, 153

Vyx Note, 286

Wagner, Richard, 208

Wałęsa, Lech, 423, 439

Wallachia, 80, 141, 158, 166, 169, 207, 211, 221, 282
   Origins, 137
   Phanariot rule, 168, 219
   Revolution of 1848, 220
   Russian protectorate, 219
   Union with Moldavia (1861), 221

Wallenberg, Raoul, 365

Wandlitz, 417

War of the Holy League (1684-99), 168

Warsaw, 247, 249, 250, 312, 332, 335, 384, 387, 388, 420, 421, 423
   Becomes capital, 174
   Destruction (1944), 336, 496
   'Miracle on the Vistula' (1920), 296
   Powązki Cemetery, 479

Warsaw Ghetto, 367

Warsaw Ghetto Uprising (1943), 335, 366, 420

Warsaw Uprising (1944), 335, 336, 496

Warsaw Pact, 387, 388, 396, 397, 403, 407, 409, 411, 412, 414, 421, 423, 441, 443

Warsaw Treaty of Friendship, Cooperation and Mutual Assistance (1955). *See* Warsaw Pact

Washington D.C., 380

Waterloo, Battle of (1815), 206, 229, 248

Wehlau, Treaty of (1657), 176, 196

Weser River, 75

Westphalia, Treaty of (1648), 2, 168

West, the, 47, 177, 189, 241, 264, 282, 286, 288, 295, 306, 310, 315, 322, 326, 330, 337, 340, 345, 346, 348, 353, 365, 380, 384, 387, 390, 398, 401, 402, 403, 404, 405, 409, 413, 421, 422, 425, 426, 428, 429, 430, 436, 440, 445, 456
   Decolonization, 386, 436
   Eastern strategic issues, 211, 264, 271, 280, 294, 315, 370, 371, 382. *See* Congress of Berlin (1878), Versailles Treaty (1919), Cold War
   Origins, 88, 92

White Mountain, Battle of (1620). *See* Bilá hora, Battle of (1620)

Wieliczka Salt Mines, 198

Wiener Neustadt, 114

Wilhelmshaven, 335

Wilhelm/William I (Hohenzollern), King & Emperor, 230

Wilhelm/William II (Hohenzollern), Kaiser, 245, 262

Wilhelm/William of Wied, Prince, 227, 283

Wilson, Woodrow (President), 263, 271, 281, 284, 291, 312

Winter War (1939-40), 303, 337, 358, 360, 370
Wisła. *See* Vistula River
Władysław I, 151
Władysław III (of Varna), King, 140
Władysław IV (Vasa), King, 175
Wolf, Markus, 389
World War I, 54, 115, 131, 153, 202, 207, 210, 218, 239, 245, 257, 258, 264, 271, 275, 281, 295, 297, 299, 362
  Albania, 283
  Armistice (1918), 262, 278, 279, 299, 301
  Austria-Hungary, 260, 262, 268, 271, 272, 273, 274, 290
  Balkan Front, 262, 268, 273, 278, 282, 283, 286
  Brusilov Offensive (1916), 262, 270, 282, 290, 304
  Bulgaria, 265, 268, 272, 273, 277, 279, 355
  Central Powers, 263, 270, 272, 277, 281, 282
  Concentration camps, 297
  Czechoslovak Legion, 290
  Eastern Front, 262, 268, 286, 290, 291, 295, 298
  Entente Powers, 262, 265, 267, 273, 277, 280, 281, 282, 286, 291, 306, 313, 343
  Estonia, 299
  Fourteen Points, 271, 312
  Hungary, 285
  Italian Front, 270, 286
  July Crisis (1914), 259
  Macedonia, 277, 278
  Marne River, Battles of (1914, 1918), 262
  Montenegro, 274
  Origins, 216, 240, 246, 328
  Ottoman Empire, 265, 267, 273
  Paris Peace Conference (1919). *See* Versailles, Treaty of (1919)
  Poland, 310
  Romania, 270, 281, 282, 346
  Russia, 259, 260, 262, 268, 286, 291, 304, 306, 310
  Schlieffen Plan, 260, 262
  Serbia, 259, 260, 262, 268, 272, 274, 278, 283, 286
  Somme River, Battle of (1917), 262
  Ukraine, 295
  Verdun, Battle of (1916), 262
  Western Front, 262
  Ypres, Battles of (1914, 1915, 1917, 1918), 262
World War II, xix, 19, 55, 102, 115, 153, 160, 221, 245, 258, 276, 294, 316, 368, 381, 386, 420, 425, 447, 456, 489
  Albania, 353, 355, 369
  Allies, 321, 331, 334, 336, 340, 341, 344, 345, 348, 349, 350, 353, 355, 357, 360, 368, 370, 385, 398, 413, 414, 415, 418, 443
  Anti-Nazi Resistance, 330, 333, 334, 338, 340, 341, 343, 349, 350, 359, 365, 387, 393, 395, 418
  Axis Powers, 280, 321, 330, 345, 347, 349, 356, 368, 385, 404
  Balkan Front, 330, 339, 348, 350, 353, 355, 357, 361, 392
  Baltics, 336, 337, 360, 361, 365, 368
  Belarus, 337, 359, 368
  Bulgaria, 330, 346, 349, 350, 355, 365, 369, 398
  Concentration camps, 333, 352
  Czechoslovak Free Air Force, 340
  Czechoslovakia, 294, 326, 330, 332, 340, 342, 368, 410
  Eastern Front, 330, 338, 341, 347, 357, 360
  Enigma (Cipher), 334
  Estonia, 326, 337, 338
  Fatalities, 321, 322, 353, 358, 398
  Gleiwitz Incident (1939), 332
  Greek Campaign (1940), 330, 353, 355

Hungary, 330, 343, 346, 348, 349, 356, 361, 362, 365, 369

Italian Campaign (1943-45), 330, 335, 355, 356

Jabłonkow Pass Incident (1939), 329

Jewish Anti-Nazi Resistance, 119, 335

Latvia, 338, 362

Lithuania, 338, 365

North African Campaign (1940-43), 330, 335, 339, 341

Operation Barbarossa, 321, 330, 337, 339, 342, 345, 347, 349, 354, 356, 359, 360, 370, 428

Operation Market Garden (1944). See Arnhem, Battle of (1944)

Origins, 328, 331

Ostland, 326, 337

Ploieşti Airraids (1943-44), 348

Poland, 326, 330, 331, 338, 340, 359, 361, 362, 366, 367, 368, 439

Potsdam Conference, 398, 413, 415, 428

Romania, 330, 341, 345, 346, 355, 356, 362, 369, 370

Serbia, 349, 351, 352, 369

Slovakia, 329, 342

Soviet Union, 147, 308, 321, 329, 332, 337, 338, 341, 343, 345, 347, 348, 350, 356, 357, 368, 381, 385, 392, 418, 426

Ukraine, 345, 347, 359, 361, 362, 368

Western Front, 330, 337, 339, 341, 346, 349, 357, 410

Yalta Conference, 398, 413, 415, 428

Yugoslavia, 330, 344, 348, 349, 355, 356, 369, 392, 393

World War III, 414

Wrangel, Piotr/Peter (General), 306

Wrocław, 107, 113
  Breslau, 21
  Vratislav, 94

Wycliffe, John, 36, 145

Xiaopeng, Deng, 397

Yalu River, 427

Yaroslav I, 100

Yaroslavl, 113

Yekaterinburg, 290, 305

Yellow Sea, 427

Yeltsin, Boris, 450, 451, 452

Yezhov, Nikolai/Nicholas, 309

Ypsilantis, Alexander, 219

Yugoslavia, 103, 271, 272, 279, 280, 288, 371, 382, 383, 399
  AVNOJ, 350, 353, 354, 371, 392
  Communist era, 274, 370, 392, 393, 396, 408, 410
  Creation, 274
  Crisis of 1948, 394, 395, 399, 405, 428
  Destruction (1941), 344, 349, 351, 352, 356
  Implosion (1990s), 129, 239, 395
  Interwar, 280, 281, 316, 343
  Kingdom of Serbs, Croats and Slovenes, 273
  Yugoslav Committee, 273, 275

Zagreb, 96, 273, 350, 352

Žalgiris, Battle of (1410). See Grünwald, Battle of (1410)

Zeta. See Montenegro, Serbia

Zheng He, Admiral, 66

Zhivkov, Todor, 399, 400, 401, 445

Zhukov, Georgi/George (General), 360

Žižka, Jan/John, 35

Zog I, King, 284, 353

Zogu, Ahmed. See Zog I, King

Zogu, Leka (Crown Prince), 284

Zvonimir I, King, 104

Zygalski, Henryk/Henry, 334

Zygmunt/Sigismund III (Vasa), King, 170, 174

Zygmunt/Sigismund II (Jagiellonian), King, 154, 173

ALSO AVAILABLE FROM NEW EUROPE BOOKS

"JOHN SHIRTING . . . STANDS IN THE GOOD COMPANY OF IGNATIUS J. REILLY, CHAUNCEY GARDENER, AND FORREST GUMP."
—ANDREI CODRESCU

KEEPING BEDLAM AT BAY IN THE PRAGUE CAFÉ

A NOVEL

M. HENDERSON ELLIS

978-0-9825781-8-6

"An ode to expatriate living, culture clashes, and the heady days of early 1990s Europe, this novel is a manic, wild ride."

—*Booklist*

"Ellis vividly re-creates the atmosphere of a city in the throes of transformation as well as the American Quixotes who populate this new frontier."

—*Publishers Weekly*

"Difficult to put down, unsettling yet addictive, the novel is a must-read for anyone who dares to peek behind the post-card image of a famously beautiful centre of European civilization."

—*Winnipeg Free Press*

New Europe Books

New Europe Books
Williamstown, Massachusetts

Find our titles wherever books are sold, or visit
www.NewEuropeBooks.com
for order information.